Adjusting Privatization

Adjusting
Privatization

CASE STUDIES FROM DEVELOPING COUNTRIES

Christopher Adam
William Cavendish
Percy S. Mistry

James Currey
LONDON
Heinemann
PORTSMOUTH (N.H)
Ian Randle
KINGSTON

James Currey Ltd
54b Thornhill Square
Islington
London N1 1BE
England

Ian Randle Publishers Ltd
206 Old Hope Road, Kingston 6, Jamaica

Heinemann Educational Books, Inc.
361 Hanover Street
Portsmouth, NH 03801-3959
USA

First published 1992

92 93 94 95 96 9 8 7 6 5 4 3 2 1

British Library Cataloguing in Publication Data
Adam, Christopher
    Adjusting Privatization: Case Studies
    from Developing Countries
    I. Title
    351.007

ISBN 0-85255-132-0 (Cloth)
ISBN 0-85255-133-9 (Paper)

ISBN 0-435-08068-7 (Heinemann)

Typeset in 10/10½ pt Times by
Colset Private Ltd, Singapore
and printed in Britain by
Villiers Publications, London N6

Contents

Part II: Country Case Studies

Foreword

Made fashionable by Britain in the 1980s, privatization is now in vogue around the world. It has become an important policy ingredient in the swing to reliance on markets which characterizes economic reforms now under way in the second and third worlds. In part this is because greater emphasis on free markets, and on privatization as a means to making markets work better, both occupy a central place in the thinking of the international donor community and feature prominently in its financial support for structural adjustment. Experience with privatization in the industrial countries is generally seen as successful though that view is not universally shared. Elsewhere, it is acknowledged as being more problematic. In cases like Argentina, Chile and Mexico, early problems are being overcome with emerging evidence of greater success with privatization and its contribution to external debt reduction. In other developing countries the fruits have yet to be harvested. Closer scrutiny of privatization experience over the past decade, in industrial and developing economies, suggests in reality that the process and its outcomes are neither as simple nor as straightforward as is often envisaged.

Developing economies have embraced privatization as a central plank of policy reform for a combination of reasons. Policy-makers in these countries have been influenced by their perceptions of the role that privatization has played in improving the performance of sclerotic industrial economies with large, undynamic and inefficient public enterprises (notably the UK). To them privatization offers the prospect of greater efficiency at the enterprise, as well as the economy-wide, level. It holds the promise of contributing to the state treasury immediately through public asset sale proceeds and eventually through higher tax revenues from more profitable enterprises which help to generate a higher level of economic activity. It also provides an opportunity for widening individual participation in corporate ownership and increasing private sector participation in economic decision-making, thus contributing to more transparent public policy-making. Furthermore, industrial countries have exerted considerable effort in inducing second and third world countries to liberalize and privatize their economies, through bilateral exhortation and their dominant influence over the lending policies and adjustment prescriptions of multilateral financial institutions. Critics in the developing world have often portrayed these two types of persuasion as political and ideological pressure improperly exercised through multilateral conditionality, especially in the heavily indebted countries. But developing countries have not embraced privatization simply because of such pressure. Extremely distressed economic circumstances in many of these countries have exerted their own imperatives in forcing them to improve fiscal, micro- and macroeconomic performance and to access external finance through all possible means including privatization.

Obviously, developing countries cannot afford either the frustration or lost time of inadequate attempts at privatizing. If privatization is to contribute to improving economic performance it is crucial that policy-makers in these countries know how a portfolio of public assets should be sold and understand the processes by which expected improvements in performance are actually achieved. Yet the empirical evidence (including the substantial contribution made by this book) suggests that implementation of privatization programmes has been weak while their outcomes have owed as much to changes in the economic environment as they have to the transfer of public asset ownership. There is therefore genuine concern in the developing world as to exactly what privatization can achieve and what role it has to play in the process of economic adjustment and transformation. More should not be expected from privatization policy than it can reasonably deliver, especially when the supporting conditions and policies which are necessary for its success are absent.

It is becoming clearer with the passage of time that privatization is much more than simply a matter of selecting public enterprises for sale, valuing them and trying to get right the sequence in which they are to be sold. All of these elements are, of course, extremely important. Considerable technical analysis and skill needs to be brought to bear on each of these problems. But even when they are handled as best as circumstances permit, the outcome of public asset sales (in terms of intended improvements in fiscal and economic performance) can be disappointing because the inadequacies of the developing economic environments in which they take place overwhelm the benefits that are supposed to result.

Privatization in developing countries has been based mainly on the experience of countries in Western Europe. But few developing countries if any possess the economic characteristics and endowments which European economies enjoy, in particular the existence of reasonably competitive domestic markets for goods and services, well-developed capital markets with considerable breadth, depth and absorptive capacity, and sound regulatory structures which have evolved over decades. The absence of these essential prerequisites makes achieving all the benefits of privatization that much more difficult. In *industrial* countries the 'success' of privatization is largely dependent on strategic and tactical choices for sale from a public asset portfolio, on proper valuation, pricing and appropriately timed sequencing. Though these same factors are equally important in *developing* countries as well, privatization success in the latter may be even more dependent on its being linked to carefully programmed steps of economic liberalization, the concomitant development of market regulatory structures and an appropriate redefinition of the 'economic borders' of the state in the country concerned. These major aspects can usually be taken for granted in more developed industrial environments.

Where competition policy, market structure and the regulatory environment are underdeveloped the transfer of asset ownership can simply result in continuing operating inefficiencies with excess rents being collected by the private instead of the public sector. Instead of the Treasury benefiting from such sales, governments often have to provide sweeteners in the form of gross underpricing of enterprise assets, price supports, subsidies or tariff protection which diminish or prevent the financial and economic returns of privatization from materializing. In undeveloped capital markets where the option of selling state-owned enterprises through public flotations is limited, developing country governments often resort to direct sales in an opaque fashion which raises questions about the probity of privatization decisions and brings the entire process under suspicion.

For all these reasons, the challenge facing policy-makers in developing countries and the donor community is to learn how to tailor the privatization process to the structure and circumstances prevailing in such economies in order to ensure its success. This book on 'Adjusting Privatization' represents an important contribution to fostering better understanding of the privatization process in developing countries and contributing to an informed debate which is pragmatic in its content. Drawing on research of the experience of selected countries in Africa, Asia, the Caribbean, and the South Pacific it provides a detailed picture of the economics and politics of the privatization process in the smaller developing economies, offering valuable insights on the key issues raised by privatization experience in the third world. Its observations and analysis are pertinent also for countries of the second world which are now placing so much reliance on privatization for the transformation of their economies.

Many developing countries, including several members of the Commonwealth, have adopted privatization policies and programmes. Others are engaged in deep internal debate on launching such programmes. All of them are anxious to have more guidance on the preparation and satisfactory implementation of these programmes and on how the promised benefits of the endeavour can be realized to the fullest extent. The time is therefore particularly ripe for more empirical contributions to improving our understanding of privatization and its management.

The Commonwealth Secretariat was therefore happy to join with the Gatsby Charitable Foundation in supporting this comparative study of privatization experiences in selected Commonwealth countries carried out at the International Development Centre, Queen Elizabeth House, University of Oxford. We are grateful to QEH (and its Director, Professor Robert Cassen), to Percy Mistry who conceptualized, organized funding for and directed the project, and to Christopher Adam and William Cavendish who carried out the research and were responsible for the text. Not enough has been written about the impact of privatization in the third world, and this book stands out as a particularly worthy effort to fill that gap. I am sure it will be received by everyone interested in privatization as an exciting and timely contribution.

Dr Bishnodat Persaud
Director & Head
Economic Affairs Department
Commonwealth Secretariat

Acknowledgements

We wish to express our thanks to the Commonwealth Secretariat and the Gatsby Foundation for providing the financial support which made this research project possible. In particular we thank Dr Bishnodat Persaud, Dr S.K. Rao and Dr Indrajit Coomraswamy of the Economic Affairs Division in the Commonwealth Secretariat for their continued assistance and support throughout the project.

We are indebted to numerous other people for their assistance and comments in the execution of the research and preparation of this book. We especially thank Cavelle Creightney for research assistance of the Jamaican and Trinidad and Tobago country studies. We would also like to thank Robert Cassen, Kara Hanson, Laurence Harris, Machiko Nissanke, Mary Shirley, Frances Stewart, John Vickers and Ganeshan Wignaraja for valuable comments and discussion on this work at various stages. We also thank Margaret Benson, Ann Kesterton and Neil Tofts for valuable administrative assistance, and Margaret Cornell for her astute and efficient editing of the manuscript.

Our foremost debt, however, is to the many officials and managers from our seven case-study countries who assisted us during our field work, and took valuable time out to answer our often naive questions. The list is too long to include in full but we wish to acknowledge the special assistance of Richard Downer, Stephen Sterling, Donna Beman, Donald Banks, David Thompson, Frank Rampersad, Nik Najib Hussein, Ismael Fariz Ali, Leva Hekwa, Tissa Jayasinghe, Dilesh Jayannatha, Terence Ryan, Harris Mule, George Kamba, Gerald Armstrong and Eunice Kazembe. None of the above, however, bear any responsibility for the interpretation of events and decisions we present in this book. Any such errors are solely our own.

OVERVIEW

1   Introduction

The debate surrounding privatization in developing countries is based on limited empirical evidence and is often grounded in a questionable analytic framework. Despite this, privatization lies at the heart of economic adjustment programmes being adopted by governments around the world. Indeed, the philosophy of privatization has been embraced to the point where the perceived superiority of the private sector in the provision of goods and services has become almost axiomatic. However, it is precisely this assumption we believe to be invalid, and it is therefore unsurprising that privatization in many developing countries has failed to meet expectations. Only through an explicit evaluation of the fundamental economics of privatization can a more balanced role emerge.

In this book we examine privatization from an explicitly economic, rather than political, standpoint. Central to our approach is a careful evaluation of the specific effects of ownership transfer on economic performance as applied to the market structures and characteristics of many developing countries. In particular, we make a clear separation between this and the impact of other forms of market liberalization on economic performance. Further, though fundamentally an economic policy instrument, at times privatization has been *omnia ad omnes*. The fact that privatization is frequently used in pursuit of diverse objectives means that an important strand of our analysis is a consideration of how the economic efficiency objectives of privatization interact with the many other, often less precise, political and economic goals.

The book is based on evaluation of the experience of seven developing countries (Jamaica, Kenya, Malaŵi, Malaysia, Papua New Guinea, Sri Lanka and Trinidad and Tobago). They are broadly typical of many low- and middle-income developing countries in Africa, Asia and the Caribbean, and provide rich evidence for our view that the channels through which privatization can be expected to affect enterprise performance in developing countries are more complex than conventional wisdom suggests. Certainly, this evidence shows that the arguments for privatization cannot be simply transferred from the industrialized to the developing world, but must be adapted to its specific economic environment.

By adopting an economic point of view, three issues become important when examining privatization in developing countries. First, an economic perspective firmly locates the key objective of privatization as that of efficiency improvement. Doing so links privatization clearly into the theory of ownership transfer, which provides a coherent framework for analysing the actual design and implementation of privatization sales in terms of this objective. It is, after all, for this reason that privatization has become an integral feature of structural adjustment, namely as one part of a programme which aims at an economic restructuring in order to improve dramatically the efficiency of resource allocation. As the fundamental goal, then, efficiency improvement must be the yardstick against which privatization initiatives are judged.

Second, when theoretical arguments for privatization, which are grounded primarily in the economic conditions of developed countries, are applied to developing countries the situation becomes much more complex. Competitive goods and capital markets, high and efficient savings mobilization, and effective regulation are the exception in developing countries, rather than the rule. Their absence thus requires an adjustment of the way in which the theoretical arguments for privatization are applied in developing countries. In particular, it is necessary to focus attention on limitations to competition, the correspondingly more extensive role for monopoly regulation and competition policy, and on constraints to privatization imposed by narrowly based capital markets.

Finally, our analysis of market structures, savings mobilization and regulatory capacity in developing countries, lead us to conclude that an adjustment is required in the role of privatization in developing countries. For both political and economic reasons, privatization has met with only limited success in achieving many of the objectives set for it, particularly those of short-term revenue enhancement and the stimulation of nascent domestic entrepreneurship and capital market development. More strongly, however, rapid attempts to prosecute privatization can be counter-productive, especially in smaller developing countries, as the pressure to sell leads to the compromise of many of the objectives which privatization was adopted to meet, and can divert resources away from other, frequently more valuable, public sector reform measures. Thus the somewhat ambitious claims made for privatization in developing countries need to be scaled down. Privatization, in our view, can best be regarded only as a medium-term supply-side policy, a logical complement to a broad strategy of private sector development, rather than as a panacea for the multitude of ills endured by developing countries.

The book is in two parts. Part I consists of an overview of the theory of ownership transfer and a summary of the main findings from the country studies. It begins with a review of the economic theory germane to the privatization debate. Thus Chapter 2 reviews the principal objectives of privatization in developing countries, and considers how theories of ownership and control, market structure and performance, and regulation provide a framework for evaluating these objectives. Chapter 3 briefly charts the growth of the state-owned enterprise sector in the seven countries, while Chapter 4 summarizes their privatization experience. In this chapter we also consider the political context in which privatization has materialized and examine the way in which the political and economic objectives of privatization often conflict, and the extent to which the latter are compromised when privatization proceeds in the face of the political uncertainty and economic crises which have plagued many developing countries during the 1980s. Chapter 5 presents the core argument of the book and considers the extent to which the implicit economic structures which underpin the popular debate on privatization are absent in many developing countries. In particular, the chapter examines the extent to which the private sector provides the basis for competition to be elicited, the ability of governments to establish credible and efficient regulatory regimes to attenuate the adverse effects of market concentration, and the capacity of the capital market to mobilize domestic savings and provide for trade in asset ownership. Chapter 6 concludes with an assessment of the role for privatization and the need to adjust privatization within the development policy canon.

Part II consists of seven country case studies. Each charts the growth of the state-owned enterprise sector and the emergence of privatization policy. Thereafter each individual programme is reviewed and assessed against both the economic objectives identified in the beginning of the book and also the specific objectives pursued by the governments concerned. Finally the case studies evaluate the structural environment in which privatization occurs and identify the constraints that this environment applies to the pursuit of successful privatization. There is a wide range of experience across the different countries in this book. At one extreme are Jamaica (Chapter 7) and Malaysia (Chapter 9) where privatization is well-established and a sizeable number of enterprises, including large utilities, have been either completely or partially sold. At the other extreme are Papua New Guinea (Chapter 10), Kenya (Chapter 12) and Malaŵi (Chapter 13) where privatization has been very limited and generally confined to the divestiture of enterprises from the portfolios of development finance institutions.

2 A Theoretical Overview of Privatization

This chapter analyses the key theoretical issues central to the privatization debate. We start by defining what we mean by privatization. The term has been used to mean distinct things to different people,[1] and in order to impose a unified structure on the book we shall propose a tight definition. We then consider how the idea of privatization has been absorbed into the policy canon of developing countries, and look at the main objectives ascribed to it. Finally, we review the body of economic theory concerned with privatization. This falls into three broad areas: first, the relationship between forms of ownership, incentives, and the internal management of the firm; second, the links between market structures, competition, and the efficient allocation of resources in the economy as a whole; and, third, the regulation of monopolistic and oligopolistic markets.

2.1 Defining privatization

The term 'privatization' has been used to describe an array of actions designed to broaden the scope of private sector activity, or the assimilation by the public sector of efficiency-enhancing techniques generally employed by the private sector. This loose description, which results in privatization often being viewed as a goal in itself rather than as simply a means to an end, can lead to confusion. Essentially privatization is only a process, and therefore in this book we choose to work with what we regard as an analytically correct definition of privatization which covers the transfer from the public to the private sector of the ownership and/or control of productive assets, their allocation and pricing,[2] and the entitlement to the residual profit flows generated by them. Consequently, under this definition we shall confine our focus to: (i) the outright, or partial, sale of assets by the state; (ii) the transfer of assets to the private sector under leasing arrangements; and (iii) the introduction of management contracting arrangements.

An alternative way of expressing this definition, and one which moves away from the emphasis on ownership, is to focus simply on the change in the supply of a service from the public sector to the private sector, irrespective of the source of its financing. This can be simply demonstrated in the following matrix (see Roth, 1987);

		THE PROVIDER	
		PUBLIC	PRIVATE
THE PAYER	PUBLIC	1	2
	PRIVATE	3	4

Under our definition, all moves to the right, from quadrants 1 and 3 to 2 and 4, represent privatizations. Moves to the left, from 2 and 4 to 1 and 3, are obviously nationalizations, whilst vertical movements do not alter the public/ private division of supply. For example, direct sales of state-owned enterprises (SOEs) can be represented by a shift from 3 to 4, whereas management contracts and other forms of contracting-out could be represented by shifts from 1 to 2.

The advantage of this scheme is that, while it fully encompasses our definition, it allows us to identify a range of policies and actions which are closely related to privatization, but which clearly do not represent a direct switch in the source of supply. In particular, we can differentiate privatization from issues of direct SOE reform, market deregulation, and broader objectives of 'state shrinkage' (see Glade, 1986). While all these policies may expose public enterprises to greater commercial pressures, they do not necessarily either alter control and ownership structures in the economy, or change the source of supply of goods and services. State shrinkage, for example, includes any activity which reduces the involvement of the state in economic activity, such as the withdrawal of the state from certain markets in the expectation that the private sector will fill the gap. It may also involve the introduction of debt–equity swaps which extinguish sovereign liabilities for private equity participation on the part of external creditors. Similarly, while direct SOE reform also interacts with privatization (all privatizations will generally involve some reform of SOE management structures) and with state shrinkage, there is also a large class of SOE reforms, mainly the adoption of private sector practices, which entail neither privatization nor state shrinkage. For example, the adoption of 'private sector-style' management systems, employment incentive structures (such as bonus payments, commission scales, etc.), balance-sheet restructuring, and debt and capital restructuring are all reforms which will bear directly on the efficiency of the sector, but they are not privatizations.

Finally, there is the important relationship between privatization and the wider issue of economic deregulation. Many aspects of deregulation, such as price liberalization, abolition of import controls, and the deregulation of factor markets, will affect the performance of public enterprises, either directly by altering the cost function of the firm itself, or indirectly through the effect of deregulation on the competitive environment in which the firm operates. In principle, the distinction between the nature and effects of the two concepts is clear, and indeed, *ex ante*, there is no logical reason why they should be connected. In practice, however, the identification of the separate effects of privatization and deregulation on performance is often very difficult.

No definition of privatization is ever likely to be watertight, and in many cases the extent to which 'privatization' has occurred is a matter of degree and interpretation. This is particularly so in developing countries, and especially in Africa. In particular, recent years have seen an enhanced role for external agents, particularly non-governmental organizations (NGOs) and other welfare or religious organizations, in the supply process for services ranging from infrastructure construction to primary health care and education service delivery. Since the source of supply of the services has changed, such initiatives should be classified as privatizations: however, they are generally not embraced by the common usage of the term. Rather, such organizations are often co-opted by the state to provide public services in the face of labour or financial resource constraints. Similarly, Build–Operate–Transfer (BOT) schemes have been increasingly used by governments as a form of non-debt financing of public sector activities through which private contractors finance the construction of capital assets (usually roads), the cost of which is recovered through user-fees. While BOTs represent a contracting-out of the process of fixed capital formation, the intention is generally that asset ownership and control revert to the public sector following a pay-back period during which the private sector operator earns the revenue from the asset. In this sense the BOT can be seen as a variant of the standard practice of public works contracting in the face of financial resource constraints, by which the remuneration system for the contractor is switched from a certain lump-sum payment to a risk-bearing payment scheme spread out over time.[3]

Clearly our purpose here is not to provide a complete taxonomy of forms of privatization,[4] but rather to establish the foundations of a coherent terminology around which the arguments and discussions of this book revolve. However, both in the analysis of Part I, and in the country studies of Part II, from time to time we shall broaden our formal definition as required. Finally, although this form of separation is analytically neat, our task, as noted earlier, clearly to distinguish the effects of privatization *per se* from those of other aspects of SOE reform and broader economic deregulation is often difficult, though not impossible. We discuss this identification problem in more detail in section 2.3.

2.2 The policy objectives of privatization

In developing countries, privatization and SOE reform emerged as policy issues amidst the debt crisis and worsening fiscal performances of the early 1980s. Many governments have embraced the broad 'message' of privatization and it has quickly found a position at the heart of programmes of economic adjustment. It has been viewed as an instrument geared towards both short-term stabilization through expenditure reduction and also medium-term supply-side improvements by promoting more efficient resource allocation. Thus from policy statements and analyses across the range of developing countries, six principal objectives for privatization emerge.

The first, and often most urgent, objective is that of public finance rationalization. In the face of significant resource flows to the parastatal sector,[5] privatization is seen as a way of reducing net budgetary transfers and of eliminating contingent external debt liabilities. Moreover, with governments under pressure to meet short-term budget deficit targets, privatization proceeds can generate valuable capital revenue, easing the pressure for expenditure cuts in other areas, and also reducing the adverse effects which deficit financing can have on domestic investment.

The second set of objectives are the economic efficiency, or supply-side, objectives. These, as noted, are closely related to the broader issues of liberalization, and are particularly relevant given the history of government intervention in enterprise management in many developing countries. Allied to these two fundamental objectives are a host of other, somewhat broader, aims associated with a programme of privatization, and which themselves are also central to current thinking on the structural adjustment debate, not least in Africa. Amongst these is the use of public sector divestiture to 'crowd-in' a nascent private sector. Similarly privatization is viewed, in a number of smaller countries, as a means through which local capital markets may be developed and domestic resource mobilization enhanced. Finally, there are a set of political and social objectives which are intimately affected by the privatization debate. These mainly involve the distributive effects of privatization, and in particular the role of foreign capital in the privatization process, and also concern the relationship between the government and its external creditors.

The way in which privatization interacts with most, if not all, of these objectives is complex. Moreover, the direct relationship between privatization and the pursuit of each objective is often clouded by the nature of the overall policy environment into which privatization fits. In this section we shall start by addressing the theoretical underpinnings of these objectives in turn, while in Chapter 4 we shall consider some of the contradictions and conflicts between the simultaneous pursuits of these multiple objectives. We start by establishing, as a benchmark, what we term the neutrality result – namely, that under certain circumstances privatization has no net effect on fiscal balances (see Hemming and Mansoor, 1988). This provides a basis for considering the way in which real effects emerge from privatization. These we classify into three groups: (i) public finance or exchange effects; (ii) reputation effects; and (iii) economic effects.

2.2.1 Privatization and public finance: the neutrality result
One of the most persistent misconceptions in the privatization debate concerns the assessment of the fiscal effects. Much of the confusion surrounding these effects stems from the idiosyncratic nature of public sector accounting practices, and the tendency of governments to approach matters of public finance from a 'flow' rather than a 'stock', or net-worth, point of view. The technicalities surrounding the problem are straightforward, and are well covered in the literature (see Hemming and Mansoor (1988), Heller and Schiller (1989), and Jones *et al.* (1990) for a full explanation). We shall therefore outline this issue only briefly in order to clear up any residual confusion which may exist, before focusing on the important fiscal effects of privatization.

In terms of their financial impact, the proceeds from privatization represent the capitalization of future net resource flows achieved by the sale of the asset. In other words, privatization is a simple liquidity transformation of the government's net worth. In the simplest baseline case of an arm's-length sale of state equity to the private sector in an economy characterized by fully efficient capital and money markets, full and costless information and neutral tax structures, the price at which the asset is sold will be the sum of the discounted future profits generated by the asset. Thus the sale will result in the public and private sectors adjusting their relative liquidity positions, but leaving their respective net worth unaltered. In particular, whilst the immediate effect of an asset sale is indeed a reduction in the current budget deficit, this must be offset against compensatingly higher deficits in the future caused by the loss of the future earnings stream from the asset sold. However, if government were to invest the proceeds in income-earning assets, and if capital markets are efficient, then the net earnings from investing the proceeds from the asset sale in, say, bonds will generate a profit stream of equal net present value. The private sector thus reduces its holdings of money (or other financial assets) and acquires equity in privatized enterprises, whilst the government reduces its equity and increases its holding of money. To emphasize the point, consider the case where the private sector sells bonds to purchase privatization equity, whilst the government uses the sale proceeds to retire outstanding bond liabilities. Since in each case the transaction involves a change only in the composition of the sectors' net wealth, and not its level, the fiscal impact must be neutral. Note also that the same arguments follow when a loss-making public enterprise is sold, except that here government pays a price to the private sector equal to the present discounted sum of future losses.[6]

The purpose of stating this neutrality result is to demonstrate that the sale of the asset itself does not necessarily generate any real effect. Rather, real effects emerging from privatization can best be seen as deviations from this neutrality position. The ensuing discussion is thus ordered around possible sources of deviations from neutrality. The classification of these effects is not exhaustive nor, importantly, is it exclusive.

Exchange effects

There are a number of non-trivial ways in which the public sector seller and the private sector buyer may have different valuations of the proceeds from an asset (even if the asset will generate the same revenue flow under either sector's ownership) and hence bring about a real effect from privatization. These we refer to as the exchange effects of privatization.

(i) Tax distortions and the value of public funds. One recent contribution argues that real fiscal effects from privatization are determined by the value of public funds in the hands of government (see Jones *et al.* 1990). The Jones, Tandon and Vogelsang (JTV) model starts from a similar basis to that of the neutrality result.[7] However, what specifically differentiates this analysis is the role accorded in the model to the direct consequence of the flow of funds from private purchasers to the fiscus. JTV argue that if, because of tax distortions and incentive effects, the value of cash from the asset sale is greater in public rather than private hands, then there is (in a static sense) a net fiscal gain to privatization. For example, if $1 revenue in the hands of government raised through taxation costs more than $1 of revenue raised through the sale of assets, then there will be a net fiscal gain to privatization, despite the fact that the apparent liquidity position is no different from the baseline case. JTV assume that this reduction in the deadweight cost of taxation will generally occur and hence that there is a fiscal, if ultimately neo-liberal, rationale for privatization. However, this assumption subsumes a host of complex issues concerning the shift of liquid assets from the private to the public sector. Vernon (1988), in commenting on the JTV model (1988), raises a number of questions about its assumptions, referring in particular to the possible crowding-out effects that such large-scale transfers may have.[8] Needless to say, the argument acquires a greater degree of complexity when the purchaser comes from the foreign private sector, where the transfer of funds will affect the fiscus not only directly but also indirectly through the sterilization requirements of changes in the balance of payments. None the less, even though the assumption of Jones and his colleagues about the nature of this effect is, by their own admission, heroic, the transfer is likely to have some real effects, and on balance we would expect these to be positive.

(ii) Other methods. There are other ways in which the sale of assets can be non-neutral, many of which are more likely to be pertinent in developing rather than industrialized countries. An obvious first example occurs when the government is credit-constrained, either domestically through controls being imposed on domestic credit expansion, or in international capital markets because of a loss of credit-worthiness. Such constraints increase the government's discount rate (reflecting its preference for current revenue) relative to the purchaser's. The purchaser can consequently pay less than the value of the future profit stream discounted at its (the purchaser's) rate of discount. The same argument applies, perhaps more strongly, where the purchaser is foreign and the government faces significant foreign-exchange constraints. Here, because of the consequent constraint on import levels, the government's valuation of current foreign exchange will be higher than that of the private sector.

Similar non-neutralities will occur in the presence of a narrow tax base or in any situation where an increase in the marginal rate of taxation would decrease government revenue as a result of 'Laffer-curve' effects. If there are differing degrees of risk aversion between the public and private sectors we may expect the same non-neutralities. Normally it would be assumed that, because of its size, the government is more able to spread risk, and will have a lower degree of risk aversion. In such circumstances the value of the asset would be higher in the hands of the government, and, *ceteris paribus*, there would be no sale.[9] However, it is possible to think of circumstances where the private sector may be less risk-averse than government and the converse would occur. This is especially likely when the buyer is able to access the foreign capital market, or is a multi-product firm capable of spreading risks widely. Finally, since the transfer of assets will, in general, alter the distribution of wealth in the private sector, this will generate second-order effects throughout the economy brought about by changes in the propensities to consume, to invest, to import and so on.[10]

There are a host of other non-neutralities which, though important in their own right, do not fundamentally alter the foregoing neutrality result. For example, the tax structure facing private and public sector companies is generally different, as is employment legislation and the degree of access to import permits, etc. In reality these issues will be important in the valuation process, but, since they represent 'policy' distortions as opposed to structural ones, they will be implicitly, and equally, built into the valuation calculus on the part of the public and private sectors. Consequently the thrust of the neutrality arguments holds in the face of these types of distortions. However, a much more interesting analysis occurs where the government has the power to alter these (implicit) terms of the sale after it has been effected. This leads us into the more complex area of reputations, information and the credibility of government.

Reputation and government credibility effects
The credibility of the government in the eyes of the private sector also plays a major role in determining the public finance effect of privatization. In this case, the problem facing the government is how to convince the purchaser that it (the government) will uphold the conditions (broadly interpreted) of the sale and thereby maintain the future value of the asset. This problem arises typically because in a privatization programme the seller, i.e. the government, has superior knowledge of the quality of the asset, and, more importantly, has the capacity to alter its post-sale value in the hands of the buyer through policy and other interventions conditional on its sovereign authority. In particular, it has the ability to default on the sale agreement by altering tax structures, changing the rules on access to foreign-exchange auctions, etc. We can easily envisage situations where the government will have an incentive to 'default' on its agreement in order to meet short-term funding requirements, and the fact that it has this capacity will reduce the amount the private sector is willing to pay for any given asset if it (the private sector) has an expectation of such a default. Consequently, if the government is interested in maximizing the revenue flow from a privatization programme, it is in its interest to create a reputation as an 'honest broker'.

This problem is of particular relevance in those developing countries which have a history of extensive state intervention in the economy, a record which has not been conducive to the maintenance of asset values in the hands of the private sector. If the private sector fears future re-nationalization or other types of default, this will depress the price it is prepared to offer, and therefore generate a structural non-neutrality in the model. Creating a positive reputation thus enables the government to signal a change in regime and to commit itself against future nationalization or other forms of punitive intervention. As Bates (1989) notes:

> Given their past ways of doing business in the developing world, governments promoting privatization need means of convincingly precommitting themselves to staying out of

politically sensitive markets. Lacking visible and unambiguous ways of signalling such intentions, governments may find that private investors will remain reluctant to place themselves at risk by entering the market place.

This form of policy credibility and reputation creation also carries over to external relationships with the donor and foreign investor community. Both private and official foreign capital flows will be determined not only by perceptions of the (direct) viability of specific projects, but also by the reputation of the government for not reneging on the terms and conditions of foreign investment. An important aspect of this is the credibility of governments in meeting the conditions of adjustment lending. Official funds are often tied explicitly to market-oriented reforms, with private capital flows being similarly but implicitly tied to the same reforms. In this respect, the credibility of government will determine the inflow of capital, but correspondingly it is a government's commitment to privatization that is viewed as a benchmark signal in the development of a less interventionist, more market-oriented policy stance. Enhanced official aid flows and improved access to international capital markets thus represent important positive externalities flowing from the successful implementation of a privatization programme. We shall return to these issues of reputation and credibility in some detail in Chapter 4.

Economic efficiency effects

Notwithstanding exchange and reputation effects, the pivotal effect of privatization follows from the main thrust of its economic rationale, namely that the profit stream that can be extracted from the asset in the hands of private owners is, *ceteris paribus*, higher than if operated under public ownership. Privatization thus increases total factor productivity in the economy, it is argued, and its real public finance impact arises out of the additional tax revenues generated from the enhanced value of the asset realized under public ownership. Moreover, the indirect effects this will have on reducing future tax distortions elsewhere in the economy represent positive second-order effects for public finance.

Clearly this argument holds only if the gains to private ownership cannot be achieved under public ownership, and it is to arguments concerning this proposition that we now turn in considering the second main objective of privatization, namely, its impact on economic efficiency. In the following section our discussion concentrates on two main features of the debate, namely, the roles of information flows and of incentives in the determination of performance.

2.2.2 Privatization and efficiency

This second set of objectives can be stated concisely: privatization is aimed at improving economic efficiency and is undertaken on the assumption that the production of goods and services is achieved more efficiently under the direction of private rather than public owners. Popular conceptions of privatization suggest that there is a clear and well-defined body of theory which explains the superiority of private over public ownership. Closer examination, however, reveals that this is not the case. Rather, the economic arguments for privatization rest on a number of hypotheses about the relationship between ownership, information and incentives, and their impact on market structure and performance. However, these arguments can be distilled down into two main ideas. Privatization, it is argued, will enhance productive efficiency (i.e. it leads to lower-cost production) and allocative efficiency (i.e. it forces down consumer prices so that they are closer to the marginal cost of production). In this section we examine the underpinnings of these assertions, and in addition consider how regulatory instruments may be introduced when market forces fail to work effectively.

Incentives and ownership: their effect on productive efficiency

Supervising management and monitoring its productivity is a costly task facing enterprise owners: costly in terms of time and human resources, especially when the objectives of an enterprise are diverse. Moreover, information on performance is hard to acquire and the link between inputs and effort on the one hand and outputs on the other are complex: the more diverse the objectives of the enterprise the less effective the monitoring of performance will be, and the lower the level of managerial efficiency.

Under public ownership, enterprises are often used by governments to pursue non-commercial objectives which are inconsistent with efficient and financially viable performance. For example, employment maximization objectives, non-commercial price setting aimed at keeping input prices low for other sectors, uneconomic investments and limited product innovation often dominate decision-making at the expense of a more commercial orientation. Concomitant to the pursuit of these non-economic objectives by the owners of the enterprise is the inefficient monitoring and control of management. Poor and equivocal direction of management blunts incentives, allows managers more flexibility to pursue their own objectives *qua* managers, and contributes to the widespread inefficiencies which characterize many developing countries' SOEs.

On the other hand, private ownership, it is argued, is equated with a higher level of managerial supervision resulting in more commercial and more timely financial decisions (in terms of pricing, investment, R&D levels, innovation, product marketing, etc). This results directly from the more single-minded profit maximization objective of private ownership which leads to a higher level of monitoring of management performance, and the institution of more effective forms of incentives. Since managerial efficiency can be more directly related to enterprise performance when the owners pursue narrower objectives, more effective efficiency-enhancing incentive contracts can be instituted.

This is the critical assumption of the privatization debate: that the switch from public to private ownership should result in more precise and more measurable objectives on the part of the owners, which in turn should create the environment and incentives to monitor and control management more effectively. This improvement derives from the concentration of property rights over the asset. Under public ownership property rights are, by definition, dispersed and no individual owner (i.e. the elector as shareholder) has an incentive to bear the costs of gathering costly information and thus to exercise control over the management of the enterprise, principally because the benefits accruing to this effort cannot (easily) be captured by that individual alone. The dissipation of property rights under public ownership thus severs the link between asset ownership and its ultimate control and management.[11] In this context the re-concentration of ownership in private hands allows the benefits of control to be internalized by the owners of the asset and thereby creates incentives to bear the costs of information gathering and management monitoring, while the tradability of these property rights (i.e. equity) allows the forces of competition to drive this level of performance monitoring to an optimal level.

This, albeit powerful, argument oversimplifies the relationship between forms of ownership and the nature of control of management in a number of respects. First, while the creation of property rights is a necessary condition for control to be exerted over management, it is not a sufficient condition. Second, notions of the public sector as a homogeneous social welfare maximizer and the private sector as a pure profit maximizer are somewhat naive: in reality neither sector conforms to these types. While these assumptions are often convenient simplifications, maintaining them in the context of privatization serves to obscure rather than clarify the links between ownership and efficiency.

It is more productive to reconsider the relationship using the well-established principal–agent theory, a framework which helps to identify the complexities which arise in reality. The basic issue is simply how the performance of managers (agents) changes when the objectives of the owners (the principals) alter, but with the following problem: as a result of incomplete information on the market, the principal is prevented from fully controlling the actions of the agent. Since it is assumed that the agent's objective function differs from that of the principal, and further, that the agent will act in a self-interested way, then the goal for the principal is to design an incentive structure such that the agent is induced to act in the principal's interests.

Approaching the issue from this angle we seek to reject the notion that the differences in enterprise performance under public and private ownership are necessarily intrinsic. Rather, we argue that such differences are grounded in the disparity between the objective functions of public and private sector owners and the different forms of agency relationships the ownership structures engender.

There are two elements to this argument. First, those who argue that differences between public and private owners are intrinsic claim that public sector owners (as opposed to managers) will always pursue non-commercial goals for political ends. While there is plenty of evidence that this often occurs, there is no intrinsic reason why it is always the case. The fact that there are many examples of SOEs (such as those operated in Singapore) which are not used in pursuit of non-commercial goals is adequate refutation.[12] The presence of non-commercial objectives is more indicative of poor management rather than an intrinsic feature of all public ownership. The removal of such objectives may be a necessary condition for altering the objective function of public owners, but it is not sufficient.

The second element of the argument is that to compare (as is often done) the 'general equilibrium' objective function of public ownership with the 'partial equilibrium' of private ownership is generally an inappropriate comparison. To explain, the attraction of the switch from public to private ownership is that it replaces a complex, 'general equilibrium' objective function of the government which includes not only static and dynamic considerations but also second-order effects in the economy (for example, the impact that actions will have on employment, trade, and fiscal balances), with a tighter 'partial equilibrium' objective function of the private sector as principal. Because of these differences it is argued that the information requirement of the public objective function is much heavier than for the private sector, and that it is the simplicity and lower informational demands of the private maximand that foster the efficiency gains.

This begs the question, however: what becomes of the additional 'general equilibrium' elements of the public sector objective function? In answering this, we encounter here the link between public and private ownership and the issue of regulation. In an ideal world where the social costs and benefits coincide with private costs and benefits, then, concomitantly, the objective functions will be equivalent and their information requirements congruent: in this case transfer of ownership will not result in a simplification of the objective function. In cases where social and private costs and benefits diverge, then further public policy in the form of regulatory practice may be necessary to achieve social welfare objectives. Consequently, the simple case of the general versus partial equilibrium comparison we started with is inappropriate. Rather, the relevant comparison is between public ownership and private ownership with regulation, and which of the two can most efficiently acquire the necessary information and put in place the incentives necessary to extract efficient performance by managers (the agents).

Once we introduce the issue of regulation, then, and acknowledge the necessary informational demands that it begets, the comparison becomes more complex. When this issue is examined in detail below the trade-off between these two ownership forms will be formalize).

The conclusions from the comparison between the maximands of public and private owners are mirrored by similar differences in the agency chain linking the ultimate principals (i.e. the electorate or the shareholders) to the ultimate agents (i.e. the enterprise management). Indeed, even if the objective functions of the principals were identical, differences in the nature of the agency chain might result in differences in enterprise performance under the two regimes.

Principal–agent relations: the public sector
Characteristically the extended relationship linking the electorate, legislature, executive and bureaucracy in the public sector provides for complex agency chains. The first link is that between the electorate as principals and the legislature and executive as agents. While political success (i.e. continuation in office) may depend *inter alia* on meeting the concerns of the electorate about SOE performance, pursuit of economic efficiency in public enterprises is actually more likely to be subordinated to meeting the concerns of specific interest groups. This is strongest when the benefits of efficiency gains to the electorate are dissipated widely, and the adjustment costs fall principally on an active political group. For example, in a situation of chronic overstaffing, the costs of adjustment will fall primarily on organized labour. The political power of such interest groups will determine how far the electorate's concerns are transmitted into political action to reform the SOEs. It is straightforward, and historically accurate, to imagine situations in which the electorate is dissatisfied with the performance of the sector, but the power of those to whom the rents from inefficient SOEs are accruing will ensure that the general concern is not addressed. However, as popular support for privatization has increased, so the electoral cost of ignoring the pressure for reform from the electorate *qua* consumers has grown so as to ensure that reform and privatization emerge at least as covert objectives of government.

Such conflicts are replicated at subsequent and lower links in the chain. The problems are similar to standard agency problems in industrial economics, namely those of asymmetric information on the effort level of the enterprise management, and of the consequent ability of the management to extract rent from their control of information. However, public sector organizations face three particular problems: the first is that traditionally there are many links in the agency chain, and agents are often responsible to more than one principal. Second, the links between inputs (i.e. effort and efficiency) and outputs (profitability) are frequently weak. This arises both from the complexity of the 'general equilibrium' objective function and also from the fact that price-setting is frequently controlled. Finally, proscriptions on the use of performance-related pay often deprive public sector organizations of one of the most important instruments available to private sector principals to influence the actions of the agent.[13]

Principal–agent relations: the private sector
How, then, will a change in the objective function of the principal, brought about by the transfer of asset ownership to the private sector, alter the performance of management? Other than the direct effect of curtailing some of the interventions that governments can make in an enterprise by strengthening the barriers between politicians and mangers,[14, 15] the arguments for private ownership are based on

the simplification and streamlining of the agency chain, and greater flexibility in the design of incentive-efficient contracts. At the extreme, if the owners are also the managers of the enterprise, or if the owners have complete information on the effects of managers' actions on enterprise performance, then it would be possible for shareholders to monitor management and sanction its actions accordingly. However, as with incomplete (or costly) information and/or multiple shareholders (as with a public share issue), the situation is less simple. Specifically there is a free-rider problem, leading to sub-optimally low monitoring of management, since no individual has the incentive to incur the cost of monitoring when s/he benefits only to the extent of his or her shareholding. A standard instrument to ameliorate this problem is the board of directors, who act for the shareholders as a whole to enforce behaviour from management consistent with profit maximization. However, the creation of executive management structures produces further principal–agent relationships: hence, the continual process of innovation in management structures in the private sector can be seen as an attempt to find the most efficient incentive contracts in the face of inherent principal–agent problems.

A second method by which shareholders can, in theory, ensure that management performs in a manner consistent with profit maximization is through the threat of takeovers. In an efficient capital market, share prices accurately reflect performance so that management inefficiency results in share values lower than the profit-maximizing level. A 'hostile bidder' could then buy the shares at this level and earn a profit on the takeover by enforcing appropriate management behaviour. Failure to perform renders the company liable to a hostile bid: hence the threat of takeover creates a self-regulating incentive scheme.[16] Thus, the effectiveness of the capital market in imposing managerial discipline requires, first, that share prices accurately reflect current asset values and, second, that the number of players in the market is sufficient for takeover threats to be credible. It should be noted, however, that empirical work done on takeovers and mergers is somewhat inconclusive, suggesting not only that post-takeover profitability improvements were negligible, but, more significantly, that the best barrier against a hostile takeover is size.[17] The larger are privatization sales relative to average market size, the weaker the takeover threat will be in automatically regulating post-privatization performance.

Before concluding this discussion on principal–agent relationships it is important to note that such relationships will not merely come into play in the management of SOEs, but also in the management of the privatization process. As demonstrated in the country studies, the power of each link in the chain to influence the actions of the other players will have an important impact on the form of the privatization process. Thus, such principal–agent problems are as much a feature of the execution of a privatization programme as they are of the direct management of enterprises.

Though we have not attempted to formalize any of these ideas, the foregoing discussion on the links between ownership and performance has illustrated how the returns to the property rights of individual owners of the enterprise can, as a result of incomplete control over the actions of agents at various levels, be easily dissipated. Intrinsically there is no difference in the fundamental mechanism through which this dilution occurs between the public and private sector. Rather, differing performance outcomes are brought about by a variety of factors concerning the nature of the objective functions of public and private owners, and the types of organizational structures through which management of the enterprises is instrumented. The difference between ownership forms is thus a question of orders of magnitude, and in assessing the impact of privatization on enterprise efficiency, the relative information requirements and the complexity of the different principal–agent relationships will be the overriding determinants.

Markets, competition and performance

Though market liberalization and the promotion of competition are neither necessary nor sufficient conditions for privatization, they are often closely linked. The link occurs because a chief determinant of information costs is the degree of competitiveness in the market. Competition generates information and lowers its cost for the owners of firms in the market (regardless of ownership), and it is the lower information costs which enhance efficiency as monitoring of management improves. Thus, changes in enterprise performance have more to do with the nature of competition than with the form of ownership. In this section we examine the effects of competition on performance: first, the extent to which the existence of a competitive market environment facilitates greater control of management through the reduction in information costs and, second, the way in which competition drives prices towards their welfare-maximizing level by eliminating monopoly profits. Finally we consider the extent to which competition can be denied, and the consequent role for market regulation.

Competition between firms in the same market means that prices and profits reveal information about the costs of an enterprise, and in particular about the efficiency of input use. With no other market referent the principal is unable to determine whether, say, a fall in profits is due to worsening demand or inefficiency on the part of management. If the market is competitive, then profit and price information from other firms will assist the principal to determine the amount of slack. Thus the information generated by competition improves the efficiency of management supervision and reward; therefore, by extension, the weaker the competitive forces, the weaker the signal of the link between inputs and outputs. It is the weakening of this information signal which leads to the view that 'the reward of monopoly is a quiet life'.

Thus competition can have direct effects on the internal efficiency of the firm. However, its main effect is the elimination of monopoly profits. A useful starting-point for an analysis of this aspect of competition is the theory of 'contestable markets' which identifies the conditions required to ensure that firms operate efficiently (both in terms of managerial or cost-reducing efficiency, and also in terms of welfare-improving pricing and investment (see Baumol et al., 1982). In essence a contestable market is one in which any firm is continuously exposed to actual or threatened competition from efficient producers who can enter the market at low cost, undercut the incumbent's price and acquire market share. The threat of this profit-reducing competition is thus the spur to efficient operations by all firms in the market.

Though contestability is evidently not a realistic description of markets in developed (let alone developing) countries, it serves as a useful benchmark against which to assess barriers to competition existing in most markets, and provides a guideline to assess the likely outcome of programmes of privatization.

Barriers to entry and maintenance of monopoly powers

Contestability relies on the threat of market entry being the catalyst for competition. Its antithesis, entry-deterrence, is thus clearly central to the maintenance of monopoly or oligopolistic profits, and to the efficiency arguments for privatization.

In some cases markets are natural monopolies where, for a given level of demand, cost and technological factors, a single firm can produce the required

required output more efficiently than two or more firms. Traditionally, many areas of SOE operation have been regarded as natural monopolies, especially in small economies: we can think in particular of the utilities, transport and communications networks, and some highly capital-intensive production activities such as steel-making and cement.[18] The key point is that, given the economics of the industry, competition will be absent regardless of the type of ownership: thus privatization *per se* may not alter performance significantly. Such a possibility leads to the issue of regulation, which we discuss later.

Barriers to entry and the maintenance of monopolistic profits can occur even when the industry is not a natural monopoly. This form of entry-deterrence – known generally as strategic entry-deterrence – allows an incumbent firm (or firms) in a market (regardless of the nature of the ownership) to maintain its (their) dominant market position in a number of ways. The industrial economics literature contains numerous studies of forms of strategic entry-deterrence, although all involve the incumbent using various instruments to increase the costs of production and market entry so as to make it unprofitable for new entrants to compete. Patenting, advertising, brand proliferation, technology choice, capital intensity, product dumping, loss-leading and predatory pricing are all used as means of deterring entry to the market.[19] In addition, there is a similarly rich literature on forms of collusive behaviour aimed at maintaining duopoly or oligopoly power. Whilst the literature on entry-deterrence is vast, the results are relatively straightforward, and are equally applicable to strategic and collusive behaviour. The scope for entry-deterrence depends on four key factors: the elasticity of demand for the product, the scope for technological substitution and cost reduction, the access to credit to allow the firm to survive through periods of intense (but unsustainable) price competition, and the enforceability of collusive behaviour. In general, the more elastic the demand for the product, and the greater the choice of production technologies, the less vulnerable is a market to strategic entry-deterrence and thus the more open it is to competition. Similarly the larger the incumbent, and the greater its access to financial resources, the more able it is to indulge in 'painful' strategic behaviour to maintain its monopoly position, while the broader the range of instruments available (and the weaker the anti-trust or regulatory regime) the more sustainable is entry-deterring collusion.

In the light of these theoretical results a number of features concerning the likely effects of competition emerge as salient to an analysis of privatization in developing countries. First, there are a significant number of sectors where SOEs dominate. Many of these are natural monopolies (at least in the medium term) and they are therefore unlikely to feel the effects of competition. Second, those which are not natural monopolies dominate by virtue of their size, and often their access to technology and credit. Thus, while there are a number of sectors where the scope for effective competition is high (for example, in the industrial, manufacturing and service sectors), significant barriers to entry, either 'natural' or strategic, are likely to prevail. Third, the number of sectors within the economy where the extent of competition is sufficient to generate efficient outcomes is small, especially in lower-income developing economies. Finally, one of the most common features of small economies is the prevalence of interlocking directorates. Often senior officials, financiers and eminent business people sit on the boards of many different public and private enterprises, and are thus in a position to promote collusive behaviour.

It is apparent therefore that privatization in smaller developing economies cannot be analysed within the simple property-rights and contestability paradigms. Changing ownership itself will not be sufficient, and may not even be necessary to elicit performance improvements. Rather, competition and regulation policy will emerge as major determinants of the effect that privatization will have on economic efficiency.

Regulation

In the previous sections we reviewed the arguments concerning how changes in ownership and the effects of competition may be expected to lead to improved monitoring of management and thus an improvement in internal efficiency. We argued that if markets are competitive and there are no externalities then there will be no difference in the information costs to public and private principals and internal efficiency will be unaffected by the form of ownership (except, perhaps, as a result of the differing complexity of the agency chain), assuming, of course, that the public owners are not pursuing non-commercial objectives. However, we then proceeded to consider the extent to which private monopoly or oligopoly positions can be created and/or maintained such that, in addition to reductions in internal efficiency, there will be losses in allocative efficiency, as prices are maintained above the marginal cost of production. The presence of monopoly means that the relevant comparison of ownership forms is between public ownership with internal regulation and private ownership operating under market regulation.

The question of regulation is thus concerned with the problem of ensuring that a firm (whether public or private) acts in a manner consistent with social welfare. Regulation of public firms is traditionally (and often sub-optimally) undertaken by fiat, through public (non-market) determination of pricing and output decisions. The regulation of private companies, in contrast, generally operates through public fiscal or legislative interventions operating within broad market-determined parameters. The essential feature of the regulatory problem is that in general the regulator (i.e. the government) does not have the same degree of information about the market as the firm itself has.[20] Thus the challenge is to design a regulatory system which creates incentives for the private enterprise to produce while at the same time curtailing monopoly power. In this sense regulation is in itself a principal–agent problem, and many of the arguments discussed above are relevant. Clearly, if the social cost of regulation of a private sector industry outweighs the internal and allocative efficiency gains from privatization, then it is not obvious that privatization should be undertaken. This consideration is of central importance in developing countries where the capacity of the (potential) regulator to put in place and maintain effective regulatory structures is usually quite limited. This is particularly pertinent when governments in smaller countries are considering the sale of enterprises to foreign companies. Frequently such governments will find themselves in a situation where the firm to be regulated is larger and more economically powerful than the government itself. In order to formalize this point we illustrate the generic regulation-choice problem by using a simple model developed by Shapiro and Willig (1990).

Regulation v. public ownership of a monopolistic enterprise

The purpose of this model is to illustrate the factors which will, *ceteris paribus*, determine the choice between retaining a monopolistic enterprise under public ownership and privatizing it and subjecting it to regulation. The model shows how this decision is based on an estimate of the relative magnitude of two principal–agent effects, namely the extent to which government can control public sector managers versus the extent to which private sector managers can capture rents from the regulatory process. We consider the information sets and incentives facing three groups, namely the government,[21] public sector officials (as managers) and private owners. There are three types of private information: (i) the externalities and political objectives attached to the enterprise's activities (e.g. consumer surplus, environmental considerations, national security considerations, etc.), denoted ψ; (ii) the efficiency-reducing private agenda of the public officials, ϵ; and (iii) the firm's cost, demand and other market conditions, θ. The model is based on the following diagram.

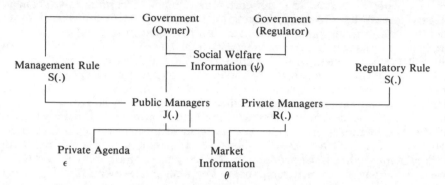

The profitability of the firm is a function of actions, x, and the nature of the cost and demand conditions, θ. Throughout we assume that profits, π, are increasing in θ and x, π_θ, $\pi_x > 0$. We can assess the two forms of ownership being considered by the government in the decision to privatize.

(i) The enterprise directly managed by public officials. Here, by dint of their role as managers of the firm, public officials have information θ on demand conditions, and under public ownership the total profits accrue directly to the treasury, $\pi(x, \theta)$. As employees of a state-owned enterprise, the managers pursue the public objectives ψ, the benefits accruing from which are S(x, ψ). Overall government welfare is thus:

$$W^G = S(x, \psi) + \pi^G(x, \theta)$$

However, the public officials also pursue their own private goals defined as J(x, ϵ), where $J_x < 0$. Total welfare under public ownership, determined by the outcome of the principal–agent game between government and the public sector managers, is thus:

$$V^G = W^G - \alpha J(x, \epsilon)$$

where α is a measure of the extent to which public officials can pursue their own agenda. $W^G - V^G = \alpha J(x, \epsilon)$ is simply the measure of enterprise inefficiency arising from the rent that public officials can extract because government cannot observe ϵ.

(ii) Regulated private enterprise. In view of this loss government may consider the alternative option, namely the privatization of the enterprise and the introduction of a regulatory procedure to ensure that the social objectives, ψ, are met. Here, for simplicity, we assume that the government directly fulfils the role of regulator.[22] Now that the enterprise is no longer directly run by the public officials, only the private owners observe θ. The regulator must therefore establish a policy which meets the social welfare objectives, but still allows the firm to cover its costs in the 'worst-case' demand environment (so that the output is actually produced). This necessarily yields the firm more profit than is optimal (i.e. if government had access to θ) in all cases where demand is higher or costs lower than in the worst case. In this situation the firm chooses its optimal response

to the regulatory rule and as a result the privatized enterprise will earn informational rents, $R(x, \rho)$, which are always greater than or equal to zero. As a result of regulated private ownership, the welfare function is:

$$W^P = S(x, \psi) + \pi^P(x, \theta) - R(x, \rho)$$

If we assume, *ceteris paribus*, that the neutrality result holds so that the dividend yield from the asset under public ownership $\pi^G(x, \theta)$ is equal to $\pi^P(x, \theta)$, the capitalized value of the sale proceeds, then the difference between the two ownership regimes can be expressed simply as

$$W^P - W^G = \alpha J(x, \epsilon) - R(x, \rho)$$

Thus the privatization decision is between two competing second-best options, namely the welfare loss of public sector managerial inefficiency on the one hand, and the welfare loss of monopoly profits accruing through informational rents on the other.

This simple result underlines the central point that, in assessing the benefits of privatization when enterprises are capable of earning monopoly or oligopoly profits, the factors determining the decision will be: (i) the extent to which the public sector officials' actions deviate from the objectives of the government; (ii) the capacity of the public sector to design cost-effective and efficient regulatory schemes; and (iii) the extent to which private managers can extract and maintain informational rents. In many instances discussed in the case studies, governments have been faced with exactly this problem, but more often than not the emphasis has been placed on the first of these factors, occasionally to the complete exclusion of the other two. One of the less benign outcomes of this narrow focus has been the transfer of ownership (and monopoly control) to foreign private companies who, because of their size, have dominated the regulation game and effectively captured the regulatory process (see the discussion on Telecommunications of Jamaica in Chapter 4).

Regulation in practice

In general regulation has focused on the rate of return as a strategic variable with which to calibrate the monopoly profits of an enterprise and to trigger the extent of regulation. In this scheme, firms are allowed to make a maximum rate of return on capital (i.e. profit) over a certain period, which will be some mark-up over the market rate. The well-established Averch–Johnson (1962) model demonstrates how under these conditions firms will make decisions affecting their capital base with a view to altering the price they are allowed to charge. In particular rate-of-return regulation leads to over-capitalization, through which the firm obtains higher absolute profit but lower internal efficiency.

Whilst this is a special case, it again illustrates the essence of the regulatory problem, namely that the firm is generally much better informed than the regulator about firm-specific and market conditions. The regulatory challenge is to design an incentive scheme to exploit this superior information available to the managers. There are two general types of result in these models of regulation. The first arises where the regulator cannot observe the cost structure of the firm, and generally sets an allowable price which exceeds the socially optimal price. In this situation the firm is earning monopoly profits on its restricted information set.[23] The second result arises where the regulator is able to use competitive forces to push firms into revealing their information. Thus one role of competition in a world of incomplete information (even with dominant-firm advantages) is to generate comparative cost and efficiency information for the regulator (information which is harder to obtain from a monopolist), which can be used to improve the efficiency of the regulatory process.

This latter result underpins the case for franchising, where, although the market being regulated may be monopolistic, efficiency can be achieved by creating competition for the 'capture' of the monopoly market. The right to supply the market (the franchise) is won through a competitive bidding process whereby the contract is offered to the company with the best price–quality package. Franchising is an attractive and widely used way of combining competition and efficiency without a burdensome regulatory framework. However, there are certain problems, chiefly the danger of uncompetitive bidding, the problem of asset handover when the franchise changes hands, and the difficulty of contract specification and monitoring. Once again, these problems may well be exacerbated in the case of developing countries. In terms of uncompetitive bidding there are two factors at work, the first being the risk of collusion between bidder and regulator, and the second being incumbent advantage positions, where the arguments for strategic entry-deterrence may still apply *pari passu*, especially if the incumbent has an information advantage. One particular issue which we shall discuss later is the apparently limited use of franchising in the privatization programmes in the countries covered here, even though market conditions may be more conducive to franchising than to other forms of privatization.

This section has covered the main economic arguments linking privatization with public finance enhancement and economic efficiency. We have argued that there is no intrinsic difference between public and private ownership, but rather that observed differences in performance are a reflection of differences in the objective functions of different owners, and in the principal–agent relationships between asset owners and managers. Consequently we have suggested that the efficiency impact of privatization will depend on the nature of product demand, the degree of competition in goods markets, and the capacity to put in place effective regulatory structures. We now turn to those objectives of privatization which, while broader in their scope, are not so closely linked to the core theoretical debate on public versus private ownership and control of assets. These objectives are private sector development, capital market development, income distribution considerations, and compliance with the conditionality of external creditors.

2.2.3 *Private sector development*

While the shrinking of the public sector and the containment of fiscal deficits frequently dominate thinking on privatization in the short run, their analogue is equally important. In developing countries privatization is seen as an instrument to 'crowd-in' a nascent private sector, and thus reverse the downward trend in aggregate private sector investment which has been such a characteristic of the 1980s. It is viewed therefore as a means not only of enhancing the marginal efficiency of existing investment (by switching its source of supply), but also as a means of increasing the total volume of investment. This 'crowding-in' argument is, of course, intrinsically linked to the broader issues of deregulation, state shrinkage, and financial liberalization policies, all of which are aimed at promoting higher domestic savings and improving their intermediation to productive investment. Part of this impetus for privatization derives from the feeling that 'getting the prices right' in terms of deregulation and financial liberalization may be a necessary condition for growth in private sector investment, but alone it may not be sufficient. Thus the creation of an enabling environment may need to be primed, in a Keynesian fashion, through the privatization of state-owned enterprises. This view is lucidly expressed in the Government of Malaysia's guidelines on privatization which link the two efficiency elements of privatization thus (Government of Malaysia, 1985):

. . . privatization is expected to promote competition, improve efficiency and increase the productivity of the services. [In addition] privatization, by stimulating private entrepreneurship and investment, is expected to accelerate the rate of growth of the economy.

The arguments surrounding the impact of privatization on efficiency of investment and service delivery have been fully discussed in earlier sections: those for 'crowding-in' are, however, less clear and less well defined. Three general arguments can be advanced. First, as a result of extensive cross-subsidization, soft budget constraints, and administrative restrictions conferring preferential market access, state-owned enterprises frequently enjoy high degrees of protection. The removal of such barriers as a result of a programme of privatization and deregulation will be accompanied by an inflow of private investment seeking to exploit these previously protected opportunities for monopoly profit. The analysis of this process has been dealt with above in relating privatization to market structures. Second, and related, if the expected rate of return to private investment is a negative function of market uncertainty, then a reduction in this uncertainty will boost investment. Frequently, public investment decisions are made by fiat. As a result, price and output levels will diverge from real resource costs, and will be unresponsive to demand conditions. Even if allocation decisions are market-based, product prices may be distorted by the web of cross-subsidization in the goods and factor markets. These non-market decisions distort price signals and consequently increase the degree of uncertainty facing private investors contemplating market entry.[24] A reversion to market price signals through privatization will thus be accompanied by a reduction of uncertainty, thereby raising the expected rate of return to domestic fixed capital investment. The third way in which 'crowding-in' is expected to occur is less precise and relies on the extent to which privatization may alter the degree of risk aversion in the economy. Often subsumed in notions of 'corporate culture' or 'market orientation', the idea here is simply that by re-establishing the link between economic risk and reward the private sector will be induced to switch from asset accumulation in the form of precautionary assets (e.g. fixed income deposits) to more risky domestic capital assets. This asset-switching effect is important when governments seek to reverse private capital flight which has occurred under earlier economic control regimes, and a number of countries have, in fact, designed their privatization programmes around attempts to promote the direct repatriation of domestic capital which had been previously exported.

2.2.4 *Capital market development*
Closely related to the previous point is the view that privatization, especially in a number of smaller countries, will serve as a means whereby local capital markets may be either developed or revitalized and domestic savings mobilization enhanced. A commonly perceived problem of many of the smaller emerging capital markets is the shortage of tradable stock, and augmentation of the supply of stock through the sale of government equity has been seen as one way through which the capital market may be effectively 'kick-started' into action. That privatization and capital market development have become fused in the minds of policy-makers is understandable, and, indeed, there can be little argument that privatization, especially if it is to occur on a large scale, will be facilitated by the presence of properly functioning capital markets. But privatization can, and often does, occur both in the absence of adequate formal capital markets and/or without the intermediation of capital markets even where such markets exist and function well.[25] Similarly, capital markets can be (and in many countries have

been) developed in quite a healthy fashion without privatization programmes. Nevertheless, privatization is often viewed as offering opportunities for linkages with capital market development. However, it can have potentially malign effects on capital market development, and can, if mishandled, weaken the capacity of nascent capital markets to intermediate and manage the risks resulting from public-to-private asset transfers. This is analysed in more detail in Chapter 5.

2.2.5 Income distribution

Privatization will rarely have a neutral effect on the distribution of income. Consequently, the perceived implications of the sale of assets for income and wealth will be a major determinant of the privatization process. In some instances the issue is made explicit, as in the case of Malaysia where one of the main stated objectives of privatization is to promote the attainment of the New Economic Programme income distribution targets. More frequently such discrimination, determining, for example, the relative access of domestic and foreign participants, is implicitly achieved through the design of the programme. For example, if divestiture is effected through private sales there will generally be a concentration of equity wealth. On the other hand, the distribution of shares freely to all electors will initially have a positive effect on wealth distribution. Indeed, one of the most common phenomena in privatization share issues in both developed and developing countries is the 'underpricing' of shares so as to achieve a favourable wealth distribution. Again this issue will be dealt with in Chapter 5.

There are other, more complex income-distribution effects at work, however. As we shall discuss in greater detail in the next chapter, one of the dominant forces leading to the creation of large SOE sectors originally was the desire to address concerns over income distribution and to redress the balance of economic power towards the government's political constituency. This was achieved through a number of mechanisms, i.e. the expansion of employment, fringe benefits, price subsidies, etc. State-owned enterprises became key instruments for the allocation of rents to favoured groups. The thrust of pro-privatization arguments lies, however, in the efficiency-enhancing removal of such rents, and thus in many cases privatization is seen as antithetical to these earlier forms of government behaviour. The key point here, as the case studies show, is that the evolution of privatization programmes has been determined by the attempts of governments to reconcile the twin objectives of maintaining control over the allocation of such rents while achieving the desired efficiency gains (see for example, Bienen and Waterbury, 1989, and Glade, 1989). This can in some cases result in the paralysis of the entire programme, or in other cases can manifest itself in the complex nature of the sale process. We shall examine these issues in more detail in Chapter 4.

2.2.6 Meeting adjustment conditionalities

The emergence of policy-based lending in the 1980s has seen privatization being drawn into the intricate relationships between developing countries and their external creditors, who rapidly embraced the policy. For example, as Table 2.1 shows, the decade to 1989 saw the World Bank involved in 143 adjustment loans directed towards SOE reform worldwide, of which half included privatization components. Put simply, in such cases governments pursue privatization in order to have access to such donor assistance, and to ensure that aid disbursements are not jeopardized. However, the relationship is rarely straightforward, and in practice, though progress in implementing privatization policies has rarely matched the expectations of the creditors, aid disbursements have not been compromised. More often, the credibility of the donors (for example, the World Bank and IMF)

Table 2.1 *World Bank lending for SOE reform and privatization*
(No. of loans by type of loan and region)

	SALs	SECALs	TALs	PELs	PETALs	TOTAL	Privatization Component	Value[c] US $m
Africa	30	17	21	9	2	79	45[a]	1,687.1
Latin America	14	4	10	5	–	33	18[b]	1,965.1
Asia & Pacific	5	3	–	1	–	9	7	870.0
Middle East & N. Africa	6	11	3	2	–	22	4	830.0
TOTAL	55	35	34	17	2	143	74	5,352.2

Source: A. Galal: 1990.

Notes
a) Includes $85m (2 SALs) to Malawi.
b) Includes $191m (3 SALs, 1 PEL, 1 TAL) to Jamaica.
c) Total value of lending with privatization component.

Key:
SAL (Structural Adjustment Loan)
SECAL (Sector Adjustment Loan)
TAL (Technical Assistance Loan)
PEL (Public Enterprise Loan)
PETAL (Public Enterprise Technical Assistance Loan)

vis-à-vis OECD governments and other developing country governments requires that slippage, non-compliance and amendment of privatization conditions are tolerated (see Mosley, Harrigan and Toye, 1991). The pursuit of privatization within this framework can, and does, create distortions and problems for its implementation, and we shall return to these issues in Chapter 4.

2.3 The impact of privatization

Despite the wealth of discussion and theoretical argument relating to the merits of public versus private ownership, actual evidence to date is less than conclusive. In this section we aim briefly to marshal the existing evidence in order to provide a background for the country studies. Moreover, the evidence focuses exclusively on the link between privatization and efficiency. No comprehensive body of evidence exists to assess either the direct and indirect public finance effects of privatization or any of the subsidiary objectives. While country-study analyses provide the detail of individual programmes, they often lack readily generalizable conclusions. Numerous attempts have been made to draw more rigorous and generalized quantitative conclusions on the issue of public versus private ownership but they have faced a number of difficulties, some of which we shall discuss here.

The first problem facing any research into privatization is that of data availability and measurement. Primarily the poor financial and technological data for SOEs prior to privatization make evaluating changes consequent on the transfer of ownership difficult.[26] Furthermore, even if the data are available, it may not be possible to draw any firm conclusions because of the time lags involved in the assessment of changes in performance. The effects of a transfer in ownership may not be felt for a period of months or years, and the translation of these effects into measurable quanta may take longer (especially given the publication lags on company accounts). While this represents a general problem, it is particularly the case in assessing the privatization experience of the 1980s: to a significant extent we are not yet in a position to evaluate fully the effect of privatization.[27]

Notwithstanding the issues of measurement and data availability, we are confronted by a more fundamental problem, namely that, as discussed above, standard economic theory in general has nothing to say on ownership *per se*. It offers no clearly defined and testable hypotheses, but rather establishes the links between ownership and performance through a series of related theories and hypotheses concerning the nature of incentives, agency problems, financial constraints and profit-maximizing behaviour. Inference is therefore necessarily complicated, and as Killick and Commander (1988: 102) stress:

> . . . while mainstream economic theory does point to the preferability of competition, it is actually silent on the ownership issue . . . there is, of course, no necessary connection between the two.

This problem is underscored by the technical complexity of distinguishing within the data the effects of privatization *per se* from the host of liberalization and SOE reform measures that have frequently accompanied privatization. One of the most complex relationships to disentangle is the relative effects of the pre-privatization 'clean-up' of the enterprise and the privatization itself. For example, Vickers and Yarrow (1988) show the extent to which in the UK major improvements in commercial performance occurred prior to privatization as the public sector prepared the enterprise for sale.

A third measurement problem arises with the construction of counterfactuals – what would have happened in the absence of privatization. In some cases this is a relatively easy issue. In the situation in which, say, the government chooses to sell one textile firm out of a number of similar firms, then the performance of the remaining public sector textile firms will provide the basis for a counterfactual. Matters are more complex in the case of monopolies, and in particular the natural monopolies where there is by definition no counterfactual comparator. Further, matters are again complicated by the effect of associated reforms, especially in terms of price deregulation and where the monopoly is a price setter in domestic markets, and thus profit cannot easily be used as an indicator of 'welfare'.

Fourth, in any form of comparative analysis, there is a problem of selection bias. For example, if, as is the case, governments embark on their privatization programme by selling the most viable enterprises, the resulting performance effects may be overstated *vis-à-vis* the impact of privatization on the SOE sector in total.

To get at the effects of ownership on performance two main methods have been employed. The first is to track an individual enterprise through time in order to assess the impact of its sale on performance. As noted, however, given that many privatization programmes are in their early stages, there are very limited data available to do justice to this method. The second approach is to abstract from the specific question of the effects of privatization as a process in order to focus more simply on the relationship between performance and ownership, since ultimately it is this that is of concern to policy-makers. In this type of empirical work researchers generally regress performance variables (financial, technical, etc.) against a measure of ownership, while controlling for a host of characteristics of the firm or industry, or country. The standard model is of the form

$$P = \alpha_0 + \alpha_1 D + \alpha_2 X + \epsilon$$

where P is the measure of performance; D the ownership variable; and X a vector of relevant characteristics, both the nature of the firm and the macroeconomic and policy environment in which it operates. The focus of the work is, essentially, to estimate the size and sign of the coefficient α_1. Of the two main approaches, the first uses direct comparisons of identified companies operating in similar markets (and thus for whom the vector of variables X is similar). A number of studies further distinguish the ownership variable between fully private companies, SOEs and joint-venture operations.

Results

The number of empirical studies following this latter method is quite vast and we shall not attempt a survey here. Comprehensive surveys, such as Vickers and Yarrow (1988) for developed economies, and Bouin and Michalet (1991) and Millward (1988) for developing countries, review these studies; here therefore we restrict ourselves to a brief summary of the main results, and focus on the problems of drawing inferences from these results for developing countries.

A number of important results come from head-to-head studies in industrialized economies, most notably with Caves and Christensen's (1980) study of the two Canadian railroad companies operating in a relatively deregulated environment, and a number of studies of the (more regulated) air transport sector in Australia (Davis, 1971, 1977; Forsyth and Hocking, 1980; Kirby and Albon, 1985). While the Canadian study suggested that in the presence of a competitive market ownership was not an important determinant of performance, the studies for Australia are less conclusive. There efficiency seemed higher in the private sector as opposed to the public, but even so the extent of the regulation so greatly reduced the overall efficiency of operations relative to similar efficiency levels overseas that the relative performance differences seemed less significant.

Similar results emerge in studies of monopolies, where the evidence suggests that, regulatory frameworks notwithstanding, there is no clear difference in performance between publicly and privately owned utilities (see Vickers and Yarrow, 1991). One of the biggest international studies (focusing only on large companies) is less ambiguous, however (see Boardman and Vining, 1989). In their study of 500 firms in 1983 (of which 419 were private, 58 public, and 23 jointly owned), they found that, in general, state-owned enterprise performance (measured only in terms of financial performance) was worse than that of private companies across a range of financial and productivity measures.[28]

Millward's (1988) review of performance studies in developing-country industries draws similar conclusions. Examining differences in technical efficiency, Hill (1982) on the Indonesian textile sector, Tyler (1979) on the Brazilian plastics and steel industry, Hughes (1990) on the Jamaican aluminium sector, and Kim (1981) on manufacturing in Tanzania, all arrive at similar conclusions: public ownership has a small, negative, but statistically insignificant effect on technical efficiency, with overall performance being principally determined by size. Strong diminishing returns to scale are frequently observed which, since public enterprises have tended to be larger than their private counterparts, becomes a key explanation of the apparently worse performance of SOEs. However, it must be noted that such results may be distorted by a sample selection bias since often enterprises have fallen under public ownership as a result of public rescue following financial crisis under private sector operation.

One relevant result which emerges from the above studies, and in particular from the analysis in Tanzania, concerns the relative efficiency of foreign-owned enterprises. Foreign capital, management and choice of technology tend to be more efficient and more profitable than domestic capital, either public or private. A qualification on this result is provided by Grosh's (1990) study of manufacturing in Kenya. Here the evidence suggests that, while there is very little difference between the performance of private manufacturing enterprises and those in which government has a majority control, neither group is as efficient as joint-venture operations in which the government takes a minority equity position, with the majority equity and management in the hands of (often foreign) private investors. This latter group (referred to as quasi-public firms) has a much lower rate of effective protection and a lower domestic resource cost than both public and private companies, whilst still retaining a higher rate of return. One of the valuable aspects of this study is the way in which it explores many of the problems noted above. For example, in the case of Kenya many of the public companies under examination have become so simply as a result of 'rescue operations' on the part of the state in order to protect employment, etc. As a result the SOE sector is dominated by old-vintage enterprises, operating in economically sub-optimal locations. This will inevitably depress their aggregate performance. In this respect we can note the ongoing work of Bhaskar (1991) in assessing the effects of ownership in the Bangladesh manufacturing sector. Here the sample selection problem is avoided since, following wholesale nationalization in 1972, the choice of which enterprises to privatize has (apparently) been made on a relatively random basis thereby providing the researcher with a relatively unbiased sample consisting of both public and private firms. Initial indications, however, fail to alter radically the conclusions from other studies.

Thus, the empirical evidence on the effect of ownership is less than categorical. However a number of conclusions emerge which reinforce the central argument of this book. The first is that, *ceteris paribus*, in relatively competitive markets the evidence suggests that private enterprise is rarely (if ever) less efficient or less profitable than public enterprise, and more frequently is significantly more efficient or profitable than comparable public enterprise. Beyond this conclusion the results are less clear, although this ambiguity serves to underline the central argument that ownership by itself is rarely the dominant determinant of performance. In particular, the influence of the regulatory and competitive environment (particularly in the utility sectors) greatly overrides the impact of ownership on enterprise performance.

2.4 Conclusions

This chapter has served to provide the theoretical economic context within which privatization can be assessed. It has outlined the major objectives assigned to privatization as a policy instrument, and has reviewed the key economic relationships which are expected to provide the transmission mechanism from privatization to enhanced performance and efficiency. In some cases this transmission is theoretically clear and precise; in others, the mechanisms are less quantifiable and turn on the broader issues of policy credibility, government reputation, investor expectations, the management of economic coalitions and the allocation of rents. We have also attempted to reflect some of the empirical evidence which has emerged in an attempt to quantify the overall efficiency impact of private ownership. The evidence is plagued by often intractable measurement problems but does suggest that there is some discernible positive effect of private ownership on the financial performance of companies. Little evidence has yet been adduced on the broader effects of privatization on macroeconomic performance. The question which remains unanswered therefore is: why, in the face of such neutral evidence, has the developing world (and its creditors) embraced privatization as such an article of faith in economic adjustment? Part of the answer lies in a search for credible alternatives in response to the evidently parlous state of the SOE sector in so many developing countries, to which we turn in Chapter 3. However, we believe that a fuller and more interesting explanation lies in the persistent failure to extract from the evidence of, and theoretical arguments for, privatization an understanding of how the key transmission mechanisms relating privatization and enterprise performance are altered when privatization is implemented within the generally thin market structures prevalent in developing countries.

Notes

1. See, for example, the definitions used *inter alia* by Pirie (1986), Glade (1986), and Berg and Shirley (1987).
2. Conditional, of course, on the constraints imposed by the economic and regulatory environment faced by the enterprise.
3. It is interesting that in Malaysia even this has been compromised by the existence of comprehensive government underwriting for the largest BOT schemes.
4. Pirie (1986) identifies some 22 different forms of privatization, many of which have only a limited relationship with the definition suggested here.
5. *World Development Report* (1988) notes that for a sample of 25 developing countries the median contribution of the SOE sector to the total public sector deficit was 48%.
6. The initial cash payment can be thought of in terms of 'sweeteners' – subsidies, debt write-offs, etc, rather than a cash payment.
7. Although, as will be discussed later, they do allow for the pure effects of the 'dynamic efficiency' of private ownership.
8. Vernon (1988) suggests that it was this form of crowding-out caused by wholesale privatization in Chile which led to the bankruptcy of many of the very enterprises that had been sold to the private sector under the programme.
9. The discounted value of the profit stream in the hands of the government would be higher than in the hands of the private sector, and thus the maximum price the private sector would be prepared to pay would be lower than the minimum the government would sell for.
10. Consider again, for example, how the collapse of much of the commercial sector in Chile in 1982–3 was accentuated by the excessive leverage of many privatized assets.
11. This form of argument derives from the work of Alchian and Demsetz (1972).
12. See, for example, Glade's (1991) discussion of the efficient operation of SOEs in Latin America.
13. For a comprehensive review of the issues of principal–agent relationships and incentive design see Rees (1985).
14. Frequent confusion arises between privatization and liberalization. There are many interventions a government can make which affect the running of the firm *after* privatization, including output price controls, penal taxation, interest- and exchange-rate policies, etc. It is often assumed that these will be removed during the privatization process, but there is no necessary reason why they have to be. Thus, the removal of government interference as a goal of privatization must restrict itself to the removal of more direct, firm-specific interventions.
15. It is sometimes the case that technocratic arms of government have used, or intend to use, privatization as a method of removing SOEs from parts of government (especially line ministries) they consider to be more prone to interference.
16. There is, however, a free-rider problem here also since a (small) shareholder receiving a bid by a raider has an immediate incentive to hold on to the shares and free-ride the capital gain brought about by the hostile bid (assuming that the share price will rise as a result of the new management). But if all shareholders attempt to free-ride the bid will not take place and thus management is not 'disciplined'. However, strategic behaviour, compulsory acquisition orders, and limited legal protection of minority shareholder interests can combine, and have combined, to dilute the effect of the free-rider problem, thereby re-establishing in part the link between internal efficiency and takeover threats.
17. This phenomenon has probably been diluted somewhat in recent years by the growth in the leveraged buy-outs and junk-bond dealings.
18. Although technological innovation has shrunk the realm of natural monopolies, especially in the telecommunications sector.
19. See for example Waterson (1984) and the references therein.
20. Clearly, if the regulator had full information and sufficient power s/he could compel the firm to act in a first-best manner all the time.

21. For simplicity we ignore the possibility of agency problems which may exist between the objectives of the electorate and the actions of the government. This does not alter the essential elements of the result.
22. In general, this will not be the case and the regulatory function will be carried out by the public officials who will retain their own private agenda. As with note 21, this is done to keep the model simple, but as a result sidesteps the important problem of *'quis custodiet ipsos custodes?'* [who guards the guardians?].
23. There are a host of more complex models which extend the simple case – see Vickers and Yarrow (1988) for a summary.
24. This phenomenon is, of course, exacerbated to the extent that the government is able to alter market conditions by fiat. One of the major elements of uncertainty facing private capital during the 1970s was the risk of government appropriation of assets and their profit stream. Combined with the effects of poor macroeconomic management and financial liberalization, this contributed to high levels of capital flight.
25. In fact, our evidence would suggest that, in terms of number and scale of enterprises sold, non-market sales predominate, even when capital markets exist and are quite well developed.
26. One of the major elements of many SOE reform/privatization programmes is an attempt to create a consistent database for the SOE sector. Under public ownership audit requirements are frequently ignored and the compilation of accurate and timely financial data is rarely a priority.
27. It may be noted that only late in 1989 did the World Bank embark on its first major post-privatization performance evaluation exercise. The final results of this study are not expected to emerge until 1992 at the earliest.
28. Note that in these studies there is no systematic attempt to take into consideration the second-order economic effects attendant on the pursuit of employment or other objectives carried by the SOEs.

3 The Origins & Growth of the Public Sector

It has been the rapid, and for long unchecked, growth in the public sector which has provided the seeds for privatization to flower as a policy. For many developing countries including those covered by this book, the dominant feature of their post-independence economic history has been the rapid growth of the public sector. Public intervention in the economy was a *sine qua non* of policy throughout the 1960s and 1970s, and the SOE sector has been one of the most common instruments used to effect such intervention. The SOE sector has traditionally been a major consumer of resources and credit; is responsible for a major share of fixed capital formation; is one of the largest employers in many economies; and accounts in many cases for a large share of the public sector deficit. However, reliable data on the sector are difficult to obtain and are often compromised by differences in definition, and biased by inter-agency transfers and other off-budget resource flows. Estimates vary widely, but some strong trends emerge. Nellis (1986) conservatively estimates that, for a sample of sub-Saharan African countries, the contribution of the SOE sector to total GDP is 17%. He notes elsewhere that this may be low, and that it also masks a huge variance, with many cases (even outside the centrally planned economies) where the sector accounts for over 50% of total GDP (Nellis and Kikeri, 1989). The sector generally accounts for a similar proportion of gross investment, although in the smaller economies, especially in Africa, the share may be higher. The considerable presence of the sector is offset, however, by the flow of funds to it from other sectors of the economy. The SOE sector is rarely a generator of surplus funds, and on average is a net debtor with respect to central government (and through the government budget to the domestic and foreign private sector). A recent evaluation by the World Bank shows that, for a sample of 25 developing countries, the median SOE contribution to the overall public sector deficit was 48%.[1] Its share of domestic credit has been estimated at around 30% (Nellis and Kikeri, 1989), with a similar share of total external debt.[2] Table 3.1 shows how this pattern is reflected in the countries studied in this book.

The SOE sector is, however, frequently highly skewed and in general a small number of SOEs account for a large share of output, total employment and net profits or losses. For example, the aggregate total performance figure for the SOE sector in Malaysia (which as a whole is profitable) is highly distorted by the size and profitability of the national oil company, PETRONAS, whose turnover alone accounts for almost 30% of the total turnover of the 1100 SOEs in the country. Behind this aggregate lie a large number of poorly performing companies. A similar example comes from Jamaica where the combined budget of the 21 largest SOEs was equivalent to the total central government budget. The sector is similarly skewed in terms of its areas of involvement, especially in Africa. SOEs generally are dominant in the utilities sector – for example, 86% of utilities in

32 Adjusting Privatization

Table 3.1 *The share of the SOE sector in the economy*

Country	Year	No. of SOEs	SOE Output as % of GDP	SOE Investment as % of Total Investment	Employment
Jamaica	1985	640	20	11	–
Trinidad and Tobago	1985	46	16	26	13
Malaysia	1989	1158	25	5	–
Papua New Guinea	1989	40	10	8	–
Sri Lanka	1988	250	20	35	40
Kenya	1984	150	15	25	15
Malawi	1984	91	25	20	8

Source: Country case studies, Chapters 7–13.

Africa and 62% in Asia are publicly owned.[3] In Africa, however, public ownership also tends to dominate in the transport (41%) and mining sectors (55%) and is also a major player in the manufacturing sector (21%). Exposure in the manufacturing sector is significantly lower in Asia and the Caribbean where the indigenous private sector is generally more buoyant.[4] The dominant presence of the SOE sector across many sectors serves to underline the fact that SOE performance is as much a matter of macroeconomic management as it is of microeconomic efficiency.

The state-owned enterprise sectors in the countries studied in this book have followed similar paths, and the specific experiences of the different countries reflect the varying stages in development of each rather than any dissimilarity in government policy. The broadly common experience reflects the main political and economic concerns facing all developing countries over the last 30 years or so. To some extent the various responses to the crisis of the SOE sector, especially privatization initiatives, follow the same pattern in which divergence of approach mainly reflects underlying circumstances rather than fundamentally different objectives. However, as discussed later, the policy concerns and constraints which resulted in the creation of a large SOE sector are just as evident today: thus the privatization debate, at least in developing countries, is significantly motivated by the search for new instruments through which these same objectives can be pursued.

The stylized facts of the growth of the SOE sector in the countries covered here and its subsequent declining viability developed as follows. The initial period following Independence and lasting until the late 1960s saw only gradual growth in the sector, with the state taking an active role in the provision of naturally monopolistic services and, to some extent, in the purchase and marketing of primary sector outputs. The pervading strategy in other sectors was one of *laissez-faire* in which foreign capital and management played a dominant role – what was known as 'industrialization by invitation' or the 'Lewis strategy', with government participation outside its core areas being driven principally by reaction and political expediency rather than by an active policy of interventionism. By the late 1960s and early 1970s political thinking, often in response to measurably worsening income distribution and rising unemployment in these new economies, shifted towards more *étatiste* economic management, in which public sector investment and employment decisions were grounded in a more explicit welfare metric, and in which the interests of the indigenous population (or sub-groups thereof) were strongly represented.[5] The particularly favourable economic circumstances of the early 1970s assisted in the promotion of a rapid (and ultimately unsustainable) growth in the SOE sector based on these ideas. Strongly pro-active intervention, based on a mixture of government investment in new commercial activities, financial 'rescue' of ailing activities, and, to a much lesser extent, outright nationalization, was financed through the combination of the favourable shifts in the terms of trade facing developing countries in the mid-1970s and a high inflow of official and commercial foreign capital. By the end of the 1970s the SOE sectors were the dominant players in many of these economies.

As we stress in this book, ownership, whether public or private, is not in our evaluation the key determinant of enterprise performance and the efficiency of resource allocation. As such, the growth of the SOE sector need not be viewed as a problem. However, as is widely seen, the growth of the SOE sector during the 1970s has been matched by a decline in its level of financial viability and a concomitant rise in the net flow of resources to the sector. Its drain on public finances and the sclerotic effect the inefficiency of this large sector had on the rest of the economy meant that the problems facing governments in sustaining the SOE sector were not merely concerns about microeconomic efficiency, but rather had substantial macroeconomic effects on both the demand and supply sides of the economy. Consequently the sector's poor performance was seen as a major contributory factor to the alarming economic crisis emerging at this time.

By the end of the 1970s, the SOE sector in many countries was performing very badly indeed. The litany of problems facing the sector is well known:[6] political interference and political appointments were widespread and yet public accountability was minimal; control of management was weak and yet administrative functions overwhelmed commercial activities; vague and often contradictory objectives dominated commercial activities; investments were excessively capital- and technology-intensive and often sub-optimal; responsiveness to market conditions was often non-existent. Many of the firms that had been taken over by government on the argument that they were being run badly by the private sector had no corporate plans for recovery and often performed even worse under state ownership than under the private ownership from which they were supposedly rescued. On top of this it was not unusual for the sector to face chronic organizational deficiencies in its relationship with central government, involving multiple controlling agencies, overlapping of functions, and an absence of performance criteria. Helped by 'soft budget constraints' SOEs were persistently long-lived, well past the point where they were making any contribution towards their fixed costs, their operations funded through taxation and increasing domestic and foreign borrowing. Thus the stage was set for reform of the sector.

In order to provide some background to the discussions which follow we conclude this chapter with a brief review of the development and performance of the SOE sector in each of the seven countries covered in this book.

3.1 Specific country experience

Three distinct phases of development in the SOE sector can be differentiated for Jamaica. The first occurred up to Independence in 1962, during which the government's role in the economy focused on the creation of a regulatory regime and the development of the key infrastructural sectors. The main areas of operation at the eve of Independence were in regulation and promotion, social and community services, and agricultural marketing. Government involvement in the manufacturing sector was restricted to indirect intervention through two development finance corporations, while all the utilities, except the railways, water, and the post office, were still foreign-owned. The second phase coincided with the era of the first post-Independence government (the JLP) and the creation of an explicit commitment to greater state participation in the economy. Although there was some growth in the size of the SOE sector during this period, the major growth did not occur until the third phase following the election of the first Manley PNP Government in 1972. Committed to a socialist economic strategy, the Manley Government adopted an aggressive industrial acquisition programme aimed at direct control of the 'commanding heights' of the economy, and the achievement of explicit income distribution goals. The growth of the public sector during the late 1970s was both precipitate and chaotic, and by 1980 consisted of approximately 640 entities in all sectors of the economy, accounting for around 20% of GDP. Loss-making enterprises abounded, accountability structures became amazingly diverse, while the financial control and monitoring system was practically moribund. Overstaffing was legion, and the intricate weave of price controls to which the sector was subject rendered rational resource allocation virtually impossible. On the eve of the election of the Seaga Government in 1980 the SOE sector in Jamaica was, in the eyes of many observers, in a parlous state.[7]

A similar three-phase development occurred in Trinidad and Tobago. The first phase, from roughly 1956 (the date of Independence) to 1970, embraced an identical non-interventionist stance which combined the active promotion of private sector-led industrialization with the creation of a regulatory framework, although a small number of enterprises came under state control, principally through bailouts. Following the 'Black Power' riots in response to increasing unemployment and worsening income distribution, the early 1970s saw a re-evaluation of the role of government intervention in the economy. This second phase witnessed the shift to active government intervention through the SOE sector. Fortuitously, this change in policy coincided with a rapid expansion of government revenues following the 1973 increase in the oil price and the discovery of natural gas offshore. The government was able to finance the expansion of the SOE sector throughout the 1970s and 1980s through a policy of both nationalization and the government-backed creation of new industries. By 1986, the government was the majority shareholder in 46 firms, in 35 of which it had 100% ownership. As in Jamaica the SOE sector now accounted for a substantial portion of GDP. By 1985, the total value added of the state enterprises and utilities was 16% of GDP; SOE employment accounted for 13% of total formal sector employment; and capital investment for 26% of the national total.[8]

As with many other aspects of the Malaysian economy, the origins of the SOE sector are intricately tied up with the New Economic Policy (NEP) developed in 1970 following race riots in Kuala Lumpur the previous year. The NEP is an affirmative action programme designed 'to reduce and eventually eradicate poverty by raising incomes and increasing employment opportunities for all Malaysians, irrespective of race' and 'to correct economic imbalances so as to reduce and eventually eliminate the identification of race with economic function'. Prior to 1970 government participation in the economy was limited to regulatory, infrastructural, and marketing operations. Central to the NEP, however, was corporate equity ownership, changes in which were achieved principally through the SOE sector. The 1970s consequently saw an unparalleled growth in equity acquisition by the government and its holding companies. As a result, though viewed as being fundamentally a market-oriented economy, by 1980 the SOE sector in Malaysia consisted of approximately 1150 enterprises, comprising the traditional core utilities – transport, communications, water supply and energy – but with massive additional exposure in non-traditional sectors such as services, finance, construction and, particularly, manufacturing. The complex holding company structures established under the auspices of the NEP dramatically blurred the public/private divide in Malaysia. As a result the overall resource-call of the sector remained hidden, but best-guess estimates suggest that by the early 1980s the sector accounted for around 25% of GDP.[9]

Economic policy in Sri Lanka since the 1940s has been directed principally towards the reduction of unemployment and the alleviation of poverty. In the first 30 years after Independence in 1947, the problem was addressed by expanding the agricultural sector, and by promoting an import-substituting industrialization strategy built around a core of SOEs. The SOE sector grew rapidly from the late 1950s through nationalization in the plantation, transport and financial sectors. The most rapid growth, however, followed the re-election of the Sri Lankan Freedom Party-led United Front Government in 1970. The Government Business Undertakings Act and the Land Reform Act of 1971 paved the way for the creation of a large number of Government-Owned Business Undertakings (GOBUs), and accelerated the process of nationalization in the plantation sector. By 1977 there were in excess of 250 SOEs covering all areas of economic activity, accounting for approximately 20% of GDP, 35% of gross investment and almost 40% of formal sector employment. However, growth in the sector had slumped and employment creation had stagnated. The collapse of the United Front and the subsequent landslide victory of the United National Party marked a radical re-orientation of the economy. Starting with programmes to revitalize the private sector, which had been virtually idle during the previous era, the '1977 liberalizations' contained the seeds for the later attempts to rehabilitate the SOE sector and to proceed towards its eventual privatization.[10]

The origins of the SOE sector in Kenya extend back to the early 1900s, with the creation of the East African railway system, linking Mombasa on the coast with the inland cities of Nairobi and Kampala. By Independence in 1963, public ownership was widespread in infrastructure, agricultural marketing, and also in the development finance sector. From Independence until the late 1970s attention shifted towards the role of the state in broader resource management, under the auspices of a political and economic philosophy known as 'African Socialism'. This combined the notion of a collective mixed economy with the goal of 'Kenyanization' – i.e. the rapid acceleration of the transfer of economic control from the hands of foreigners and Kenyan Asians to Kenyan Africans. These two aims melded within an interventionist economic policy, one key element of which was public ownership. By the 1980s the SOE sector in Kenya consisted of some 150 entities, accounting for approximately 15% of GDP in the late 1970s and a similar proportion of gross capital formation, 30% of all public sector employment and 50% of public sector capital formation. Once again, the downturn in the terms of trade, coming on the heels of the collapse of the East African Community in 1977, revealed the critical state of the SOE sector.

Although the SOE sector in Malaŵi is small in the absolute number of enterprises (it consists of some 24 wholly-owned entities), it accounts for a major share of GDP (approximately 25% in 1984). The SOE sector has evolved in a manner almost identical to that in Kenya, adopting many of the implicit objectives, if not the rhetoric, of the philosophy of 'African Socialism'. Thus, from a base of infrastructural and development finance immediately after Independence, there followed a more interventionist stance pursued in the early 1970s and implemented through the operations of three large holding companies, the Malaŵi Development Corporation (MDC), the Agricultural Development and Marketing Corporation (ADMARC), and the Press Corporation,[11] which were rapidly involved in the promotion of the manufacturing and services sectors. As with Kenya, the 1970s were characterized by relatively favourable terms of trade which combined with persistently low producer prices to generate large cash balances in the hands of ADMARC. These were invested in the non-traditional sector. More often than not, these investments were not self-sustaining and the terms-of-trade reversal in the early 1980s again exposed the inherent weaknesses in the sector; in particular, these weaknesses transmitted themselves into the broader problems of macro-economic management.

The SOE sector in Papua New Guinea is the smallest in the countries covered here, both in absolute terms and relative to GDP. The sector accounts for approximately 10% of GDP, 8% of total capital formation, and a similar proportion of formal sector employment. It consists of approximately 40 entities, covering commodity marketing boards, Commercial Statutory Authorities (CSAs) which cover the main utility sectors and finance, and a number of smaller commercial enterprises. In general the sector is relatively profitable and, most evidence suggests, technically efficient given the environment in which it operates. The challenge facing the SOE sector in Papua New Guinea in the 1980s was somewhat dissimilar to that of the other economies. Papua New Guinea is a mineral-based economy and stands to enjoy a substantial boom in that sector. The challenge for the non-mineral sector (which includes the bulk of the SOE sector) is how to manage the consequences of a mineral boom so as to avoid the worst excesses of the Dutch Disease phenomenon. Policy towards the SOE sector, and latterly in respect of privatization, has turned on this key issue: it has been more an issue of optimal management for the future than one of response to failures in the past.

3.2 Conclusions

Perhaps with the exception of Papua New Guinea, the fiscal and debt crises of the early 1980s began clearly to expose the excessive size of the SOE sectors in these seven countries and to identify the extent of their call on public finances, while concurrent examination began to reveal their relative inefficiency and excessive staffing. Despite the breadth of activity undertaken, there remained a heavy dependence on primary commodity production and export. The fall in most commodity prices from 1980 to 1982, combined with sharply rising real interest rates worldwide, imposed a severe squeeze on the already fine margins being earned by the sector. Financial crisis spread rapidly through the sector as a result of the close linkages between enterprises and in consequence through the domestic credit and fiscal systems. Thus SOE reform, which hitherto had been of periodic concern, emerged as a serious macroeconomic priority for most governments, who, catching the 'winds of change' from around the world, embraced privatization as the central instrument for such change.

Notes

1. *World Development Report* (1988), Chap. 8.
2. Identifying the true share of the sector in external debt is notoriously difficult, since in many cases flows to the SOE sector are in the form of external loans on-lent by central government.
3. Short in Floyd *et al.* (1984).
4. There are obvious exceptions, however, for example Sri Lanka and Bangladesh.
5. For example, the ideas of Kenyanization, the New Economic Programme in Malaysia, the Trinidad and Tobago response to the Black Power riots, etc. reflected these concerns.
6. See, for example, Shirley (1983).
7. See Chapter 7.
8. See Chapter 8.
9. See Chapter 9.
10. See Chapter 11.
11. See Chapter 13 which also provides a discussion of the particular nature of the Press Corporation.

4 Privatization: Outcomes & Evaluations

4.1 Introduction

The purpose of this chapter is to describe and analyse the implementation and progress of divestiture in the seven countries studied in this book. The details of each programme are covered in the case studies in Chapters 7 to 13, while here we draw out the main themes from the cross-country experiences. However, two important caveats must first be mentioned. The first is that, as with any study of systems in which change is in progress, we are inevitable hostages to fortune. The country studies were carried out in 1990, and in a number of the countries under examination, principally Jamaica and Malaysia, sizeable sales have occurred since the time of this research.[1] It is the case, however, that developments since 1990 do not fundamentally alter our conclusions, and we stress that our study is not primarily concerned with a simple cataloguing of sales but rather with assessing, first, the way in which privatization as a policy option has been adapted to meet the constraints and characteristics of developing countries and, second, the way in which these (often necessary) adaptations affect the capacity of privatization to fulfil the objectives set out for the policy. The second caveat relates to the discussion at the beginning of Chapter 2 concerning the definition of privatization. Our definition will of necessity exclude some actions which may be described in other parts of the literature as privatization, especially the deregulation/contracting out of social sector services and the detailed restructuring of commodity marketing boards.

Section 4.2 presents a factual report on the extent and characteristics of privatization across the seven countries, and contrasts this with the financial results from SOE reform programmes. From this analysis we derive a set of structural features which we regard as intrinsic to privatization in the economies under discussion. However, a substantial portion of the literature on privatization in developing countries has focused not on these issues, but rather on the narrower debate concerning 'getting the process right'. We describe some of the salient features of 'process' issues in section 4.3. Hence, this section considers the adoption of privatization as a goal, the development and adequacy of structures implementing privatization, the different methods of sale open to government, and the management of privatization programmes. These issues clearly play some part in determining success or failure, but it is our argument that the fundamental determinants of privatization outcomes lie in the structures of economies and the nature of privatization programmes as political processes. Along with the inherent conflicts between the objectives of privatization, these factors serve to delineate a comparatively small domain for 'programme issues'. Discussion of the structural features of economies – which essentially involves making explicit the implicit assumptions of the developed-country privatization model – follows in

Table 4.1 *Number of privatizations by country and by method of sale*

	Total	Public Sale	Private Sale Domestic	Private Sale Foreign	Private Sale Joint	MC & Lease Domestic	MC & Lease Foreign	MC & Lease Joint
Jamaica[a]	41	3	15	6	4	2	1	9
Kenya[b]	1	1	0	0	0	0	0	0
Malawi[c]	17	0	8	9	0	0	0	0
Malaysia[d]	24	4	12	0	2	6	0	0
Papua New Guinea[e]	4	0	0	4	0	0	0	0
Sri Lanka[f]	6	3	1	2	0	0	0	0
Trinidad and Tobago	5	2	0	2	0	0	1	0
TOTAL	98	14	36	23	6	8	2	9

Source: Country case studies, Chapters 7–13.

Notes
a) Details on some smaller sales are missing. Sales of hotels have been treated individually. Land sales have been entered as one item under Private Sale–Domestic and land leases have been entered as one item under MC (Management Contract) & Lease–Domestic. Each component of multiple-transaction privatizations is treated separately.
b) Excludes the abortive sale of Uplands Bacon Factory.
c) Excludes MDC/ADMARC/Press Holding share swap and small estate sales.
d) Excludes BOT projects and corporatizations.
e) Includes sales by Agbank in 1987.
f) Sale of United Motors was part-domestic part-foreign and is treated as two sales.

Chapter 5. The remainder of the present chapter covers issues of programme management in section 4.3 and the politics of privatization in section 4.4. First, however, we briefly describe the extent of privatization in the seven countries.

4.2 A progress report 1980–90

Progress in privatization in the seven countries has been slower than hoped. As noted at the beginning of this chapter, while our listing of privatization transactions cannot be totally comprehensive, we believe that it is accurate enough, and certainly captures the most important transactions. In compiling the figures we have tried to adhere closely to our own definition of privatization, and have made certain assumptions. First, we have included only sales (public and direct), leases and management contracts. Within these we include sales of equity (either total or partial) owned by government, even when this equity is held through development finance or other institutions, but have, however, chosen to ignore closures of plant as privatization. Moreover, in many cases we have excluded transactions which accord with the relevant government's definition of privatization but not with ours.[2] Having said this, however, the country studies later in the book distinguish many of these complexities. The purpose at this stage is to draw out only the main features of the programmes as far as the size, scope and extent of resource shifts are concerned.

In Tables 4.1–4.8 we identify the patterns of the privatization programmes that have occurred from the start of the policy up to July 1990. All proceeds are expressed in US dollars and as a proportion of GDP so as to facilitate cross-country comparison. Another possibility is to express them as a proportion of the budget deficit. However, this causes problems because the 1980s, for all our case study economies, were a period of considerable fluctuations in public finances

Table 4.2 *Privatization proceeds by country and method of sale*[a] *(US$m.)*[b]

| | Total | Public Sale | Private Sale | | |
			Domestic	Foreign	Joint
Jamaica	*230.7*	*66.2*	*36.8*	*117.5*	*10.2*
Kenya	*9.1*	*9.1*	*0.0*	*0.0*	*0.0*
Malaŵi	*7.2*	*0.0*	*2.2*	*5.0*	*0.0*
Malaysia	*180.3*	*85.9*	*40.4*	*0.0*	*54.0*
Papua New Guinea	*4.5*	*0.0*	*0.0*	*4.5*	*0.0*
Sri Lanka	*10.7*	*2.9*	*0.0*	*7.8*	*0.0*
Trinidad and Tobago	*94.5*	*9.6*	*0.0*	*84.9*	*0.0*
TOTAL	537.0	173.7	79.4	219.7	64.2
No. of Privatizations[c]	79	14	36	23	6
AVERAGE VALUE	6.8	12.4	2.2	9.6	10.7

Source: Country case studies, Chapters 7–13.

Notes
a) The values of some of the small sales (inc. land sales) listed in Table 4.1 are missing.
b) Converted at the exchange rate applicable at the date of sale.
c) Not including management contracts or leases.

thanks largely to the impact of the debt crisis, commodity price shocks and intense adjustment measures. Thus, the proceeds from privatization expressed as a proportion of the deficit are uninformative: they generally say more about the movement in the deficit than they do about the proceeds from privatization. Moreover, only the gross proceeds from the sale are reported here and no attempt is made to identify the costs of privatization (either the direct costs such as transactions fees, or the indirect costs such as write-offs and other pre-privatization costs). The tables therefore may overstate the short-run revenue flows from privatization: once again, however, the country studies attempt to clarify these issues in more detail.

For the seven countries we have identified only 98 enterprises which have been (totally or partially) privatized through sale or leasing, out of a total of approximately 2,000 SOEs (Table 4.1). In addition, the privatization process has tended to be concentrated in the smaller enterprises (see below), leaving the larger concerns untouched: in short, privatization has to date only skimmed the surface of state sector holdings.

As a corollary, the proceeds from privatization have not generally been large (the only exception to this being Jamaica). Privatization proceeds during the period total a mere US$537 million, of which US$411 million or 77% is accounted for by Jamaica and Malaysia (Table 4.2). As a proportion of GDP, only in Jamaica and Trinidad and Tobago has the accumulated sum of privatization proceeds reached a proportion of GDP greater than 1% (Table 4.3). It is particularly interesting to note that in Malaysia, a country popularly regarded as being in the vanguard of developing-country privatization, the volume of privatization revenue remained minuscule during the 1980s.[3]

Another common thread is the concentration of transactions in certain types of enterprise. The majority of enterprises that have been privatized have been commerce, manufacturing and service enterprises – 63 out of 98 – with the next largest number being from the agricultural sector (though this is dominated by the small tea estates sold by ADMARC in Malaŵi) (Table 4.4). However, proceeds from commerce, manufacturing and service enterprise sales were less than 30% of

Table 4.3 *Privatization proceeds by country and by method of sale*[a] *(% of GDP)*[b]

			Private Sale		
	Total	Public Sale	Domestic	Foreign	Joint
Jamaica	7.20	2.25	1.10	3.56	0.29
Kenya	0.09	0.09	0.00	0.00	0.00
Malaŵi	0.61	0.00	0.19	0.42	0.00
Malaysia	0.55	0.27	0.12	0.00	0.16
Papua New Guinea	0.18	0.00	0.00	0.18	0.00
Sri Lanka	0.15	0.04	0.00	0.11	0.00
Trinidad and Tobago	2.34	0.24	0.00	2.10	0.00
AVERAGE	1.59	0.41	0.20	0.91	0.06

Notes
a) Not including the value of management contracts or leases.
b) The figures represent the total of privatization proceeds to date as a sum of the proportions of those proceeds to GDP in the respective years of sale.

total proceeds, and less than half of those from sales of transport and communications enterprises (Table 4.5). Furthermore, the average sale value of privatization in this type of enterprise is only US$2.6m. The great majority of privatizations to date have, as noted earlier, been concentrated in the smallest government enterprises, which are generally located in the industrial sector and may be amongst the more competitive companies in the public sector portfolio. The only large enterprises dealt with have tended to be either banks or telecommunications firms, with a small number of sales in the latter category dominating the figures for total proceeds. (The transport and communications sector accounts for US$330m. out of total proceeds of US$537m., with an average sale value of US$33m.)

The story is similar when it comes to looking at method of sale (Table 4.6). The largest number are accounted for by direct sales to domestic buyers, after which direct sales to foreign enterprises and public sales through capital markets are roughly equal in number. However, the value of private sales to domestic enterprises is very low: an average sale value of US$1.7m. per enterprise, versus an average value of US$12.4m. for public sales, and an average US$9.6m. for sales to foreign enterprises. Importantly, direct foreign involvement (excluding foreign

Table 4.4 *Number of privatizations by country and by function of enterprise*[a]

	Total	Commerce, Manufac- turing & Services	Finance & Banking	Transport & Communications	Water & Energy	Regulatory & Marketing	Agri- cultural
Jamaica	41	30	1	5	0	0	5
Kenya	1	0	1	0	0	0	0
Malaŵi	17	10	0	0	0	0	7
Malaysia	24	13	2	4	0	0	5
Papua New Guinea	4	2	0	1	0	0	1
Sri Lanka	6	6	0	0	0	0	0
Trinidad and Tobago	5	2	2	1	0	0	0
TOTAL	98	63	6	11	0	0	18

Note
a) Including management contracts and leases.

Table 4.5 *Privatization proceeds by country and function of enterprise*[a] *(US$m.)*

	Total	Commerce, Manufac- turing & Services	Finance & Banking	Transport & Communications	Water & Energy	Regulatory & Marketing	Agri- cultural
Jamaica	230.7	104.2	16.1	110.3	0.0	0.0	0.1
Kenya	9.1	0.0	9.1	0.0	0.0	0.0	0.0
Malaŵi	7.2	5.4	0.0	0.0	0.0	0.0	1.8
Malaysia	180.3	18.6	8.7	133.5	0.0	0.0	19.5
Papua New Guinea	4.5	0.8	0.0	1.0	0.0	0.0	2.7
Sri Lanka	10.7	10.7	0.0	0.0	0.0	0.0	0.0
Trinidad and Tobago	94.5	6.3	3.3	84.9	0.0	0.0	0.0
TOTAL	537.0	146.0	37.2	329.7	0.0	0.0	24.1
AVERAGE VALUE	6.8	2.6	6.2	33.0	0.0	0.0	4.0

Note
a) Excluding management contracts, leases and closures.

participation in joint ventures) in the privatization programmes of the seven countries accounts for almost 40% of total sales value.

Clear links emerge between type of enterprise, method of sale, and source of finance (Tables 4.7–4.10). Direct domestic private sector participation has been concentrated exclusively in the smaller end of the commercial, manufacturing and service, and agricultural sectors, where it accounts for 50% of all sales. Larger sales, and in particular those in the finance and banking, and transport and communications sectors, depend on direct foreign involvement and public share issues. The higher average size of joint-venture sales as a method of sale in the commercial, manufacturing and services sector is also notable and their presence in the transport and communications sector. In general once the scale of enterprise sales rises foreign participation seems a necessary component.

A significant comparison which is not often made involves the short-term impacts on fiscal balances of privatization *vis-à-vis* SOE reform. Our data suggest that, in those countries where serious attempts have been made to address the problems of the public sector, the immediate public finance position has been

Table 4.6 *Number of privatizations by method and function of enterprise*

	Total	Public Sale	Private Sale			MC & Lease		
			Domestic	Foreign	Joint	Domestic	Foreign	Joint
Commerce, Manufacturing & Services	63	7	26	13	4	4	1	8
Finance & Banking	6	4	1	1	0	0	0	0
Transport & Communications	11	3	0	5	2	1	0	0
Water & Energy	0	0	0	0	0	0	0	0
Regulatory & Marketing	0	0	0	0	0	0	0	0
Agricultural	18	0	9	4	0	3	1	1
TOTAL	98	14	36	23	6	8	2	9

Table 4.7 *Value of privatizations by method and function of enterprise*[a] *(US$m.)*

		Public Sale	Private Sale		
	Total		Domestic	Foreign	Joint
Commerce, Manufacturing & Services	146.0	41.9	54.2	39.7	10.2
Finance & Banking	37.2	32.6	4.6	0.0	0.0
Transport & Communications	329.7	99.2	0.0	176.5	54.0
Water & Energy	0.0	0.0	0.0	0.0	0.0
Regulatory & Marketing	0.0	0.0	0.0	0.0	0.0
Agricultural	24.1	0.0	20.6	3.5	0.0
TOTAL	537.0	173.7	79.4	219.7	64.2

Note
a) Excludes management contracts and leases.

improved to a much greater extent by direct SOE reform measures. It is conceptually difficult to identify the exact magnitude of public finance effects arising from SOE reforms; the figures presented here are therefore indicative rather than definitive. By analysing public finance accounts we have attempted to identify those changes in the flow of funds between central government and the SOE sector which can be ascribed to SOE reforms. This exercise is notoriously difficult, however, for a number of reasons. First, where SOEs predominate in the tradable goods sectors (e.g. through primary production or marketing of export crops), their financial performance is heavily determined by exogenous factors, and in particular changes in the terms of trade. The 1980s were an era of volatile international price movements, and in such cases identifying changes attributable to reform is difficult. A second, and related, point is the perennial problem of relating profit (or surplus) to efficiency in situations of imperfect competition. Improved (short-term) cash flow to government from a monopolistic marketing board can be as much the result of a reduction in producer prices as it is of improved efficiency.

These caveats notwithstanding, we have attempted to identify the fiscal effects of SOE reform in the countries studied. As in the earlier section, these changes are expressed in terms of GDP rather than of the budget deficit itself. For example, in Trinidad and Tobago the set of reform measures introduced in the mid- and late-1980s reduced government transfers to the SOE sector by a cumulative amount of 10.5% of GDP between 1982 and 1988, as compared with cumulative privatization receipts of 2.3% of GDP. In Sri Lanka, the reduction of government

Table 4.8 *Average value of privatizations by method and function of enterprise*[a] *(US$m.)*

		Public Sale	Private Sale		
	Average		Domestic	Foreign	Joint
Commerce, Manufacturing & Services	2.38	5.98	2.08	3.05	2.55
Finance & Banking	6.20	8.15	0.00	0.00	0.00
Transport & Communications	29.97	33.07	0.00	35.30	27.00
Water & Energy	0.00	0.00	0.00	0.00	0.00
Regulatory & Marketing	0.00	0.00	0.00	0.00	0.00
Agricultural	1.26	0.00	2.29	0.88	0.00
AVERAGE	7.01	12.40	2.27	9.55	10.72

Note
a) This table excludes the value of management contracts and leases, the UPSAK sales in Malaysia, some smaller privatizations in Jamaica, and Trinidad and Tobago's sale of DFC.

Table 4.9 *First-day excess demand/excess supply data*

							Revenue (Loss)/Gain	
Company[a]	Country	Currency	Issue Price[b]	Opening Price[c]	Shares Offered	Shares Sold	Local[d] Currency (000s)	% on Par[e]
CCC	Jamaica	J$	2.00	1.90	111,945,488	78,690,000	7,869,000	3.51
NCB	Jamaica	J$	2.95	4.94	30,600,000	30,600,000	(60,894,000)	−67.46
Seprod	Jamaica	J$	2.50	−	3,000,000	3,000,000	−	−
TOJ	Jamaica	J$	0.88	0.90	126,500,000	126,500,000	(2,530,000)	−2.27
MAS	Malaysia	M$	1.80	3.50	70,000,000	70,000,000	(119,000,000)	−94.44
MISC	Malaysia	M$	2.40	5.00	84,985,000	84,985,000	(220,961,000)	−108.33
TW	Malaysia	M$	1.10	2.30	15,000,000	15,000,000	(18,000,000)	−109.09
CMS	Malaysia	M$	1.30	2.48	5,000,000	5,900,000	(5,900,000)	−90.77
UMSL	Sri Lanka	SL Rupees	10.00	10.00	10,000,000	3,300,000	0	0.00
NCB	Trinidad	TT$	0.69	−	3,410,000	3,410,000	−	−
TCL I	Trinidad	TT$	0.75	−	12,000,000	12,000,000	−	−
TCL II	Trinidad	TT$	0.85	−	21,000,000	21,000,000	−	−
Average Revenue Loss/Gain							Mean	−52.09

Source: Country case studies, Chapters 7–13.

Notes
a) Full details of companies in country case studies.
b) Issue Price = price at which shares offered in primary issue.
c) Opening Price = price at end of first day's trade.
d) Revenue Loss/Gain = Premium (discount) times shares sold.
e) Revenue Loss/Gain expressed as percent of total Par = issue price times shares offered.

transfers equalled 6.4% of GDP between 1982 and 1988, as against privatization receipts of 0.2% of GDP. In Papua New Guinea, the net cash flow from government to SOEs was reduced as a proportion of GDP by 1% between 1982 and 1987 as against privatization receipts of 0.04% of GDP. These aggregate figures are substantiated in the case studies by empirical evidence from individual publicly-owned companies undergoing reform programmes within the public sector, as well as those being 'cleaned up' in advance of privatization. Such firms often show dramatic improvements in their financial positions vis-à-vis government. This evidence would suggest, then, that governments in developing countries facing (often tough) budgetary targets earn a far higher return to their scarce reform effort when concentrating on improving poor SOE performance rather than divesting enterprises.

One further point needs mentioning. The country case studies show that few SOEs other than the smaller National Investment Bank of Jamaica (NIBJ) sales in Jamaica were brought to market without first undergoing a major financial and managerial reconstruction, if they were not already profitable.[4] Strictly speaking, if we seek to identify only the effects of the change in ownership on performance, then the effect of such 'clean-ups' must be excluded. However, the counter-argument is often expressed that such changes can only be initiated and maintained when a commitment to privatization is credible and therefore these 'clean-ups' represent an integral part of the privatization process. This argument is motivated by the observation that, in the past, a number of countries have pursued similar reform measures under public ownership with no intention of privatization: although such efforts were frequently successful in the short run, their effects have not been sustained. Thus it is suggested that only with the credible threat and hence eventual realization of an ownership change can such improvements be 'locked in'. As Shapiro and Willig (1990: 4) note:

Table 4.10 *Three-month excess demand/excess supply data*

Company	Country	Currency	Adjusted Issue Price	Issue Price[a]	3-Month Price	Shares Offered	Shares Sold	Revenue Loss (−)/Gain (+) Local Currency (000s)	Percent on Par[b]
CCC	Jamaica	J$	2.00	1.85	1.51	111,945,488	78,690,000	26,754,600	12.92
NCB	Jamaica	J$	2.95	3.47	4.60	30,600,000	30,600,000	(34,578,000)	−32.56
Seprod	Jamaica	J$	2.50	3.98	6.65	3,000,000	3,000,000	(8,010,000)	−67.09
TOJ	Jamaica	J$	0.88	0.93	0.90	126,500,000	126,500,000	3,795,000	3.23
MAS	Malaysia	M$	1.80	1.70	2.63	70,000,000	70,000,000	(65,100,000)	−54.71
MISC	Malaysia	M$	2.40	3.81	7.20	84,985,000	84,985,000	(288,099,150)	−88.98
TW	Malaysia	M$	1.10	1.40	1.93	15,000,000	15,000,000	(7,950,000)	−37.86
CMS	Malaysia	M$	1.30	1.41	2.05	5,000,000	5,000,000	(3,200,000)	−45.39
UMSL	Sri Lanka	SL Rupees	10.00	9.43	11.00	10,000,000	3,300,000	(5,181,000)	−5.49
NCB	Trinidad	TT$	0.69	–	–	3,410,000	3,410,000	–	–
TCL I	Trinidad	TT$	0.75	–	–	12,000,000	12,000,000	–	–
TCL II	Trinidad	TT$	0.85	–	–	21,000,000	21,000,000	–	–
							Mean		−26.33

Source: Country case studies, Chapters 7–13.

Notes
a) Original issue price adjusted for movement in market index since issue.
b) Revenue Gain/Loss calculated relative to Adjusted Issue Price times shares offered.

In terms of *real politique* [sic] needed reforms of public sector control may be infeasible, and the drama, shock, and coalition-creation of privatization may be the only effective route for real change.

This argument is difficult to accept *in toto*, since we are sceptical of the implicit assumption that the public sector is everywhere and always an intrinsically bad enterprise manager. However, it does point to an important theme that reappears later in the case studies. While privatization programmes in developing countries have not yet altered radically the public/private balance, the 'threat effect' of privatization has brought a halt – in some cases dramatic – to the rapid expansion of the SOE sector evident in the 1970s. Thus, in Malaysia, where during the 1970s government enterprise acquisition and creation was running at almost three per week, the 1980s saw the creation of new SOEs fall to almost zero. A similar story can be told for Jamaica, Kenya and Sri Lanka. Furthermore, the widespread acceptance of the 'philosophy' of privatization, especially amongst populations and electorates dissatisfied with public enterprise performance, has made it easier for governments to undertake SOE restructurings that would previously have faced broad political opposition. Hence, our evidence supports the claim made elsewhere that the insinuation of the ideas and threat of privatization into policy-making and control processes has imparted a notable degree of flexibility into these economies, and in this sense alone has contributed to the supply-side responsiveness pursued under adjustment programmes.

This discussion of short-term public finance effects should not, however, obscure the lessons of the data on the first decade of privatization. These are that privatization has proceeded slowly; it has only marginally reduced the size of the public sector; it has raised comparatively small volumes of funds; the majority of sales have been small and concentrated by sector; and there has been a pronounced dualism linking sale size, enterprise sector and method of sale whereby small divestitures of commerce/manufacturing/services enterprises are managed through direct sales to the domestic sector, whereas large sales of banks and utilities are carried out through public share sales or direct sales to foreign firms. It is these facts that we shall address both in the remainder of this chapter, and in Chapter 5.

4.3 Privatization methods and management

Privatization began to be promoted as a solution to the ills of the SOE sector in the early 1980s. At that time the expansion of the SOE sector had reached its apogee and it was increasingly clear that the sector's growth, let alone its overall size, was unsustainable. Thus at a time when many countries – not least the UK – were embracing the idea of privatization as part of a broader political philosophy aimed at reducing the role of the state, many developing countries saw privatization as a quick and efficient means of averting or solving the impending crisis of the SOE sector. Though in many cases privatization was embraced principally as a solution to an immediate fiscal crisis, it must also be acknowledged that many countries accepted it as an integral part of a shift towards greater market orientation of economic policy.

4.3.1 Privatization structures
In all the countries covered here governments began to move towards privatization in the early 1980s with the creation of various institutions (either *ad hoc* or statutory) charged with managing the divestiture process. The main developments were as follows:

Privatization Legislation and Structures

Jamaica	NIBJ Divestiture Committee	1981
	NIBJ Divestiture Secretariat	1982
	National Hotels and Properties Divestment Unit	(not known)
	Agro 21 Divestment Secretariat	(not known)
	PM's Cabinet Submission on Privatization	1986
	Cabinet Sub-Committee on Privatization	1990
Trinidad and Tobago	Bruce Committee	1979
	Bobb Committee	1984
	Rampersad Committee	1984
Malaysia	'Malaysia Inc.' Policy	1983
	Cabinet Privatization (Main Committee)	1985
	Privatization Secretariat/Economic Planning Unit (EPU)	1985
	Privatization Guidelines	1985
	UPSAK	1987
	Privatization Masterplan	1990
Papua New Guinea	National Executive Council (NEC) Policy Statement on Privatization I	1987
	NEC Policy Statement on Privatization II	1988
Sri Lanka	Parliamentary Committee on Public Enterprises	1980–7
	Presidential Commission on Privatization	1987
	Presidential Commission on People-ization	1989
	Public Investment Management Board	1989
Kenya	Ndegwa Committee on Statutory Bodies	1979
	Working Party on Government Expenditure (WPGE)	1982
	Task Force on Divestiture	1986–90
Malaŵi	Department of Statutory Bodies	1982
	World Bank Structural Adjustment Loans (SALs) I–III	1981–6

Source: Country case studies, Chapters 7–13.

The enthusiasm with which the ideas were adopted differed quite dramatically between countries. For example, while in Kenya the Ndegwa Committee Report on the Statutory Bodies of 1979 and the Working Party on Government Expenditure (WPGE) of 1982 took a cautious view of privatization, viewing it primarily as a minor adjunct to the broader aim of imposing greater discipline on the SOE sector, in Malaysia privatization was enshrined as part of the 'Malaysia Inc.' policy promoted by Prime Minister Dr Mahathir bin Mohamed in 1983, as a central element in the restructuring of the entire economy. To an extent these differences reflected the nature of the crisis facing the respective economies, and also the relative balance between the political and technocratic impulse for privatization, with higher profile programmes being associated with greater political support for the programme. Thus in Kenya privatization enjoys technocratic support but has consistently been regarded with suspicion by politicians, and the work of the Ndegwa Committee and the WPGE has not received wholehearted support from the executive.[5] In Malaysia, however, privatization emerged as the personal standard of Dr Mahathir whose enthusiasm ensured that the programme has achieved a profile higher than is perhaps warranted, and has done so against significant opposition from technocrats and other groups.

Similar phenomena exist in Sri Lanka where President Premedasa has formulated a particular brand of privatization policy known as 'People-ization', and in Jamaica where in the mid-1980s privatization was a crucial line of political schism between the government of then-Prime Minister Seaga and the opposition.[6] The profile of Malaŵian privatization has been high, especially outside the country.

Malaŵi has frequently been held up by the donor community as the prime example of privatization in action in Africa: it is not clear whether this view is held as strongly within the country itself. Finally in Papua New Guinea and Trinidad and Tobago the profile has been more modest. In the case of Papua New Guinea, privatization was overshadowed by the macroeconomic management of the incipient mineral boom, while in Trinidad and Tobago the government of the National Alliance for Reconstruction has been distinctly ambivalent about privatization. It has remained committed to it for pragmatic rather than ideological reasons, but still emphasizes the importance of the SOE sector in raising employment and meeting ethnic balance objectives.

A typology of structures

Three main models/structures for privatization exist amongst the countries studied. The first is a centralized structure where the privatization/SOE reform process is handled exclusively by a single institution within government: the institution may be either an existing department of government, usually within the Ministry of Finance, or a specifically created institution. This type of structure exists in Malaŵi, where the co-ordination of SOEs and their privatization is managed entirely by the Department of Statutory Bodies (DSB),[7] in Trinidad and Tobago, where privatization is managed by a committee within the Ministry of Finance, and, latterly, in Papua New Guinea, where privatization is the responsibility of the Commercial Investment Division (CID) of the Ministry of Finance. The polar case, that of complete decentralization, where each relevant holding institution is responsible for the privatization of elements of its portfolio, more clearly characterizes the situation in Kenya. Here each minister with SOEs in his/her portfolio is responsible for the management of privatization in that sector. Sri Lanka followed a similar path in the early phase of its privatization programme, as did Papua New Guinea during the first, and ultimately unsuccessful, phase of privatization when a similar structure prevailed.

The third model is the hybrid in which there are a small number of institutions or bodies with a relatively broad scope of functional responsibility. Jamaica most clearly represents this type of model. Although, formally, privatization was supposed to be managed by the Divestment Secretariat of the National Investment Bank, in fact major portions of the programme were carried out by agencies that had previously been responsible for the (mis)management of the asset they were privatizing. This 'gamekeeper turned poacher' approach proved surprisingly successful. The hybrid model is also present in Malaysia (where the 'mainstream' privatization programme is managed by the EPU, while the divestiture of smaller industrial sector SOEs comes under the ambit of UPSAK, the Ministry of Finance Public Enterprise Monitoring Unit) and in Sri Lanka, where the Public Investment Management Board (PIMB) and the Commercialization Division have separate spheres of responsibility.

Though these three types can be distinguished, they are not static structures, so as programmes mature (or at least acquire a higher profile) structures have tended to become more centralized. To an extent this reflects a learning process. As will emerge in section 4.3.3 and in the country studies, most countries found that without inter-agency co-ordination (and co-option) the process of privatization became not only extremely protracted but also undermined by significant problems. The country studies are replete with examples of weak co-ordination of agencies resulting in poorly implemented programmes.[8] Consequently over the decade there have been a number of revisions to privatization structures aimed at improving co-ordination. Under the Privatization Masterplan in Malaysia, for example, the activities of UPSAK and the EPU are gradually being merged. Similarly in Sri Lanka the previously decentralized structures – through which line ministries dominated the process – have been replaced by a more organized system.[9] And again, in Papua New Guinea, the fiasco of the attempted sale of the Niugini Insurance Company has led to moves to strengthen the structures, with all initiatives being channelled through and co-ordinated by the CID. However, it is not invariably the case that centralization will improve the speed of programmes, even if it improves efficiency. For example, in Jamaica the current Peoples Nationalist Party government has moved to centralize the structures it inherited from the previous Jamaican Labour Party administration. Some Jamaicans close to the privatization programme fear, however, that this will slow progress, since it will result in greater power to a bureaucracy that is still ambivalent about divestiture.

One of the more obvious ramifications of these various organizational structures concerns the way in which programmes are developed. What has tended to happen throughout the decade and across countries is that the more centralized the privatization system has become, the more clearly a 'privatization pipeline' emerges by which government clearly announces its intentions, the companies identified, the method and proposed timetable for sale. This approach stands in contrast to a more reactive approach to privatization whereby government, having endorsed the principle of privatization, has proceeded on a relatively *ad hoc* basis with candidates being selected sequentially and often in response to immediate financial crises. Exemplifying this latter approach is the Kenyan situation where the notion of 'privatization by default' has gained currency (see Chapter 12). Here the catalyst has been the financial collapse of the SOE (generally one in which government has a minority stake held through a development finance institution), which has forced the official receiver to identify a private sector purchaser to take over the company.

Thus the latter 1980s witnessed the disclosure of comprehensive arrays of privatization candidates presented as a 'shopping list' to the domestic and foreign private sector. The most comprehensive so far has been the Malaysian Privatization Masterplan which, unveiled in 1990, provides a 5-year plan of action aimed at divesting approximately 430 enterprises. Similar pipelines have been developed by the governments of Sri Lanka (in this case the pipeline is linked explicitly to IDA adjustment credits), Jamaica, Malawi, and Papua New Guinea. Of course, the development of these ambitious plans does not ensure that sales occur on target: we return to an assessment of this likelihood in Chapter 6.

4.3.2 Methods of sale
There is virtually no limit to the different methods of sale open to governments, and experience worldwide has shown that privatization has spawned a considerable number of innovative selling techniques. However, most of the countries have inextricably linked the privatization of state assets to public share issues through a formal stock exchange. Indeed, in each of the five countries in which a formal capital market/stock exchange exists[10] sales through the stock exchange have occurred and have often been used to raise the profile of the programme. This is particularly the case in Jamaica and Malaysia where the National Commercial Bank (NCB) and Malaysian Airline System (MAS) sales respectively were central to establishing the credibility of the privatization programme. Moreover, this method of sale has been used to effect (part of) the largest sales undertaken across all the countries, namely the M\$136.3m. (US\$54m.) sale of MISC in

Malaysia and the J$110.0m. (US$20m.) sale of Telecommunications of Jamaica (ToJ) in Jamaica.[11]

While it is the case that such share issues have featured strongly in the countries considered in this book, other methods of sale have been numerically dominant. In fact, the single most common method has involved the direct sale of the enterprise (or part of it) to a domestic or foreign purchaser, or to a joint-venture consortium of both. In general, the purchasers have been either third parties, or (in the case of the sale of government equity in joint ventures) the existing incumbent shareholders. One of the dominant, if not particularly surprising, features of the work reported in this book has been the limited extent to which the domestic private sector has emerged as a major player in this process. This, more so in the case in the smaller economies, tends to question the assumption of a private sector hitherto 'crowded-out' by large-scale SOEs,[12] and raises questions about the 'crowding-in' capacity of privatization. This point is reinforced by an analysis of the way in which sales are managed. While there have been some cases where competitive bidding has been possible for enterprises sold to domestic capital (e.g. smaller NIBJ and some hotel sales in Jamaica), in most other cases the seller (i.e. the government) has not been in a position to invite rival bids for the enterprise: usually, then, it has been faced with a situation where there is a single buyer, able to exploit this monopsony power. (This situation was actually institutionalized in the 'first-come, first-served' early sales of the Malaysian programme.) Buyers tend to be existing enterprises and are often competitors in the same domestic, or often export, market; frequently they are companies which have had up- or down-stream linkages with the government company and use the purchase to integrate their operations; and, in some (admittedly fewer) cases, they are 'fly-by-night' companies able to exploit the unique set of circumstances surrounding the privatization process. Furthermore, given the lack of competitive auctions and the consequent monopsony rents, it is no surprise that many purchasers of privatized assets in developing countries believe that they have clinched a 'good deal'. What has failed to occur in general through the private sale process has been the introduction of new domestic venture capital into the market. We shall return to these aspects of the privatization debate in Chapter 5.

One ramification of this dormant private sector has been that enterprises have rarely been sold directly to the existing management, or the employees of the firm.[13] A characteristic of most public share sales has been the allocation, often at preferential terms, of shares to employees and managers, but in general this has constituted only a small proportion of total equity (often around 5%), and has been aimed at ensuring managerial and employee co-operation in the sale. (We return to an analysis of Employee Share Schemes (ESSs) as methods of transferring income to employees later in this chapter.) In general, however, the absence of such buy-outs highlights two of the key questions which will affect not only this form of ownership transfer, but also the privatization process more generally in developing countries. First there is the issue of the risk of ownership, and whether a traditionally risk-averse public sector labour force will be able, or even wish to be able, to become a risk-loving private sector owner. And secondly, bearing this point in mind, there is the concern that the domestic financial sector will be reluctant to absorb the risk of lending to finance this form of new ownership. In view of relatively low levels of personal wealth, employee or management buy-outs will generally be highly leveraged, and given the acknowledged risk aversion of the financial sector in developing countries the prospects for obtaining such risk capital are limited.

The foreign sector is a dominant player in the privatization process in developing countries, particularly in Africa, Oceania, and the Caribbean where the domestic private sector has traditionally been thin. Foreign capital has always played a major role in these economies, either in terms of debt financing of public sector investment, or by way of foreign direct investment, and foreign participation in privatization programmes is therefore a logical extension of this process. However, such participation has engendered ambivalent attitudes. In some cases, foreign capital has been seen as the only way in which debt-distressed and hence credit-constrained economies may be able to access the capital, technology and managerial expertise necessary to generate the supply-side responses essential to adjustment. This consideration has been critical in the Jamaican programme, not only in the privatization of the only two telecommunications firms to Cable and Wireless (UK) but also in planning the divestiture of a number of large, but persistently poorly-performing, SOEs (e.g. Air Jamaica, the international airline; JPSCo, the electricity utility; and JRC, the rail company) to other foreign buyers or managers.

In other countries, however, such transfers of ownership are regarded as implying a loss of sovereignty, and foreign participation has therefore been highly regulated.[14] Nevertheless, foreign participation through direct sales (often as a result of existing shareholdings) has been an important feature of privatization in all the economies studied. As the tables above indicate the foreign sector has accounted for over 40% of all sales, and has predominated in the acquisition of larger assets by direct sale. In Papua New Guinea, Trinidad and Tobago, and Sri Lanka all direct sales of assets have been to foreign investors, while in Malaŵi the same result has only been attenuated by the sale of a number of small enterprises to local entrepreneurs; by value foreign capital has dominated in the programme. As a footnote to this point, while foreign capital has still dominated in all the programmes reviewed, its presence has further ramifications, to the extent that it has been the opposition to foreign capital which has so severely retarded many of the programmes. In numerous cases (particularly in Kenya, Malaŵi, Papua New Guinea) sales have been forestalled as attempts have been made to identify domestic purchasers of assets, rather than having to rely on the actual demand from foreign capital.

To an extent, it has been politically easier to access foreign capital through direct sales than through capital market sales. None the less, foreign ownership through equity participation in public share sales has been considered. One of the key instruments for this is the debt–equity swap, which, though developed in Latin America, has not been a major feature in other developing countries. Elsewhere, however, policies on foreign participation have been seen to alter in response, *inter alia*, to the demands of the privatization programme. For example, in Sri Lanka the punitive 100% withholding tax on foreign share transactions was waived for Mitsubishi of Japan's equity participation in the 1989 sale of United Motors, and eventually abolished entirely in 1990; similarly a small portion (approx. 3%) of the equity in STM (the Malaysian telecommunications company) has been allocated to foreign investors – the first time in Malaysia that foreign participation in privatization issues has been countenanced.[15] This sale was expected to occur some time in 1991.

Although this book takes as its main focus the transfer of assets through sale and leases, a number of other methods of transfer of control have occurred. The most common has been the relatively widespread use of the contracting-out of management, either as a precursor to full divestiture or as an end in itself. This type of reform/restructuring has been particularly prevalent in the airline industry (Air Lanka, Air Malaŵi and Air Niugini have all entered short-term management contracts with overseas airlines), and also in some of the manufacturing sectors. For example, in Trinidad and Tobago's steel industry, in the textile industry in

Sri Lanka, and in the cement industry in Jamaica, the management contractees have gone on to become eventual owners of the enterprise. A further method of privatization to emerge, as yet only in Malaysia, has been the build–operate–transfer method of financing capital projects, used extensively in Malaysia to finance the construction of a toll-road network and elements of the water treatment and sewerage system. The procedure has been plagued by a number of political problems, and to a large extent the 'privatization' element of the venture has been compromised by the network of guarantees and underwriting arrangements necessitated.

Finally, again in spite of its theoretical attraction and its satisfactory use elsewhere in the world, there has been no widespread use of franchising arrangements to introduce competition into the monopoly supply of markets. While the regulatory structure designed to accompany the sale of STM in Malaysia (and the equivalent proposal in Sri Lanka) envisages the use of franchising in the supply of value-added networks, this has not as yet been developed to any sizeable degree. Especially given the transfer of monopoly telecommunications firms, this represents a substantial welfare-improving opportunity forgone. We return to this issue in Chapter 5.

4.3.3 Programme management

The final technical/institutional issue concerns programme management. Programmes have failed where governments have not ensured that the agency (or agencies) responsible for the implementation of privatization has been given sufficient powers in relation to other agencies in the bureaucracy around them, and where line ministries (or ministers) are well placed to derail sales programmes. More importantly, implementing agencies have often been inadequately staffed to carry out the time-intensive process of privatization, and sales have proceeded too rapidly for the capacity of the institutions to manage the sale. This was a feature of the United Motors sale in Sri Lanka where the enterprise was sold with the important issues of the transfer of pension rights unresolved. Similarly, the abortive sale of Niugini Insurance Corporation was so rushed that, though the Act establishing the corporation as an SOE was repealed, its 'successor company' legislation was not passed and the corporation was *ultra vires* for almost 18 months. Finally, the failed transfer of the Uplands Bacon Factory and Kenya Meat Commission to the private sector was in large measure due to the combination of pressure from donors to meet adjustment conditionality and weak domestic management of the sale.

Many of these problems stem from a tendency on the past of governments and external donors to underestimate the resource cost of managing the privatization effort: it is one of the ironies that the management of privatization can in fact involve an extensive call on the time and resources of the public sector. This is manifested in a variety of ways, and governments have generally underestimated the extent to which the details of individual privatization transactions have to be dealt with before asset sales can go ahead. For instance, it is often the case that major changes need to be made to the legal standing of SOEs before privatization can occur, involving delays as complicated legislation is drafted and promulgated.[16] Recapitalization of enterprises is another issue where handling the details of such transactions is found to take much longer than expected, while the identification and screening of suitable buyers have proved an extensive process for reasons we discuss in Chapter 5.

Moreover, privatizations require a great number of smaller issues to be addressed, especially relating to the contractual terms and conditions of the post-privatization labour force, the transfer of their pension entitlements, and the restructuring and renegotiation of their trade union status and recognition (if any). In some countries, underestimation of these requirements has led to two specific problems. First, countries are frequently involved in adjustment programmes which have time-specific privatization components. Delays in the completion of privatization transactions sometimes result in countries breaking loan conditions.[17] Second, important aspects of the programme are decided either during or after the privatization itself. We have already noted the problems this may cause for the future successful regulation of monopolies, but in other cases, as with United Motors, *ad hoc* provisions have had to be introduced to cope with the fact that certain procedures had not been promulgated prior to the sale of the enterprise.

Amongst smaller developing countries, one of the main resource costs associated with privatization has been the lack of experienced domestic technical expertise, which has resulted in many of them having to import expensive foreign consultants to help structure and implement the details of each transaction. Only in the case of Kenya has the government not resorted to the use of external consultants in the design and management of the programmes. Aside from the direct costs of this form of technical assistance, there is a concern that, though the capacity of the consultants is not questioned, much of their experience has been gained in the management of the UK privatization programme, and there has been a tendency for this to emerge in the form of homogeneous programmes across countries, frequently placing a great emphasis on the use of public share sales. Moreover, the use of external consultants often reinforces concerns on the part of anti-privatization coalitions that the exercise is fundamentally about the sale of national assets to (footloose) foreign investors. Whether correct or not, such concerns have an important effect on the way in which privatization is promoted as an adjustment policy.

4.4 The politics of privatization

Privatization, involving as it does a redrawing of the public/private boundary, is an inherently political process. It should therefore be no surprise to find political objectives playing an important role in shaping what is usually presented as a 'neutral', efficiency-enhancing, tool. In fact, the interface between political and economic objectives is an intrinsic determinant of the shape and success of privatization programmes in all countries. Furthermore, this interface engenders a whole range of conflicts in objectives which derive from the *omnia ad omnes* nature of privatization in developing countries. In this section we examine how the broad political objectives of governments have determined the overall profile of privatization programmes (including an extended discussion of reputation, credibility and precommitment), the way in which the satisfaction of political goals affects the design of transactions, and how conflicts in the multiple objectives of privatization result in eventual trade-offs between competing second-best objectives.

4.4.1 The orientation of governments

At its broadest and most charitable, the government's objective function can be characterized as maximizing the welfare of the greatest number of citizens. In this case, the emergence of privatization can be seen as a response to general dissatisfaction with SOE performance, just as in this perspective the creation of SOEs was a response to concerns about domestic asset distribution and establishing national economic control. In a number of countries, shifting perspectives about the merits of SOEs on the part of the public have made privatization programmes politically possible – most notable examples being Jamaica, Malaysia and Sri Lanka. This possibility is reinforced from the government's point of view by the observable popularity of privatization programmes in other countries and hence the potential political advantage to be gained from 'successful' privatization. These considerations clearly interact: political support for privatization programmes is often a direct function of the 'success' they enjoy. Success in this sense usually means the extent to which the domestic constituency enjoys, or expects to enjoy, participation in the privatization process, the most obvious indication of shared success being through public share issues where it is clear that the 'riches are being shared'. Thus we find that the profile of the programme is higher in Jamaica and Malaysia where the use of public share sales has been a feature, while in Sri Lanka President Premedasa's 'people-ization' initiative is attempting to bring a similar degree of popular support by directly linking the programme to wider share participation. In other environments where the potential beneficiaries are less obvious, or not obviously central to the government's domestic constituency (such as foreign capital), the public level of support is more limited, and the programme of lower profile.

However, while this public change of opinion can provide the enabling environment for privatization, our case studies suggest that the exact form of each programme is determined by a far narrower government objective function, concerned more with the promotion of specific groups' welfare than with the common weal. Thus, viewed in this light, privatization is a tool through which the government can attempt to achieve the same objectives as motivated the original creation of the public sector; the difficulty lies in achieving control of the distribution of rents to favoured groups while addressing other goals, most notably the improvement of enterprise efficiency.[18] In developing countries, more often than not these favoured groups are ethnic. The classic example here is Malaysia, where the overarching principle determining the design and implementation of the programme was conformity with the distributional objectives of the New Economic Policy, namely the promotion and protection of the Bumiputra's relative asset holdings. These aims were realized in the sales of MAS and MISC, for example, through the design of preferential entitlements to purchase equity, in the design of a government golden share that retained a substantial degree of control over the companies after their 'privatization', and the pre-placement of substantial amounts of equity with public sector institutions predominantly concerned with the enlargement of Bumiputra wealth. Indeed, the rent-transferring objectives of the Malaysian Government have consistently resulted in a refusal actually to transfer risk and a consequent stymieing of the objectives of improved efficiency and private sector development.

In some cases, the government has an even narrower objective function. This is the case in Malaŵi, where the privatization exercise has largely concentrated on restoring the financial viability of Press Holdings, the country's largest single company, wholly owned by the President. In other cases, the inability of government to adjust privatization as a new method of achieving old objectives has slowed programmes, even where general public support would be forthcoming. In Kenya the failure of the government to institute a distribution scheme that would ensure the allocation of assets to Kenyan Africans rather than Kenyan-Indians and yet simultaneously raise sufficient revenue has retarded the programme. In Papua New Guinea, the government's inability to sell to the domestic sector and the political sensitivity of selling to the foreign sector following the Bougainville riots has paralysed the programme, and, in Sri Lanka, entrenched bureaucratic opposition to privatization harmed certain transactions. The key point of this discussion, though, is that in general the adjustments made to privatization programmes in order to accommodate or implement these goals are revenue- and efficiency-reducing. By restricting access (and thereby raising rents), they drive a wedge between the actual and potential revenue yield from the asset, incur the dead-weight loss of rent-seeking activity, and depart from optimal resource allocation. Despite this, political imperatives appear such that the trade-off is made. This pattern is repeated when we look at the design of individual sales.

4.4.2 Political goals and individual transactions

It is often the case that the initial phase of a privatization programme is politically controversial. This is especially so when privatization represents part of the political agenda of a newly elected party, or when it is espoused by a recently victorious wing of a party in power. In these circumstances, when debate over privatization is characterized by political conflict, the first transaction with substantial publicity is required by the government to be 'successful': in effect, it becomes a bell-wether sale. The political importance of privatization leads, however, to the government adopting a risk-averse stance, and hence the requirements for political success do not fit easily with the economic rationales for privatization. The exemplar of this type of transaction is the public sale of NCB shares in Jamaica. The intense opposition (subsequently modified) of the PNP to the sale[19] meant that the JLP had to find a formula that would be politically attractive: this is found in the promotion of wider share ownership. In order to achieve this aim, the government shaped the transaction so that (i) there was a 7.5% limit on the total shareholding to be acquired by any individual, (ii) the share allocation mechanism in the event of excess demand would strongly favour the smaller investor and (iii) the issue was priced conservatively. While this strategy was successful in attracting a large number of new players into the equity market, for reputational reasons (see below), the government had to specify the ownership restriction extremely tightly. This reduced NCB's potential efficiency by locking in a sub-optimal level of management monitoring (resulting from the free-rider problem in information collection implicit in a widespread shareholding). Furthermore, one of the obvious effects of underpricing the issue was to forgo potential revenue. Thus, two key objectives were compromised by the government's response to the political dynamics of the sale.[20]

Another example arose in the sales of United Motors Limited in Sri Lanka. Here, the sale of the enterprise was speeded up on account of political considerations in spite of (or perhaps because of) the worsening security situation in the country, and the resulting lack of attention to the design of the issue (application forms were not delivered on time, the prospectus was poorly prepared, etc.) was a primary cause of the issue's failure. Moreover, in order to ensure that sale of equity would go ahead regardless of public demand, the government arranged for a group of public sector financial institutions to underwrite the issue. In the event, the sale was a disaster, and these underwriters took up 70% of the equity issued. Following privatization, there were only three trades of equity in the following year, and it is clear that the underwriters were colluding in managing the stock so as not to destabilize the share price. It is difficult to see how this outcome is contributing either to improving efficiency within the firm, or to the development of the stock exchange.

The fact that governments aim to raise political capital from privatization gives leverage to groups able adversely to affect the sale. In public share sales in particular, such leverage accrues to the managers and labour force of the enterprise to be privatized. These groups can and do use their bargaining power over government to extract rent-creating concessions. Such behaviour on the part of managements explains the frequency of efficiency-reducing measures incorporated in the terms of sale (e.g. post-privatization preferential market access and tax exemptions, the retention of unprofitable parts of a portfolio within the public sector, etc.). Suppliers of labour have at times extracted extreme concessions: an interesting case is the Malaysian railways, which the government has offered to sell for M$1 if the purchasers commit themselves to forgo any retrenchment of the labour force. More frequently in public share sales, Employee Share Schemes (ESSs) are established which offer equity at a discount. ESSs are often justified on the economic grounds that they extract higher effort levels from labour by tying reward to profitability via dividends. However, the quantitative importance of these links is dubious, and they are in any case strongly attenuated by free-rider problems and high monitoring costs. Rather, the main function of ESSs in privatizations seems to be to transfer rents to employees, principally to reward loyalty or to avert their opposition, especially in cases where retrenchment is expected. If underpricing exists, then ESSs, which give employees secure access in the allocation system, will guarantee against employees 'missing out' on any windfall profits made as a result of undervaluing the net worth of their past and future labours. In some cases, the transfer process can become somewhat extreme. In the case of Seprod, a Jamaican company privatized in 1985, 33% of the total share issue was reserved for employees at a price of J$1.50 against a market issue price of J$2.50. The option to purchase these shares was exercisable at any time for five years. Given that the share price of the firm never dropped beneath its issue price, and at one point reached J$8.50 per share, substantial opportunities existed for capital gains. Not surprisingly, nearly all the Seprod ESS shares were taken up.

Another feature of making a 'success' of privatization involves attracting buyers. At times, risk aversion on the part of governments means that they prefer to compromise revenue objectives rather than lose sales. As noted in section 4.1, most SOEs brought for sale have been involved in pre-privatization clean-ups, with often substantial capital restructurings and/or loss write-offs being undertaken at the government's expense. The pre-sale debt write-offs in the textile mills in Sri Lanka, the substantial investments in telecommunications and the recapitalization of MISC in Malaysia, the huge write-offs in Malaŵi, and the assumption of exchange-risk on CCC's loans in Jamaica are all examples of this. In some cases, these transactions are sufficient virtually to eliminate the short-term revenues to the government: while it is the case that SOEs often need some reform before sale (at government's expense), the size of these transactions suggests that they may be another form of rent distribution.

In this class of actions, and in public share sales specifically, underpricing of public assets is the most ubiquitous method of attracting buyers. However, we suggest that underpricing may lessen the expected benefit of sales on other goals of privatization, specifically revenue-raising, capital market development and efficiency objectives. We deal in Chapter 5 with the issue that such privatizations can be detrimental to capital market development, due to adverse selection and moral hazard problems in attracting new players. For the moment, we note that from the general record of privatizations via public share issues, it is clear that underpricing is not a random event, but is systemic to such sales. In terms of first-day pricing, of the eleven sales for which we have detailed enough data, nine were underpriced and five substantially so.[21] For the two issues which were not underpriced, the timing of the Sri Lankan sale was widely criticized, while the over-pricing of the Jamaican CCC issue was a direct result of the over-enthusiasm generated by the response to the previous (underpriced) NCB offer.[22] The story is generally unchanged when three-month prices are examined.[23] That our sample is not unusual is suggested by the fact that other countries (e.g. France, Japan and the UK) show a similar history of underpricing in stock market sales (see Vickers and Yarrow, 1988: Chap. 7). The revenue loss to governments consequent on underpricing is clear from Tables 4.9 and 4.10 (*see pages 43 and 44*), from the moderate in Trinidad and Tobago to the outstanding in the case of Malaysia.

With regard to the impact on capital market development, it is clear that the persistence of underpricing reflects the attempt by governments to satisfy certain objectives through the sale of shares. The key goal here is that of wider share ownership. Underpricing encourages share applications from small agents in two ways, first through lowering the cost of a given asset bundle in the presence of wealth and credit constraints, and secondly when underpricing is signalled well in advance. In this event, the riskiness of investment is intentionally reduced and this will induce more risk-averse agents to apply for shares. The wider share ownership objective is then made instrumental through the government's choice of share allocation scheme.[24] However, we would argue that underpricing is a costly and inefficient method of achieving the objective of wider share ownership. If this is the government's true objective, then the 'give-away' option should be explored more fully.[25]

It may be the case, though, that the government has the secondary aim of creating a class of buyers antagonistic to the renationalization of the enterprise. This clearly involves some mix of sunk investment in asset acquisition combined with a capital gain, so that the repurchase of the firm is not only costly but also unpopular. Thus, to hark back to the earlier discussion, one would expect to find motives for underpricing to be particularly strong where privatization is politically controversial. For example, the Jamaican Prime Minister's comment on the NCB privatization (which, as we noted, was at the time strongly opposed by the PNP) was:

> . . . [in achieving its objective] to democratise the ownership by as wide a cross-section as possible . . . [this] will make it virtually impossible for any government to renationalise . . . [this act] is irreversible . . . no power on earth can change it.

Given the strongly political nature of divestment, it is quite probable that underpricing will remain embedded in capital market sales, with the attendant negative externalities for capital market development. Allied to underpricing has been the stipulation of restrictions on the extent of individual share ownership, principally to head off concerns about the reconcentration of ownership in the hands of private sector elites. Such restrictions, which are present in virtually all public share issues in the countries studied here, generally limit any individual shareholding to a maximum of 10% of the total equity. Though such measures may have a political *raison d'être* (as in the case of NCB), they do so only at the cost of further institutionalization of the efficiency-reducing free-rider problems associated with widely dispersed equity ownership.

In conclusion, detailed analysis of the evolution and design of privatization programmes suggests that a key place must be accorded to the innately political nature of divestiture. Governments seek to achieve political objectives, especially distributional ones, while at the same time trying to ameliorate the crisis in the SOE sector and respond to the set of normative arguments forming the case for privatization. Much of the evidence cited above implies that, when they have the power, governments respond to trade-offs in these competing objectives by sacrificing goals other than the political. This conclusion, though, is modified by three considerations. First, the risk aversion of governments, caused by fear of failure, is lessened as controversy decreases. This allows consideration of economic goals to predominate.[26] It is interesting to contrast here the experience of Jamaica and Malaysia. In the former, political convergence on broad economic policy and on the merits of privatization in particular have allowed the current government to concentrate far more on the economic adjuncts of privatization, namely consideration of competition and regulation, and the revenue-maximizing design of sales. In Malaysia, on the other hand, the continuing desire to meet the goals of the New Economic Policy (NEP) has led to a situation in which though asset ownership is broad, assets are systematically underpriced and risks massively underwritten by public sector institutions, thereby compromising the underlying fiscal, efficiency, private sector and capital market objectives of the programme. However, the new phase of the NEP and the Privatization Master-plan does suggest that this ultra-cautious stance may be relaxed somewhat in the future.

Second, it is erroneous to regard the economic objectives of privatization as forming a consistent set. In reality, there are conflicts within this set just as there are between political and economic objectives. These conflicts are discussed in section 4.4.4. However, finally, the above analysis assumes that the government is in control of all the relevant variables that determine the outcome and pay-off of privatization transactions. In an important class of cases, this is not an accurate characterization. This brings us to an analysis of reputation, credibility and pre-commitment in the following section. This section is somewhat more technical and may be skipped without any great loss of continuity.

4.4.3 Reputation, credibility and pre-commitment

In discussing the objectives of privatization programmes in Chapter 2, it was briefly noted that a government's reputation with the private sector and its desire to signal intent to external donors would be important determinants of the price and shape of transactions. Reputational considerations derive from two innate features of privatization transactions, namely asymmetric information, and uncertainty in the enforceability of contract. As we shall show, a situation where a government has a poor reputation results in a sub-optimal outcome from both the public finance and the social welfare perspective. In this section, we present a simple model illustrating this problem, and discuss different ways in which governments have adapted privatization programmes using pre-commitment and reputation-creation strategies to get round the problem.

The main focus of the reputation issue concerns policy-making (i.e. privatiza-tion) over time. However, we begin by considering the problem and its solution (i.e. the Nash solution in which agents' best responses, conditional on beliefs about the behaviour of other agents, are consistent with those same beliefs) in a static, one-shot, situation. For this we use a simple, highly stylized, version of the model developed by Backus and Driffill (1985).[27] The essential feature of this model is that once the sale of an asset has been finalized the government is able to renege on its conditions of sale in order to earn additional revenue. This could be achieved in a number of ways, for example by changing the tax structure for the industry, by altering the conditions for access to the foreign-exchange auction, by imposing price controls on the industry, by changing remittance conditions for profits in the case of foreign-owned companies, by changing the regulatory framework, or ultimately by re-nationalization or expropriation. Furthermore, when the govern-ment has provided 'sweeteners' to the purchaser, there will be a cash incentive not to honour these, and thereby increase its pay-off. The government's perceived pro-pensity to renege on the sale contract (some of whose elements may be implicit) will affect the amount the private sector is willing to pay for the asset.

We consider a government which, facing some (unspecified) credit constraint, seeks to raise revenue. This it can do through the sale of an asset, but it can also augment this revenue through post-sale default. However, the private sector pur-chasers will take into account the likelihood of the government default in deciding whether to accept the offer for sale. We assume that no sale will occur if the maximum price the private sector will pay is less than the offer price. The government's anticipated total revenue from the sale is q = p + r, where p is the revenue raised at the time of sale, and r is the revenue raised through future default. We define the government's (sub)utility function as:

(1) $U_g = f(r, (r - r^e))$
     $\quad (-) \quad (+)$

where the first argument implies that the government gets utility from revenue now rather than later (for a given split between p and r), while the second argument suggests that the government none the less derives extra utility in the situation where the monetary value of its default is greater than the purchaser had expected (labelled r^e).[28] Intuitively we see that, while government wishes to maximize short-term revenue by maximizing p, it also has an incentive to 'fool' the private sector.

We assume that the private sector's (sub)utility function is defined as:

(2) $U_p = g(r - r^e)$, where $|r - r^e| > 0$
     $\quad (-)$

which simply states that for a given p (where p = q − r), the private sector does not like to be fooled.[29] Following Backus and Driffill (1985) and Vickers (1986), we simplify the analysis by choosing an arbitrary functional form for (1) and (2):

(3) $U_g = -\alpha r^2 + \beta(r - r^e)$

(4) $U_p = -(r - r^e)^2$

From this the Nash equilibrium solution can be derived as follows:

(5) $\delta U_g/\delta r = -2\alpha r + \beta = 0 \Rightarrow r = \beta/2\alpha$

(6) $\delta U_p/\delta r = 2(r - r^e) = 0 \Rightarrow r = r^e = \beta/2\alpha$

Substitute back into the utility functions U_g and U we get government and total (social) utility $U_g = U = -\beta^2/4\alpha$. These are clearly lower than would be the case if the government were able to set $r = r^e = 0$, such that $U_g = U = 0$, which is a Pareto improvement on the Nash solution. However, it is clear that the Nash solution is a direct result of the inability of the government to commit itself to a no-default scenario. Given the nature of its utility function, where it has an incentive to default in order to 'fool' the private sector, then the private sector will expect this default and consequently not accept the asset at the higher price. This is a standard example of the 'prisoners' dilemma' problem. Hence, if government could somehow convince the private sector that it was not going to default on its privatization agreement, the private sector would be induced to pay a higher current price for the asset. The government, then, has a clear economic incentive either to improve its reputation or to circumvent the credibility problem by designing binding contracts. Given the (known) structure of the government utility function, this is not possible in a one-shot sale, as above. However, once we consider a dynamic setting, the issue of policy credibility and reputations becomes clearer.

Credibility and reputation in a dynamic setting
To motivate this discussion, we need a realistic model of how the private sector might eventually come to trust the government. We suggest that an appropriate characterization of this dynamic can be found in a Bayesian framework, in which, rather than trusting the government *ab initio*, the private sector updates its assessment of the government's nature over time in response to its observations of the

government's actions. Suppose that, in contrast to the Nash solution, the nature of the government's utility function is unknown at the beginning of the process, but that the private sector makes some *ex ante* estimate of the government's 'honesty', p. The corresponding *ex ante* likelihood of default is then $(1 - p)$. If the government defaults on the initial sale then p will fall to zero (as it has revealed its true nature), and thereafter the private sector will expect a default and its offer price will fall accordingly. If, however, the government does not default, then the private sector will revise its assessment, p, according to a Bayesian updating rule. Letting the no-default state be N, the honest government be H and the dishonest D, the Bayes theorem states that the purchaser's revised estimate of the government being honest is the conditional probability that it is honest given that it did not default in this period. This is expressed as

(7) $p_{t+1} = prob(H|N)$

$$= \frac{prob(N|H)prob(H)}{[prob(N|H)prob(H) + prob(N|D)prob(D)]}$$

Under such a scheme the private sector gradually revises its estimate of the government's honesty as each sale unfolds. The result of such trust updating, and an illustration of the policy issue facing government, is presented in Fig. 4.1. This shows a case where the private sector initially sets $p = 0.25$. If after three sales no default has occurred the Bayesian rule would see the private sector's probability estimate of the government's honesty rise to 65%, and after 10 sales with no default the value of p exceeds 99%. If, however, the initial probability was 75% then the 99% certainty level would be reached after 6 sales. Clearly the initial probability estimate is crucial in determining the speed with which the government approaches full credibility and hence maximum revenues. Thus, in a world where offer prices by the private sector reflect their *ex ante* probability estimates, then it will be in the interest of government to act so as to influence this estimate.[30] One instrument for doing this lies in the design of privatization programmes.

Accelerating the reputation process through the design of privatization
In the world outlined above, the government faces a time path as in Fig. 4.1, and its objective is then to minimize the area above the Bayesian trajectory (i.e. the revenue loss). In this section we return to the experience of privatization to demonstrate two ways in which governments have attempted to minimize revenue loss. The first approach involves signalling strategies which increase the slope of the Bayesian trajectory. The main examples here concern the underpricing of shares and the sequencing of sales. The second method is the use of instruments through which government can short-circuit the gradual reputation trajectory by jumping to p* instantaneously. The chief strategies here are government pre-commitment and consideration of post-default punishment options. These will be dealt with in turn.[31]

Underpricing and sequencing
As demonstrated above, underpricing of shares in the primary market is an endemic feature of the privatization process in a large number of countries. While it is true that underpricing is used to achieve a number of objectives (as discussed in the previous section), it is also widely viewed as a way of enhancing a government's credibility and reputation. Reputations are perceived to be made on the basis of 'successful' sales, where success is measured in terms of the over-subscription for shares and the premium revealed on first-day trading. In terms of Fig. 4.1, the implicit argument is that the first-day trading premium generated

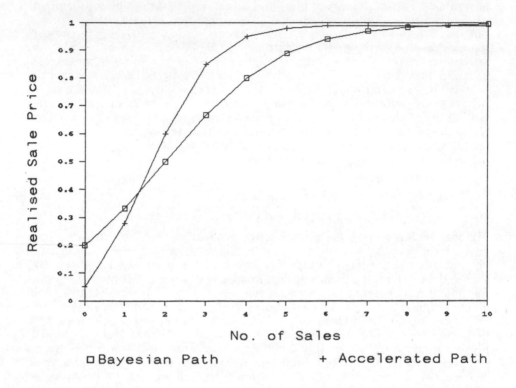

Figure 4.1 *Privatization share price and reputation*

by pricing shares below the Bayesian trajectory in the initial sale will serve to signal the government's reputation and therefore raise the price the private sector is prepared to pay for later sales more rapidly than otherwise. Using underpricing in this manner is problematic, however, since it has adverse effects on other privatization objectives and also is often an inefficient strategy for creating a reputation. First, as shown above, it can have a number of serious distributional effects, since it represents a cumbersome method of effecting a lump-sum cash transfer from the issuer to lucky share applicants implemented through the equity market. Second, it may have adverse effects on the development of the capital market operating principally in terms of moral hazard and adverse selection effects; we defer discussion of this point to Chapter 5. Third, and more importantly for the discussion here, there is the problem that underpricing may become self-defeating in that, as a result of either the adverse selection problem or political dynamics, it becomes locked into the privatization process. It is then possible that the 'underpricing' trajectory never crosses the Bayesian trajectory, and thus the government must accept a permanently lower level of revenue.[32]

If the price itself cannot be relied on to signal reputations sufficiently, an alternative route may be to use the sequencing of the sale of assets, by concentrating in the early stages on the sale of assets in sectors where the scope for default is more limited. Typically this would entail competitive as opposed to monopolistic sectors, sectors open to greater foreign participation, and also sales of relatively small assets. We showed above that, out of some 95 privatizations in our study countries, 63 were in the manufacturing, commerce and services sectors, and only in the two countries where privatization was well entrenched in the policy corpus had the programme moved significantly into the sale of utilities. This pattern of sales is corroborated by broader reviews of privatization: for example, the World Bank states (Berg and Shirley, 1987: 3–4)

> Sales have tended to affect SOEs that are small in terms of assets and employment, [and] privatization appears to have occurred most frequently in manufacturing and services sectors.

While we argue that this pattern of sales predominantly reflects the weakness of the domestic private sector, it is also a response to the private sector's unwillingness to commit large investment funds in an environment of policy risk. This unwillingness is one part of the difficulty governments face in selling off larger SOEs. Eventually, however, investing in a reputation through careful sequencing may bring a return by allowing privatization of these larger enterprises.

Pre-commitments and punishment

More fundamentally, though, using the sale price both to indicate the intrinsic value of the asset and to create a reputation may not be possible (or if possible may operate too slowly). When neither the quality of the asset nor the quality of the seller is known the private sector faces a signal extraction problem, since it observes only one piece of information, namely the price. Faced with this signalling problem, the government can use non-price instruments to boost credibility. Indeed, these instruments may well offer it the easiest way of maximizing revenues in dynamic sales by eliminating the information overload problem of price signalling and allowing it to jump to p* (in Fig. 4.1) almost immediately.

These non-price instruments can be divided into pre-commitments by the vendor (legal or otherwise) against future default, and punishment options by the seller or by other agents in the event of such default. Although these are conceptually separate, it is natural to see them as linked issues, on the grounds that only if the buyer is able to punish the vendor after the breaking of a pre-commitment will that punishment be credible. Thus, it may be optimal (i.e. intertemporally revenue-maximizing) for the government to introduce 'full' or 'perfect' punishment possibilities into privatization sales in order to make its pre-commitments credible. As suggested above, this is essentially a method of circumventing the reputation problem by eliminating the uncertainty that asymmetric information introduced into the sale process.

Broadly speaking, pre-commitments and punishment possibilities can be classified into two main sorts: (i) those that are instrumented through third parties, and (ii) those that are implicit or explicit to a bilateral contract. An example of the general form of third-party pre-commitment is the recently created Multilateral Investment Guarantee Agency (MIGA) and other investment promotion schemes which provide insurance against loss of earnings as a result of non-commercial risk (including re-nationalization). In privatization, though, these would mostly impact only on sales to foreign investors. Another more common example comes through the exigencies of IMF and World Bank adjustment lending which attempt to bind government policy actions.[33]

In general, for reasons such as these, third-party strategies are rare. More typical are pre-commitments and punishment possibilities built into the individual sale contract. However, although these offer the most rapid way of dealing with the reputation problem, they frequently compromise other objectives of the privatization programme. To document this point, we present two examples of explicit pre-commitment/punishment provisions from the Jamaican privatization programme.

The National Commercial Bank (NCB) sale, as noted above, was critical to the whole Jamaican privatization programme. The ramifications of political controversy for the design of the sale have already been analysed: here we focus on the government's methods of pre-commitment with respect to potential buyers. While the NCB itself was a consistently profitable institution (implying that, as a private firm, an appropriately priced share issue would have been enthusiastically received), the Jamaican Government still had a reputation for extensive intervention in the private sector. Thus one of the key means in persuading individuals to buy shares would consist of designing a visible and credible method of locking the government out of future interventions in the running of the NCB.[34] This was made all the more important by the decision to sell only 51% of the equity, leaving the government in control of 49% after the sale. Hence, reputation issues would be central to the success of the privatization programme in Jamaica.

Ultimately the government chose a pre-commitment option which tied its hands by rendering certain entrenched provisions of the company virtually immune to alteration. These were (i) that the government's remaining 49% share was declared non-voting, and (ii) that any individual's shareholding could not exceed 7.5% of total equity. These provisions could only be changed by unanimous agreement at a meeting of more than 90% of shareholders with voting rights. The Memorandum of Association of the bank was similarly entrenched. These restrictions, which far exceeded normal private sector practice in Jamaica, indicated the seriousness of the government's desire to signal its intention not to default. This conclusion is underscored by the fact that when the government was considering the inclusion of a 'golden share' arrangement its advisers warned that such an action would raise fears of future intervention and thus render the NCB unsaleable. The government consequently dropped the idea.[35]

If the privatization of NCB was important politically, the sale of Telecommunications of Jamaica (ToJ) was regarded by the government as equally crucial for economic growth, since by 1988 telecommunications was regarded as a critical bottleneck in the restructuring of the economy. In order to obtain the necessary quantity and high quality of capital investment required to overhaul the telecommunications sector, the government had to sell the company to a foreign operator. Given the size of the new investment proposed (approximately US$300m. over a 5-year period), the government needed to convince the buyer that the investment would not be jeopardized by default in the future (either by way of re-nationalization or through price controls), even if there was a clear short-term economic incentive to do so. The methods chosen in this case were a combination of legal pre-commitment and the prescription of a punishment process. In brief, these were as follows:

i) ToJ was granted an exclusive (i.e. monopoly) 25-year licence for domestic and foreign telecommunications in Jamaica which would be renewed automatically for another 25 years unless, with 2½ years notice, the government acquired all ToJ assets at a fair market value as determined by a firm of valuers acceptable to both parties.

ii) In the event of a revocation of the licence, ToJ was allowed two years to sell its assets. If it was unable to do so, the government would be obliged to purchase the assets at a fair market price.

iii) In the event of such a repurchase the government was obliged to pay either in cash or up to 95% of the total in promissory notes denominated in US dollars or UK sterling over a period of 15 years at 2% above London Inter-Bank Overnight Rate (LIBOR) for similar sized deposits.

iv) ToJ price-setting regulations guaranteed the company an annual 17.5–20%

return on shareholders funds. Further, the design of the regulatory regime made no attempt to impose cost savings on the firm.

Essentially, these provisions offered the foreign owners of ToJ an investment free of expropriation risk, with a guaranteed return. These extraordinarily detailed agreements, in fact, offer a example of almost perfect pre-commitment since the Jamaican Government specified a punishment strategy that would leave the putative owner of ToJ indifferent between holding ToJ equity and accepting government compensation.

Interesting as these transactions are in themselves, the key point for the discussion here is that these pre-commitment/punishment strategies, motivated by the revenue-maximization objective of the government, served to reduce economic efficiency below the optimal position. In the case of the NCB, shareholder control of management was compromised by the entrenched provisions, while for TOJ a 50-year monopoly position was locked in under the simple rate-of-return regulation.[36] That these punitive pre-commitments were deemed necessary to establish the government's credibility in the privatization programme is an indication of the extent to which confidence in the 'honesty' of the Jamaican Government had been eroded during the previous decades. It also suggests that there are costs to poor reputation other than bad economic performance, namely the costs of re-establishing reputation or of devising procedures to circumvent the problem of lack of credibility. These costs may emerge as explicit trade-offs in the implementation of privatization programmes, especially in countries where governments have interventionist reputations but wish to embark on privatization programmes of substantial size.

The second form of bilateral pre-commitment/punishment strategies are implicit commitments, the main one being the creation of a wide share ownership base. Put simply, the larger the number of shareholders, the greater will be the political cost of default. Wider share ownership binds the government into a large number of individual contracts with its electorate, each of which is able to punish default. The logical implication of this is, of course, the 'give-away' option, now popular in Eastern Europe, through which shares in SOEs are distributed free to all taxpayers, voters or citizens. This form of privatization can be seen as a means of effectively achieving a number of the main objectives of privatization. Aside from the creation of a near-perfect reputation and important reputation externalities in other areas, the method also facilitates a rapid and cheap divestiture on the part of the state. In doing so it quickly allows for a private market valuation to emerge, with consequent implications for the development of capital market trading and optimal resource and risk allocation; it avoids the re-concentration of wealth in the hands of those investors who have the liquidity and luck to purchase privatization shares; and it represents a 'pure' form of privatization by giving back to the private sector the freedom to choose how to allocate the asset bundle which has hitherto (nominally at least) been held in its name.[37] While, in many of the countries which have sold enterprises through public issues, wider share ownership has been used as a political and reputational tool, no governments in our country studies have explored the 'give-away' option.

The impact of reputation and policy credibility issues on the design and implementation of privatization programmes has rarely been explored in other studies of privatization in developing countries.[38] This may once again be the result of the importation of developed-country models – where credibility in government policy is not such an important issue – to the developing-country context. However, our line of analysis suggests that, though often unremarked, governments are obliged to take account of policy credibility considerations when implementing sales – especially when divesting large enterprises and/or involving foreign buyers. Inasmuch as a number of countries are seeking to expand their programmes and start privatizing utilities, we would expect methods of securing private sector credence in government policy to become more important. However, as noted above, across the scope of our research, the use of pre-commitment and punishment contracts have emerged as the most widespread and most effective methods for enhancing a government's reputation. While these may be revenue-maximizing (when compared to the base case of reputational updating), they run the risk of locking in inefficiencies over the long term and hence vitiating the key objective of the sale.

4.4.4 Other conflicts in objectives

In the last three sections, we have discussed the ramifications of the innately political nature of privatization. We examined ways in which governments' attempts to instrument political objectives in privatization have shaped both programmes and individual sales, and analysed strategies which governments have employed to overcome reputational constraints that are outside their direct power to change. In both cases, however, we noted that these actions caused friction with other, publicly professed, goals of privatization and that, in general, political aims were those chosen to be directly instrumented. As the disjunction between the thrust of political and other objectives increases, so the achievement of the main aims of privatization is made increasingly less likely.

However, there are also tensions within the publicly professed objectives of privatization, which we delineated in Chapter 2. These would exist even if the government were a social welfare maximizer with no political agenda of its own. Here we consider some of the more problematic conflicts in objectives which have already been encountered in the countries studied (the discussion of capital market impacts is deferred to Chapter 5). Of course, what we refer to here as 'conflicts in objectives' may not be regarded as such by those undertaking the privatization process. What we observe are publicly expressed objective functions, not privately held rankings (which may be internally consistent). However, these two rankings may differ substantially, and what we observe as a conflict may be a tension between the two positions.

A fundamental conflict facing all governments is that of achieving the economic objectives of privatization in the light of ancillary objectives, particularly the desire to improve fiscal balances (often in response to external pressure). This is particularly troublesome in developing countries where privatization often takes place in the midst of a fiscal crisis in which the government is confronted simultaneously by the urgency of loan conditionality on the one hand, and growing domestic political dissatisfaction on the other. Given this framework, the temptation is for governments to emphasize the short-run liquidity transformation (i.e. cash for equity) aspect of privatization. Thus, an overriding goal of programmes tends to be the rapid reduction of fiscal deficits by the quick sale of enterprises, and the decision to sell a function of the forces leading a government to prefer cash to equity. This, however, clashes in a number of ways with the rationale most often put forward for privatization, namely the enhancement of efficiency. Firstly, often only the most profitable enterprises are sold, since they are the easiest to divest quickly. Not only are these enterprises generally net contributors to current revenue, but they are likely to be operating efficiently (in an internal sense). Sale of these enterprises is unlikely to result in greatly enhanced efficiency. The limiting example of this type of dynamic was the fourth tranche sale of ToJ, which gave the foreign shareholder a majority equity stake for the first time. This sale was carried out solely to earn foreign exchange so that the government could pass a quarterly IMF performance test. Second, we find that in a number of cases the profitability of SOEs is a function of their monopoly power (either natural, strategic or administratively determined). As stressed earlier, sale of public sector monopolies to the private sector invariably means a transfer of monopoly profits to the private sector: there is no inevitability of efficiency gains in this case. Too often the desire to bring enterprises to market and maximize immediate revenue has resulted in pressures to proceed with the divestiture of monopolistic enterprises, while the issue of the post-privatization regulation of private monopolies is either ignored until after the sale has occurred or at best inadequately considered.[39]

The specific problem of conflict between revenue maximization and efficiency enhancement forms one part of a broader conclusion on the attainability of these two goals. Although improvements in public finance and gains in efficiency are espoused as the two most important objectives of privatization, we suggest that in many developing countries they have at best been only partially fulfilled. In all seven countries studied, efficiency gains and revenue improvements have not been, or may not be, substantial, for a variety of the reasons expounded above (i.e. as a result of the types of enterprises sold, the lack of regulatory systems to accommodate the widespread presence of market dominance, or more basic political pressures). The majority of firms that have been privatized are ones which have already been running relatively efficiently, either over a long period of time, or due to pre-privatization clean-ups.[40] This is especially true of share sales to the public, where it is generally assumed that the offer for sale of loss-making SOEs would not attract private investors.[41] In these cases, it may well be that the net long-run impact on public finance will be negative. On the other hand, there are clear examples of genuine and measurable success in terms of post-privatization efficiency gains, although these are more common in other types of privatization (i.e. direct sales to the domestic and/or foreign private sector, and management leasing), such as the textile mills in Sri Lanka, Iron and Steel Company of Trinidad and Tobago (ISCOTT) and hotel leasing/sales, bus route tenders, and agricultural marketing board sales in Jamaica. In these cases, the net long-run impact on public finance has been (and will be) positive.

A second conflict concerns revenue maximization and private sector development. The pronounced dualism of privatization sales was emphasized in our review of the experience of privatization to date. Concentration on the sale of larger enterprises through public share sales or foreign purchase may result in higher revenues in each budget, but as successive country studies show, they will do little to 'crowd in' the small- and medium-scale domestic private sector, which lacks the resources to become a player in this type of programme. The problem is reinforced by the fact that short-term revenue maximization involves the sale of monopolies as they are: in many cases, governments have let slip the opportunity of creating competitive markets or breaking up Leviathan enterprises through a strongly pro-competitive policy, though both would have a positive effect on the development of the domestic private sector. A more common occurrence, however, is the creation of private sector entry-deterring oligopolies and monopolies.

There is also a tension in privatization programmes caused by the necessity of meeting adjustment conditionalities. This tension is made manifest through pressure from external agencies to proceed with divestiture as rapidly as possible. However, speed of sale is seldom conducive to the full realization of the potential of privatization. First, there is pressure on governments to privatize enterprises before they are ready for sale. Increasingly, multilateral agencies have come to realize that both SOE reform and privatization programme issues are time-consuming, and that three-year adjustment loans are excessively blunt instruments for implementing privatization. As the World Bank notes (Galal, 1990):

> it has been noted that most attempts to reform public enterprises have used SALs [Structural Adjustment Loans] . . . yet public enterprise problems are complex and SALs generally have been selective and macro-oriented . . . It has also been noted that several components of public enterprise reforms take longer to implement than permitted under a typical SAL disbursing period.

Second, privatizations undertaken at high speed or under intense pressure are often poorly designed. For example, in Kenya the Uplands Bacon Factory sale was pursued in response to the moratorium on disbursements of a previous adjustment loan. Though UBF's sale was not directly part of any adjustment conditionality, and ultimately was not successful, the government clearly felt it would restore its credibility (Mosley *et al.*, 1991: Vol. 2, Chap. 10). In the event, however, design faults arising from excessive haste caused the sale to fail. Similarly in Jamaica, privatization of the Caribbean Cement Company (CCC) was undertaken with extreme rapidity. As Chapter 7 documents, however, certain avoidable mistakes in the construction of the sale had a negative impact not only on the firm's post-privatization performance but also on the net revenues from the transaction received by government. Of course, design problems are not only caused by external pressure. In the case of the land leases in Jamaica, failures arose where there was a conflict between improving the yield on agricultural land (an efficiency objective), and the government's desire to diversify the agricultural sector through the promotion of non-traditional crops (a private sector development objective, broadly interpreted).

This last trade-off reasserts itself in another way. In some countries, the goal of private sector development has been concerned with involving the private sector in projects which have previously been the province of the state, rather than being concerned with promoting the assumption by the private sector of entrepreneurial (i.e. more dynamic, risk-taking) behaviour through the encouragement of competition. Thus, 'crowding-in' the private sector can take the form merely of enticing the private sector into new areas of economic activity, through substantial government underwriting of commercial risk. The classic example of this is the Malaysian Build–Operate–Transfers (BOTs), where the creation of 'safety net' guarantees by government to protect private sector operators against future revenue shortfalls effectively undermines the whole purpose of BOT in the first place.[42] However, the implication of such transactions is that competition is stifled and hence expectations of efficiency gains are downgraded.

4.5 Conclusions

Analysis of the record of a decade's privatization in our country studies showed that actual outcomes had been quantitatively disappointing. Privatization to date has played only a small role in the reform of the SOE sector. However, aggregating across the programmes revealed certain common salient features. Most importantly, the analysis delineated how the design and outcomes of individual transactions and privatization programmes are strongly influenced by (i) the attempt by governments to address political issues, or gain political capital from privatization; (ii) the need to ensure credibility in privatization policy; and (iii) the intrinsic tensions in the broad goals assigned to privatization. The satisfaction of these constraints, however, can result in a failure to attain other objectives. Specifically, it is the goal of improved efficiency – which after all provides the central economic argument for privatization – which is most often subordinated (whether deliberately or through oversight) when trade-offs occur.

Of course, governments in developing countries could adopt far more rigorous competition and regulatory policies. The adoption of such policies could result in a far stronger concern with efficiency enhancement in privatization transactions. This, indeed, is one of the issues discussed in the next chapter. However, we believe that even if governments oriented privatizations purely around economic/technocratic issues, the nature of economic structures in developing countries would often have a powerful limiting impact on the potential of privatization. Documenting this claim is the subject of the next chapter.

Notes

1. The most important is the M$2.35bn sale of 24% of the equity in Syarikat Telekom Malaysia in November 1990. A number of smaller but controversial transactions have occurred in Jamaica.
2. For example, we exclude (in this section) the Malaysian BOT contracts, the 'corporatizations' which have occurred in Sri Lanka, the tendering of various local government services in Jamaica, and the closure of SOEs in a number of countries.
3. However, the privatization of telecommunications in Malaysia in late 1990 dramatically changes this result (see Chapter 9).
4. In the case of Sri Lanka, for example, this stage has been formalized through the process of 'corporatization' whereby government-owned business undertakings (GOBUs) are restructured into public companies in which government retains 100% of the equity prior to sales to the public. Similarly, the sale of equity in MISC by government was preceded by a M$125m. rights issue in which government participated.
5. Indeed, it has been suggested that the extensive use of such committee structures and the guidelines which have emerged from them have been employed to retard any privatization initiatives. The fact that there have been virtually no asset sales in Kenya throughout the entire decade would support this claim.
6. This reflects a similar dynamic to the programme in the UK. In both countries, privatization came to symbolize extreme differences in economic policy between the government and the opposition.
7. This, of course, does not exclude, as indeed occurs, the possibility of the body contracting out of work by the DSB to private sector consultancies.
8. Good examples are the United Motors sale in Sri Lanka, the Port Klang sale in Malaysia, the Niugini Insurance Corporation sale in PNG and the land lease programme in Jamaica.
9. Although, as discussed in the case study, the situation in Sri Lanka is complicated by a bifurcation of roles brought about in no small measure by the intransigence and opposing objectives of external donors.
10. Only Malawi and Papua New Guinea are without formal stock exchanges.
11. As will be noted in the case studies, though these sales were effected ostensibly through the capital market, to the extent that the shares were listed, the bulk of the issue was handled through private placements to institutions prior to sale.
12. There are many other reasons for the lack of private sector development.
13. This feature is not unique to the countries studied, but is an absence observed elsewhere amongst developing countries. Despite the theoretical attraction of the management or employee buy-out option, the phenomenon has not caught on. One of the few projects of this kind amongst developing countries is a 'greenfield' project between Goodyear tyres and an Egyptian tyre manufacturer. This is not a completely appropriate example, however, since two of the fundamental problems encountered in projects of this sort in low-income economies – namely labour shedding and financing of the share purchase – have been overcome by the fact that the project is new and financed by an external donor at concessional rates. (Information provided to the authors by the Centre for Privatization, Washington, in 1989.)
14. In Trinidad and Tobago, an extreme case, foreign ownership of traded equity was until recently illegal unless a specific exemption had been granted by the President.
15. These shares are to be sold at M$7 per share (as opposed to the offer price for domestic investors of M$5 per share), and will be effected through the sale of exchangeable foreign-exchange bonds by the Bank Negara. The bonds will be redeemable for STM equity.

16. In Jamaica, SOEs were given a new legal standing under the Public Enterprises Act, while in Sri Lanka the process of SOE corporatization took five years from the first suggestion of the move to its legislative completion.

17. On account of this problem, concern has been expressed that World Bank SALs are not appropriate mechanisms for encouraging privatization. See S. Kikeri, *Bank Lending for Divestiture: A Review of Experience*, World Bank Working Paper Series No. 338, 1990.

18. Note that in some cases it was realized that the SOE sector was a very inefficient method of favouring certain constituents. While employment could be targeted, prices and output were less easy to direct specifically at chosen groups.

19. The government was sufficiently concerned about this opposition to take the unusual step of noting the PNP's stance in the share offer document. See Chapter 7 for more details.

20. It is worth noting that the recent development of a domestic political consensus in favour of privatization in Jamaica has allowed much more attention to be paid to economic and technical issues rather than political concerns in the design of the programme.

21. We define underpricing to be a situation where the offer price is less than the post-sale revealed market price.

22. In fact, this Jamaican experience offers evidence of the potential dynamic costs of underpricing.

23. Note that these are a less reliable guide to under- or overpricing due to the effect of intervening noise on the share price.

24. In the event of oversubscription, almost all sales have involved an at times extremely heavy weighting of the allocation scheme towards the smaller investor.

25. This option is being explored most fully through the universal voucher schemes of Central and Eastern European post-communist governments.

26. Hence the paradox that the costs of departures from efficiency orientation in privatization programmes are raised by the presence of opposition to the programmes themselves.

27. They use the Barro–Gordon 'surprise supply function' model to argue that the extremely tight monetary and fiscal policy in the UK in the early 1980s was adopted by the new Conservative Government to create a reputation for toughness. Vickers (1986) uses the model in an extension of the monetary policy problem to examine the case where 'wet' governments may wish to masquerade as 'drys', while 'drys' seek to signal their 'dryness' early in their term of office.

28. In other words by expecting a lower level of r, the private sector is prepared to buy at a higher level of p, but consequently following default the total 'cost' is $p + r = q^* > q$.

29. For simplicity this condition rules out the situation where $r^e > r$, in which case the price the private sector would be prepared to pay would be less than the offer price and thus no sale would be effected.

30. The characterization here is somewhat oversimplified, since in reality privatization occurs in conditions where information is not readily available and is frequently ambiguous. Hence it may not always be clear to the private sector whether a post-privatization deterioration in, say, profits, is due to the default on the part of the government or to other (possibly external) factors. In such cases, less mechanistic punishment strategies are likely. Assume that, although the players may not be able to observe true states of nature, they can make judgements about their probability distribution. Then the punishment strategies employed will be more sophisticated and involve consideration of Type I and Type II errors. However, the essential results outlined above will remain unaltered.

31. In some countries – mostly Central and Eastern Europe – a third method of establishing a reputation has come about as a by-product of wholesale systemic changes. Incumbent, post-communist, governments innately possess widespread public trust thanks to the circumstances of their emergence. The range of possible economic policies was enormously expanded by the collapse of communism, including a dramatic reduction of the costs of establishing a reputation in privatization programmes.

32. Evidence on this 'lock-in' effect is ambivalent. On the one hand, the UK privatization programme has been characterized by persistently large discounts on public share sales. This has conditioned investor psychology to such an extent that applications now appear to depend on the expectation of immediate and significant capital gains. On the other hand, the three Jamaican public share sales have been marked by progress towards a zero discount position. Malaysia lies between these two extremes.

33. However, there are a number of problems with this latter form of pre-commitment. First, there is frequently a lack of precision in loan conditions. Second, there are difficult principal–agent problems in which the principals (the shareholders of the purchasing firms) are unable to ensure that the agents (the multilateral institutions) will safeguard them against default by the government. Third, in such cases the third party may have an incentive to collude with the government to obscure defaults on the part of the latter. Fourth, these third parties may act in ways which the

purchasers perceive as compromising their interests, for example, by imposing conditionalities about devaluation and import compression.

34. Importantly, the government of the day was concerned not just with tying its own hands but also with eliminating the possibility of intervention by a future government hostile to private ownership.

35. Interestingly, as a result of the success of the NCB sale, by the time of the next public issue (of the Caribbean Cement Company) the government's reputation had improved to such an extent that a 'golden share' was included with no apparent objections from the private sector.

36. The inefficiency of this type of regulation as a result of the Averch–Johnson effect, whereby rate-of-return regulation creates incentives for the firm to over-invest in capital, has been widely noted (Vickers and Yarrow, 1988).

37. This hides a plethora of complex public finance effects. For example, the transfer of wealth from public to private will have non-neutral consumption and savings effects, while the impact of taxation will be similarly distortionary.

38. One may contrast this with the applied and theoretical literatures on structural adjustment and trade shocks, where credibility and consistency of government policy are of great importance.

39. Note that efficient regulation, by lowering the expected profit stream to the enterprise, lowers the sale price and thereby deprives government of immediate revenues.

40. This observation arises from the 'paradox of privatization', namely that governments wish to sell loss-making enterprises, for which there are no buyers, and hence are forced to sell profitable enterprises only.

41. In a number of cases – especially Malaysia – companies are required to demonstrate a dividend record before listing is achieved.

42. This conclusion is particularly strong in an economy such as Malaysia where the government is not seriously credit constrained.

5 Privatization & Economic Structure

In our review of the theory underpinning privatization, we suggested that three factors were crucial in determining the economic impact that privatization will have. The first is the structure of the enterprise and the nature of the market into which it is sold. We suggested that the size of the firm relative to its competitors, the inelasticity of demand for its output, and its capital intensity are major factors in determining the firm's ability to deter entry into the market and to earn monopoly profits. The second is the ability of the capital market, in addition to mobilizing savings for investment, to provide price signals to enhance resource allocation and impose market discipline on enterprise management. The third is the nature and capacity of regulation and competition policy, through which the adverse effects of private sector monopoly power may be attenuated. Much of the policy formulation and implementation of privatization in developing countries has proceeded as if these factors were not material. We suggest, on the contrary, that, though there are many political forces which shape the process of privatization in the short run (cf. Chapter 4), it is in fact these constraints that have been the ultimate determinant of the pace and structure of privatization in developing countries over the medium term, and which therefore determine the fundamental value of privatization in such economies. In this view, it is no surprise that privatization has been less successful in the low-income economies of Africa and in Sri Lanka, or in the narrow oil- and mineral-based economies of Trinidad and Tobago and Papua New Guinea, than in the larger, more diversified, economies of Jamaica and Malaysia. The pace of progress is fundamentally determined by the economic structure of the economy, while the likely efficiency impact of privatization is similarly determined by market structures and regulatory capacity.

In this chapter we attempt to consider in detail how the structure of the domestic private sector interacts with privatization. Section 5.1 examines the extent to which the domestic private sector in the seven economies can both provide a competitive environment through which the economic efficiency gains expected to flow from privatization can be realized, and also generate the resources to absorb privatization sales (this latter point being generally omitted in the privatization debate). Section 5.2 focuses on the twin roles of the capital market in the privatization process, namely savings mobilization (from the domestic and foreign sectors), and the imposition of discipline on management. Section 5.3 considers the issue of regulatory capacity and its likely impact on the post-privatization environment. As noted in Chapter 2, privatization objectives have included the 'crowding-in' of the private sector, and the 'kick-starting' of the capital market. Throughout this chapter we therefore consider both the constraints that economic structure imposes on privatization and the feedback from privatization to these structural factors.

Table 5.1 *Macroeconomic characteristics*

Country	Pop. (mn)	GNP/capita (US$ 1988)	Urban Pop. (% of Total)	GDI[a]	GDS[b]	Budget Deficit (% of GDP)	Manufacturing (% of GDP)
Jamaica	2.5	1,070	52	27	19	(5.0)	22
Trinidad	1.3	3,350	69	18	21	(4.1)	10
Malaysia	17.9	1,940	43	26	36	(8.0)	24
Sri Lanka	17.2	420	21	23	13	(12.8)	16
PNG	3.9	810	16	26	21	(1.9)	9
Kenya	24.0	370	24	26	22	(6.6)	11
Malaŵi	8.8	170	12	16	8	(8.6)	11

Source: World Development Report, 1991.

Notes
a) Gross Domestic Investment.
b) Gross Domestic Savings.

5.1 Private sector constraints and limits to competition

The countries covered in this book differ quite markedly in the size and structure of their economies, not least the maturity of their domestic private sectors. In this section we describe the structure of the industrial sector and the extent to which the forces of competition are present, the relative size and economic power of SOEs within this sector, and finally the capacity of the domestic and foreign sectors to mobilize the resources necessary to acquire privatized assets.

Throughout we face the problem of evaluating arguments on the basis of only limited evidence. As shown in Chapter 4, the extent of sales to the domestic private sector has been extremely limited, and especially so in the smaller economies. It is unlikely therefore that any appreciable 'crowding-in' has yet occurred. It is, by extension, difficult to conjecture about the effect of future privatization efforts on private sector investment, whether by crowding-in or by altering perceived investment uncertainty. We start by considering the nature of the private sector (mainly the non-agricultural sector), first in terms of market structures, competitiveness and concentration, and then in terms of its savings mobilization capacity. Finally, we consider the relationship between the domestic and the foreign private sectors.

5.1.1 The domestic private sector and competition
Table 5.1 summarizes some aspects of the economic structure of the seven economies. The countries fall into three main sets. The first is Malaysia and Jamaica which, despite their difference in population, have similar fundamental characteristics in terms of income levels, urbanization, market depth, and the share of manufacturing in total GDP. The second set is Trinidad and Tobago and Papua New Guinea which are small mineral-exporting economies[1] in which the manufacturing sector accounts for a relatively small proportion of total output. Although they have very different levels of per capita incomes these two economies are both narrowly based and heavily import-dependent. The third comprises the two African economies of Kenya and Malaŵi. In some respects these are two very different economies – Kenya is the most industrialized East African economy, while Malaŵi remains fundamentally a poor agricultural economy – but as the case studies will show, they share many characteristics typical of other economies in Africa. Finally, there is Sri Lanka which conforms to its reputation as one of the outliers amongst developing economies: a low-income country, but one boasting a highly structured and relatively industrialized economy. Though

Table 5.2   *Size and concentration in the domestic manufacturing sector*

	Share of Manuf. in GDP	Capacity Util.	EPR[a]	Employment[b]	Market Concentration[c]
Jamaica	22%	60%	75%	16%	–
Trinidad	10%	–	–	13%	57%
Malaysia	24%	85%+	14%	18%	16%
Sri Lanka	16%	–	100%	12%	90%
PNG	9%	–	–	10%	80%
Kenya	11%	40–90%	30%	13%	65%
Malaŵi	11%	45%	140%	8%	89%

Source: Country case studies, Chapters 7–13.

Notes
a) Effective protection rates based on average rates across all subsectors.
b) Manufacturing employment as percentage of total.
c) Market concentration ratios defined as proportion of employees in firms with less than 50 employees (Malaysia, PNG, Sri Lanka); sales concentration ratios based on Hirfindahl index (Kenya and Malaŵi, Trinidad and Tobago).

the sample is small, these countries represent reasonable archetypes for many low- and middle–low-income developing countries (outside the Southern cone), and hence the common characteristics of their domestic private sectors go a long way to explaining the nature of the privatization process in many similar developing economies.

Data on the structure of the private sector are usually limited, partial, and more dependent on infrequent external analyses[2] than on data produced regularly by statistics bureaux. In general we are compelled to rely on survey data and casual observation: however, these both delineate a consistent picture. As the country studies show, a large proportion of firms are small measured by employment and turnover, are owner-managed, with limited access to long-term finance, and have a restricted risk-spreading capacity. Moreover, there remains a severe dearth of indigenous joint-stock companies in most of the economies. Markets are frequently concentrated, being dominated by one or more large public sector or foreign-owned enterprises accounting for the major proportion of output, or, if not by these, then by a small number of family or tribally-owned enterprises.

In addition, we have tried to identify some more quantitative data on the structure of the domestic private sector. Table 5.2 assembles some of the survey evidence on the structure of the domestic manufacturing sector in order to illustrate some features on the size distribution and degree of concentration prevalent in the seven countries.

Though sketchy, this evidence is informative. First, with the exception of Malaysia, the industrial (non-agricultural) sectors tend to be characterized by low levels of capacity utilization (often due to foreign-exchange rationing), and high levels of effective protection. Moreover, the evidence suggests that the sector is also highly concentrated. Limited statistical data exist on concentration rates but those which do are supported by casual observation. The Hirfindahl indices of concentration for Kenya and Malaŵi indicate very high market dominance by monopoly and oligopoly firms (many of which are SOEs), while employment-based evidence from other economies replicates this.

In the smaller economies in this study, the bulk of private sector employment is generated in micro-enterprises, while the small number of firms with a work-force of more than 50 people contain most, if not all, of the SOEs. In Sri Lanka, for example, most private sector firms are very small, with over 85% of all firms in the manufacturing sector employing less than 5 people. Less than 1% of firms employ more than 100 people, and within this group are found virtually all SOEs and all foreign-owned companies (USAID, 1988). A comparable picture emerges in the Caribbean, where for Trinidad and Tobago and Jamaica research suggests that market dominance is significant in a wide range of sectors, and that dominant firms in these sectors are frequently state-owned (Ayub, 1981; Crichton and Farrell, 1988). In Kenya the manufacturing sector is similarly concentrated, with 50% of all firms employing less than five people, and only 10% employing over 50, while average SOE size in the Kenyan manufacturing size is approximately 120 employees (Grosh, 1986).

Though not universal, SOE sectoral domination is widespread. Whilst this may be expected, for example in the oligopolistic transport, energy, communications, and possibly finance sectors, we have noted that it also emerges in what are usually regarded as traditionally more competitive sectors, such as manufacturing, agriculture, and services. This suggests that these economies are significantly different from those implicit in the models of competition underpinning the privatization debate. Only in the largest country in the sample, namely Malaysia, is there evidence that the private sector in general is deep enough to provide a sufficient degree of competition in the industrial sectors, although, even there, the relative balance is still in favour of public enterprises. This raises issues of competition policy and regulation to which we shall return in section 5.3.

The advantages of size and capital intensity as instruments for enforcing market dominance are, in many cases, compounded by the presence of interlocking directorships which enhance the capacity of large firms, especially oligopolistic ones, to act collusively. It is a common feature of smaller developing countries that a small number of individual owners and directors sit on a large number of company boards. Sometimes these companies exist in the same market so that tacit market-sharing can be easily enforced. More often, though interlocking directorships are less direct, they are equally important, such as directors of industrial enterprises being also board members of financial institutions. In addition, such directors may also hold seats on important advisory committees to government on matters such as taxation and trade policy. Such situations are by no means illegal,[3] but they clearly impart important advantages to the interlocked firms, even simply because of the improved flows of information. This phenomenon is more prevalent in smaller economies: Malaŵi is the most extreme case with the interlocking shareholdings and directorships between Press Holdings and the two public sector holding companies, ADMARC and MDC, but it is also a traditional feature in Jamaica, Sri Lanka and Kenya.

These characteristics of the private sector in our country studies translate naturally into concerns about a lack of post-privatization competition. There is one caveat to these concerns, however. In the industrial sector of a number of countries (for example, Malaysia, Sri Lanka, and Kenya) public ownership extends over a number of enterprises operating in similar sectors. Divestiture of these enterprises together may well, of itself, provide the basis for a competitive market regardless of the structure of the private sector *ex ante*. Similar situations exist in other sectors. For example, the simultaneous privatization and deregulation of urban bus transport systems in Sri Lanka and Jamaica have created efficient and (highly) competitive markets. An identical situation arises in the agricultural sector in the Caribbean, where wholesale sales of land (Jamaica) and sugar plantation land (Trinidad and Tobago) could provide the basis for a competitive market. The discussion of individual country experiences will pursue this point further.

To a large extent the characteristics of the private sector outlined above were responsible for stimulating the growth of the SOE sector in the first place. State intervention was justified on the grounds of exploitation of scale economies of production. Indigenous private sector entrepreneurs were not in a position to mobilize sufficient funds for investment, or, if they were, did not appear prepared to absorb the high risks involved in investment in commodity-dependent economies. Moreover, the formal financial system, which was principally geared towards the financing of export trade, was rarely sufficiently diversified to provide venture capital for capital-intensive development. Large-scale investments, not only in infrastructure but also in the traditionally more competitive manufacturing and processing sectors, were not forthcoming from the domestic private sector, and were in fact provided by the public and foreign sectors. However, the form of intervention chosen to address this structural weakness of the private sector has also served to exacerbate the problem. As noted in Chapter 3, the growth of many developing economies in the 1960s and 1970s was based on a combination of foreign direct investment and public sector import-substituting investment, a strategy which has had significant implications for the development of a competitive economy. In a number of cases (most obviously Jamaica and Malaysia) the growth in the public sector has been complemented by growth in the indigenous private sector: in others the public sector has substituted for the private. In these countries, therefore, SOE dominance of the industrial sector by legislative fiat, and by their preferential access to domestic credit, foreign financing and import licences, has effectively 'crowded-out' the indigenous private sector. Most importantly, however, governments rarely addressed the issue of private sector development, and in some cases have acted deliberately to suppress private sector activity. Thanks to these actions, indigenous private sectors are still very weak.

Moreover, the economic capacity of putative post-privatization firms to maintain monopoly profits is often enhanced by the political negotiations underpinning the privatization process. The first and most direct example is the pre-sale 'readying' process which, as a result of debt write-offs and refinancings, contributions towards contingent pension liabilities, labour force adjustments and so on, endows the enterprise with a favourable capital or asset structure yielding competitive advantage at the taxpayer's expense. Less benign are agreements to maintain 'most favoured' status in terms of tariff and trade policy, foreign exchange access, access to government contracts, etc.

The clear implication of the foregoing is not only that the structure of the private sector limits the scope for privatization, but that the development of the domestic private sector requires a comprehensive strategy to reverse all these constraints. Privatization of itself cannot be expected to lift the constraints of the private sector, and can only hope to be a medium-term component of the private sector development strategy.

5.1.2 Mobilization of domestic savings

A second limiting factor is the extent to which the private sector can generate an adequate supply of savings for investment. Although this issue is never directly addressed in the theoretical literature on privatization, it is clearly a necessary, if not sufficient, condition for successful privatization. Savings can be generated from two sources: domestic and foreign. Savings behaviour has been at the centre of much research concerning the performance of developing economies. In particular, the extensive debate on financial liberalization revolves around concerns that repressed financial systems combined with loose monetary and fiscal policies have distorted the process of savings. In many low-income economies aggregate savings are low, poorly intermediated, and often held in non-financial forms. Moreover, financial repression has contributed to an extensive

Table 5.3 *Domestic savings and the proceeds from privatization*

Country	GDS (% of GDP)	Manuf. (% of GDP)	Proportion of proceeds from foreign sector[a]
Jamaica	19%	22%	53%
Trinidad	21%	10%	93%
Malaysia	36%	24%	9%
Sri Lanka	13%	16%	72%
PNG	21%	9%	100%
Kenya	22%	11%	–
Malaŵi	8%	11%	65%

a) Assume proceeds from joint sales are split 50 : 50 between domestic and foreign.

growth of capital flight, and the preference for holding non-financial assets. The pool of domestic savings available for long-term fixed capital formation or equity investment is thus frequently shallow. Table 5.3 indicates that there is a substantial range in the levels of aggregate gross domestic savings among the sample countries; this correlates quite closely with an observed split between foreign and domestic participation in the privatization programmes in the various economies.

In addition to a low average propensity to save, savings patterns in these smaller economies, especially from the household sector, are highly skewed and subject to extreme variability over time.[4] Mosley *et al.* (1991, Vol. 2: 271) describe this characteristic aptly by quoting the remark of a former Kenyan politician that Kenya is 'a country of ten millionaires and ten million beggars'. Moreover, the domestic savings pattern in many low-income developing countries is dominated by seasonal effects and is broadly precautionary, aimed at consumption smoothing in the face of uncertain agricultural income streams[5] rather than being long-term and speculative, as required for privatization. Such savings patterns are rarely conducive to large-scale risky capital investment.

There are also often marked differences in savings patterns between urban and rural communities. Rising incomes and a switch from subsistence (rural) to contract-wage (urban) structures are likely to generate increasingly higher levels of speculative savings, a point which is supported by the evidence in Tables 5.1 and 5.2. These conditions are likely to be necessary to ensure that there will be a sizeable degree of domestic savings mobilized for equity investment.

An additional factor worth noting concerns the way in which the macroeconomic environment influences the mobilization of savings for privatization. The environment in which privatization has been instituted in most countries has been characterized by deep economic crises, frequently accompanied by severe income compression, upward price adjustment for basic commodities, and considerable reductions in real wages. Privatization has become an integral element of adjustment programmes designed to rectify such macroeconomic disequilibria, but its success is compromised by the presence of conditions which are not at all conducive to savings mobilization and equity investment. This is a second paradox of privatization: the conditions which have necessitated privatization are those which are militating against its effective implementation. The exception to this trend is the foreign sector, for which the period of macroeconomic adjustment has improved its relative purchasing power. Although there is evidence that the supply response of foreign capital to structural adjustment is weak, exchange-rate devaluations, weak competition from the domestic sector, and the 'desperation' of the seller all combine to give foreign investors a strong advantage in taking up privatization issues. We now turn to the link between the foreign and domestic private sectors.

5.1.3 The foreign sector and privatization

If the domestic private sector cannot, in general, provide either the competition necessary to ensure efficient performance of former SOEs, or the resources to absorb them, this may be provided by the foreign sector, either through foreign-owned companies operating directly in the domestic economy, or through import penetration. However, across most of our countries controls on foreign direct investment are tight, and effective protection in most sectors is high. While policy towards foreign participation has been liberalized recently in a number of countries, foreign participation is generally welcomed only in the export-oriented sectors, and direct competition with domestic producers is not widely encouraged. Consequently programmes of incentives have been developed aimed at attracting foreign direct investment, which centre around the creation of Export Processing Zones and other enclave-based initiatives. If foreign entrepreneurship is indeed a conduit for increased competition, then in many cases it has been thwarted through the effective segmentation of this section of the economy.

Similarly, our evidence points to the use of quantitative restrictions and levels of effective protection which limit the impact of competition from imports.[6] In a number of cases there are structural factors which provide natural barriers to competition for the domestic economy. The most striking examples are Papua New Guinea and Malaŵi, where transport costs drive a significant wedge between fob and cif prices. In the case of Malaŵi this has been estimated to be in the region of 60% of the fob price (see Chapter 13). Structural constraints notwithstanding however, most countries have instituted trade and tariff reform policies aimed at the abolition of quantitative restrictions and the equalization and reduction of nominal rates, often under the auspices of World Bank lending, as in Jamaica, Kenya, Malaŵi, Malaysia and Sri Lanka. Though the level of overall protection is falling on average, and is relatively moderate in, say, Malaysia, average effective protection rates remain strikingly large. World Bank studies variously report Effective Protection Rates for the manufacturing sector in Jamaica of 1.75 (1986), (where 1.00 represents neutral protection); 1.39 for Malaŵi (1987); 2.07 (1987) for Sri Lanka; and 2.12 (1987) for Kenya. These figures also mask an extremely wide range of protection, with some sectors hiding behind virtually impenetrable barriers to entry.

Finally, the serious debt crisis faced by many developing countries limits their access to foreign savings as a source of financing investment. Private lending to developing countries virtually ceased during the 1980s, and governments have been faced with the prospect of having to sell assets in their entirety in order to have access to foreign savings.

Consequently, the extent to which the foreign sector can provide an effective spur to competition in the domestic market remains limited. While some SOEs operating in international markets are already exposed to competitive forces,[7] in general the continued protection of domestic sectors limits the impact of foreign competition on all enterprises regardless of ownership structures. Taken together these observations suggest that, in general, the degree of competition afforded by the domestic private sector in a number of developing countries is limited. In the context of privatization policy our central argument – that a change in ownership without both reform of private market structures and the enhancement of regulatory capacity will not necessarily generate efficiency gains – is thus of prime importance in developing countries.

Though the economics of foreign participation in the privatization process are relatively straightforward, the politics of foreign participation are, for good reason, much more complex, and, even if the economic arguments for greater foreign participation are compelling, these cannot be unequivocally translated into political action.

At a basic level, the sale of assets, and, more importantly, the sale of monopoly entitlements, to the foreign sector involves the transfer of control and monopoly rents from the domestic to the foreign economy. This is an absolute economic 'loss' to the economy. In an 'ideal' privatization, the net effect of the sale would be positive: the net foreign-exchange proceeds accruing to government, combined with the positive externalities generated by higher levels of operational efficiency, would lead to higher social welfare.

It is of little surprise, then, that in most countries there is an unwillingness to sell major assets to non-nationals.[8] This sensitivity is frequently the result of a colonial/imperial experience, and indeed localization was frequently one of the main reasons for the original nationalization programmes, especially in Africa and the Caribbean. However, given the sizes of the foreign and domestic private sectors relative to the size of the larger SOEs (see Tables 4.2 to 4.4), it has become clear that foreign participation in the privatization process has become a necessary condition for its progress, and a reluctance to involve this sector will act as a major brake on privatization in the countries concerned.

This conclusion raises a fundamental 'neo-colonialist' problem of privatization: without a robust domestic private sector, direct foreign participation will be the only method of generating the efficiency gains of privatization. However, if the concerns about direct foreign participation which prompted the growth of the SOE sector remain, then it is likely that government will be reluctant to privatize those enterprises whose poor performance generated the desire for privatization in the first place. This reluctance shows through in the experience of a number of countries, where – despite much debate – the progress of privatization has been very slow indeed.[9]

5.1.4 Conclusions on private market structures

Since privatization is only a process, the relevant domain for an investigation of its effects is the structure of the economy in which it occurs. Here we have explored two main lines of enquiry, namely the competitiveness of the domestic economy and its absorptive capacity. On competitiveness, much of the debate takes the privatization of monopolies as the exception to the norm. In many smaller developing economies, however, the nature of the domestic private sector and the limits to foreign competition mean that the converse holds: across a wide range of economies SOEs are either the dominant firms in their markets or between them wield considerable oligopoly power. The implications of this for privatization policy are clear: competitive-market effects alone will not be sufficient to realize efficiency gains, and thus the design and implementation of regulation structures and competition policy are of paramount importance. The irony is, as we shall discuss in the next section, that the need for regulation is greatest in economies which have the most limited capacity to manage it effectively.

On absorption, while theory often ignores concerns about the absorptive capacity of the purchasing sector, this oversight is untenable in reality. Weaknesses in domestic savings levels (especially during periods of economic stabilization) and deficiencies in their mobilization mean that absorptive capacity will be found predominantly in the foreign sector. This again raises issues about regulatory policy and the capacity to regulate large foreign-owned enterprises, but also highlights the role of the domestic financial system, and in particular the capital market, in the mobilization of domestic savings for investment. We shall discuss the interaction between capital markets and privatization in section 5.3.

5.2 Post-privatization regulation and competition policy

Regulation is essential for the successful management of a market-based economy where actual and potential monopoly positions exist. However, one of the persistent misperceptions of privatization in developing countries is that the process of selling state assets absolves the public sector from this challenge of economic management. Regulation of monopoly power and the creation of an 'appropriate' enabling environment in which the forces of competition will flourish are thus essential adjuncts to privatization. This is particularly important in smaller developing economies where, as noted earlier in this chapter, competition in many markets is so weak that without appropriate regulation the hypothesized benefits of privatization can be quickly dissipated through the creation and maintenance of monopoly profits. Despite this, post-privatization regulation of utilities and other monopolies has remained a distinctly low-profile activity. The countries in this study are not alone, however, since it is only recently that attention has focused on utility regulation and competition policy in many industrialized economies. The difference, though, is that, in many industrialized economies such as the UK, privatization proceeds in an economic environment which not only is more competitive but also has a stronger tradition of market-based regulation and competition policy. For many developing countries privatization is occurring contemporaneously with a fundamental reorientation of the economy, in which governments are being required to move away from earlier anti-competition forms of regulation based on direct controls, towards more market-oriented, pro-competition regulation. In most of the countries in this book this transformation is under way, and efficient regulation and competition policy is beginning to emerge as an important element of adjustment programmes and of privatization. However, this development is in its early stages and it remains difficult to assess the capacity of these economies to succeed in such a transformation.

The main purpose of this chapter is to evaluate the regulatory capacity in the seven economies. We do this by reviewing the past history of regulation, and describe the extent to which privatization is being accompanied by the development of new regulatory structures. However, since there has been only very limited regulatory innovation in any of the countries studied, it is not easy to draw firm conclusions on their actual regulatory capacity from this evidence alone. We therefore supplement this evaluation by adducing evidence on the capacity for regulation from other areas of public policy. It is important to note that it is not our purpose to examine in detail competing regulatory rules or the detailed design of regulation systems: our interest is only in assessing the capacity of these countries.

5.2.1 The regulatory experience

In general, there is very little explicit regulation of the SOE sector in developing countries – an experience broadly shared by the countries in this book. There is often a wide array of regulatory bodies, but these are mostly involved in regulating other private sector activities, such as commodity production and trading. It has been much less common for regulatory bodies to include within their ambit commercial and industrial SOEs. The main exception is, of course, in the financial sector where explicit arm's-length regulation by the central bank of both private and state-owned financial institutions is commonplace.

Utility regulation has usually been 'internalized' by central governments, although an exception to this is found in the Caribbean where utility regulation has come under the aegis of Public Utilities Commissions (PUCs) in both Jamaica and Trinidad and Tobago. In Jamaica, the PUC was established in 1966 to oversee the pricing and commercial performance of the major utilities, many of which were foreign-owned at the time (see Chapter 7). The regulatory relationship was tense and plagued both by difficulties over information disclosure and verification, and concerns on the part of the PUC that the utilities were engaged in sizeable transfer-pricing. However, following nationalization of these utilities in the early 1970s, the PUC was disbanded and its functions absorbed within central government, principally under the aegis of the Ministry of Public Utilities and Transport. The PUC in Trinidad and Tobago was established in the same year and remains in operation. However, it has signally failed to exercise a satisfactory degree of regulatory control, not least because political interference in SOE management and direct price controls rendered the regulatory process redundant. The PUC has been the subject of extensive review, aimed at trying to erase the more egregious weaknesses in the regulatory process (see Government of Trinidad and Tobago, 1979).

The problems of Trinidad and Tobago's PUC stand out only because regulation is explicit and its weaknesses consequently exposed. In other countries, where the regulation of SOEs has generally been internalized by central government, the same weaknesses proliferate. The main features of internalized regulation have been, first, the preponderance of quantity controls rather than price instruments as the principal regulatory instrument, and, second, decentralization, with individual line ministries being responsible for the regulation of the SOEs in their portfolio. This form of internalized regulation has resulted, across all countries, in a standard array of problems and weaknesses. In addition to a lack of policy co-ordination between SOEs operating in similar markets but under different ministerial portfolios,[10] there have been the traditional problems of protracted review procedures; vague and often contradictory guidelines; erratic price adjustments; frequently ineffectual powers of enforcement; and an absence of flexibility. This heavy-handed and incentive-numbing form of regulation was principally directed towards maintaining low output prices for politically strategic goods, but at the cost of the internal efficiency of the firm, and of the efficient allocation of resources in the economy as a whole.

To the extent that privatization is one response to the problems of the SOE sector then regulation is an important component. In the case of natural monopoly SOEs (principally the utilities), the objective is to design new arm's-length regulatory schemes which will meet the twin objectives of providing the utility with a regulatory regime which is sufficient to promote efficiency-enhancing behaviour while at the same time guarding against welfare-reducing pricing. However, this is only part of the story for most developing economies, since to a large extent the privatization programme will be dominated by the sale of enterprises that are not natural monopolies but are likely to enjoy monopoly or oligopolistic positions. This introduces the broader question of competition policy and the capacity to guard against excessive concentration and monopoly in the private sector.

In general, prior to the development of privatization programmes none of the countries studied here operated a body of competition policy aimed at addressing the adverse effects of market dominance. Private sector regulation was either ignored or, depending on the product, was subject to heavy-handed regulation via extensive price or quantity controls. Even in those areas of regulation which seemed more market-oriented, the ethos was similar, with either no regulation at all or regulation through quantitative control. Thus in the financial sector there was generally a combination of restrictions on interest rates and direct credit allocations, and completely unregulated securities and exchange activities. For example, in Jamaica, Kenya and Sri Lanka there coexisted financially repressed commercial banking sectors side by side with equity markets operating without any form of regulation.[11] Similarly, while foreign direct investors frequently met with a very tight regulation of access to the domestic economy (implemented through quantitative restrictions and licences), once in the country such investors found their monopoly positions rarely challenged. Evidence suggests that this form of regulation has created considerable disincentive effects, and has often not even been successful in reducing the extent of monopoly (see Grosh, 1990).

5.2.2 Privatization and new developments in regulatory instruments

Partly as a result of privatization, a number of the countries studied have attempted to develop more arm's-length, market-based regulatory systems. There are four areas where this has occurred: the institution of regulatory structures specifically linked to individual transactions; developments in private sector competition policy; securities legislation; and the development of arm's-length relationships between the government and the SOE sector itself.

Explicit post-privatization regulation has only appeared in the telecommunications sector. Three countries have privatized telecommunications utilities (Jamaica, Trinidad and Tobago and Malaysia), while one, Sri Lanka, has transformed the telecommunications department into a public company operating under an explicit arm's-length regulatory structure. However, the approaches to the regulation of the privatized telecommunications enterprises differ markedly between the Caribbean countries and Asia. In Jamaica the regulatory structure was built into the terms of the 25-year licence granted to Telecommunications of Jamaica in 1988, and is based exclusively on a rate-of-return measure (see Chapters 4 and 7). Though the details are much less clear, a similar rate-of-return structure has emerged following the sale of TELCO in Trinidad and Tobago. In contrast, the regulatory structures in Sri Lanka and Malaysia have been established by legislation (the Telecommunications Act) which establishes statutory regulatory bodies, and stipulates the form of the regulatory regime. In both cases the regulatory rule is based on the RPI-X formula pioneered in the UK which links allowable price increases to the consumer price index rather than to the rate of return on the company's capital. The Government of Malaysia is currently considering a unified regulation structure for all privatized utilities to be based on the same price-index form of regulation.[12]

New developments in competition policy have appeared only in Kenya and Jamaica in recent years. In 1989 the Government of Kenya introduced the Restrictive Trade Practices, Monopolies and Price Control Act, which perfectly exemplifies the shift away from direct regulation through control of prices. While the Act allows some continued domestic price control, it also establishes a procedure to control against predatory pricing, other forms of strategic entry deterrence and collusion, and to empower statutory investigations of 'excessive' concentration of economic power (see Chapter 12 for details). The proposed Competition Act for Jamaica (which was to be placed before parliament in 1991) contains the same essential elements: prohibitions against collusion and strategic entry deterrence, and the promotion of consumer interests within a non-interventionist regulatory framework. In neither Kenya, where the emphasis since 1989 has been on the price decontrol aspect of the legislation, nor Jamaica is it yet possible to assess the likely success of these initiatives. Both embody essential elements of a good 'hands-off' regulation policy, but whether the policy can be a valuable instrument in promoting economic efficiency through competition depends more on effective monitoring, implementation and punishment than on the promulgation of legislation. Without these elements, competition policy will lack credibility. As we shall discuss below, this issue of credibility will be of particular importance with regard to the inflow of foreign direct investment. By the late 1980s many governments were in the process of (or considering) the further relaxation of restrictions on foreign direct investment, and it is clear that, if domestic competition policy cannot effectively constrain the activities of generally large and economically powerful foreign investors, not only are some of the gains from foreign participation jeopardized, but the credibility of competition policy in the eyes of other, domestic, investors may be undermined.

The third area of innovation is the financial sector, and in particular equity trading which, as noted before, in many countries had been virtually free of formal regulation. In Sri Lanka, Kenya, Trinidad and Tobago and Jamaica the late 1980s have seen the introduction of new securities legislation designed to provide for increased transparency in securities trading, to introduce investor protection provisions and to limit the extent of insider-trading in what are generally accepted as extremely collusive markets. In Malaysia, on the other hand, where regulation of the industry has been in place since the Securities Industry Act of 1973, there have been periodic revisions to keep pace with new developments. Finally, in Malaŵi and Papua New Guinea, where there are as yet no formal markets in equities, proposals for the development of capital markets are combined with regulatory schemes of varying formality.

In general, this rash of developments in capital market regulation in the smaller economies has derived from broader moves towards financial sector liberalization. However, in the Caribbean, these changes have also been a response to concerns that failure to impose regulatory structures on hitherto extremely collusive markets would seriously undermine the credibility of privatization public share issues.

Finally we come to other, pre-privatization developments in regulation. Responding to the chronic failure of internal regulatory structures, the focus of SOE reform efforts has been on the creation of arm's-length relationships between SOEs and governments. The key feature of these changes has been an attempt to replace the uncertain and heavy-handed features of internal regulation with less interventionist, efficiency-oriented structures. Thus under the aegis of the Department of Statutory Bodies in Malaŵi, the Public Investment Management Board in Sri Lanka and the Commercial Investment Division of the Ministry of Finance in Papua New Guinea, steps towards market-based regulation, relying on rate-of-return regulation, medium-term corporate plans, and target-based performance monitoring have been instituted.[13] As indicated in the country studies, these developments have often been successful, and have contributed to better medium-term planning and performance in the SOE sector.

5.2.3 *Evaluation and conclusions*

Many of the countries studied in this book have been slower in acknowledging the importance of regulation than in embracing privatization, despite the fact that the costs of weak regulation are likely to be high in developing countries with narrowly based private sectors. Of course, the developments in terms of competition policy, securities regulation, and public-sector performance targets outlined above are encouraging. Even with improved regulation, though, the problem remains of trying to gauge the trade-offs between efficiency gains and informational rents highlighted in the Shapiro and Willig model presented in Chapter 2. Recent developments in privatization and regulation policy have clearly gone some way to eliminating the worst problems of internal regulation, but the extent to which governments can minimize the informational rents lost in arm's-length regulation is still unclear. A number of reasons for uncertainty remain.

First, although consideration of regulation (eventually) accompanied the privatization of state-owned telecommunications enterprises, similar regulatory considerations were absent both in the sale of other monopoly concerns (for example, the cement industries in the Caribbean) or in the proposed sale of monopolistic enterprises in the other countries. This 'oversight' is symptomatic of one of the weaknesses of regulation process, namely the 'copy-cat' phenomenon, where regulatory structures are borrowed from other, structurally very different, economies. Both Malaysia and Sri Lanka have implemented regulatory structures for telecommunications virtually identical to the UK Telecommunications Act (1984), while in Papua New Guinea the wholesale import of rate-of-return regulation for the Commercial Statutory Authorities has created some quite harmful disincentive effects for the utilities. While it may in some circumstances be optimal to borrow the design of regulatory structures from a developed country technological shelf, in general it is not. Regulation needs to be designed in response to the structure of the industry and the nature of other regulatory instruments in the country in which it operates. It does not follow, for example, that, because the RPI-X formula was deemed to be appropriate in the UK in the mid-1980s, it is appropriate for Sri Lanka in the 1990s.

Second, there remains a concern about the resource costs of information collection and analysis required for effective regulation. The case studies indicate that the resources allocated to regulation are often limited, and, as yet, are virtually non-existent for the implementation of competition policy. Governments are improving their data collection for state-owned enterprises, but the capacity to collect and analyse data on private enterprises is negligible. One of the recurring features of the country studies is the dearth of information available on the structure of the private sector:[14] without even the basic data on markets and their structures, the ability and, perhaps more importantly, the credibility of regulators efficiently to evaluate claims of market dominance and strategic behaviour is undermined.

Third, there is the problem of private enterprises being able to capture increasingly large informational rents through the regulatory process. This is of particular import for small economies' negotiating power *vis-à-vis* large foreign players who will tend to dominate privatization programmes. Because of its greater access to, and control over, information on market conditions, cost of capital, technological factors of production, etc., the firm is in a position to negotiate (or re-negotiate) regulatory schemes which allow it to capture more of the monopoly profits from the operation than would occur if the regulator had full information. When combined with the difficulty of obtaining, analysing and processing the required information from the regulated firm, effective regulation can become a major task. Many of the associated problems facing the regulator, such as the problem of (optimal) regulatory lag, the problem of 'after-the fact' regulation, and the adequate specification of pricing rules, further underline the difficulty of efficient regulation.[15] Moreover, these points warrant particular attention in the case of a multinational, multi-product monopolist, where the regulator's control strategy may only weakly affect the monopolist's actions, and where the acquisition of accurate cost data is made more problematic by the possibility of transfer-pricing. This is likely to be of particular concern in the Caribbean and Africa, where large multinational enterprises are emerging as players in the privatization programme.

The challenge of undertaking effective regulation and competition is thus substantial, and in many respects is a much greater challenge than that of actually implementing the privatization programme itself. The early evidence would suggest that, while regulatory structures are emerging, the capacity to make them effective is limited and the costs of regulation have been downplayed in many of the countries considering privatization. Without adequate resources (both financial and human), the risks of regulatory capture and losses of credibility will increase dramatically, and may undermine gains from privatization. Forcing the pace of privatization in the context of ineffective and non-credible regulation may thus ultimately be self-defeating.

5.3 Privatization and the role of the capital market

This section examines the linkages between the management of a programme of privatization and the stock market. We start by considering the extent to which the presence of the capital market assists in the privatization process: how it facilitates the mobilization of savings; the extent to which it 'packages' investment bundles; and also the extent to which, through secondary market activity, it values the assets and provides for their tradability. The second objective is to analyse the extent to which privatization can fulfil the objectives of capital market development specified in Chapter 2, and in particular how the promotion of privatization impacts on the nature and speed of development of the capital market. This issue is rarely addressed in the literature on privatization in industrialized economies,[16] but in developing countries, where privatization frequently runs in tandem with capital market development, it acquires a higher profile. We start by briefly describing the characteristics of the capital markets in the seven countries.

Table 5.4 *Market capitalization as % of GNP*

	1980	1981	1982	1983	1984	1985	1986	1987	1988	1989
Study Countries										
Jamaica	2.0	4.3	5.4	3.1	6.0	13.2	21.9	21.6	23.3	24.6
Kenya	–	–	–	–	–	–	–	–	5.6	0.0
Malaysia	50.6	61.2	51.9	76.1	57.2	52.0	54.2	58.6	67.1	106.3
Sri Lanka	–	–	–	–	–	6.1	6.6	9.1	6.7	6.1
Trinidad	–	17.2	17.0	13.0	10.7	6.3	7.8	8.4	6.5	11.0
Other Countries										
India (Bombay)	4.4	6.4	6.1	4.1	4.0	6.8	5.8	5.6	8.5	10.2
Nigeria	3.0	3.2	1.6	3.3	3.4	3.0	1.8	3.4	3.1	4.6

Source: IFC, *Emerging Stock Markets Factbook*, 1991.

5.3.1 Characteristics of capital markets

Of the seven countries studied five have existing capital markets (namely Jamaica, Kenya, Malaysia, Sri Lanka, and Trinidad and Tobago), while both Malaŵi and Papua New Guinea are actively examining options for the creation of formal stock exchanges. With the exception of Kenya, all have used the capital market in their privatization programmes, although to varying degrees. Tables 5.4 to 5.7 describe these markets in detail.[17]

Apart from Malaysia, where market capitalization since 1980 has consistently represented over 50% of GNP, the capital markets in these countries are small. Market capitalization generally averages less than 20% of GNP (Table 5.4), which

Table 5.5 *Market turnover (as % of GNP)*

	1980	1981	1982	1983	1984	1985	1986	1987	1988	1989
Study Countries										
Jamaica	0.11	0.07	0.18	0.14	0.29	1.04	2.78	2.50	0.73	2.32
Kenya	–	–	–	–	–	–	–	–	–	–
Malaysia	10.50	13.99	5.19	11.34	6.56	7.48	4.25	12.10	7.55	18.37
Sri Lanka	–	–	–	–	–	0.05	0.08	0.16	0.17	0.04
Trinidad	–	0.28	2.90	1.94	0.97	0.83	1.09	0.54	0.53	1.85
Other Countries										
India (Bombay)	1.60	4.01	2.68	1.16	1.94	2.34	4.63	2.63	4.35	6.46
Nigeria	0.01	0.01	0.01	0.02	0.02	0.02	0.03	0.02	0.02	0.02

Source: IFC, *Emerging Stock Markets Factbook*, 1991.

is somewhat lower than the average for all emerging markets of around 25%–30%. Turnover has been similarly modest: apart from Malaysia (where turnover has been on average 8% of GNP), it has generally been less than 2% of GNP (Table 5.5). Moreover, the depth of trade on these markets[18] (even including Malaysia) is low, especially in comparison with mature markets, and, more appropriately, with the Newly Industrialized Countries.

The record of these markets in the 1980s has been mixed. In most cases markets have deepened, especially in the latter half of the decade. Thus, in Jamaica, Malaysia and Sri Lanka, capitalization has generally risen as a percentage of GNP, turnover rates have mostly increased (notwithstanding the effect of the 1987 stock market crash in more developed markets), and a greater number of stocks are traded now compared to a decade ago (Table 5.6). The most dramatic example of an expanding market has been the Jamaican Stock Exchange, where market capitalization has risen from 2% of GNP in 1980 to 25% in 1988. However, in other cases, notably Trinidad and Tobago, the reverse has occurred: capitalization has fallen as a percentage of GNP, and the number of firms listed has been reduced. It is worth noting, though, that in real terms only the Jamaican Stock Exchange has grown: the other five have remained virtually constant or declined.

Also, in a number of markets, especially the more dynamic ones of Malaysia and Jamaica, there have been significant developments in the introduction of new instruments, players and techniques. In Malaysia for example, a Second Board was instituted in 1989, traders now deal using a real-time computer-based over-the-counter system, and new markets have been established in corporate bonds,

Table 5.6 *Number of listed companies*

	1980	1981	1982	1983	1984	1985	1986	1987	1988	1989	1990
Study Countries											
Jamaica	38	36	35	36	36	38	40	43	44	45	44
Kenya	54	55	54	54	54	54	53	53	55	57	56
Malaysia	182	187	194	204	217	222	223	232	238	251	282
Sri Lanka	–	–	–	–	–	171	171	168	176	176	175
Trinidad	–	29	34	34	36	36	33	33	33	31	30
Other Countries											
India	–	2,114	3,358	3,118	3,882	4,344	4,744	5,560	5,841	5,968	6,200
Nigeria	90	93	93	93	93	96	99	100	102	111	131

Source: IFC, *Emerging Stock Markets Factbook*, 1991.

Table 5.7 *Capital market privatization and the increased supply of equity*

	1984	1985	1986	1987	1988	1989	1990[a]
JAMAICA							
Privatization share value as % of market capitalization	0.00	0.67	2.87	4.51	2.52	0.00	
Privatization share value as % of prior-year turnover	36.76	76.01	43.90	27.13	0.00	0.00	
Privatization share value as % of prior-year new issues							
TRINIDAD AND TOBAGO							
Privatization share value as % of market capitalization						0.65	
Privatization share value as % of prior-year turnover						13.35	
Privatization share value as % of prior-year new issues						100.00	
MALAYSIA							
Privatization share value as % of market capitalization		0.11	0.00	0.18	0.01	0.00	1.51
Privatization share value as % of prior-year turnover		1.11	0.00	4.01	0.11	0.09	13.03
Privatization share value as % prior-year new issues		2.70	0.00	32.45	0.73	0.39	97.57
SRI LANKA							
Privatization share value as % of market capitalization						0.59	
Privatization share value as % of prior-year turnover						56.18	
Privatization share value as % of prior-year new issues						49.63	

Source: Country case studies, Chapters 7–13.

a) To June 1990 only.

commodity futures, and mortgage bonds, as well as equities and government paper. While not nearly as dramatic, there have been some similar developments in the other markets in our studies, especially concerning the drafting of new securities legislation.

5.3.2 *Capital market constraints on privatization*

At the most basic level, the absence of a capital market limits the government in its choice of privatization method to direct sales. The existence of a weak capital market pushes the government in the same direction, with the capacity of the market determining the number and size of sales that can be absorbed. While there are positive reasons why the government may choose to divest through direct sales (they are speedier, more covert, allow more room for negotiation by the seller, etc.) 'forced' divestiture through direct sales, caused by the non-existence of capital markets or the presence of thin ones, imposes potentially significant costs on the government. These can be broadly classified as problems of resource mobilization; tradability and performance monitoring; and policy transparency.

Resource mobilization

There are a number of separate issues involved in assessing the capacity of capital markets to mobilize domestic resources, the first of which is search costs. The essence of the capital market is to provide the mechanism through which the aggregate demand of a large number of small buyers can be channelled into the supply of entitlements to a small number of large assets. In the absence of such a market, sellers (i.e. the government in the case of privatization) incur extensive search costs in identifying individual buyers with sufficient resources and capacity to acquire the assets.

Second, in cases where the distribution of wealth is highly skewed, direct sale of assets to only those agents that have accumulated resources, can exacerbate the adverse welfare effects of concentration of asset ownership. These adverse effects of ownership concentration can, without appropriate regulation, lead to situations where dominant agents/firms act to limit the economic effects of privatization in terms of pricing and production. A number of countries which do not have developed capital markets have found that the scope of privatization is limited by the inability to mobilize domestic resources from a sufficiently wide base to avoid an increase in ownership concentration. In other words, the absence of a capital market not only creates difficulties in the sale of large assets (usually those whose sale will have the greatest economic impact), but, when other types of sales occur, can lead to the exacerbation of monopoly power in the domestic private sector.

Third, capital markets can assist in eliminating one of the major barriers to fixed capital accumulation by reducing the minimum size of investment in financial assets for any individual agent, and simultaneously provide the mechanism for its tradability. Privatization programmes, which claim the broadening of economic participation as one of their objectives, confront a significant barrier in the absence of a capital market. This feature of capital market privatization sales is of particular importance in cases where income and asset distribution assumes a strong political dimension, as in Kenya, Malaysia, and Trinidad and Tobago.

Fourth, an extension of this issue is where foreign savings represent an alternative source of demand for privatized enterprises. Here the politics of divestiture to the foreign sector are difficult, and, as we have noted repeatedly, there are numerous cases where governments have found that foreign investors have represented the only source of capital sufficiently large for privatization. Governments have mainly viewed the advantages of foreign participation in the domestic economy in terms of technical and management expertise. Foreign ownership is still perceived as a disadvantage. When capital markets do not exist, it can be difficult to acquire these management services except at the cost of the sale of the majority of assets. Where they do exist, then, by tapping into a broader domestic capital base and, significantly, by offering a market through which foreign investors' equity stakes can be liquidated in the future, foreign participation in the privatization programme is facilitated and its worst effects attenuated.

Fifth, capital markets permit governments to deal with the 'lumpiness' of asset sales, especially through the use of multiple tranches in the divestiture of the same enterprise.[19] This has the benefit of reducing the demand on domestic resources by any single tranche (thereby avoiding dramatic relative price changes and subsequent crowding-out) and allowing the smoothing of government revenues, and establishes more accurate pricing of assets, thereby avoiding revenue losses through 'accidental' underpricing.

Tradability and efficiency

These five features deal exclusively with the role of capital markets in facilitating the primary sale of assets, but secondary trading capacity is also essential. As noted in Chapter 2, the tradability of property rights is an important mechanism through which the efficiency gains of privatization can be extracted and maintained. Moreover, secondary trading facilities clearly enhance the perceived liquidity of equity, and in economies where investment uncertainty is high, this will increase the purchaser's valuation of the asset. Thus by providing tradability of property rights through the equity market the government can increase the revenue yield from the sale. In addition, listing on a capital market acts as a positive signalling mechanism to the banking sector, thereby enhancing the company's access to credit. Secondary trading facilities also provide a market-based mechanism (as described in section 2.3) whereby the initial efficiency gains expected from privatization can be locked in. Share-trading in a company provides a direct valuation of the net worth of the enterprise, and movements in the share price (relative to appropriate indices) can generate information to shareholders on management performance. Hence, capital markets can provide appropriate incentive and monitoring environments for continued efficiency improvements after sale. In the absence of capital markets or, more commonly, in the presence of capital markets which do not actively carry out these functions (especially markets where the threat of takeover is weak and where the share price can be manipulated by large players), the costs of performance monitoring and the creation of appropriate incentive structures will be higher.

Policy transparency

Finally, the capital market can affect the management of a privatization programme. In general, public share issues on established markets impose the legal conditions of clarity, transparency, and consistency on the vendor. Although this is not necessarily the case, since it is possible to sell assets in poorly regulated markets, repeated use of weak markets is not sustainable, especially if the participation of foreign capital is required. For example, public share issues require independent statements of valuation of the firm to be sold, full dissemination of information, a declaration of actual and contingent liabilities, clear statements of corporate policy, and future disclosure obligations. The government is also impelled to specify clearly its intended future policy towards the firm. Such conditions are not characteristic of direct sales, which provide opportunities for less overt mechanisms.[20] This is not to argue that there is no role for private market sales, but to suggest that the establishment of government policy credibility in privatization can be enhanced through public share sales. A privatization programme based solely on private direct sales can be consistent with being an 'honest broker': however, it is less easy for the government specifically to create such a reputation using this approach.

Thus the presence of a functioning capital market will to a large measure impact on the structure, speed and management of privatization programmes. As noted in Chapter 4, in those countries where the capital market is relatively well developed (Malaysia and Jamaica), the privatization programme has been more comprehensive and, within it, the capital market has been quite widely used. Too many other factors are at work to argue any direct causality, but the importance of the market for privatization is clear. We turn now to the issue of the reverse causation from privatization to the development of the capital market.

5.3.3 *The impact of privatization on capital market development*

The principal function of a capital market in any economy is to intermediate and allocate commercial risk, and this capacity will develop over time depending upon the nature of asset flows through the market. However, a privatization programme based on a programme of asset sales through the capital market will, in general, affect the nature of the risk intermediated by the market, and also the capacity with which the market manages this intermediation.

It is clear that most of the effects of privatization on the development of nascent capital markets are not unique to privatization *per se*. However, the nature of privatization inevitably adds a particular dimension to the discussion.[21] First, privatization issues are often large in relation to other equity issues and to the market itself. Second, the assets sold through privatization may have characteristics different from those prevailing in the market. For example, they may be concentrated in certain sectors (e.g. transport and communications), be of a similar capital vintage, and be of larger than average size. Third, privatization issues have a higher profile than other issues and tend to involve a greater number of players, many of whom are new to equity trading. Fourth, privatization programmes are often used as a way of stimulating other market developments, such as the launch of new instruments and the development of securities market regulation. Finally, since privatization programmes are viewed by vendor and purchasers as dynamic processes, the success or failure of the programme has important reputation and policy credibility implications for the government. These features suggest that the impact of privatization on capital markets will not be neutral, and that the dynamic impact of privatization on capital market development needs close attention.

It is widely believed, by governments and donors, that an increase in equity supply through the sale of privatization shares will 'kick-start' a capital market. As the country studies for Sri Lanka, Papua New Guinea, Malaŵi, Kenya and Trinidad and Tobago show, the policy debate on privatization is intimately linked with the capital market objectives. However, this notion is unduly narrow and ignores many of the more important dynamic linkages between the two phenomena.

Privatization affects the capital market in four main ways: (i) it increases the volume of equity listed on the market; (ii) it alters the number and type of players on the market; (iii) it imposes demands on the technological, regulatory, and operational capacity of the market; (iv) it will constitute a significant (if short- or medium-term) intervention by the government in the capital market. The last of these points has been dealt with in the discussion in Chapter 4 on reputation creation, underpricing and sequencing. These issues have important short-term implications for capital market development, but this section focuses only on the medium-term implications flowing from the first three.

Privatization and the supply of equity on the market

Privatization through capital markets clearly increases the volume of equity listed, and as such may be expected to have positive effects on the functioning of the market. A greater supply of equity may mean improved opportunities for portfolio composition and risk-spreading opportunities, a higher volume of trade (since there are now more relative prices in the market), more accurate asset pricing and valuation, a broader sectoral spread of assets, and generally improved information flows within the market and elsewhere throughout the economy.

In addition, an increase in the supply of equity enhances the liquidity of the equity market relative to other markets, and may lead to improved asset composition across the financial system as a whole. Specifically, greater equity market liquidity can provide an avenue for both public and private sector contractual savings institutions to reduce their exposure to long-term government paper and diversify their asset portfolio, which is a much discussed issue in Malaysia, Kenya, and Papua New Guinea.

Finally, increased equity market depth and liquidity may be expected to induce a switch from real and informal asset holdings into financial assets. In the absence of developed equity markets and with generally low real interest rates, a large proportion of private sector savings are often held in non-financial forms. The monetization of savings can lead to greater efficiency in resource mobilization and allocation. For example, perceived equity market weaknesses in Sri Lanka and also in Africa have contributed to a relatively high level of informal sector savings.

These three arguments have featured strongly in the privatization debate in a number of countries in our study (see Chapters 7, 9, 10 and 11) and, though it is premature to draw definite conclusions, some evidence does exist to suggest that these phenomena will occur. In our study the most dramatic developments have been witnessed in Jamaica where, over the five years from 1985, when the capitalization of privatized firms rose from 4% to 26% of total market capitalization, indicators of market competition – in particular, capitalization and turnover concentration ratios – suggest that the new privatization issues have significantly influenced the market structure, with the four-firm concentration ratio by capitalization falling from 55% to 43% in 1985–9.

Notwithstanding the above points, a number of problems arise, the most important of which concerns the risk profile of the market. In a first-best situation, an increase in the supply of equity through privatization may be expected to improve the risk profile of the market, and at worst would leave it unchanged. In reality, however, most small markets are likely to be skewed in terms of their risk profile,[22] and, given the tendency for privatization issues to be large in relation to the average size of the listed companies, in many cases privatization will have significant effects on the risk profile as well as the structure of the market. Table 5.7 shows the scale of privatization issues in relation to various measures of market absorptive capacity. Even in the deepest of the markets covered in our study, new privatization issues account for a significant proportion of new equity investment. Again in Jamaica, for example, such was the size of the privatization programme that by 1988 privatization stocks accounted for 37% of market capitalization, and 26% of value of turnover, while 4 of the 10 largest listed companies were privatized.[23] A similar picture is beginning to emerge in Malaysia where the government has begun to list three large utilities on the market.[24]

It is not inevitable that this type of equity injection should be distortionary, but there are certain characteristics which give grounds for concern. The first and most important is the sectoral concentration of privatization issues. If privatization issues are concentrated in the same sector this can enhance the degree of risk covariance within the market. The case of Malaysia is illustrative. Up to mid-1990 92% of the value of privatization share issues through the Kuala Lumpur Stock Exchange (KLSE) was in the transport and communications sector. Since the value of these issues so far has been small in relation to the size of the market, there is no particular problem of risk distortion. However, subsequent sales of the telecommunications and electricity companies would mean that privatized enterprises in the transport, communications and utilities sector could account for up to 15% of total market capitalization. It is plausible to assume that these enterprises follow a similar path over the business cycle; this event alone will have a far from trivial effect on the risk structure of the KLSE. In view of the size of the KLSE, the Malaysian experience is likely to be mild in comparison to many thinner markets, where single privatization issues could account for much higher percentages of market capitalization.

The second way in which increased equity supply has wider implications is through the potential crowding-out of other forms of saving. While there may be unambiguous wealth effects from privatization (in which the realizable value of an asset in the private sector is greater than when it is in the public sector), an increase in the supply of equity will also induce portfolio adjustment within the equity market itself and across other markets. This may have crowding-out implications for the equity market and for the bond and money markets.

Concern about equity market crowding-out is present in Malaysia, where, prior to the listing of the first tranche of equity in the state telecommunications company (which was (correctly) anticipated to raise the equivalent of almost 100% of the previous year's total new issues on the KLSE), the central bank imposed a moratorium on rights issues by existing listed companies. Anecdotal evidence also abounds from other markets of investors and issuers holding off on new issues in anticipation of privatization issues. Crowding-out of other markets can also occur. In theory, privatization is in essence an asset swap between the government and the private sector: thus crowding-out in other asset markets is inevitable. This outcome assumes an efficient capital market, and in reality the effects of increased equity supply are likely to be less direct and may even have benign effects on other markets. In particular, as noted above, greater activity in the equity market will draw funds away from the market for government securities, the effect of which will be to induce greater competition in the market for government paper, with attendant benefits in encouraging greater market determination of interest rates. However, less welcome may be the extent to which short-term speculation in privatization stocks crowds out money and financial markets. A noted case of this phenomenon occurred with the share issues by the three largest commercial banks in Kenya (one of which was publicly owned), all of which issued new equity on the Nairobi Stock Exchange from 1986 to 1989. In each case the shares were generously priced and the issues heavily over-subscribed. The monetary statistics show clear drops in balances held on deposit with the banking sector in the months that these issues were made as investors switched large amounts of resources from deposit accounts into equities.

The implications of the above are twofold. First, though privatization can be a quick way of increasing the volume of stock in the market, there are clear indications that the risk profile of privatization issues may not be optimal for a fragile developing market. It is therefore important that, if privatization programmes are to foster capital market development, the volume and sequencing of equity issues must be such as to ensure that the overall risk profile of the market remains balanced and not excessively exposed to trade or other exogenous shocks. Second, it is likely that there will be some degree of crowding-out of savings elsewhere in the financial sector. In particular, attention must be given to the extent to which the privatization programme constrains the raising of funds through the equity market by the private sector, and also the extent to which the programme may impinge on the other financing requirements of government.

Privatization and new market players

The concept of wider share ownership is at the core of virtually every privatization programme. While this has more to do with the politics than the economics of privatization, there are a number of important economic channels through which a broader base of players will influence the development of the capital market. In general, whilst there is evidence concerning the acquisition of shares in privatization issues by new shareholders, the more relevant issues in terms of general equity market development are the extent to which privatization alters the behaviour of existing players; what type of (rather than how many) new players are attracted by the issue; and the way in which the privatization issues shape new investor perceptions about future privatization and other share issues.

The positive effects of more players in the market are relatively straightforward. As with the effect of an increase in the supply of equity on the market, an increase in the number of players may be expected to reduce the degree of concentration and increase the degree of competition within the market. In addition, there exists the view that broader equity participation in the economy will foster a market-oriented ethic in the economy at large which will have positive macro-economic benefits in areas as diverse as wage bargaining, investment policy, and internal economic efficiency.[25]

These ideas are impossible to quantify, and it is far from clear that privatization is the most efficient way to foster this ethic. More germane to the issue of capital market development is the extent to which privatization may be expected to influence the performance of the important existing players on the market.

In most capital markets the key players tend to be the long-term savings and pension institutions. In a number of programmes (Malaysia, Papua New Guinea, Kenya, and Sri Lanka) a key element in the privatization and capital market debate has been the promotion of greater equity participation by these institutions. The commonly held view is that, faced with very thin secondary markets in government paper and negligible markets in corporate bonds, these players have tended to adopt extremely risk-averse investment policies based on the accumulation of long-term government paper and fixed-term deposits. The deepening of the capital market through privatization stocks, combined (often) with revision of the policy objectives and investment guidelines of these institutions to increase equity participation, is seen as one of the most important externalities of the privatization and capital market debate. The extreme risk aversion of the long-term contractual savings institutions (and their propensity to hoard stock) has long been identified as one of the major constraints on the development of the capital market in many, especially African, developing countries. Consequently, the stimulus that privatization issues seem to be giving to these institutions may have far-reaching effects for the financial system as a whole.

Another key group of new players, and the one which has attracted much attention amongst the donor community, is foreign investors. The attraction of foreign participation in privatization programmes has been alluded to earlier, but there are other discernible externalities arising from the inflow of foreign investors into the equity market, both directly and through portfolio equity participation. First is the belief that foreign investors are more dynamic than domestic investors and will induce closer monitoring and control than may otherwise occur. Second, especially in the case of foreign portfolio investment, foreign investors may be more active in the secondary market as their portfolio choices are determined across a wider range of assets. Greater foreign portfolio investment will thus particularly deepen the secondary market.[26] Third is the view that greater orientation towards foreign participation results in attention being directed towards revision of securities legislation, and in particular foreign investment conditions, both of which could be expected to induce greater direct foreign inflows into non-privatization assets.

The most obvious, and possibly least important, set of drawbacks from a large increase in equity in the market is the impact on players who, for whatever reason, find themselves in captive underwriting positions. For example, a number of Jamaican private sector underwriters were obliged by the government to subscribe for 50% of privatization issues in order to destroy the incentive for these underwriters, as investors, to see the issue fail. More generally, in a number of countries, major public sector institutions are expected to fulfil investment as well as underwriting functions for new, large, privatization issues. The undoubted conflict of interests generated not only affects the role of these players in the market, but also feeds back on the design of the privatization programme itself in cases where such underwriter/investor players are major public enterprises, as in the case of Permodalan Nasional Berhad (PNB) in Malaysia. The PNB is, however, somewhat peculiar in that one of its main functions has traditionally been to act as a buffer against commercial risk being passed on to individual shareholders. Until late 1989, PNB operated a unit trust scheme, known as the Amanah Saham Nasional (ASN), in which all downside commercial risks were underwritten by PNB (see Chapter 9). More recently, however, concerns have been raised that the objectives of the privatization programme and this underwriting function will be unable to coexist, and recent developments within the PNB have attempted to reduce the extent of the risk-underwriting function by ensuring that commercial risks are passed on to investors.

As noted, privatization has frequently included, as one of its objectives, the promotion of wider individual share ownership through public issues. One of the main instruments used by any issuer of shares, particularly in privatization sales, is the allocation/pricing process through which government can directly influence the composition of players in the primary market. Evidence suggests, however, that, in some markets – most noticeably the KLSE, this allocation distribution is not sustained, particularly when the issue price diverges significantly from the market price. What occurs is that the share distribution rapidly contracts as successful individual applicants realize capital gains through sales (usually) to institutions which seek to hold assets for long-term purposes, but which were rationed in the primary allocation. This phenomenon does little to the structure of market players, but rather represents a cumbersome method of effecting a lump-sum cash transfer from the issuer (government) to lucky share applicants, instrumented through the equity market.

The prevalence of this behaviour on the part of new players raises an important second-order effect, operating principally in terms of moral hazard and adverse selection effects. Consistent share underpricing on the part of the government represents an imperfect form of risk insurance for investors. The presence of such insurance induces market participants to act in otherwise excessively risk-assuming ways (the moral hazard effect). In addition, it will attract players into the market who would not otherwise participate in an 'un-insured' equity market (the adverse selection problem). It seems clear that, however desirable this form of insurance may be from a political point of view, it is doubtful that it serves to develop the equity market. More sharply, the issue is raised of whether an influx of investors who see equity participation in privatization issues as a low-risk, speculative activity is consistent with balanced capital market development.

This phenomenon is, however, not universal. One particularly noticeable feature about new players attracted by privatization issues in many countries is the relative lack of sophistication of their portfolios. Even in the UK, a large majority of the new shareholders, attracted by the underpriced privatization issues, tend to hold very narrow portfolios consisting of only the shares of privatized companies, where their portfolio composition is determined principally by the vagaries of the allocation process rather than by any other portfolio choice criteria.

Though not an inevitable consequence of privatization *per se*, this occurrence is likely to be prevalent in markets where sophistication in share dealing is relatively low. The phenomenon is very clearly seen in Malaysia (Table 5.8), although a striking counter-example is found in Jamaica, where share underpricing has not

Table 5.8 *Distribution of shareholders*

Company	Number of Shareholders	
	At Issue	*End 1989*
CCC (Jamaica)	c. 23,000	24,408
NCB (Jamaica)	30,606	30,307
ToJ (Jamaica)	17,168	17,426
MAS (Malaysia)	25,000	11,500
MISC (Malaysia)	60,000	5,000

Source: Chapters 7 and 9.

been accompanied by a rash of profit-taking by successful applicants in the primary issue.

In Jamaica, the new entrants, though numerous, are relatively unsophisticated and tend not to trade in the secondary market, which neutralizes the positive effect of an increase in equity supply. Moreover, this lack of secondary trading also raises problems concerning the control and discipline of management by shareholders. This is a variant of the general free-rider problem of widespread share ownership. Since the benefits of monitoring become a public good amongst all shareholders, there will be incentives for small shareholders to free-ride on the monitoring effort of larger shareholders. In the case where there is a large number of small passive shareholders (as in Jamaica), or when the bulk of shares are held by passive investment funds, this free-rider problem can become sufficiently strong for a sub-optimal level of monitoring of management to ensue. The most worrying scenario is in the case of large, powerful enterprises in which the widely spread, passive, domestic small shareholders exercise no effective control over either dominant overseas shareholders or the enterprise management.

Though attracting a large number of new players through privatization may be seen as having independent political benefits, capital market development on the other hand is determined by the quality of new investors. Pricing policies which introduce only risk-averse new players attracted by the prospect of certain capital gains clearly do not augur well for long-term, sustainable development of the market. New players attracted to equity markets on the promise of virtual zero downside risk not only will continue to expect significant underpricing in future privatization issues, but may also prove to be volatile players when the market assumes a less distorted risk profile. Consequently information and education about equity participation become essential not only for this reason, but are also necessary to ensure that the market is not hindered by equity hoarding on the part of passive shareholders.

Privatization and equity market management capacity
It is clear that equity market management capacity will evolve gradually with any non-privatization increase in equity. However, the large scale and the bunching effects of privatization sales will have a catalytic effect on the market institutions and their capacity to maintain and improve the functioning of the market. Similarly, privatization has proved to be a stimulus to the revision of financial sector regulation. Both effects influence the performance of the financial services sector as a whole. In the countries we have studied market capacity has improved in four main areas.

First is the revision (or in some cases the introduction) of capital market regulatory structures. In Malaysia the securities legislation was overhauled by the 1983 Securities Industry Act; in Sri Lanka a Securities Council was established in 1987 to provide for orderly market trading and investor protection; in Kenya the Capital Market Development Authority was created in 1989 in an attempt to create a market environment in which the (as yet dormant) privatization programme could progress; and in Papua New Guinea the government has been involved in establishing a regulatory framework for a capital market through which privatizations can be floated. The story in Jamaica is characteristic of many similar markets. The Jamaican Stock Exchange (JSE) has, since its inception, operated without any form of securities legislation, to the extent that concern has been repeatedly expressed about insider trading and the manipulation of the market. The influx of new players, including the prospect of greater international participation in the Jamaican equity market, has undermined the integrity of the self-regulating structure, and has resulted in a build-up of pressure on the market authorities to jettison this image and overhaul their legal and regulatory framework. It is widely believed within the market that the introduction of an effective regulatory framework is imperative, if the privatization process and the integration of the JSE into the broader Caribbean stock exchange initiative is to be achieved.

Second, a related development has been the stimulus that the introduction of foreign players to the privatization process has had on tax policy and policy towards foreign equity participation. For example, in Sri Lanka's first stock market listing (of United Motors) 5% of the equity was sold to the Mitsubishi Motor Company. To effect this sale, however, the government was obliged to issue a waiver on the 100% tax on non-resident share transactions, originally enacted in 1963. As the privatization programme has unfolded, however, moves have been made by the government to repeal this 100% tax wholesale, first for privatization share issues, and then more widely. Similarly, in the Trinidad Cement Limited sales the Ministry of Finance relaxed the otherwise heavily regulated licensing system for foreign participation. And in Malaysia, as the privatization programme has expanded, and particularly as increasingly larger issues are being considered, formerly strict conditions on direct equity participation by foreign investors have weakened, in anticipation of the forthcoming sale of STM (the Malaysian telecommunications company) equity to the foreign sector.

Third, the anticipation (and realization) of heavier trading volumes associated with the privatization programmes has resulted in technological development in trading and settlement systems, and the promotion of expertise in support services. For example, both Sri Lanka and Malaysia have seen the introduction of new trading and settlement systems since 1989, while in most countries undertaking privatization there has been a discernible decrease in reliance on external technical assistance in areas such as underwriting, valuation and management of privatization issues.

Fourth, the push for privatization has seen the development of new financial instruments, aimed at bundling privatization stocks so that markets can be made. The most common instrument being considered at present is a unit trust composed specifically of shares in privatized companies.[27] To date no such trusts have been launched in the countries studied, but proposals are in progress in Sri Lanka, Malaŵi, Kenya and Trinidad and Tobago.

Generally, the impact of privatization on this aspect of capital market development has been, and is likely to be, positive. However, there remains a risk that the pressures on the market and its supporting infrastructure to process the large volumes of trade associated with a rapid programme of privatization may undermine its credibility and integrity.[28] Since the loss of credibility in the capital market will not only jeopardize the privatization programme itself, but will clearly set back the overall process of capital market development, it is important that the

push for privatization through the capital market does not exceed the technical
capacity of the market to manage the sales.

Conclusions
The main purpose of this section has been to suggest that the links between
privatization and capital market development are strong and can be mutually
reinforcing. The presence of a deep and well-functioning capital market dramatically widens the scope for implementing privatization, for promoting equitable
(initial) wealth distributions, and for accessing foreign equity participation in
a politically neutral way. Moreover, developed secondary trading capacity can
promote the efficient monitoring of management, while the tradability of equities
enhances their liquidity and hence their value.

We have argued that privatization can make a major contribution to the deepening of equity markets, but the 'kick-starting' paradigm in itself is oversimplified. In doing so we have attempted to identify a number of key issues which need
to be addressed if progress in privatization and capital market development are to
remain congruent over the medium term. First, there is the need to ensure that
sudden increases of equity on the market do not adversely warp its risk profile
in a way that compromises its capacity to absorb and spread risk. Second, it is
important to consider the extent and direction of the crowding-out effects of large
equity flotation. Third, in attempting to increase the number of players in the
market, consideration must be given to the quality and sophistication of the new
players attracted, and the impact that pricing and allocation policies will have on
their market behaviour. Fourth, greater attention than has hitherto been the case
must be paid to education and information about equity participation. And, fifth,
the pace of privatization needs to be matched to the technical capacity of the
market.

5.4 Conclusions

In this chapter we have examined the interactions between the structure of the
private sector, the capital market, and the regulatory regime and the implementation of privatization. In general we have seen that the economies studied here
have been characterized by narrowly-based private sectors with high levels of
effective protection and widespread domination of many sectors by state-owned
enterprises. Capital markets are generally small and their absorptive capacity
limited, while the capacity for efficient and credible regulation is weak. While
it is the case that there are feedback effects from privatization to the development of the private sector, to the deepening of the capital market, and to
the enhancement of regulatory capacity, in the short run the dominant effect is
from the structural constraint to the nature of the programme. As such these
constraints severely limit the options for and value of privatization as an active
adjustment policy. Moreover, the lifting of these constraints represents a goal
of the development process in general, rather than merely an impediment to the
privatization process in particular, and it is no accident that countries which have
run at least moderately successful programmes, namely Jamaica and Malaysia,
are on most measures far more 'developed' than those where the programmes
have stumbled, such as Kenya, Sri Lanka, Malaŵi and Papua New Guinea.

Notes

1. As will be detailed in the country studies, PNG is set to enjoy a mineral and petrochemical boom which will in all likelihood eclipse that enjoyed in the 1970s by Trinidad.
2. The most valuable sources are World Bank Industrial Sector Memoranda.
3. In Jamaica, however, legislation is being passed to outlaw 'unnecessary' interlocking directorates.
4. See, for example A.S. Deaton, 'Savings in Developing Countries', *World Bank Research Observer* (1989).
5. Ibid.
6. It is a common feature of World Bank-supported trade liberalization that tariffs on directly competing final goods are the last and slowest to be reduced. See Mosley *et al.* (1991).
7. Their performance may, of course, still remain inefficient as a result of 'soft' budget constraints, as in the case of Kenya Airways, etc.
8. The cases of the Kuwait Investment Office's purchase of BP shares and the frequent rejections of foreign vehicle manufacturers' bids to purchase the British Leyland group are good examples of the prevalence of these concerns in the UK.
9. A classic example is the commitment by the Government of Trinidad and Tobago to retain the large oil- and gas-based industries in public ownership. Given the size and technical nature of these firms, sale could only be to the foreign private sector.
10. Problems in transport policy co-ordination are particularly common. See Chapter 9 on Malaysia and Chapter 12 on Kenya.
11. Indeed, observers have argued that in all three countries the equity markets existed only because there were no regulatory restrictions on such activities as insider-dealing.
12. Plans are under way to sell, in addition to the telecommunications utility, railways and electricity generation.
13. Under trigger-based schemes, medium-term performance targets are set in line with the agreed corporate plans. Only if the enterprise's performance fails to meet these targets is active intervention by government triggered.
14. In fact, in most cases, the most detailed information on market structures is collected by external agents such as the World Bank.
15. See Vickers and Yarrow (1988), Chapter 4, for a discussion of these specific regulatory problems.
16. One exception to this being Vickers and Wright's (1988: 19–22) discussion of the capital market constraint on privatization in Europe.
17. All data presented here come from the IFC, *Emerging Stock Markets Factbook* and our own studies.
18. Measured by market turnover as a percentage of market capitalization.
19. As in the case of the sale of NCB in Trinidad and Tobago.
20. Across developed and developing country cases, there are numerous cases where the apparent reporting and disclosure conditions are significantly weaker for non-market sales. In Kenya none of the sales have been through the capital market, and all have been shrouded in mystery; in Malaysia the initial first-come, first-served contracts and Build–Operate–Transfer Schemes have been attacked for their tendency to 'cronyism'; in Sri Lanka, there are the cases of the sales of the government-owned tile factories and textile mills.
21. When privatization is accomplished through direct sales, such divestiture creates pressures for the future tradability and liquidity of private claims.
22. For example in Sri Lanka, of the top five companies, which accounted for 53% of total turnover in 1988, three were in the financial sector, and the other two in the services sector.
23. Including the largest company on the Jamaica Stock Exchange in 1988, Telecommunications of Jamaica.
24. The first M$2.35bn tranche of the sale of STM (Malaysian Telecommunications) occurred in November 1990, after the completion of this study. Proposals for the sale of further equity in STM and in the electricity utility are under way.
25. In Jamaica, for example, there is anecdotal evidence of much greater interest on the part of chief financial officers and accountants in the performance of their companies' shares relative to competitors.
26. Generally in the countries in this study foreign portfolio investors' participation in privatization issues has been prohibited, although they are able to participate in the secondary market in some countries. A recent development in this area is the decision by the Malaysian Government to sell

a small tranche of STM equity directly to foreign investors (at an issue price 40% above the domestic issue price).

27. In particular, these unit trusts have been conceived of as a vehicle for the partial divestiture of the asset portfolios of government-owned development finance institutions.

28. For example, though not associated with the privatization programme *per se*, the KLSE suffered from a serious credibility problem associated with the loss of a significant amount of scrip in early 1990 on the change-over to its computerized reporting and settlement system.

6 Adjusting Privatization

Background

For many developing countries the 1980s was the decade of adjustment, as countries underwent painful programmes of economic stabilization and embarked on measures designed to bring about medium-term improvements in the structure of the economy, particularly on the supply side. Privatization lay at the confluence of these goals. Many governments embraced the idea of privatization as a possible solution to the dire straits into which the SOE sector had fallen, and as a means of stanching the flow of funds to these SOEs from the public sector as a whole. Further, privatization has been instrumental in policy programmes aimed at broader adjustment issues. In part, this was because privatization became viewed as an integral part of a reform package including trade liberalization, price deregulation, fiscal stabilization and the like, even though these policies were conceptually quite separate. More logically, however, privatization became part of adjustment because of its close links to the longer-term objectives of private sector and capital market development.

Governments also embraced privatization because the SOEs had disappointed in their role as distributors of rents towards favoured income and ethnic groups. The *laissez-faire* approach to the efficient management of SOEs had fostered a small group of rentiers for whom the distributional effects of state ownership were positive and often sizeable, but at the cost of falling efficiency in operations and increasingly unsustainable fiscal disequilibrium. Second, attempts to spread benefits more widely through price controls and cross-subsidization not only were excessively blunt, but were also undermined by poor output quality, erratic service and the emergence of rationing. Thus, while privatization in some sense represents a jettisoning by governments of earlier welfare considerations, it can also be a method of achieving those same considerations, both through the provision of improved services and also through realizing wealth transfers more efficiently.

Outcomes

Despite the apparent priority accorded to privatization by governments and donors, the results by and large have not supported initial expectations. In part, this is because many of the expected effects will only be manifest in the medium term, but more important is the fact that much less progress in actual implementation has been made than was initially envisaged. With the exception of Jamaica, there has in general been no substantive shift in ownership of national wealth from public to private sectors, and even in Jamaica the cumulative proceeds of privatization from 1981 to 1989 constituted only 7.2% of GDP. Elsewhere, notably in Malaysia, which quickly acquired a reputation as a major privatizer, the scale of privatization in the 1980s was small.

There has, however, been some measurable improvement in the overall performance of the SOE sector during the period. For one thing, the creation of new SOEs has come to a virtual halt, not least in areas such as manufacturing and services. But, more importantly, SOE reform has directly contributed much more to the rationalization of public finances than has privatization, and indeed has been an important factor in the overall improvement of fiscal balances. Price and tariff restructuring, production rationalization, restructuring of management and capital, corporate planning, and the introduction of arm's-length control and monitoring schemes between the SOEs and central government have featured strongly in this period.

Whereas accounting for the flow of funds from the privatization exercise is relatively straightforward, the identification of efficiency gains is more difficult. In many cases the sale of the asset has been too recent to expect any such gains to be clear, but more often the nature of the sale and the environment in which it proceeded have served to negate any positive effects which might have been expected. In Chapter 2 we showed how privatization has almost as many objectives as the policy it was supposed to supplant, namely state ownership of the means of production. As in the case of state ownership, simultaneous achievement of all these objectives is not possible. Thus one of the key findings from Chapter 4 was that government's internal ranking of the multiple goals of privatization usually greatly down-played the importance of attaining efficiency improvements. In particular, we examined the way political factors, public finance needs, and the pressure from external creditors shaped sales in a manner unconducive to the achievement of this core objective.

Concerning privatization and its broader objectives, namely private sector and capital market development, changing income distribution and the meeting of loan disbursement conditions, achievements have been limited. Countries have made progress in attaining these objectives, but this has not in general been due to privatization. Private sectors have become more competitive during the decade, but this was principally as a result of trade policy reform and domestic price liberalization rather than explicitly because of privatization. Similarly, capital market development and the pursuit of wider share ownership have depended more on financial liberalization and broader economic deregulation than on the stimulus created by the supply of equity in privatized enterprises. In both cases, there have been some positive impulses from privatization, but, as we have argued, these are limited by the structural constraints that weak private sectors and thin capital markets have themselves placed on privatization.

Income distribution (both international and inter-ethnic) has proved to be one of the most binding constraints on the entire privatization process. In a number of countries it has effectively suffocated all other aspects of the debate, while in others, where privatization has turned on the complexities of these concerns, it has induced significant distortions in the design and implementation of programmes. In the case of foreign ownership, these problems have been particularly acute. Faced with limited domestic demand, many governments have faced the choice of either selling assets to the foreign sector and incurring heavy political losses, or continuing to hold them in the public sector. Furthermore, the management of sales to the foreign sector has raised complex (and often unresolved) issues of regulation.

Finally, the evidence of the 1980s has shown that privatization sits uncomfortably within the disbursement conditions of policy-based lending. Many countries have embarked on programmes of privatization within the framework of structural adjustment programmes, and the pressure to meet these criteria has, on occasion, led to poor programme management and inadequate preparation of enterprises for sale. More common, however, has been the tendency for donors to tolerate slippage of loan conditionality as it became clear that the rapid implementation of privatization during a period of often quite severe stabilization measures could be a costly exercise. Despite the rhetoric of policy-based lending, rarely was a failure to privatize an enterprise a sufficient reason to halt the disbursement of aid flows.

Evaluation

Though our work is based on a small sample of countries, in which privatization has in some cases been a marginal activity, it is becoming increasingly clear that the problems and issues we have identified in these seven countries provide appropriate archetypes for a wide range of economies. Though the problems faced in Eastern Europe of reorientating an entire economy are of a different type, for most other developing countries the issues raised here are germane, if of differing orders of magnitude. Supporting this is the fact that a number of the more recent works which touch on privatization have echoed the conclusions of our own work (see, for example, the conclusions and findings of Chapter 7 of the *World Development Report*, 1991, Glade, 1991, and Shirley and Nellis, 1991).

In trying to explain the very significant shortfall between the experience of privatization and original expectations, we have focused on two important aspects. First, and most fundamentally, we have argued that the speed, form and economic effects of privatization will be ultimately determined by the structural and regulatory limitations of the economy. However, privatization does not occur in a vacuum, and thus the second important argument of the study highlights the pervasive effects that political considerations have had on the design and implementation of privatization programmes. Consequently, it is the tensions between the economics and politics of privatization, and also between the various objectives of privatization itself, that have shaped privatization history in the 1980s, and which will determine the short-term outlook for programmes in the next decade.

Concerning our first argument, the thrust of the analysis in Part I of this book has been to make explicit the theoretical underpinnings of arguments for privatization, which rely significantly on assumptions about economic structure that are more appropriate for developed than developing countries. Comparing these with the features of our country studies gives us a basis for deciding how to adjust our notions of what privatization can and cannot be expected to achieve in low- to middle-income countries.

Significantly, economic theory highlights the importance of information flows and incentive mechanisms for efficient management, and of market structure and regulation for the efficient allocation of resources. In developing countries, however, information flows are frequently weak. Under public ownership, performance indicators have tended to be denominated in quantitative terms (such as employment, output, physical assets) and prices themselves, often set by fiat and layered with extensive cross-subsidization, rarely transmitted information on true resource costs. Moreover, these distortions frequently pervaded all economic sectors regardless of ownership, through the effects of widespread domestic price controls and complex trade policy. Transfer of ownership may eliminate some of the more extreme elements of the weak internal processing of information, but this will be of only limited value if broader price distortions remain.

Similarly, limited market size (which means that 'natural' monopoly becomes a common occurrence), extensive concentration of economic power, institutional linkages, and limited import penetration in certain sectors have served to limit competition on the supply side. Monopolistic and oligopolistic enterprises thus dominate the domestic economy, many of which (especially in the smaller economies) are state-owned. Privatization of such enterprises without restructuring of the enterprise itself or without associated changes in market structure may have no measurable impact on enterprise performance. These structural limitations of the domestic economy in developing countries are so pervasive that effective regulation of markets against the adverse effects of monopoly and oligopoly power becomes an essential adjunct to virtually all substantial privatization initiatives, rather than, as in many industrialized economies, a specific requirement in respect of the sale of a small number of monopoly utilities. One of the most worrying features of privatization in developing countries is the extremely low priority accorded to market regulation and competition policy. However, even if this were reversed, the evidence suggests that a number of countries have some way to go before the capacity would exist to implement efficient and credible regulation.

Furthermore, the absence of efficient means of savings mobilization for equity investment remains an important constraint to broader implementation of privatization objectives in a number of the poorer developing countries, such as Malawi and Papua New Guinea. Governments in these countries are constrained in the form and size of sales: what is more, without tradability of assets they face lower realizable prices for them; and by being unable to 'unbundle' asset entitlements they face the prospect of reconcentration of asset ownership in the hands of a small private sector elite.

There are, of course, feedbacks from privatization to the development of private sector, capital market and regulatory structures, but these are weak, and the process of trying to accelerate privatization may be ultimately harmful. Overburdening the absorptive capacity of the economy, and the administrative capacity of government, may ultimately result in privatization becoming a welfare-reducing activity as rents are captured by powerful buyers, capital markets are distorted, and the loss of regulatory credibility produces negative externalities in other areas.

Our second argument concerned the importance of the nature of the political environment and the political objectives of the government in crucially shaping the privatization programme in the short run. Privatization has been a politically contentious policy, often regarded either as a line of demarcation between political parties in pluralistic countries, or as a threat to the economic well-being of rentiers in single-party systems. Its implementation has, as a result, often been undertaken as an article of political faith, but at the same time with an extreme sense of caution. Moreover, in many developing countries it is closely combined with a range of other related adjustment policies and political objectives, and has been pursued in the midst of painful stabilization measures. Conflicts abound, and for risk-averse or cautious governments, often lacking credibility in the eyes of the domestic electorate and foreign donors and investors, this has meant that the economic objectives of privatization are frequently compromised (or even completely ignored) as a result of political expediency. While such expediency may in some cases be economically rational in a dynamic sense (in that it is necessary to create a reputation with buyers to ensure market receptivity for the future), it does underline the important fact that putting privatization in the van of reform can often be achieved only with significant revenue and efficiency costs. Similarly, though privatization is essentially concerned with the transfer of commercial risk to the private sector, this is often compromised by implicit underwriting of the private sector in privatization sales by a politically cautious government.

Not surprisingly then, the reality of privatization in developing countries has not met expectations. It remains a priority, however, and as many countries move into a second decade of privatization it is valuable to consider what adjustments to the policy are required for privatization to play a useful role in medium-term economic reform in developing countries.

Outlook – adjusting privatization for the 1990s

There is no doubt that in the current wave of 'market-friendly development' privatization will remain a major component of economic policy packages in the 1990s. Moreover, as we have seen in Jamaica and Sri Lanka, as political opposition to the policy diminishes, programmes of privatization are likely to be less politically motivated and less designed around the narrow objective of securing political 'success'. This, it is hoped, will allow a more balanced view of the role of privatization to emerge.

The first adjustment required if privatization is to be effective in achieving its efficiency-enhancing objectives is that it be clearly regarded as a medium-term supply-side policy, a logical complement to broader private sector development. The ultimate goal of developing countries is a vibrant and competitive private sector, and as goods and capital markets and regulatory capacity develop and deepen so privatization can become a valuable policy instrument. The scope for privatization is inevitably going to be greater the higher the level of development in the economy. Consequently, the objective of policy should be the development of the private sector and the capital market. Privatization should fall within these broader objectives, with more attention being paid to the direct economic objectives, and allowing the politics to die away.

Second, and conversely, it is doubtful that privatization can play any major role in the short run in the face of adverse structural economic conditions. Endemic investment uncertainty, problems of policy credibility, and the political forces impinging on governments as they attempt to bring about economic stabilization are not conducive to the success of privatization, and in such cases privatization for the short run should be downgraded, and governments and donors should reassess its role within adjustment programmes. Judicious privatization, especially through the sale of smaller enterprises, is still valuable, but attempts to accelerate privatization programmes will vitiate the goals they are supposed to achieve, on two fronts. Not only will the programme come up against the binding constraints of the economy, but also the political intervention required to secure the success of privatization in periods of crisis may actually 'lock-in' welfare-reducing elements. Underwriting and underpricing arrangements, guarantees on market access, and over-generous restructuring, which are required to see sales proceed in such circumstances, are precisely such impediments to efficiency-enhancing privatization.

Third, in view of these concerns, it is essential that the current capacity of the domestic private sector to absorb public asset sales, and therefore expectations of the scale of privatization programmes is re-assessed. Privatization 'pipelines' are still extremely optimistic, and across a number of countries they have already been seen to slip, or to be implemented in a hurried and sub-optimal way. Only a fraction of the Sri Lankan pipeline for 1990 and 1991 has been implemented, while the same is the case with the ambitious Privatization Masterplan in Malaysia and the second wave of privatization in Jamaica and Trinidad and Tobago.

These views obviously beg the question: how, then, ought governments to proceed in tackling the still prevalent short-term crisis of the SOE sector? We argue that direct reform of SOEs, combined with broader, market-based regulatory frameworks, will offer much more fundamental adjustments in resource use than will rapid privatization. An oft-cited argument in favour of privatization was that SOE reform would not persist and that it was only with the 'threat' of privatization that efficiency gains could be 'locked-in'. However, though this argument had currency in the early 1980s, it seems less powerful now. First, there is evidence that the 'threat' effect has been established: governments have abandoned the creation of SOEs as major tools of economic policy, and the prevailing political sentiment is firmly based in the demand for efficient services from SOEs. Secondly, having established privatization as a medium-term option, SOE reform measures acquire a definite context. SOE reform within a broader framework of market development is consistent, in a way that it was not in an environment of non-market pricing and control. Thus the establishment of market-based regulatory structures for the SOE sector allows governments to 'practise' and develop their regulatory capacity, to implement appropriate (and effective) competition policy, and to create the information and incentive structures that will be robust enough to ensure that, eventual privatization can be successful. Paradoxically, then, given the constraints placed on immediate privatization by the economic structures of many developing countries, one policy for strengthening market orientation in these economies is the intelligent reform of the SOE sector, structured around sound economic principles. In combination with a reduction in the urgency currently assigned to privatization and the revision of programmes around a medium-term, efficiency-oriented framework, this will allow governments to assess more clearly the relative costs and benefits of competing policy alternatives in pursuit of the efficient supply of goods and services in a manner consistent with the ultimate welfare objectives of government and society.

II COUNTRY CASE STUDIES

7   JAMAICA

7.1 Introduction

The privatization programme in Jamaica has been the largest of all our country studies. It has involved the greatest number of enterprises, and has had the most substantial impact on fiscal balances. It therefore offers a fascinating opportunity to explore the issues outlined in the first six chapters of this book. In general, the highlight of the Jamaican programme has been its diversity, both in terms of the economic sectors in which privatized enterprises operate, and the size and methods of sale. In some cases, privatization in Jamaica has clearly been a success, both in that it satisfied the objectives of the government and, more importantly, in that it achieved the fundamental rationale of privatization, namely efficiency-enhancement. There is also evidence that the privatization programme had a positive impact on the Jamaican Stock Exchange. However, in other cases, and especially in the larger, more visible transactions, the success of privatization has been constrained by three factors. The first, naturally, has been the structure of Jamaica's private sector, which remains largely oligopolistic. The second constraint has been the tendency of the Jamaican Government in the 1980s to view privatization as a goal rather than as a means to an end. This concentration on the transaction rather than the result has led to insufficient attention being paid to competition and regulatory policy, the necessary adjuncts to an economically successful programme of privatization. The third constraint was the fact that, by the mid-1980s, privatization was a focal point of the political schism that then existed between the two main political parties. The controversy surrounding certain sales adversely affected the design of privatization, in contrast to those sales which were not the subject of political attention. However, in this regard, the Jamaican privatization programme has also been a success in that political convergence on the desirability of divestiture has meant that, like the selfish gene, privatization has ensured its own survival.

7.1.1 Macroeconomic background

Jamaica's economy is primarily determined by its position as a medium-sized island in the Caribbean. That is to say, its economic structure has grown out of its history as a colony, and the need to trade consequent on its small size. Thus, at Independence, Jamaica was an open economy, with production concentrated in the sectors which predominated during the colonial period, namely export crops (sugar, coffee and bananas) and agroprocessing, and extensive foreign ownership of the key economic sectors. Like most developing countries, Jamaica recorded appreciable growth rates in the 1960s, with real growth in the period 1965–1970 of over 5% per annum. In Jamaica's case, this was the result of favourable agricultural producer prices, the development of the bauxite mining sector, and growth in tourism and in non-traditional manufacturing. Broadly speaking, the government followed the 'industrialization by invitation' strategy then common in the Caribbean. Despite high growth, however, domestic discontent arose with this economic strategy because of widespread foreign ownership and rising unemployment.

As a result, a more radical government of the PNP under Michael Manley was elected in 1972 with a far more socialist economic orientation. However, the next eight years were disastrous ones for Jamaica, with a decline in real GDP of 21% between 1974 and 1980. In part, this was due to external shocks, especially the rise in oil prices and a decline in tourism. However, domestic economic policy also contributed to negative growth. One part of the reorientation of economic policy involved an excessively rapid expansion of state ownership, as outlined below. More broadly, though, the Manley Government of 1972–80 instituted wide-ranging price and trade controls, raised marginal tax rates considerably, and substantially expanded government spending through a rapidly increasing public sector labour force and rising transfers. Real interest rates were negative, and incentive structures became increasingly oriented against exports. Macroeconomic indicators generally worsened: a deteriorating external balance was funded through reserve depletion and external borrowing while import controls were tightened; price controls were extended to over 100 products and the exchange rate became increasingly uncompetitive.

Although social spending was raised during the period, the crisis in the domestic economy was severe enough to result in the election in 1980 of the Jamaica Labour Party (JLP) under Edward Seaga with an economic programme of a completely different hue. The broad outlines of this programme, which included commitments to both privatization and the reform of the SOE sector, are discussed where appropriate in subsequent sections. Here, however, we note that, despite a decade of often intensive structural adjustment, the Jamaican economy remains in a precarious position. As Table 7.1 shows, growth in the 1980s was intermittent, in part due to the persistent shortages of foreign exchange caused by the country's crippling debt burden. Policy reform has affected many areas, especially trade and price liberalization, exchange-rate devaluations, and fiscal retrenchment (in particular, a dramatic reduction in the number of employees working for the government). However, structurally the Jamaican economy ended the 1980s largely unchanged, in that economic growth is still heavily dependent on international commodity prices and US tourism, and foreign investment is still critical to meeting the capital needs of important sectors of the economy.

7.2. The SOE sector

The key date for the SOE sector was 1980, when the new JLP Government of Edward Seaga was elected on a platform which included both the reform of SOEs and the transfer of some of the government's holdings to the private sector. By this time, the government had acquired extensive ownership in a variety of the most important productive sectors, and the issue of the performance of the public enterprises sector had become increasingly important in the determination of the overall performance of the economy. As in most other countries, it is in the context of dissatisfaction with the economic performance of the SOE sector that the option for privatization has become a policy priority. This section therefore traces the origin and development of the SOE sector in Jamaica, presents evidence of its performance before 1980, outlines the various reform programmes put in place since the beginning of the 1980s, and attempts to evaluate the effects of these reforms on public enterprise performance.

Table 7.1 Jamaica: Macroeconomic data

		1977	1978	1979	1980	1981	1982	1983	1984	1985	1986	1987	1988	1989
GDP	(J$bn)	3.0	3.7	4.3	4.8	5.4	6.1	7.6	9.9	12.5	14.5	16.3	18.3	22.1
Private consumption	(% of GDP)	65.7	63.4	63.0	65.4	70.2	69.5	66.6	66.4	72.9	67.3	62.5	62.7	60.3
Public consumption	(% of GDP)	20.7	20.1	19.3	20.3	20.7	22.0	20.1	16.6	15.7	15.4	14.6	16.1	14.1
Investment	(% of GDP)	12.2	15.0	19.2	15.7	20.4	20.9	22.3	23.0	25.0	18.5	22.6	25.9	29.1
Domestic savings	(% of GDP)	11.3	11.7	13.3	9.5	7.7	8.7	12.0	9.9	10.0	13.5	17.4	n.a.	n.a.
Exports of G&NFS	(% of GDP)	29.8	41.4	48.1	51.1	47.2	37.8	33.2	52.9	57.9	53.2	54.8	47.2	47.4
Imports of G&NFS	(% of GDP)	28.4	40.2	50.4	52.8	58.5	50.1	42.2	61.9	71.5	54.4	54.5	52.5	51.3
Real GDP growth	(%)	-2.4	0.5	-1.8	-5.7	2.6	1.2	2.3	-0.9	-4.6	1.8	6.2	1.5	4.6
Real priv. cons. growth	(%)	-7.5	-6.8	-3.5	-3.0	1.5	2.6	2.0	5.7	-2.3	0.1	5.9	11.9	0.1
Real pub. cons. growth	(%)	1.0	3.9	-1.3	-3.8	2.4	3.5	-1.0	-6.7	-2.8	-0.6	1.7	15.6	-9.6
External public debt	(US$bn)	1.0	1.2	1.5	1.9	2.3	2.7	3.0	3.2	3.6	3.7	4.0	4.0	4.3
Debt service	(US$bn)	0.2	0.2	0.3	0.3	0.4	0.4	0.4	0.4	0.5	0.6	0.8	0.8	0.6
External public debt/GDP	(%)	33.3	55.8	60.5	70.0	77.2	81.8	82.6	135.8	180.3	150.2	140.4		112.5
Debt service/X of G&NS	(%)	16.4	14.7	23.5	19.3	31.3	32.8	30.7	31.5	43.4	47.8	49.4		
Central gov. deficit	(J$bn)	-0.5	-0.5	-0.5	-0.8	-0.8	-0.9	-1.2	-0.6	-0.8	-0.4	-0.5	-1.1	
Public sector balance	(J$bn)					-0.9	-1.0	-1.5	-1.5	-1.8	-1.0	-1.4	-2.5	
Central gov. deficit/GDP	(%)	-17.3	-14.2	-12.4	-17.5	-15.7	-14.0	-15.7	-6.5	-6.2	-2.4	-2.9	-6.0	
Public sector balance/GDP	(%)					-15.9	-15.6	-19.6	-15.2	-14.2	-6.6	-8.3	-13.4	
Employment in public administration (000s)		108.6	99.4	107.9	105.6	101.5	101.0	102.0	100.5	81.1	79.9	72.8	74.1	n.a.
90-Day T-bill rate	(% p.a.)	7.2	8.3	9.2	9.9	9.8	8.6	12.4	13.3	19.0	20.9	18.2	18.4	19.1
Inflation rate	(% p.a.)	11.5	35.0	28.8	28.2	12.0	6.5	11.3	27.8	26.0	14.8	6.7	8.2	14.4
Unemployment rate	(%)	24.5	22.9	24.2	27.9	26.3	27.0	25.9	24.5	24.4	25.0	21.2	18.4	

7.2.1 *The development of the state sector up to 1980*

The development of the state sector in Jamaica occurred in three relatively distinct phases. The first was the pre-Independence period. Before Independence in 1962, the government's general strategy was to assign to the private sector the responsibility for economic production, and to itself the responsibility for regulation and the development of some parts of the infrastructure – the 'industrialization by invitation' development path, widely adopted in the Caribbean prior to independence. Thus, during this period the government made few interventions to secure direct ownership but instead concentrated on establishing regulatory institutions, agricultural marketing agencies, and institutions for industrial financing. Strikingly, most major utilities were foreign-owned, and no domestic regulatory body had yet been established to monitor or examine their performance.

The second phase lasted from Independence to the election of the PNP in 1972. The rise in economic aspirations surrounding Independence brought pressure for increased government involvement in the economy, and a commitment to state participation in the productive sectors was incorporated in the 1963–8 Five-Year Plan. Despite these pressures, however, the involvement of government in production expanded slowly, with most of the expansion still involving the creation of new bodies rather than the takeover/nationalization of existing ones. However, during this period, some powerful agencies were established, such as the Prices Commission, the National Water Agency, the Port Authority and the Urban Development Corporation, which had substantial roles to play in the economy (see Brown and McBain, 1983). Furthermore, the government began to set up or take over bodies which would be of some importance in the privatization programme. For example, it took control of three sugar factories when they were facing closure, and set up the Sugar Industry Authority. In the tourism sector, it established the Hotel Corporation of Jamaica Ltd as part of its policy of encouraging the construction of large, convention-type hotels. By the end of 1971, the government already owned, or had a stake in, five hotels and was active in the development of resort areas.

In the utilities, the single most important step towards more widespread government control came with the creation of the Public Utilities Commission, which was given the power to examine the performance and profitability of the electricity company (JPS) and the domestic telephone company (JTC), both monopolies, and the Passenger Transport (Corporate Area) Board, with the power to examine the Jamaica Omnibus Service (JOS) with a view in both cases to approving or rejecting proposed rate increases. The outcome of the rate applications hearings held under the auspices of these regulatory bodies was that these companies were found to be operating in contravention of their licences and to be involved in highly questionable accounting practices with a view to earning supernormal profits.[1] As a result, the government decided to acquire equity interests in the companies. Thus, it bought JPS in 1969, JTC in the early 1970s, and JOS in 1974 – a transaction which, although carried out under the following government, was effected largely as a result of the deficiencies revealed at this time.

The third, and most dramatic, phase was the PNP Government of 1972–80. This government was committed to a socialist economic strategy and an assault on the power of the 'plantation elite'; it therefore favoured a rapid expansion of public ownership, including the acquisition or nationalization of the 'commanding heights' of the existing private economy. From 1974 onwards, as public revenues were swelled by the bauxité levy on mining companies, the government was able to proceed with its ambitious acquisition plans. The explicit aims

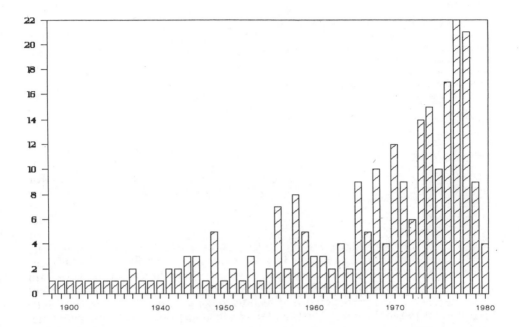

Figure 7.1 Creation of public enterprises (1900–80)
Source: Brown and McBain, 1981.

of the programme were to maintain, via government ownership, buoyant growth in certain critical areas of the economy, and to use public control of major industries to redistribute incomes. The acceleration of the public ownership programme can be seen in Fig. 7.1, where the mid-1970s saw a considerable increase in the number of public enterprises created. However, this period differed in two important respects from the previous periods, namely in that the government was taking over a large number of enterprises rather than creating them, and that public sector activities were being expanded into the core productive sectors of the economy.

Thus, for the first time the government became a significant player in the mining sector, with takeovers of bauxite, aluminium, petroleum and cement companies. Public ownership expanded in the sugar sector such that by 1980 the government owned 8 out of 12 sugar factories, producing 75% of Jamaica's sugar output, and in hotels, where, following a rash of threatened failures, it acquired 50% of total room capacity. Moreover, it began actively to take over manufacturing enterprises, nationalized Barclays Bank to form the National Commercial Bank, set up a number of other public financial institutions, and created the State Trading Corporation to make the state a major importer (a function through which it would be able to influence pricing and investment decisions). Finally, some new utilities were established, and the PUC was abolished on the assumption that public ownership was a sufficient condition to ensure that monopolies acted in the public interest.

Table 7.2 *Sectoral analysis of public enterprises in 1980*

Type of enterprise	Number
Regulatory, distribution and promotional enterprises	49
Social and community services	20
Services to agriculture, forestry and fishing	10
Communications	3
Financial services	18
Agricultural distribution services	25
Sugar industry enterprises	18
Mining	7
Manufacturing enterprises	43
Utilities and transport	17
Tourism	26
Other enterprises	13
TOTAL	249

Source: Brown and McBain, 1983.

7.2.2 *The performance of the state sector before the 1980s*

As a result of the rapid expansion of public ownership under the Manley Government, by 1980 Jamaica had a large public sector by world standards. However, or perhaps as a consequence, the government did not have even the minimum information on the number or size of its holdings,[2] their performance, the financial flows between the government and the state enterprise sector, the number of persons employed in the firms it owned, the amount of domestic and foreign debt incurred, the efficiency of these firms, their importance in various markets, etc. It is therefore impossible to provide firm statistical evidence on the overall nature or performance of these enterprises by the 1980s.

The only detailed analysis of the public sector we have is from 1980, by Brown and McBain (1983). The derived figure for public sector bodies by enterprise type is given in Table 7.2; however, it is certain that this understates the size of the sector by 50%. Nevertheless, it demonstrates that, through its expansion programme, the government now owned enterprises in almost every important sphere of economic activity. SOE performance was therefore crucial in determining macroeconomic growth: although the data are inexact, in 1984 the public enterprise sector alone (i.e. excluding central government) accounted for 21% of GDP, 11% of employment, 11% of investment and 19% of the country's capital stock (World Bank, 1987a). A different source estimates the gross assets of Jamaican SOEs to have been J\$4.4bn in 1980 as against 1980 GDP of J\$4.8bn (Mills, 1981).

There is, though, general agreement that, by the end of the 1970s, the SOE sector was performing very badly indeed, and that this poor performance played its part in bringing about the alarming collapse of the economy that occurred at that time. Evidence suggests that the Jamaican SOE sector was suffering from the standard litany of problems of public sector enterprises in developing countries. Political interference and political appointments were widespread but public accountability was minimal. SOEs were being run according to highly questionable economic criteria whereby the objective of saving employment allowed excessive wage increases and overemployment, which resulted in a sharp increase in government subsidies. In an attempt to control inflation or to achieve distributional objectives, many firms were continually refused the price increases needed to make them financially viable. Many of the firms that had been taken over by government on the argument that they were being run badly by the private sector had no plans for recovery and often performed even worse under state ownership.[3]

7.2.3 *Reform of the SOE sector*

The Seaga Government, newly elected in 1980, faced a severe economic situation. The economy was recording negative growth, facing high unemployment and low capacity utilization, had experienced a punishing flight of skilled labour and capital, was suffering high inflation, a binding foreign-exchange shortage, a deep public sector deficit and soaring external indebtedness. There was an extensive system of controls on imports, wages and prices plus a highly distortionary tax regime. In its election manifesto, the JLP had offered a (then) radically conservative strategy, comprising economic deregulation, trade liberalization and a markedly more pro-free enterprise attitude. By then, the JLP had become convinced that the public sector was not the key to rapid growth, but rather harked back to the earlier view of the private sector as the engine of growth, with the government acting as enabler and regulator.

As a result, the government was involved in an intensive process of macroeconomic reform that lasted throughout the 1980s. Because of the pressing need to reduce dramatically the public sector financial deficit, issues of public sector reform were central to the various adjustment plans agreed with the International Monetary Fund and the World Bank. This reform involved not just the implementation of central government revenue-raising measures, expenditure control, and revision of the tax regime, but also an increasing focus on the SOE sector as a major determinant of the consolidated public deficits. And it should be remembered that this was being carried out amid a general and major reform of the macroeconomic environment.

The actual reform effort can most tractably be broken down into two parts, namely the general reforms of the SOE sector, and the specific and more detailed reform programme for the 21 largest SOEs picked out for special attention by the multilateral lenders. (The privatization component of these reforms is discussed in section 7.3.)

With regard to general reforms, because of the rapid expansion of the 1970s, the public enterprise sector lacked many of the requirements of bureaucratic rationality. First, the information base on SOEs was extremely poor. Second, as a result of the *ad hoc* nature of their establishment, SOEs were operating under different legal frameworks, with unclear ownership. For example, some SOEs found themselves classified as private enterprises in terms of the Companies Act, while others operated under specific enabling legislation. The former group were operating under a legal system which had no provisions for reporting requirements or audit criteria. With regard to ownership, as late as 1985 it was the case that shares in (identified) SOEs were held by 44 different organizations, 24 of which were subsidiaries of the remaining 20.[4] In some cases, different ministries owned shares, leading to uncertainty as to which line ministry was in control, while in other cases, a parent corporation and its subsidiary reported to different ministries. Fourth, SOEs generally had no clearly defined functions or an adequate system of administrative oversight. The result was extremely poor financial performance and the acquisition of contingent liabilities outside the public sector capital budgeting procedures.

Certain reforms have been enacted to deal with these problems, but the weaknesses have not been resolved. For example, while a public enterprise list was set up by the Ministry of the Public Service, the list remains incomplete and the information collected on each SOE inadequate. In the absence of such information, the change to the legal framework of the SOEs embodied in the Public Enterprises

Act is of little consequence. Ownership centralization has been attempted under the auspices of the National Investment Bank of Jamaica:[5] however, a number of the larger enterprises remain untouched. Finally, to improve the performance monitoring of the SOEs, a Public Enterprise Division (PED) was set up in the Ministry of Finance, responsible for drawing up management plans to define the functions and operations of SOEs. Aside from the larger enterprises discussed below, however, this measure has not fully solved the problem, since the PED is not large enough to cope with the size of the SOE sector, with the result that in 1990 it was still ignorant of the existence of a number of SOEs.

To sum up, then, the government has not dealt adequately with the general reforms of the SOE sector. This is in contrast to the group of larger SOEs, which have been subject to sometimes intensive reform effort.

Reform of the 21 major SOEs

Most of the reform effort of the Jamaican Government has gone into improving the 21 largest SOEs,[6] whose performance was also weak. In 1980, for example, their combined operating surplus was only J$4.5m. on sales of more than J$1.5bn, including net transfers from government of J$147.2m. Poor performance in these SOEs was a structural impediment to macroeconomic reform and growth since they were operating in key areas, e.g. power, water, telecommunications, trade (especially importation), and the ports.

From the early 1980s onwards, a reform programme was set up intended to deal, both generally and on a case-by-case basis, with the problems of these SOEs. Much of the impetus for this programme came out of the policy conditionality of the multilateral lending organizations. The concern of the World Bank and the IMF arose from the fact that the 21 enterprises selected for attention had a consolidated budget larger than that of the government itself. In terms of their financial programming exercises, it was crucial to bring these enterprises 'on line' in order to give credit ceilings and deficit targets some macroeconomic meaning.[7] Thus, part of the purpose of adjustment lending was the incorporation of these largest enterprises into the government budgetary process. Furthermore, supported by World Bank lending specifically for the public enterprise sector, each enterprise had its own reform plan to restore it to a state of financial viability and improved efficiency. These generally involved investment plans, rating reforms, and management reorganizations aimed at the commercialization of the enterprises.

The aggregate outcome of this reform effort can be seen in Table 7.3. In the period 1981/2–87/8[8] there was a considerable improvement in the consolidated financial performance of these SOEs. Their current operating balance moved from −1% to 6.9% of GDP over the period, reflecting both revenue-raising measures and expenditure control. Net transfers from the central government moved from 4.5% to −1.3% of GDP, or a cumulative improvement of 21.8% of GDP. Although their capital expenditure programme was expanded, their overall balance reached 1.8% as against −0.4% of GDP at the beginning of the period. Their debt position dramatically worsened: government-guaranteed debt rose from 10.2% to 15% of GDP at the same time as overall external debt expanded far more rapidly.

However, there are doubts about the effectiveness of the reform programme, in part because of the continuing poor performance of some of the most important utilities. For example, both the electricity and the water utilities currently face notable operational difficulties, as do the railways and the airline. These remain problem areas after up to a decade of reform attempts. As we shall see below, this poor performance has impinged on the progress of their privatization. Further, the main criticism of the programme is that it has concentrated exces-

Table 7.3 *Summary operations of selected SOEs*[a] *(J$m.)*

	1981/82	1982/83	1983/84	1984/85	1985/86	1986/87	1987/88	1988/89
Current operating balance	−51.5	95.0	130.7	368.0	800.4	844.0	1,129.9	729.9
Transfer from CG[b] (net)	239.1	152.4	144.1	262.8	−57.8	−17.5	−212.7	197.1
Capital expenditure	211.3	373.7	368.2	764.4	880.1	582.6	631.2	1,044.3
Overall balance	−23.7	−126.3	−93.4	−133.6	−137.5	243.9	286.0	−117.6
Financing	23.7	126.3	93.4	133.6	137.5	−243.9	−286.0	117.6
Foreign financing (net)	89.9	126.4	41.0	206.1	300.6	−157.0	74.2	458.6
Domestic financing (net)	−66.2	−0.1	52.4	−72.5	−163.1	−86.9	−360.2	−341.0
o/w Banking system	−63.5	−5.3	−43.5	−88.9	−89.3	135.3	−288.3	n.a.
Government Guaranteed debt in J$ (Dec.)	546.2	525.7	882.4	1,451.9	1,812.8	1,585.0	2,438.7	2,437.2
Ratios	(percentages)							
Operating balance/ GDP	−1.0	1.5	1.7	3.7	6.4	5.8	6.9	4.0
Transfers from CG/ GDP	4.5	2.5	1.9	2.7	−0.5	−0.1	−1.3	1.1
Overall balance/GDP	−0.4	−2.1	−1.2	−1.4	−1.1	1.7	1.8	−0.6
Operating bal./CG deficit	6.1	−10.9	−10.9	−56.8	−102.2	−235.2	−235.7	−64.2
CG transfers/CG deficit	28.2	17.5	12.0	40.5	−7.4	−4.9	−44.4	17.4
Overall bal./CG deficit	2.8	14.5	7.8	20.6	17.6	−68.0	−59.7	10.4
Government Guarantee debt/GDP	10.2	8.6	11.6	14.7	14.5	11.0	15.0	13.3
Memorandum items:								
GDP	5,350.2	6,142.9	7,576.5	9,856.3	12,496.1	14,456.9	16,307.1	18,292.1
CG deficit	−849.1	−868.5	−1,196.3	−648.4	−783.3	−358.9	−479.4	−1,136.0
CG deficit (% of GDP)	−15.9	−14.1	−15.8	−6.6	−6.3	−2.5	−2.9	−6.2
Government Guaranteed debt in US$ (Dec.)	306.6	295.1	269.2	294.5	330.8	289.2	443.4	444.8

Sources: World Bank (1989a), Bank of Jamaica Statistical Bulletins.

Notes
a) Air Jamaica Ltd, Airports Authority of Jamaica, Jamaica Broadcasting Corporation, Jamaica Commodity Trading Corporation, Jamaica Merchant Marine Ltd, Jamaica Mortgage Bank Ltd, Jamaica Public Service Company Ltd, Jamaica Railway Corporation, Jamaica Sugar Holdings Ltd, Jamaica Telephone Sector Accounts, Jamaica International Telecommunication Ltd, Jamaica Telephone Company, National Hotels and Properties Ltd, National Housing Corporation, National Investment Bank of Jamaica, National Water Commission, Petroleum Sector Accounts, Petrojam Ltd, Petroleum Corporation of Jamaica, Port Authority, Sugar Industry Authority, Urban Development Corporation.
b) CG refers to Central Government.

sively on the financial performance of the SOEs rather than on improvements in operational efficiency. For example, the pricing reforms have tended to follow a cost-plus approach, which has, according to the World Bank: 'helped to mask . . . operational inefficiencies and monopoly situations'.[9] As a consequence of this emphasis on financial performance, the reform programme left untouched two SOEs (JCTC and Petrojam) which were profitable thanks to monopoly control rather than efficient operations, and which generated very substantial rents (close to 12% of GDP). As we shall see, this emphasis on financial performance rather than efficiency permeated the privatization programme as well.

7.3 The privatization experience

Jamaica has undertaken a substantial programme of privatization, and this breadth of experience offers a fascinating wealth of lessons. In this long section documenting the record, we take the opportunity to comment on various components of the programme as we present them rather than making conclusions *en masse*.

7.3.1 The emergence of privatization

The emergence of privatization as official policy in Jamaica can be traced to the early 1980s, and represented one strand of the policy reversal that was (rhetorically at least) put into practice following the 1980 election.[10] Several factors contributed to the incorporation of privatization in the government's policy canon. The first was the growing disenchantment with the performance of the SOE sector. Not only were SOEs inefficient and a major drain on public resources, but they were also not successfully meeting the goals of maintaining growth and reducing unemployment. Hence, even the PNP was beginning to rethink their usefulness.

The second major impetus came from the involvement of international agencies in the policy-making process in Jamaica, of which the most important have been the IMF, the World Bank, and the US Agency for International Development (USAID). In view of the parlous state of the economy, the multilateral lenders had significant policy leverage over the Jamaican Government from the late 1970s onwards. The IMF became involved in short-term adjustment lending as early as 1977, and throughout the 1980s the World Bank and the IMF together had almost continuous structural adjustment lending programmes.[11] These loans have had both public enterprise reform and divestiture components, reflecting the speed at which the policy of privatization became incorporated in adjustment policy overall. USAID, Jamaica's major bilateral lender, has also strongly promoted privatization through the terms attached to the disbursement of concessional funds and through the financing of parts of the divestment process, especially the hiring of foreign technical assistance.[12]

The third and most crucial impetus towards privatization, however, was the election of the JLP under Edward Seaga in 1980. Seaga, who had been Finance Minister in the previous JLP administration, was far more pro-free enterprise than the PNP, and had the reputation of being a competent technocrat. The JLP campaigned in 1979–80 on a manifesto that included a commitment to privatization as part of an overall restructuring of the state sector, and of a more widespread programme of economic liberalization and deregulation.[13] Clearly, this programme was adopted independently of the international organizations, and reflected a response both to the economic problems characteristic of the Jamaican economy in the late 1970s, and to the change in the international intellectual environment. It is certainly the case, though, that this ambitious programme of privatization could not have occurred without the strong support of the Prime Minister. Thus, the pressure to privatize coming from the international organizations mostly acted to reinforce a domestic policy shift that had already occurred. Despite this, the involvement of these organizations was still controversial and, in order to avoid the politically dangerous accusation that Jamaica was being sold out to foreign interests, their role was downplayed.

7.3.2 Privatization policy and aims

The JLP Government moved relatively swiftly after 1980 to start its privatization programme. By 1981, it had set up a Divestment Committee (DC) and had established guidelines and procedures for the DC to follow. These guidelines (quoted in Mills, 1988) stressed two fundamental principles, namely:

i) the policy of divestment of equity and control in commercial enterprises at prices based on commercial criteria after taking into account the nation's interest (this would exclude the public utilities);
ii) the intention to discontinue operating enterprises which were not commercially viable (though viability would be attempted through private sector participation).

The priorities for sale would be based on the budgetary impact, the economic impact, employment linkages, and the social impact.

However, between 1981 and 1985, the programme progressed relatively slowly. Only two small firms were sold, most agricultural marketing boards had been restructured, some hotels had been leased, and some municipal services had been contracted out. Although some 30 SOEs had been selected for divestiture, none had yet gone ahead. While some of this delay reflected genuine problems in selling off enterprises, the Prime Minister clearly felt a new initiative needed to be made. Thus, in spring 1986, he presented a new divestment policy paper to the Cabinet, which redefined the aims of the policy and authorized the sale of enterprises through the local capital markets. The revised aims were (in order of importance): to improve the efficiency of the economy by placing more productive capital under private control; to develop the local capital market and stimulate 'the involvement of a large number of citizens in the free market system'; to encourage more private investment and reduce the 'crowding-out' effects of state ownership; to reduce the fiscal deficit; and to raise foreign exchange in those cases where foreign investors would be permitted to participate (Leeds, 1987).

These aims were standard to developing country privatizations, and were hence subject to the conflicts described in Chapter 4. Finally, rather than develop a privatization blueprint with a time-specific programme, Seaga made it clear that he thought a case-by-case selection method would be the most likely to succeed in Jamaica. However, in terms of the scope of privatization it still appeared to be government policy to restrict sales to enterprises other than utilities: for example, in his Budget Speech for 1986/7, Seaga stated:

> . . . the government will divest its ownership in commercial enterprises which it is felt can be successfully run by the private sector. This includes banking, hotels, industry, agriculture, selected air and sea transportation. The government will not, however, divest its ownership in the utilities, the petroleum industry, the mining industry, telecommunications and major air transportation. This group of enterprises . . . must always be run in the public interest.

In fact, by the end of the 1980s, this position had changed somewhat, as we shall see.

7.3.3 Privatization structures

The structures associated with privatization carry out three main functions: selection, evaluation and implementation. The method of selection of initial enterprises for privatization in Jamaica is not clear, but generally seems to rely on line ministries suggesting likely candidates for sale to the Cabinet. Evaluation and implementation were carried out by the Divestment Committee, subject to the approval of the political directorate. The 6-strong Divestment Committee consisted of representatives of the Bank of Jamaica, the Ministry of Finance, the Attorney-General, and the National Investment Bank of Jamaica from the public sector, plus two private sector representatives. While it had undoubted technical ability, there were organizational problems which obstructed its operations; crucially, none of the members worked for the committee on a full-time basis and all had other heavy responsibilities. Given the complexity of most divestitures, then, 'the Committee became bogged down in fact finding' (Downer, 1986).

In order to circumvent these problems, the Divestment Committee obtained a Divestment Secretariat, which was established as a separate section of the National Investment Bank of Jamaica, and financed by USAID. Its task was to undertake fact-finding, to advertise and to negotiate privatizations, including the important function of evaluating the net worth of an enterprise. Though headed by the director of a successful private sector enterprise and with two full-time staff, it has very much associated itself with the mechanics of the privatizations that it has been involved in, rather than with any evaluations.

Whereas the Divestment Committee was originally set up to co-ordinate all privatizations, in fact it has been responsible only for the sale of industrial and financial enterprises. There are two main reasons for this: a lack of time and a lack of co-ordination. As a result, other sales have been instrumented by other agencies. The leasing and sale of the hotels (a programme which had substantial revenue impact) was carried out by a group comprising employees of National Hotels and Properties Ltd, under the authority of the Ministry of Tourism. A land divestment programme was instituted in the agricultural sector, tied in to the Crop Diversification Programme. The agency responsible for land leasing is the Divestment Secretariat of Agro 21, a specialized agency set up to promote export and non-traditional agriculture. Land sales, in contrast, have been handled by the Registrar of Lands, without any reference to the leasing programme. Finally, the franchising of bus routes in the Kingston metropolitan area from JOS to private concerns was organized by the Ministry of Public Utilities and Transport, without reference to the Divestment Committee.

Thus, privatization structures in Jamaica have been uncoordinated and decentralized. Assessment of this essentially decentralized approach to privatization is difficult. On the one hand, the current PNP Government appears to be of the opinion that a more ordered and comprehensive approach is needed, and that new structures should be created to oversee the programme (see below). On the other hand, some involved in the privatization process to date have felt that a more centralized programme would merely have led to stronger bureaucratic obstruction and hence that Jamaica would have not have achieved its relatively extensive privatization record.

7.3.4 The privatization record

A history of the privatization programme up to the middle of 1990 is given in Table 7.4. The early phase of the privatization programme (i.e. in the first half of the 1980s) moved slowly. Apart from the hotel leasing programme (see below), there were only three other divestitures. The first was the sale of Versair Inflite Services Ltd in 1981, a small company that supplied food and beverages for all airlines operating in Jamaica, and the restaurants and bars at both international airports.[14] It had been taken over by the government in 1977, but was very badly managed and was suffering from large financial losses. The revenue from the sale was small, being only J$1.2m. (US$0.7m.). However, the most important feature of the sale was that it was made to a consortium of local, Caribbean and US companies, namely Grace Kennedy (Jamaica), Goddard (Barbados) and Marriot (US). The involvement of both domestic and regional as well as US capital was important in the 'selling' of this first privatization to the domestic audience. A second, smaller privatization was the sale of Southern Processors Ltd in 1982: like Versair,

Table 7.4 *Summary of privatizations*

Name	Date	Method & Purchaser	Sector	% Equity Gov-Owned: Pre-Sale	Post-Sale	Proceeds (J$m.)	(US$m.)	Agency
1) Sales								
Versair	1981	Private – Joint	Services	100	0	1.2	0.7	NIBJ
Southern Processors Ltd	1982	N/K	Manufacture	100	n.a.	n.a.	n.a.	NIBJ
Seprod Ltd – I	1985	Private – Domestic	Manufacture	100	55	30.0	5.4	CIB
Seprod Ltd – II[a]	1985	Public	Manufacture	55	38	9.8	1.8	CIB
Banana Company[b]	1985	Private – Domestic	Agriculture	n.a.	n.a.	n.a.	n.a.	Min of Ag
Rural Ice & Cold Storage Ltd	1986	Private – Domestic	Services	100	0	0.5	0.1	NIBJ
Hanover Spices Ltd	1986	Private – Domestic	Manufacture	100	0	0.1	0.0	NIBJ
Hellshire Fish Farm Ltd	1986	Private – Domestic	Fishing	100	0	0.3	0.1	NIBJ
Zero Processing & Storage Ltd[c]	1986	Private – Domestic	Services	100	0	4.0	0.7	NIBJ
Jamaica Oxygen & Acetylene Ltd	1986	Private – Foreign	Manufacture	47	n.a.	2.0	0.4	NIBJ
National Commercial Bank Ltd (NCB)	1986	Public	Banking	100	49	88.7	16.1	NIBJ
Caribbean Cement Company – I[d]	1987	Private – Foreign	Manufacture	100	90	25.0	4.5	NIBJ
Caribbean Cement Company – II	1987	Public	Manufacture	90	27	157.4	28.6	NIBJ
Telecommunications of Jamaica – I[e]	1987	Private – Foreign	Communications	83	72	102.3	18.6	NIBJ
Telecommunications of Jamaica – II[e]	1987	Private – Foreign	Communications	72	53	183.5	33.4	NIBJ
Royal Caribbean Hotel	1987	Private – Joint	Services	100	0	15.4	2.8	NHP
Serge Island Dairies Ltd	1988	Private – Joint	Manufacture	30	0	1.8	0.3	NIBJ
Telecommunications of Jamaica – III	1988	Public	Communications	53	40	108.5	19.7	NIBJ
Fantasy Resorts (Hotel)	1989	Private – Domestic	Services	100	0	22.4	3.7	NHP
Inn on the Beach (Hotel)	1989	Private – Domestic	Services	100	0	0.7	0.1	NHP
Wyndham Rose Hall Beach (Hotel)	1989	Private – Foreign	Services	100	0	132.0	22.0	NHP
Eden II Hotel	1989	Private – Domestic	Services	100	0	60.0	10.0	NHP
Jamaica Jamaica Hotel	1989	Private – Domestic	Services	100	0	96.0	16.0	NHP
Telecommunications of Jamaica – IV[e]	1989	Private – Foreign	Communications	40	20	231.8	38.6	NIBJ
W.I. Pulp and Paper Ltd	1989	Private – Joint	Manufacture	81	0	38.1	6.4	NIBJ
Jamaica Gypsum and Quarries[f]	1989	Private – Domestic	Mining	100	0	4.0	0.7	NIBJ
Trelawny Beach Hotel	1990	Private – Domestic	Services	74	0	n.a.	n.a.	NHP
Hedonism II (Hotel)	1990	Private – Domestic	Services	100	0	n.a.	n.a.	NHP
Montego Inn	1990	Private – Domestic	Services	100	0	n.a.	n.a.	NHP
Land for Agriculture[g]	1985–90	Private – Domestic	Agriculture	100	n.a.	n.a.	n.a.	RoL
TOTAL						1,315.5	230.7	

Table 7.4 continued

Name	Date	Method & Purchaser	Sector	% Equity Gov-Owned: Pre-Sale	Post-Sale	Proceeds (J$m.)	(US$m.)	Agency
2) Leases/management contracts								
Jamaica Omnibus Services (JOS)[h]	1984	Lease – Domestic	Transport	n.a.	n.a.	n.a.	n.a.	Min of PU
Jamaica Sugar Holdings[j]	1985	MC – Foreign	Agriculture	100	100	n.a.	n.a.	Agro 21
Port Antonio Marina	1988	Lease – Domestic	Services	n.a.	n.a.	0.0	0.0	NIBJ
Various Hotels	1982	Leases – Both	Services	n.a.	n.a.	1.7	0.9	NHP
Various Hotels	1983	Leases – Both	Services	n.a.	n.a.	9.1	4.8	NHP
Various Hotels	1984	Leases – Both	Services	n.a.	n.a.	24.0	6.1	NHP
Various Hotels	1985	Leases – Both	Services	n.a.	n.a.	50.1	9.0	NHP
Various Hotels	1986	Leases – Both	Services	n.a.	n.a.	46.9	8.5	NHP
Various Hotels	1987	Leases – Both	Services	n.a.	n.a.	66.1	12.0	NHP
Various Hotels	1988	Leases – Both	Services	n.a.	n.a.	75.9	13.8	NHP
Various Hotels	1989	Leases – Both	Services	n.a.	n.a.	74.9	12.5	NHP
Land for Agriculture[g]	1985–90	Leases – Both	Agriculture	100	n.a.	n.a.	n.a.	Agro 21
TOTAL						348.7	67.6	

Notes
a) Of 16.5 million shares sold, 10.5 million were new equity. 15 million shares were sold at J$2.50, 1.5 million at J$1.50.
b) The Banana Company was closed, and the boxing plants and growing plants were divested.
c) Sold to Seprod Ltd.
d) Sale of 10% of equity to Scancem.
e) Sold to Cable and Wireless (UK) Ltd.
f) Sold to Caribbean Cement Company.
g) 35,000 acres sold to small farmers and 30,000 acres leased for commercial production by March 1989. Receipts are small.
h) Value of the ten leases not known.
j) Tate & Lyle are paid J$7.2m. over a 10-yr period to manage sugar fields and two 100% government-owned sugar factories.

Abbreviations:
CIB – Coconut Industry Board
Min of Ag – Ministry of Agriculture
Min of Pu – Ministry of Public Utilities and Transport
NHP – National Hotels and Properties Ltd
NIBJ – National Investment Bank of Jamaica
RoL – Registrar of Lands

this divestiture was akin to a 'reprivatization' since it had only been taken over by the government in 1973.

The third privatization of this period was the leasing of routes of the Jamaica Omnibus Service (JOS) to private operators. As noted in section 7.2, JOS had been taken into public ownership as a result of a number of operational irregularities. However,there was no effective regulatory framework established to supervise JOS after nationalization so that its performance worsened until, by 1980, an annual loss of J$11m. was being made and by 1982, cumulative losses were greater than the total equity of the company.

The government therefore decided to curtail the direct carrier responsibility of JOS by auctioning off primary passenger routes (mainly in Kingston) to private operators who would either lease buses from JOS or run their own buses. Bids were received from 31 organizations, of which 8 were successful in being allocated routes.[15] Although there is no specific empirical evidence, it is generally accepted that privatization of buses has greatly improved performance. However, while the changes made to JOS certainly represented a divestiture, they did not represent a full liberalization of urban transportation. First, JOS itself was not scrapped, but survived with certain regulatory functions. These included the ability to prescribe fares for all routes, the responsibility for monitoring the roadworthiness of the private buses, and the right to withdraw licences if the appropriate conditions were not met. Furthermore, the entry of other bus companies into the new market was circumscribed, thus providing the 'newly enfranchised' operators with only limited competition from other owners. On account of this, in some ways JOS represents the paradigmatic Jamaican privatization, i.e. a transaction where the transfer of ownership is made, but where other factors encouraging or discouraging efficient operations are given less attention.

These three privatizations were the only results of the first years of the JLP Government. After 1985, however, the programme accelerated dramatically and we present these divestitures thematically as follows: first, larger sales involving the capital market; second, the smaller sales carried out by NIBJ; third, the hotel divestment programme; fourth, the land privatizations and divestitures in the agriculture sector.

Sales involving the capital market

Seprod

The sale of Soap and Edible Products Ltd (Seprod) in 1985 was in many ways a precursor of the three biggest single sales of the Jamaican programme to date, namely NCB, CCC and ToJ, in that it shared a similar programme design and faced similar problems. However, this sale was undertaken on the advice and urging of Seprod's principal owners, who were an amalgam of public sector and private farmer interests brought together in the form of the Coconut Industry Board. Thus, it did not form part of the central government's programme, but was rather relatively autonomous.

History of the company and reasons for sale. Seprod, a firm involved in processing the products of the indigenous coconut industry into edible oils and soaps, was acquired by the Coconut Industry Board (CIB) in 1944. Throughout the 1950s and 1960s, Seprod expanded continually through takeovers, the installation of new production technology, and the conclusion of manufacturing agreements with foreign companies, although, as a result of the decline of the domestic coconut industry, it became increasingly reliant on imported inputs. In the 1970s and early 1980s, the firm was adversely affected by the general downturn in the Jamaican economy. More importantly, though, the government stipulated that Seprod purchase its imports through the State Trading Corporation (STC) and introduced price controls on its main products, namely edible oils, soaps and margarine. The impact on the firm of these price controls was predictable. Profitability was depressed as a result of the government's desire to hold down prices, efficiency was affected by the management's lack of freedom to vary inputs flexibly, and the firm developed only cyclically, as determined by the timing of price increases. Finally, management time was spent almost exclusively on survival rather than longer-term planning for the firm.

However, as a result of historical strength, strategic behaviour by the firm and protection from foreign imports, by the mid-1980s, Seprod still maintained a strong position in the domestic markets in which it operated.[16] Furthermore, the advent of the JLP Government in 1980 led to the gradual removal of price controls on factory prices which was completed in 1983. This had an important effect on Seprod's financial performance. Turnover more than tripled between 1980 and 1985, while pre-tax profits rose from J$7.5m. in 1981, Seprod's worst year, to J$23.2m. in 1985.[17] Simultaneously, though, the government was dismantling (albeit slowly) the system of import licensing that allowed Seprod such dominant market shares, and replacing it with duty tariffs at less protective levels. Faced with the constraint of competition, most particularly from other CARICOM producers such as Unilever in Trinidad and Tobago, Seprod clearly needed to enhance working capital and increase its investment level. With low profits, no access to capital from its parent company and a worsening debt–equity ratio, the firm sought an equity injection, both through the sale by CIB of some of its existing shares and also through the issuing of new equity. This proposition was assented to by both the CIB and the government.

Privatization. The capital structure of Seprod was as follows: J$50m. authorized shares, J$16m. issued and fully paid shares, and a long-term debt of J$39m. The entire issued share capital was owned by the CIB: consequently, of 12 directors making up the Board, 9 came from the CIB. Hence, the privatization of Seprod was planned as follows. First, the CIB would sell 6 million shares at J$2.50 each to private sector institutional investors, who would also subscribe for 6 million new shares at the same price. Second, there would be a public offer through the Jamaica Stock Exchange for a further 3 million new shares, also priced at J$2.50 per share. Third, 1.5 million shares would be reserved for the staff of the company under an Employee Share Scheme (ESS). These shares would be sold at J$1.50, and any which were not immediately sold would be held as options to be purchased by employees at any time over the next five years. Finally, after the sale, 6 CIB Board members would resign to make way for directors elected by the new shareholders.

All parts of the privatization proceeded as planned. The main purchasers of the institutional shares were a consortium of Seprod's distributors. Although the full subscription was made, there was some 'behind the scenes' action by the management to persuade some of the more reluctant buyers. The public sale through the JSE represented the first new issue on the market for 16 years: despite this, the issue was oversubscribed and a share allocation scheme triggered which favoured the smaller investor. Following these transactions, public ownership was indeed reduced to minority status. The Coconut Board owned just 37.7% of Seprod's equity, while private institutional investors owned 45.3%.

As a result of this sequence of transactions, Seprod achieved its immediate aims. First, it raised J$22.5 million in fresh equity. Second, it thereby reduced the debt–equity ratio to more manageable levels. Third, control of the company was passed to a more competitively constituted board. Finally, on account of the transfer from public to private, Seprod found it could access new sources of capital via the commercial banks.

Post-privatization performance.   Immediately after privatization, Seprod used its expanded access to capital to proceed with a five-year investment programme aimed at updating its production technology in order to meet increasing competition in the domestic marketplace. The basic strength of the company and its prospects was reflected in the large jump in its share price over the year following sale: from J$2.50 per share at the time of sale in December 1985 to a peak of J$8.50 in January 1987. Relative to the performance of the JSE as a whole, the stock appreciated by 80% in value over the same period. Furthermore, pre-tax profits in 1986, at J$33.7m. were 30% up on the previous year.

After 1986, however, performance worsened, as Table 7.5 shows:

Table 7.5   *Seprod's financial performance 1985-9 (J$m.)*

	1985	1986	1987	1988	1989
Turnover	467.6	497.6	558.1	623.9	656.3
Pre-tax profits	23.2	33.7	24.0	22.9	10.7
Taxation	10.9	12.9	5.5	5.1	1.5
Post-tax profits	12.3	20.8	18.5	17.8	9.2
Current assets	132.3	131.4	155.5	159.3	177.8
Current liabilities	86.2	81.3	101.3	113.3	162.1
Long-term debt	28.8	20.1	26.2	15.3	13.1
No. of shares (mill.)	25.0	25.6	29.9	30.2	35.1
Price–earnings ratio	3.62	8.31	8.02	4.86	9.62
Earnings per share[a]	0.69	0.80	0.63	0.59	0.26
Closing stock price	2.50	6.65	5.05	2.87	2.50

a) For comparative purposes, figures have been adjusted to reflect a bonus issue in July 1989.

Although the growth in turnover remained strong, profitability was persistently squeezed until, by 1989, post-tax profits were below their nominal level in 1985, the year before privatization. Other indicators tell a similar story, although the company has been successful in reducing its long-term debt. The chief reason for the decline in profitability was the reimposition in 1987 of price control on many of its products. The dramatic impact this had on the stock market's valuation of the firm can be seen from Fig. 7.2, which demonstrates the collapse of Seprod's share price in the year after July 1987, from J$8.50 (340% of the sale price) to J$2.80 (110% of the sale price) in August 1988. Since then, it is worth noting, Seprod has increasingly underperformed the JSE overall index.

Key issues.   First, the substantial rise in the share price in the first year after privatization suggests a revenue loss to the firm through the underpricing of the asset. As shown in Chapter 4, underpricing of public share sales is endemic and represents a revenue loss to the public weal. However, in the case of Seprod, gauging the extent of the loss is complicated by evidence that demand from institutional investors almost exactly matched the supply of shares at the price of J$2.50 even though this turned out *ex post* to have undervalued the net present value of the firm's assets. Why the institutions undervalued Seprod so dramatically is not clear; interestingly, though, the managing director of Seprod has subsequently commented that in the light of experience, a management buy-out would have been preferable to the sale of equity,[18] suggesting that the management also underestimated the net worth of the firm at the time of privatization.

Second, the public finance effects of the privatization were complicated by the reimposition of price control. Privatization is often seen as a method of relieving budgetary pressures especially through reducing debt exposure, cashing-in

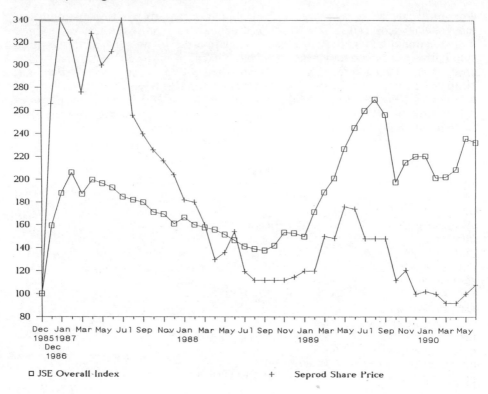

Figure 7.2 *Seprod share price vs JSE Index (Dec. 1985 = 100)*

non-liquid equity, and raising future taxation following efficiency gains in the enterprise. The first two effects were negligible in Seprod's case. The third involves apportioning efficiency changes either to the ownership transfer or to other changes in the market environment occurring simultaneously. We discuss this later, but note here that the decline in profitability after 1986 also hurt government tax revenues: interestingly, in 1986 the government collected more company tax from Seprod than it did in total for the next three years. It would appear, then, that the government deliberately reduced potential fiscal gains from privatization by its own actions.

Third, the Seprod story involves the government reneging on an implicit privatization contract, as described in Chapter 4. In Seprod's case, the government was able to default with no apparent adverse effects on its reputation in later sales (i.e. after the default) as a result of Seprod's small size, and the fact that the loss of share value consequently on default was borne by a group who were effectively politically captive to the then JLP Government.

Fourth, the Seprod Employee Share Scheme turned out to be a particularly complex way of transferring capital gains to the labour force. The motivation for this is unclear: the managing director expressed the ESS as a way of ensuring that the workforce did not 'miss out' on the potential benefits of divestiture, although another interpretation is that the guarantee of ESS-style lump-sum transfers is generally intended to buy off potential union opposition to the sale. In any case, as Fig. 7.2 shows, Seprod's share price has never fallen below J$1.50 (i.e. 60% of the sale price) and thus employees were able to make immediate capital gains *at any point* during the lifetime of the ESS. Indeed, the hyper-rational (or hyper-lucky) agent, who bought at the time of sale and sold when the share price was at a peak, could have made a capital gain of J$7 per J$1.50 share. That Seprod employees have not been unaware of these opportunities is shown by two facts. First, at the closure of the ESS in December 1990 only 5% of the 1.5 million shares remained unsold. Second, the ESS shares have, according to the management, had a high rate of turnover. Thus, while the economic arguments for employee share ownership programmes are usually couched in terms of appropriate incentives for labour effort, in the Seprod privatization the motivations were quite different. As we shall see, the use of ESSs in other capital market sales in Jamaica follows the Seprod example rather than that of economic efficiency.

Fifth, it is often claimed that privatization will improve enterprise efficiency. In the case of Seprod, it was not possible to obtain any direct measures of efficiency; however, there is indirect evidence suggesting that efficiency has been improved since the divestiture. There has been a certain amount of labour-shedding, contiguous with higher production volumes. This was caused by the implementation of the five-year capital investment programme, carried out in order to improve the antiquated production processes of the pre-divestment period and to allow Seprod to compete effectively with other CARICOM producers. As we saw earlier, this was the chief motivation for divestiture. However, this begs the question of why it was not possible for Seprod to carry out such a programme while it was still in the public sector. Clearly, the answer is that the public sector no longer had access to sufficient capital to allow Seprod to modernize; such capital could only be accessed by Seprod as a private sector body. So, in some senses, one might regard Seprod's divestiture as a response to the credit-constrained nature of Jamaica's public sector. This link will reappear in later privatizations.

The National Commercial Bank (NCB)

The NCB sale represented the first substantial sale directly planned by the government following the new impetus to the privatization programme occasioned by the Prime Minister's paper to the Cabinet in 1986. As such, the divestiture was highly visible, and the success or failure of the sale would be crucial in determining the future of the government's political and divestiture programmes. The high-profile nature of the NCB sale had a profound impact on several key decisions concerning the divestiture, including the pricing of the asset and the post-privatization structure of the company, as we outline below.

In order to execute what it regarded as a critical sale, the government brought in certain special consultants to head the NCB privatization team. The 'key player' (Leeds, 1987) was Richard Downer, a senior partner in Price Waterhouse, Jamaica, and an adviser to the Prime Minister who has already worked on methods of accelerating the divestiture process in Jamaica. The others were John Redwood, a merchant banker at N.M. Rothschild, UK, who had been Margaret Thatcher's principal adviser on privatization, and his deputy, Oliver Leitwin, both of whom had substantial direct experience from their work in the UK of the technical and the political sides of implementing divestitures, especially through public offerings.[19] The remainder of the team comprised other private-sector specialists from Jamaica working on the legal, financial and marketing aspects of the transactions. In fact, the nature of the group selected to instrument the sale had an important impact on the smoothness with which it eventually went ahead, the crucial elements being the access to and trust of the PM that Downer enjoyed, and the 'vast reservoir of practical and technical knowledge' (Leeds, 1987: 17) of the Rothschild team.

Table 7.6 *NCB's financial performance, 1982–9 (J$m.)*

	1982	1983	1984	1985	1986	1987	1988	1989
Turnover	121.8	183.7	265.7	407.5	508.1	536.4	628.1	732.0
Pre-tax profits	16.7	26.4	34.8	38.4	36.0	52.0	76.9	108.1
Taxation	7.6	12.1	19.0	20.1	18.5	25.3	34.4	43.1
Post-tax profits	9.1	14.3	15.8	18.3	17.5	26.7	42.5	65.0
Total assets	1,101.0	1,373.0	1,815.0	2,250.0	2,732.0	3,247.0	3,728.0	5,029.0
Deposits	869.0	1,127.0	1,500.0	1,880.0	2,193.0	2,602.0	2,847.0	3,511.0
Advances	617.0	822.0	987.0	1,128.0	1,452.0	1,794.0	2,046.0	2,859.0
No. of shares (mill.)	10.0	10.0	10.0	10.0	10.0	60.0	60.0	60.0
Price–earnings ratio	n/a	n/a	n/a	n/a	12.67	8.41	5.56	4.68
Earnings per share	0.91	1.43	1.58	1.83	0.39	0.44	0.71	1.08
Gross profit margin	13.71	14.39	13.09	9.42	7.18	9.69	12.25	14.76
Closing stock price (J$)	n/a	n/a	n/a	n/a	4.94	3.70	3.95	5.05

History and performance prior to privatization.   The origins of the NCB stretch back to 1837, when the Colonial Bank of London first set up operations in Jamaica. After slow expansion and acquisition by Barclay's Bank in 1925, its assets were taken over by the government in 1977 and it was renamed the National Commercial Bank. At the time, NCB was the second largest banking operation on the island. Following nationalization, the NCB grew strongly and by 1986, the year of privatization, it had become the largest commercial banking operation in Jamaica with 33 branches, 6 agencies, 5 service centres and various administrative departments. As Table 7.6 shows, it was consistently profitable in the early 1980s, and by September 1986 had built up assets of J$2.7bn and employed over 1,800 people.

The strong performance of NCB during its period of state ownership is largely explained by two factors. First, the government did not intervene in any significant way in the management of the bank (though the Board of Directors was politically determined). In general, NCB received no significant preferential treatment compared to other competing financial institutions. One small difference from other private sector banks is that for a long time NCB was in breach of banking legislation by being undercapitalized.[20] It was for this reason that, prior to privatization, NCB's equity was transferred to NIBJ, which effected a substantial expansion of its capital base via an injection of J$20m. in return for shares, thus increasing NCB's equity from 10 million to 60 million shares (Table 7.6). Furthermore, with the government as its shareholder, NCB was not required to pay a dividend on its equity, thus increasing the capital available for reinvestment.

Second, the banking market in Jamaica was (and is) relatively competitive, comprising eleven commercial banks, a number of large building societies, and two development banks (see section 7.5). While the two largest institutions (namely the Bank of Nova Scotia and NCB) control about 70% of total bank deposits, evidence suggests that there has been a steady increase in competition since the 1970s, especially in the area of labour-hiring and product innovation. Jamaican banks also resisted the aggressive intrusion of US banks in the early 1980s, suggesting a relative dynamism in the financial sector. It was in this environment that NCB, though state-owned, was operating, which ensured that it either competed effectively or shrank.

The selection of NCB and government aims for its privatization.   Given the above history and operational performance of NCB, the reasons why the government chose it as the first sale in the revitalized privatization programme are obvious. As a consistently profitable firm and (joint) market leader in a 'safe' market, NCB would be very attractive to private investors. Furthermore, as the largest bank with a substantial rural network, NCB was a nationally recognized name with a reputation for a politically neutral management. This visibility was also aided by the fact that government salary cheques in both urban and rural areas were paid through NCB.

Alongside the general objectives of the privatization programme, the government had certain specific aims for the sale of NCB. The key aim, of course, was that the sale should be a 'success', defined largely in political rather than in economic terms. In 1986, privatization was still highly controversial, with the opposition PNP firmly opposed to sales of public assets on the grounds that it would result in the reconcentration of asset ownership and the abandonment of the fruits of public ownership. Thus, the key political goal for the NCB divestiture had to be the blunting of the PNP's objections through the successful encouragement of a substantial share application by smaller investors, which would have to be achieved despite fears about future renationalization. Success in this endeavour would simultaneously provide the JLP with a political victory, and potentially (on UK lines) recruit voters to the JLP's side. The importance of the political debate surrounding the sale resulted in the (unusual) inclusion in the NCB share offer document of a section entitled 'Attitude of the People's National Party', stating

> The President of the People's National Party has made a number of statements opposing divestment of NCB Group, as have other members of the Party. The attention of applicants is drawn to these statements, which have included suggestions that public control would be re-established over NCB Group. In a later statement, the President of the Party stated that he would not oppose the sale of up to 49 percent of the issued share capital provided that the resulting shareholding is widespread.

In the following section we shall see how the JLP Government's political objectives affected the conditions of the offer. However, aside from the political issues, there were a number of other specific aims:[21] (i) to 'democratize' the ownership of major Jamaican enterprises; (ii) to aid the process of capital market development. It was expected that the NCB sale would enlarge the JSE by 10% and also bring in a new class of investors, thus demonstrating that Jamaica did not suffer from a shortage of domestic savings and encouraging private companies to raise capital via the equity market; (iii) to act as a demonstration of the effectiveness and possibilities of privatization, thereby giving impetus to the government's (ambitious) long-term programme; (iv) to produce a more efficient NCB; and (v) to reduce what Prime Minister Seaga saw as the inappropriate involvement of the government in commercial banking.

Interestingly, public finance considerations did not constitute one of the specific objectives of the NCB sale. In fact, the government argued that, apart from the initial cash-flow from the sale, it was unlikely that there would be any major impacts on the budget arising from NCB's divestiture.

Shaping the sale. It was decided by the government that NIBJ would offer for sale 30.6 million ordinary shares in NCB Group, i.e. 51% of the issued share capital of the company. This decision left the government with two problems: first, what would it do with its own 49% remaining share? and, second, how would it ensure wide ownership of the 30.6 million shares on sale?

With reference to the first problem, the key issue was to allay worries that the government might be able to intervene in the running of the company by using its sizeable minority stake. This very real fear amongst institutional and small investors arose from the interventionist reputation of past Jamaican governments.

In order to dispel such fears, the government had to make a binding and credible pre-commitment concerning the remaining 49% of the equity. Hence, the government declared, first, that the shares retained by NIBJ would not be sold before at least 6 months after the initial tranche sale and, more importantly, that the remaining shares would 'not carry voting rights if retained by GoJ or NIBJ'.[22] The government also terminated its power to appoint members to the Board of Directors.[23]

Concerning the goal of a wide subscription of the shares, the government introduced two important institutional arrangements. The first was to impose restrictions on ownership. Thus, it was decreed that shares could be acquired only by Jamaican citizens and, critically, that individual ownership of shares would be limited to 7.5% of the total voting shares.[24] Any shares owned over this amount would result in the entire share ownership being declared non-voting until the excess was sold. The second was a share allocation scheme which, in the event of excess demand, would weight the allocation of shares in favour of smaller bids. In fact, the issue was oversubscribed, and hence the following weighting came into effect (Leeds, 1987).

NCB share allocation scheme

No. of shares requested	Number of shares received	
1,000– 1,500	1,000 plus 85.0% of additional	500 shares
1,500– 2,000	1,425 plus 70.0% of additional	500 shares
2,000– 3,000	1,775 plus 45.0% of additional	1,000 shares
3,000– 4,000	2,225 plus 35.0% of additional	1,000 shares
4,000– 5,000	2,575 plus 25.0% of additional	1,000 shares
5,000– 7,500	2,825 plus 20.0% of additional	2,500 shares
7,500– 10,000	3,325 plus 12.5% of additional	2,500 shares
10,000– 50,000	3,638 plus 9.0% of additional	40,000 shares
50,000–100,000	7,238 plus 9.0% of additional	50,000 shares
100,000 and above	11,739 plus 8.5% of the remainder applied for	

Thus, an investor applying for 1,500 shares would receive 95% of the total demanded, while an investor applying for 100,000 shares would receive only 11.7% of the total demanded.

In order to reinforce the credibility of these commitments (especially the declaration of the government 49% share as non-voting and the 7.5% ownership restriction), and hence encourage a substantial application from smaller investors, the government installed these undertakings as Entrenched Provisions in NCB's Memorandum of Association and, in addition, put in place an unusually tight set of restrictions on alterations to these provisions. In the share offer document, it declared: 'These provisions will only be able to be amended, removed, suspended or altered if there is unanimous agreement at a shareholders' meeting at which at least 90% of shareholders are present in person or by proxy.' Since it was extremely unlikely that these conditions would ever be met, this restriction implied that a change to the Entrenched Provisions could be made only via legislation.

As noted above, the government had multiple objectives for the NCB sale, and clearly the attraction of a large number of small shareholders satisfied more than one of these. Specifically, it would achieve the aim of 'democratizing' the ownership of NCB, and also introduce a large number of new players to the JSE and thereby, it was hoped, 'kick-start' the equity market into a new phase of sustained growth. However, while these represent potentially laudable aims, we argue that the main motivations for the restrictions outlined above, which had as their goal the attraction of a large number of shareholders, were political, namely the problem of the government's general lack of credibility and the JLP's specific desire to spike the PNP's guns. This view is borne out by the Prime Minister's oft-quoted remark on the NCB privatization (Mills, 1988):

> . . . [in achieving its objective to] democratize the ownership by as wide a cross-section as possible . . . [this] will make it virtually impossible for any government to renation-alize . . . [this Act] is irreversible . . . no power on Earth can change it.

Finally, the government enacted an Employee Share Scheme, as in the Seprod sale. Under the ESS, approximately 13% of the shares offered for sale (i.e. 3,916,440) were reserved for full-time employees of NCB Group and its subsidiaries. The preferential allocation scheme was as follows:

Employee share scheme allocation method

Shares	Minimum purchases & multiple of purchase	Price
20 Free Shares	20	Free
350 Matching Shares	50: 25 free and 25 purchased	1 Free for each share purchased at offer price
850 Discounted Shares	50	10% discount on the offer price
850 Priority Shares	50	Offer Price
2,070 in total		

The purchase in each category was conditional upon the employee taking up the full complement of shares in the previous category. A special purchase scheme was also set up, in which NCB made a J$10m. loan to the ESS Trustees to enable them to take up the entire block of shares offered under the scheme, with the shares themselves as collateral for the loan. Employees would then pay the Trustees either in cash or by an Easy Payment Plan of salary deductions over a 2-year period. However, this was a potentially risky arrangement, in that, had the secondary market price fallen, NCB could be in the embarrassing position of repurchasing substantial amounts of its own equity.

Given an eventual sale price of J$2.95 per share, potentially the ESS offered employees the following opportunity for static financial gain:

Comparative cost: ESS shares vs normal shares (J$)

Shares	Running Total		ESS/Normal	Effective share price	Financial gain
	ESS cost	Normal cost			
20 Free	0.00	59.00	0.0%	0.00	59.00
350 Matching	516.25	1,091.50	47.3%	1.40	516.25
850 Discounted	2,773.00	3,599.00	77.0%	2.27	250.75
850 Priority	5,280.50	6,106.50	86.5%	2.55	0.00
2,070 total					826.00

Thus, an employee who purchased free and matching shares for an outlay of J$516.25 would end up owning an asset worth J$1,091.50, i.e. a capital gain of 111%. However, in recognition of this possibility, the government restricted the tradability of the ESS shares so as virtually to eliminate the likelihood of trading and thereby eradicate the possibility of significant capital gains. In the event, the ESS was received enthusiastically by the Bank's employees, with roughly 98% purchasing shares under the scheme, with the result that the workforce became the largest single group of shareholders in the privatized NCB. On the debit side, though, Leeds (1987) estimates that the cost to government of the free and discounted shares in the ESS was roughly J$1.2m.

The privatization sale.   Of the sale itself, two features were particularly important, namely the marketing campaign and the pricing decision. The marketing campaign is well described in Leeds (1987), and only a brief description is given here. Essentially, the principal aims were to demystify the stock market in order to encourage a new class of investors, and to reduce political opposition to the sale, especially from organized labour. To these ends, substantial campaigns were launched, with both advertisements in the national press offering 'question-and-answer' explanations of the JSE, and selected key groups targeted for special attention. The marketing campaign was broadly successful, in that public opposition and/or scepticism was reportedly reduced, as indeed was antagonism from the unions.

In the case of NCB, the pricing of the asset posed a particularly complex dilemma, the solution of which would be critical to determining the success of the sale. The complexity arose from the substantial uncertainties involved in estimating a demand curve for the asset, due both to the substantial weight the issue was placing on the mobilization of savings through the JSE and also to the credibility and pre-commitment problems discussed above. On balance, the government decided that the goal of broader share ownership and the demonstration of the merits of privatization through the success of the sale were more important than the object of revenue maximization; hence the NCB share price was set with these objectives in mind. An indicator of this decision is that, after making a comparison between NCB and its main competitor, BNS, the government set a share price of J$2.95 per NCB share, representing a price/earnings ratio of approximately 7.6 against a BNS p/e ratio of 14.0 and an average of 9.3 for the other major commercial banks.

Unsurprisingly, the share price turned out to be extremely attractive to both small and institutional investors. Over 30,000 Jamaican citizens and institutions applied for shares and, as a result, the offer was 170% oversubscribed, thereby triggering the allocation scheme described above. In view of the strength of demand for the shares, the first-day trading in NCB shares was vigorous and by the close of trading the price had risen to J$4.94, a 67.5% increase on the opening price. In total, the revenue received by the government for the sale of NCB shares was as follows:

NCB sale revenues

1) Public share issue	26,683,560 shares @J$2.95	= J$78.7m.
2) Employee Share Scheme	3,916,440 shares	= J$10.0m.
TOTAL	30,600,000 shares	= J$88.7m.

This was comfortably the largest privatization transaction in the programme to date.

Post-privatization performance.   Table 7.6 shows that NCB has grown substantially since its return to the private sector. Compared with 1986, by 1989 its total assets had nearly doubled (in nominal terms), and both pre- and post-tax profits had trebled. However, this order of growth was the norm in Jamaica's commercial banking sector during the period in question, and thus NCB seems not to have excelled in terms of growth. A comparison of the movement of NCB's share price against the overall JSE index in Fig. 7.3 displays a remarkable correspondence

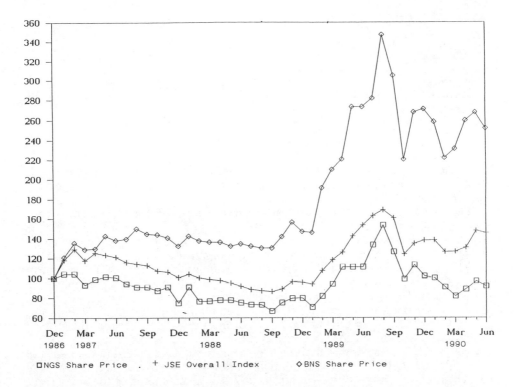

Figure 7.3 *NCB share price vs JSE Index and BNS (December 1986 = 100)*

between the two (at least until the end of 1989), suggesting that NCB was not out-performing the average firm listed on the JSE.[25] A more pertinent comparison is with the share price of NCB's chief competitor, BNS. This shows that NCB's share price has substantially *under*performed its rivals, as a result of BNS's faster profit and asset growth. Naturally, this is not sufficient information upon which to base any firm conclusions about the impact of privatization on NCB's performance. However, the tentative conclusion that the change of ownership *per se* has had little effect is confirmed by the Managing Director of NCB, Donald Banks, who locates the critical change as being the removal of the fear of government interven-tion in NCB's management.

Since the privatization transaction, the government has attempted to dispose of its remaining holding, as it indeed pledged to do at the time of sale. In this, however, it has not been successful (until recently – see below). The main attempt came in 1988, when the government advertised the sale of the whole of its 49% stake by a tender to institutions, who the government felt had lost out in the original sale. However, the great majority of the bids came in at well below the prevailing market price for NCB shares, yet centred around a common mean; hence, the government and NCB management claimed that there had been collu-sion between the main buyers. It therefore cancelled the offer, and its 49% stake remained unsold.

Key issues.   The sale of NCB was primarily intended to accomplish two goals, namely to spur on the growth of the capital market in Jamaica and to act as a demonstration of the possible success of a privatization programme. The inter-actions between the privatization programme and capital market development

Table 7.7 *NCB shares 1986–90*

Date	NCB share price	Total number of NCB shareholders[a]
Sale of Shares	J$2.95	c. 30,000
December 1986	J$4.94	30,606
December 1987	J$3.70	31,200
December 1988	J$3.95	29,790
December 1989	J$5.05	30,309
June 1990	J$4.55	30,451

a) JSE, private communication.

are analysed more fully in section 7.5, incorporating evidence from all the public share sales. Preliminarily, however, we examine certain issues germane to the NCB privatization.

The first is that the NCB sale clearly demonstrates the conflicting role of the government as both promoter and arbiter of the sale. This is at its most acute in the relationship between the government and small investors. On the one hand, the government wishes to encourage as many applications as possible, since the level of oversubscription is the usual way in which the 'success' of a sale is most immediately measured. On the other hand, the government also has an obligation to provide the smaller, less knowledgeable and less experienced investor with accurate information concerning the risks of equity investment and, ideally, some idea of how to form judgements about the promotional literature that the government itself is producing. While consideration of this point might suggest that the privatization process should itself be privatized (or at least placed in the hands of an impartial body), in fact the political importance of divestiture is such that governments do not wish to relinquish their role as promoter of the sale. Thus, governments tend to opt for the solution that involves offering investors a one-way risk only, i.e. by underpricing the asset. This conflicts, however, with another normative role of government, namely that of revenue maximizer. In the NCB case, a pricing of the asset at the less conservative, but still reasonable, price of J$3.50 per share would have raised an extra J$14.7m. while selling at the 'revealed' market price of J$4.94 per share would have produced an extra J$53.1m.[26]

Second, the government was intent on expanding the number of direct shareowners.[27] In this it achieved considerable success, in that it attracted roughly 30,000 new players on to the market. Furthermore, despite the opportunity for capital gain that the rise in the share price offered, in fact there has not been a rapid contraction of the number of NCB shareholders, in contrast to the experience of other countries (most notably the UK in developed countries and Malaysia in developing countries). The implication of this ownership pattern for the JSE is examined in section 7.5.

Third, the government had as its objective a more efficient NCB. This goal was stymied, however, by the ownership restrictions introduced to satisfy another aim of the sale, namely dispersed ownership. Furthermore, a legally imposed restriction also reduces the pressure on management coming from predatory shareholders on the JSE. Table 7.7 demonstrate how the number of shareholders has remained roughly constant. Equally important, though, is the fact that the 7.5% limitation makes illegal the concentration of larger shareholdings which could effectively monitor management. The position of the largest shareholders is given in Table 7.8. Noting that the NCB Share Scheme comprises a large number of small employee holdings, it can be seen that the ownership of shares is effectively dispersed. In the view of both the NCB's Managing Director and the technical architect of the privatization transaction, Richard Downer, the ownership restriction

Table 7.8   *NCB ten largest shareholders at 30 December 1989*

Name	No. of Shares	% of Non-Gov Shares	% of Total Shares
West Indies Trust Company	2,368,863	7.74	3.87
Eagle Merchant Bank	2,260,000	7.38	3.69
NCB Employee Share Scheme	1,546,608	5.05	2.53
Scotiabank Jamaica Ltd	1,110,301	3.63	1.81
Jamaica Mutual Life Assurance Co.	1,073,714	3.51	1.76
Anthony Ferrari	353,698	1.15	0.57
Jamaica National Building Society	261,470	0.85	0.43
Life of Jamaica Ltd	253,318	0.83	0.41
Mutual Security Merchant Bank Ltd	173,105	0.56	0.28
Manchester Pension Trust Fund Ltd	169,164	0.55	0.28
Total	9,570,241	31.28	15.64

Source: JSE ownership listings.

has a negative effect on the privatized firm, a direct result of the trade-off between the (in)efficiency of the ownership structure and the political acceptability of the sale. Downer in particular argues that the restrictions, although undesirable, were probably necessary as a form of binding pre-commitment against future intervention and a signal that the government was serious about selling the enterprise.

Finally, the NCB sale has been regarded by many, especially in developing countries, as a clear example of the success of privatization. In assessing NCB as a stand-alone sale, however, such a judgement clearly depends on the definition of success used. In many ways, the NCB sale did seem an outstanding achievement, especially in a technical and a political sense. However, one of its crucial features from an economic perspective was the way in which economic-type goals (revenue maximization, efficiency) were partially subordinated to political ends (programme continuity, success against the opposition). It is in this qualified context that the NCB privatization should be viewed.

Caribbean Cement Company
After the NCB sale, the government wanted to divest another large firm through the mechanism of a public offering as speedily as possible. Plans for the sale of the Caribbean Cement Company (CCC) were therefore rapidly drawn up by roughly the same team as had been responsible for the NCB transaction, the main change being that Redwood and Leitwin were unavailable and were replaced by another Rothschilds' consultant. However, in this sale the team was unable to repeat its earlier 'success'.

History and pre-privatization performance.   The Caribbean Cement Company was incorporated as a private company in 1947, was granted an exclusive right to manufacture Portland cement in 1949, and started commercial operations in 1952, initially producing 100,000 tons of clinker[28] per annum. The company expanded capacity in 1956, when production doubled, and in 1964, when production again doubled to 400,000 tons. The company also actively sought registration on various Stock Exchanges with the result that it listed shares in the USA in 1962, on the Toronto Stock Exchange in 1964 and on the newly opened JSE in 1969.

In 1977 the Manley Government announced its intention to take over the company CCC, as Leeds (1987) notes, presented an inviting target for nationalization: not only was it generally profitable, it was also part of the 'commanding heights' of the economy which the PNP had pledged to take into public ownership, and

Table 7.9 *CCC's performance, 1982–89 (J$m.)*

	1982	1983	1984	1985	1986	1987	1988	1989
Turnover	56.9	66.5	97.5	113.5	122.0	150.7	195.4	243.5
Interest payments	n/a	n/a	n/a	n/a	n/a	8.4	8.0	55.7
Pre-tax profits	1.5	−1.9	6.7	3.1	17.5	29.2	39.6	−12.6
Taxation	0.0	0.0	0.0	0.0	0.0	0.0	0.0	0.0
Post-tax profits	1.5	−1.9	6.7	3.1	17.5	29.2	39.6	−12.6
No. of shares (mill.)	38.0	38.0	38.0	96.0	96.0	125.0	125.0	125.0
Shareholder's equity	5.4	3.5	30.5	101.6	119.1	204.1	237.5	265.3
Long-term debt	37.9	76.5	132.5	207.8	351.0	489.2	515.8	522.4
Debt–equity ratio	7.02	21.79	4.34	2.04	2.95	2.40	2.17	1.97
Price–earnings ratio	n/a	n/a	n/a	n/a	n/a	6.23	5.05	−11.88
Earnings per share	0.04	−0.05	0.18	0.04	0.18	0.26	0.32	−0.10
Gross profit margin	2.64	−2.85	6.88	2.70	14.33	19.38	20.29	−5.19
Closing stock price	n/a	n/a	n/a	n/a	n/a	1.60	1.60	1.20
Cash dividend	0.00	0.00	0.00	0.00	0.00	0.00	6.25	12.50
Dividend per share	0.00	0.00	0.00	0.00	0.00	0.00	0.10	0.10
Production (tons):								
Local	229.7	271.7	255.9	233.1	229.7	286.8	363.0	405.6
Export	0.0	0.5	0.0	3.0	4.5	11.0	9.1	23.5
Import	29.8	9.9	0.0	0.0	0.0	0.0	12.3	27.0
Total	259.5	282.1	255.9	236.1	234.2	297.9	384.4	456.1

Sources: CCC, *1989 Annual Report*; JSE, *1989 Stock Exchange Handbook*.

was a company owned by the island's wealthy. The takeover was a lengthy process, completed only in 1980 when NIBJ acquired 90.3% of the issued share capital by issuing debentures in exchange for ordinary stock units of the company.[29] NIBJ subsequently expanded its shareholding to 99.4% by a similar offer to non-resident owners.

During the period of government ownership, the company suffered a reversal in performance brought about by slow economic growth and price control. However, two important steps were taken in this period. The first was the signing of a bilateral treaty between the Jamaican Government and Norway, whereby A/S Norcem, the only Norwegian cement company and later to be an important player in the CCC's privatization, would provide technical assistance to CCC. The second was the signing of a US$57.2m. loan agreement between the government and the Inter-American Development Bank (IDB) concerning CCC which had as its aim the enhanced economic efficiency of the firm, especially in export markets. This expansion and modernization project involved a US$50m. input from CCC, and was carried out between 1983 and 1987. CCC's productive capacity was increased to 800,000 tons of clinker per annum, an output requiring the export of a proportion of production if capacity was to be used to the full.

The performance of CCC in the period up to 1987 is shown in Table 7.9. While CCC was profitable for all years except 1983, its gross profit margin was very low and its performance was clearly inadequate. As a result of the financing of its expansion plans, the company accrued a large US dollar-denominated debt relatively rapidly, which, in Jamaican dollar terms, increased almost tenfold between 1982 and 1986. However, the debt/equity ratio was reduced by means of successive expansions of shareholders' equity.

Finally, throughout the period of state ownership, CCC retained its monopoly status. The small size of the domestic market and the high entry barriers caused by large initial investment needs were sufficient to maintain its position as the sole domestic producer of cement, and, while in principle it faced competition from imported cement (since the duty was small), in fact transportation and handling charges meant that it retained its natural monopoly.

Selection of CCC and aims for the privatization.   Leeds (1987) reports the following as the main reasons for the selection of CCC as the follow-up candidate to NCB for a public share sale: (i) the transaction would be large enough to warrant a public offering, and would therefore contribute to the development of the capital market; (ii) the company's performance was improving and projections suggested good future profitability; (iii) the company was not operating in a politically sensitive area; (iv) the management of the firm was enthusiastic about divestiture.

The last factor was one of the more important. The managers of CCC had several reasons for supporting a return to the private sector. While, as the Financial Controller of CCC confirmed, the Seaga Government did not intervene in the running of the company, the existence of CCC in the public sector placed the firm under certain constraints which limited its freedom in the areas of salary negotiations[30] and financial management (especially its inability to tap into Jamaica's commercial banking network). This was regarded as particularly important following the substantial amount of new investment that had gone into the company, combined with the impetus from the new management team.

Shaping the sale.   Consequent on the retention of most of the NCB team and the perceived success of the NCB sale, many similar features were retained in the design of the CCC divestiture. For example, the fact that the PNP once again opposed the sale of NCB meant that the government was again keen to emphasize the potential benefits to the smaller investor, and hence put in place an allocation scheme that would direct shares to smaller-sized applications in the event of oversubscription. However, there were problems intrinsic to CCC that had to be overcome before sale could be countenanced.[31]

The first of these was the *financial restructuring* of the firm. The impact of the modernization and expansion programme combined with the devaluation of the exchange rate on CCC's debt was noted above. The government was concerned lest this debt discourage applicants by raising doubts about the sustainability of the firm's future cash flow (this was despite internal projections which suggested that, barring one particular year, the repayment schedule looked manageable[32]). Thus, on 21 May 1987, the government redenominated US$62m. (JS$340m.) of CCC's debt into the domestic currency with unchanged interest and repayment terms, and assumed the exchange risk on the loans itself. Furthermore, in order to improve the company's debt/equity ratio temporarily and thereby improve its balance sheet, NIBJ purchased 16.5 million shares from CCC, the repayment of which would be made from the proceeds of the public offer. The government justified this financial restructuring as relatively costless, and as playing an important role in making CCC an attractive proposition for investors. However, the full cost of the debt redenomination would depend on the future path of the exchange rate and, as we shall see, the costs involved here turned out to be not insignificant.

Second, in order to fill the one-year financing gap mentioned above, and also act as a 'sweetener' to the privatization transaction, the sale included a system of *subscription warrants*. These were to be issued to every shareholder on the basis of one warrant for every five shares held, and would confer on the holder the right to subscribe for shares in CCC at a subscription price of J$2.30 per share (as against an actual sale price of J$2.00 per share) at any time before 31 December 1988.[33] The warrants would be tradable instruments on the JSE, and represented the only form of new money coming into the company as a consequence of the sale. Critically, the success or failure of the subscription warrants was constructed to depend on a rise in the secondary market price of CCC shares.

The third crucial move was the sale of equity in advance of the public offer to CCC's *foreign partner*, Scancem (formerly Norcem). This was regarded as advantageous by both sides. From Scancem's point of view, CCC was a potential tool in its aims to control the US East Coast cement market: its expansion plan for CCC, coming into fruition by 1987, had been in part a strategy which would allow it to increase its exports to this region. An equity stake in the company would formalize the arrangement between the two partners. From CCC's point of view, Scancem had been instrumental in the revitalization of the firm and employees from Scancem occupied four leading positions in the company. 'Locking-in' Scancem's participation via an equity stake was seen as a way of ensuring the high quality of CCC's performance. Furthermore, it was believed that the sale of a portion of the shares to the foreign partner would act as a signal of assurance to domestic investors as well. However, the eventual sale price negotiated for the 10% stake – J$2.00 per share – was definitely on the high side, and had implications for the eventual public issue.

As in the NCB sale, the government's aims of widening share ownership led it to introduce ownership restrictions on CCC shares. Under these provisions, the maximum shares that could be allotted to any one applicant were 10% of the issued share capital, raised from the 7.5% of the NCB sale on account of the agreement already made with Scancem. Similarly, in the event of undersubscription it was declared that any shares remaining with the government or NIBJ would carry non-voting rights. There was, however, one important way in which the ownership restrictions differed, namely that in this sale the government created a special share for itself which could only be issued to and held by the Accountant General on behalf of NIBJ. This 'golden' share meant the Accountant General would be entitled to attend and speak at shareholder meetings, but the share was non-voting and had no right to the capital or profits of the company. However, the provisions meant that the consent of the Special Shareholder would be required before any of the entrenched provisions in CCC's Articles of Association could be altered. These relate to: (i) the voluntary winding-up of the company; (ii) the creation of an additional Special Share; (iii) the disposal of any of the company's assets; and (iv) the creation of a new class of shares of more than 10% of the issued share capital. The interesting point is that the government felt able to write such a share into the CCC issue soon after it had been advised during the NCB sale that any such government involvement would be disastrous. We conjecture that this represents a substantial rise in public confidence in the government's credibility on account of the well-managed NCB sale.

Finally, the government once again reserved stock for an employee share scheme, which was given special import in the Prime Minister's 1987 budget speech (Leeds, 1987):

> It is central to the ideological position of this government that workers should have a share in ownership to boost personal motivation and to spread ownership of assets in the economy.

The scheme reserved 4,840,000 shares (or 3.9% of the total) for full-time employees of the company, with provisions for purchase broadly similar to those of NCB. However, there were tightenings in the provisions which, though small, suggest that the government was responding to the criticism of the NCB sale on the grounds that it had offered stags excessively easy capital gains. These tightenings were a hardening of the trading restrictions on concessional shares, and a

5% premium on any unallocated shares subsequently sold to employees if the secondary price had risen by 20% over the offer price.

The privatization sale.   As in the NCB case, the two most important features of the sale were the marketing campaign and the pricing decision. The marketing of CCC followed the pattern of the previous sale, and aimed at both educating potential investors about the JSE and raising the profile of CCC. This latter task was more problematic than for NCB since CCC was not a well-known company, its product was not particularly marketable, its historical financial performance was not nearly as strong and its future performance was dependent on the uncertain outcome of an export drive. In the event, post-sale market research revealed that CCC 'name-recognition' had increased substantially during the media blitz, although this does not reveal whether the campaign also persuaded more investors to apply for the issue.

The crux of the CCC sale, however, was the decision concerning what level of total subscriptions to aim for. This involved two related decisions, namely (i) what proportion of equity should be sold? and (ii) at what price should it be offered? The easier decision involved the proportion of equity to be sold. Both the managers of CCC and Scancem took the view that all the government's shareholding should be sold, since both were afraid lest a future government might renege on its commitment not to intervene in the company, and use its remaining equity to realize this. Furthermore, the advisers had noted the adverse impact that NCB's 49% overhang had on the secondary price, thanks to investors' fears about future sales of large chunks of equity. Thus, although Seaga had at one point talked of selling 50–70% of CCC's shares to the public, in fact the decision was made to offer 100% of the government's equity in the company.

The pricing decision, though, was considerably harder, with several factors contributing to the final decision. The first was the difficulty of making a market valuation of CCC. Whereas with NCB valuation could be made on the basis of historical performance, in CCC's case it was essentially based on future profit in view of the less impressive past profitability. It was not clear, however, whether risk-averse investors would regard the probability of improved performance in the future in the same light as a solid record in the past and hence be prepared to pay the same amount. Furthermore, the banking market offered a comparable firm with a public listing with which to compare NCB, whereas, as a monopoly producer, no such comparison was available for CCC, thus making detailed financial comparisons impossible.

Second, there was the impact of the NCB sale. Despite the above, it was clear that, at any reasonable price, the CCC sale would be aiming to raise roughly double the amount of the NCB transaction. In other words, the pressure on the absorptive capacity of the JSE would be correspondingly higher. Worries about this, though, were undoubtedly lessened by the fact that the unfilled demand for NCB shares had been in the region of J$160m. which the advisers believed would be available for purchasing the CCC equity. Moreover, the government was sensitive to the allegation that public funds had been squandered through the underpricing of NCB and was keen not to repeat the mistake.

Despite these uncertainties, in the end the relatively ambitious Scancem price was the one agreed upon, namely J$2 per share. On the basis of this offer for sale price, CCC's capitalization was J$250m. and its price–earnings ratio 8.70 on prospective 1987 earnings and 10.98 on historic 1986 earnings – not an unattractive offer. Pulling the above threads together, then, the CCC sale was as follows.

CCC pre-sale capital structure

Authorized		150,000,000	J$0.50 shares = J$75.0 million
Issued	Scancem	12,499,995	
	ESS	4,840,000	
	Minority	554,512	
	For public sale	107,105,488	
		124,999,995	J$0.50 shares = J$62.5 million
Reserved for warrants		24,999,999	
		149,999,994	

The offer for sale was hence for 111,945,488 J$0.50 ordinary shares, divided into 107,105,488 for public sale at J$2 each (or 85.6% of the total issued capital), and 4,840,000 for the Employee Share Scheme (ESS), at an average price below J$2 per share. As a final point, the sale was conditional on applications for at least 52 million ordinary shares, i.e. 50% of the offering.

In the end, the offer was undersubscribed and, in many people's eyes, was regarded as a failure. By the end of the offer period, 78.69 million shares (representing 72% of the equity offered to the public) were sold to roughly 23,000 investors; 99% of employees became shareholders under the ESS, although total demand did not exhaust the shares available; the remaining 28% of the stock was retained as non-voting shares by NIBJ. The lack of full subscription led to the conclusion that the sale had been overpriced and, as one would expect, the secondary price suffered an immediate fall in its value to J$1.90 per share at the end of the first day's trading. However, while the CCC issue did not raise all the capital hoped for by the government, the volume of shares purchased meant that the CCC offering was by far the largest public offering in the history of the JSE. Furthermore, the complete CCC transaction produced substantial revenues for the government.

Receipts from the CCC sale

21/5/87	Scancem	12.5 million shares @J$2.00	J$ 25.0m.
24/6/87	Public	78.7 million shares @J$2.00	J$157.4m.
24/6/87	ESS	<4.8 million shares	n.a.
	Total		>J$182.4m.

Thus, gross revenues to the fiscus were at least twice as large as in the case of NCB.

Post-privatization performance.   CCC has expanded production dramatically since 1987, and there has been a concomitant increase in sales (Table 7.9). For example, in 1989 CCC recorded the highest volume of production in its history at 405,600 tons and saw the highest volume of sales, which itself represented a 19% increase over the record figure of 1988. While most of these sales were to the domestic market, some 23,500 tons were exported to the Eastern Caribbean. However, little of this improved performance can be attributed to the privatization. The production figures clearly reflect the extensive modernization and expansion investment that occurred from 1983 onwards, while CCC itself explains the sales improvement as due to the (unexpected) buoyancy of the construction industry (especially following Hurricane Gilbert), a new CCC marketing thrust, and its improved production capability. In fact, as noted earlier, Scancem bought into CCC largely in order to service the US cement market, but found it was unable

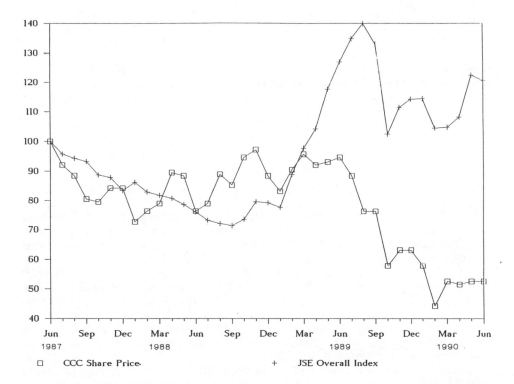

Figure 7.4 *CCC share price vs JSE overall index (June 1987 = 100)*

to diversify into this export market because of the extremely strong growth in domestic demand.

In contrast, financial performance has not matched this impressive sales record. While profitability rose significantly in 1988, exceeding privatization forecasts, in 1989 the company made a loss of J$12.6m. despite a substantial rise in turnover from J$195.4m. to J$243.5m. due to both increased sales and increased prices.[34] The financial performance of the firm is clearly reflected in the relative movement of CCC's share price *vis-à-vis* the JSE overall index (Fig. 7.4). In 1987, it drifted steadily down from its 'revealed' market price, reaching a low of J$1.38 in January 1988. It picked up in 1988, but 1989 saw a dramatic worsening. Not only did CCC miss out on the JSE boom in the first half of the year, but the share price also collapsed from June 1989 to February 1990, reaching a low of J$0.84 as against the original share price of J$2 and the revealed price of *c.* J$1.90.

The causes of this weak performance were fourfold. First, there were problems in the start-up of new kilns, resulting in a production loss of 60,000 tons, an increase in costs and a loss of profits estimated at J$22m. Second, there were other cost increases caused by a rise in the prices of fuel and imports due to an adverse change in the exchange rate. Third, a 20% stamp duty was imposed on coal, in contravention of what CCC thought was an implicit government undertaking to keep CCC fuel imports duty-exempt. This affected CCC since it had just completed its conversion from oil- to coal-fired kilns.

However, a fourth important reason was the failure of the warrants to raise the cash that CCC had expected. All unconverted warrants expired on 31 December

1989 – 24,971,044 out of a total issued of 24,999,999. This was not surprising. As noted above, the effectiveness of the warrant scheme depended on a rise in the secondary market price of CCC's equity to J$2.30; however, the share price never reached par throughout the warrant period. Unfortunately, the health of CCC's cash flow had been predicated on the securing of J$50m. through the conversion of these warrants. The failure of the warrant programme thus necessitated the company seeking replacement finance from the commercial banking sector, which had a considerably higher interest rate than its previous long-term debt. This development has put pressure on CCC's financial performance, as the company accounts demonstrate, especially through a dramatic rise in interest payments from J$8m. in 1988 to J$55.7m. in 1989. This almost single-handedly accounts for the magnitude of the shift from profit to loss in those years.

Key issues. As shown above, the aims of the CCC privatization largely constituted capital market development and a reinforcement of the demonstration effect of NCB. The most surprising omission was any consideration of efficiency. In the event, the sale reflected this apparent lack of concern in several ways. First, CCC was and is a domestic monopolist both as a public and as a private firm, and in theory an appropriate regulatory structure should have been put in place after the sale to ensure allocative efficiency. CCC itself argues that it faces potential competition from imports: however, others claim that it operates dominant-firm strategies, especially price wars, that leave it as the only realistic importer of cement, thereby reinforcing its monopoly. Whether CCC operates in a competitive market or not is a question that would need more detailed analysis: what is surprising is that, given this uncertainty, the issue of regulation was never discussed in the privatization programme.

Second, there is also the potential for the capital market to impose discipline on the firm. However, as in the NCB sale, the introduction of an ownership restriction limits the effectiveness of shareholder monitoring by introducing free-rider problems into the acquisition of information. Even though the restriction in CCC's case was 10% rather than 7.5% of the equity, these problems are still institutionalized, as the following list of shareholders owning more than 5% suggests:

CCC Shareholder list

	No.	*%*
NIBJ (non-voting)	33,188,995 shares	26.6%
Dyoll Merchant Bank Ltd	12,729,995 shares	10.2%
Scancem (prearranged)	12,499,995 shares	10.0%
Mutual Security Merchant Bank & Trust Co.	11,588,218 shares	9.3%

Only two shareholders, other than those prearranged, own more than 5% of CCC shares. Furthermore, despite the price decline, small investors have apparently not been aggressive players: the number of shareholders three years after the sale was 24,408 as against *c.* 23,000 at the time of sale. The result is, as the Financial Controller of CCC confirmed, that there is little pressure on the company's management arising from the JSE.

Finally, though it was argued that the ESS would involve the labour force in a contract that would induce extra effort from workers, there is no evidence from the firm that any such change has taken place.[35] In conclusion, then, it does *not* appear that the transfer of CCC's ownership from public to private *per se* has had any major positive impact on the efficiency of the firm. As Leeds notes (1987: 67–8):

The privatization of CCC entailed the transfer of ownership from a public sector monopoly to one in the private sector . . . as with NCB, there was scant justification for privatization on the basis of its effects on the company's efficiency.

Another important issue arising from the CCC experience is clearly that of pricing. Due to the uncertainties and pressures outlined above, the government overpriced the CCC issue and hence less than the full offer was sold. However, in a static sense, overpricing is in symmetrical relation to underpricing: while the latter results in oversubscription, and is thus regarded as a success but in fact also implies a revenue loss to government, overpricing results in undersubscription, is thus regarded as a failure but also implies a revenue gain to government. In CCC's case, the government sold 78.7 million shares at a price that was higher than the revealed market price, and hence raised more than the market value of the assets. Of course, overpricing also contributed to the failure of the warrant. However, the main problem here was not pricing, but a design fault in the warrant which assumed a secondary market price rise. Thus, inasmuch as the current problems of CCC are the result of financial difficulties, it was the design of the privatization that was at fault.

Finally, the CCC sale offers an interesting example of the cost in some privatizations of 'sweeteners', which often take the form either of pre-privatization restructurings, the cost of which is borne by government, or of special privileges offered to share purchasers. The main factor in the CCC lease was the government's assumption of exchange risk on US$62m. of debt via a debt redenomination into Jamaican dollars. Without this restructuring, the government felt the enterprise would not be sellable. However, in the event this restructuring proved costly. The great majority of the debt started repayment from 1989 onwards, by which time there had been a sizeable depreciation in the exchange rate from J$5.50 to J$8 per US$ (the exchange rate subsequently collapsed to J$19–21). Thus, the local currency value of the CCC debt increased by J$152m. to J$492m. while CCC's liability to government for the same debt remained constant. This considerable rise in the value of the debt was almost sufficient to eliminate any net financial gains from CCC's privatization.

Telecommunications of Jamaica (ToJ)
The ToJ privatization remains the most ambitious single sale of the entire programme in Jamaica. The four separate transactions raised a total of J$626.1m. which, to put the figure in perspective, represents 37.6% of total privatization receipts to date, or roughly 3% of 1989 GDP. The privatization also involved the transfer of a key infrastructural service to the foreign private sector and as such represented the antithesis of the philosophy that had guided the government in the 1970s. However, the ToJ sale was marked by a totally inadequate consideration of post-privatization regulation, an error which, given the contract the government has entered into, may affect the performance of the enterprise for as long as 50 years.

History and pre-privatization performance. ToJ itself was incorporated only in 1987, and was set up in order to facilitate privatization of the telecommunications sector by acting as the holding company for the two already existing companies, namely Jamaica International Telecommunications (Jamintel), and the Jamaica Telephone Company (JTC), which had been responsible for international and domestic telecommunications respectively. Historically, JTC had run the gamut of ownership arrangements, ending up in 1975 in public ownership. Its performance as an SOE was not distinguished, however. The rate of connections was poor, with substantial recorded unmet demand, and JTC was widely held to be one of the most inefficient of the utilities. In the 1980s, a reform programme produced some improvements in the quantity of service: however, by 1987 the density of the network was still only 3.55 telephone outlets per 100 inhabitants, satisfying only 63% of recorded demand,[36] while the average waiting time for a residential connection was 156 weeks.[37] Jamintel had a different record. Since 1970, the company had been jointly owned by the government (51%) and Cable and Wireless (UK), and by 1987 was providing international telephone services, telex services, telegraph services, leased circuits, facsimile services, international data access, circuits for satellite television, and so on. It had a record of consistent profitability, and had declared a dividend in every year of operations except 1977.

Selection of the sector and government aims for its privatization.   As late as 1986 the Prime Minister had announced in his budget speech in Parliament: 'The government will not . . . divest its ownership in . . . telecommunications . . . This [enterprise] must always be run in the public interest.' Yet within two years this pledge was reversed. The reasons for this volte-face were threefold. First, the government now viewed telecommunications as a key sector for its economic plans, especially the encouragement of foreign investment and the emergence of a competitive exporting sector linked to the US economy. Second, it concluded that one of the main causes of JTC's poor performance, when compared to Jamintel, lay in its constrained access to technology, finance and foreign exchange. Jamintel, through its link with Cable and Wireless (C&W),[38] was in a much better position both to access the latest in technological advance and also to arrange the finance and foreign exchange necessary for its importation via credit guarantees from C&W. JTC, on the other hand, relied on the financing ability and creditworthiness of the Jamaican Government. This meant that in the 1980s it was unable to renovate its capital stock at the rate required. By the end of the 1980s, it was clear that a substantial investment programme was needed in domestic telecommunications for which the government would be unable to provide either the investment funds or the foreign exchange.[39] Finally, as two of the 21 largest SOEs incorporated into the government's budgeting under IMF credit ceilings, both JTC and Jamintel found their capital expenditure plans subject to last-minute vetoes determined by quarterly macroeconomic targets rather than long-term firm-level planning.

Simultaneous consideration of these problems led the government to one solution: sale of the entire telecommunications sector to a foreign investor. This would concurrently release both firms from arbitrary budget decisions, and, more importantly, would give JTC access to the capital, technology and foreign exchange it needed to modernize its system through importing capital.[40] By coincidence, the equity agreement between the government and C&W in Jamintel was up for renegotiation, which gave the government the opportunity to restructure the entire sector.

Shaping the sales.   The sale of the sector was made in several tranches. The main moves beforehand comprised the transfer of the equity of JTC and Jamintel to a single holding company, ToJ,[41] and the creation of a regulatory structure for the company that would exist after the sales. Although, as part of the purchasing package, decisions on these were bound up with the sales themselves and were the outcome of bargaining between the government and C&W (the principal actors), for clarity of exposition and because the chronology is at times obscure, the two are separated here.

First, ToJ was created with the aims of establishing corporate objectives, co-ordinating acquisition and allocation of resources, and arranging finance for the group. With almost breathless speed, ToJ became the sole owner of JTC and

Jamintel. Thus, ToJ was incorporated on 19 May 1987 with an authorized share capital of J$1bn, acquired Jamintel's equity via a share swap in June and purchased all JTC's shares with its own equity (following a professional valuation of the latter company) between July and November of the same year.

The second move was the establishment of a regulatory structure that would determine access to, exit from, and pricing in the monopoly after the ownership transfer had occurred.[42] Whereas the objective of regulatory policy is usually the protection of the consumer from excessive extraction of surplus, in this case the regulatory regime had an important additional goal, namely the enticement of C&W to commit substantial investment resources to Jamaica and hence also the guarantee of the security of such commitments. (This, after all, was the main reason that the government had decided to sell JTC and Jamintel.) Thus, the regulatory structure put in place for Jamaican telecommunications has a different flavour from those usually encountered.

With regard to access and exit, on 31 August 1988, the government granted ToJ an exclusive 25-year licence for both domestic and international services, which ToJ then assigned to JTC and Jamintel respectively. This licence would be subject to the following conditions:

i) It was (and is) renewable for a further 25 years (subject to the same conditions as the original licence apart from the renewal provisions) unless, 2½ years prior to the end of the licence, the Minister of Public Utilities and Transport (MPUT) notified ToJ that the government intended to acquire the telephone undertakings of either JTC or Jamintel. In this circumstance, the government must revoke the telecommunications licence of the other firm, and acquire its assets as well. In the event of such a decision, it was stipulated that the acquisition must be at a fair market value, as determined by an independent firm of appraisers.

ii) The licence could also be revoked if MPUT determined that the licensee had failed to comply with its terms (including carrying out the prearranged capital development programme noted above), after a reasonable opportunity had been given to the licensee to remedy this failure.

iii) In the event of revocation, the licensee has a two-year period in which to sell its telephone undertakings. However, if it fails to do this, then within 12 months of the end of the 2-year period, the government *must* buy the assets at a fair market price.

iv) Any such government acquisition will occur in accordance with a prescribed regime whereby it may elect to pay by cash, or up to 95% in promissory notes denominated either in US$ or UK£, payable by half-yearly instalments of principal and interest over a 15-year period, bearing interest at 2% above the six-month LIBOR for equivalent-sized deposits.

As far as pricing was concerned, the regulations specified that JTC and Jamintel are entitled to charge rates sufficient to result in post-tax consolidated earnings for ToJ of not less than 17.5% and not more than 20% in consolidated shareholders' equity at the end of the preceding financial year. Such rate adjustments as ToJ might wish to make will be made via an application to MPUT, who may approve a new rate or refer the matter to a referee for determination of an appropriate rate, this referee to be appointed by the Minister, in consultation with ToJ, from the present or former members of the Jamaican Supreme Court.

Examining the terms of this in some ways extraordinary licence suggests that, in effect, the government was granting ToJ a risk-free monopoly position in Jamaican telecommunications with a guaranteed rate of return on its investment

Table 7.10 *ToJ privatization of share capital (J$)*

	Start	23 Jul 87	02 Oct 87	28 Sep 88	QIII 89
Number of shares owned:					
GoJ	798,718,838	696,381,990	512,902,030	368,402,030	193,265,300
C&W	90,799,952	193,136,800	376,616,760	376,616,760	569,753,490
Public	76,164,858	76,164,858	76,164,858	76,164,858	202,664,858
As % of total shares:					
GoJ	82.7	72.1	53.1	40.0	20.0
C&W	9.4	20.0	39.0	39.0	59.0
Public	7.9	7.9	7.9	21.0	21.0

Sale revenues (J$m.):

23/07/87 – GoJ sells 102,336,848 shares at J$1.00 per share	=	102.3
02/10/87 – GoJ sells 183,479,960 shares at J$1.00 per share	=	183.5
28/09/88 – GoJ sells 126,500,000 shares at J$0.88 per share	=	108.5
Q III/89 – GoJ sells 193,136,730 shares at J$1.20 per share	=	231.8
Total:		626.1

for as long as 50 years. The implications of this regulatory regime are returned to later.

The privatization sale. The first two tranches of the ToJ privatization were concomitants of the equity restructuring documented above. As part of this, the government and C&W had agreed to various transactions concerning ToJ shares. Under ToJ's Shareholder's Agreement, it was stipulated that C&W would hold at least 20% of the issued share capital of ToJ. Thus, on 23 July 1987 as Table 7.10 shows, the government sold 102,336,848 ordinary ToJ shares to C&W at J$1 each in order to bring C&W to this agreed limit. Three months later, on 2 October, a further 19% was sold to C&W at the same price. The result of these transactions was to reduce the governments shareholding in ToJ to 53%, and increase C&W's to 39%. Subsequent events suggest that the government obtained a good price from C&W for these two tranches.

Following the government's policy goal of broadening share ownership and giving small shareholders a stake in the largest national enterprises, a portion of ToJ's equity was offered to the public by means of a share sale through the JSE.[43] Thus, on 28 September 1988, 126,500,000 ordinary shares, comprising some 13% of the issued ordinary share capital of ToJ, were offered for sale to the public by the government at J$0.88 per share, with no limit on the number of shares that any individual could buy. This price represented only a small discount on the price C&W had been prepared to pay in the earlier transactions, and endowed the firm with a reasonable historical price earning ratio of 4.3 and an expected dividend yield of 10%.[44] As Table 7.10 shows, as a result of this transaction, the government would truly have privatized ToJ, in the sense that it would no longer have a straight majority of the equity, although by a small margin it would still be the single largest equity owner. In order to make clear that it sought to preserve this position, the government declared in the Offer for Sale document: 'The current intention of government is not to reduce its share-holding [in ToJ] beneath the 40 percent level.'

In accordance with another government policy aim, namely the involvement of the workforce, 21,100,000 shares of the total public offer, or 2% of the issued share capital, were reserved for employees of the group via an Employee Share Scheme, on terms similar to those of the NCB sale.

A final, and unusual, facet of the ToJ public tender concerned the underwriting arrangements for the issue. The entire offer was domestically underwritten by a consortium of 14 financial intermediaries: however, these were the same firms (i.e. institutional investors) from whom the government was expecting substantial demands. Hence, this was potentially an incentive-incompatible contract, in that it was in the collective interest of the underwriters to let the offer fail and then pick up what was essentially good stock cheaply thereafter. In order to circumvent this problem, the government insisted that, as a condition for underwriting the issue, each institution involved would apply for half the shares which they were underwriting, called Provisional Placed Shares, so that a minimum demand of 52,700,000 shares was guaranteed from the underwriters of the issue. These applications for Provisional Placed Shares, which could not be withdrawn, would also have to be accompanied by a post-dated cheque for the full amount of the transaction. In this way, the government camouflaged its concerns by presenting this regulation as a method of credit checking. The government thus made sure that the issue would not be manipulated by a powerful group of financial institutions.

In the end, despite the appearance of Hurricane Gilbert at the same time as the sale, the public issue was mildly oversubscribed: 11,114 applicants applied for a total number of 152,379,450 shares. As a result, a share allocation rule was triggered which, while acting as usual in favour of the smaller applicant, did not have a steeply declining schedule. The immediate premium on the shares was a very modest J$0.02 per share, i.e. well below the normal premium on private share issues. Hence, although the government decided to sell the equity at a price below that it received from C&W, the evidence suggests not only that it accurately priced the public issue, but also, as noted above, that it had got a good deal on its earlier sales. In total, the government received J$108.5m. from the ToJ JSE offer. Although this was not as much as for CCC, it was larger than the investment tapped in the NCB sale. Thus, the comfort of this sale suggests that the capacity of the capital market was now substantially larger than it had been at that time.

Although, as noted above, the Offer for Sale document asserted that the government would not reduce its shareholding below the 40% level, in fact there was one further sale of ToJ equity to C&W in the third quarter of 1989.[45] In this transaction, 193,136,730 ordinary shares, or 20% of ToJ's issued share capital, were sold at a price of J$1.20 per share, bringing the government a further J$231.8m. The significance of this deal was that it gave C&W straight majority control of the company. As such, one might have expected either the government to extract a higher price for the sale, or for there to have been a compelling reason for it. In fact, the trade occurred because the government looked like failing a quarterly IMF test, and desperately needed foreign exchange.[46]

Post-privatization performance. Since the privatization of ToJ has occurred so recently, there is very little evidence on post-privatization performance. Furthermore, as the chief reason for the privatization was the need for substantial investments in JTC, one would not expect performance to improve greatly in domestic telecommunications until this programme was nearing completion. In the interim, two facts can be noted. First, ToJ's share price has remained curiously static since the public offer, not breaking out of the narrow range J$0.70 to J$0.95 and trading mostly in an even more limited range. As Fig. 7.5 shows, this means that ToJ missed out on the JSE boom of the first half of 1989, and in general the ToJ price has lagged well behind the JSE overall index. However, since only a small proportion of ToJ's equity is traded on the JSE, and since the firm is not looking to domestic equity markets for substantial capital funding, this is not a particularly

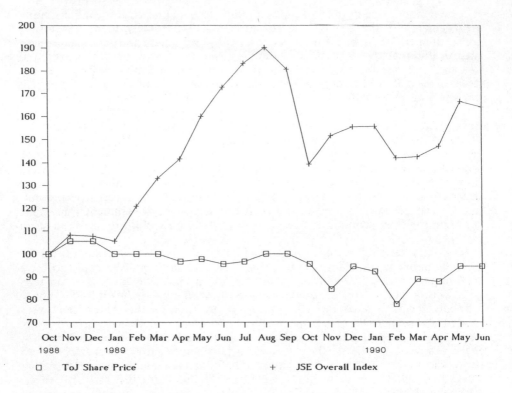

Figure 7.5 *ToJ share price vs JSE overall index (October 1988 = 100)*

good indicator of performance. Second, C&W has become very involved in the management of the companies, having put its own personnel in place in both ToJ and JTC. This, combined with the substantial investment resources that C&W has agreed to commit, suggests that privatization may lead to a substantial improvement in JTC's performance compared to its previous history, at least over the medium term.

Key issues. In some sense, the ToJ privatization was a more narrowly focused sale than those discussed previously, in that it had as its aim one overriding objective, namely the establishment of the conditions whereby JTC could receive a major capital infusion. However, the government's concern with this goal led it to ignore other important aspects of privatization, especially the goal of increased efficiency. Options for involving competition from other firms, instituting competition between JTC and Jamintel, and promoting contracting-out were not considered. That the government not only failed to give consideration to pro-competition policies in the telecommunications sector at the time of privatization, but also 'locked-in' the monopoly arrangement through the granting of exclusive licences, would appear to have been a substantial missed opportunity.[47]

Given that the ToJ monopoly was created, however, the government was obliged to set up an adequate regulatory framework. This, we contend, it did not succeed in doing. Examination of the regulatory regime outlined above suggests two problems. The first concerns the simple rate-of-return price regulation that ToJ currently faces. The benefit of this type of arrangement is that the information requirements of the regulator are small, meaning that an elaborate and highly trained regulatory staff is not needed at present. However, on the negative side, the inefficiencies of rate-of return regulation are well established (see Vickers and Yarrow, 1988; Chap. 4). The inadequacy of the current formula means that ToJ does not face sufficient incentive for efficiency improvements. Other methods were suggested during the negotiations with C&W, especially the RPI-X formula used in the UK, but the company strongly resisted these: the feeling on the Jamaican side was that C&W did not want to establish a regulatory precedent for other developing countries.

The second problem is that the majority of the regulations are in fact oriented towards providing C&W with security on its investments, i.e. they are addressing the issue of pre-commitment by the government. Indeed, the detailed specification of repayment regimes in the event of either non-renewal or revocation, including stipulations concerning foreign currency transactions, combined with a possible 20% annual return on investments, provides C&W with a near-riskless investment opportunity, and hence almost perfect pre-commitment by the government. While reputational weakness and absence of bargaining strength mandated a favourable regulatory regime for C&W, the final agreement suggests that C&W managed to extract almost perfect monopoly rents from the government. It would appear that, if the government had paid more attention to competition policy and the regulatory process during the privatization, it could have heightened the expected benefits from the transfer of ownership.

Sales through the NIBJ
At the same time as these larger sales were progressing, the NIBJ's Divestment Secretariat was also proceeding with a number of smaller sales. These had very different characteristics from the public share sales. First, their relative invisibility meant that the sale conditions were not shaped by political objectives. Indeed, the head of the Divestment Secretariat (DS) described them as 'privatization through the back door'[48] on account of the low publicity that both the JLP and PNP Governments have accorded them. Thus, the DS was free to sell the enterprises on the terms they felt were most favourable to the government. Second, their revenue impact was bound to be small, and therefore there was no pressure to sell quickly in order to meet budgetary targets. This gave the vendor more power in negotiations with prospective purchasers. Third, for these sales the DS did not have the need of outside consultants, but instead managed the process itself, bringing in outsiders only for specialized tasks such as assessing the net worth of enterprises.

The selection of firms for privatization under the DS was done by the relevant line ministry, with Cabinet approval.[49] After the DS received authorization, it went ahead with two valuations of both the firm's physical assets (land and machinery) and its equity. Unlike other agencies in other countries, the DS made no attempt to 'clean up' the firms in advance of sale, but rather privatized them whether they were profit- or loss-makers. Not only did this policy probably speed up the privatization process, but it also raised the anticipated post-sale efficiency gains. Following valuation, the enterprise was tendered and the 'best' offer selected (where best comprised a mix of the highest offer and an assessment of the ability of the tenderer to run the firm). The DS then bargained with the tenderer to try and extract the highest price possible. This could be a lengthy process, but meant that the DS could not be accused of selling state assets on the cheap. Once the sale was concluded, there were no restrictions on the new owner, who could shed labour or close the enterprise if it appeared necessary.

One quirk of these sales is that two of the firms were bought by Jamaican enterprises that had themselves been previously privatized. This intriguing pattern (of

Table 7.11 *Post-1985 privatizations through the NIBJ*

Date	Name	Sector	Nationality of Purchaser	% Equity Govt-Owned: Pre-Sale	Post-Sale	(J$m.)
1986	Rural Ice & Cold Storage	Services	Domestic	100	0	0.5
1986	Hanover Spices Ltd	Manufacturing	Domestic	100	0	0.1
1986	Hellshire Fish Farm	Fishing	Domestic	100	0	0.3
1986	Zero Processing & Storage[a]	Services	Domestic	100	0	4.0
1986	Jamaica Oxygen & Acetylene	Manufacturing	Foreign	47	n.a.	2.0
1989	Serge Island Dairies	Manufacturing	Joint	30	0	1.8
1989	W.I. Pulp and Paper	Manufacturing	Joint	81	0	38.1
1989	Jamaica Gypsum and Quarries[b]	Mining	Domestic	100	0	4.0
Total						50.8

Notes
a) Sold to Seprod Ltd.
b) Sold to Caribbean Cement Company.

'gamekeeper turned poacher') appears in a number of countries. Thus, Zero Processing and Storage was acquired by Seprod only one year after Seprod had itself been privatized, while Jamaica Gypsum and Quarries was bought by CCC.

A summary of NIBJ sales is presented in Table 7.11. This demonstrates the generally small nature of the transactions involved, and the concentration of sales in the manufacturing and services sector.

There is no firm evidence on the impact of divestiture on the firms involved. NIBJ itself is reviewing the progress of its programme, and part of this will involve a follow-up study of the firms already sold in order to gauge the impact on output, sales, productivity, and efficiency. As yet, though, this information is not available.

Hotels
Other parts of the privatization programme fell outside the purview of the NIBJ. Of these, the most important were the hotel privatizations, both in terms of the number of transactions and also their fiscal impact. Government involvement in hotels derived from the late 1970s, when it acquired a raft of hotels on the verge of closure which had government-guaranteed debt under the hotel incentive programme, such that it owned or controlled hotels accounting for 50% of total room capacity. These were placed under the control of National Hotels and Properties Ltd (NHP), a wholly-owned subsidiary of the Urban Development Corporation. However, at no point were the operations of NHP profitable or successful, and by 1982 the Auditor's Report for the company stated:[50]

> . . . the company and eleven of its subsidiary companies have sustained substantial operating losses for 1982 and prior years and nine of those subsidiaries had substantial deficiencies in assets at March 28, 1982. The continuation of the company and those subsidiary companies as going concerns is dependent upon financial support from the parent corporation and ultimately upon future profitable operations.

Thus, the JLP Government inherited a familiar situation. The hotels were not profitable, and thus required annual government subventions. Furthermore, in order to aid profitability, the government had granted a substantial number of hotels exemption from income tax, thus reducing government revenues. At the same time insufficient investment in the sector meant that the quality of most hotels was deteriorating and capital expenditure was required. Unless an overhaul was made, the tourist industry would continue to decline. However, privately-run

Table 7.12 *NHP hotel operations history*

	79/80	80/81	81/82	82/83	83/84	84/85	85/86	86/87	87/88	88/89	89/90
Total number of NHP hotels	17	18	18	16	16	19	17	17	17	17	17
o/w: Operated by NHP	10	9	3	5	4	4	2	2	3	3	3
Leased	6	8	14	10	11	14	15	15	13	13	5
Sold to private sector (cum.)	0	0	0	0	0	0	0	0	1	1	9
Other	1	1	1	1	1	1	0	0	0	0	0
Number with income-tax exemptions	6	8	9	9	8	6	6	5	5	3	n.a.
Value of leases (J$m.)	0.0	0.0	1.6	9.1	24.0	50.1	46.9	66.1	76.0	74.9	n.a.
Value of sales (J$m.)	0.0	0.0	0.0	0.0	0.0	0.0	0.0	0.0	15.4	0.0	311.1
Leases as % of govt revenues	0.0	0.0	0.1	0.5	0.9	1.6	1.1	1.4	1.4	1.0	n.a.
Sales as % of govt revenues	0.0	0.0	0.0	0.0	0.0	0.0	0.0	0.0	0.3	0.0	4.2

Source: NHP Ltd *Annual Accounts*, 1979–1989, and interview with NHP's Director of Finance, December 1989.

hotels existed and were profitable in a competitive market and, furthermore, foreign hotel chains could be enticed into the market. Finally, the government wished to reorient its role away from ownership in the tourism sector, and towards promotional activities under the auspices of the Jamaica Tourist Board. Thus, the motives for the privatization of the hotels were the classic ones: to boost efficiency, to improve the government budget, to allow a redirection of government expenditure, and to raise foreign exchange. (The importance of this latter objective is shown by the fact that domestic purchasers of hotels have to pay half the sale price in foreign exchange.) To carry out this programme, a group of employees within NHP itself was organized into a privatization unit – another example of gamekeepers (rent extractors) turned poachers (sellers).

The hotel privatization programme unfolded in two stages. Summary data on the programme are contained in Table 7.12. In the first half of the programme, the emphasis was on leasing hotels or awarding management contracts. This orientation was the result of the government's unwillingness to sell the hotels outright. In terms of numbers, the leasing programme peaked in 1986, when a total of 15 out of 17 hotels were being operated in this fashion. The NHP divestment unit showed itself capable in this period of reorganizing the hotel sector relatively rapidly, and both local and foreign companies were involved in leasing arrangements. As the programme continued, however, the disadvantages of leasing were discovered, namely that the lessees had insufficient incentive to invest and/or were operating the enterprises for short-term profit. Thus, the failure of some of the arrangements led the government from 1986 onwards to revitalize the programme by focusing more effort on sale. The method of sale was simple: an outright cash sale of the whole equity, with no special arrangements or concessions involved. Although sales were initially slow, a substantial number of hotels were sold in 1989 and the remainder were expected to be sold soon after. Ultimately, following the privatization of all its holdings, NHP itself would be liquidated and would, in some sense, have abolished itself.

What was the impact of the hotel privatizations? First, there is the effect on NHP itself, for which a set of accounts are presented in Table 7.13. This shows relatively clearly the financial impact of the leasing programme. Lease income

Table 7.13 *Summary of NHP accounts, 1979–1989 (J$m.)*

Year end March:	1979	1980	1981	1982	1983	1984	1985	1986	1987	1988	1989
Revenue	42	65	65	69	59	81	124	108	117	179	187
o/w Lease Income	0	0	0	2	9	24	50	47	66	76	75
Expenditure	28	41	49	51	35	36	35	30	21	43	49
Interest	16	20	21	21	15	17	26	33	41	50	44
Other expenses	25	31	31	38	32	43	68	81	44	78	85
Operating profit/(loss)	(27)	(29)	(36)	(42)	(23)	(15)	(6)	(37)	11	7	9
Profit/(loss) attrib. *to parent company*	(83)	(57)	(46)	(49)	(20)	(64)	(53)	(39)	10	10	(12)
Long-term liabilities	76	68	63	76	71	79	143	135	122	111	99

boosted total revenues substantially: by the mid-1980s, it was providing 40% or more of total NHP revenue. On the back of this rise in revenues, NHP finally recorded an operating profit in 1987, after more than a decade of losses. As a result, both the profit and loss account and long-term liabilities peaked in the mid-1980s and started to decline thereafter. From 1985 onwards, NHP even started paying taxes to the central government.

More broadly, though, there is the impact on both the government and the hotels themselves. Of the nine hotels sold, only two have been closed. However, in both cases, the purchasers intended alternative uses for the properties: in one case, to build a residential complex, in the other to turn the hotel into a furniture warehouse. There is no reason *ex ante* why these are not more efficient uses of the assets, and hence these closures cannot be presumed to be signs of failure. In the remaining hotels, NHP asserts that substantial new investments have occurred, especially where the sale was to foreign buyers. Furthermore, even though there were no restrictions on post-sale labour-shedding, in fact employment levels have not been reduced. Finally, since 1980 there has been substantial growth in the Jamaican tourist industry, with tourist arrivals exceeding 1 million for the first time in 1987 and estimated tourism revenues rising by 10% per annum between 1980 and 1988. While this can be explained in part by the government's renewed promotional efforts (see below), an important additional cause was the refurbishment and improvement of properties that occurred thanks to the leasing programme.

With regard to the impact on government, the outcome has been almost completely positive; the only area in which the government was disappointed was in its failure to attract more foreign buyers. Concerning budgetary issues, Table 7.12 measures both the lease and sale revenues as a proportion of total government revenues. By the peak of the leasing programme, the hotels were providing over 1% of government revenues each year. In quantitative terms, the annual revenues were equivalent to the amount raised in the NCB sale; and as lease revenues, unlike sales, they meant that the government's net wealth was not being reduced. The revenue from the sale of the hotels was also surprisingly large, at least J$311.1m.[51] in 1989, or the equivalent of 4.2% of total revenues. Taken together, then, these sales were even larger than the final ToJ transaction, and one of them – the sale of the Wyndham Rose Hall Beach Hotel – raised almost as much revenue as CCC. Obviously, given the size of the funds raised from the whole programme, the fiscal impact was quite substantial. This would have been augmented (though we cannot quantify this) by the reduction in government concessions to the hotel sector. As Table 7.12 shows, the number of hotels with income-tax concessions was reduced from a peak of 9 in 1982 to 3 by 1989. Thus, the hotel divestiture also allowed the government to be fiscally 'harder' and restore a fairer tax regime. Finally, the government was able to redirect expenditures towards promotional activities; thus, in real terms, the budget of the Jamaican Tourist Board rose by 150% between 1980 and 1987.[52]

In conclusion, the hotel privatization programme is an example of a policy which, although pursued quietly, had an impact almost as large as the 'headline' sales that have been more traditionally associated with and analysed in the Jamaican privatization programme. Moreover, there is little evidence of the type of political interventions in sales that has tended, in other parts of the Jamaican privatization programme, to reduce expected efficiency gains. Indeed, as we argued in Chapter 4, the two facts were related, so that the absence of a political spotlight on the hotel privatization, which could otherwise have been a contentious policy, allowed a more efficiency-oriented and revenue-maximizing programme to be implemented.

Privatizations in the agricultural sector
Although the agricultural sector in Jamaica provides only a small proportion of GDP (between 7.5% and 9%, 1977–87), as in many developing countries it accounts for a disproportionately large share of total employment (between 33.1% and 36.6%, 1977–87). Developments in this sector thus have significant implications for welfare, especially of the rural poor. The 1980s witnessed a range of policy reforms in the agricultural sector aimed at increasing rural incomes and employment, reducing rural–urban migration, promoting non-traditional crops and rehabilitating traditional export crops. These reforms comprised improvements in land-use policy, the overhaul of export marketing, attention to institutional reform, and the liberalization of price controls and domestic marketing. Privatization initiatives in the agricultural sector were taken in order to fulfil the above objectives, and they therefore form only one section of a broad agricultural reform programme.[53]

Regarding land-use policy, one of the key aims was to put the large, and largely idle, government land holdings to productive use. (These properties had ironically been acquired from the private sector in the 1970s under the Idle Land Law.) This was attempted through land leasing and land sales to private agents. In the case of land sales, not much is known about the programme, other than that the Registrar of Land claims to have sold roughly 30,000 acres. However, government revenues from the sales and the impact on agricultural yields are not known.[54] In respect of the leasing programme, the government vested responsibility for oversight in Agro 21, an agency established to promote the development of non-traditional crops, an objective which was an integral part of the leasing programme itself. Broadly, the structure was as follows. Before a lease could be granted, the lessee had to present a farm plan for the property that satisfied Agro 21. If successful, the leases would be granted for a 49-year period, and the responsibility of Agro 21 was to provide adequate delineation of the property and infrastructural facilities. Following the assumption of the lease, the lessee had to adhere to the farm plan, or else s/he could be found in breach of contract and stripped of the lease. By 1990 Agro 21 had leased out roughly 31,000 acres for a variety of different projects.

However, quite a high proportion of the agricultural leases failed to become sustainable projects. This reflected a number of weaknesses in the administration and fundamental orientation of the leasing programme. First, the lessees' agricultural production was not adequately co-ordinated with the rest of Jamaica's agricultural policies. In particular, insufficient extension services were offered by the Ministry of Agriculture, partly as a result of the general weaknesses of the Ministry, and partly due to lack of co-ordination between the Ministry and Agro 21. Second, because of the weak rights that the lease gave the lessee,[55] the commercial banks refused to regard the lease as collateral. This led to lessees having difficulty in obtaining access to adequate working capital, with concomitant problems when cash-flow shortages emerged. Third, on account of the link with the promotion of non-traditional crops, a frequent problem was the selection of inappropriate crops for a given piece of agricultural land and inability to adapt non-traditional crops to Jamaican conditions. Leases involving traditional crops were less likely to fail than those involving non-traditional crops. Fourth, and related, the terms of the lease gave very little flexibility to the lessee, especially concerning crop choice. For example, the legal lease document contained a provision whereby the lessee agreed 'not without the *written* consent (such consent not to be unreasonably withheld) of the Lessor to farm or cultivate on the leased land any crop other than the zoned crops or in any other way to vary the farm plan'[56] (our italics). Thus, where poor crop choice was a problem, the only solution was the rewriting of the lease.

For these multiple reasons, as the Managing Director of Agro 21 stated, 'the programme hasn't really worked'. On account of lack of information on revenues and yields, it is difficult to make an economic evaluation of the programme. While, on the one hand, crop yields on the leased land could not be less than the zero yield of idle land, on the other hand, the leasing programme absorbed some portion of the US$75m. that USAID earmarked for the promotion of non-traditional crops and land leasing, and hence there are opportunity-cost considerations for the public funds used to promote the programme.

The other main areas of agricultural reform involving privatization concerned two of Jamaica's most important cash crops: bananas and sugar. Both these sectors had experienced export declines in the 1970s. Rehabilitation efforts concentrated on pricing reforms, reorganization of marketing boards, and limited divestiture. In the banana sector, this package – involving, *inter alia*, the divestiture of the boxing factory – was basically successful, with export recovery and new investments in the sector. Rehabilitation of the sugar sector has proved more elusive, however, and in particular the government has not been successful in improving the performance of the sugar factories it acquired in the 1970s. Reform attempts have involved closing down the National Sugar Company (NSC), which had previously run its factories, and in its place establishing Jamaica Sugar Holding (JSH) to oversee its two remaining factories,[57] which were then placed under the management of Tate and Lyle (the pre-nationalization owners) for a period of 2 years. However, while the privately-owned factories have remained profitable with high rates of capacity utilization, there has been little improvement in the publicly-owned factories. JSH still produces sugar at 66% higher cost than international competitors, both factories suffer from severe operational problems, there is too much capacity in the industry and an insufficient supply of cane with the result that the government-owned factories operate at very low levels of capacity utilization. Consequently, like NSC before it, JSH has a weak financial position, losing J$102.7m. in 1988/89 and J$84.2m. in 1989/90, and relies on borrowings from its parent corporation, the Sugar Industry Authority. The only viable solution to the industry's problems lies in rationalization and the general privatization of a sector where there is little compelling reason for public ownership. This the government has been reluctant to do, however, because of the substantially increased unemployment that such a move would entail.[58] Thus, despite a decade of reform, including limited divestiture, there has been no great improvement in the sugar industry.

The agricultural privatizations, then, have a more chequered pattern than others. This reflects the more complex nature of the agricultural sector and the fact that the reasons for success or failure of privatization initiatives often lie outside the programme itself. For example, while poor policy design was important in explaining the disappointments of the land leasing programme, so also were the fundamental problems and weaknesses of the agricultural sector, which privatization by itself could not address. Similarly, the political imperative of employment retention in the sugar industry virtually guaranteed that privatization would be unsuccessful.

7.3.5 Recent[59] and future privatizations

Apart from the continuation of programmes started under Seaga, something of a hiatus has occurred in the Jamaican privatization programme since the advent of the new PNP Government in 1989. Indeed, the few privatizations which have occurred have been very controversial, and it is fair to say that privatization under the PNP has made a doubtful start. For example, the government's remaining equity holding in ToJ was sold to C&W, but without any opportunity for the minority shareholder (the public) to participate. Similarly, 10% of the goverment's NCB equity was sold to NCB employees, reducing the government's stake to 39%. However, these employee purchases were subsidized by NCB via an easy payment plan and below-market interest rates, at the expense of existing shareholders who were not consulted. Further, the government sold Workers Bank in a transaction notable for its opacity. Finally, a number of land sales have been strongly criticized both for low prices and potential illegalities.

While these transactions have been somewhat ill-conceived, the hiatus in privatization does not reflect an anti-privatization stance on the part of the PNP. In fact, the PNP has radically changed its economic ideology since the 1970s in areas of importance to the privatization programme. For example, it is now enthusiastic about private sector development, encourages foreign investment, and is prepared to work with the multilateral institutions that have made divestiture part of adjustment conditionality. Thus, the pause that has occurred has resulted not from a desire to halt or reverse the programme, but rather from the PNP's intention to review the progress of privatization under the JLP. From this review[60] two main policy conclusions have emerged. First, the PNP has moved to centralize the institutions responsible for privatization, in contrast to the previously decentralized approach. This has involved locating all privatization activity within the NIBJ, as well as the establishment of a Cabinet Sub-Committee on Privatization, chaired by the Prime Minister himself. Second, and far more substantively, the PNP has attempted to place the privatization programme in the context of a private sector development strategy involving a much more serious approach to competition and regulation policy (or deregulatory policy where appropriate). This has occurred despite the controversial transactions that the PNP has so far effected. Hence, the expressed motives for privatization under the Manley Government tend to derive more from the desire to create a competitive domestic economy rather than just to alter ownership structures.

In fact, proposals currently being considered by the government envisage, if implemented, a considerable expansion of the Jamaican privatization programme, as Table 7.14 shows. For example, the Cabinet has approved the sale of several of the larger SOEs, and the (not inconsiderable) task remaining is to locate buyers and negotiate appropriate terms and conditions. Similarly, a substantial number of smaller enterprises and government services have been identified for sale or contracting out.

However, this list of proposed privatizations suggests an important but often overlooked facet of the privatization programmes, namely the length of time that elapses between the privatization decision and the actual sale. Many of the

Table 7.14 *List of enterprisess to be privatized, mid-1991*

Name	Sector	% Govt Ownership	Method of Privatization
1) Proposed privatizations involving the larger SOEs			
Air Jamaica	Air Transport	100%	Minority equity sale to international investor
Caribbean Cement Company	Manufacturing	29%	Public sale of remaining shares
Donald Sangster Airport Terminal	Services	100%	Build–own–operate terminal
Jamaica Public Services Company	Electric utility	100%	Creation of private sector generating capacity
Jamaica Railway Corporation	Transportation	100%	Lease of assets & franchise
National Commercial Bank	Banking	39%	Sale of remaining equity
National Water Commission	Water utility	100%	Sale of sewerage processing + asset leases
Petrojam	Manufacturing	100%	Sale of shares
Trans-Jamaican Airlines	Air Transport	100%	Sale of shares
2) Proposed NIBJ privatization of smaller enterprises			
Abbatoirs	Agribusiness	100%	Lease
Agricultural Mechanical Services	Agribusiness	100%	Sale of assets
Antillean Food Producers	Manufacturing		Sale of assets
Ariguanabo Company	Manufacturing	100%	Sale of assets
Caribbean Steel Company	Manufacturing	51%	Sale of shares
Cornwall Dairy Development	Agribusiness	100%	Sale and lease of assets
Darliston Community Foods	Agribusiness	100%	Sale of shares
Ethanol Dehydration Plant	Manufacturing	100%	Lease or sale of assets
Government Printing Offices	Services	100%	Contracting out
Grains Jamaica	Agribusiness	51%	Sale of shares
Highgate Foods	Agribusiness	38%	Sale of shares
Hospital Services	Services	100%	Sale of assets and contracting out
Infirmary Catering	Services	100%	Contracting out
Innswood Vinegar	Agribusiness	51%	Sale or lease of assets
Jamaica Bauxite Mining Company	Mining	100%	Lease of assets
Jamaica Export Trading Company	Trading	100%	Sale of shares
Jamaica Fisheries Complex	Agribusiness	100%	Lease of assets
Jamaica Soya Products	Manufacturing	60%	Share sale
Kingston Dry Dock	Services	100%	Sale and lease of assets
KIW International	Manufacturing	42%	Public sale of shares
Motor Vehicle Repairs–Local Government	Services	100%	Contracting out
National Cassava Products	Agribusiness	100%	Sale or lease of assets
National Rum	Agribusiness	100%	Sale of shares
National Tool & Die Co.	Manufacturing	100%	Sale of assets or shares
Parking Meters/Traffic Flow Monitoring	Services	100%	Contracting out
Port Authority of Jamaica	Services	100%	Sale and lease of assets
Postal Services/Package Delivery	Services	100%	Contracting out
Road Maintenance	Services	100%	Contracting out
Standard Building Products	Manufacturing	100%	Sale of assets
West Indies Glass	Manufacturing	62%	Sale of JSE listed shares
3) Proposed privatizations in the tourism sector			
Bath Fountain Hotel	Tourism	100%	Lease of asset
Forum Hotel	Tourism	100%	Sale of assets
Milk River Hotel & Spa	Tourism	100%	Lease of assets
Montego Freeport & Subsidiaries	Tourism	n.k.	Sale of assets
Negril Cabins	Tourism	100%	Sale of assets
Negril Royal Palm Resort	Tourism	100%	Lease of assets
Oceana Hotel	Tourism	100%	Sale of assets
Pegasus Hotel	Tourism	60%	Sale of shares

Table 7.14   *continued*

Name	Sector	% Govt Ownership	Method of Privatization
4) Proposed agricultural privatizations			
Black River Upper Morass Development Co.	Agriculture	100%	Sale or lease of assets
Eastern Banana	Agriculture	n.k.	Sale of shares
Font Hill Farms	Agriculture	100%	Sale of assets
Lydford Farms	Agriculture	100%	Sale of assets
Minard Estates	Agriculture	100%	n/k
Montpelier Property	Agriculture	100%	Sale and lease of assets
Shettlewood Property	Agriculture	100%	Sale and lease of assets
St Jago Farms	Agriculture	100%	Sale and lease of assets
Victoria Banana	Agriculture	100%	Sale of shares

Sources: Various government documents plus interviews.

putative larger sales involve enterprises that have been slated for privatization for as long as a decade,[61] and have been undergoing restructurings for at least as long. Even after such an intensive reform effort, however, there are still some doubts about the attractiveness of certain enterprises to the private sector (Air Jamaica, Jamaica Railway Corporation, and Petrojam). This story is repeated when it comes to the smaller sales. In this case, the delay has arisen not because of restructuring, which is not undertaken, but simply on account of the time needed to arrange the various aspects of a deal. Especially with the larger enterprises (which have the most substantial budgetary impact), but also with the smaller, privatization takes time, and speeding up the process may lead to sales which are poorly thought out and designed, resulting in a stymieing of hoped-for benefits. A critical issue here concerns utility regulation: although it is likely that private sector operators will be licensed in electricity generation, there is no evidence that the government is attaching a priority to the simultaneous creation of a regulatory structure for the sector. The ambitious PNP programme will need to deal with these problems if it is to be successfully implemented.

7.3.6 An assessment of the privatization programme

As a large programme, with sales on which we have some quite detailed information, the Jamaican experience is not easy to summarize. In doing so, we inevitably miss some of the nuances that make Jamaica a fascinating case study of privatization. These have been presented, however, in the analysis of privatization experience above and, to some extent, in the first half of the book, where we drew heavily on the Jamaican case study. In broad summary, three main strands can be drawn out of the Jamaican experience.

First, because of its size, the Jamaican programme in aggregate has had a greater financial impact on the government than that of any of the other country studies. Evidence on this is presented in Table 7.15, which shows that the cash flow from privatization in the latter half of the decade has at times been appreciable in size. In 1987 – the peak year in proportional terms – receipts accounted for over 11% of total government revenues, and as much as 3.4% of GDP; substantial flows were recorded in 1989 as well. In cumulative terms, revenues from sales and leases up to and including 1989 equalled 9.5% of GDP and, if more recent transactions were included, would be well over the 10% mark. In international terms, this represents a substantial programme. However, despite this, it has not decisively changed the private/public sector balance. While it is true that SOE creation has largely come to a halt, due to the change in policy orientation of which privatization was a part, the forty or so transactions which make up the record of Jamaican privatization are still small when compared to the size of the remaining SOE sector. (As a corollary to this point, we note that privatization receipts equal less than one half of the public finance improvement brought about by reform of the 21 largest SOEs, at 9.5% versus 21.8% of GDP respectively.) This is, of course, reflected both in the size of the PNP's privatization pipeline, and in the fact that a significant number of the major public enterprises remain in government ownership, despite concerted attempts at sale.

Second, the Jamaican story clearly indicates the importance of programme design in achieving successful privatization, especially when multiple objectives coincide and conflict. We have analysed these issues in detail both in Chapter 4 and in section 3.4 of this chapter. Here we summarize by suggesting that the government has focused excessively on privatization as an end in itself, rather than as a means to raising efficiency in the firm and the economy as a whole. While some efficiency-enhancing sales have undoubtedly been achieved, in important cases privatizations have been designed in such a way as to reduce their long-run welfare-raising potential. Most important has been the lack of attention paid to competition and regulation policy: without a more serious effort here, the programme will remain flawed. Also of interest is the interaction between the politics and economics of privatization. On the one hand, there is evidence that personal commitment from Prime Minister Seaga was important in galvanizing the programme in the second half of the 1980s. On the other hand, the political controversy surrounding privatization and the reputational weakness of the government were critical sources of elements in the design of transactions that departed from the economic optimum. But, finally, in some senses the major success of privatization in the 1980s in Jamaica was that it established itself as part of the political consensus, allowing a more technocratic orientation to emerge by the beginning of the 1990s.

Third, analysis of aggregate data highlights some of the important structural features of privatization in Jamaica. (These data were consolidated in Chapter 4, and are not shown separately here.) Looking at privatization proceeds by method of sale, over half of privatization revenues (excluding leases) have come from private sales to foreign investors, with public share sales comprising roughly 30% of total revenues, and sales to the domestic private sector comprising only 15%. This is in spite of the fact that, of 29 public and private sales, 15 were to the domestic private sector and only 6 were to foreign buyers. A similar skewedness is found in privatization proceeds by function of enterprise. Here, although revenues from sales of commerce/manufacturing/services and transport/communications enterprises are roughly half each of total revenues, 21 of the former were sold as against 4 of the latter. Combining these two categorizations shows that Jamaican privatization has rested on three main mechanisms. The highest number of sales has been of commerce/manufacturing/services enterprises to the domestic private sector: these, however, have been of small size on average. For larger sales measured by average size of proceeds, the government has relied either on public share sales or sales to the foreign sector. In the latter case, sales of telecommunications have figured prominently. This pattern of sales reflects the constraints that the structure of the Jamaican economy has placed on the programme. Most notably, while mobilization of domestic savings has not yet been a problem in public share sales, it seems clear that the domestic private sector is not of sufficient size to absorb or manage the larger firms that the government wishes to sell. For this, it has had to call on foreign entrepreneurship. Documenting these points is the subject of the following two sections.

Table 7.15 *Jamaican privatization cash flow*

		1981	1982	1983	1984	1985	1986	1987	1988	1989	1990	Total (Cumul.)	Average 1986–9
Number of transactions[a]		1	2	1	2	5	7	6	4	9	3	40	7
Receipts (J$m.)	Sales	1.2	0.0	0.0	0.0	39.8	95.6	483.6	110.3	585.0	n.a.	1,315.5	318.6
	Leases	0.0	1.7	9.1	24.0	50.1	46.9	66.1	75.9	74.9	n.a.	348.7	66.0
	Total	1.2	1.7	9.1	24.0	89.9	142.5	549.7	186.2	659.9	n.a.	1,664.2	384.6
As % of total govt revenues	Sales	0.08	0.00	0.00	0.00	1.27	2.19	9.95	2.02	7.82	n.a.	23.33	5.75
	Leases	0.00	0.10	0.51	0.90	1.59	1.08	1.36	1.39	1.00	n.a.	7.93	1.19
	Total	0.08	0.10	0.51	0.90	2.86	3.27	11.31	3.41	8.82	n.a.	31.26	6.94
As % of GDP (market prices)	Sales	0.02	0.00	0.00	0.00	0.32	0.66	2.97	0.60	2.64	n.a.	7.21	1.79
	Leases	0.00	0.03	0.12	0.24	0.40	0.32	0.41	0.41	0.34	n.a.	2.28	0.37
	Total	0.02	0.03	0.12	0.24	0.72	0.99	3.37	1.02	2.98	n.a.	9.49	2.16
Memorandum Items (J$m.):													
Total Govt Revenues[b]		1,502.7	1,649.5	1,790.9	2,667.9	3,143.3	4,361.1	4,861.6	5,466.3	7,477.7	n.a.		5,541.7
GDP[c]		5,350.3	6,142.9	7,576.5	9,856.3	12,496.1	14,456.9	16,307.1	18,292.1	22,133.4	n.a.		17,797.4

Notes
a) This counts the number of separate transactions rather than the number of firms sold. See Table 7.4 for details. Land leases and sales are excluded. One hotel lease counted for each year.
b) Govt Revenues for 1988 are preliminary and for 1989 are estimates. Sources: World Bank and Bank of Jamaica.
c) Estimate for 1989. Source: Jamaica Five Year Development Plan, 1990–95.

Table 7.16 *GDP by sector of origin, 1986*

	Current price J$m.	%
Agriculture, Forestry & Fishing	820.0	6.2
Mining & Quarrying	901.7	6.8
Manufacturing	3,028.5	22.7
Electricity & Water	403.5	3.0
Construction & Installation	1,018.3	7.6
Distribution	2,811.2	21.1
Transport & Communications	1,084.1	8.1
Finance & Insurance	964.1	7.2
Real Estate & Business Services	1,089.5	8.2
Government Services	1,292.2	9.7
Miscellaneous Services	593.4	4.5
Non-Profit Institutions	111.3	0.8
Imputed Service Charges	−787.6	−5.9
GDP at market prices	13,312.1	100.0

7.4 The structure of the private sector and limits to competition

As argued in the opening chapters of this book, the private sector's characteristics are a crucial feature in determining the scope and effectiveness of privatization. The size, breadth, depth and openness of the sector affect both the privatization options available to a government and the performance of an enterprise after sale by determining the intensity of competition. However, in common with almost all developing countries, information on the structure of Jamaica's private sector is unsatisfactory, making a detailed analysis impossible. The limited disaggregated data that are available refer solely to the manufacturing sector, and have a historical/policy perspective rather than focusing on structure and concentration. As a first cut, though, before turning to manufacturing, we can draw some broad conclusions from aggregate GDP data. Analysis of Table 7.16 and knowledge of Jamaica's larger SOEs lead to the conclusion that, for some important sectors of the economy, SOEs dominate. For example, output in the electricity and water sector is provided exclusively by a small number of SOEs (JPSCo and NWC), as was the case in transport and communications until the privatization of ToJ and, less importantly, JOS. In some parts of agriculture, in mining and in distribution, a small number of SOEs play important, though not monopolistic, roles. Naturally, this is not the case in all sectors; as we saw earlier, both the finance and tourism sectors have a sufficient number of firms to promote competition, and in the urban transportation sector the government simultaneously privatized and deregulated, thereby creating a competitive market. The key point is that for a major portion of Jamaica's GDP, output is dominated by firms which have substantial market power, in contradistinction to the perfectly competitive paradigm. This market power would exist whether the said firms were publicly- or privately-owned unless a strong pro-competition framework surrounded the asset transfers.

Broadly speaking, then, a number of Jamaica's sectors appear monopolistic or oligopolistic.[62] More detailed information, though, is available for the largest sector: manufacturing.

Table 7.17 *Salient data for Jamaica's manufacturing subsectors, 1978*

Subsector	Number of Large Establishments[a]	Subsectors % of 1978 Value Added	Imported Inputs % of Total Sales 1964	1978
Food processing	157	23.0	15.4	49.8
Beverages	8	15.8	7.2	39.5
Tobacco	7	12.2	18.6	64.5
Textiles	136	4.4	36.9	34.0
Footwear	29	2.7	52.0	19.0
Leather products	4	0.7	52.0	30.8
Furniture	44	2.3	23.2	31.3
Paper and paper products	57	4.6	60.0	32.5
Metal products	119	11.4	64.4	59.7
Chemicals	78	10.7	35.4	33.2
Other	114	12.2	n.a.	n.a.
Total/Average	753	100.0	18.7	43.4

Sources: Ayub, 1981 and authors' calculations.

a) Firms with more than 10 employees and sales in 1978 greater than J$500,000.

Since independence, the manufacturing sector has increased in importance and range.[63] In 1950, it accounted for just 11.3% of GDP: this share rose to 15.7% in 1970, 18.2% in 1977 and 22.7% in 1986, at which time it employed 131,000 persons, or 12.2% of the labour force. Its most impressive feature, though, is its relative diversity. For a country of only 2.5 million inhabitants, the range of products is impressive. Although much of Jamaica's output is concentrated in the traditional developing country comparative-advantage goods (i.e. textiles, footwear, food processing), there are significant machinery and electrical equipment industries. Furthermore, as Table 7.17 shows, in some of the most important industries (i.e. food processing, textiles, metal products and chemicals) there are a considerable number of large establishments, suggesting, at first glance, a depth to the manufacturing sector unusual for a developing country of Jamaica's size.

However, this appearance of diversity covers a variety of structural problems that are rooted in the sector's historical development. Broadly speaking, the growth of Jamaican manufacturing was shaped by two government policies, namely industrial incentives legislation and a vigorous policy of import substitution. Industrial incentives legislation was instituted in the 1950s, and took the form of income tax exemptions, duty-free imports, generous depreciation allowances and tax-free dividends. By all accounts it was important in providing the initial impetus to industrial activity: in the 1950s, manufacturing grew at an average annual rate of 7.6%. Continued growth of the sector, though, was increasingly explained by the policy of import substitution, for which the chosen

Table 7.18 *Number of items under import restrictions, 1961–82*

Product	1961	1964	1968	1973	1979	1980	1982
Consumer goods	44	58	128	164	272	310	314
Raw materials & intermediate goods	3	5	15	16	26	30	22
Capital goods	3	9	15	21	36	40	30
Total	50	72	158	201	334	380	366

Sources: Ayub, 1981 and World Bank, 1989a.

policy instrument was an increasing array of quantitative restrictions (QRs) rather than tariffs, which remained at moderate levels. As Table 7.18 shows, the number of items under import restrictions grew rapidly in the 1960s. Although growth rates initially remained high, by the early 1970s, the manufacturing sector slowed down until, in the late 1970s, it started to contract (between 1974 and 1980, average annual growth in manufacturing was -4.6%). This contraction was the result both of the general macroeconomic crisis of the time and of the specific structural weaknesses of the sector arising from these government policies.

Government policy oriented the sector in the following ways. First, duty-free imports of capital goods, depreciation allowances, and QRs on final products induced a high capital intensity of manufacturing production, in a country which is labour-abundant. Second, by the mid-1970s, Jamaican manufacturing had become characterized by low domestic value-added, and a high import dependency. As Table 7.17 shows, the average import intensity of manufacturing increased from 18.7% in 1964 to 43.4% in 1978. This was a response both to the duty-free import rule and to the increasingly overvalued exchange rate. Third, the structure of protection led to a bias in production in favour of domestic and CARICOM markets. Effective protection coefficients calculated for 1978 were 1.68 for domestic sales, 1.19 for exports to CARICOM, and 0.90 for other exports. This anti-export bias arose from the nature of the government's trade policies and was worsened by the exchange-rate appreciation. These characteristics resulted in a manufacturing sector which was very vulnerable to the shocks of the 1970s. Simultaneously, low domestic demand and a shortage of foreign exchange for imports caused the sector to shrink, as it was unable to redirect production to exports. By the end of the 1970s, these problems resulted in low rates of capacity utilization: as Ayub reports, in 1978 the mean rate of capacity utilization in manufacturing was only 56%.

More importantly for our study, government policies aimed at the growth of manufacturing also strongly affected the extent of industrial concentration. The key instrument here was the method of granting QRs on individual products. According to Ayub (1981: 34–5):

> . . . The size of the quota has been determined by the gap between domestic demand and domestic supply. Thus, where an approved firm's installed capacity can meet domestic demand, it is subject to no foreign competition. In addition, it is rare for more than one firm to be approved for the same product . . . [hence] there are powerful barriers to domestic competition once the initial firm has been established.

The outcome of such a regime was the creation of a mostly monopolistic and oligopolistic rather than a competitive manufacturing sector. For a large number of products, domestic production was accounted for by either a small number of firms or only one firm. Of the major subsectors, only clothing, furniture and footwear had low levels of industrial concentration in terms of both sales and employment, and imports accounted for a significant fraction of consumption in only a few products.

Given the structural problems of the sector and the reversal in the 1970s of some of the progress made in the previous two decades, it was clear that reform was required. Thus, in the 1980s the government attempted to strengthen the sector through institutional reform of supporting agencies, the Modernization of Industry Programme, and revision of corporate taxation legislation. Most important, though, was the reform of trade policy aimed at promoting export-led growth via the elimination of anti-export biases and abandonment of the strategy of import substitution. To this end, QRs were progressively abandoned, import licensing was phased out, price controls were lifted, import duty exemptions were

Table 7.19 *Growth rates of manufacturing subsectors*

	1977–80	1980–83	1984	1985	1986	1987
Food	−32.7	16.7	8.3	−7.3	10.6	5.7
Sugar, molasses & rum	−17.0	−12.0	−6.8	11.5	−3.7	−7.8
Beverages	2.7	−14.3	−5.7	4.6	7.8	2.9
Tobacco & products	4.9	8.7	−5.2	−1.3	−12.8	10.9
Food and agribusiness	−12.2	1.8	−0.8	−1.2	2.0	5.3
Textiles & apparels	−35.2	−21.0	30.1	19.4	29.5	36.5
Leather & products	0.0	66.7	−20.0	40.0	14.3	−12.5
Footwear	−49.5	−13.0	−6.4	0.0	−15.9	0.0
Wood & wood products	−40.3	−15.0	8.8	13.5	7.1	4.4
Furnitures & fixtures	−51.5	24.5	18.0	−5.6	−16.2	12.3
Paper & products, printing	5.4	1.9	7.6	−8.8	14.8	−2.2
Petroleum refining	−10.2	13.9	−41.6	48.8	0.0	−32.3
Chemicals & plastics	−19.5	35.4	−5.0	−5.5	10.1	13.6
Non-metallic products	−48.9	68.1	−3.3	−1.7	6.1	3.3
Metal products	−31.8	37.0	−12.7	−8.4	−4.1	7.7
Other	−33.3	30.0	−3.8	20.0	0.0	3.3
Total	−19.7	10.5	−4.2	0.5	3.7	5.2

Source: Statistical Institute of Jamaica.

discontinued and the exchange rate was successively devalued. As Table 7.19 shows, these reforms appear to have had some effect, in that manufacturing value-added in general grew between 1980 and 1987. However, in the most buoyant sector – textiles – most growth occurred in the Free Zones which were designed explicitly for the export sector and contribute little to the efficiency or competitiveness of the domestic sector at large. In fact, despite the government's reform package, there appears to have been very little structural change in the sector in the 1980s. Shares of value-added have, with the exception again of textiles, remained broadly constant, with manufacturing continuing to be dominated by the agribusiness subsector.

This failure of the reform programme to make a dramatic impact is not altogether surprising. One problem has been that, despite the changes in trade policy, by the mid-1980s, the protection regime had worsened. Table 7.20 documents the point. The cause of this failure lay in the partial way in which trade liberalization was implemented. Widespread *ad hoc* exemptions from import duties were granted to a large number of firms, with the result that less than half of all imports were liable for duties. Where imports might compete with domestic industry, the reference prices on which duties were assessed were set at artificially high levels so that, in some cases, actual duty charged could be as high as treble the cif price. This device afforded a high degree of protection to food and steel producers.

Despite the dearth of recent data on the current structure and concentration of the manufacturing sector, the above evidence suggests that there has been little

Table 7.20 *Effective protection coefficients*

	Domestic sales	*Caricom sales*	*Other markets*
1978	1.68	1.19	0.90
1986	1.75	1.30	0.90

Source: World Bank, Operations Evaluation Department, 1989.

change from the pattern of the late 1970s. Casual empirical evidence reinforces this suggestion. Examples of oligopolistic price-fixing in domestic markets are often cited by government officials and the press; in some cases, as with bread, these have occurred after the decontrol of prices. It appears, then, that the manufacturing sector reflects in miniature the structure of Jamaica's GDP, i.e. although some markets are competitive, an important subset are monopolistic or oligopolistic. As suggested in Chapter 2, these markets will not provide privatized firms with the environment in which maximum economic efficiency and welfare will be attained.

Another source of competition can come via foreign investment. Jamaica's history of foreign investment regulation mirrors that of most developing countries. After a period of openness, the more 'nationalist' economic policy of the 1970s aimed to capture the 'commanding heights' of the economy from foreign control. However, the arrival of the JLP government resulted in a fundamental reorientation of policy, and under successive structural adjustment programmes various measures were undertaken aimed at promoting direct foreign investment. For example, in 1981 the government set up an investment promotion agency, the Jamaica National Investment Programme, and later consolidated it (with the Jamaica Industrial Development Corporation and the Jamaica National Export Corporation) into JAMPRO, a 'one-stop' promotion agency. Other aspects of the bureaucratic process were also streamlined. Rules governing the repatriation of dividends and profits were gradually liberalized over the decade, and the banning of foreign investment from certain sectors was eventually scrapped. The government signed both the OPIC Agreement and the MIGA Convention. The JLP and the current PNP Governments both made it clear that they welcomed direct foreign investment. Despite these efforts, though, new direct foreign investment has remained small, with only two years of positive net inflows in the period 1980–88. Thus, although the government would welcome the competitive impulse of direct foreign investment, it seems that foreign capital will not play a major role in broadening or deepening private sector market structures in the near to medium term.

7.4.1 Summary and new policy directions
We have seen that Jamaica's private sector does not provide a generally competitive environment, nor is the threat of foreign investment sufficient to enforce competitive behaviour through contestability. Although certain sectors and subsectors stand out as counter-examples, the main feature of both the manufacturing sector and the primary and services sectors is a sufficient degree of market concentration to allow firms to wield market power via strategic behaviour, with the attendant negative consequences for efficiency and welfare. While, thanks to the poor database, there is no matching of SOEs to economic subsectors, the implication for the privatization programme is clear. To the extent that the government can (i) privatize into an already competitive market, (ii) enhance market competition through simultaneous sales in a sector, or (iii) create a competitive market through deregulation carried out as part of the privatization package (or vice versa), then it can expect efficiency gains to be realized. In Jamaica, as we showed in section 7.3, all of these are possible and in some cases have been implemented – an example of (i) is NCB, of (ii) are the hotels, and of (iii) is JOS. However, given the nature of the private sector, options (i) and (ii) appear limited essentially to agribusiness and land sales, and hence the conclusion of section 7.3 is reinforced: if privatization is to fulfil the goal of raising economic efficiency, the government must pay substantially more attention to competition policy. What an analysis of the private sector adds to this conclusion, though, is that this should be done

not just in order to improve the privatization programme, but for the much more important reason of general private sector development.

To its credit, this is precisely the direction that the current government is taking. The PNP's shift toward a policy (and associated legislation) oriented around competition and deregulation reflects two motives. The first is to respond to criticisms of the privatization programme to date. The second is that an active pro-competition policy can be portrayed as radical and anti-elitist (and thus in the political tradition of the PNP) since its aim is to break up oligopoly markets, whose participants have in the past held substantial economic power in Jamaica. Thus, this type of policy can be located at a curious convergence point between conservatism (= free markets) and socialism (= anti-elitism). The PNP's statement on competition maintains the following as objectives:[64]

1) to provide for competition, rivalry in markets and to secure economic efficiency in trade and commerce,
2) to promote consumer welfare and to protect consumer interests, and
3) to open markets and guard against undue concentration of economic power.

To attain this, the government intends to pass a Competition Act, and to establish a Fair Trading and Monopolies Commission. After making it clear that there will be no legal impediment to 'normal aggressive commercial behaviour', a pledge repeated several times, the government proposes that the features of the Competition Act will be:

1) prohibitions on agreements among competitors that restrict competition and injure customers;
2) prohibitions on those mergers that create or enhance dominant firms, and
3) prohibitions on practices by dominant firms that create or maintain artificial barriers to entry or unfair market position.

In particular, it intends to address the problems of restrictive business agreements and practices, consumer unfairness practices, mergers and dominant market positions, and interlocking directorates. The Act would thus make illegal cartel-type arrangements (formal or informal) to fix prices, divide or restrict output and rig bids, as well as prohibiting a firm's use of market power to engage in predatory conduct or other actions aimed at frustrating competition. Although public utilities are exempted from the terms of the proposed Act, the new Commission will have the authority to investigate utilities with the aim of recommending policies in the sectors that would promote competition. Furthermore, if passed, the Act and the Commission would provide a useful framework for scrutinizing proposed privatizations from the standpoint of competition, and thus maybe avoid the privatization of un- (or inadequately) regulated enterprises, as has occurred in the past. Of course, while the legislation appears a promising start, competition policy will only be successful if the new Commission is given adequate power in practice and is supported by the political leadership.

7.5 Privatization, resource mobilization, and capital markets

In contrast to the private sector, better information is available on resource mobilization and the financial sector. For a low–middle-income country, Jamaica has a well-developed financial sector and a reasonably-sized capital market. On account of the priority accorded to capital market (i.e. the Jamaica Stock Exchange) development in the programme, Jamaican privatization offers an interesting study of its dynamic effects on the JSE. Despite imperfections in the

Table 7.21 *Savings and investment, 1977–87 (J$m.)*

	Average 1977–80	1981	1982	1983	1984	1985	1986	1987
Investment	623.4	1,077.2	1,224.4	1,556.6	2,154.5	2,786.2	2,468.4	3,558.4
Foreign savings	175.0	668.2	712.8	720.4	1,226.2	1,672.3	675.3	828.9
Domestic savings	448.4	409.0	511.6	836.2	928.3	1,113.9	1,793.1	2,729.5
o/w – Public	−209.8	−212.6	−603.1	−139.0	−110.0	606.1	672.3	879.6
– Private	658.2	621.6	1,114.7	975.2	1,038.3	507.8	1,120.8	1,849.9
As % of GDP								
Investment	15.5	20.4	20.9	22.3	23.0	25.0	18.5	22.6
Foreign savings	4.1	12.6	12.1	10.3	13.1	15.0	5.1	5.3
Domestic savings	11.4	7.8	8.8	12.0	9.9	10.0	13.4	17.3
o/w – Public	−5.4	−4.0	−10.3	−2.0	−1.2	5.4	5.1	5.6
– Private	16.9	11.8	19.1	14.0	11.1	4.6	8.3	11.7

Source: World Bank, 1989a.

latter, evidence suggests that these are being dealt with through general reforms, and that privatization has in general had a positive impact on the stock exchange's development.

7.5.1 Domestic savings and the financial sector

Unlike Malaysia, Jamaica has traditionally not had a high rate of total domestic savings, and a sizeable portion of investment has been financed out of foreign savings. Although a variety of structural adjustment measures implemented in the 1980s aimed at raising savings rates, the problem has not been solved. As Table 7.21 shows, despite a substantial turnaround in the public sector, the performance of total domestic savings in the first half of the 1980s was worse than that of the late 1970s.

One might assume from this that the efficiency of resource mobilization was weak. In fact, the opposite is the case. Jamaica possesses an impressive array of financial institutions acting as intermediaries between savers and users of savings. Apart from the central bank, as at June 1990 there were 11 commercial banks (total assets J$16.1bn), 21 merchant banks (total assets J$4.3bn), 5 finance houses, 3 trust companies, 9 life insurance companies, 18 general insurance companies, 6 building societies, 2 development banks, 2 unit trusts, 91 credit unions and 1 recently established venture capital company (Iton, 1990). Furthermore, in contrast to other developing countries, the commercial banking sector is mostly domestically-owned,[65] and is oriented towards domestic rather than low-risk, developed-country money markets. On account of the range of institutions, there is also little of the lending dualism that plagues financial systems in other developing countries. These facts betoken a level of financial sophistication unusual for a country of Jamaica's size and income, which is clearly advantageous to a carefully planned programme of privatization.

7.5.2 The Jamaica Stock Exchange (JSE)

Within this financial sector, the key institution for privatization has been the JSE, the strengthening and deepening of which has been an important goal of policy in the 1980s. According to Iton (1990), organized trading in corporate securities started in 1961, when the Kingston Stock Market Committee was set up under the Bank of Jamaica. The JSE superseded this committee in 1969, having been incorporated in 1968 as a private company owned by its broker members. Three types of securities have been listed on the JSE: ordinary shares, preference shares and

Table 7.22 *JSE market performance 1980–90*

		Market Index	Trading Value (J$ '000)	Trading Volume ('000)	Market Capitalization (J$m.)	No. of Firms Listed
1980		66.58	5,101	7,390	124.1	
1981		152.23	3,332	4,196	225.8	
1982		211.16	10,156	5,542	316.0	
1983		240.38	9,820	5,185	359.2	32
1984		461.10	26,027	9,744	697.7	31
1985		941.50	116,679	37,641	1,456.6	32
1986		1,499.87	358,512	59,252	3,085.8	35
1987		1,515.09	399,971	71,876	3,468.7	39
1988		1,439.22	136,738	43,521	4,297.1	40
1989		2,075.85	516,431	95,215	6,228.4	40
1990	QI	1,904.43	40,405	8,974	5,485.9	
	QII	2,191.75	39,190	9,202	6,319.1	40

Source: Stock Exchange Yearbooks 1980–84, 1986, 1988 & 1989, Bank of Jamaica Annual Reviews, Mayberry Investments Ltd and Iton, 1990.

corporate bonds. However, in general there has been very little activity in the latter two, and hence we focus our attention on the ordinary share sector.

The record of the JSE as a primary market has been disappointing. As Table 7.23 shows, few companies have chosen to use it as a source of new capital. The record is worse in the 1970s, when only 4 companies issued new shares on the JSE. In general, firms have preferred to expand equity through stock bonuses and rights issues. The reasons for this general lack of new issues are as follows. First, business financing has historically been dominated by the commercial banking sector, so that firms had little need to access capital through the JSE. This dominance was reinforced by the prevalence of interlocking directorates between financial and non-financial enterprises. Second, the tax regime has in the past been biased against equity financing, both through the tax deductibility of interest charges and through double taxation of dividends, so that firms had little incentive to use the JSE.

However, Table 7.24 also suggests that, in this area, privatization has had a positive impact on equity markets. The Seprod, NCB and CCC transactions were

Table 7.23 *New issues on the Jamaican Stock Exchange*

Company	Year	J$m.
Life of Jamaica Ltd	1970	0.76
Workers Saving and Loan Bank	1973	0.50
Guiness Jamaica Ltd	1973	0.78
Gleaner Company Ltd	1978	4.00
Royal Bank of Jamaica Ltd	1982	2.92
Carreras Group Ltd	1982	3.16
Seprod Group Ltd	1985	39.80
NCB Group Ltd	1986	88.70
Caribbean Cement Co. Ltd	1987	157.40
Hardware and Lumber Ltd	1987	8.00
CIBC Jamaica Ltd	1988	31.00
ToJ Ltd	1988	108.50
Mutual Security Bank	1989	32.00
Jamaica Citizens Bank	1990	20.00

Sources: Iton, 1990, and own data.

Table 7.24 *Top ten companies by market capitalization: 1985, 1988 and 1989*

Ass. with Priv.	1988 ranking and name	(1989 rank)	Value (J$m.)		
			1985	*1988*	*1989*
*	1. Telecommunications of Jamaica Ltd	(2)	–	917.40	820.83
	2. Bank of Nova Scotia	(1)	203.28	569.18	1,048.92
	3. Desnoes and Geddes	(3)	100.00	479.17	415.48
*	4. National Commercial Bank	(7)	–	237.00	303.00
*	5. Caribbean Cement Ltd	(13)	–	210.04	150.04
	6. Wray and Nephew Group	(9)	180.00	180.00	248.70
	7. Carreras	(4)	91.02	166.11	391.39
	8. Grace Kennedy and Company	(8)	278.69	153.28	277.16
	9. Lascelles	(5)	136.80	144.00	386.40
*	10. Jamaica Banana Producers' Association	(11)	132.80	133.96	218.69
	Other:				
*	Seprod Group		62.51	85.82	88.34
*	W.I. Pulp and Paper		2.24	4.68	21.26
	Total market capitalization (J$m.):		1,456.60	4,297.07	6,228.40
	Firms associated with privatizations as % of total		4.4	37.0	25.7
	Value of four largest capitalizations (J$m.):		798.77	2.202.75	2,676.62
	Value of ten largest capitalizations (J$m.):		1,383.13	3,190.15	4,423.80
	Four-firm concentration ratio by capitalization:		54.8%	51.3%	43.0%
	Ten-firm concentration ratio by capitalization:		95.0%	74.2%	71.0%
	Four-firm concentration ratio by volume of equity traded:		60.2%	36.9%	43.9%
	Ten-firm concentration ratio by volume of equity traded:		75.8%	59.5%	71.1%

Sources: Stock Exchange Yearbook 1988, Mayberry Investments Ltd, authors' work.

instrumental both in reasserting the possibilities of primary issues on the JSE and in substantially raising estimates of the market's capacity. The fact that other firms subsequently issued new shares on the JSE is considered by many to be an important achievement of the privatization programme.

As a secondary market, the JSE has shown a similar trajectory. After remaining broadly constant in the years 1969–72, the JSE market index dropped considerably during the unpropitious 1970s on the back of declining trading volumes and values and a fall in the number of listed firms, due to delistings following nationalizations and takeovers. During the 1980s, a decade-long bull market emerged. The market index rose from 53.71 at the end of 1979 to 2,075.85 at the end of 1989 – a 3,700% nominal gain. Similarly, the volume and value of transactions and the number of listed companies all increased. Most importantly, there was a considerable deepening of the JSE: market capitalization as a percentage of GDP rose from 2.5% in 1980 to 28.1% in 1989, and the number of individual shareholders increased by roughly 30,000, thanks to the privatization issues. As we saw in Chapter 5, the JSE was the only stock exchange in our country studies to make significant real gains in the 1980s.

Despite this impressive performance, the JSE was afflicted by important weaknesses. Although trading intensified in the 1980s, there was very little aggressive equity acquisition of the sort consistent with the existence of a plausible takeover threat. Also, while the number of firms listed increased, few of these were the medium-sized firms that the JSE was hoping to attract in order to bring a greater diversity and dynamism to the market. Furthermore, it is widely accepted that prices on the JSE are essentially managed by a narrow cartel of brokers – the result of the key institutional deficiency of the JSE, namely the absence of securities legislation. While, as a self-regulating body, the JSE has some power over its members (i.e. brokers and listed companies), there is inadequate investor protection and no legal sanction against insider trading. As a consequence, it is admitted by those within the exchange that insider trading and market manipulation are rampant. This has had the effect of keeping potential investors away from the market and limiting the trading of the tranche of new investors introduced to the JSE in the 1980s. In a 1989 survey of the latter group (Stone, 1989) 65% of dissatisfied investors gave market manipulation as the cause of their disquiet.[66]

7.5.3 *The impact of privatization on the JSE*

As we have emphasized throughout, capital market development was high among the priorities of Jamaican privatization. This was on account of both the free market orientation of the JLP Government and also the opportunities for political capital to be made from wider share ownership. In contrast to other countries, the capital market has not proved a binding constraint on the Jamaican privatization programme. Of course, the substantial recourse to the JSE that the Jamaican Government has made has meant that the privatization programme has brought the weaknesses of the JSE into sharper focus: this has, however, forced policy-makers to look more seriously at strengthening the institution than they otherwise might have done. We look at the various effects of the privatization programme on the JSE in turn.

First, privatization has clearly had a substantial impact on the value of equity traded on the JSE. As Table 7.24 shows, at its peak in 1988, the capitalization of firms associated with the privatization programme comprised 37% of total market capitalization. Similarly, the same firms comprised 26 and 39% of stocks traded by value and volume respectively. Thus, privatization reinforced the bull-run that was already occurring in the 1980s. From Table 7.23, it is clear that Seprod, NCB and CCC were the first sizeable new issues on the JSE – in the case of CCC involving a value of equity equal to more than 5% of the then market capitalization. Not only did public share sales encourage private firms to arrange primary issues, as mentioned earlier, but they also decisively raised the accepted absorptive capacity of the market. However, doing this involved risks, and it is likely that only a privatization issue, which is underwritten by government, could have achieved this result.

Privatization has also been associated with increases in the volume and value of secondary trading in the second half of the 1980s. Trading volumes rose tenfold over the period 1984–9, an unambiguous sign of greater dynamism in the market. Though causality cannot be established, JSE officials suggest that the nature of privatization equity as 'blue chip' stocks and the demonstration effect of the primary issues were significant factors in explaining this dynamism. Furthermore, despite the substantial size of sales, the privatization programme has not adversely skewed the risk structure of the JSE in the manner of other countries discussed in Chapter 5. As Table 7.24 shows, the privatization programme has been associated with declines in the four- and ten-firm concentration ratios of market capitalization, from 55 to 43% and from 95 to 71% respectively. With regard to trading volumes, equivalent concentration ratios show similar declines. This broadening of both capitalization and trading is potentially an important development, as it betokens a transformation from an underdeveloped and underused capital market to one where risks are being genuinely intermediated.

In one respect, though, the positive impact of privatization on the JSE has not been as great as claimed, namely the effect of the introduction of a large number of new players into the market. Before the mid-1980s, JSE individual stockholders were overwhelmingly from the higher income segment of the population, namely top managers and company directors. However, through a combination of asset under-pricing (in the NCB sale) and a share distribution scheme which dramatically favoured the smaller investor (NCB, CCC and ToJ), the government succeeded in introducing almost 30,000 new investors into the market in the period 1985–7. These new investors came from a lower income bracket, were mostly clerical, secretarial and technical employees, and – perhaps surprisingly – were predominantly female. Thus the government succeeded partially in one objective, namely the democratization of share ownership. However, it was also believed that these new investors would become aggressive market players, and thereby raise the efficiency of risk intermediation through the JSE. There is firm evidence, though, that this has not materialized. First, according to the JSE, trading remains dominated by pension funds and other institutional investors. Second, despite opportunities for making considerable financial gains (or averting losses in the case of CCC), very little trading in privatized equity by small investors has occurred. Indeed, the number of shareholders in NCB, CCC and ToJ has remained remarkably constant at around 30,000, 24,000, and 17,000 respectively.[67]

Third, evidence from AGMs of the privatized companies suggests that a substantial number of shareholders have little conception of the nature or tradability of the asset they are holding.[68] We discussed in Chapter 5 the problems that attracting this type of player pose for capital market development, and will not repeat that discussion here. However, the Jamaican case highlights the role of public education in ensuring the smooth development of the capital market. While the pre-privatization media blitz of NCB was clearly successful in attracting buyers, it was not sufficiently informative about the concept of equity and an equity market. The JSE itself believes this will require an ongoing campaign of public education, unrelated to the exigencies of any particular privatization transaction.

Furthermore, certain features of the design of privatizations through the JSE have worked to lessen the expected benefits of sales on capital market development. First, with regard to the underpricing of the NCB shares, the same arguments concerning moral hazard and adverse selection follow through from Chapter 5. Second, the ownership restrictions specified in the NCB and CCC public issues expressly work to limit the possibilities of aggressive speculation and takeover by making the latter illegal. This restricts the JSE's function as an efficiency-inducing weapon, and retards its development as a risk intermediator. Significantly, the current government, with the support of the JLP and the bank itself, is looking at ways of reversing by law the ownership restrictions embodied in NCB's Articles of Agreement.

Finally, the volume and close sequencing of the public share issues raised the profile of certain technical and institutional limitations of the JSE. While reform of these limitations would have occurred naturally given a gradual development of the JSE, the scale of privatization transactions gave reform a new urgency. On the technical side, increases in trading volumes and in the value of new placements inevitably demand evolution in market capacity. Thus, the JSE lengthened the trading week from 2 to 3 days (one hour per day), and is moving to automate the clearing and settlement system, which at the moment is done on a manual, call-over basis. It has also tightened its monitoring rules, by instigating quarterly reporting for listed companies, and introducing the compulsory disclosure both of directors' equity involvement and of the ten largest shareholders of a listed company. It is also putting pressure on the government finally to pass securities legislation (after 20 years of promises) so as to eliminate activities such as insider trading which sour the reputation of the exchange. Lastly, there have been developments in broadening the JSE. The JSE itself has examined the creation of new instruments to develop the capacity of capital markets to allocate risks competitively. This was supported by the government in its 5-Year Development Plan (1990–94) which announced its intention to develop a secondary market in government securities. More important have been regional developments, namely the creation in 1991 of the Caribbean Stock Exchange linking the three equity markets of Barbados, Jamaica and Trinidad and Tobago. If successful, this should increase both the volume and the competitiveness of financial intermediation in the region, with attendant benefits for the JSE as the dominant market of the troika.

In conclusion, then, the Jamaica story has largely been one of complementarities between privatization and capital market development. In general, equity markets have not constrained divestitures and will not do so except for sale of all the equity in a few of the largest SOEs. The privatization public share issues have been associated with a strengthening of equity markets, other than the disappointing performance of new players attracted to equity ownership. Furthermore, ongoing reforms and regionalization suggest that well-chosen, well-timed and well-managed sales could bring stronger benefits to the JSE. However, there has been one critical area of failure, namely the weak regulatory capacity of the JSE. This brings us to our final section.

7.6 Regulatory capacity and privatization

In Chapter 2, we presented at some length the case for regarding the regulatory capacity of government as of importance in determining the gains to be expected from a programme of privatization. In this brief section, we try to determine this capacity in Jamaica, although this exercise is difficult because the evidence is only fragmentary. Regulatory experience of the type discussed in Chapter 2 (i.e. of monopolies and oligopolies) is generally absent. Of course, this in itself is indicative of the lack of attention historically paid to such issues by the Jamaican Government. As effective regulation of enterprises is a complex operation with considerable learning-by-doing benefits, this lack of regulatory 'practice' in Jamaica betokens a certain weakness. However, where such relevant experience does exist, there is no great evidence of regulatory sophistication. Regulatory experience of a different sort is more common, but, as we suggest below, it is difficult to draw conclusions from this.

As in Trinidad and Tobago, at one point the government did institute a regulatory body for monopoly utilities.[69] This was the Public Utilities Commission (PUC), set up in 1966 specifically to regulate the operations of the power company (JPS) and the domestic telephone company (JTC), both of which, at that time, were foreign-owned. Regulatory control was set up on the basis of the North American example, specifically the Federal Power Commission. While initially the relationship between the PUC and the regulated firms was harmonious, this ceased after both firms applied for rate increases. The hearings to investigate the rate applications became increasingly adversarial, and were characterized by many of the problems that have featured in regulatory experience elsewhere. Both firms were found to have inflated their rate bases through questionable accounting practices in order to earn higher profits under rate-of-return regulation. Establishing an accurate measure of the rate base took up a substantial amount of the PUC's time during the hearings. Having done so, though, the PUC twice rejected proposed rate rises which it might otherwise have granted. The PUC hearings were also characterized by difficulties in obtaining the necessary information from the regulated firms. This in part explains the increasingly adversarial nature of the hearings. Finally, the PUC did not last long enough to solve the problematic issue of regulatory power. Although it was able to refuse rate increases, this was a very blunt instrument for getting the regulated utilities to carry out the investment programmes they were contractually obliged to undertake, and to improve the efficiency of their operations. The 'resolution' of these problems adopted by the then government was nationalization. However, this was clearly not a solution, not only did public ownership *not* improve the efficiency of the firms' operations but, more fundamentally, public takeover did not resolve the problem of regulatory power over foreign monopolists; it merely abolished it. Finally, the PUC itself was abolished in 1975 on the assumption that regulatory issues had been settled by the inauguration of state ownership.

While it is clearly invalid to suggest that the Jamaican Government's bureaucratic ability, and hence regulatory capacity, has remained at the same level as in the late 1960s, the experience of the PUC does at minimum suggest that monopoly regulation will be more problematic than is currently appreciated in the privatization programme. The issues that arose in the history of the PUC are similar both to those of regulatory experience in Trinidad and Tobago and in countries with a more extended regulatory record. In this regard, the way in which the Jamaican Government has dealt with the issue of monopoly regulation in the privatization programme to date does not inspire confidence. Not only was the question completely ignored in the CCC sale, but also – as repeatedly mentioned in earlier parts of this book – the new regulatory structure set up for ToJ was inadequate, and there seems no compelling reason why the disputes that plagued the PUC experience should not reappear under the current structure of telecommunications regulation. However, as noted in section 7.4, the promulgation of competition legislation also means that issues of monopoly regulation are gaining in importance in Jamaica, and it is therefore to be hoped that any future privatizations of monopoly enterprises will take these issues into account.

The regulation that the government has carried out in other sectors of the economy has not provided the basis for the effective regulation of monopolies. This is not to say that regulation elsewhere has been bad, merely that it has not provided appropriate experience. For example, as shown in Table 7.2, by 1980 there were at least 49 regulatory, distributional and promotional enterprises in existence in Jamaica (Brown and McBain, 1983). Few of these carried out activities that are usually regarded as the core regulatory responsibilities of government. Indeed, these core regulatory responsibilities have often been ignored, as shown with reference to the JSE in section 7.5 and to the public utilities above. Furthermore, those agencies with have an explicitly economic orientation have often carried out their regulatory responsibility in a manner ill-suited for transfer to monopoly regulation. A classic example of this is the Prices Commission, which conducted a blunt programme of price controls applied largely without regard to an enterprise's static costs or dynamic incentives. Similarly, regulation of foreign exchange, investment and trade controls essentially involved enforcement of quantity rationing schemes aimed at restricting access to rents. It is questionable whether a bureaucracy steeped in this type of control experience can rapidly make the transition to the more flexible, price-based systems intrinsic to monopoly regulation.

In conclusion, evidence of regulatory capacity in Jamaica is extremely sketchy. Although the current government is paying far more attention to competition and regulatory policy, the little evidence that does exist suggests at minimum that regulatory capacity is not strong. With regard to privatization, then, it would seem clear that in the case of sales of enterprises with actual or potential market power, very careful attention needs to be paid to the issue of regulatory design in order both to avoid the problems of the previous period of active regulation and to ensure that the expected allocative efficiency gains of privatization do indeed materialize. Such a strategy may involve a strong degree of caution before government locks itself into an egregious contract of the sort exemplified in the ToJ privatization.

7.7 Conclusions

In contrast to the enigmatic nature of privatization in Malaysia, the Jamaican programme offers an abundance of quirks and findings. In some sense, as we have suggested throughout, this abundance is in itself one of the lessons of the Jamaican case study. Despite a private sector of only limited depth and competitiveness, a capital market which up to the beginning of the programme had intermediated only small transactions, and a generally hostile macroeconomic environment, the Jamaican Government has been able to carry out a programme not only substantially larger than that of any other country in our sample, but also in proportional terms as large as that of the UK, the queen of privatizers. Furthermore, none of the transactions were marked by the outstanding failures documented in other countries. In many cases, especially the smaller NIBJ sales and hotels, privatization met the goals set for it by the government. In particular, there appear to have been mutual complementarities between the privatization programme and the development of the Jamaican Stock Exchange, through which most of the larger sales were instrumented. Thus, the diversity of the Jamaican programme suggests that political commitment and attention to programme design can provide the background for quite substantial programmes of privatization (in a quantitative sense) even in a relatively unpropitious environment such as the small island economy of Jamaica.

However, equally importantly, the Jamaican programme demonstrates just as validly the constraints to privatization consequent on the economic structures of low- and middle-income developing countries. The first of these is the length of time effective privatization can take, both in the sense that certain SOEs have been involved in more than a decade of reform effort and yet are still not sellable, and in the sense that rushed transactions may contain design faults sufficiently severe to compromise the objectives of sale. Second, as shown in section 7.3, the record of privatization in Jamaica shows that the programme has had to be built round the low absorptive capacity of the domestic private sector, with a bifurcated pattern of sales whereby small sales involve direct sale to domestic entrepreneurs, whereas large sales involve either public share issues or foreign participation. We have also tried to clarify the difference between a successful programme judged by the quantity of sales and one measured against the normative objectives of privatization. As is clear from the Malawi study, if a government is willing to focus on the goal of sale alone, then there is no reason why it should not be able to dispose of its entire equity holdings extremely rapidly. While this is clearly not the Jamaican case, there have been elements of this 'transactions-dominance', most notably in inadequate consideration of competition and regulation policy, especially given the weakness of regulatory capacity in the government as a whole, and a willingness to subordinate efficiency goals to other, less compelling, objectives of privatization.

Ultimately, though, privatization in Jamaica will stand or fall not by the multiplicity of its subsidiary objectives, but by its net contribution to welfare through its long-term impact on enterprise performance and efficiency. While our presumption is that, in a number of cases, privatization in Jamaica will achieve this goal, hard evidence is not yet available; hence, in this sense at least, the jury is still out.

Notes

1. The performance of the PUC and its implications for regulation policy in Jamaica are discussed further in section 7.6.
2. In fact, estimates of the number of enterprises varied widely, from a minimum of 249 to a maximum of 643.
3. As examples, consider the following. Despite making persistent losses, partly due to labour feather-bedding, the JRC was forbidden to raise fares or to retrench staff. JPSCo and JOS both faced substantial wage awards immediately after their acquisition by government (71% and 96% respectively), while being refused applications for increased rates. As a result, JPSCo's unit costs rose substantially after nationalization, while by 1980 JOS had only 165 operational buses out of a fleet of 598. Air Jamaica was a persistent loss-maker, and by 1980 was employing 1,194 staff for only 9 planes. In the sugar sector, the co-operatives that the government had set up on purchased sugar estates were adjudged by an official investigation to be virtually bankrupt and suffering from overerstaffing and poor management. JIDC, the umbrella organization for development of the manufacturing sector, was found in 1975 to be collecting 13% of rent on factory shells, had paid no interest or principal on its J$11m. loans from government, and was nurturing employment-intensive, loss-making enterprises.
4. Source: the Public Sector Register 1984/5 produced by the Administrative Staff College, Ministry of the Public Service, Government of Jamaica.
5. Note that the NIBJ was also given the responsibility for investigating and implementing the government's privatization strategy. Paradoxically, the ownership of NIBJ itself was obscure, as the capital structure of seven shares was owned by seven different private individuals. Not only was this an illegal arrangement, but it also made the NIBJ a private, not a public sector body.
6. For a list, see note to Table 7.3.
7. It is interesting to note that this close control of SOEs has provided an impetus towards privatization, in that enterprises would then be free from the (sometimes arbitrary) capital expenditure restrictions that fiscal austerity entailed, and able to have access to new sources of capital.
8. It is unclear whether the worsening of performance in 1988/9 reflects a diminution of the reform effort or the effect of Hurricane Gilbert. It has therefore been excluded from the analysis.
9. World Bank, *Program Performance Audit Report: Jamaica, Structural Adjustment Loans II and III*, Washington DC, 1989.
10. For an argument that, in practice, the Manley and Seaga Governments' economic policies differed far less than their rhetoric would suggest, see Harrigan's analysis (Mosley, Harrigan and Toye, 1991).
11. It should be noted that the adjustment loans of the early 1980s have come in for heavy criticism from the World Bank's own internal policy review body, the Operations Evaluation Department (OED). This concluded that poor loan design was 'costly to Jamaica's economy in terms of the income forgone, of the enormous build-up of foreign debt that now burdens the economy and of the prolonged human hardship'.
12. It was claimed by Jamaican government officials that USAID was pushing for very rapid privatization, more so than the multilateral bodies. Although USAID recognized that faster sale might mean forgoing substantial public revenues, it argued that the policy of privatization was more important than maximizing the fiscal impact.
13. It must be acknowledged, however, that the JLP's pro-free enterprise stance was sufficiently flexible to permit two significant expansions of the state sector during the early 1980s, namely the purchase of the oil refinery to avoid closure by Esso, and the increase from 6% to 50% in the GoJ's equity ownership of Jamalco after Alcoa also announced closure. The political cost of the implied rise in unemployment was clearly too high. Interestingly, the government's investment in and management of Jamalco proved so successful that by 1987 the original owners were negotiating for a return of control of the company to them.
14. Details from Kennedy, 1986.
15. For details, see Government of Jamaica Ministry Paper No. 45 (1984), *Kingston Metropolitan Region - Transport System*.

16. Figures for domestic market shares in 1984 were as follows:

Seprod market shares

Edible oils	90–95%
Margarine and shortening	100%
Toilet and household soaps	60–70%
Powdered detergents	90% (+ 50% of the Barbados market)
Animal feeds	25%
Cornmeal	100%

Source: Seprod Ltd, 'Share Prospectus – Offer for Sale', Kingston, 1985.

17. *Seprod financial performance*

	1980	1981	1982	1983	1984	1985
Turnover	101,285	115,162	117,935	157,958	228,957	324,225
Pre-Tax Profit	(2,847)	(7,190)	(6,171)	1,689	10,731	23,207
Post-Tax Profit	(3,670)	(7,441)	(6,171)	1,689	8,648	11,826

Source: Seprod (1985).

18. Interview, July 1990.
19. The bill for these professionals' services was paid by USAID.
20. Bank supervision is the responsibility of the Bank of Jamaica (BoJ). Although in general the BoJ's Bank Supervision Department is regarded as an efficient regulator, NCB is not the only financial institution to have gained from BoJ's less strict application of banking legialation: the Worker's Bank has been bankrupt, but as a result of political pressure has not had its licence removed.
21. This information is derived from Leeds (1987), and from interviews with Richard Downer and the Managing Director of NCB, Donald Banks.
22. NCB Group, '1986 Offer For Sale', NIBJ, Jamaica.
23. Interestingly, during the process of shaping the sale, it was proposed that the government should include a 'golden share' arrangement which would give it the power to intervene over strategic decisions in the firm after the sale of the majority of the equity. However, the government was advised that, if any such arrangement were made, small investors would simply not purchase equity, thereby frustrating the main objective of the sale.
24. Equal to 4.5 million shares, or 15% of the equity actually being sold.
25. Note that the calculation of the series for NCB takes as its starting-point the 'revealed' market price of the asset, as established at the end of the first day's trading. This removes any over- or under-pricing effect from the comparison.
26. One Jamaican civil servant described NCB underpricing as a subsidization of the socially-desirable goal of wider share ownership.
27. The existence of a public enterprise sector means that every citizen is an indirect shareholder.
28. Clinker is an intermediate product which, when combined with gypsum, produces cement.
29. Paradoxically, these are still tradable on the JSE alongside the privatized equity of CCC.
30. Through the requirement that CCC salaries be on the same scale as other parts of the public sector, the company found it was unable to match comparable private sector wage levels. Thus CCC appears to have been a case where salaries in an SOE were too low.
31. Note that the following discussion makes no attempt to stick to a chronological ordering. It is also useful to remember that all the preparations for the sale had to be completed in an extremely short time, between the announcement of the sale in January 1987 and completion in June of the same year.
32. Source: Interview with Richard Downer. Downer in fact expressed the opinion that the government offered too much to the company in the form of restructuring.
33. Later extended to 31 December 1989.
34. CCC raised its prices by 7.5% in June 1989 and by 20% the following November. This followed a period during which prices had been held constant or had risen by less than the rate of inflation.
35. In any case, this argument is theoretically implausible.
36. Telecommunications of Jamaica Ltd, 'Offer for Sale', the Accountant General, Kingston, 1988.
37. *Telephony* (1985), quoted in Roth (1987).
38. A UK firm that had itself been privatized in 1981.

39. For example, the 'Offer For Sale' document talks of a 5-year investment programme in JTC worth J$1.99bn. Not only would the government not be able to generate these funds, but furthermore a capital expenditure programme of this size could not have occurred under public ownership as it would have fallen foul of IMF restrictions.
40. The impetus to privatization from the need to tap into international technology and capital in the context of a credit-constrained government is present in a number of SOEs that have not yet been sold. See section 7.3.5, on future privatizations.
41. ToJ's nature as a holding company is demonstrated by a breakdown in 1988 of the 2,700 people employed by the three companies.

ToJ Group Employment

	ToJ	*JTC*	*JAMINTEL*
Engineering & Technical	0	1,102	62
Operators	0	427	42
General Administration	5	840	151
Total	5	2,369	255

42. Of course, telecommunications should have been regulated effectively while in public ownership where it was also a monopoly. In this case, privatization had the benefit of forcing the government to consider action it should already have taken.
43. Less charitable commentators argue that the public share offer was made in order to avoid charges of 'selling out'.
44. ToJ, 1988.
45. By this time, it may be noted, the JLP Government had been replaced by a PNP Government again headed by Michael Manley, but with a much-reformed political and economic orientation.
46. Confirmed by the Financial Controller of Jamintel.
47. In fact, the current government is being advised by the multilateral agencies to try to unstitch the agreement with ToJ in order to introduce competition in some of the areas suggested above.
48. Interview with the authors, July 1990.
49. The long time needed actually to sell the firms means that there has always been a substantial divestment pipeline.
50. Touche, Ross, Thorburn and Co., 'Auditors' Report to the Members of National Hotels and Properties Limited', Kingston, 1982.
51. Although there were 8 hotel sales in 1989, the price of only 5 of these sales are known to us. This figure is, therefore, an underestimate.
52. World Bank, *Jamaica: Adjustment Under Changing External Conditions* , Report No. 7753-JM, Washington DC, 1989.
53. Much of the information here is taken from World Bank (1989a)Annex I on agriculture.
54. It is unclear whether this information exists in the Government of Jamaica either.
55. For example, the lessee had no right to buy the property eventually, and was contractually forbidden to build on the land.
56. Section 3(d)(ii) of 'Lease Under the Registration of Titles Act' contained in *Agro 21, Land Divestment Policy Manual, 1989*.
57. Of its other three factories, one was closed, one was sold to Petrojam in an unsuccessful attempt to convert it to ethanol production, and one was leased to farmers and factory personnel.
58. For example, one analysis of the Jamaican sugar indistry which taken into account the impact of the likely reduction of EC sugar quotas concludes that the whole industry may well be unviable in its present form.
59. These sales occurred after the research for this book was undertaken. Thus, though some of them involve enterprises discussed above, we do not have sufficient detail to include them in section 7.3.4.
60. This has been carried out in conjunction with the World Bank, another example of the changed orientation of the PNP Government.
61. As an example, the sale of JRC was first mooted in 1978 under the previous PNP administration.
62. This conclusion is strengthened by the persistent problem of interlocking directorates in the private sector at large, which makes relatively competitive sectors less so.
63. In the following we draw heavily on secondary literature, and in particular Ayub (1981). Although much of his work refers to 1978, as Table 7.16 shows and as we argue below, there was little real growth in the manufacturing sector between 1978 and 1987 and no suggestion of substantial

structural change. We assume, therefore, that his discussion and conclusions hold for the 1980s as well.

64. *Government of Jamaica, 'Proposals for a Competition Act 1991'*, which replicates the speech made by the Minister of Industry, Production and Commerce when presenting draft legislation to the legislature on 9 April 1991.

65. Ownership of the commercial banks' equity in 1989 was as follows: Jamaican public, 71.6%; foreign banks, 22.5%; GoJ, 5.9%.

66. This, the only survey of its kind, used telephone interviews with randomly chosen sample of 2,055 middle and upper income earners in order to elicit information about the characteristics and motives of shareholders in Jamaica.

67. *Jamaican privatization stocks: numbers of shareowners.*

	NCB	CCC	ToJ
December 1986	30,606		
December 1987	31,200	c. 23,000	
December 1988	29,790		
April 1989			17,168
December 1989	30,307		17,367
June 1990	30,451	24,408	17,426

We are grateful to Ms Donna Beman of the JSE for providing these data.

68. An extreme case of this is a shareholder at an AGM who believed that his equity ownership imposed an obligation on CCC to fund his son's education at a US university.

69. Much of this information comes from Swaby, 1980, which, though somewhat partial in its sympathies, provides an interesting history of the rate applications processed under the PUC.

8 TRINIDAD & TOBAGO

8.1 Introduction

Privatization in Trinidad and Tobago (T-T) can in many ways be regarded as an expanded version of the Kenyan programme – that is to say, while T-T's programme has been larger, it has shared many of the same features. Most notable of these in T-T are the length of time that privatization has been a policy option compared to the little that has actually been achieved, and the importance of political factors in limiting the government's ability to divest enterprises. Thus, although privatization as a policy has been espoused since 1972, only 5 enterprises have – on a generous interpretation of the term – actually been privatized.

There are three powerful constraints to privatization in T-T. The first is the structure of the economy which, perhaps more than in any of our country studies, has delineated the scope for privatization. T-T is a classic mineral-based economy, with an oil and gas sector largely run by government. The state-owned enterprise sector is dominated by a number of large hydrocarbon industries that the government established with mineral rents in an attempt to diversify the productive base of the economy. In terms of privatization, this economic structure means that state enterprises often dwarf the absorptive capacity of the private sector. In addition, the domestic private sector over the last twenty years has been significantly weakened by 'Dutch Disease' effects. Second, in the 'decade of privatization', the 1980s, T-T has been hit by a devastating macroeconomic collapse. Coping with this has involved a period of intense fiscal and macroeconomic adjustment that has not been conducive to administering privatization. Finally, privatization in T-T has been stymied by the delicate ethno-political position in the country. T-T is a society with strong ethnic, political and economic conflicts, the resolution of which was one of the strongest causes of the expansion of the state sector in the 1970s and early 1980s, by which the government accepted responsibility for maintaining employment and ensuring an equitable distribution of income. Furthermore, sensitivities about national ownership of key economic sectors is high, resulting in an ambivalent attitude to sales to foreign enterprises. The inability of privatization to surmount these concerns is a major reason for its as yet limited trial in T-T.

However, like a mutating organism, privatization has recently returned to the forefront of policy, although for very singular reasons (see section 8.3.4). If this recent programme goes ahead, then, despite the above constraints, T-T may become – perhaps to its own surprise – a major privatizing nation.

8.1.1 Macroeconomic overview

After rapid economic growth in the 1970s, due largely to the country's position as an oil exporter but also thanks to development of natural gas, the 1980s have seen much more difficult times for the economy. Average annual real growth during the period 1976–82 was as high as 7%: however, after 1983 T-T registered six successive years of negative real growth, the result of which has been a contraction of the real domestic economy of more than 25% since the peak year of 1983 and an even sharper contraction of per capita incomes.

The proximate cause of this negative growth was the decline in the real oil price in the early 1980s, combined with the spectacular price collapse of 1986, which resulted in a contraction in the petroleum sector. The resultant fall in the value of exports and government revenues from the oil sector led to the familiar adjustment problems of external and fiscal deficits, a decline in net foreign assets, and an increase in external debt. In order to combat these, the government attempted to squeeze domestic demand and reduce imports through expenditure reductions and exchange-rate devaluations. However, the fall in domestic demand also had an impact on other sectors of the domestic economy, which have fallen as fast if not faster than the petroleum sector, and resulted in a sharp rise in the unemployment rate to 22% by 1986.

Following an extended period of office of the People's National Movement (PNM), in 1986 a new, more right-wing, government of the National Alliance for Reconstruction (NAR) was elected. This government has broadly speaking followed orthodox stabilization policies. However, due to the continuing parlous state of the country's reserves and the pressing need for a rescheduling of the foreign debt, it negotiated with the IMF a Compensatory Financing Facility purchase of US$114m. in November 1988 and a Stand-By Arrangement for US$128m. in January 1989. In these agreements it pledged to continue the process of fiscal reform, with some emphasis on continuing to improve the performance of the SOE sector through both internal reform and limited privatization. Despite a decade of adjustment, though, the economy still remains highly dependent on changes in international commodity prices.

As far as privatization is concerned, two facets in particular of macroeconomic performance have been important, namely the growth and sectoral development of the economy, and the swingeing fiscal cuts of the 1980s. We deal with these in turn.

8.1.2 Growth and sectoral developments in the economy

The overall performance of the economy has been largely determined by developments in the petroleum sector, which very roughly comprises a quarter of total GDP and a substantial share of exports. The 1970s were boom years for T-T as the value of oil production and exports rose rapidly in response to the rises in the international oil price that occurred in the middle and latter parts of the decade. The then PNM Government was well aware of the dangers inherent in a mineral-dependent economy, and avoided the trap of consuming windfall revenues by saving 70% of them in the period 1974–8 (Gelb with Auty, 1988).

Instead, in an attempt to safeguard growth, encourage the diversification of the domestic economy and exports, and promote interlinkages in domestic production, the government invested a sizeable share of the oil rents in gas-based industries such as steel, fertilizers, and methanol. (As we show in section 8.2, it also used increasing fractions of revenue to take over declining industries.) However, while the new investments had the potential to contribute strongly to growth, in fact their impact was lessened by difficulties in plant start-up and weaknesses in international prices resulting in low returns to these investments.

Further, as the experience of other oil exporters shows, such a commodity boom is not an unambiguous benefit because of attendant 'Dutch Disease' impacts on the non-oil tradables sector. Thus, the period 1974–81 saw industrial production shrink as a proportion of non-oil output, and the viability of non-hydrocarbon manufacturing exports undermined by the persistent appreciation of the exchange rate, especially after 1979. By 1981, then, the domestic manufacturing sector was relying heavily on domestic markets. In the agricultural sector, though, the government was unwilling to sanction a structural shift towards non-tradables, resulting in a build up of subsidies and price controls. In summary, as Gelb with Auty (1988) note, on the eve of the oil price declines of the 1980s:

> Three chronic problems – low investment quality, high consumption levels, and a seriously weakened non-mining economic sector – became apparent.

Since 1982, however, the economic position has been bleak, with real GDP and real per capita GDP declining at alarming rates (Table 8.1). These annual data show the severity of the contraction that T-T has undergone since the peak of the country's economic performance, including the dramatic declines in per capita incomes that the protracted recession has forced on the populace.

An analysis of GDP by sector of production reveals that it is not just the oil sector that has contracted (Table 8.2). As is clear, the decline in petroleum sector output is matched by the fall in non-oil output, with especially dramatic declines in the manufacturing, construction and financial sectors. In manufacturing, both the gas-based industries and the other manufacturing subsectors have performed poorly, contributing to a sectoral reduction in output in real terms of 30%. The hydrocarbon industries have been hit both by low international prices for their output and by start-up problems. Non-hydrocarbon manufacturing should have benefited from the reversal of Dutch Disease effects consequent on the fall in oil prices. However, as noted above, this sector was increasingly dependent on domestic demand, the compression of which has led to severe difficulties. Further,

Table 8.1 *GDP, real GDP and real GDP per capita, 1980–89*

	GDP, Market Prices	Real GDP	Real GDP Per Capita	Annual Percentage Growth		
				GDP, Market Prices	Real GDP	Real GDP Per Capita
	TT$m.	TT$m.	TT$			
1980	15,031	15,031	13,727	35.0	10.4	8.5
1981	16,433	15,723	14,101	9.3	4.6	2.7
1982	19,128	16,351	14,652	16.4	4.0	3.9
1983	19,054	17,202	15,102	−0.4	5.2	3.1
1984	18,610	15,980	13,658	−2.3	−7.1	−9.6
1985	17,813	15,133	12,847	−4.3	−5.3	−5.9
1986	17,372	14,891	12,451	−2.5	−1.6	−3.1
1987	17,376	13,894	11,463	0.0	−6.7	−7.9
1988	17,227	13,296	10,970	−0.9	−4.3	−4.3
1989	17,213	12,804	10,556	−0.1	−3.7	−3.8

Sources: Republic of Trinidad and Tobago, *Restructuring for Economic Independence: Draft Medium-term Macro-Planning Framework 1989–95*, 1988; Ministry of Finance, *Review of the Economy 1989*, 1989.

Note: For all real data, 1980 = 100.

Table 8.2 *GDP of Trinidad and Tobago by major sectors*[a] *(TT$bn, Constant price 1980 = 100)*

	1984	1985	1986	1987	1988	1989	Cumulative Change 84–89
GDP, market prices	16.0	15.1	14.9	13.9	13.3	12.8	−19.9%
Petroleum sector	3.8	4.1	4.0	3.7	3.6	3.6	−4.7%
Agriculture	0.3	0.3	0.3	0.3	0.3	0.4	24.2%
Manufacturing[b]	1.3	1.1	1.2	1.1	1.0	0.9	−30.4%
Construction & Quarrying	2.1	1.7	1.3	1.2	1.2	1.1	−48.8%
Distribution[c]	1.8	1.5	2.0	1.7	1.6	1.3	−25.7%
Transcomms	1.5	1.4	1.4	1.3	1.3	1.3	−15.6%
Fin./Ins./Real Estate	2.0	1.9	1.7	1.4	1.3	1.2	−42.3%
Government	2.4	2.3	2.4	2.3	2.3	2.3	−4.2%
Other	0.8	0.8	0.7	0.9	0.8	0.8	0.2%

Source: Ministry of Finance, *Review of the Economy 1989*, 1989.

Notes
a) GDP is allocated according to T-T's System of National Accounts rather than the ISIC.
b) Excludes oil refining and petrochemical industries, which are included in the petroleum sector.
c) Excludes distribution of petroleum products, which is included in the petroleum sector.

domestic manufacturing has been heavily overprotected and consequently inefficient; hence it was unable to divert output to exports. The poor performance of this sector has ramifications for privatization which are explored in section 8.4. The fall in the construction industry's value-added is also a direct result of poor demand conditions, but also has been affected by smaller than expected linkages between the steel plant and construction output.

Thus, T-T has suffered an immense macroeconomic shock, for which it was ill-prepared at the beginning of the 1980s. As a consequence, it has been involved in a long period of adjustment, and most notably, an extended programme of fiscal retrenchment.

8.1.3 Fiscal policy
The macroeconomic shock of the 1980s particularly affected government as the main recipient of windfall revenues. As Table 8.3 demonstrates, revenues have declined both in absolute terms and as a proportion of GDP. At their peak in 1982, total revenues to the government stood at TT$7,067m., up from TT$2,772m. in 1978 due to the oil boom of 1979. However, since then total revenues have fallen to TT$4,978m. in 1989, a fall of nearly 30% in current prices alone. The main cause of this fall was a decline in oil revenues, which dropped from 27.6% of GDP in 1980 to only 9.4% in 1986, while the share of non-oil revenue in (a declining) GDP has remained roughly constant.

In response to this revenue crisis, the government has had to cut expenditure, and total expenditure has in fact been reduced for seven consecutive years, 1982–89. However, much of this reduction has been confined to capital expenditure, which has fallen from TT$3,375m. in 1982 to TT$409m. in 1989, a massive drop of 88%. Despite an active programme of reduction in subsidies to the parastatal sector pursued by both the previous and current governments (see section 8.2), recurrent expenditures have declined much less slowly, from TT$6,038m. in 1982 to TT$5,279m. in 1989. One pressure on recurrent expenditure has been a rise in interest payments on T-T's debt, caused both by an increase in interest rates and successive devaluations.

Table 8.3 *Summary of Central Government Fiscal Operations (TT$m.)*

	1980	1981	1982	1983	1984	1985	1986	1987	1988	1989	% Change 1982–89
Total revenue & grants	6,403	7,051	7,067	6,552	6,613	6,665	5,456	5,300	4,948	4,978	−29.6
Total expenditure & net lending	5,355	6,624	9,414	8,768	8,269	7,582	6,468	6,312	5,931	5,687	−39.6
Current expenditure	3,135	3,550	6,038	6,238	6,273	6,038	5,591	5,066	5,335	5,279	−12.6
Capital expenditure & net lending	2,220	3,075	3,375	2,530	1,996	1,545	878	1,246	596	409	−87.9
Recurrent (deficit)/surplus	3,268	3,501	1,029	314	340	627	(135)	234	(387)	(301)	
Overall surplus/(deficit)	1,048	426	(2,347)	(2,216)	(1,656)	(917)	(1,012)	(1,012)	(984)	(710)	
As % of GDP:											
Total revenue & grants	42.6	42.9	36.9	34.4	35.5	37.4	31.4	30.5	28.7	28.9	
Total expenditure & net lending	35.6	40.3	49.2	46.0	44.4	42.6	37.2	36.3	34.4	33.0	
Current expenditure	20.9	21.6	31.6	32.7	33.7	33.9	32.2	29.2	31.0	30.7	
Capital expenditure & net lending	14.8	18.7	17.6	13.3	10.7	8.7	5.1	7.2	3.5	2.4	
Recurrent (deficit)/surplus	21.7	21.3	5.4	1.7	1.8	3.5	−0.8	1.3	−2.2	−1.7	
Overall surplus/(deficit)	7.0	2.6	−12.3	−11.6	−8.9	−5.2	−5.8	−5.8	−5.7	−4.1	
Memorandum item:											
GDP at market prices	15,031	16,433	19,128	19,054	18,610	17,813	17,372	17,376	17,227	17,213	−10.0

Source: ibid.

As a result, fiscal deficits have persisted throughout the 1980s, although as a proportion of GDP they were cut from their peak of 12.2% in 1982, and stabilized at around 5.5% (1986–9). However, the current government was unsatisfied with this performance, and therefore embarked on a policy of tax reform[1] combined with further expenditure reduction measures (i.e. a 10% cut in wages and salaries) with the intention of both reducing the deficit and stimulating a return to growth. As we shall see in section 8.3.4, though, the reinstatement of the privatization programme derived indirectly from this renewed reformist vigour.

We have dwelt on the macroeconomic background at some length in order to make two points. The first is to accentuate the link between the structure of T-T's GDP and the creation of its SOE sector. This link we explore in more detail in the next section. The second is to highlight the truly substantial programme of macroeconomic reform that successive governments have been obliged to undertake. In terms of both their negative impact on investor confidence and the government's ability to manage the time-consuming process of privatization, these macroeconomic developments do not provide a conducive background for a broad programme of privatization.

8.2. Analysis of the SOE sector

As suggested in the introduction, the expansion of the state sector in the 1970s and early 1980s and its performance during that period provide a delineation both of the reason why privatization policy developed in T-T, and also the reason for its somewhat circumscribed domain. Thus, in section 8.2.1 we examine the history of the SOE sector since Independence and its position in the economy in the early 1980s, while in sections 8.2.2 and 8.2.3 we describe the performance enterprises and the policy shift of the 1980s.

8.2.1 History

Broadly speaking, the history of the SOE sector in T-T can be divided into 3 phases. The first, from roughly 1956 (the date of Independence) to 1970, was characterized by non-interventionism in accord with the government's 'industrialization by invitation' strategy. Thus, during this period the government had no active policy of direct involvement in production through state ownership, and intervened only in response to the threat of closure of a large enterprise or vigorous lobbying by domestic pressure groups for such a move. Because of this piecemeal approach, the government had, by 1972, a comparatively small presence in the ownership of the economy. It had investments at this time in 32 companies, of which 4 were 100% owned, a further 10 were majority-owned, and combined investments were worth approximately TT$60m.

However, by 1970 this broad economic strategy was perceived domestically to have failed. First, employment expansion had not been sufficient to absorb a growing labour force, and unemployment was rising with a consequent increase in labour unrest. Second, there was little evidence that localization was occurring: the largest enterprises in the economy remained in foreign hands. Third, and perhaps most importantly, the increase in inequality over the period exacerbated racial divisions so that the 'losers' – mostly the blacks and East Indians who in 1970 comprised 43 and 40% of the population respectively – became increasingly antagonistic to the government and its economic policy.[2] The result of these developments was the 'Black Power' riots of 1970 and the near-toppling of the government in an army coup attempt the same year. These events led the government to undertake a fundamental shift in its economic strategy. This accepted that the government should play a far more active role in promoting economic growth, arguing that the private sector

> could not be relied upon alone to produce the kind of momentum which the country required to safeguard its economic independence and provide additional jobs, economic growth and an equitable distribution of the national income.[3]

The government, then, embraced the notion of public ownership under the guise of localizing the economy, accelerating the development process, rationalizing the provision of public services, and aiding the development of non-traditional production sectors. However, there was also an important political goal to the expansion of the SOE sector, namely the involvement of the black and Indian populations in economic growth, both through the establishment of new industries and through the protection of jobs in non-profitable industries that were threatened by the Dutch Disease effects of the oil boom.

Somewhat fortuitously, this change in policy coincided with the rapid expansion of government revenues consequent on the 1974 increase in the oil price and the discovery of new natural gas reserves. Thus the government was able to put its plans into effect, and the SOE sector was expanded throughout the 1970s and early 1980s through a policy of both nationalization and the government-backed creation of new industries. By 1985, the government was the majority shareholder in 48 firms, in 37 of which it owned 100% of the equity. There was one firm in which it had a 50% share, a further 17 in which it was a minority shareholder, and a group of five utilities (Table 8.4). Furthermore, the total value of the government's shareholding had by 1986 reached over TT$4bn (excluding the utilities), and some of the companies were significantly larger than the largest in the private sector. A list of the largest companies by nominal value of shareholding is as follows:[4]

Name:	% Gov. Shareholding	Nominal Value of Gov. Shareholding (TT$)	Output of Enterprise
1) ISCOTT	100	2,314,941,000	Steel
2) BWIA	100	552,360,590	Airline
3) TIMC	100	417,259,500	Methanol
4) T-T Urea Co.	100	340,264,244	Fertilizer
5) TRINTOPEC	100	261,232,000	Oil
6) TELCO (pre-sale)	100	257,820,361	Telecommunications
7) CARONI Ltd.	100	177,287,760	Sugar
8) TCL	81	152,530,323	Cement
9) Arawak Cement Co.	49	147,474,785	Cement
10) TRINTOC	100	105,788,425	Oil

The SOE sector now accounted for a substantial portion of GDP: in 1985, the total value-added of the state enterprises and public utilities was TT$2.9bn or some 16% of GDP. In the same year, total employment in the sector was 53,700, or c. 13% of total formal sector employment, and capital investment was TT$1bn or 26% of national capital investment (Henry, 1989).

The sectoral distribution of the majority-owned SOEs shows that the government had indeed achieved its aim of taking over the 'commanding heights' of the economy by acquiring enterprises in the petroleum, agricultural and finance sectors which had previously been foreign-owned. Sectorally, the expansion of ownership occurred in two ways. First, the government used windfall revenues for industrial diversification. The clearest examples of this are the firms set up to

Table 8.4 *Number of government enterprises by sector, 1985*[a]

Govt Share-holding	Total No. of Cos.	Petrol & Related Inds.	Agric & Related Inds.	Manu-fac-turing	Transport, Comms. & Broad-casting	Hotel & Related Inds.	Finance, Banks, & Insurance	Other
100%	37	9	7	9	4	1	1	6
51–99%	11	2	1	–	2	1	5	–
50%	1	–	–	–	1	–	–	–
< 50%	17	–	2	8	2	2	3	–
Totals	66	11	10	17	9	4	9	6

Source: Mills, 1988.

a) Excluding the utilities.

maximize the downstream benefits of T-T's gas reserves (i.e. steel, fertilizers and methanol). In these industries, the government believed that a long-term comparative advantage could be developed, but that it would have to assume the costs and risks of start-up. Substantial investment funds were committed by the government, with an estimated US$1.5bn spent on establishing the various projects. Although some of these were successful – especially those conducted as joint ventures with foreign participation – a number were plagued with problems, including cost overruns, construction delays, and completely inadequate projections of global demands and prices. Thus, the productivity of many of these investments was often low, and, even if technically efficient, the firms often lost money because of low international prices. Finally, in terms of their impact on the domestic economy, few of the expected upstream and downstream benefits actually materialized.

Increasingly, though, the government chose a second route, namely nationalization, as, for example, in cement, commercial banking, oil refineries, sugar and telecommunications. Often the prime motivation was simply to avoid the job losses that would result from impending closure. Between 1974 and 1978, the government spent TT$1.67bn to acquire forty companies, which included the dominant sugar company (CARONI), Shell's oil refinery (renamed TRINTOC), and the cement company (TCL) (Gelb with Auty, 1988). However, difficulties emerged in the operation of these enterprises almost immediately. The result was a steady increase in SOE loans and subsidies from government to cover rising operating losses.

8.2.2 SOE performance in the early 1980s

By the early 1980s it became increasingly clear that the SOE sector was not operating as had been intended, but rather was suffering from the same problems that emerged in state sectors in many other countries at this time. While there were significant differences in the SOEs' performance in T-T, the problems were broadly as follows. As Tables 8.5 and 8.6 show for the state enterprise and public utility sectors separately, financial performance was poor. For example, the public utilities had a cumulative deficit of TT$900m. between 1974 and 1979. With the collapse of the fiscus after 1982, such deficits became an excessive burden on public finances. This was worsened by the impact of the oil price decline on the profitability of the oil sector, which reduced the overall profits of the state enterprise sector. While in 1984 the state enterprise sector's overall balance was still positive, by 1986 this had turned into a deficit of −3.3% of GDP (TT$589m.).

Table 8.5 *Consolidated accounts of major SOEs*[a] *(TT$m.)*

	1984	1985	1986	1987	1988	Est. 1989
Operating revenues	3,482.2	4,557.7	4,612.9	6,119.6	7,044.3	7,181.7
Operating expenditures	2,872.4	4,157.0	4,614.3	5,749.2	6,343.8	5,992.8
Wages and salaries	666.0	926.4	968.0	1,058.0	1,121.1	1,025.7
Interest payments	192.9	279.6	336.2	387.3	442.8	327.1
Other goods/services	2,013.5	2,951.0	3,310.1	4,303.9	4,779.9	4,640.0
Operating balance	609.8	400.7	(1.4)	370.4	700.5	1,188.9
Current transfers from gov.	526.6	408.1	133.0	122.3	147.0	131.0
Other income	73.7	80.5	70.9	66.6	64.3	42.3
Other current expenditure	278.2	95.2	71.5	81.9	119.1	13.4
Taxes	457.9	486.9	660.0	705.9	581.1	665.0
Current account balance	474.0	307.2	(529.0)	(228.5)	211.6	683.8
Capital transfers from gov.	534.2	228.5	327.3	283.4	154.6	99.4
Capital contributions	11.9	33.1	15.3	1.0	0.8	82.6
Capital expenditures	451.4	800.2	402.5	617.6	446.8	706.3
OVERALL BALANCE	568.7	(231.4)	(588.9)	(561.7)	(79.8)	159.5
Total transfers from gov.	1,060.8	636.6	460.3	405.7	301.6	230.4
Taxes to gov.	457.9	486.9	660.0	705.9	581.1	665.0
Memorandum items:						
Net transfer from gov.	602.9	149.7	(199.7)	(300.2)	(279.5)	(434.6)
Operating revenue as a % of operating expenditure	121.2%	109.6%	100.0%	106.4%	111.0%	119.8%
Wages as a % of operating expenditure	23.2%	22.3%	21.0%	18.4%	17.7%	17.1%
Current transfers from gov. as a % of total current revenue	12.9%	8.1%	2.8%	1.9%	2.0%	1.8%

Source: Ministry of Finance, private communication.

a) Comprises CARONI, TRINTOC, BWIA, TRINTOPEC, ISCOTT, DFC, Trinidad Cement Ltd., National Fisheries, National Gas Co., T&T Methanol Co., T&T Urea Co., Fertrin, Tringen, T&T Nat. Petroleum Marketing Co Ltd., SCOTT

In the public utilities, the overall balance peaked at a deficit of −2.3% of GDP (TT$414m.) in 1985.

As a result, SOEs were reliant on government transfers. Once again, even before the worst period of the early 1980s, the scale of transfers was significant: in the early 1970s (before the first oil boom) they were equal to approximately 30% of government recurrent expenditure. However, the situation became clearly insupportable in the 1980s. Between 1979 and 1984, total loans, advances and subventions to SOEs were TT$5.8bn and in 1984 itself total transfers (capital and current) stood at 9.8% of GDP. However, these transfers did not completely cover deficits, with the result that the external debt of the SOEs (which is guaranteed by government in the event of repayment difficulties) reached TT$2.5bn by the end of 1986, or 42% of T-T's entire external debt. Similarly, private domestic claims on the SOEs rose from TT$121m. in 1980 to TT$947m. in 1984, and TT$1,229m. by 1986.

These woeful overall financial indicators were caused by the problems referred to above. However, in the context of a prolonged recession, it was clear that the government could no longer afford to subsidize loss-making and/or inefficient

Table 8.6 *Consolidated accounts of the public utilities*[a] *(TT$m.)*

	1984	1985	1986	1987	1988	Est. 1989
Operating revenues	588.7	681.5	803.5	899.6	939.7	1,059.6
Operating expenditures	1,227.8	1,196.7	1,235.5	1,238.9	1,253.8	1,389.7
Wages and salaries	776.5	723.5	703.3	649.0	668.2	561.5
Interest payments	121.5	142.3	155.0	170.0	195.8	236.7
Other goods/services	329.8	330.9	377.2	419.9	389.8	591.5
Operating balance	(639.1)	(515.2)	(432.0)	(339.3)	(314.1)	(330.1)
Current transfers from gov.	513.0	561.2	406.1	355.4	252.8	200.0
Other income	0.0	0.0	0.0	0.0	0.0	0.0
Other current expenditure	0.0	0.0	0.0	0.0	0.0	0.0
Taxes	0.0	0.0	0.0	0.0	0.0	0.0
Current account balance	(126.1)	46.0	(25.9)	16.1	(61.3)	(130.1)
Capital transfers from gov.	206.5	95.1	98.3	46.4	1.3	42.3
Capital contributions	48.7	24.0	7.8	4.9	4.7	0.0
Capital expenditures	477.0	579.0	246.9	220.2	69.1	136.7
OVERALL BALANCE	(347.9)	(413.9)	(166.7)	(152.8)	(124.4)	(224.5)
Total transfers from gov.	719.5	656.3	504.4	401.8	254.1	242.3
Taxes to gov.	0.0	0.0	0.0	0.0	0.0	0.0
Memorandum items:						
Net transfer from gov.	719.5	656.3	504.4	401.8	254.1	242.3
Operating revenue as a % of operating expenditure	47.9%	56.9%	65.0%	72.6%	74.9%	76.2%
Wages as a % of operating expenditure	131.9%	106.2%	87.5%	72.1%	71.1%	53.0%
Current transfers from gov. as a % of operating revenue	87.1%	82.3%	50.5%	39.5%	26.9%	18.9%

Source: Ministry of Finance, private communication.

a) Comprises Water and Sewerage Authority, Electricity Commission, Public Transport Corporation, Port Authority and Trinidad and Tobago Telephone Company.

state enterprises. As a result of budgetary crisis, then, reform of the SOEs was implemented.

8.2.3 Change in policy towards the SOEs

Reform of the SOE sector began under the PNM, which instituted a hard budget constraint for those enterprises which the government felt were strong enough to operate with a reduced subsidy. Thus total transfers to state enterprises and public utilities were reduced from TT$1.8bn or 9.8% of GDP in 1984, to TT$1bn or 5.9% of GDP in 1986. However, reform gathered pace following the electoral victory of the NAR in 1986, which was more sympathetic to the private sector than the previous government. The NAR set up a State Enterprises Committee to examine the whole question of the SOE sector and come up with proposals for the reform of each enterprise. The NAR adopted an essentially pragmatic approach to the issue of ownership, regarding the SOE sector as having produced some notable benefits (especially the localization of decision-making), while noting the inability of the private sector to carry out the management of some of the larger enterprises in the government portfolio. However, it had a pressing need to reduce the SOE sector's call on declining government revenues, and therefore developed a plan for SOE rationalization based on the following principles:[5]

   i) a reduction of shareholding in those enterprises with the potential to be operated viably by the private sector (i.e. privatization);
  ii) winding up of those companies with no real prospect of becoming commercially viable and whose continued existence cannot be justified on the basis of social return;
 iii) rationalization of service enterprises;
  iv) a restructuring of the capital base and improvement of management personnel, systems and practices in those enterprises which, because of their strategic national importance, will remain under state ownership and control, to ensure they operate at a high level of efficiency and with little or no financial dependence on the Treasury.

In the context of these principles, the 45 wholly or majority-owned SOEs were classified into three groups, with 12 to be divested wholly or in part, 6 to be disbanded, and 21 to remain in public ownership as 'strategic enterprises'.

Privatization policies are examined in section 8.3. However, the programme occurred slowly enough to mean that the SOE clean-up was applied to almost all the SOEs that the NAR inherited in 1986. The details of the SOE reform programme were similar to those observed in other countries, and we therefore do not describe it here.[6] With regard to the results of the programme, little is known on enterprise efficiency. However, we do have data on financial performance, which suggest that the reforms brought generally positive results. As Tables 8.5 and 8.6 show, the period 1986–8 saw a very healthy rise in total operating revenue, from TT$5.5bn, or 31.4% of GDP, to TT$8.1bn, or 51.6% of GDP. While some of this rise was a result of oil price increases after 1986, to a greater extent it was the result of price liberalization and the government's insistence on improved revenue collection. Furthermore, recurrent expenditures had a slower rate of increase, from TT$6bn in 1986 to TT$7.7bn in 1988, thanks to the impact of labour-shedding on slowing the rise in wages and salaries (total employment in major state enterprises fell from 25,635 in 1986 to 22,770 in 1988). The result was a shift from an operating deficit in 1986 to a position of surplus of TT$0.4bn in 1988. The government reduced its total transfers from TT$1bn in 1986 to TT$0.6bn (now only 3.9% of GDP), and the consolidated deficit of the SOEs improved from −TT$0.8bn to −TT$0.2bn.

Thus, these aggregate figures suggest that a substantial improvement was achieved in the operations of the SOE sector following the reforming intentions of the NAR Government.[7] Analysis at the disaggregated level, however, suggests that the NAR has still had to respect the same political considerations that gave birth to the SOE sector in the first place. The classic example of this is the agricultural SOE, Caroni. This is predominantly a sugar producer and marketer, accounting for two-thirds of T-T's cane output, and 100% of processing and marketing. However, according to the World Bank, T-T 'supports a seriously obsolete sugar industry that produces sugar at about 10 times the world price'.[8] It survives only thanks to protection, but imposes a substantial cost on the economy equal to over TT$360,000 per sugar worker or farmer per annum, or TT$360 per capita.

It is therefore unsurprising to find that Caroni performed badly (Table 8.7). Its operating revenue has been only half its expenditure, meaning that, even with substantial government transfers (roughly TT$200m. per annum) and paying no tax, Caroni usually runs a deficit. However, reform efforts have been stymied by the politics of employment in Caroni. Caroni is the largest single employer in the SOE sector, with c. 10,000 employees out of a total of c. 25,000 in the major

Table 8.7   *Caroni Ltd Summary Accounts, 1984–88 (TT$m.)*

	1984	1985	1986	1987	1988	Est. 1989
Operating revenues	124.6	163.8	209.7	251.9	263.2	348.6
Operating expenditures	381.5	423.5	374.6	407.9	459.6	520.1
Wages and salaries	229.6	262.4	237.9	235.9	257.2	223.1
Interest payments	6.3	10.6	15.5	23.3	26.7	26.4
Other goods/services	145.6	150.5	121.2	148.7	175.7	270.6
Operating balance	−256.9	−259.7	−164.9	−156.0	−196.4	−171.5
Current transfers from gov.	275.0	197.8	115.0	105.8	147.0	121.0
Other income	0.0	0.0	0.0	0.0	0.0	0.0
Taxes	0.0	0.0	0.0	0.0	0.0	0.0
Current account balance	18.1	−61.9	−49.9	−50.2	−49.4	−50.5
Capital transfers from gov.	10.0	0.0	0.0	0.0	0.0	0.0
Other	14.6	14.1	11.2	6.4	4.9	1.3
OVERALL BALANCE	14.1	−63.0	−55.7	−56.6	−54.3	−51.8
Total transfers from gov.	285.0	197.8	115.0	105.8	147.0	121.0
Taxes to gov.	0.0	0.0	0.0	0.0	0.0	0.0
Memorandum items:						
Net transfers from gov.	285.0	197.8	115.0	105.8	147.0	121.0
Operating revenue as a % of operating expenditure	32.7%	38.7%	56.0%	61.8%	57.3%	67.0%
Wages as a % of operating expenditure	60.2%	62.0%	63.5%	57.8%	56.0%	42.9%
Current transfers from gov. as a % of total current revenue	68.8%	54.7%	35.4%	29.6%	35.8%	25.8%

Source: Caroni Ltd.

SOEs. The majority of these employees were East Indians, who were heavily dependent on the sugar sector. Caroni sugar workers were also highly organized and had managed to demand an 80% rise in real wages between 1975 and 1981 at the same time as capacity fell by two-thirds. Thus, while the reform programmes of the PNM and NAR did succeed in reducing employment in Caroni, there was unanimous agreement that substantial subsidies should remain in order to (artificially) maintain employment.

8.2.4 Conclusions

Along with the macroeconomic environment delineated in section 8.1, the structure of the SOE sector and the reasons surrounding its development are major determinants of the scope for privatization in T-T. In particular, we suggest two dominating features. The first is the origin of SOE expansion in the political troubles of 1970, and the role that SOEs still play in instrumenting employment objectives, combined with the strong political sentiment in T-T in favour of the localization of asset ownership. These interact with the second feature, namely the size and specialization of the large SOEs that the government established with boom revenues. These considerations have oriented the government towards continuation of the SOE sector and away from sales of the large SOEs to the domestic private sector or the foreign sector. This is reflected in the government's own classification of 21 SOEs as strategic and therefore to be kept in the public domain. However, as also noted above, privatization has been a policy objective in T-T for almost twenty years, and it is to this that we now turn.

8.3. The privatization experience

8.3.1 Privatization policy

The development of privatization policy in T-T has essentially fallen into two phases, namely the period 1972–86, and from 1986 onwards. In the first phase, the government's policy on privatization was drawn from the same 1972 White Paper[9] that had presented the policy change which underpinned the massive expansion of state ownership in the 1970s. This seeming inconsistency was reconciled by the government's insistence that state ownership was merely a method of holding assets in trust for the population at large, assets which would be directly sold to the population when circumstances permitted. In particular, state ownership was presented as a natural (if rather paternalistic) half-way house between foreign control and domestic ownership of the 'commanding heights'.[10] Thus, inasmuch as privatization was genuinely a goal of the government in the 1970s, the issue was framed in terms of the localization and equal distribution of asset ownership, i.e. the same combination of nationalism and egalitarianism that underlay the expansion of government ownership.

However, actual divestitures were limited in this period, and confined to the three NCB transactions that we outline later on. Instead, the orientation of privatization policy changed as views of the SOE sector altered in response to its economic failings. As early as 1979, a committee was set up under then Central Bank governor Bruce to make recommendations on the divestiture of shares to the public at large. This was followed by a further committee in 1984 chaired by Bruce's successor Bobb, which had as its mandate a review of the policy of public participation in industrial and commercial enterprises. In the light of the poor performance of the SOEs and the general macroeconomic crisis, this committee concluded that 'some of the rationale for the objectives of state ownership enunciated were no longer valid'.

However, nothing was done with reference to these committees' suggestions. Finally, in 1986 the NAR set up the State Enterprises Committee under Frank Rampersad, which recommended privatization as one part of an overall restructuring plan for SOEs. This marked the transition to the second period of privatization, namely one when the emphasis moved away from issues of national control and towards issues of operational efficiency and the appropriate location of the public/private ownership boundary. Thus, T-T's professed objectives for privatization began to incorporate those more commonly expressed in other countries, and the decision to privatize could therefore be made under any of the following conditions: (i) the judgement that the objective of state ownership had been achieved; (ii) the pursuit of a more balanced distribution of income and wealth; (iii) the government's needs for financial resources; and (iv) the realization that a particular activity might be best left in the hands of the private sector.

As suggested above, the NAR's commitment to privatization was essentially pragmatic rather than ideological: that is to say, the NAR believed in a mixed economy, and saw privatization as one way of pulling itself out of a fiscal mire.

8.3.2 The experience of privatization

The Rampersad Committee drew up a list of 12 enterprises that were recommended for privatization. Of these, however, only 5 privatizations have been completed to date. By a curious coincidence, the first three transactions in T-T occurred in firms which mirrored the major privatizations of Jamaica, namely commercial banking (NCB/NCB), cement (TCL/CCC) and telecommunications (TELCO/ToJ).

The National Commercial Bank (NCB)
The privatization of NCB has been unusual in that the government's gradual shedding of its equity stake has taken place over a decade, and is still not concluded. Furthermore, the privatization of NCB seems to have had few objectives other than the slow transfer of equity to T-T citizens.

NCB was originally a branch of a foreign-owned bank, the Bank of London and Montreal, until the government acquired a controlling share in 1970. It has traditionally provided the standard range of branch-based commercial banking services and additionally set up two finance companies (NCB Trust Company and Trinfinance Limited) in the 1970s. Performance at NCB has in general been good: even in the macroeconomic decline of the 1980s, it managed to increase its total revenues and remain profitable without the help of government subventions. This is in large part explained by the fact that NCB operates in the reasonably competitive commercial banking sector, which by 1986 had 8 banks operating 117 branches.

The privatization of NCB has been a gradual process. NCB was the only company to have equity divested during the first phase of the privatization programme. As Table 8.8 shows, equity in NCB was sold by the Ministry of Finance via public share sale in April 1978 and October 1980, raising TT$4.3m. and TT$2.3m. respectively, at the same time as NCB was offering subscriptions to new equity. According to NCB itself, in all cases the offers were fully subscribed. However, at the end of these transactions, the government still owned a majority of the equity. In choosing to sell limited amounts of equity in such a fashion, the government was almost aping the development of smaller stock exchanges, where the first equity issues are traditionally small tranches of equity in solidly performing commercial banks.

There were no further developments between 1981 and 1987. In 1988, NCB was technically 'privatized', in the sense that the government's total equity holdings were reduced to less than 50% of the issued equity. However, this occurred not as a result of a public sale, but followed NCB's purchase in September 1988 of 1,580,996 shares from government to establish an Employee Share Acquisition Scheme. As Table 8.8 shows, this reduced the government's holdings in NCB to 46.4% of the issued equity. Finally, in December 1988 the Ministry of Finance offered for sale a further 10% of NCB's total equity (i.e. 3.4 million shares) at a fully paid price of TT$0.69 each. Reflecting the government's desire to ensure asset distribution to workers and the small investor, the allocation scheme's ranking of the importance of applications was as follows: (i) up to 20% of the issue could go to employees; (ii) up to 10% could go to the T-T Unit Trust Company; (iii) to individuals citizens; (iv) to local companies; (v) to resident aliens; and (vi) to non-resident aliens. In the end, the offer was oversubscribed, with 3,977 applicants for a total of 5,936,872 stock units.[11] As a consequence there was a small rise in the secondary market price to TT$0.71 per share at the end of the first day's trading. It may be noted, however, that the pricing of this NCB issue was easy, in that there already existed equity traded on the TTSE which provided a valuation of the firm.

Trinidad Cement Limited
If the NAR's privatization of NCB represented the continuation of a previous programme, then TCL was the first 'new' privatization, in that it was carried out more

Table 8.8 *NCB (Trinidad and Tobago)*

1. History of Share Capital (TT$)

	30/11/87	*30/06/87*	*10/10/88*	*31/12/88*
Public	15,190,005	16,704,854	16,704,854	20,114,854
Bank Staff (ESAS)	0	· 0	1,580,996	1,580,996
Minister of Finance	15,809,995	17,390,991	15,809,995	12,399,995
Total issued	31,000,000	34,095,845	34,095,845	34,095,845
Public	49.00%	48.99%	48.99%	59.00%
Bank Staff (ESAS)	0.00%	0.00%	4.64%	4.64%
Minister of Finance	51.00%	51.01%	46.37%	36.37%
Total issued	100.00%	100.00%	100.00%	100.00%

2. Privatizations & Subscriptions

PRIVATIZATIONS

Date	From	To	No. of shares	Price (TT$)	Value (TT$)
Apr 78	Ministry of Finance	Public	2,400,000	1.80	4,320,000
Oct 80	Ministry of Finance	Public	870,000	2.60	2,262,000
Dec 88	Ministry of Finance	Public	3,410,000	0.69	2,352,900
Total			6,680,000		8,934,900

SUBSCRIPTIONS

Date	From	To	No. of shares	Price (TT$)	Value (TT$)
Apr 78	NCB	n.a.	5,000,000	1.80	9,000,000
Oct 80	NCB	n.a.	3,000,000	2.60	7,800,000
Nov 81	NCB	n.a.	8,000,000	2.75 ·	22,000,000
Total			16,000,000		38,800,000

clearly for reasons of poor enterprise performance. However, in the privatization of TCL, it appears that the policies of efficiency improvement and wider asset ownership were being addressed by two separate features of the government's reform plan. That is to say, improving enterprise performance seems to have been addressed by a management reorganization that was not intrinsic to privatization, whereas asset ownership goals were again achieved through a public share sale.

Following the government's acquisition in 1976, TCL's performance was poor. By 1981, its output had dropped to one-half of capacity, and its production costs were twice those of an efficient North American producer (Gelb with Auty, 1988: 276). As a result, TCL has been reliant on substantial subsidies, followed by the accumulation of large losses after the removal of the subsidy from 1984 onwards. The poor performance was principally the result of the government's policy of keeping cement prices low despite inevitable increases in production costs. This both resulted in low sales revenues and gave the firm no incentive to invest in new plant to replace its 22-year-old capital stock. By the end of 1987, then, TCL's accumulated losses were TT$91.2m., and net indebtedness to the government was TT$137m.

Following the decision to privatize the company, the government instituted a rapid 'clean-up' programme. This was characterized first by the introduction of a new Board of Directors and a new General Manager in early 1987, with a mandate to improve the efficiency of the firm, and second by output price decontrol. TCL's reform strategy involved the achievement of the following: rapid gains in processing and manufacturing cost efficiencies; manpower reductions (employment at TCL fell to 413 by 1988 as against 699 the year before); and export market penetration (TCL started exporting in 1987 for the first time since 1974 – export earnings were TT$9.6m. in 1987 and TT$25.5m. in 1988).

However, another key element was a balance-sheet restructuring of the company, the hallmarks of which were a capitalization of 50% of TCL's outstanding debt, including the conversion of long-term government debt into 5% redeemable preference shares, and a 50% reduction in ordinary share capital (which occurred between the two public share sales). As a result of these reform measures, TCL returned to profit in 1988 following an impressive increase in operating revenues (aided by a 20% rise in the price of cement in September 1988), and a reduction in operating expenditures, as Table 8.9 shows. With this profit, TCL was able to pay a dividend on its shares in 1988 of TT$3.9m.

At the same time as these improvements, the government announced its intention to sell its entire ordinary shareholding in TCL in three tranches. Two of these have been implemented to date. Phase I of the sale was in January 1989, when 12 million TT$1 shares were offered at TT$0.75 per share, payable in full. Phase II occurred in January 1990, when 21 million TT$1 shares were offered at the slightly higher price of TT$0.85 per share, which reflected a rise in the price of the

Table 8.9 *Trinidad Cement Ltd Summary accounts, 1984–9 (TT$m.)*

	1984	*1985*	*1986*	*1987*	*1988*	*Est.* *1989*
Operating revenues	76.1	72.5	70.8	69.8	90.1	108.5
Operating expenditures	81.9	71.5	77.9	92.7	82.4	86.0
Wages and salaries	35.0	30.0	31.0	28.3	23.6	22.2
Interest payments	1.0	1.9	6.5	9.0	1.8	1.3
Other goods/services	45.9	39.6	40.4	55.4	57.0	62.5
Operating balance	−5.8	1.0	−7.1	−22.9	7.7	22.5
Current transfers from gov.	0.0	0.0	0.0	0.0	0.0	0.0
Other income	0.0	0.0	0.0	0.0	0.0	0.0
Taxes	0.0	0.0	0.0	0.0	0.0	0.0
Current account balance	−5.8	1.0	−7.1	−22.9	7.7	22.5
Capital transfers from gov.	1.3	0.8	1.7	7.7	0.0	0.0
Capital revenues	0.1	0.1	0.1	0.8	0.5	0.0
Capital expenditures	4.1	6.1	3.7	2.8	7.6	14.9
OVERALL BALANCE	−8.5	−4.2	−9.0	−17.2	0.6	7.6
Total transfers from gov.	1.3	0.8	1.7	7.7	0.0	0.0
Taxes to gov.	0.0	0.0	0.0	0.0	0.0	0.0
Memorandum items:						
Net transfer from gov.	1.3	0.8	1.7	7.7	0.0	0.0
Operating revenue as a % of *operating expenditure*	92.9	101.4	90.9	75.3	109.3	126.2
Wages as a % of *operating expenditure*	42.7	42.0	39.8	30.5	28.6	25.8
Current transfers from gov. as a % of *total current revenue*	0.0	0.0	0.0	0.0	0.0	0.0

Source: TCL.

secondary market stock that had occurred during the period. Both share sales were a success in that they were both oversubscribed. In the first offer, there were 3,064 applicants for 21,016,650 stock units, while in the second there were 3,575 applicants for 40,615,550 stock units.[12] In both cases, then, there were immediate rises in secondary markets, with prices at the end of the first day's trading of TT$0.83 and TT$0.91 per share respectively. As a result of these two sales, the government's equity holding in TCL was reduced to 34% of issued capital.

The design of both share sales was affected by the government's goal of achieving the widening of wealth ownership. Three methods in particular were used. First, in both sales, the same allocation scheme for shares was used as had been instituted in the NCB sale. In the event of full subscription, this gave employees and small shareholders a minimum of 30% of the equity on offer. Second, in the manner of the Jamaican programme, the government placed in the company's Articles of Association a restriction that the total share ownership of any individual must not exceed 10% of total issued equity. Finally, the government strongly promoted employee share ownership in TCL. To do this, it both established an Employee Incentive Scheme, whereby employees could purchase up to 10,000 shares during Phase I at a 10% discount on the offer price, and an Employee Share Ownership Plan, to which the government donated 1,958,571 shares as an initial allocation.

With reference to issues in the privatization debate, it is clearly too early to know whether the transfer of ownership *per se* has had any impact on the efficiency of the firm. However, given our discussion of theoretical issues in Chapter 2 and the general lack of aggressiveness of trading on the TTSE, it would be extremely surprising to find that the widely dispersed shareholders of TCL were in a position to discipline the enterprise management and enforce efficient behaviour. Rather, as we suggested at the beginning, the public share issues appear to have been designed more with the aim of widening asset distribution, with management changes and price deregulation more important in explaining improvements in TCL's performance.

T-T Telephone Company Limited (TELCO)
TELCO, in common with the other utilities, had a poor record in the 1970s and early 1980s. It was a persistent loss-maker, and provided a poor service to customers. As a public utility and a domestic monopolist, it was subject to regulation by the Public Utilities Commission (PUC): as we describe in section 8.6, however, this regulation was extremely weak. Reform efforts from 1984 onwards, including rate revisions granted by the PUC, improved the utility's financial performance. Between 1984 and 1988, operating revenues increased from TT$151m. to TT$371m., a more rapid expansion than expenditures, resulting in a decline in the operating deficit. The government was also able to remove all transfers to TELCO during this period. However, operational performance was still not satisfactory, and the firm's overall balance was still in deficit to the tune of TT$45m. in 1988. In order to access international technology and involve the private sector in the management of telecommunications, the government took the decision to divest itself of a portion of TELCO's equity, which would clearly involve sale to a foreign buyer. Finally, to make the firm more attractive to potential buyers, the government wrote off one-third of TELCO's debt.

The TELCO sale was advertised worldwide and, after four offers were received, bidding and negotiations ensued until the government decided to accept the offer from Cable and Wireless (UK),[13] which offered the best deal in terms of foreign exchange, expertise and technology.[14] Thus, during 1989, an agreement was made with C&W for the purchase of 49% of the equity, at a price of TT$361m.

with the government holding the remaining 51%. Hence, the TELCO sale was not a privatization in the strict sense of the word, although it clearly involved the introduction of new elements into the management of the firm. The first equity instalment of 85% of the sale price was paid in November 1989 and the remaining 15% was due in March 1990. The funds were to be used to retire part of the company's external debt obligations and government advances to the company, and to finance a portion of its development programme.

However, since TELCO still has a domestic monopoly, the government has continued to regulate the company. It proposed the establishment of a new Telecommunications Authority to carry out this function, but the structure of this proposed authority is unclear. As in other countries, however, it is the case that the government did not adequately deal with the regulation issue before it sold its equity.

Iron and Steel Company of Trinidad and Tobago (ISCOTT)
This company represents the government's largest single holding of equity, at TT$2,315m., or almost half of its total equity holdings. It is also the greatest failure in the government's industrialization programme. After withdrawing from a joint venture with three multinational partners, the government began its own steel operation in 1977. During the construction of the plant, a change in plans led to construction cost overruns of 30%, the financing of which imposed a heavy burden on ISCOTT. With only a small domestic market, production was targeted at the southern United States: however, in these markets ISCOTT was competing with the most efficient mini-mills in the world. Unable to undercut US producers, ISCOTT was left with 'woefully inadequate markets . . . the worst-case projection for ISCOTT quickly became overly optimistic' (Gelb with Auty, 1988: 283).

Thus, ISCOTT never exceeded 29% capacity utilization in its first five years of operations, has persistently made financial losses, and has required substantial government support, as Table 8.10 shows. By 1985 (probably the worst year), its operating revenues had sunk to only 32% of operating expenditures and it had built up an unmanageable debt, with interest payments equal to 97% of operating revenue. After considering the option of closing the company, the government decided that it was possible to reform it only through private sector involvement.

Hence, in January 1986 the government entered into a two-year management contract with New Hamburg Steel and Vorst Alpine, with the aim of corporate break-even by 1989 and complete self-financing by 1991. This plan achieved some success, with production increases in all the company's products in 1986 followed by a 24% rise in output in 1987. Furthermore, despite intense competition, ISCOTT's export performance improved significantly, with exports rising 41% in 1987. However, these improvements in efficiency were not sufficient to make a profit, and the company remained saddled by a large debt burden caused by past losses.

In 1988 therefore the government decided to reschedule or refinance the outstanding debt obligations of ISCOTT. Furthermore, after the end of the first management contract, it opted to lease the assets of ISCOTT to ISPAT, an Indian steel firm. Under the terms of the contract, the government of T-T receives an annual lease payment, as well as a percentage of any profits. While ISCOTT's outstanding liabilities continue to be guaranteed by the government, it is expected that under this lease arrangement ISCOTT could make a positive net contribution to the budget within the next few years. An offer by ISPAT to buy the company outright is also under consideration.

While it is too soon to judge the impact of the leasing arrangement, it seems that the first contract did improve the performance of ISCOTT. However, it remains

Table 8.10 *ISCOTT Summary accounts, 1984-8 (TT$m.)*

	1984	1985	1986	1987	1988
Operating revenues	132.8	114.0	254.9	316.3	396.3
Operating expenditures	316.4	353.6	471.4	554.3	589.5
Wages and salaries	35.0	35.0	49.8	54.4	54.3
Interest payments	55.0	110.6	103.0	116.6	101.8
Other goods/services	226.4	208.0	318.6	383.3	433.4
Operating balance	−183.6	−239.6	−216.5	−238.0	−193.2
Current transfers from gov.	0.0	0.0	0.0	0.0	0.0
Other income	11.5	3.6	5.3	2.7	3.1
Taxes	0.0	0.0	0.0	0.0	0.0
Current account balance	−172.1	−236.0	−211.2	−235.3	−190.1
Capital transfers from gov.	379.2	98.2	237.7	217.2	76.2
Other	3.5	−7.8	58.9	6.5	11.9
OVERALL BALANCE	205.8	−129.9	−33.8	−24.6	−125.8
Total transfers from gov.	379.2	98.2	237.7	217.2	76.2
Taxes to gov.	0.0	0.0	0.0	0.0	0.0
Memorandum items:					
Net transfer from gov.	379.2	98.3	237.7	217.2	76.2
Operating revenues as a % of operating expenditure	42.0	32.2	54.1	57.1	67.2
Wages as a % of operating expenditure	11.1	9.9	10.6	9.8	9.2
Current transfers from gov. as a % of total current revenue	0.0	0.0	0.0	0.0	0.0

Source: ISCOTT.

to be seen whether the company can be made commercially viable by the private sector.

The Development Finance Company (DFC)

DFC is a financial institution which makes concessional loans for larger investments. In 1989, its capital base was restructured after approaches were made to local and foreign investors. The strategy here was to give lending institutions an equity interest in the DFC so as to strengthen their commitment to providing technical assistance, monitoring loan funds and improving DFC's efficiency and effectiveness. In the end, three international development financial institutions bought equity. Before the restructuring, the government owned 94.2% of DFC equity and the National Insurance Board owned 5.8% Since the divestment this has become: government, 38%; the International Finance Corporation (an arm of the World Bank), 34%; and the remainder is held by the NIB, the Commonwealth Development Corporation (of the UK) and the German Finance Company for Investments in Developing Countries.

According to the Chairman of the Divestment Committee, however, these private sector partners are not interested in managing the company: their equity investment ensures them only a presence on the board. The management of DFC has not changed, and the foreign equity participants are acting not on the basis of profit but out of a desire to assist the development process. Thus, whereas in TELCO there was a change in management control without a change in ultimate ownership, in the case of DFC the reverse has been the case. Although technically a privatization, then, the DFC transaction had none of the objectives associated with divestiture.

8.3.3 Key issues of T-T's experience with privatization

The main characteristic of T-T's privatization programme is the slowness of its implementation. During the first phase of privatization, only two transactions occurred. Under the NAR, a party more well-disposed to the private sector, there was a brief flurry of activity in 1988/9, then another period of inaction. Aside from the TELCO sale, the transactions involved have been small (Table 8.11), and have therefore had little impact on fiscal balances.

Furthermore, this list overstates the extent to which 'privatization' in the 1980s sense of the word has really occurred. Certainly, it is difficult to regard the DFC transaction in this light. Neither in the case of TELCO nor in that of ISCOTT has there been a transfer of the majority of asset ownership: rather, these transactions were more concerned with tapping into private sector management expertise and practices. Finally, while the NCB transactions ultimately involved a reduction in government equity holdings to less than 50%, this occurred not, it seems, because of a belief that such an action would improve the operations of the bank, but more as part of a programme of gradual asset transfer.

It cannot be said, then, that the NAR has expedited the privatization programme. Indeed, of the 12 enterprises originally slated for privatization in 1986, by 1991 7 still remained untouched by the programme, and in 9 the government still owned a majority of the equity. Despite this, there has been criticism of the programme from trade unions and political opponents of the NAR. In general, these focus on the accusation that privatization will facilitate a reconcentration of asset ownership. This criticism draws strength from some of the public share sales, where secondary market price rises have resulted in short-term profit-taking and a reduction in the distribution of the shares.[15] In fact, as shown in Chapter 4, though underpricing has occurred in all T-T's share issues for which we were able to obtain the relevant data, it has not been a spectacular phenomenon. Indeed, the secondary market price rises have been of a size very similar to those observed in private sector equity issues on developed-country stock exchanges. In some sense this is unsurprising, since T-T has used the 'tranche sale' method suggested elsewhere (see Vickers and Yarrow, 1988) as a means of establishing sale prices and avoiding underpricing.

The political reaction to such a small programme of sales, though, explains why the NAR Government in the third NCB tranche and both TCL tranches concentrated far more on asset distribution issues than on expected efficiency gains. All these tranches have been too recent to make any categorical statement about the

Table 8.11 *Privatization revenues*

Date	Enterprise & Tranche	Number of shares	Share price (TT$)	Revenues (TT$m.)	% of GDP
1978	NCB I	2.4 million	$1.80	4.32	0.05
1980	NCB II	0.9 million	$2.60	2.26	0.02
1988	NCB III	3.4 million	$0.69	2.35	0.01
1989	TCL I	12.0 million	$0.75	9.00	0.05
1990	TCL II	21.0 million	$0.85	17.85	0.10
1989	TELCO			361.00	2.10
1988	ISCOTT	(lease)		n.a.	n.a.
1989	DFC	(equity restructuring)		n.a.	n.a.
Total				369.78	2.33

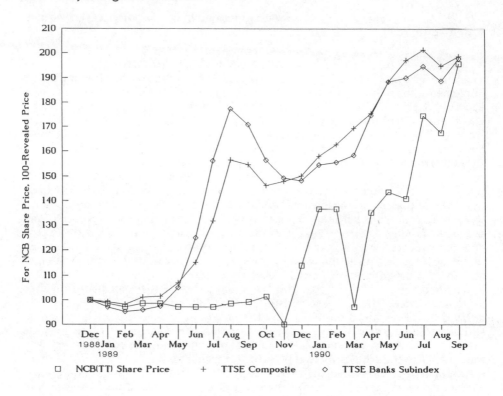

Figure 8.1 *NCB share price vs TTSE indices (December 1988 = 100)*

impact of ownership transfer on enterprise performance in T-T. The only impressionistic evidence we have derives from the performance of the two firms' share prices against the rest of the TTSE (Figs 8.1 and 8.2). Especially for TCL, the correlation between the firm's equity prices and overall market movements suggests at minimum that they are not dramatically outperforming other enterprises in the rest of the exchange. However, a longer period of time will need to elapse before efficiency impacts can be judged.

The concentration on allocation issues was undoubtedly a response to strong domestic concerns about income distribution. Two other facets of T-T's privatization programme can also be viewed as a response to the economic and political constraints outlined in sections 8.1 and 8.2. The first is that there has been no transfer of ultimate ownership to foreign enterprises, although this could have occurred in both the ISCOTT and the TELCO transactions. This is unsurprising, given the strong opposition to any policy that would reverse progress in localization in T-T. Second, there have been no direct sales of enterprises to the domestic private sector. The weakness of this sector has already been mentioned in section 8.1, and a fuller analysis is given in section 8.4. Finally in this section, however, we present the new developments in privatization policy that are likely to result in a substantial increase in the privatization programme in T-T.

8.3.4 Recent developments and the future of privatization

As is traditional, the government of T-T developed a pipeline of enterprises for sale. This comprised at most ten firms, all of which were small apart from the

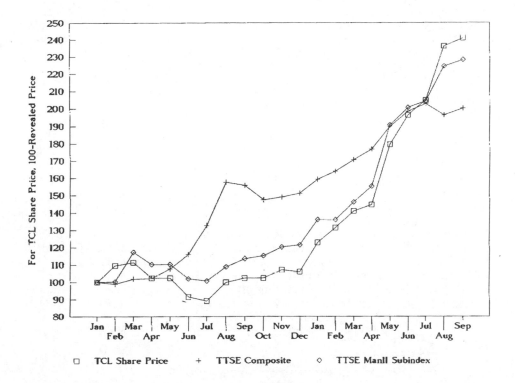

Figure 8.2   *TCL share price vs TTSE indices (January 1989 = 100)*

national airline, BWIA, and Arawak Cement Limited. As noted above, though, progress in divesting this pipeline was slow. Instead, domestic developments have led the government to adapt privatization for a rather unusual purpose.

In 1986, as part of fiscal cuts, the government suspended the cost-of-living adjustments made to civil servants' salaries and, in 1989, it implemented a nominal 10% cut in civil servants' wages. The real value of public wages thus fell dramatically during the period. In response, the civil servants sued the government in the courts, and won their case. The courts ordered the back payment of lost salaries, and in addition awarded an additional cost-of-living adjustment. This immediately created a substantial government liability of TT$1.7bn (or *c.* 8% of GDP) owed to its own workforce. While it has declared itself unable to pay this liability in the short run, it is under a legal obligation to do so.

The government has decided to use its equity holdings to pay off the liability. It has therefore created the State Unit Trust Fund in a new institution called the National Investment Company, whose assets will consist of shares in the ten to twelve most profitable public enterprises.[16] The government will sell a portion of these units to institutional investors in T-T, and use the proceeds to pay off part of its debt to public employees. The remainder of the debt will be paid by simply distributing units directly to public employees. The units will be tradable on the TTSE, and will pay dividends. Through this mechanism, then, the government is planning to instrument a privatization that will dwarf anything that has gone before in T-T.

In terms of the goals of privatization, this is the public finance objective instrumented at its most extreme. In some senses, although brought about in an unusual way, it represents a logical step forward to privatization in a country which is unwilling to sell assets to foreigners, but where the majority of the state's holdings are large and involve unique management knowledge such that direct sale to the domestic private sector is not an option. However, if instrumented, it will be one of the stranger causes of privatization in our study.

8.4 The private sector

This section focuses on the private industrial/manufacturing sector. This, of course, overlooks the agricultural sector, which is important on account of its share of aggregate employment and its role as employer of last resort in an economy afflicted by high unemployment rates in the formal sector. However, the structural inefficiency of T-T's agricultural sector is well attested, and needs no further discussion here.[17] Furthermore, it is clear that little privatization activity will take place in this sector thanks to the political need to support the operations of Caroni. It is therefore somewhat irrelevant to our analysis.

The private manufacturing sector in T-T consists largely of light manufacturing plants established to provide goods for domestic and regional markets. These can be categorized as assembly products, building materials, components for motor vehicles, food processing, garment manufacturing and certain household products. These industries are in general highly import-dependent, and are characterized by poor domestic linkages. In the following two sections, we analyse the structure and efficiency of this domestic industry in order to establish the potential of the private sector to provide a competitive environment for privatized enterprises.

8.4.1 Structure of the manufacturing sector

As is typical in developing countries, information on the structure of the manufacturing sector is weak. *Ex cathedra* pronouncements about elites and oligarchs abound, especially in the Caribbean. In order to gauge the accuracy of such statements, we rely on the little published material that has appeared on both the structure and the efficiency of the manufacturing sector as a whole.[18] While this material has the drawback of not separating out public and private sector manufacturing, it does give a good picture of market conditions across the entire sector even if in some areas the number of monopolies is inflated by the presence of the SOE sector in the data. The published material on the structure of the manufacturing sector relates to industries' competitiveness by relying on the structure–conduct–performance hypothesis. This assumes, somewhat simplistically, that firms behave according to the market structure in which they find themselves.[19] Market structure in this sense refers to the number of firms operating in a particular market, and the relative size of these firms. Thus, analysis of market structure traditionally starts with an assessment of market concentration in different industries.

With regard to concentration ratios, Table 8.12 classifies T-T's 42 manufacturing subsectors into high-, medium-, and low-concentration industries (HCIs, MCIs and LCIs) by sales, using a four-firm measure of concentration. In HCIs, the four largest firms account for 70% or more of total sales (including imports), in MCIs they account for between 35 and 69% of total sales, and in LCIs for less than 35%. Thus, 42% of the total number of industries can be classified as HCIs, 31% as MCIs, while only 27% fall into the LCI category (although employment ratios show that it is the LCIs that take the greatest share of employment). In the HCIs, one important characteristic is that the number of business establishments in each industry is relatively small: only one industry has more than nine firms in

Table 8.12   *Classification of industries by concentration category, 1982*

	Industries		Employment	
Concentration Category (Sales)	Number	Percent of total	Number	Percent of total
High (70% and over)	19	42.2	9,924	32.5
Medium (35 to 69%)	14	31.1	8,229	27.0
Low (34% and under)	12	26.7	12,371	40.5
Total	45	100.0	30,524	100.0

Source: Crichton and Farrell, 1988, p. 164.

it, six have between five and nine firms, a further six have between two and four firms, while five industries are monopolies (two of which are SOEs). As these sales concentration ratios include imports, the above figures suggest that firms in HCIs operate behind significant entry barriers (whether natural or caused by high rates of effective protection) and are thus shielded from competition. MCIs and LCIs both display a far greater variance in the number of firms in each industry, and also show increasing evidence of import competition as concentration ratios decline.

Table 8.13 shows the concentration ratios calculated by industry group. The average of all the groups is 57%. On an individual industry basis, out of a total of 45 industries, roughly 29 have a concentration ratio greater than this average, while 19 have concentration ratios of over 70%. From these data, Crichton and Farrell (1988:174) conclude 'generally, and on average, concentration in the manufacturing sector in Trinidad and Tobago is high'.

Table 8.14 combines the analysis of manufacturing by concentration with an analysis of industry structure, looking at the number of firms in an industry, and the size ratios of those firms. In terms of the debate about firms' performance, it is possible to think of a continuum running from monopoly and oligopoly situations (HCIs, few firms, large size ratios), through various combinations of indicators suggesting that firms have some market power, to a perfect competition situation (LCIs, many firms, small size ratios). It is in the latter situation where one would expect firms to be operating efficiently from an economic rather than an allocative point of view.

Based on Table 8.14, we can conclude the following. In the 13 HCIs with few

Table 8.13   *Concentration of sales (adjusted for imports) and employment by industry group, 1982*

	Total Number of Industries	Sales Concentration Ratio	Employment Concentration Ratio
Food Processors	14	65.3	67.2
Drink and Tobacco	3	94.9	95.0
Textiles & Garments	4	16.6	39.6
Printing & Publishing	2	67.0	37.4
Paper Converters	1	31.3	18.1
Wood & Related Products	2	10.9	20.3
Chemicals & Non-Metallic Minerals	9	96.0	92.0
Pharmaceuticals	1	46.9	42.3
Assembly-Type and Related Industries	6	59.9	80.1
Other Metal Industries	3	52.4	71.0
TOTAL	45	57.0	

Source: Crichton and Farrell, 1988, p. 173.

Table 8.14 *Distribution of industries according to degree of concentration, ratio of establishments, and number*

	Large Size Ratios		Small Size Ratios		
Concentration Category	Few Units (≤10)	Many Units (>10)	Few Units (≤10)	Many Units (>10)	Total
High (70% and over)	13	0	6	0	19
Medium (35 to 69%)	6	6	2	0	14
Low (34% and under)	2	8	1	1	12
Total	21	14	9	1	45

Source: Crichton and Farrell, 1988, p. 177.

firms and large size ratios, and the 6 HCIs with few firms and small size ratios, monopoly power or oligopolistic competition or collusion can be expected to exist. In the 6 MCIs with few firms and large size ratios, the 6 MCIs with many firms and large size ratios, and the 2 MCIs with few firms and small size ratios, conditions are similarly favourable for oligopolistic competition or collusion, although this is increasingly offset by the presence of some import competition. Finally, in the SCIs there are still industries where such oligopolistic behaviour is possible. In the 12 SCIs with many firms and small size ratios, firms are closer to the position of 'pure competition', although even here, as Crichton and Farrell report, firms are involved in both price and non-price competition. In general, they conclude that 'there are . . . several markets where there may be a strong disposition toward the exercise of significant market power' (p. 186).

The nature of the private sector in T-T therefore appears to call for a strong pro-competition policy combined with regulation of the worst excesses of monopoly. We return in section 8.6 to the government's capacity to carry out such a programme. In terms of the privatization debate, however, the importance of such conclusions on industrial structure are clear, namely that the efficiency gains consequent on privatizing into the domestic sector may not be that great. This conclusion from an examination of the structure of the manufacturing sector is reinforced by an examination of evidence on the sector's efficiency.

8.4.2 Efficiency of the manufacturing sector

It is generally accepted that the private manufacturing sector in T-T is weak. Before the oil booms of the 1970s and early 1980s, the sector was generally characterized by the production of consumer durables and non-durables for domestic requirements in areas where the domestic market was of a sufficient size for plants to be set up with minimum efficient scale. However, these industries were supported by the provision of a variety of incentives such as duty-free concessions on imported inputs and price and non-price protection of the domestic market from import competition.

As a result of this structure of development, the private manufacturing sector came to be typified by the following characteristics: a low level of transformation in import-substituting manufacturing; a low level of linkages with the rest of the domestic economy; as a consequence, heavy reliance on imported goods; in the absence of competition due to protection, the quality of local goods was lower than that of comparable imports, while prices were higher; and a weak export performance. The sector was a heavy net user of foreign exchange and came to rely on the foreign-exchange earnings of the oil sector.

This fragility meant that the manufacturing sector was ill-prepared for the twin shocks it suffered, namely the boom-induced Dutch Disease of the 1970s, and the declines in foreign-exchange availability and in domestic demand that occurred after the early 1980s. It was hit especially badly as a result of the latter problems. For example, output of motor vehicles fell from 22,900 units in 1984 to 11,900 units in 1985, output of fridges fell from 21,800 to 6,400 in the same period, while between 1983 and 1985 output of textiles, garments and footwear fell by 30%. Importantly, the decline in domestic demand was not accompanied by a switch into export production, confirming that much of the domestic manufacturing sector is simply not competitive in world markets: manufacturing exports have accounted for only 5% of total exports in recent years. By the end of the 1980s, the situation of manufacturing had not greatly improved, so that the World Bank could conclude:[20]

> All three leading manufacturing subsectors [food processing, assembly industries and petrochemicals] are flawed, and none furnishes a sure foundation for rapid expansion of production.

Thus, due to the factors outlined above, the manufacturing sector has also remained small. As a proportion of GDP, the whole sector (i.e. public and private) barely increased between 1973, when it was 11% of GDP, and 1985, when it was 12% of GDP. In fact, this aggregate figure masks a decline in the relative contribution of the private manufacturing sector, since this period includes the setting-up of the large gas-based industries.

The picture of the domestic manufacturing sector in T-T is clear enough. It is, in general, of small size, is performing weakly, and is characterized by extensive monopoly and oligopoly positions. The implications for privatization are twofold. First, in the estimated 14 industries where SOEs exist but are not monopolists, efficiency gains from transfer to the domestic private sector may be much smaller than expected. It would appear to make sense for the government to copy Jamaica's example and start to focus on pro-competition policy rather than the simple transfer of assets. Second, there are important industries in which SOEs are monopolists. This is especially the case with the gas-based manufacturers. Alternative management teams cannot be found in T-T itself: only through the involvement of the foreign sector could the private sector be brought in in any way other than the packaging of equity for public sale or for transfer to civil servants.

8.4.3 The foreign sector

As has been emphasized throughout this chapter, the main constraint here is not whether foreign enterprises will be able to buy or operate privatized firms, but whether the government will allow portions of domestic production to be owned by non-residents. As in most Caribbean countries, T-T has experienced significant amounts of foreign investment from North America, especially in the pre-Independence era and in the first stage of economic policy-making. However, as noted in section 8.2, the whole policy of freedom for foreign investors came under attack after the 1970 riots. Localization of asset ownership became a key goal of government policy, and restrictions on foreign investment were introduced. These included the Alien Landholders Act, which prohibited foreigners from holding equity in a company without express permission from the President.

With the faltering of growth in the 1980s, though, the new NAR Government adopted a more welcoming attitude to foreign investment. This included the revision of the foreign investment code, and the elaboration of new regulations in the Investment Policy document produced by the Industrial Development Corporation. This outlined the creation of the Investment Co-ordinating Committee (the 'One-Stop Shop') and the ratification of MIGA as proof of the government's new policy on foreign investment. While the Investment Policy document expressed a preference for joint ventures, it allows 100% foreign ownership of firms if the foreign investor provides 100% of the capital and technology, and either exports 75% or more of its output, or uses substantial supplies of local raw materials, or generates significant employment.[21] Finally, in response to the creation of the Caribbean Stock Exchange, the government repealed the Alien Landholders Act and replaced it with the more liberal Foreign Investment Act of 1991.

Given this more relaxed attitude to the issue of foreign investment, it is possible that privatization via the selling of SOEs directly to the foreign private sector may be a way of getting round the constraint of the domestic sector's small size and weakness. Indeed, to some extent this has already occurred in the TELCO deal, and perhaps will occur in the case of ISCOTT. Furthermore, T-T is well used to the joint-venture approach to its industrial development. As noted in section 8.2, the more successful of the gas-based industries were those in which the government went ahead with an experienced foreign partner, while some of the least successful were those where foreign enterprises had bailed out of the project at an early stage.[22] This history suggests a pattern of sales where the government holds on to a strategic portion of equity, while handing over management control to the foreign firm (e.g. TELCO).

However, it would be foolish to ignore the still considerable domestic political constraint to a wholesale programme of sale of state assets to the foreign private sector. As noted earlier, while the SOE programme may now be perceived as something of an economic failure, it has fulfilled some important political objectives, namely the localization of decision-making and the promotion of African and (to a lesser extent) Indian aspirations. Gini coefficients and disparity ratios confirm that there was a substantial reduction in inequality during the period 1970–82 (Henry, 1989). There is now a genuine fear that privatization, whether to the local or foreign private sector, will reverse that trend. Thus, while it seems that the government could allow a certain number of enterprises to be bought by foreign firms, it is likely that there is a limit to the number of enterprises that could be sold this way.

8.4.3 Conclusions

Turning to the question posed at the beginning of this section, namely whether the private sector is large enough and competitive enough to ensure that a transfer of ownership from public to private will bring about efficiency gains, the answer must be – in some limited cases. We have seen that the domestic private sector is small, often monopolistic, and both weak and inefficient, and thus unlikely to produce substantial efficiency gains after privatization. Domestic direct sales may thus have to be confined to some smaller industrial SOEs where competitive markets already exist. As to the foreign sector, we have seen that, while the current government is more accommodating to foreign investors than the previous one, there are political constraints that would curb any widespread privatization initiative.

8.5 Resource mobilization and capital markets

A further issue in the privatization debate relates to the ability to carry out the privatization of SOEs through the local capital markets. The main capital market, the Trinidad and Tobago Stock Exchange (TTSE), is one part of a financial system which is fairly well-developed. As at 1986, it comprised 8 commercial banks operating 117 branches, 8 finance companies, 6 trust companies, 4 thrift institutions, 3 building societies, 43 active insurance companies, 3 development finance institutions, 2 merchant banks, over 300 credit unions, over 140 pension funds and a stock exchange. While, as we saw in section 8.1, the financial sector suffered severely in the macroeconomic collapse of the 1980s, it has remained broadly-based and financial intermediation therefore remains a broadly competitive activity. As a chief instrument for privatization in T-T, the TTSE is described in the following section, while section 8.5.2 discussses some of the issues surrounding its interaction with privatization.

8.5.1 *The size and characteristics of the TTSE*
The TTSE as an institution is relatively young. Before 1981, an informal securities market existed that was overseen by the Ministry of Finance and the Central Bank. This achieved some prominence following the government's decision to localize the foreign-owned banking and manufacturing sectors of the economy. The stock market as a formal body has been in existence only since the passage of the Securities Industry Act of 1981.

There are six member firms of the Exchange, although one of these was suspended from April 1988, and another is a non-active member. Trading takes place on three days a week, when securities are traded in alphabetical order, on a call-over basis. The Exchange operates on a cash basis, and the settlement period is now 5 days. Only domestic securities are traded, i.e. no foreign bonds or shares are listed, and as at the end of 1988 there were 33 listed companies with 39 listed issues. Thanks to the Alien Landholders Act, until recently shareholders generally had to be T-T residents (whether individuals or companies), although aliens can be granted a licence by the President authorizing them to hold shares. Once granted, this licence allows the freedom to trade in and repatriate foreign exchange.

The performance of the Stock Exchange since 1981 is summarized in Table 8.15. This shows clearly the pertinent development, namely that the Stock Exchange experienced a continuous decline between 1982 and 1988. Market capitalization by the end of 1988 had fallen to about one-third of its 1982 value, from TT$3.2bn to TT$1.1bn. The annual value of shares traded had fallen even faster, from TT$0.6bn to TT$0.1bn, over the same period, and the local market index fell accordingly from 145.9 at the end of 1982 to 32.4 at the end of 1988. Aside from a temporary blip in 1986, the decline in the TTSE was also associated with a fall in the number and value of new issues raised on the Exchange. Thus, whereas TT$81m. was raised from 11 issues in 1982, only TT$9m. was raised from 1 issue in 1989.

While the main cause of decline was clearly the poor performance of the ecoonomy, there were other reasons why the TTSE declined so rapidly. First, profitable firms have limited their recourse to equity funding because of excessively harsh disclosure requirements, and the size of the Exchange has been limited by tight listing requirements. Second, investor confidence has been hit by heavy capital losses caused by the price declines of the secondary market. These capital losses also led institutional investors to prefer government bonds or straight bank deposits, as interest rates on these have been more stable and more attractive. In order to counter some of the technical issues amongst these problems, the Stock Exchange has proposed an amendment of the Securities Industry Act, which would, *inter alia*, improve disclosure standards, relax listing requirements, and move towards the registration of public companies and the creation of facilities for trading in unlisted shares. This should have a positive impact on strengthening the TTSE. Another source of confidence is that the position of the Stock Exchange has started to improve from 1989. Over the whole year, the overall index increased by 49% to 48.7% (with the rise in the market index continuing into 1990), while total market capitalization increased from TT$1.1bn to TT$1.7bn.

Table 8.15 Trinidad and Tobago Stock Exchange performance

1. Market performance 1981–90

	Market Index[a]	Trading Value (TT$'000)	Trading Volume ('000)	Market Capitalization (TT$m.)	Market Capitalization (US$m.)	Market Dividend Yield (%)	Price/Earnings Ratio	Price/Book Value Ratio	No. of Firms Listed	No. of New Issues	Value of New Issues (TT$'000)
1981	122.40	45,977	11,161	2,821	1,175		12.43	2.3	29	1	22,000
1982	145.90	556,592	90,280	3,258	1,357	3.53	9.20	1.5	34	11	81,084
1983	71.60	362,212	71,576	2,427	1,011	5.92	7.30	0.8	34	5	19,563
1984	59.60	182,973	55,655	2,022	843	7.82	7.10	1.0	36	2	7,533
1985	49.10	148,565	48,483	1,668	463	7.69	9.21	0.9	36	1	3,462
1986	38.30	186,040	85,003	1,346	374	7.81	4.97	0.7	33	3	62,824
1987	39.46	11,600	9,200	1,398	388	5.85	10.35	0.7	33	0	0
	38.96	18,400	19,900								
	40.73	33,400	19,800								
	39.96	27,200	27,200								
1988	37.62	49,300	20,700	1,136	268	6.29	8.30	0.6	33	1	2,346
	32.84	16,300	8,300								
	33.72	39,800	27,400								
	32.41	9,200	5,800								
1989	32.78	19,100	13,400	1,748	411				31	1	9,000
	37.34	8,400	6,500								
	50.13	98,400	39,900								
	48.68	167,500	82,800								

Sources: TTSE, *Annual Reports* (various), IFC, *Emerging Stock Markets Factbook*, 1990.

a) October 1981 = 100.

2. Impact of privatization stocks on TTSE, 1989

	Total Market Capitalization (TT$m.)	Trading Volume ('000)
TTSE total	1,748	142,561
NCB	28	1,544
TCL	44	2,235
NCB & TCL as % of TTSE total	4.10	2.65

Source: TTSE, *Factbook*, 1989.

8.5.2 *Privatization and the stock market*

The first question to be confronted is whether or not the Stock Exchange is sufficiently large for a programme of domestic share sales of public companies to be a viable option. It is clear that, compared to other countries where share issues have been more frequently used, T-T's stock market is relatively small. For example, the market capitalization in 1988 was only 6.6% of GDP as against a figure of roughly 50% in Malaysia and 25% in Jamaica. Furthermore, despite the fact that public shares have accounted for 5 out of the 8 separate transactions comprising the privatization programme to date, in terms of revenues public share issues have accounted for only TT$36m. out of total privatization receipts of TT$370m. The impact of the NCB and TCL sales on the TTSE has not been substantial: as Table 8.15 shows, in 1989 they accounted for only 4.1% of total market capitalization and 2.7% of trading volume. Thus, the privatizations to date have not significantly tested or expanded the market's capacity.

In addition, the size of potential privatizations is very large when compared to the current market capitalization of the Stock Exchange. For example, if the government were to decide to sell its entire stake in Arawak Cement Co. via a public share issue, then the value of the shares for sale would be equal to more than 10% of total market capitalization. In the case of the largest of the 'strategic' industries, TTMC, the nominal share value of the company represents 37% of the total market capitalization of the Stock Exchange. Sale of such large issues would clearly be ill-advised. Of course, the TTSE could receive a substantial expansion of its capitalization if plans to list the State Unit Trust Fund go ahead. In this case, though, there would be no call on savings mobilization through the Exchange, since the plan is to give the shares away to civil servants in lieu of their back wages. However, such an expansion might place severe strain on the technical capacity of the market to undertake the volume of trading that would occur following the unit trust's listing.

Thus, the absorptive capacity of the TTSE is limited. This suggests that privatization by way of public share issues will have to be restricted either to small firms or to a gradual programme of tranche sales in the larger enterprises. Furthermore, the small number of listed firms and the nature of trading make the TTSE an ineffective institution for enforcing efficient behaviour by firms. First, there are few comparator firms on the Exchange, so that the information costs to the small investor of monitoring a firm's performance are not significantly reduced by a Stock Market listing. Second, there is virtually no history of predatory behaviour or aggressive takeovers on the Exchange, so that market discipline remains very weak.[23] Finally, it is traditional for trading on the TTSE to remain in very narrow bounds. For example, TTSE *Annual Report* for 1989 reported:

> 91.5% of transactions on the floor of the Exchange took place at either no change in price from the previous transaction or at the minimum variance of $0.01, and 98.2% of all transactions occurred at a price variation of $0.05 or less. In 1988, the corresponding figures were 92.9% and 98.1% respectively.

This is not a pattern of trading consistent with a market that will impose discipline on enterprise managements by punishing departures from profit-maximizing behaviour.

Thus, it seems likely that privatization through public share issues will retain the orientation of the programme to date, namely as a method of spreading direct share ownership to workers and smaller investors rather than of improving the efficiency of a firm's operations. This may go some way towards tackling the criticism expressed in T-T that privatization is only about the reconcentration of asset ownership. Part of this criticism derives from the fact that historically the

Table 8.16 *Distribution of stock owwnership on the TTSE in 1985*

Number of shareholders in an enterprise	Number of such enterprises listed
< 500	11
500 to 5,000	20
5,000 to 10,000	3
10,000 to 20,000	3
> 20,000	1
Total	38

Source: Henry, 1989.

distribution of stock ownership has not been very wide, as Table 8.16 shows.

These data derive from 1985, before the recent NCB and TCL transactions which should presumably have lessened the degree of concentration. Under an asset-broadening strategy, then, it is likely that the government will try and attract new purchasers into the market. Whether these new investors contribute to the market or whether – in line with the Jamaican experience – they become largely passive shareholders will determine the future impact of privatization on the TTSE.

For the moment, though, for the reasons outlined above it does not seem that the TTSE is an institution through which major transfers of ownership could be instrumented.

8.6 Regulatory issues and constraints

8.6.1 The need for regulation

The analysis of section 8.4 suggested that a significant proportion of T-T's SOEs and privatized firms operate in industries that are either monopolistic or oligopolistic. In response, a welfare-maximizing government has two options: it can try to encourage competition or deregulate the industry in order to approximate more closely the position of perfect competition, or, if competition is not possible (in the case of natural monopoly and in industries characterized by minimum scale efficiencies), it can choose the regulatory option.

In common with most developing countries, T-T has not had a policy on competition *per se*. However, various policy actions have undoubtedly affected levels of competition in the economy, the most important of which has been trade policy and the creation of protected markets. Moves to reduce protective barriers, then, are probably the most important way of encouraging efficiency through competition, although such policies are strongly opposed by the domestic manufacturing sector which stands to lose rents in the process. T-T has reformed its trade policy in the 1980s by devaluing the real exchange rate, by reforming the tariff system, and by slowly reforming the negative list of import goods which require licences. While these developments should go some way to introducing more competitive forces into the economy, there is clearly a limit in T-T's case to how far domestic deregulation is an option. First, there are a number of industries which are natural monopolies (especially the utilities). Second, there are a further group of industries where domestic competition is not an option because of market size (especially the heavy industries).[24] Thus, in T-T there is clearly a need for regulation, a need which exists independently of whether the industry is in public or private hands. T-T is one of the few countries in our study which has a lengthy and continuous history of regulation, and it is to an examination of this that we now turn.

8.6.2 The experience of regulation

Regulatory experience in T-T is confined to regulation of the public utilities by the Public Utilities Commission (PUC).[25] As noted earlier, this was set up in 1966 to review utility rates, and given sufficient powers to succeed in its objectives through its statutory right to demand information from the utilities concerned. However, its early performance was far from satisfactory, as the Report of the Committee to Review the Role and Functions of the Public Utilities Commission of 1979 discovered. The reasons cited there for its failure were: (i) the excessive length of cases caused by the over-judicialization of the rate review procedure; (ii) the lack of Ministerial support for the PUC and lack of full co-operation from the utilities themselves; (iii) poor appointments to the PUC (it lacked a Chairman between 1974 and 1979); and (iv) lack of clear guidelines for utility pricing, and pressure from government for utilities to make decisions aiming at the maximum availability of services rather than profitability.

These are reasons, of course, why utility regulation has commonly failed in other countries. As a result of the failure of the PUC, the utilities turned in very poor performances, with extremely low, regulated prices resulting in poor revenues, poor quality of services, and a heavy reliance on government transfers.

Following the Committee's report (Government of Trinidad and Tobago, 1979), the government introduced legislative changes to strengthen the PUC. It was given an explicit pricing goal after the report of a further task-force in 1983, which gave consideration to the principle of utility self-sufficiency and recommended that, while some subsidies should exist in the case of social benefit, utilities should aim to cover all their recurrent expenditures and a portion of their development budgets. Thus, from 1982 onwards, utilities were permitted to approach the PUC for rate setting, in the context of a push for greater efficiency.

These rate rises have largely been awarded, and the PUC has been more active in monitoring service quality. In certain cases, it has succeeded in improving the performance of the utilities: for example, in both TELCO and TTEC between 1984 and 1988, the utilities satisfied the condition that they reduce their financial dependence on government, while also slowly bettering the quality of the service to consumers. In the case of TELCO, the PUC used consumer surveys to monitor consumer satisfaction with the company so as to check that rate rises were being accompanied by operational improvements. In the case of TTEC, the PUC also distanced itself from its previous history as a subsidy-approving body when, in response to allegations that its approved rate rise was too high for the poor, it argued that subsidizing electricity was a legislative rather than a rate-setting function.

However, in the cases of the Port Authority, PTSC and WASA, the PUC has had very little success. The Port Authority and PTSC have been described as 'utilities . . . [remaining] . . . in the horse and donkey cart age' (Ryan, 1985). PTSC was awarded a rate increase in 1985, but from such a low level of revenue that the financial situation was barely improved (Table 8.17). An investigation of PTSC by the PUC showed that the corporation was in a very poor state, and unable to offer the public a reasonable level of service. Passenger numbers were in decline, despite heavy expenditure on new buses, an increase in fleet size, and a large increase in the labour force, while new buses made little difference to the volume of service provided. It was clear that PTSC needed far more than just a rate adjustment in order to improve its performance, and that the powers of the PUC were insufficient to deal with the problem. The Port Authority has been described (Ryan, 1985) as . . . 'the Augean Stables of the utilities', where the PUC has sought to use its rating mechanism to 'nudge the Port Authority into an orbit where sanity would prevail' through quantifying inefficiencies in the authority's

Table 8.17 *Public Transport Service Coporation summary accounts, 1984–9 (TT$m.)*

	1984	1985	1986	1987	1988	Est. 1989
Operating revenues	17.4	24.2	25.7	24.8	21.8	16.9
Operating expenditures	181.7	178.8	175.3	156.0	148.0	175.1
Wages and salaries	124.0	123.2	121.0	102.6	99.7	87.4
Interest payments	0.0	0.0	0.0	1.3	0.9	0.0
Other goods/services	57.7	55.6	54.3	52.1	47.4	87.7
Operating balance	−164.3	−154.6	−149.6	−131.2	−126.2	−158.2
Current transfers from gov.	159.6	162.7	132.3	141.5	137.0	120.0
Other income	0.0	0.0	0.0	0.0	0.0	0.0
Taxes	0.0	0.0	0.0	0.0	0.0	0.0
Current account balance	−4.7	8.1	−17.3	10.3	10.8	−38.2
Capital transfers from gov.	21.0	25.8	9.5	6.4	0.0	2.0
Capital revenues	0.0	0.0	0.0	0.0	0.0	0.0
Capital expenditures	31.8	42.9	13.6	4.0	2.3	0.0
OVERALL BALANCE	−15.5	−9.0	−21.4	12.7	8.5	−36.2
Total transfers from gov.	180.6	188.5	141.8	147.9	137.0	122.0
Taxes to gov.	0.0	0.0	0.0	0.0	0.0	0.0
Memorandum items:						
Net transfer from gov.	180.6	188.5	141.8	147.9	137.0	122.0
Operating revenue as a % of operating expenditure	9.6	13.5	14.7	15.9	14.7	9.7
Wages as a % of operating expenditure	68.2	68.9	69.0	65.8	67.4	49.9
Current transfers from gov. as a % of operating revenue	917.2	672.3	514.8	570.6	628.4	710.1

Source: PTSC.

operations worth roughly TT$27m. per annum. However, there has been little impact on the actual performance of the utility. Finally, WASA is the most inefficient water authority in Latin America and the Caribbean.

Thus, on balance the experience of regulation by the PUC of these particular utilities does not point to a particularly sophisticated regulatory capacity within T-T. In particular, the PUC has been unable to overcome the problems of regulatory lag, the hiding of sensitive or critical material by the utility under review, the obstruction of the regulator by late submission of material, and the fact that the PUC only has the power to regulate 'after-the-fact', i.e. after investment decisions have been taken. This latter difficulty has meant that the PUC has found itself having to sanction a rate rise on account of poor investment decisions that have already been made. Thus, a review of the PUC experience in T-T does not suggest that the government would be able to carry out a more widespread regulatory role effectively, unless significant efforts were made to improve current capabilities. As we argued in Chapters 5 and 6, this should place a limit on the speed at which the government privatizes enterprises which economic welfare suggests should be the subject of regulation.

8.7 Conclusions

Comparing the experiences of the two Caribbean countries in our study presents what at first blush appears a paradox, whereby Jamaica has carried out a programme of privatization far more extensive than T-T's but with a much lower per capita income. However, our analysis suggests that the possibilities for privatization in T-T have been strongly determined both by the nature of the economy and by the history and political attitudes that led to the original creation of the SOE sector. T-T's mineral economy, the nature of the government's attempts to diversify the productive base, the origins and policy goals of the SOE sector, and the domestic consensus in favour of localization have all served to reduce both the economic rationale for privatization and political commitment to it as a policy. In a normal sense, then, we would not expect privatization to progress at any great speed in Trinidad and Tobago. However, it is possible that a pressing budgetary need will now lead to a quite dramatic transfer of core SOEs to the government's own workers. If this transaction goes ahead, it will be one of the more singular privatizations among our case studies.

Notes

1. Most notably a reduction in marginal tax rates and the introduction of a value-added tax in 1990.
2. Harewood, J. and R. Henry, *Inequality in a Post-Colonial Society: Trinidad and Tobago, 1956–1981*, St Augustine: ISER, The University of the West Indies, 1985, calculate that the Gini coefficient of income inequality moved from 0.43 to 0.51 between 1957/8 and 1971/2.
3. Government of Trinidad and Tobago, *White Paper on Public Participation in Industrial and Commercial Activities*, Government Printer, Port-of-Spain, 1972.
4. Source: Ministry of Finance, personal communication. Note that the value of nominal shareholdings is a very poor guide to the net worth of the firm, especially when an enterprise has substantial accumulated losses.
5. NAR, *Medium Term Macro Planning Framework, 1989–95*.
6. For a comprehensive discussion of SOE reform programmes, see Shirley and Nellis (1991).
7. Note that the aggregate figures are biased by the fact that 6 loss-making companies were closed down after the government concluded that they were economically non-viable, and, for some of them, that their functions could be better filled by the private sector. However, these enterprises were in general small and their removal does not detract from the overall results.
8. World Bank, *Trinidad and Tobago: A Program for Policy Reform and Renewed Growth*, World Bank, Washington DC, 1988.
9. Government of Trinidad and Tobago, *White Paper on Public Participation in Industry*.
10. In other words, the government was presenting nationalization as the first stage of privatization.
11. Private communication from TTSE.
12. Private communication from TTSE.
13. C&W had recently completed the purchase of Telecommunications of Jamaica – see Chapter 7.
14. Source: interview with Frank Rampersad, January 1990.
15. Interview with Hamid O'Brien, Chairman of the Divestment Committee, Ministry of Finance.
16. The exact composition is not decided at the time of writing.
17. For a good exposition, see World Bank, *Trinidad and Tobago: A Program for Policy Reform and Renewed Growth*, World Bank, Washington DC, 1988, pp. 77–92.
18. In particular, Crichton and Farrell (1988) who derive their results from the Central Statistical Office's 1982 survey of business establishments.
19. Crichton and Farrell express their own concern with this paradigm as an essentially static analysis with insufficient attention paid to the issue of feedbacks and to the decisions of the firm concerning which market to locate in.
20. World Bank, *A Program for Policy Reform*, op. cit.
21. It also declares certain activities out-of-bounds for foreign investors, namely land development, petroleum marketing, small-scale enterprise, the distributive trades, advertising and the media, management services, auditing, handicrafts, furniture, insurance, cement manufacture, taxi

services, and tyre retreading. Some of these are, of course, substantial subsectors of the economy.

22. As Gelb (1988) comments, 'One lesson from Trinidad and Tobago's experience is that foreign investors are important in screening projects, diversifying risk, and securing market access for large, export-oriented, resource-based industries.'

23. Although one company, CLICO, 'emerged during the year [1989] as a corporate raider' according to the *Trinidad and Tobago Sunday Express*.

24. Competition, of course, exists in export markets for these firms.

25. There are five public utilities, namely the Port Authority, the Public Transport Service Corporation (PTSC), the Trinidad and Tobago Electricity Commission (TTEC), the Trinidad and Tobago Telephone Company (TELCO), and the Water and Sewage Authority (WASA).

9   MALAYSIA

9.1 Introduction

Malaysia has frequently been portrayed as one of the standard-bearers
of privatization amongst developing countries. As early as 1985 the *Euromoney*
business magazine claimed that 'outside the UK, Malaysia's programme of selling
off huge chunks of the public estate is probably the most extensive of its kind in
the world'.[1] In this chapter we argue that, throughout the 1980s at least, this
reputation was unwarranted. Though the programme has had a high profile and
has involved a considerable volume of resources, its net impact on the relative
balance of the public and private sectors has been minimal. It has been more
closely linked with other government policy objectives than with the basic
economic objectives assigned to privatization. This is somewhat ironic since,
among the countries in this study, Malaysia has the strongest economic base on
which privatization can thrive. It is the largest economy, has the most sophisticated capital market, and a thriving private sector. However, much of the potential of the economy, including the effects of the privatization programme, have
been constrained by government intervention, in the main through the structures
and consequences of the New Economic Policy (NEP), the ethnically-based
affirmative action programme which has shaped the conduct of economic policy
in Malaysia since the early 1970s.

9.1.1 Macroeconomic background

Malaysia is a lower-middle-income economy of approximately 16.5 million
people, of whom 60% are Malay (known as the Bumiputra) and the remainder
non-Malay (principally Chinese and Indian). GNP per capita in 1988 was
US$1,940 (*World Development Report*, 1990). The two decades since 1970 have
witnessed a period of significant growth in the Malaysian economy, in line with
other emerging Newly Industrialized Countries (NICs). However, during the early
1980s the economy faced a severe recession, following a 17% deterioration in the
terms of trade between 1981 and 1982. The current account deficit grew
dramatically during the period, the public sector deficit, which had averaged
approximately 10% of GDP during the first NEP decade, reached 21.7% of GDP
in 1982, and between 1984 and 1985 real growth fell from 8% to −1%. The subsequent 1985–7 recovery programme saw the economy return to pre-recession levels
of activity, with real GDP growth rates of 5.3%, 8.7% and 7.6% being recorded
for the years 1987–9 respectively (Fig. 9.1).

   Gross domestic savings levels in Malaysia are particularly high, averaging
approximately 29% of GDP over the NEP period (Table 9.1), and exceeding 33%
in 1990. However, much of this saving is contractual. In particular, the largest
single savings institution, the Employees Provident Fund (EPF), accounts for

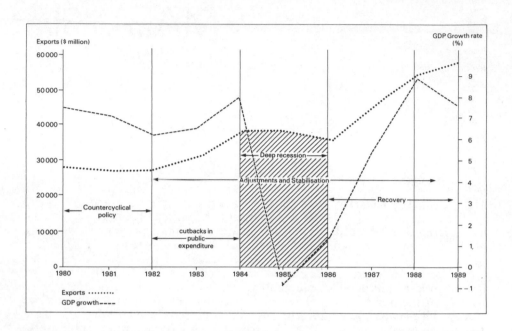

Figure 9.1 *Malaysia: Growth, recession and recovery, 1980–89*
Sources: Fifth Malaysia Plan 1986-1990 and the Mid-Term Review of the Fifth Malaysia Plan 1986-1990.

approximately 20% of total employment income, whilst the investment trusts of the Permodalan Nasional Berhad (PNB) (see section 9.2), and the Islamic savings institutions attract a further large proportion of these savings.

As Table 9.1 indicates, the investment to GDP ratio has risen rapidly since Independence, and currently averages approximately 31% of GDP, having exceeded 40% in 1982-3. Since the emergence of the NEP, the public sector share total investment has risen dramatically, reaching a peak during the construction boom of the early 1980s, when, for the only time since Independence, public sector investment[2] accounted for 50% of total investment in the economy. The economic restructuring programme, combined with the development of a more private sector-oriented development strategy, has seen public sector investment drop back sharply since 1986.

Malaysia is a resource-rich economy, both in terms of oil and natural gas as well as non-mineral resources, yet despite this its development since Independence in 1957 has been based on a broadening of its production and non-traditional export sectors. At Independence the economy was dominated by the agricultural sector, which accounted for over 40% of GDP, 60% of formal sector employment, and almost 70% of export earnings. In particular, Malaysia was the world's largest producer of natural rubber and tin. Over time, however, though remaining a world leader in these two commodities, the country has successfully diversified activity across its broad resource base, and has seen the emergence of the hydrocarbon industry and other manufacturing activity which between them now dominate the economy.

Table 9.1 *Composition of Gross Domestic Product (%)*

	1956–60	*1961–65*	*MP1*[a] *1966–70*	*MP2 1971–75*	*MP3 1976–80*	*MP4 1981–85*	*MP5 1986–90*
Real GDP growth	4.10	5.00	5.40	8.00	8.60	5.20	4.60
Functional composition (% of GDP)							
Agriculture	40.20	31.50		27.70		20.80	21.10
Mining	6.30	9.00		4.60		10.50	10.60
Manufacture	8.20	10.40		16.40		19.70	24.10
Construction	3.00	4.50		3.80		4.80	3.20
Services	42.30	44.60		47.50		44.20	41.00
Economic classification (% of GDP)							
Consumption	79.20	80.50	80.30	77.70	69.50	72.50	69.00
Public	14.70	16.00	17.80	17.50	16.40	17.40	16.80
Private	64.50	64.50	62.50	60.20	53.10	55.10	52.20
Investment	12.60	18.90	16.70	24.40	27.40	36.30	27.50
Public	2.70	8.40	6.40	7.80	10.00	17.30	11.20
Private	9.90	10.50	10.30	16.60	17.40	19.00	16.30
Gross national savings (% of GDP)	16.60	17.80	18.30	20.80	30.00	27.50	31.30
Savings – investment (% of GDP)	4.00	−1.10	1.60	−3.60	2.60	−8.80	3.80

Source: Bank Negara Malaysia.

a) MP = Malaysian National Plan.

Real growth in the manufacturing sector averaged 10% per annum from Independence until the early 1980s, and although the sector's growth declined during the economic slowdown and recession from 1982 to 1986, recovery since 1986 has been rapid, with growth rates again reaching the pre-recession period.

Throughout the period from Independence until the late 1960s, the emphasis was on import substitution, but during the 1970s there was a shift towards labour-intensive and high-technology export-oriented production, to the extent that manufactured exports now account for over 50% of all exports. The 1980s saw an even greater emphasis on the manufacturing sector, especially as Malaysia has developed an increasingly outward-looking stance, although there is evidence of a reorientation towards the growing domestic market, especially in the capital-intensive and consumer durable sectors. The severity of the recession of the mid-1980s added extra stimulus to the need for even greater diversity in the economy, and has been followed by renewed measures aimed at greater liberalization of the domestic economy, the reduction of the role of the public sector in the economy, and the rejuvenation of foreign participation in the domestic economy.[3]

9.1.2 Structural constraints and the New Economic Policy

One of the most pervasive problems of the economy, and one which has widespread implications for the privatization programme as a whole, is the extent to which political structures create barriers to efficient intermediation of commercial risk. Consequently domestic risk aversion is exacerbated, leading to low levels of investment in productive activities (relative to aggregate savings). Investment opportunities abound in Malaysia; there are skilled human resources, both industrial and managerial, and a sophisticated financial sector, capable of raising capital domestically and internationally. In addition, the economy is well served by transport and other communications systems. Despite this, however, and as a result of historical factors and the philosophy underpinning the New Economic Policy, the economy, and the financial system in particular, function so as to divert risk capital away from private sector investment towards non-productive, public sector activities. Furthermore, even when funds are directed towards domestic investment, business licensing and employment practices create barriers to efficiency and competition in the private sector. The details and implications of these constraints will be dealt with in detail in sections 9.4–9.6, but at this stage it is necessary to establish the context for much of the analysis to follow by outlining the origins of the New Economic Policy, and its impact on the economy.

9.1.3 The New Economic Policy

From Independence until 1970 the political economy of Malaysia was shaped by the so-called 'Bargain of 1957'. This was an agreement between Malay and non-Malay (i.e. Chinese and Indian) interest groups which allowed the latter a relatively free hand to pursue their commercial interests while the Malays retained political control, through which a degree of positive discrimination was exercised (mainly through public sector employment policies). However, following race riots in Kuala Lumpur in May 1969, sparked off by growing resentment of Chinese domination of the economy, the predominantly Malay government moved quickly to develop an economic programme of affirmative action towards the Bumiputra. The New Economic Policy was the embodiment of this affirmative action programme and was immediately integrated in the Second (1971–5) and subsequent Malaysian National Plans.[4] In doing so it fundamentally altered the course of macroeconomic policy-making for the next two decades. The NEP outlines the objectives of economic policy as '(i) the promotion of national unity and integration; (ii) the creation of employment opportunities; and (iii) the promotion of overall economic growth', noting that 'the economic objective of national unity may be expressed as the improvement of economic balances between the races or the reduction of racial economic disparities' (NEP quoted in Faaland et al., 1990: 307).

Though the NEP embodied a broad range of socio-economic objectives such as employment, housing, education, and an exclusive civil service recruitment policy, the litmus-test was, and remains, the distribution of corporate asset ownership as the indicator of wealth distribution. In 1970 62% of all corporate assets were owned by foreigners, 34% by non-Bumiputra (i.e. Chinese and Indian) Malaysians, and 4% by the Bumiputra (PNB, 1990). The NEP consequently set target equity ownership levels of 30% foreign, 40% other Malaysian, and 30% Bumiputra to be reached by 1990. Aggressive programmes were instituted in pursuit of this target, including the compulsory transfer of shares to the Bumiputra and the creation of specialized financial institutions (see discussion of the role of the PNB in section 9.2 below). By 1980 (half-way through the NEP period), the distribution of equity ownership had improved quite markedly, but was still a long way off the original NEP target, being foreign 43%; other Malaysian 45%, and Bumiputra 12% (of which 7% was institutional). By 1985 it had reached foreign 25%, other Malaysian 57%, and Bumiputra 18% (8% institutions). It is interesting to note that the main beneficiaries have been the non-Bumiputra Malaysians – a reflection principally of the dynamism and risk-assuming savings and investment behaviour of this group which had also fuelled its growth during the era of the Bargain of 1957.

Though corporate equity distribution was the central element of the NEP, the programme was (and is) central to all other aspects of economic life in Malaysia. Most importantly, government policy towards the SOE sector during the 1970s, and, perhaps counter-intuitively, the push for privatization in the 1980s, has been driven by the needs of the NEP. The relationship between the NEP, the public sector, and the privatization programme will be dealt with in sections 9.2 and 9.3.

The NEP expired in 1990, and the debate surrounding its future has been intense. Aside from the equity distribution targets, evidence over the two decades of the NEP has been mixed. While real GDP growth has been impressive and the standard of living of the Bumiputra as a whole has improved dramatically, the overall performance of the economy has been only modest by regional standards. It has been widely argued that growth has been hampered by the NEP. When it was introduced, Malaysia ranked second only to Japan amongst the ASEAN nations in terms of GDP per capita; by 1990 it had fallen behind South Korea, Taiwan, Hong Kong and Singapore, and was only marginally above Thailand. Had growth not been constrained by the NEP, it is argued, the economic performance and welfare of the Bumiputra would have been even more greatly enhanced. Moreover, it is argued, the NEP has contributed to a serious degree of 'cronyism',[5] especially with regard to government contracting and licensing procedures. Preferential access to publicly funded business has reduced public sector efficiency and raised concerns about the transparency of government policy-making and implementation.

The politics of the NEP aside, its predominant effect has been to assign an extremely broad role for government intervention in the economy. It is, perhaps, this issue alone which most singularly characterizes the recent economic history of Malaysia, and, most certainly, which has shaped the privatization programme. The NEP is an instrument of positive discrimination and, as such, its primary feature has been to attempt to shield the Bumiputra from the ravages of commercial risk. This principle can be seen not only to operate in the acquisition of wealth-creating assets for the Bumiputra, and the expansion of the public sector in the 1970s and early 1980s, but has been assimilated into the privatization programme. As Vickers and Yarrow (1991) argue 'just as political agendas influence SOE behaviour so do they also influence the conduct of privatization programmes'. This chapter argues that this has been one of the overriding features of the Malaysian privatization programme.

9.2 The SOE sector: origins, structure and development

9.2.1 Introduction and definition of the SOE sector

For an economy which is viewed as being fundamentally market-oriented, Malaysia's SOE sector is surprisingly large. Indeed, it is among the largest in the world outside the centrally planned economies, with over 1,100 SOEs comprising both core utilities – transport, communications, water supply, energy and finance – and also a large exposure in non-traditional sectors such as services, construction and, particularly, manufacturing. The origins and development of the SOE sector in Malaysia are central to an understanding of the politics and structure of the current privatization programme.

Definition. Within Malaysia itself there are a number of different definitions of what constitutes an SOE, and frequently in official statistics only the largest, wholly-owned SOEs are acknowledged. For the purposes of this section, however, we embrace the entire range of government equity holdings, both direct and indirect, whether it be a majority or minority interest. Since Malaysia is a federal state, this definition includes not only those SOEs in which equity is held directly by the central federal government, but also where equity participation is through either state governments or one of the many pan-regional development authorities.[6]

Two measurement problems are encountered when assessing the size and scope of the SOE sector. First, in the national accounts, enterprises are not analysed in terms of ownership; consequently there is no comprehensive measurement of the overall contribution of the sector to GDP. All measures reported in official statistics are thus only approximations. This is most noticeable with official statistics on the so-called 'consolidated' public sector financial performance, in which the federal and state government financial position is consolidated with that of approximately 50 of the larger wholly-owned SOEs.[7] Second, the collection of detailed financial data on the SOE sector is a comparatively recent phenomenon in Malaysia. Following growing concern about the lack of a comprehensive database the government contracted the Permodalan Nasional Berhad (PNB) to provide a financial data collection and monitoring system for the SOE sector. The unit, known as Central Information Collection Unit (CICU), began operations in 1985, and although it has not fully established its database (there remain a small number of companies (98) on which it has only limited data), it does provide an impressive array of data, allowing us to build a reasonably comprehensive picture of the SOE sector in Malaysia.

9.2.2 Origins of the SOE sector

The *laissez-faire* implications of the 'Bargain of 1957' were closely adhered to. During the period up to 1970 government intervention in commerce and industry was virtually non-existent and Malaysia maintained a minimal SOE sector covering the transport, energy, communications, utilities and commodity marketing sectors. Following the Kuala Lumpur riots, it became widely accepted (amongst the ruling Bumiputra) that economic discrimination was endemic and, if rapid economic advancement amongst the Bumiputra was to be achieved, broader state intervention was required. Yusof (1989) notes:

> The market could no longer be trusted to overcome the many forms of discrimination. The employment and ownership-restructuring targets, of which the latter was the most contentious, had the greatest influence on the shape of state intervention in the economy. So in the Malaysian case state intervention explicitly was motivated as a means of accelerating Bumiputra participation in industry and commerce. Because the Bumiputra were still disproportionately engaged in low income, agricultural and rural activities, a massive transfer to the industrial and urban occupations to close the gap between them and the non-Bumiputra would require state intervention.

The 1970s therefore saw an unprecedented expansion in SOE participation in the commercial, industrial and service sectors and well as in the emerging oil- and gas-based exploration sector. It was spearheaded by the federal government but all the state economic development agencies also increased their equity participation. The expansion was so rapid that, while the SOE sector was growing at a rate of over 100 enterprises per year by the mid-1970s, there was virtually no concomitant growth in the control or monitoring systems. Not only did this result in the creation of a huge class of companies whose managements were *de facto* acting independently of any effective shareholder control, but it also meant that the government remained ignorant of the extent of its assets and liabilities as shareholder of a significant proportion of the economy.[8] Only with the onset of economic crisis – in the form of the first recession in post-Independence Malaysian history – was the government galvanized into action on the SOEs. With the election of Dr Mahathir bin Mohammed in 1980 the creation of new SOEs came to an abrupt halt (see section 9.3).

9.2.3 Size and structure of the SOE sector

Official estimates suggest that the output of the SOE sector accounts for around 25% of GDP (World Bank, 1989c: 58), while CICU records show that, as at the end of March 1990, there were 1,158 SOEs (78% of them operational), with a total

Table 9.2 SOE distribution 1990

Industry	Sector	Active[a]	Non-op[b]	Liq/Rec[c]	Shell[d]	Total	GOVERNMENT OWNERSHIP			Capital M$m.	Av Cap M$m.	Cap as % of Total	Frequency as % of Total
							100%	Maj	Min				
AGRIC	Forestry	19	5	0	1	25	6	5	14	58.77	2.35	0.25	2.16
	Liv/Fish	21	5	0	1	27	12	11	4	120.35	4.46	0.50	2.33
	Plantation	75	13	3	4	95	45	30	20	3,923.25	41.30	16.39	8.20
	TOTAL	115	23	3	6	147	63	46	38	4,102.37	27.91	17.14	12.69
BUILD & CONSTRUCT	Building	25	2	4	1	32	10	16	6	72.91	2.28	0.30	2.76
	Mech & Elec	2	1	0	0	3	2	1	0	1.16	0.39	0.00	0.26
	Property Dev	76	11	2	8	97	30	38	29	1,250.42	12.89	5.23	8.38
	TOTAL	103	14	6	9	132	42	55	35	1,324.49	10.03	5.53	11.40
EXTRACTIVE	Mining	18	9	3	0	30	6	14	10	372.44	12.41	1.56	2.59
	Petroleum	4	0	0	0	4	0	4	0	150.75	37.69	0.63	0.35
	TOTAL	22	9	3	0	34	6	18	10	523.19	15.39	2.19	2.94
FINANCE	Comm Bank	9	0	0	0	9	0	7	2	3,209.01	356.56	13.41	0.78
	Dev Bank	4	0	0	0	4	2	2	0	369.33	92.33	1.54	0.35
	Disc Hse	1	0	0	0	1	0	1	0	12.00	12.00	0.05	0.09
	Factoring	2	0	0	0	2	0	2	0	12.00	6.00	0.05	0.17
	Finance Co	8	0	0	0	8	0	4	4	182.23	22.78	0.76	0.69
	House Credit	2	0	0	0	2	1	0	1	176.42	88.21	0.74	0.17
	Insur. Co	12	0	0	0	12	1	6	5	186.51	15.54	0.78	1.04
	Invest. Cos	62	12	2	2	78	30	25	23	4,270.91	54.76	17.85	6.74
	Invest. Trust	4	0	0	1	5	3	1	1	41.02	8.20	0.17	0.43
	Leasing	5	2	0	0	7	0	5	2	37.00	5.29	0.15	0.60
	Merch Bank	5	0	0	0	5	0	3	2	86.25	17.25	0.36	0.43
	Unit Trust	1	0	0	0	1	0	1	0	32.00	32.00	0.13	0.09
	TOTAL	115	14	2	3	134	37	57	40	8,614.69	64.29	36.00	11.57
MANUFACT	Basic Metals	10	0	1	0	11	2	3	6	825.82	75.07	3.45	0.95
	Fab. Metals	46	7	5	0	58	9	14	35	946.82	16.32	3.96	5.01
	Food Bev Tob	32	11	8	0	51	11	19	21	743.62	14.58	3.11	4.40
	Non-met mins	37	6	3	1	47	14	14	19	598.28	12.73	2.50	4.06
	Paper & Print	8	0	0	0	8	2	2	4	410.97	51.37	1.72	0.69
	Petro-Chems	61	5	5	0	71	10	26	35	1,646.88	23.20	6.88	6.13
	Textiles	12	4	0	0	16	7	4	5	93.52	5.85	0.39	1.38
	Wood Prods	40	9	2	6	57	37	11	9	241.82	4.24	1.01	4.92
	TOTAL	246	42	24	7	319	92	93	134	5,507.74	17.27	23.02	27.55

Table 9.2 Continued

Industry	Sector	Active[a]	Non-op[b]	Liq/Rec[c]	Shell[d]	Total	GOVERNMENT OWNERSHIP			Capital M$m.	Av Cap M$m.	Cap as % of Total	Frequency as % of Total
							100%	Maj	Min				
SERVICES	Commod. Bkrs	1	0	0	0	1	0	0	1	0.25	0.25	0.00	0.09
	General Serv	77	14	6	1	98	28	53	17	951.34	9.71	3.98	8.46
	Trading (Cons)	29	7	3	0	39	14	12	13	120.38	3.09	0.50	3.37
	Trading (Inds)	33	12	3	1	49	26	16	7	295.32	6.03	1.23	4.23
	Hotels	42	2	1	1	46	22	13	11	896.22	19.48	3.75	3.97
	Insur Bkrs	6	2	0	0	8	4	1	3	3.25	0.41	0.01	0.69
	Mgmt Servs	56	7	2	1	66	37	21	8	366.81	5.56	1.53	5.70
	Money Bkrs	2	0	0	0	2	0	0	2	0.37	0.18	0.00	0.17
	Restaur	1	2	0	0	3	1	2	0	6.33	2.11	0.03	0.26
	Surveyors	2	0	0	0	2	0	1	1	0.23	0.12	0.00	0.17
	TOTAL	249	46	15	4	314	132	119	63	2,640.49	8.41	11.03	27.12
TRANSPORT	Airlines	4	0	1	0	5	0	2	3	470.60	94.12	1.97	0.43
	Haulage	12	1	0	0	13	1	8	4	96.60	7.43	0.40	1.12
	Public T'port	28	1	0	1	30	12	16	2	67.74	2.26	0.28	2.59
	Shipping	9	2	1	8	20	4	12	4	575.90	28.79	2.41	1.73
	TOTAL	53	4	2	9	68	17	38	13	1,210.84	17.81	5.06	5.87
OTHER IND	Others	0	3	0	6	9	6	3	0	6.70	0.74	0.03	0.78
	Pub. Utils	0	1	0	0	1	1	0	0	0.00	0.00	0.03	0.86
	TOTAL	0	4	0	6	10	7	3	0	6.70	0.67	0.03	0.86
TOTALS		903	156	55	44	1,158	396	429	333	23,930.51	20.67	100.00	100.00

Source: PNB/CICU Database.

a) Trading; b) Dormant or pre-operational; c) In liquidation or receivership; d) Shell companies – paid up capital of M$2m. but no activity.

Table 9.2a *Largest SOEs by turnover*

Company	Sector	Capital (M$m.)	Govt Equity (%)	Turnover (M$m.)
1. PETRONAS Bhd	Petroleum	100	100	6,726
2. Malaysia Discount Berhad	Finance	12	100	5,150
3. Malaysia LNG Berhad	Petroleum	600	65	2,521
4. Malaysia Airline System Bhd	Airlines	350	60	1,895
5. Syarikat Telekom Malaysia Bhd	Telecom	500	100	1,699
6. Malaysia Intl Shipping Corp Bhd	Shipping	500	58	1,530
7. PETRONAS Dagangan Bhd	Petroleum	50	100	1,473
8. Perbadanan Kilang Feld	Food Manuf	146	77	1,319
9. Bank Bumiputra Malaysia Bhd	Finance	1,376	100	1,209
10. Perbadanan Perusahaan Penapisan	Food Manuf	20	77	811
11. Permodalan Nasional Berhad (PNB)	Finance	100	100	805
12. Malaysian Rubber Development Corp Bhd	Rubber Manuf	125	100	758
13. Perbadanan Getah Felda	Petroleum	7	77	603
14. United Malayan Banking Corp Bhd	Finance	333	74	477
15. Perusahaan Otomobil Nasional (PROTON)	Vehicle Manuf	150	70	450
16. Sabah Gas Industries Bhd	Petroleum	372	100	442
17. Rakyat Berjaya Bhd	Forestry	1	100	422
18. Sabah Marketing Corporation Bhd	Services/Holding	15	100	364
19. PETRONAS Carigali Bhd	Petroleum	50	100	348
20. Perwira Habib Bank Malaysia Bhd	Finance	405	86	301
TOTAL		5,212		29,303
% of Total SOE		22		57

Source: PNB/CICU Database.

paid-up capital of M$23.9bn (Table 9.2). Of these companies, 396 (or 34%) were 100% government-owned; a further 429 (37%) majority owned; in the final 333 (30%) government had only a minority equity stake. The government equity share in the sector accounted for 70.3% of the total, amounting to M$16.7bn.

Malaysia's SOEs are broadly spread across all sectors, with finance, services, and manufacturing dominating in terms of simple number of enterprises, accounting for 12%, 27%, and 28% of all SOEs respectively. In terms of capitalization, a similar picture emerges, with the finance and manufacturing sectors accounting for approximately 60% of total capitalization. The sector is extremely concentrated: the largest 20 SOEs (less than 2% of the total) have a combined capitalization of M$5.2bn (5% of GDP and almost 22% of total SOE capitalization) and a combined turnover of M$29bn (57% of the estimated total turnover of the sector for 1988) (Table 9.2a). The majority of the SOEs are small, however. Excluding the top 20 (whose average capitalization was M$260m.), average capitalization is only M$18m. (US$6.7m. at 1988 prices), and most enterprises operate in relatively competitive markets. Table 9.3 classifies the SOE sector between federal, state, and regional agencies, by capitalization, and by source of debt as at February 1990.

SOEs in Malaysia are held almost equally between the federal and the state governments, with only a few (4%) by the regional agencies. Their sectoral distribution (Table 9.4) indicates that state SOEs predominate in the primary sectors – agriculture, extractive industry, plantation agriculture, and logging – while the transport and finance sectors are dominated by federal SOEs. A further feature is the large number of state manufacturing and service SOEs, most of which were created as direct elements of the NEP, as an attempt to reduce regional income inequalities. Federal SOEs tend to be significantly larger than those held

Table 9.3 *SOEs by paid-up capital, size and source of borrowing*

1. SOEs by paid-up capital

	Number of Companies	Total Capital (M$m.)	Govt Equity (M$m.)	Govt Equity as % of Total Capital	Average Capital (M$m.)
Federal	556	18,521	12,738	68.78	33.3
State	553	5,048	3,829	75.85	9.1
Regional	49	241	170	70.54	4.9
TOTAL	1,158	23,810	16,737	70.29	20.6

2. SOEs by size

	Number of Companies	Capital >M$20m.	Capital M$1m.–M$20m.	Capital M$1m.–M$5m.	Capital <M$1m.
Federal	556	135	117	106	198
State	553	52	114	150	237
Regional	49	4	9	11	25
TOTAL	1,158	191	240	1	460

3. SOEs by source of borrowing

	Number of Companies	Govt Loans	Foreign Loans	Domestic Loans	Total Loans	Debt/ Total Capital
Federal	556	21.38%	27.54%	51.08%	100.00%	184.89%
State	553	34.67%	24.28%	41.05%	100.00%	169.53%
Regional	49	41.35%	11.81%	46.84%	100.00%	98.34%
TOTAL	1,158	24.13%	26.81%	49.06%	100.00%	180.73%

Table 9.4 *Distribution of SOEs by sector*

Sector	Federal	State	Regional	Total
Agriculture	5	19	3	27
Construction	8	26	1	35
Extractive	6	27	1	34
Finance	100	33	1	134
Manufacturing	153	155	14	322
Plantation	22	61	12	95
Property	44	53	1	98
Services	162	135	16	313
Logging	0	25	0	25
Transport	56	12	0	68
Others	0	7	0	7
TOTAL	556	553	49	1,158

by state or regional agencies (both in terms of debt and equity capital), accounting in total for 78% of total equity capital and 79% of debt capital. State and regional SOEs are significantly smaller, and are much less likely to raise capital from sources other than the government. Whereas the average debt capitalization of federal SOEs was M$61m. from all sources, that for state SOEs was only M$15m.

and for regional SOEs less than M$5m. The federal SOEs also had, on average, much larger exposure in the domestic and foreign financial markets (accounting for 51% and 27% of total debt respectively), while for state and regional SOEs the principal debt was to the government. The overall SOE debt–equity ratio of 180% is significantly higher than the average private sector ratio (estimated to be approximately 100%),[9] although the implications of this are not clear since, while government can (and does) extend cheap credit to SOEs, it is also a less demanding shareholder in terms of dividend requirements.

9.2.4 Performance of the SOE sector

Aggregate performance figures for the SOE sector are determined to a significant degree by the performance of PETRONAS and its subsidiaries, which is closely tied to external conditions, and in particular the world oil market and the exchange-rate policy of the government. The 1980s were a period of considerable volatility for the world oil price, which fell from US$39 per barrel in 1981 to a low of $US14.8 per barrel in 1986 before improving again towards the end of the decade.

Using official data from the Ministry of Finance[10] Table 9.5 shows that, despite relatively poor operating performance, the sector has undertaken extremely high levels of development expenditure. The generally weak performance is masked, however, at least in the early years of the decade, by high profits from PETRONAS and its subsidiaries (whose surplus alone (M$3.5bn) reached 5% of GDP in 1982). The expansion of development expenditure during the Fourth Plan period, combined with the fiscal expansion from 1981 to 1984, was accompanied by a rapid expansion in development expenditure by the SOEs, which rose from 4.2% of GDP in 1981 to almost 10% in 1984.

This dramatic growth in the capital expenditure of the non-financial public enterprises reflected a general surge in public sector capital expenditure, which for the three years 1981–3 was consistently in excess of 25% of GDP, and which led to an unprecedented construction boom. The overall deficit of the sector rose concomitantly, touching 3.5% of GDP by 1984. Recession hit the sector hard, with revenues being depressed by low oil and other commodity prices as well as by a fall in Malaysia's export competitiveness. The bulk of the adjustment within the sector came with the contraction of development expenditure, from M$7.7bn in 1984 to M$2.9bn in 1987, leading to a modest overall surplus for the sector in 1987. More recently, however, reduced operating surpluses combined with increased development expenditure have again returned the sector to a situation of overall deficit.

Table 9.5 *Non-financial public enterprise performance (M$m.)*

	1981	1982	1983	1984	1985	1986	1987	1988	1989	1990
Operating Surplus	2,304	3,423	4,306	5,005	5,649	2,825	3,574	3,616	3,725	3,961
Capital Expenditure	2,419	4,006	6,127	7,762	6,186	3,850	2,885	3,730	4,464	4,900
Surplus/(Deficit)	(115)	(583)	(1,821)	(2,757)	(537)	(1,025)	689	(114)	(739)	(949)
As % of GDP										
Operating Surplus	4.00	5.47	6.16	6.29	7.28	3.94	4.48	3.98	3.70	3.66
Capital Expenditure	4.20	6.40	8.76	9.76	7.98	5.37	3.62	4.11	4.44	4.54
Surplus/(Deficit)	−0.20	−0.93	−2.60	−3.47	−0.69	−1.43	0.86	−0.13	−0.73	−0.88
Memorandum:										
GDP (Mkt Prices)	57,613	62,579	69,941	79,550	77,547	71,729	79,711	90,806	100,650	107,948
Oil Price (US$/bl)	39.0	36.3	30.7	29.3	27.6	15.1	19.6	15.9	19.6	24.4

Source: Ministry of Finance, *Economic Report 1989/90.*

Table 9.6 *SOE financial performance (M$m. and %)*

	1980	1981	1982	1983	1984	1985	1986	1987	1988
Gross turnover	24,172	22,910	22,868	26,013	32,870	34,468	34,076	42,849	51,026
Operating profit	11,378	9,751	8,764	8,022	10,273	10,478	9,133	8,738	11,277
Interest charges	536	697	912	1,218	1,673	1,643	2,099	2,820	3,103
Post-tax profit	7,368	5,285	4,465	3,208	5,096	4,731	3,553	3,217	5,096
Dividends	440	496	2,082	2,711	2,504	3,001	3,075	3,014	3,608
Gross fixed capital formation	0	3,612	4,642	5,784	5,407	2,713	2,233	8,093	1,620
Overall balance	6,928	1,177	(2,259)	(5,286)	(2,815)	(983)	(1,754)	(7,890)	(132)
External debt									
Debt to govt (o/s)	3,218	4,917	5,253	5,247	5,247	4,569	4,589	9,590	8,658
External debt (o/s)	4,483	5,964	7,345	8,672	8,578	10,031	9,744	9,542	9,669
Domestic debt (o/s)	2,560	2,904	3,536	3,317	3,698	4,085	4,623	4,397	4,147
TOTAL DEBT	10,261	13,785	16,135	17,235	17,523	18,685	18,956	23,529	22,504

SOE Performance as % GDP	1980	1981	1982	1983	1984	1985	1986	1987	1988
Gross turnover	45.3	39.8	36.5	37.4	41.3	44.4	47.9	54.5	56.2
Operating profit	21.3	16.9	14.0	11.5	12.9	13.5	12.8	11.1	12.4
Interest charges	1.0	1.2	1.5	1.8	2.1	2.1	2.9	3.6	3.4
Post-tax profit	13.8	9.2	7.1	4.6	6.4	6.1	5.0	4.1	5.6
Dividends	0.8	0.9	3.3	3.9	3.1	3.9	4.3	3.8	4.0
Gross fixed capital formation	0.0	6.3	7.4	8.3	6.8	3.5	3.1	10.3	1.8
Overall deficit	13.0	2.0	−3.6	−7.6	−3.5	−1.3	−2.5	−10.0	−0.1
External debt									
Debt to govt (o/s)	6.0	8.5	8.4	7.5	6.6	5.9	6.4	12.2	9.5
External debt (o/s)	8.4	10.4	11.7	12.5	10.8	12.9	13.7	12.1	10.7
Domestic debt (o/s)	4.8	5.0	5.7	4.8	4.6	5.3	6.5	5.6	4.6
TOTAL DEBT	19.2	23.9	25.8	24.8	22.0	24.1	26.6	29.9	24.8

Source: Permodalan Nasional Berhad Central Information Collection Unit.

Mindful of the narrowness of the Ministry of Finance database, however, we have attempted to create a broader picture of the SOE sector's aggregate financial performance, using CICU's regular evaluations (Table 9.6).[11] The general pattern, in particular of the overall deficit, more or less reflects the picture of Table 9.5, although, importantly, Table 9.6 puts the scale of the sector as a whole into perspective, indicating SOE turnover accounting for between 40% and 50% of GDP, whilst the same pattern in operating profits and fixed capital formation emerges. Table 9.6 also shows a considerable rise in overall interest costs, which account for about 6% of turnover and 3.5% of GDP.

On the basis of these two tables, the SOE sector is, in aggregate, a net consumer of public resources and, were it not for the presence of the petroleum sector which was highly profitable during most of the late 1970s and 1980s, the financial burden would be sizeable. This general conclusion can be supported by detailed data from CICU, which tracks the profitability of companies in the data base (Table 9.7). Though there is a clear cyclical pattern, with the percentage of profitable SOEs falling sharply in 1985 and 1986, approximately 40–45% of all SOEs have been unprofitable throughout the 1980s. Of these, almost half (or 25% of all SOEs) had negative shareholders funds[12] – a condition which would be unlikely to persist under private ownership.

Finally in this section, Table 9.8 analyses the relative performance of the SOEs over time according to general performance criteria based on enterprise profitability relative to capitalization. Although this table does not reflect the relative

Table 9.7 *Summary of profitable and unprofitable SOEs*

	1980	1981	1982	1983	1984	1985	1986	1987	1988
Profitable[a]	61%	60%	54%	58%	58%	52%	52%	53%	60%
Unprofitable	39%	40%	46%	42%	42%	48%	50%	47%	40%

Source: CICU Report, February 1990.

a) Reporting net operating profit.

Table 9.8 *Relative performance of SOEs 1980–88 (%)*

	SICK[a]	WEAK[b]	SATISFACTORY[c]	GOOD[d]
1980	12.53	26.24	10.88	50.35
1981	13.19	26.74	9.63	50.44
1982	15.25	29.15	9.86	45.74
1983	12.12	30.12	10.04	47.72
1984	14.02	26.98	11.80	47.20
1985	16.79	30.20	11.09	41.92
1986	18.95	29.54	13.31	38.20
1987	19.23	27.43	13.87	39.47
1988	16.67	24.15	14.42	44.76

Notes
a) Companies with negative shareholders funds.
b) Loss-making companies with shareholders funds <200% of paid-up capital.
c) Shareholders funds <100%, but currently profitable.
d) Shareholders funds >100% and profitable.

size of 'sick', 'weak', 'satisfactory' and 'good' companies, it does indicate the persistence of a very large number of unprofitable companies drawing on taxpayers' funds. Even at the height of the public sector boom in 1981 and 1982, over 40% of all SOEs were either 'sick' or 'weak', which underlines one of the main criticisms of SOEs, namely that they are allowed to survive when commercial market conditions would have caused closure and reallocation of resources to more profitable activities.

9.2.5 Sectoral performance
Despite the breadth of the SOE sector, three groups play a particularly important role in the sector as a whole. These are the petrochemicals, manufacturing, and finance sectors.

The petrochemical sector. Malaysia is a medium-sized, non-OPEC oil exporter, producing high-grade crude oil, and liquefied natural gas (LNG). Approximately 80% of crude oil and condensates are exported, principally to Japan, Singapore and Korea, while 95% of LNG is exported to Japan. Petroleum exports (crude and LNG) accounted for approximately 22% of total Malaysian exports in 1989, a slight fall from the 27% share in 1984.

This sector is dominated by Petroleum Nasional Sdn Berhad (PETRONAS) and its subsidiaries. Under the Petroleum Development Act 1974, PETRONAS has full monopoly powers and privileges in the exploitation and development of on-and off-shore petroleum resources, which it manages through a system of up-and downstream licensing arrangements,[13] principally with foreign multinationals. A total of 22 upstream Production Sharing Contracts (PSC) are currently in force – mainly with Shell, Exxon, and BP.

PETRONAS is the single largest, and by far the most profitable, of the Malaysian SOEs, with a turnover in 1988 of M$6.7bn and profits of M$3.8bn. Moreover, the PETRONAS group as a whole (including Malaysia LNG Berhad) consists of 10 companies (4 of which are in the 20 largest SOEs), with a combined estimated turnover of M$12.6bn, approximately 27% of total SOE sector turnover. PSCs and standardized international practices mean that, as well as being financially robust, PETRONAS is also an internally efficient domestic monopoly, which operates as a price-taker in international markets. Domestic financial performance is therefore determined principally by world market prices and, in particular, domestic exchange-rate management. PETRONAS has consequently remained outside the SOE reform ambit and, furthermore, in view of its strategic nature, it has not been considered in the privatization debate.

The manufacturing sector.   Despite the paucity of hard data, survey and sample evidence suggests that manufacturing SOEs arc, on the whole, less profitable and less efficient than private sector counterparts.[14] Poorer performance in the SOE sector is due principally to the standard catalogue of problems facing SOEs: poor project evaluation; pursuit of non-commercial objectives; weak, relatively passive, management; and a persistent tendency to have weak capital structures. Evidence from CICU on manufacturing SOEs suggests that SOE debt/equity ratios are consistently higher than those prevailing in the private sector.

Profitability in the manufacturing sector has been consistently and significantly lower in SOE operations. This low profitability, combined with high leverage brought about by erosion of the equity base and the accumulation of external debt (much of which was contracted to finance expansion during the early construction boom period of 1981–2), has resulted in an extremely large number of unprofitable companies. Inappropriate capital structures are not the only problem, however, since, as CICU notes, 87% of firms with negative net profits in 1989 also had negative operating profits, suggesting that the financial weakness in the sector is more fundamental than merely weak gearing.

The Bumiputra financial institutions.   State involvement in the financial sector in Malaysia is significant, more especially in terms of the specific functions undertaken by public sector financial institutions rather than their actual share of the market. Whilst the vast majority of public sector institutions operate relatively efficiently within a competitive environment, particular attention needs to be paid to the role of the Permodalan Nasional Berhad (PNB), which enjoys a unique position within the financial sector, and is central to the privatization process.

Early initiatives of the NEP in pursuit of equity participation targets involved direct compulsory share transfers to Bumiputra individuals and companies, and the creation of the MARA unit trust (later to become the Bumiputra Stock Exchange). However, in the face of persistent profit-taking on the part of recipients of equity (through the resale of equity to non-Bumiputra), the government developed the concept of 'ownership-in-trust' by establishing an investment trust dedicated to the Bumiputra. This trust, the Yayasan Pelaburan Bumiputra (YPB), was established in January 1978, under a Board of Trustees chaired by the Prime Minister. In order to implement these objectives YPB established the Permodalan Nasional Berhad (PNB) in March 1978. PNB serves as the executive agency for YPB, evaluates, selects and purchases shares in public and private sector companies, and distributes selected shares to Bumiputra individuals through the Amanah Saham Nasional (ASN) unit trust. The ASN was established by PNB in May 1979 as a subsidiary company to administer and market a unit trust scheme directed specifically towards equity participation amongst Bumiputra.

In January 1981, Prime Minister Tun Hussein Onn launched a 'Scheme of

Transfer of Shares held by Government Agencies to Bumiputra Individuals' through the PNB. This share transfer proceeds in two stages. First, shares in (profitable) SOEs are transferred to PNB at par value. Up to October 1986 the shares of 37 companies with a par value of M$1,300m. had been transferred to PNB, while data for March 1990 show that the equity of a total of 93 companies was by then held by PNB. The second stage involves the transfer of some of these shares to ASN, which then issues par-value units against the ASN share portfolio as a whole (which also includes other non-SOE equity). The relationship between ASN and PNB means that shares can be (and are) moved in and out of the ASN portfolio, since PNB directly manages the ASN portfolio, whilst ASN itself only manages a unit trust.

ASN is open only to Bumiputra. Investments are denominated in M$1 units, with each unit holder allowed a maximum of M$49,900. Savings are mobilized through an extensive network of agencies, and take-up of units has been rapid and widespread: by 1982 there were over 1 million individual unit-holders, and by 1989 this had risen to 2.44 million (out of 12 million Bumiputra), by which time the value of units outstanding was M$4.04bn. It is now estimated that, in terms of unit holders, the ASN is one of the biggest unit trust schemes in the world. The popularity of the ASN owes much to the fact that it offers risk-free investment opportunities, whereby, in addition to enjoying generous tax exemptions on dividends and bonus shares (i.e. capital gains), all downside capital risk is effectively eliminated, since poor performing equities are removed from the unit by the PNB. Because of the attractiveness of the ASN, the fund almost reached saturation point in terms of membership. It was proposed therefore that ASN would be floated in early 1991, allowing the value of units to be directly market-determined. However, a second, 'lifeboat' fund, the Amanah Saham Bumiputra (ASB), has been created to fill the role now occupied by the ASN. The funding for ASB will again be from PNB companies, and it is expected that it will increasingly include shares from major privatization issues – most notably the STM and LLN issues (see section 9.3 below).

These Bumiputra financial institutions currently play a major role in the economy, and this role is likely to expand as the privatization programme proceeds. Their presence does, however, introduce distortions and anomalies into the capital markets. The most obvious distortion is the extent to which these institutions divert Bumiputra savings away from other (higher-risk) investment instruments through the cross-subsidization from other public resources. In addition, PNB's privileged access to all new issues[15] gives it a dominant role as shareholder, and it is a matter of debate whether this is beneficial to the efficient operation of the capital market (see section 9.5 below). Thirdly, there is increasing concern among many of the SOEs that PNB has, through its CICU contract, a strategic advantage in acquiring commercial assets for its own portfolio at less than their market and/or social value. Finally, and perhaps most importantly in terms of the privatization programme, there is a concern that PNB's position as a major player in the capital market and as a key instrument of the NEP may lead to serious compromises in the management of privatization. Essentially, conflict arises when the argument for privatization on the grounds of improved efficiency through competition (i.e. the arguments being advanced for the privatization of telecommunications and electricity) conflict with the desire on the part of PNB to maintain the portfolio value through shareholding in enterprises earning monopoly profits. This issue has been discussed in detail in Chapter 4.

9.2.6 Assessment of SOE sector

Only in the last few years has concern been raised about the overall performance of the SOE sector in Malaysia, in response to the realization that, as far as the NEP objectives are concerned, asset acquisition will engender changes in wealth distribution only if the value of these assets are maintained. Reflection over the first twenty years of the NEP seems to suggest that government intervention in the enterprise sector has, with a few exceptions when natural or other monopoly conditions prevailed, failed to maintain the value of assets appropriated for the Bumiputra. Restoring the value of these assets (in terms of the income stream they generate) has thus become a priority.

One of the effects of the establishment of CICU is that this fact has become obvious to government and the general public for the first time. The thrust of criticism has been directed more towards internal microeconomic weaknesses in the sector itself rather than the failure of the macroeconomic environment in which SOEs operate. Foremost amongst the concerns have been that in many cases management weaknesses exist, principally because of poor or non-existent shareholder discipline, arising from the fact that until the late 1980s the government did not have even the most basic knowledge of the activities of the enterprises in which it was the major (or even sole) shareholder. Moreover poorly designed incentive structures have created severe agency and accountability problems. These problems have been exacerbated by access to soft finances leading to poor resource allocation decisions and frequent operational inflexibility.

The government's response to the need to enhance internal efficiency has been threefold: first, a marked change in the development expenditure programme, with a switch away from using the SOE sector to implement development objectives; second, a direct attack on individual SOE enterprise performance; and, third, the privatization programme itself. It is to the third of these objectives that we now turn.

9.3 Privatization policy and practice

9.3.1 'Malaysia Inc.' and the genesis of privatization

The earliest references to privatization in Malaysia are found in discussions in 1983 of what was known as 'Malaysia Incorporated', Prime Minister Dr Mahathir's concept of the country as a corporate entity in which the government provided the enabling environment in terms of infrastructure, deregulation and liberalization, and overall macroeconomic management, but where the private sector assumed the role as the main engine of growth (see also the Fifth Malaysian Plan (1986–91).[16] Central to 'Malaysia Inc.' was an extremely ambitious programme of privatization. The specific stimulus for the nature and style of the privatization policy seems to have come from the UK, and, as will be noted below, many of the decisions and methods have mirrored contemporaneous moves in the UK programme.

The emergence of the policy reflected two concerns. The first was growing disillusionment with the performance of the SOE sector. Though this was less prevalent during the public sector boom of 1981 and 1982, it became particularly important more recently, and has progressed to the fore since the recession in 1985–7.

The second force behind the emergence of the policy was the re-assessment of the role of the NEP. At first glance privatization may seem a peculiar volte-face, in which the government has swung from public sector asset acquisition to an emphasis on private ownership as the key to pursuing Bumiputra asset ownership. However, a closer examination of the concept of public and private ownership in the Malaysian context reveals consistency in the policy. The motivating factor behind the rapid growth of the SOE sector in Malaysia stems almost exclusively from the issue of distribution. Successive governments have remained ideologically neutral on wider issues of collective state control versus private control (outside the sphere of essential services), with the only relevant division being Bumiputra and non-Bumiputra. Consequently the process of asset acquisition by a Bumiputra government was viewed more as an off-budget activity directed to meeting the private objectives of its constituency. The implicit ideology remained one in which government acted as trustee for Bumiputra institutions, through the YPB and its associated institutions, the PNB and ASN. Against this background the apparent change in attitude towards the concept of asset ownership seems less perverse: the desire for ownership to reach the 30% target has stimulated a need for not only a greater supply of asset stock to the Bumiputra, but also to ensure that asset values are maintained through the promotion of a higher overall level of growth and profit within the economy. As will be noted below, the eventual methods of asset sale employed have tended to emphasize the close link between the objectives of the NEP and the privatization programme.

9.3.2 Defining privatization
The *Guidelines on Privatization* (1985), employs a relatively standard definition of privatization, encompassing principally asset sales, including partial sales. However, it also includes leasing management contracting and contracting-out of services or other activities, including the increasingly popular Build–Operate–Transfer (BOT) schemes for large capital investment.[17]

Privatization policy in Malaysia consists of two main, currently independent, elements. The first is the mainstream reform process co-ordinated by the Economic Planning Unit (EPU) of the Prime Minister's Office, and is the programme which is promoted (and widely acknowledged) as the sole privatization programme. The EPU programme has included all the major assets sales and the corporatization of SOEs for future sale, has co-ordinated the deregulation, licensing and BOT aspects of the programme, and in addition has developed the Privatization Masterplan (see section 9.3.9 below).

Privatization also appears as an important element of the work of the Unit Pengawasan Syarikat and Agensi Kerajaan (UPSAK) or the Unit for Monitoring Government Agencies and Enterprises. UPSAK, which was created in 1987 following a report by the Auditor General highlighting the parlous state of the SOEs, is principally responsible for SOE reform measures. It is an advisory unit and is charged with advising the Finance Division of the Treasury on reform and restructuring of (mainly smaller) SOEs. In addition, it provides small-scale consultancy services to many of the SOEs with a view to stimulating self-funded restructuring, some of which may involve privatization.[18]

9.3.3 EPU privatization policy framework
The Guidelines. The centrepiece of privatization in Malaysia is the Economic Planning Unit's *Guidelines on Privatization*. Issued in 1985, these establish the government's privatization objectives, identify key sectors for privatization, and outline the administrative structures to be employed. They cite five objectives to be pursued through privatization: (i) reduction of the financial and administrative burden of government; (ii) promotion of competition and increased productivity of SOEs; (iii) stimulation of private entrepreneurship, investment and growth; (iv) reduction in the role of the state; and (v) promotion of the objectives of the NEP through increasing the supply of private equity.

Typically, privatization programmes involve a selection by government of enterprises for privatization, most frequently within a well-defined framework of targeted and proscribed sectors. Sequencing is determined by the government and the programme is managed on a tender or public sale basis. In a departure from this method, the Malaysian Government initially adopted an 'invitation' approach. All private sector initiatives were welcomed, with no sectors or activities being explicitly ruled out,[19] and with the enticement that consideration would be given on a 'first-come-first-served' basis. Approval of submissions was to be based on a number of criteria, principally that privatization proposals were profitable and viable; that any social objectives being previously carried out by SOEs be continued; that employees were 'not disadvantaged' by privatization; and that the cost–benefit analysis directly addressed the needs of the NEP. Bumiputra participation thus emerges as a central element of the privatization process. There is a clear preference for private Bumiputra participation, but as the *Guidelines* state (p. 8, para 33):

> priority will need to be given to private Bumiputra interests. Depending on circumstances, however, Government will also consider allowing trust agencies, or other government companies [sic], to participate initially in the ownership of the privatized enterprises.

Similarly, foreign and non-Bumiputra participation is allowed, but subject to strict ownership conditions in accordance with the NEP (Malaysian ownership must be 70% of the total, of which 30% must be Bumiputra).

Administrative structures. Following the publication of the Guidelines the institutional arrangements for managing the privatization programme were established.[20] The main advisory body, reporting directly to Cabinet, is the Privatization (Main) Committee under the chairmanship of the Director General of the EPU and consisting of the Directors General from the main ministries (Finance, Energy, Communications, and the Implementation Co-ordination Unit). The executive body below the Main Committee is the Privatization Secretariat, established within the EPU, and consisting of between 10 and 15 staff. Private sector submissions received by the EPU are initially sent to the relevant technical committees, after which successful applications are reviewed by the Main Committee and sponsors are called to give evidence prior to final recommendation being sent to Cabinet. Successful privatization proposals are then co-ordinated by the EPU, at which point external assistance is traditionally employed, generally from amongst the numerous institutions in the Kuala Lumpur financial sector.

In addition to the 'invited' submissions, the Secretariat also initiates, plans and manages the large-scale privatization projects which have emerged directly from government policy initiatives (for example, the proposed Telecommunications, Railways and Electricity sales). To date, this aspect of identification and selection has been extremely *ad hoc*, relying more on personal whim and precedent from other countries than on structured proposals.

Assessment of privatization structures. The approach to the planning of privatization adopted in Malaysia has met with a mixed response. Whilst international observers have welcomed the clear structures, in particular the publication of a concise and accessible set of guidelines setting out the government's own objectives and implementation strategies, there is severe criticism about the policy structures from within the country.

The most pervasive criticism is that the 'first-come-first-served' approach, which was initially promoted as a way of accelerating the process of privatization and also a mechanism whereby the private sector had an incentive to submit projects, lacks transparency and has had the effect of perpetuating the 'cronyism' which has pervaded the NEP era (see *Malaysian Business*, 1 December 1987). The problem came to a head over the awarding of a BOT contract for the prestigious North–South Highway, a M$1.6bn road project through Peninsular Malaysia linking Thailand with Singapore, to United Engineers, a company with a poor financial track record and limited experience with road construction but in which the government party, UMNO, held a significant equity stake. The second main concern arising out of the lack of transparency in the policy is the opportunity this extends to the significant bureaucratic elite opposed to privatization. Opposition is grounded principally in a concern to maintain rent-seeking capacities and is apparent not only amongst officials of the federal government but, perhaps more vigorously, within the state governments, where privatization is seen as synonymous with increased centralization of economic power in the hands of a Kuala Lumpur elite (see *Malaysian Business*, 1–15 September 1989).

Third, there is an increasing perception on the part of the private sector that opposition to privatization comes from the highest levels within the civil service, and not merely from those directly affected by the loss of rent-seeking opportunities. In particular the view is widely held that it is only the personal commitment of Dr Mahathir which maintains the momentum of the programme. The Prime Minister has taken personal charge of the 'Malaysia Inc.' programme and also the privatization process, and, as will be noted below, his personal interventions have shaped a number of the larger initiatives. It is strongly believed that, without Dr Mahathir, privatization in Malaysia would peter out.[21] The widespread uncertainty about the government's broader political commitment to privatization has meant that enticements and other reputation costs emerged as a constant feature of the programme during the 1980s.

To a significant extent, the force of these criticisms has been acknowledged, and prompted the development of the Privatization Masterplan (PMP) which is seen as an attempt both to re-establish the momentum of privatization (there were no large-scale asset sales from the time of the sale of MISC in 1987 until the STM sale in late 1990) and to address the criticisms of 'cronyism' and lack of transparency by strengthening the 'government initiative' aspect of the policy relative to the 'invitation' element. Concern that the bureaucracy still retains strong incentives to sabotage the policy has, however, been inferred by some observers from the immense delays is bringing the PMP to Cabinet.

9.3.4 Mainstream privatization initiatives

By mid-1990 there had been approximately 24 major privatization initiatives handled by the EPU, and listed by the government as privatizations. As noted above, the Malaysian Government uses a broad definition of privatization which includes various liberalization and deregulation measures and BOT projects, as well as asset sales. This section will reflect all these initiatives, but the focus will be mainly on the asset sales and leases. Sections 9.3.5 and 9.3.6 will describe the major privatizations in detail, and section 9.3.7 will identify key policy and design issues which have emerged.

Table 9.9 summarizes the EPU privatizations to mid-1990.[22] Of the asset sales the 4 largest are all in the transport and communications sector, although of these only in the Klang Container Terminal sale did the government sell a majority of the equity.[23] There have been four public issues in the programme, although only MAS and MISC have been of any appreciable scale, and it is noticeable that these two sales occurred early in the programme (prior to the 1987 stock-market crash).

Since early 1987, although there have been a number of smaller EPU sales (including the public issue of equity in Cement Sarawak and the finance company

Table 9.9 EPU monitored privatizations[a]

	Date	Sector	Method	Amt Sold[b]	Capitalzn[c] M$m.	Proceeds[d] M$m.	Adviser[e]	Completed
1. Completed sales								
Klang Container Terminal (KCT)	1985	Transport	Private	51%	111.6	56.9	ASSEAM	Yes
Sports Toto	1985	Services	Private	70%	30.0	35.5	AMMB	Yes
Malaysian Airline Systems (MAS)	1985	Transport	Public	20%	350.0	63.0	MIMB	Yes
Aircraft Repair & Overhaul Dept (AIROD)	1984	Transport	Private	49%	6.8	72.8	EPU	Yes
Malaysian Int'l Shipping Corp. (MISC)	1987	Transport	Public	11%	500.0	136.3	AMMB	Yes
Tradewind Berhad	1988	Finance	Public	7%	140.0	10.7	AIMB	Yes
Syarikat Gula Padang Terap Sdn. Bhd	1988	Agric./Sugar	Private	100%	–	51.0	EPU	Yes
Cement Sarawak	1989	Manufact	Public	16%	32.0	6.4	AMMB	Yes
Cawangan Percetakan Keselematan	1989	Printing	Private	100%	–	5.0	EPU	Yes
TOTAL PROCEEDS						437.6		
2. Licensing/contracting/BOT								
TV3	1983	Services	Licence	–	–	44.1	CIMB	Yes
Kuching Interchange	1987	Roads	BOT	–	–	86.0	EPU	Yes
North Klang Bypass	1987	Roads	BOT	–	–	20.5	EPU	Yes
Kuala Lumpur Interchange	1987	Roads	BOT	–	–	300.0	EPU	Ongoing
Labuan Water Supply	1988	Water	BOT	–	–	126.5	EPU	Yes
North–South Highway	1988	Roads	BOT	–	–	4,300.0	EPU	Ongoing

Larut Matang Water Supply	1989	Water	BOT	—	339.0	EPU	Ongoing
Ipoh Water Supply	1989	Water	BOT	—	308.0	EPU	Ongoing
Labuan–Beaufort Interconnection	1989	Roads	BOT	—	80.0	EPU	Yes
Garbage Disposal	1990	Services	BOT	—	50.0	EPU	Ongoing
Marketing of Airtime	n.k.	Services	MC	—	–	EPU	Ongoing
RISDA Marketing	n.k.	Services	MC	—	–	EPU	Ongoing
Tube Wells	n.k.	Services	MC	—	–	EPU	Ongoing
Semenyih Dam	n.k.	Water	MC	—	–	EPU	Ongoing
Abattoir	n.k.	Livestock	Leasing	—	–	EPU	Ongoing
TOTAL CONTRACT VALUE					5,654.12		

3. Corporatizations

Syarikat Telekom Malaysia Berhad (STM)	Jan 1987	Telecoms	Public[f] 49%	equity[f]	500.0	EPU	Yes
Lembaga Lektrik Negara (LLN)	Due 1990	Power	Public[f] 49%	equity[f]	–	EPU	Ongoing
TOTAL					14,800.0		

Source: EPU.

Notes
a) Excludes all divestitures handled by UPSAK.
b) Amount of government equity to be sold.
c) Paid-up capital as reported to CICU.
d) Proceeds accruing to government only for asset sales. Value of contract for contracts/licences and BOT.
e) AMMB: Arab Malaysian Bank. AIMB: Asian International Merchant Bank.
   MIMB: Malaysian International Merchant Bank. CIMB: Commerce International Merchant Bank.
f) Proceeds exclude costs of divestiture process.

Tradewinds), the emphasis has switched towards contracting-out and in particular the negotiation of BOT contracts – especially in the road sector and the provision of water treatment facilities. Included within this group of initiatives is the North–South Highway project which at M\$4.3bn is the single largest BOT project undertaken to date.

Table 9.9 also lists two major privatizations-in-waiting, the telecommunications department, STM (which was converted from a government department into a public company in 1987, and planned for sale starting late 1990), and LLN, the electricity department, whose corporatization was expected by late 1990.

One of the striking features of the EPU privatizations is that the majority have been in sectors which are traditionally not tackled early in privatization programmes elsewhere. Whereas in most programmes (see for example Jamaica and the UK) sales of utilities followed a period in which smaller, more competitive firms were sold, in Malaysia the pattern seems to have been somewhat reversed. Transport, roads, telecommunications, and water supply have been sectors targeted for early attention. However, as discussed in greater detail below, this impression of monopoly privatization may not be entirely appropriate.

Though the overall scale of the EPU privatization process is small, the individual asset sales have been important in defining the shape of future policy. Section 9.3.5 briefly describes the individual enterprise sales in chronological order, while section 9.3.7 considers in detail the key issues of policy implementation and programme management, employment guarantees, risk sharing, and, in particular, the impact of the ownership objectives of the NEP.

9.3.5 Privatization projects

Port Klang Container Terminal (1983–6)

The privatization of container handling at Port Klang was central to the development of privatization techniques in Malaysia. Not only was it the first major privatization initiative following the government's explicit commitment to the policy but it also served as a trial for future sales. It laid down guidelines in the areas of employment and pensions legislation, labour relations, and land sales, and provided the government and the civil service with the opportunity to acquire expertise in handling privatization efforts.

The privatization process.[24] The Klang Port Authority (KPA) is a wholly government-owned enterprise which manages the largest port in Malaysia. It was established under the Ports Authority Act 1963, and in 1973 established a container terminal. Throughout its history KPA has been a profitable enterprise, though since 1973 the container terminal has been the most profitable part of the port. Despite this KPA was perceived to be performing inefficiently, and concerns were expressed that Port Klang would be boycotted by international shippers, raising the uncomfortable spectre of an even greater proportion of Malaysia's trade being routed through Singapore. Consequently, though the decision to privatize the container operations at Port Klang was taken very suddenly (allegedly in an attempt to find something to privatize in order to create some credibility for the programme), there was a clear efficiency motive for it.

The privatization process began in November 1983 when the Prime Minister (personally) selected the container terminal as Malaysia's inaugural privatization transaction. In June 1984 a local merchant bank, Aseambankers, was selected as lead consultants in a team which included two UK firms with privatization experience, Price Waterhouse and Kleinwort Benson. The submission of the consultants' report to the government led to the immediate creation of the EPU (Main) Committee on Privatization to review it. Offers were subsequently invited, with four bids finally being accepted for consideration, all of which were joint ventures with foreign companies. The winning bid was accepted in March 1985, and came from a consortium Konnas Terminal Kelang (KTK) which was specifically created as a joint venture between a Malaysian company, Kontena Nasional (80%), and P&O Australia (20%). Under an amendment to the Ports Authority Act 1963, a separate company Klang Container Terminal (KCT) was created with an authorized capital of M$500m. KCT issued the total equity to KPA for M$111.6m. (for the movable assets of the terminal, and a lease fee for the immovable assets, land and buildings of M$16.9m. per annum.)[25] KTK then purchased 51% of these shares from KPA (for M$56.9m.), and became the managing partner of KCT. KCT began operating as a private company in March 1986.

Kontena Nasional is a Malaysian company in which a number of larger SOEs have an equity holding, and consequently the change in ownership structure of the container terminal is as follows:

KCT Share Ownership

Pre-Sale		Post-Sale		
Klang Port Authority	100%	*Klang Port Authority*		49%
		Konnas Terminal Kelang		51%
		of which		
		Kontena Nasional	80%	
		P&O Australia	20%	
	100%			100%

Kontena Nasional Share Ownership

Permodalan Nasional Berhad	82 %
MISC	7.5%
PERNAS Shipping	7.5%
Other	3 %
	100 %

Indirect Shareholding in KCT

Klang Port Authority	49.0%	(SOE)
Permodalan Nasional Berhad	33.5%	(SOE)
MISC	3.1%	(SOE)
PERNAS Shipping	3.1%	(SOE)
P&O Australia	10.2%	(FOREIGN)
Other Private Sector	1.1%	(PRIVATE)
	100.0%	

Clearly, in terms of ownership, there is very little by way of pure privatization, since KCT remains 88.7% owned by government-owned enterprises. The key issue was not the transfer of ownership of KCT to the private sector, but rather the fact that the equity injection from P&O Australia effectively purchased a management contract, through which P&O staff now occupy the posts of Chief Executive Officer, Acting General Manager, and Chief Engineer. The extent to which the efficiency turnaround can be attributed to this rather than the change in ownership *per se* is considered below.

Further privatization of KCT. In the initial agreement between KPA and KTK, it was recommended that KCT should, within a period of two years, seek a public listing on the Kuala Lumpur Stock Exchange, involving a dilution of KPA's holding in KCT from 49% to 20%; that of KTK from 51% to 40%; the creation of a 5% employee participation scheme; and the balance sold to the market (subject to the usual NEP provisos). This listing had not occurred by mid-1990, but was expected to occur sometime later in 1990/91. Tentative estimates suggested a 100 million M$1 share issue at M$3 per share, raising M$300m. in new capital, which would be used to finance future expansion at the port.[26] This, to be known as the West Port, would be given over exclusively to containerization, and under the management agreement/memorandum of understanding between KPA and KCT, the latter has a first-right-of-refusal on any new containerization activity within Port Klang. This clearly would establish KCT as the major operator within Port Klang, and, moreover, in proscribing competition in the port, would leave KCT in a domestic monopoly position.

Sports Toto Malaysia (August 1985 and July 1987)
Sports Toto Malaysia was established by the government in 1969 for the purpose of running Toto (lottery) betting activities in terms of the Pool Betting Act 1967. The company started operations with an authorized share capital of M$1m., and an initial paid-up capital of M$200. It performed successfully throughout the 1970s, and was not affected by the recession in the mid-1980s. In 1983 the share capital was raised to M$1,000,200 by a bonus issue of M$1 million out of retained earnings.

In August 1985, following an offer by interested private sector investors (the first-come-first-served approach), the Minister of Finance (Incorporated) sold 70% of the equity to a private company, B&B Enterprises Berhad, for M$35m. At the same time B&B passed on 10% of the equity to the Melewar Corporation Berhad. The sale conditions included payment in perpetuity of a 3% royalty to the government and 10% of pre-tax profits to the National Sports Council. In early 1987 a rights issue was made for M$29m. (29 for 1) paid in cash by all shareholders, raising total paid-up capital to M$30m. Following this Sports Toto sought a public listing on the KLSE concurrent with a public offer of 5.25 million existing shares (17.5%) by the two private sector shareholders, at M$2 per M$1 share. In accordance with practices in other public issues, the company also issued a Special Rights Share to the government, allowing it to be represented with observer status at AGMs, to grant or withhold prior consent on issues of merger, takeover, asset disposal, or amalgamation, and to appoint three directors including the Chairman, in addition to its rights as an ordinary shareholder.

Of the 5.25 million shares, 1.5 million (28%) were allocated to directors, employees, and Toto agents, 1.125m. to approved Bumiputra institutions, and 2.625m. to Malaysian companies and citizens, subject to the restriction that no single holding (other than by the government or anyone acting on its behalf) was to exceed 10% of total issued capital.[27] The public issue raised M$10.3m. which accrued to B&B (M$9m.) and Melewar (M$1.3m.), leaving the post-sale share distribution as follows:

Sports Toto Share Ownership

	1983	1985 (Sale)	1987 (Pre-Listing)	1987 (Post-Listing)
Minister of Finance	1.0m (100%)	0.3m (30%)	9.0m (30%)	9.0m (30.0%)
B & B Enterprises		0.6m (60%)	18.0m (60%)	13.5m (45.0%)
Melewar		0.1m (10%)	3.0m (10%)	2.3m (7.5%)
Bumiputra Insts				1.1m (3.8%)
Employees & Agents				1.5m (5.0%)
Other Malaysians				2.6m (8.7%)
	1.0m (100%)	1.0m (100%)	30.0m (100%)	30.0m (100%)

Interestingly, though the 1987 sale of equity in Sports Toto is often referred to by the Malaysian authorities as a privatization, there has been no dilution of the government holding since its original sale in 1985, although the 1987 sale did provide for the issue of a 'Golden Share'. We shall discuss this further in section 9.3.6.

Malaysian Airline Systems Berhad (MAS) (1985)

MAS was created in 1972 out of the Malaysia–Singapore Airlines Limited (MSA), following the separation of the two governments in 1971.[28] Throughout the 1970s the airline performed well, mainly concentrating on the domestic and regional network, although by 1978 it was beginning to expand its operations significantly, especially into the international market. The early 1980s were difficult times and, although capacity utilization remained reasonable (at around 66%), MAS was hit by high interest rates and high fuel costs, and in 1981/2 turned in a loss of M$35m. It paid no dividend the to government during the five years to 1985 (Table 9.10).

It was in response to these conditions that the company decided to strengthen its capital base so as to boost its cash flow and finance fleet modernization. It approached the government with a request for M$250m., which was not initially approved. However, and, it is argued, probably in response to the successful publicity surrounding the privatization of British Airways in the UK, the government later recommended that the MAS capital requirement should be met through a public share issue, part of which would consist of a sale of government equity in the airline. The privatization of MAS was thus embedded in a broader capital restructuring and listing of MAS shares on the KLSE.

The initial share capital of MAS at the time of its incorporation was 5 million shares, all held by the government. This was gradually increased to 70 million in 1979 through progressive cash injections from the government. Prior to listing, a revaluation was carried out on all assets, leading to a revaluation surplus which, along with M$131 million from the General Reserve, added a further 210 million shares, leaving the issued capital of the company prior to listing and the new issue at 280 million shares.[29]

The MAS capital issue/privatization occurred in October 1985 with the issue of the first privatization prospectus in Malaysia. It established the objectives of the sale and outlined the share allocation procedures to be adopted. In terms of the Prospectus, the sale was to have four main objectives, namely: (i) to implement the government's policy of privatization; (ii) to provide an opportunity for government approved institutions, Malaysian investors and eligible employees of MAS and its subsidiaries to participate in the equity of the company in accordance with the objectives of the NEP; (iii) to raise capital for the MAS fleet expansion; and (iv) to obtain a public listing for the company.

The listing of MAS stock on the KLSE consisted of three elements. First the company issued 70 million M$1 shares (priced at M$1.80). Second, the government sold 35 million of its own equity to approved institutions (through private placement). Finally, the company issued a M$1 Special Rights Redeemable Preference Share to the government. This 'Golden Share' gave the government the right of veto over the acquisition of the airline by a third party, the acquisition of other companies by MAS, and any major sale of assets. In addition the Golden Shareholder also had the right to appoint six of the eleven board members.[30]

The share allocation was determined in line with Capital Issues Committee procedures (see section 9.6), established to ensure that, in the primary issue at least, the distribution of equity ownership accorded with the objectives of the NEP. The 70 million new share issue was distributed as follows: employees of MAS and its subsidiaries 17.5m. shares (25.0%); approved Bumiputra institutions 3m. shares (4.3%); and Malaysian companies and citizens 49.5m. shares (70.7%). The issue

Table 9.10 Malaysian Airline System – financial and operation performance

	1979/80	1980/81	1981/82	1982/83	1983/84	1984/85	1985/86	1986/87	1987/88	1988/89
Total revenue (M$m.)	581.5	825.7	995.3	1,183.5	1,237.3	1,314.4	1,326.0	1,432.7	1,613.9	1,939.2
Total expenditure (M$m.)	562.5	817.1	1,028.9	1,170.8	1,140.1	1,179.7	1,218.8	1,316.9	1,458.5	1,738.9
Pre-tax profit/(loss)	19.0	8.6	(33.6)	12.7	97.2	134.7	107.2	115.8	155.4	200.3
Rate of profit (%)	3.3	1.0	−3.4	1.1	7.9	10.2	8.1	8.1	9.6	10.3
Passenger load factor	69.0	68.2	70.3	70.2	70.9	74.6	72.9	70.8	75.9	77.0
Overall load factor	67.5	67.3	70.9	65.1	69.8	73.8	74.0	72.9	77.0	76.9
Real revenue per employee (constant 1985 M$000s)	74.5	91.5	99.8	118.8	123.5	124.1	123.0	125.6	135.3	150.0

Source: MAS, Annual Report, 1988/89.

and sale (which was heavily oversubscribed) generated gross proceeds to MAS of M$126m. (M$121m. after expenses), while the government placement yielded M$63m. in privatization procccds. Following the public issue the distribution of shareholders was as follows:

Malaysian Airline System Share Ownership

	Pre-Sale		Post-Sale	
Minister of Finance (Incorporated)	252m	(90%)	217.0m	(62%)
State of Sarawak	14m	(5%)	14.0m	(4%)
State of Sabah	14m	(5%)	14.0m	(4%)
Bumiputra institutions (PNB etc.)			38.0m	(11%)
Employees of MAS			17.5m	(5%)
Other Malaysians and companies			49.5m	(14%)
	280m	(100%)	350.0m	(100%)

The government remains the single major shareholder and the public sector as a whole (including the Bumiputra institutions) still controls 81% of the equity. Moreover, the shareholder control by government is underwritten further by the Special Rights share.

AIROD – Aircraft Maintenance (1985)
AIROD is a M$73m. joint-venture company, employing 200 people and providing maintenance and repair services for the Royal Malaysian Air Force. It was incorporated in late 1986 with the shareholding split between Lockheed Aircraft Services International of the USA, who hold the management contract and 49% of the equity, and Aerospace Industries of Malaysia (AIM), who holds 51% of equity. AIM is owned jointly by MAS (33.3%), the Minister of Finance Inc. (29.2%), and United Motor Works (Malaysia) Holdings (37.5%).[31] Though initially involved only in repair work, AIROD has moved into commercial and overseas defence contracting, and has also begun 'black-box' assembly for Lockheed. The company has a relatively short financial history and, though no comprehensive financial statistics are available, it is known that AIM's contribution to MAS group profits has been positive and rising over the period 1987/88 to 1988/89.

Malaysia International Shipping Corporation (1987)
The Malaysian International Shipping Corporation was incorporated in 1968 as a joint venture between the government, the public sector (the Lembaga Urusan & Tabung Haji)[32] and the private sector (Frank Tsao (Liberia) Ltd, and Kuok Brothers Berhad). MISC has subsequently developed as the major shipping line in Malaysia, and indeed has acquired the status of the national shipping company.[33] Growth has been rapid and, prior to the public issue in January 1987, the MISC fleet consisted of 41 vessels with a deadweight tonnage of 1.38 million tons.
MISC's fleet expansion up until 1986 had been financed partly through increases in shareholder equity (from the original shareholders and new, principally public sector, shareholders) from M$7m. in 1969 to M$100m. by the eve of the public issue, but mainly through borrowing through the domestic financial sector. High interest rates, combined with the world trade recession of the early 1980s, severely depressed MISC's financial performance (Table 9.11). No dividends were paid from 1981 to 1985, losses were recorded in 1982 and 1983, and by 1984 the company's debt–equity ratio had reached an extremely high level of 22:1 (average debt to equity for all SOEs was only 2:1).
By 1986, though the company had returned to a position of profitability

Table 9.11 *Malaysian International Shipping Corporation – Financial and operation performance*

(M$ million)	1979	1980	1981	1982	1983	1984	1985	1986	1987	1988
Total revenue (M$m.)	349.9	573.4	600.8	482.1	651.3	892.7	974.4	1,217.1	1,383.8	1,534.4
Pre-Tax Profit/(Loss)	28.9	56.7	16.4	(58.5)	(60.9)	57.5	163.1	243.1	288.3	391.6
Rate of Profit (%)	7.3	9.9	2.7	(12.1)	(9.4)	6.4	16.7	20.0	20.8	25.5
Dividend	2.5	2.5	0.0	0.0	0.0	0.0	22.5	37.5	62.5	75.0
Debt–Equity Ratio	–	–	–	–	–	21.8	10.4	6.0	2.5	1.5
Earning per Share (Sen)	–	–	–	–	–	57.5	163.1	92.9	57.3	78.0
Real Revenue Per Employee	–	–	–	–	–	351.0	347.9	435.6	522.1	577.0

Source: MISC, *Annual Report 1988/89*.

(principally due to success in winning a lucrative 20-year LNG transportation contract with Japan, which now accounts for 50% of the total profit), it still required a significant equity injection to support its proposed M$1bn fleet expansion. It consequently agreed with the government the following financing proposal, only part of which involved the sale of government equity to the private sector:

i) A special issue of 25 million M$1 shares to the Minister of Finance (Incorporated), 'in appreciation of Government's support to the company',[34] fully paid and financed from retained earnings. This step raised the issued share capital from M$100 million to M$125 million;

ii) A M$125 million one-for-one bonus issue to all shareholders, financed out of retained earnings. This raised the issued share capital to M$250m.;

iii) A M$250 million one-for-one rights issue at par to all existing shareholders (including the government). This raised issued capital to M$500m. and generated M$247m. net proceeds for MISC;

iv) A M$1.00 Special Preference Share issued to the Minister of Finance (Incorporated), which allows the government to attend general meetings as a non-voting member (above and beyond its rights as an ordinary shareholder), and to grant or withhold prior consent on issues of merger, takeover, asset disposal, and amalgamation;

v) An application to the KLSE for the public listing of the entire equity of MISC;

vi) A public share offer by the 11 major shareholders in MISC of 84,985,000 shares, at an offer price of M$2.40 per share. The proceeds of the sale were to accrue directly to the shareholders and not to the company.

A number of objectives were achieved by this restructuring programme. First, MISC raised an additional M$247m. towards its capital expansion programme (step (iii)). Second, by expanding its capital base by 400%, the company dramatically improved its debt–equity ratio (steps (i), (ii) & (iii)). Third, the corporation achieved a public share quotation.[35] Fourth, the government divested some of its equity in the SOE (step (iv)), although through steps (i)–(iv) it had actually increased its equity in MISC. And, fifth, the government concurrently acquired a 'golden share' in the company.

The mechanics of the share sale are complex but to understand the way in which the Bumiputra and government-owned institutions are involved in the programme, it is important to clarify the exact mechanics of the privatization element of the MISC transaction. The 85 million shares were to be allocated as follows: Bumiputra institutions (by private placement) 25.0m. (29.4%); Malaysian employees of MISC 3.0m. (3.5%); Bumiputra institutions and individuals 17.1m. (20.1%); other private sector 39.9m. (46.9%).

Malaysian International Shipping Corporation Share Ownership

Name	Type	Pre-Sale (mill.)	Post-Sale (mill.)	Proceeds M$m.
Min. of Fin.	Federal Gov.	184.0 (36.8%)	147.2 (29.4%)	88.3
Sabah	State Gov.	20.0 (4.0%)	16.0 (3.2%)	9.6
Sarawak	State Gov.	20.0 (4.0%)	16.0 (3.2%)	9.6
Johor	State Gov.	20.0 (4.0%)	16.0 (3.2%)	9.6
Pahang	State Gov.	20.0 (4.0%)	16.0 (3.2%)	9.6
Pinang	State Gov.	20.0 (4.0%)	16.0 (3.2%)	9.6
AMMB	Bank	20.0 (4.0%)	16.0 (3.2%)	9.6
LUTH	Bank	46.1 (9.2%)	36.8 (7.4%)	22.3
Other private		74.8 (14.9%)	59.9 (12.0%)	35.8
Total		424.9 (85.0%)	339.9 (68.0%)	204.0

Source: MISC, Annual Report, 1988/89.

A comparison of their shareholdings before and after the share sale shows the number of shares that each sold. Of the shares sold, 66.8% were sold by the public sector, and 33.2% by the private sector. M$88m. accrued to the federal government, M$48m. to state governments, and M$68m. to the private sector. The most striking feature of the sale was that, though the public sector (i.e. the federal plus state governments) as a whole relinquished its majority shareholder position, the ownership structure of the company changed relatively slightly, with the federal government remaining the single major shareholder, and the public sector as a whole still controlling 45.4% of the equity. By 1989 that position had not changed, although it may be noted that the public sector institutions (ASN and the Employee Provident Fund) held a further 5.8% of the equity, bringing the consolidated public sector equity ownership in MISC to over 51%.

Tradewinds Malaysia Berhad (1988)
Tradewinds Malaysia Berhad is an investment holding company with interest in oil palm, cocoa, sugar refining, life and general insurance. It was incorporated in 1974 as a private limited company with a paid-up share capital of M$2.00m. (authorized M$500,000), held by Perbadanan Nasional Berhad (PERNAS), itself a 100% government-owned holding company.[36] During the subsequent decade private sector partners were attracted and by 1987 the issued share capital was M$140m. held by PERNAS (66.25%), Grenfell Holdings (Malaysia) (30.54%), and 3.21% held by employees of the company. The shareholders then sought a public share listing in line with the precedent established by MAS and MISC.

The KLSE listing, in February 1988, was accompanied by a sale of 15 million existing ordinary shares of M$1.00 each at M$1.10, with 10 million to be sold by PERNAS, and 5 million by Grenfell Holdings. The share allocation process followed the now standard pattern, with the 15 million shares being allocated: 6.7% to employees of Tradewinds and its subsidiaries; 28% to approved Bumiputra institutions; and the remaining 65.3% to Malaysian companies and citizens, subject to the standard restriction that no single holding, other than by the government or anyone acting on its behalf, could exceed 10% of the shares.

The sale generated net proceeds of M$16m., of which M$10.7m. accrued to PERNAS, and M$5.3m. to Grenfell Holdings, and resulted in a post-sale share distribution as follows:

Tradewinds Share Ownership

	Pre-Sale		Post-Sale	
PERNAS	92.75m	(66.25%)	82.75m	(59.11%)
Grenfell Holdings Sdn Berhad	42.75m	(30.54%)	37.75m	(26.96%)
Employees of Tradewinds	4.50m	(3.21%)	5.52m	(3.94%)
Bumiputra Institutions	—		4.20m	(3.00%)
Other Private Sector (incl 30% to Bumiputra)	—		9.79m	(7.00%)
	140.0m	(100%)	140.0m	(100%)

Cement Manufacturers Sarawak Berhad (1989)

CMS was incorporated in 1974 as a joint-venture company owned equally by the Development Corporations of Sabah and Sarawak. The company manufactures portland cement, and from 1978 to 1986 enjoyed a protected monopoly position in both Sabah and Sarawak. Following the establishment of a low-capacity cement mill in Sabah in 1986 (set up by the Sabah Development Corporation), CMS now only supplies the Sarawak market, where it enjoys a monopoly position, since high transport costs serve as effective external barriers to entry to peninsular Malaysia despite its excess capacity. Though the sector was hit hard by the recession of 1985–7, the company remained profitable, and has enjoyed an increasingly buoyant market since 1988, supported by high levels of spending by the state government in the tourism and construction sectors.

The decision to divest equity in CMS, and to seek listing on the KLSE followed the same pattern as the other public-issue privatizations. The main objectives of the sale, cited in the prospectus, were not divestiture *per se*, but rather the wish to obtain a public listing and also to facilitate share distribution in accordance with the ownership objectives of the NEP. At the time of issue the equity in CMS was held 35% each by the Sabah and Sarawak Development Corporations, and 30% by Permodalan Nasional Berhad. The share sale took place in January 1989, and involved (in addition to the public listing) the sale of 2.5 million shares (7.8%) by both the Sarawak and Sabah Development Corporations, at a price of M$1.30 per M$1.00 share.

Allocation of shares was in accordance with now standard procedures, with 8.8% allocated to employees, 27.4% to approved Bumiputra institutions, and the remainder (63.8%) to Malaysian companies and citizens (of which 30% must be Bumiputra). The sale generated gross proceeds of M$6.5m. (M$6.347m. net) to Sabah and Sarawak Economic Development Corporations, and resulted in the following post-sale share distribution:

Cement Manufacturers Sarawak Share Ownership

	Pre-Sale		Post-Sale	
Sarawak Development Corporation	11.200m	(35%)	8.700m	(27.2%)
Sabah Development Corporation	11.200m	(35%)	8.700m	(27.2%)
Permodalan Nasional Berhad (PNB)	9.600m	(30%)	9.600m	(30.0%)
Employees			0.444m	(1.4%)
Bumiputra Institutions			1.367m	(4.3%)
Malaysian Public			3.189m	(9.9%)
	32.000m	(100%)	32.000m	(100%)

Syarikat Gula Padang Sugar and Cawangan Percetakan Keselamatan Printing (1989)
Two small private sales have also been undertaken directly by the EPU, both involving total equity sale to approved (i.e. Bumiputra) purchasers. Both were sales of companies into relatively competitive market sectors: sugar-growing and printing. Since both sales were undertaken as private 'first-come-first-served' transactions, no publicly available data exist on the details of the transactions, the companies involved, or the post-sale performance of the enterprises. It may, however, be noted that both are relatively small concerns.

Build–Operate–Transfer Projects (1987–90)
As noted above, one feature of the Malaysian privatization programme is the extent to which methods other than direct asset sale predominate. In addition to a series of licensing agreements and deregulation activities (for example TV3 and various marketing undertakings[37]), Malaysia has pioneered the use of Build–Operate–Transfer (BOT) contracts for infrastructural development. These schemes, which involve in effect an extension of standard public works tendering by transferring financing risks to the contractor rather than the client, have featured strongly in two sectors: road-building and water supply. Contracts have typically been extended on the first-come-first-served basis discussed earlier, and have embodied relatively standard conditions. The earliest BOTs were in the roads sector and began following the passing of the Federal Roads (Private Management) Act 1984. Contracts generally involve local contractors (although foreign joint-venture contractors are also considered), with contract fees and toll-setting arrangements negotiated on a case-by-case basis.[38] Water supply contracts, which cover only water treatment, with distribution and final consumer billing remaining a government activity, are relatively homogeneous, in terms of both contract conditions and also of the companies bidding for the contracts. Again details on the structure of agreements are sparse.

Casual evidence suggests that the privatization effect of the BOT method has been severely compromised in Malaysia. BOT methods can really only be considered as privatization if there is a transfer of commercial risk from the government to the private sector. In the case of the road sector BOTs, the governments' concern over creating credibility for the programme resulted in high degrees of underwriting of the private sector contractors by the provision of revenue guarantees against falling toll collection. Clearly, in a situation of full underwriting, the BOT scheme merely represents a variation in funding schemes for public works projects. The contractor faces a different (but certain) payment process, whilst, in guaranteeing the toll, the government faces the same liability as if it were operating a standard user-cost recovery public road project. This problem is exacerbated in the Malaysian case by the apparent 'capture' of the government by the contractors, especially on the larger projects. This was alluded to earlier in the discussion on cronyism. More recently the contractors were forced to suspend toll collections on a section of the highway serving as a major commuter link between a suburb and central Kuala Lumpur following violent opposition from the predominantly Chinese community who use the road. The government has compensated the toll contractor in full (Hoon Lim Siong, 1990).

9.3.6 The Federal Treasury and UPSAK reforms
Running parallel to the EPU privatization programme has been a smaller programme of SOE reform and divestiture managed by the Federal Treasury through UPSAK. Starting in 1989, UPSAK prepared an audit on all the major ailing non-financial SOEs.[39] 106 SOEs in all were identified, although 17 were excluded

from the sample as they were either minority-owned, or were State-(as opposed to Federal-) owned. Of the remaining 89, government-financed rehabilitation programmes, executed under the direct aegis of the Federal Treasury, were instituted for the largest 10 major ailing companies – those with a capital base in excess of M$70m.

Table 9.12 summarizes the ten major ailing enterprises. The rehabilitation programmes are still under way and consequently no details are available on each individual reform, although most include management and production rationalization and financial restructuring, financed through renewed government equity injections.[40] One particularly revealing aspect of this reform programme is the particularly poor performance of large capital-intensive enterprises operating in the outlying states (Sabah, Kedah, Trengganu), all of which were created by state governments in the period of rapid expansion from 1970 to 1983.

The reform programme of the remaining 79 enterprises has been carried out, (without sizeable capital injection from the Treasury), by UPSAK (and its private sector contractors). As noted above, UPSAK serves principally as an advisory and co-ordinating unit, and consequently it only recommends that restructuring exercises be carried out. Implementation and, importantly, the financing of restructuring remain the responsibility of either the federal government (as in the case of the 10 major companies) or the relevant holding agency, and consequently comprehensive details of the individual reform programmes are not available. However, of the 79 companies covered 17 required no further restructuring, 12 required further restructuring but were considered viable operations, 18 were recommended for sale, and 22 for closure. As at June 1990, 9 companies had been sold to the private sector, 2 had been leased, and 6 had been closed (Table 9.13). The proceeds (or costs) of the restructuring process are not known, nor are any details of the purchasers.

UPSAK's role is expected to widen so that the review and appraisal procedures eventually cover all the SOEs[41] and, as noted in section 9.3.8, the audit and restructuring work of UPSAK is to be integrated into the second phase of privatization heralded by the Privatization Masterplan.

9.3.7 Assessment of the privatization programme 1983-90

The first seven years' experience of privatization in Malaysia provide a considerable body of information with which to assess privatization policy. The experience reveals much about the relative importance of the various objectives cited in the Guidelines for Privatization, and raises some more fundamental issues relating to ownership and performance in Malaysia.

Summary of privatization outturns and objectives

Table 9.14 details the gross cash flow generated by EPU privatizations over the period 1984-9, expressed in terms of the government revenue and GDP. Even ignoring the costs to government in pre-sale rights issues, the immediate impression from the Table is that, as a percentage of GDP, the proceeds from privatization have been surprisingly small. Even in 1985 and 1987 – the high points so far in the privatization programme – total proceeds from asset sales amounted to only 0.2% of GDP, while the cumulative proceeds from all asset sales from 1984 to 1989 totalling M$437.6m. are equivalent to less than 0.1% of GDP. When one considers that SOE sector output is estimated to be approximately 25% of GDP, the EPU privatization programme has so far been of only very modest size in terms of revenue-raising divestiture – despite its relatively high profile. The position in terms of government revenue is, not surprisingly, similar, with proceeds reaching

Table 9.12 Federal Treasury reform programme 1989: target enterprises

Company	Kedah cement	Perak Hannjoong Simen Bhd	Perwaja Trengganu Sdn. Bhd	Malayawata Steel Bhd	Malaysian Shipyard & Engineering	Sabah Forest Industries	Sabah Gas Industries	Kumpulan Fima Bhd	PERNAS Group	Perbadanan Nat. Shipping Line Bhd
Sector	Cement	Cement	Steel Billets	Steel Bars	Shipbuilding & Repair	Paper Manufacture	Methanol from Natural Gas	Investment Holding Co.	Investment Holding Co.	Shipping
Shareholding (%)										
Federal Govt	35.0	60.0	81.0	40.0	77.9	100.0	100.0	99.5	100.0	100.0
State Govt	25.0		19.0	36.0	7.4			0.5		
Domestic Private	30.0	40.0		24.0						
Foreign Private	10.0				14.7					
Financial Performance (1988) (M$m.)										
Turnover	108.1	92.9	143.0	157.6	187.0	257.6	449.8	178.0	39.9	77.1
Op. Profit/(loss)	8.8	6.3	(184.0)	10.5	14.7	11.6	60.2	1.2	23.6	2.1
Interest	49.2	38.6	111.0	15.8	9.0	90.9	90.9	11.5	36.2	17.0
Net Profit/(Loss)	(73.2)	(55.3)	(295.0)	(5.0)	5.7	(137.5)	(27.2)	(35.2)	(20.6)	(16.5)
Paid-up capital	180.0	149.6	250.0	67.2	100.0	388.2	371.9	189.3	751.0	49.0
Acc. losses	(217.6)	(80.5)	(558.0)	(115.5)	(125.0)	(114.6)	(918.0)	(20.7)	(27.2)	(23.0)
Shareholders funds	(37.6)	69.1	(308.0)	(48.3)	(25.0)	273.6	(546.1)	168.6	723.8	26.0
Long-term loans	592.6	428.8	1,370.0	44.1	212.0	1,113.7	1,226.0	166.4	588.9	222.1
Op. Profit/ Turnover	8.1%	6.7%	−128.6%	6.6%	7.8%	4.5%	13.3%	0.6%	59.1%	2.7%
Interest/ Turnover	45.5%	41.5%	77.6%	10.0%	4.8%	35.2%	20.2%	6.4%	90.7%	22.0%
Debt/Equity Ratio	3.2	2.8	5.4	0.6	2.1	2.8	3.3	0.8	0.7	4.5

Source: UPSAK, *Snapshot Review of Major Ailing Companies,* 1989.

Table 9.13 UPSAK Restructuring programme 1989

Company	Sector	Capital Acc. M$m.	Losses M$m.	Shareholders Funds M$m.	UPSAK Recommendation	Action as at Mid 1990
Pernas Holding Chain (Selangor)	Services	67.6	52.9	14.7	No action required	–
Pernas Edar	Manufacturing	16.3	23.6	(7.4)	Restructure	Under-way
Pernas Engineering	Manufacturing	10.0	67.7	(57.7)	Restructure	Under-way
MKIC Security	Services	1.0	0.9	0.1	Sell	Sold
MKIC Amlak	Services	1.0	3.6	(2.6)	Wind-up	Wound-up
Bajakimia Industries	Manufacturing	2.7	2.7	0.0	Wind-up	?
Jean Simons Wigs	Manufacturing	0.2	0.3	(0.1)	Wind-up	?
Malaysia Timber Exports	Manufacturing	0.5	0.7	(0.2)	Wind-up	?
Malaysia International Palm Oil	Manufacturing	25.0	27.9	(2.9)	Wind-up	?
Pernas Hall Engineering	Manufacturing	0.5	2.5	(2.0)	Wind-up	Under-way
Pernas Mining	Mining	12.5	18.6	(6.1)	Wind-up	Under-way
Pernas Electronics	Manufacturing	2.5	13.9	(11.4)	Wind-up	Under-way
Malaysian Titanium	Mining	20.0	63.7	(43.7)	Already in receivership	–
Associated Motors	Services	10.0	18.9	(8.9)	Sell	Sold
Berger Paints	Manufacturing	8.8	12.7	(3.9)	Sell	Sold
Kubota Agriculture Machinery	Manufacturing	10.0	10.8	(0.8)	Sell	Sold
Steelform Industries	Manufacturing	15.0	1.1	13.9	Sell	Sold
Fimajaya Foods	Ag. Process	1.5	(3.5)	5.0	Restructure	Under-way
Fima Mr. Juicy	Ag. Process	0.1	0.2	(0.1)	Restructure	Under-way
Ladang Fima	Ag. Process	2.4	3.7	(1.3)	Restructure	Under-way
Fima Fraser Hill	Ag. Process	0.5	2.2	(1.7)	Lease	Under-way
Makan Ternak Fima	Ag. Process	1.3	3.4	(2.1)	Wind-up	Under-way
Fraser Hill Mushrooms	Ag. Process	0.1	0.2	(0.1)	Wind-up	Under-way
Ayam Fima	Ag. Process	0.2	0.9	(0.7)	Wind-up	Under-way
Cashew Industries of Malaysia	Ag. Process	2.1	(10.1)	12.2	Wind-up	Under-way
Fima Rantei	Ag. Process	1.5	3.8	(2.3)	Wind-up	Under-way
Fima Timuran	Ag. Process	2.6	6.8	(4.2)	Already in receivership	–
Pembangunan Reality Corp	Finance	1.0	(2.6)	3.6	Restructure	?
Koko Malaysia	Finance	17.7	5.1	12.6	Sell	Sold
Syarikat Bandar Baru	Services	0.1	0.4	(0.3)	Restructure	?
Mardec Irving Moore	Manufacturing	4.3	4.7	(0.4)	No action required	–
MTIB Holdings	Manufacturing	2.0	6.7	(4.7)	Wind-up	?
Pengkalan Eksport	Ag. Process	0.2	1.9	(1.7)	Already in liquidation	–
Pengkalan Eksport Shapadu	Ag. Process	1.3	2.4	(1.1)	Sell	Sold

Kima	Services	20.3	6.9	13.4	No action required	—
Ladang Mara	Services	17.1	10.3	6.8	No action required	—
Batek Malaysia	Services	8.5	7.1	1.4	No action required	—
Kenderaan Langkasuka	Services	0.1	0.2	(0.1)	No action required	—
Kenderaan Sri Kedah	Services	0.4	0.4	0.0	No action required	—
Molek Express	Services	0.2	0.2	0.0	No action required	?
Starise	Services	0.1	0.1	0.0	No action required	?
Kenderaan Manik	Services	0.8	0.6	0.2	Restructure	?
Masmara Tour & Travel	Services	4.2	2.8	1.4	Restructure	?
SKMK-Star	Services	0.1	0.4	(0.3)	Sell	?
Lori Malaysian	Services	10.6	17.5	(6.9)	Sell	
Syarikat Mawar	Services	0.3	1.1	(0.8)	Wind-up	
State Ria	Services	1.5	2.3	(0.8)	Sell	Sold
State Franchise	Services	3.2	2.9	0.3	Sell	Sold
Syarikat Perniagaan Peladang	Agriculture	0.9	0.9	0.0	No action required	
Syarikat Perindustrian	Agriculture	0.0	1.3	(1.3)	No action required	?
Pempena	Tourism	41.7	5.3	36.4	Liquidate	?
Tanjung Jara Beach Hotel	Tourism	20.7	11.1	9.6	Sell	?
Motel Desa	Tourism	1.6	0.9	0.7	Sell	?
Holiday Village of Malaysia	Tourism	13.1	7.5	5.6	Sell	?
Pangkaut Rel Melaka	Tourism	0.1	0.1	0.0	Liquidate	
TDC Duty Free	Tourism	0.5	0.8	(0.3)	Already in liquidation	—
Sawira	Manufacturing	35.0	6.3	28.7	No action required	?
Pahangbit	Manufacturing	3.8	7.8	(4.0)	Restructure	?
Pasarnika	Manufacturing	1.0	1.2	(0.2)	Restructure	?
Dara Ornamental Minerals	Manufacturing	0.7	1.1	(0.4)	Wind-up	?
Dara Wood	Manufacturing	1.0	6.8	(5.8)	Already in receivership	
Kuari Kerisek	Manufacturing	0.6	1.0	(0.4)	Lease	Leased
Binadara	Manufacturing	0.9	3.6	(2.7)	Lease	Leased
Ladang Petri Tenggara	Agriculture	9.3	14.2	(4.9)	No action required	
Pertanian Johor Tenggara	Agriculture	8.0	5.8	2.2	No action required	—
Kejora Avi	Tourism	9.0	11.3	(2.3)	Sell	?
Kejora Golf & Realty Dev	Property	4.5	2.8	1.7	Sell	?
Desaru	Tourism	0.4	2.2	(1.8)	Sell	?
Johor Tenggara Hotel	Tourism	4.3	9.3	(5.0)	Sell	?
Rakyat Keteng	Agriculture	7.0	2.6	4.4	No action required	
Ketengah Pewira	Agriculture	28.5	10.3	18.2	No action required	—
Ketengah Jaya	Agriculture	20.6	5.3	15.3	No action required	—
Kesedar Inn	Tourism	1.1	0.1	1.0	No action required	—

Table 9.13 *continued*

Company	Sector	Capital Acc. M$m.	Losses M$m.	Shareholders Funds M$m.	UPSAK Recommendation	Action as at Mid 1990
Syarikat Majutani	Manufacturing	1.1	8.5	(7.4)	Liquidate	?
Kedawan Engineering Corp.	Manufacturing	0.1	0.2	(0.1)	Wind-up	?
Keda Pallet	Manufacturing	0.2	0.3	(0.1)	Wind-up	?
Syarikat Gabungan Risda	Ag. Process	7.0	5.1	1.9	Restructure	?
Smallholders Aqua Farm	Ag. Process	3.2	3.8	(0.6)	Lease	?
Narsco Properties	Ag. Process	0.8	0.2	0.6	Wind-up	?
TOTAL		536.6	539.2	(2.7)		

SUMMARY

Recommendation	No.	Action
No action [a]	22	
Sell [b]	22	11
Liquidate	3	
Wind-up	19	9
Restructure	13	5
TOTAL	79	25

Source: UPSAK

Notes
a) Includes already in liquidation.
b) Includes lease.

Table 9.14 *Privatization cash flow*

(EPU Privatizations only)		1984	1985	1986	1987	1988	1989	Curr. Tot.
Asset Sales	M$ million	72.80	155.40	0.00	136.30	61.70	11.40	437.60
	% Revenue	0.35	0.74	0.00	0.75	0.34	0.05	0.35
	% GDP	0.09	0.20	0.00	0.17	0.07	0.01	0.09
Licensing/BOT/Contracting	M$ million	0.00	0.00	0.00	406.50	4,426.50	727.00	5,153.50
	% Revenue	0.00	0.00	0.00	2.24	24.40	3.31	4.11
	% GDP	0.00	0.00	0.00	0.51	4.87	0.72	1.03
Total	M$ million	72.80	155.40	0.00	542.80	4,488.20	738.40	5,454.80
	% Revenue	0.35	0.74	0.00	2.99	24.74	3.36	4.35
	% GDP	0.09	0.20	0.00	0.68	4.94	0.73	1.09
Memorandum Items	M$ million							
	Federal Govt Revenue	20,805	21,114	19,518	18,143	21,967	23,863	125,410
	GDP (Market Prices)	79,550	77,547	71,729	79,711	90,806	100,650	499,993

Source: Economic Planning Unit.

Note: Contracts included at full value in year of commencement.

a maximum of only 0.75% of total revenue; and, in cumulative terms, proceeds amounted to only 0.35% of total revenue over the period 1984–9.

The picture is somewhat different when the other privatizations are considered. In reviewing these figures it should be borne in mind that we report the full contract value for BOTs and licencing agreements in the year the contract was signed. The reason for taking the contract value as a measure of 'proceeds' is that it represents the amount which would have had to be raised out of the public development budget had the contract not been undertaken by the private sector. And, second, since details of the payment arrangement are not known with any degree of certainty the total contract value is recorded in the year in which it was awarded, which clearly tends to overstate the impact of these contracts in their initial year, especially in view of the fact that a number of the road contracts have a long gestation period. However, notwithstanding these points, it is clear that the BOT programme eclipsed the asset sale programme in the period 1987–90, and represents a significant private sector contribution to the overall development budget, in line with the commitment made in the Fifth Malaysian Plan.

In order to assess these outcomes it is helpful to summarize, in a stylized manner, what the objectives of each sale were.[42] This is represented in Table 9.15. Most striking is that, with the exception of the KCT sale – which was a flagship sale – the only majority asset sales have been those in which the government has responded to direct bids from the private sector. Government-managed sales (which have been predominantly through public issues) have generally involved the sale of only a minority equity holding, have involved the creation of Special Rights Shares for the government, and have tended to emphasize the pursuit of NEP objectives and a capital market listing as the principal objectives of the sale. Striking, however, is the extremely limited role of employee share participation, which is present in only three sales, and then only in the case of MAS was the allocation of shares a significant percentage of the total equity. In the following subsections we attempt to analyse the cause and effect of these stylized effects.

Programme management and implementation

The government cut its teeth on the KCT privatization. To date it remains the only sizeable asset sale which has involved a considerable degree of management change, but as will be noted below, many of the issues raised and lessons learnt from the KCT privatization are of more relevance to the privatization proposals for the large utilities than for the asset sales during the 1980s. Although the initial sale plan envisaged a transfer of the fixed assets and land from KPA to the new company KCT, it later emerged that this was impossible since the land was not in fact owned by KPA but had been granted to it by federal government fiat. Further investigation revealed this to be the case with most SOEs. As an interim measure for the KCT sale, a leasing agreement was therefore drawn up pending a constitutional amendment. This amendment was eventually passed in 1989 and allowed statutory bodies to transfer or lease land to private operators through privatization. At the same time a further constitutional amendment was passed to allow statutory bodies to transfer their operations to non-statutory bodies. This again was an issue which had been overlooked in much of the thinking about privatization, which had initially been conceived in terms of equity dilution in public limited companies.

Privatization and employment policy

A coherent policy on employment and privatization emerged in an *ad hoc* manner from the KCT sale, although the publicity associated with it has entrenched the arrangements in the canon of privatization practice in Malaysia. Again the issue did not arise in the partial privatizations that succeeded the KCT sale,[43] but has become central to the corporatization/privatization programmes for the utilities.

Table 9.15 *Malaysian asset sales: analysis of stated objectives*

	Nature of Sale						Sale Objectives					
Enterprise	First-Come[a]	Direct Sale	Public Issue	Majority Sale	Minority Sale	Golden Share[b]	Privatization[a]	NEP[b]	ESOP[c] (%)	Balance Sheet[d]	Listing[e]	Improved Efficiency[f]
Klang Container Terminal		X		X			X					X
MAS			X		X	X	X	X	5.00	X	X	
MISC			X		X	X		X	0.00	X	X	
AIROD	X	X			X							X
Sports Toto	X	X		X		X		X				
Tradewinds			X		X			X	0.70		X	
Cement Sarawak			X		X			X	1.40		X	
Gula Padang	X	X		X								
Cawangan Percetakan	X	X		X								

Source: Sale Prospectuses.

Notes

Nature of Sale:
a) First-Come: asset sold following direct approach by private sector.
b) Golden Share: sale accompanied by issue of Special Rights share to government.

Sale Objectives
a) Privatization: implementation of privatization cited as specific objective of sale.
b) NEP: pursuit of asset ownership in terms of NEP objectives cited as objective of sale.
c) ESOP: percentage of total equity in enterprise reserved for application by employees.
d) Balance Sheet: improvement in balance sheet gearing cited as objective for share issue.
e) Listing: share listing on KLSE cited as objective of sale.
f) Efficiency: improved operating efficiency cited as reason for sale.

In the negotiations over the KCT sale, CUEPACS, the civil service union which represented the workers at KPA, initially took a strong anti-privatization line and consequently negotiations were protracted. The underlying principle behind the policy which emerged strongly supported employees and stated that 'employees will not lose in any way the benefits they enjoyed while being employed by Government'. Three options were available to all employees:

i) Depending on their employment status, workers could opt to retire with generous lump-sum severance pay and entitlement to early pension benefits.
ii) Employees could opt not to join KCT, regardless of their function. KPA would be obliged to retain these people without loss of pay, conditions, grade, etc.
iii) Workers could choose to terminate their contract with KPA (and the civil service) and join KCT, the new company, on terms no less favourable than before. KCT employees could not be fired for a period of 5 years, except in disciplinary cases.

In addition to option (iii), the government amended the Pension Act of 1980 to ensure that employees of the new company would not lose accumulated civil service pension rights. Given these conditions, 99% of all container terminal employees opted to join KCT, with the support of their former union (in which they were entitled to remain).

In view of the fortuitous improvement in trade volumes from 1986 onwards, the agreement reached with the unions did not pressurize the financial performance of KPA or KCT, since the demand for labour has remained high. However, many of the privatization proposals in the pipeline – in particular electricity and railways – are of enterprises which are grossly overstaffed. Sale of such assets under the above employment conditions is likely to prove extremely difficult, and it was this factor which in 1986 led the Finance Minister to announce that the government was prepared to sell the entire railway system for one Ringgit (M$1.00) on condition that it was operated as a going concern without employment cuts (*Malaysian Business*, 15 May 1989). The Railway Union of Malaya has already demanded KCT employment conditions as a minimum in the debate over the privatization of KTM, the national railways. The delay in bringing STM to a public issue was due in part to the high labour costs (STM employs 28,000 people), and analysts envisage that labour productivity is unlikely to grow sufficiently to avoid wide-scale retrenchment on the expiry of the 5-year redundancy moratorium in 1992.

The second issue related to employment policy and privatization concerns the role of employee share participation in the case of public share issues. As noted in Table 9.15, the use of employee share participation is relatively limited, and (as we shall suggest below) seems to be used more as a management incentive scheme than as an employee incentive. Employee share participation in Malaysia, unlike Jamaica for example, does not involve free share allocations, share discounts, or soft financing for equity participation. To date shares have been allocated in minimum bundles of 1,000 shares at issue prices ranging from M$1.10 to M$2.40, with applications generally payable in full; this represents a high proportion of average wages in the non-managerial sector. As discussed below, a link between privatization and wealth distribution does exist, but the mechanisms employed to achieve wider share participation were such that ESSs were hardly used.

Privatization and enterprise performance
Identifying causal effects in efficiency gains from privatization is difficult. In general, changes in performance can emanate from three sources: changes in

demand conditions; changes in market structures as determined by the degree of competition and/or regulation; and changes in the internal efficiency of the enterprise brought about by changes in ownership and management. It is the third that is relevant in assessing the impact of privatization.

In the case of all the privatizations surveyed above, available evidence points to improved performance following privatization, although frequently the improvement preceded the actual sale. Such improvements can be seen not only in financial measures (profits, turnover, dividend payments, etc.), but also in a variety of operating and productivity measures. For example, improved operating efficiency in KCT is most easily measured in the reduction in turnaround times for container operations; in 1985 it was 11.6 hours, by 1989 it had fallen by 23% to 8.9 hours. Similarly for the port as a whole, the average stay has fallen from 8 to 3.8 days, throughput was up, and Port Klang moved up from 11th to 7th position in terms of worldwide container port performance. In MAS, load factors have risen steadily since 1985/6, while revenue per employee rose by 20% in real terms between 1985/6 and 1988/9. Similar improvements are evident in MISC where real revenue per employee rose by 32% in the two years following privatization, and the company began to pay dividends for the first time since 1981 (Tables 9.10 and 9.11).

The problem of separating the causes of these improvements is difficult since most sales have occurred during a period of rapid economic recovery following the 1985–7 recession. Given also the fact that a number of the enterprises sold are in sectors with high pro-cyclical elements (cement, external trade, investment, finance), the ability to discern measurable efficiency improvements is made more complex. Finally, it must also be noted that in only four cases was the privatization more than partial, such that it involved a change in ownership and control. In fact only in the case of Sports Toto, Port Klang, and the two 100% sales has there been any change in management.

These caveats notwithstanding, there are clear areas where the privatization process has had an impact. The first is in the financial structure of companies. As noted, a number of the privatizations stated that capital restructuring, along with the pursuit of a KLSE listing, was a motivating factor. Reduced dependence on government funding gives the enterprise greater financial flexibility, while the process of asset sales (in particular through public sales) tends to impose an external discipline on the balance sheet, enables the company to improve its debt/equity ratio, and therefore improve its access to credit from the financial sector. This factor prompted the capital issues by MISC and MAS, and in the former case assisted the company in reducing its debt/equity ratio from 22 : 1 in 1984 to 1.5 : 1 in 1989. In addition to the initial stimulus or capital injection, the simple fact of being listed and actively traded on the KLSE provides disciplining forces through which the company's performance can be measured. The monitoring and disciplining role of a capital market listing can thus be a major advantage by removing control from the hands of a traditionally passive shareholder (i.e. the government).

A partial indicator of post-privatization performance may be found in the share performance of the public issue sales relative to the overall market index, the KLSE composite index. Table 9.16 and Fig. 9.2 show the performance of these shares relative to the KLSE. In general, all the companies' share prices have outperformed the market average, although the results are distorted quite dramatically by the worldwide stock-market crash in October 1987. The market as a whole fell dramatically at this time (see section 9.6), but MISC and MAS share prices stayed relatively steady, driving up the index of relative performance shown in Figure 9.2. Post-1987 share performances are less dramatic, although privatization shares have all consistently outperformed the market. The performance of MAS has been the most dramatic, outperforming the market index by 100% over

Table 9.16 *Post-privatization share price performance relative to KLSE index*

	Issue Price	1985 Q4	1986 Q1	1986 Q2	1986 Q3	1986 Q4	1987 Q1	1987 Q2	1987 Q3	1987 Q4	1988 Q1	1988 Q2	1988 Q3	1988 Q4	1989 Q1	1989 Q2	1989 Q3	1989 Q4
MAS Price (M$)	1.80	2.24	2.81	3.12	3.38	4.06	4.36	6.05	5.80	4.10	5.00	6.50	6.20	6.65	6.90	7.95	10.50	11.10
Index		100.0	125.4	139.3	150.9	181.2	194.6	270.1	258.9	183.0	223.2	290.2	276.8	296.9	308.0	354.9	468.7	495.5
Price/KLSE		100.0	133.1	180.7	163.8	167.6	113.6	145.0	241.8	163.6	157.4	185.6	190.7	193.9	175.5	186.0	220.6	204.6
MISC Price (M$)	2.40						5.25	7.30	8.95	5.40	6.00	6.90	6.65	6.95	8.65	9.05	9.15	9.10
Index							100.0	139.0	170.5	102.9	114.3	131.4	126.7	132.4	164.8	172.4	174.3	173.3
Price/KLSE							100.0	127.9	272.8	157.5	138.1	144.0	149.5	148.2	160.9	154.8	140.5	122.6
TRADEWINDS Price (M$)	1.10										1.65	2.12	2.05	2.26	2.67	2.90	2.78	2.88
Index											100.0	128.5	124.2	137.0	161.8	175.8	168.5	174.5
Price/KLSE											100.0	116.5	121.4	126.9	130.7	130.6	112.4	102.2
CEMENT SARAWAK Price (M$)	1.30														2.20	2.30	2.90	4.06
Index															100.0	104.5	131.8	184.5
Price/KLSE															100.0	96.1	108.9	133.7
KLSE (1977=100)		233.5	220.0	180.0	215.0	252.4	400.0	435.0	250.0	261.2	331.0	365.0	338.8	357.4	409.7	445.5	496.1	565.3
		100.0	94.2	77.1	92.1	108.1	171.3	186.3	107.1	111.9	141.8	156.3	145.1	153.1	175.5	190.8	212.5	242.1

Source: KLSE Research Department.

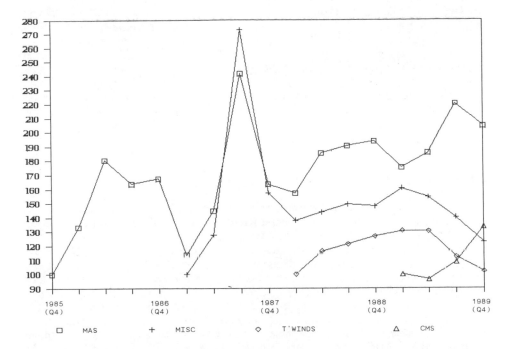

Figure 9.2   *Privatization Share Performance (Share Price vs. KLSE (KLSE-100))*

the first five years since its listing, even though its privatization did not bring a change in management. MISC, on the other hand, despite the significant capital injection it enjoyed at the time of privatization/public listing has seen its share price converge back towards the market average.

The second major area where privatization has had an impact is its effect on management incentives, and the extent to which the change of ownership can solve the principal–agent problems which frequently characterize SOEs (see Chapter 2). Evidence following the KCT privatization (the only important sale in the 1980s which altered management structures) suggests that a major impact was indeed felt through changes in management attitudes and structures (including payment structures), following the replacement of a public sector management structure with a commercial-form management system. It is less clear, however, that the new ownership structures in Malaysian privatizations so far have addressed the principal–agent problem. This is due principally to the extent of institutional shareholding, and the particular nature of ESSs. We shall return to this in section 9.6, but in general the process of share-pricing has tended to result in many shares reverting to large, frequently passive, state-owned institutions. Even those shares reserved for management – which might be thought to provide financial incentives for managers to perform efficiently – were rapidly traded as the initial recipient exploited the extremely high potential capital gains to be had in early trade in privatization stocks.

Privatization and government policy
Many governments view privatization as a means of raising short-term finance through capitalizing future revenue streams from the sale of assets. This becomes

a particularly relevant option in an environment, such as Malaysia (see World Bank, 1989c), where there exist concerns about the limits to domestic debt financing. Combined with the fact that the privatization programme began when the government was experiencing sizeable fiscal deficits, it may have been expected that asset sales would be used to support short-term revenue-raising efforts. However, in general, the percentage of equity sold in each public issue has been low – the only exception being MAS, where 30% was sold – even though there is no evidence that the capital market's absorptive capacity was a constraint. The government could easily have raised a significantly larger amount of revenue through public sales. Moreover, as will be noted below, there has been a tendency on the part of government to discount new share issues heavily on the KLSE, thereby further reducing the potential revenue flow. Short-term revenue considerations thus seem not to have been a feature of the Malaysian privatization programme.

A feature unique to Malaysia among the countries studied in this book is the relatively widespread use of the Special Rights or 'Golden' Share in privatization sales. The 'Golden Share' concept, which has been a feature of a number of UK privatizations, operates in principle as an entrenched provision allowing the holder powers of veto over fundamental decisions of the company (usually involving any major change to the basic orientation and scope of the enterprise) irrespective of the Special Shareholder's ordinary shareholding. It is essentially a guarantee which becomes operable when the holder is a minority shareholder, and is usually prevalent in cases where the enterprise is deemed to be of strategic or social importance. In Malaysia three of the assets sales have involved the use of Golden Shares – MAS, MISC, and Sports Toto. With MAS and MISC, however, the entrenchment of Golden Shares would, possibly, indicate the government's intention to dilute its shareholding further, so that it indeed becomes a minority shareholder. If this is not likely, the so-called privatizations of MAS and MISC become very difficult to rationalize: the government sells a very small part of its equity, such that there is no change whatsoever in the effective ownership structure of the enterprise and no change in the management, yet strengthens its control on an otherwise commercial company through the creation of a special share. In the case of Sports Toto, even though the government sold a majority of its equity holdings (it still holds 30%), the rationale for a Golden Share is much less clear.[44]

One final issue which is of relevance to understanding the government's objectives is the restriction on all public share sales that no one shareholder (other than government) can hold more than 10% of the stock. This is echoed by the 1985 *Guidelines on Privatization* which state: 'as far as possible the ownership of share capital of companies involved in privatization should be equitably distributed so that no one interest will hold an absolute majority'. Whilst this constraint is, presumably, driven by a need to limit concentration away from Bumiputra investors, it raises the familiar problem of shareholder free-riding and the failure of the shareholders adequately to monitor and control the enterprise management. If each shareholder has a small equity stake, then no one shareholder will be prepared to assume the costs of monitoring management since the benefits will be shared by other shareholders. It is conceivable, then, that, rather than exposing enterprises to the rigours of shareholder monitoring by profit-maximizing shareholders, privatization through public issue with ownership restrictions may in fact ensure the perpetuation of sub-optimal shareholder monitoring, particularly as ownership is re-concentrated in the hands of state-owned institutions.

Privatization and the NEP

The evidence of the first seven years of privatization in Malaysia suggests that privatization has been driven almost entircly by the NEP. We noted at the beginning of this section that the *Guidelines* stated clearly:

> Privatization will be implemented within the context of the NEP, indeed, privatization is expected to open up new opportunities for furthering the progress of the NEP.

The asset sales to date (with the possible exception of the KCT sale) have consisted, to a large degree, of the distribution of equity to the Bumiputra or their institutional representatives. Privatization thus represents a second phase in the NEP, through which the asset accumulation by government on behalf of the Bumiputra is redistributed to individual Bumiputra and Bumiputra institutions. In all the public share issues, a tranche of the issue is reserved specifically for Bumiputra institutions (and in many cases is allocated through a private placement), while the 'open' sale is subject to the requirement that a further one-third of shares are taken up, in the primary issue, by Bumiputra individuals and institutions. This segmentation of the share allocation process may explain to a degree the limited emphasis put on employee ownership as a means of widening share ownership. Unlike other economies, the instruments that influence the asset distribution already exist and the share allocation process uses these institutions rather than, for example, ESSs or other options.

The striking conclusion that emerges from this review of the first decade of privatization in Malaysia is how widespread the subjugation of the objectives set out in the *Guidelines* is to those of the NEP, and consequently it is difficult to conclude that the privatization process itself has elicited any fundamental efficiency changes. However, recent developments in the design of the second phase of privatization may serve to dilute this conclusion.

9.3.8 The future of privatization

Possibly the single most important element of the Malaysian privatization programme is the proposed corporatization and eventual divestiture of three major utilities – telecommunications, electricity, and the railway network – all of which were originally government departments. If these three privatizations are carried out (the first sale of 24% of equity in the telecommunications company started in late 1990), it will not only take the Malaysian programme into a new phase in terms of type of enterprise divestiture, moving away from commercial, relatively competitive, sectors into the traditional natural monopolies, but will also represent a major increase in scale. Estimated proceeds from the sale of telecommunications and electricity alone are expected to total M$15bn, or 13.7% of GDP, some 35 times greater than the combined value of all divestitures to date. We shall briefly discuss these in turn.

Telecommunications

Prior to 1987 telecommunications services in Malaysia were supplied exclusively by government through Jabatan Telekom Malaysia (JTM) in terms of the Telecommunications Act 1950. Early in the privatization programme, and again, as with the decision to privatize MAS, following the lead set by the UK, the decision was taken to embark on the eventual privatization of telecommunications. Arab Malaysian Merchant Bankers were contracted as consultants and proposed that privatization be carried out as a two-stage process, starting with the 'corporatization' of JTM to be followed later by a public issue of shares. Corporatization was executed in terms of the Telecommunications Services (Successor Company) Act 1985, which established the encompassing legal framework for the

creation of the new telecommunications enterprise. JTM was eventually corporatized on 1 January 1987, and became known as Syarikat Telekom Malaysia
(STM).

Many of the legal technicalities surrounding the corporatization of STM had
been previously encountered during the sale of the container facilities at Port
Klang – most noticeably the transfer of pension rights and land holding from the
public to the corporate sector – although the introduction of the instrument of the
'Successor Company' Acts was pioneered with telecommunications, and is likely
to be employed with the corporatization of electricity and railways, and other
future privatizations.

Following corporatization, the bulk of the 30,000 former JTM employees were
transferred to the new company STM, with a small group remaining with JTM to
form the putative regulatory body for telecommunications. Employees were
transferred in terms of the conditions established by the KCT sale, with STM being
committed to provide each individual with terms of service at least as good as conditions enjoyed in the public service, and agreeing to a five-year moratorium on
retrenchment.

STM has embarked on significant reforms of its operations, most noticeably in
the areas of billing, bad debt recovery and marketing. Repair and service backlogs
have been dramatically reduced and cash flow substantially improved, while
capital expenditure is expected to be reduced to approximately 75% of its pre-
corporatization levels (Table 9.17). Competition has also been introduced, with
private firms competing with STM in the supply of corporate value-added networks, such as computer lines and systems.

Electricity

Privatization plans for Lembaga Letrik Negara (LLN), the electricity department,
are not as well advanced as for telecommunications, although the general pattern
for privatization is likely to be similar: the department will be corporatized, staff
transferred on the now established terms – with a number retained in the public
sector to manage the regulatory structure for the industry – and, following a
period of financial restructuring, the enterprise will be considered for sale through
public issue to approved institutions. Corporatization was due to occur on
1 September 1990 (the new company was to be known as Syarikat Lektrik
Malaysia (SLM)), and press releases by the Minister for Energy have indicated
that SLM may make the transition from corporatization to privatization in as
little as one year. Foreign participation will also be encouraged, possibly from the
UK.

The Privatization Masterplan

During the first seven years privatization policy proceeded on an *ad hoc* basis.
Candidates emerged through the first-come-first-served basis, with little apparent
guidance from EPU (although the decision to pursue the privatization of the larger
utilities was determined within the government). Conscious of this problem, the
government commissioned a 'Privatization Masterplan' (PMP) for Malaysia.
Commissioned in 1985, it was undertaken jointly by J.Schroder Wagg of London
and Arab Malaysian Merchant Bank. It identifies approximately 430 enterprises,
with a market capitalization of M$15bn to 20bn, for privatization over a period
of 5 years.

The essence of the PMP, which at the time of writing remained under embargo,
is to replace the current approach to privatization with a coherent and integrated
programme covering the entire spectrum of the SOE sector, and bringing together
the currently separate operations of the EPU (which is under the Prime Minister's
Office) and UPSAK (under the Ministry of Finance). The PMP establishes not

Table 9.17 *Telecommunications of Malaysia pre-corporatization performance*

	1975	1976	1977	1978	1979	1980	1981	1982	1983	1984	1985	1986
Financial Indicators (M$m.)												
Total Earnings	221.4	282.7	296.3	368.2	439.4	522.7	636.1	771.7	970.9	1,231.9	1,430.4	1,558.7
Operating Profit	90.8	139.1	107.1	165.5	199.0	225.3	272.5	344.8	316.1	509.3	585.7	565.9
Interest	4.9	8.2	6.7	27.5	19.9	14.5	13.1	80.7	116.8	227.6	284.3	405.9
Net Profit	85.9	130.9	100.4	138.0	179.1	210.8	259.4	264.1	199.3	281.7	301.4	160.0
Rate of Return (%)			12.3	13.7	13.3	11.6	11.2	11.7	9.4	15.4		
Return on Capital (%)			11.0	14.0	16.0	16.2	16.3	18.0	18.7	26.3		
Debt/Equity (%)			42.0	57.0	63.0	83.1	78.8	89.0	153.5	128.4		
Operational Indicators												
Subscribers (000s)	169.5	194.2	227.6	271	325.1	395.6	488.7	585.4	700.1	849.1	958.6	1,042.8
Revenue per Sub (M$)	936.8	997.4	940.9	960.8	969.9	983.6	1,003.8	1,022.9	1,056.4	1,126.2	1,185.4	1,226.6
Lines/Employee	9.94	11.07	12.82	14.85	15.22	15.65	18.12	19.64	23.49	28.08		

Source: Salim (1990a).

only the enterprises to be identified for privatization, but also outlines a possible sequencing; 246 are scheduled for sale in the first year of the programme, 69 within two years, 107 within five years, and the remainder in the sixth year. In addition to the identification of candidates for privatization, the PMP is reported to have assessed the issues of savings mobilization (the programme requires mobilization of up to M$4bn per annum over the five-year programme) and of regulation of the monopolies, both of which will be picked up again in sections 9.5 and 9.6 below.

9.3.9 Conclusions

The first phase of privatization in Malaysia has established the programme in the centre of macroeconomic policy-making, and particularly as a complement rather than a challenge to the NEP. The progress to date has been relatively slight, with the impact being threefold. First, in the view of many observers, the main effect of the privatization programme has been to put the brake on SOE expansion and creation, and make explicit the debate over the appropriate role of the state in the economy. Second, the programme has been used as a component of the 'Malaysia Incorporated' push to enhance and rejuvenate the NEP prior to its renegotiation. Thirdly, however, it may also be argued that the first years have been used by government to establish its credibility, mainly with the Bumiputra, to outline the principles which will be followed in future privatizations, and to acquire the technical expertise for the large-scale programme heralded by the Masterplan.

Having firmly established the programme and, possibly, having signalled the government's commitment to the policy, conditions are set for a major second-phase programme under the auspices of the PMP. Implementation of Masterplan proposals will involve an unprecedented shift of resources from the public to the private sector over a short space of time. Whilst, at one level, this raises the issue of government capacity to manage this transfer, the more important debate focuses on the structural constraints which may impinge on the programme. To date the programme has not 'challenged' the absorptive capacity of the Malaysian economy. The final three sections of this chapter therefore attempt to marshall the available evidence on the issues of the private sector's ability to provide a conducive environment for competition and the realization of efficiency gains, the financial sector's capacity to mobilize savings for private sector investment, and finally the government's capacity to regulate private sector monopolies effectively.

9.4 The structure of the private sector

In general, the private sector in Malaysia is dynamic and relatively competitive. A liberal trade regime ensures that the domestic private sector is open to competition, even in the heavily regulated sectors such as petroleum. The development trajectory of the private sector has followed that of South Korea and Singapore, with strong growth from the medium-scale enterprises serving both domestic and export markets. In addition, Malaysia has an active policy towards foreign investment, and is currently favourably placed to benefit from the growth of the other Asian NICs, over which it enjoys a factor-cost advantage.

The private sector consists of three groups: the small enterprise sector, the medium- and large-scale domestic private sector, and the foreign private sector. Table 9.18 shows the size distribution in the manufacturing sector alone, which indicates the extent to which large firms dominate the sector. Firms with more than 200 employees account for 52% of total employment in manufacturing, 61% of total value-added, and 62.5% of fixed assets, while the small firm sector (i.e. employing less than 50 people) accounts for only 9% of sector value-added. In

Table 9.18 *Size and structure of the manufacturing sector*

Size by Employment	Total Employment (000s) 1978	1985	Number of Establishments 1978 (%)	1985 (%)	Avg. Value of Output (M$m.) 1978	1985	Avg. Value of Assets (M$m.) 1978	1985
Below 50	–	161	66.3	58.4	12.6	8.8	11.7	9.3
50–99	–	146	16.3	19.3	13.6	12.4	14.2	11.1
100–199	–	172	8.7	12.6	18.5	25.9	17.8	18.6
200 and above	–	521	8.7	9.7	55.3	52.9	56.2	61.1

Source: Survey of Manufacturing Industries, Department of Statistics.

general, however, industrial concentration is low, with most industrial sectors being relatively competitive. Whilst this is in line with industrialization developments in other NICs, it is very different from the size distribution in other countries in this study, where there is a high level of industrial concentration, and is one important reason why, *ceteris paribus*, efficiency gains may be more likely to be forthcoming from privatization in the Malaysian context.

The small enterprise sector (which is dominated by the Bumiputra and Chinese-Malaysian firms) is constrained by economic structures elsewhere in the economy. Although, in general, the sector is efficient in production, it faces significant difficulties in creating linkages into the rest of the economy in the presence of domination by foreign and large-scale integrated operations. It has consequently been in decline over recent years. The medium-scale, labour-intensive sector, on the other hand, is where Malaysia's comparative advantage in manufacturing currently seems to reside. Malaysia has progressively captured an increasing share of the manufacturing assembly market, and is a major assembler and exporter of electrical and electronic goods, measuring and scientific equipment, textiles, footwear and clothing. Evidence suggests that these sectors are competitive (internationally) and, moreover, are not characterized by high levels of concentration and entry deterrence. In terms of privatization it is noticeable that a large proportion of the SOEs covered by the UPSAK reforms and the Privatization Masterplan fall into this category. Again this is in quite marked contrast to many of the other countries in this study where SOEs are often the dominant firm(s) in their sector.

The relatively high degree of competition in the domestic economy is augmented by the effects of foreign competition. The average level of nominal tariff protection is relatively low in Malaysia compared to other countries in South East Asia and developing countries in general. Average nominal tariffs in 1985 were 14% compared to 23% for Indonesia, 22% for Korea, 28% for the Philippines, and 34% for Thailand (World Bank, 1989c). Tariff reform is currently under consideration, with the focus of attention being on the removal, in the first instance, of excessively distortionary effective protection rates. Combined with relatively free access and a non-distortionary exchange-control regime, competition within the Malaysian economy is thus not subject to extreme protectionism.

The foreign sector

In addition to competition through imports, foreign capital has historically played a major part in the Malaysian economy – indeed to a significant degree it was foreign participation which precipitated the NEP – and currently accounts for approximately 32% of total paid-up capital in the manufacturing sector (Ministry of Finance, *Economic Report*, 1989–90). A recent survey of foreign capital by the Malaysian Industrial Development Authority (MIDA), which serves as the central investment co-ordination office, suggests that the main growth sectors for foreign capital arc petroleum, non-metallic mineral products, and electronics, accounting for 48%, 31% and 57% of the share capital in each subsector respectively. The bulk of foreign capital inflows, which totalled M$5bn in 1987, originates in Singapore (29%), Japan (20%), and the UK (16%). Singaporean investment is concentrated in food processing, non-metallic minerals and textiles, Japanese in textiles and electronics, and UK investment in the petroleum sector. In terms of ownership, 60% of all approved investment since 1980 was in the form of joint ventures with Malaysian majority control. Up to 1986, only in about 10% of cases was there total foreign ownership, but following changes in 1987 which allow 100% foreign control when the company exports more than 80% of its products (or when there are no suitable local partners), this share rose to 36% in 1988. The same waiver is expected to be announced for foreign participation in privatization issues, if no suitable Bumiputra buyer can be found (*Business Times*, 6 October 1990).

Subject to the constraints of the NEP, foreign participation is thus welcomed in Malaysia. Applications are considered by the Foreign Investment Committee (FIC), and are granted if: (i) the investment does not adversely affect control or ownership structures in the economy; (ii) it leads to benefits in terms of Bumiputra participation and employment; (iii) it has a positive effect on export earnings, diversification, and local resource use; and (iv) it does not have environmental or other strategic implications. These guidelines apply to any acquisition of Malaysian assets by foreign companies, any domestic acquisition which increases the foreign ownership share, and any joint venture or management contract which increases foreign control of the economy. This clearly covers privatization bids from foreign companies, although the FIC has granted a specific exemption to BOT contracts. Once FIC approval is granted foreign investors face relatively light foreign-exchange restrictions. Free repatriation of capital and profits is permitted, and foreign-exchange accounts can be maintained in Malaysia. Furthermore, there are no foreign-exchange restrictions on non-resident portfolio investments.

Constraints to competition in the private sector
Although measures of concentration and import penetration indicate that the private sector is relatively competitive, there are a number of constraints to its efficient functioning, most specifically the system of industrial licensing managed by MIDA. Licences are required for the import of capacity-enhancing (or labour-substituting) equipment and for the introduction of new products or processes. Licences apply only to medium-scale companies and, despite substantial liberalization in recent years, have been identified as one of the main barriers to competition.

The licensing system is integral to the NEP, and a licence is approved subject to the maintenance of NEP equity and employment criteria. Licences are granted liberally and relatively quickly in cases where the Bumiputra participation criteria are met, and though the intention of the scheme does not seem to be to alter the supply process, the presence of the system is seen to impact on internal efficiency in a number of ways – other than in the most obvious sense of causing delays and increasing administrative costs. The general thrust of opposition to the scheme centres on the way in which the use of the licensing scheme to meet the goals of the NEP (Bumiputra equity participation, regional wealth redistribution, and employment) creates efficiency loss by discriminating against projects able to exploit economies of scale and concentration through expansion. Similarly the difficulty in finding Bumiputra investors prepared to supply sufficient capital to large-scale projects can lead to licences not being issued, despite the fact that non-Bumiputra investors elsewhere may be prepared to absorb the commercial risk on the project. Finally, the licensing scheme acts as an additional barrier to entry for incumbent firms, denying contestability to markets, and permitting the continuation of monopolistic operations.

Conclusions

The evidence from the structure of the private sector seems to suggest that of itself there is ample capacity within the sector to provide a competitive economic environment in which the efficiency gains from privatization are likely to emerge. The economy is relatively open to foreign competition and subject to low levels of protection. As a significant exporter of manufacturing goods – especially in the medium-scale assembly sector – economies of scale exist, yet barriers to entry are low. However, structural rigidities in the economy may preclude the attainment of higher levels of competition. Segmented labour markets (based on the NEP objectives) have led to an upward drift in real wages, and an erosion of unit labour competitiveness; the industrial licensing system reduces flexibility and permits an unwelcome degree of entry-deterrence in some sectors; and policy towards foreign participation is distorted by NEP considerations which may compromise the achievement of otherwise attainable levels of efficiency. Notwithstanding the above issues, however, the most fundamental problem facing the private sector is the low level of productive investment despite the high level of aggregate savings in the economy, which has been occasioned by the rigid interventionist nature of public sector savings institutions in the savings mobilization process. It is to this point that we now turn.

9.5 The capital market and resource mobilization

9.5.1 *The structure of the capital market*

Unique amongst the countries covered in this book, Malaysia has a large and well-developed equity market, regarded by many investors as one of the more dynamic emerging stock markets in the world (although it remains overshadowed by its NIC neighbours in Hong Kong, Taiwan, and Singapore).[45] It consists of two trading exchanges, the Kuala Lumpur Stock Exchange (KLSE) and the Bumiputra Stock Exchange (BSE), although the latter is virtually dormant. [46] The KLSE was established in 1973 following the dissolution of the Malaysian and Singapore Stock Exchange, and by the end of 1989 had an annual turnover in equities of M$18.5bn (17% of GDP) and a market capitalization in excess of 150% of GDP (Table 9.19). The period 1981–9 saw a significant upswing in activity on the market, especially through new issues (Table 9.20). There were 64 new issues (valued at M$4.4bn) in 1984 alone, as the corporate sector shifted away from bank credit in response to the prevailing credit squeeze.

Table 9.19 *Kuala Lumpur Stock Exchange*

	1980	1981	1982	1983	1984	1985	1986	1987	1988	1989	1990
Market Capitalization (M$bn)	27.5	34.3	32.3	53.3	47.1	39.4	39.2	46.1	63.1	107.5	131.2
Market Capitalization (US$bn)	12.4	15.3	13.9	22.8	19.4	16.2	15.1	18.5	23.3	39.8	48.6
Capn as % GDP	50.8	61.2	51.9	76.3	57.2	51.9	54.3	58.5	67.1	106.1	112.2
No. of Listed Cos.	185	187	194	204	217	222	223	232	238	251	282
Trading Value (M$m)	5,600	8,059	3,252	7,934	5,714	6,180	3,369	10,078	6,858.1	18,638	29,391
KLSE Composite Index	366.7	380.8	291.4	401.6	303.6	233.5	252.4	261.2	357.4	565.3	505.9

Source: IFC, *Emerging Stock Markets Factbook.*

Table 9.20 *Malaysian capital markets: new issues*

	1961–65	*1966–70*	*1971–75*	*1976–80*	*1981–85*	*1986–87*	*1988*
Ordinary Shares	124.9	276.2	291.9	638.9	5,470.9	1,904.4	2,840.2
Public Issues	107.5	115.3	101.1	77.4	929.1	343.1	169.0
Private Placements	5.4	22.2	27.6	21.2	0.0	76.6	0.0
Rights Issues	12.0	138.7	163.2	387.3	3,234.8	937.2	668.0
Special Issues[a]	0.0	0.0	0.0	132.6	1,307.0	222.5	94.2
Bond Issues	0.0	0.0	0.0	20.0	0.0	325.0	1,909.0
Loan Stocks	14.5	9.0	57.3	0.0	579.0	70.0	36.3
MGS (net)	888.9	1,744.7	3,878.6	9,383.4	19,821.6	11,868.8	6,105.1
TOTAL	1,028.3	2,029.9	4,227.8	10,021.9	25,871.5	13,843.2	8,981.6

Source: Bank Negara Malaysia.

a) Special share issues to Bumiputra institutions.

Secondary trade turnover has shown a similarly dramatic rise during the 1970s, with a peak of M$8bn in 1981. Trading and market value fell back in the mid-1980s following the construction boom of 1982 and 1983, culminating in an emergency closure of the exchange for three days in December 1985.[47] The market rallied in 1987, although it was not untouched by the 1987 worldwide stock market crash, when capitalization fell by approximately 36% in 14 days. The market remained intact, however, and since 1987 turnover has been bouyant. The KLSE is dominated by industrial shares (48% of total equity on the market), finance and property sector shares (approximately 15% each), with the remainder accounted for by commmodity stocks (oil palm, tin, rubber). The major players on the market are nominee companies and other corporate bodies (including PNB) which hold almost 70% of total equity, although individuals still hold a relatively high proportion of stock (19%).

The KLSE is a relatively sophisticated market. It has 53 members, and in 1989 introduced a secondary trading board to encourage greater venture-capital participation. The market also deals in corporate bonds, and a secondary market in mortgage bonds has recently been developed by Cagamas, the national mortgage corporation. In addition, the Exchange has introduced a real-time computerized share price reporting system, and established research and surveillance systems to improve security.

Finally, one of the most significant features of the KLSE in recent years, and one which sets this market apart from others covered in this study, is the attraction of international portfolio investments. There are currently 49 country-funds investing in Malaysian stocks, including the IFC's Malaysia Fund Inc., which is listed on the New York Stock Exchange with an initial capital of US$87m. Such investment funds have, so far, been excluded from participation in the privatization programme (as they have been from other primary issues), although the sale of equity in STM includes a tranche (2.5%) reserved for foreign participation. This is to be effected through the sale of foreign-exchange bonds by the central bank which will be redeemable for STM equity at an agreed rate, set 40% above the price at which STM equity was sold on the domestic market.

9.5.2 Capital market regulation
Developments in the capital market have generally been shadowed by regular revision of regulatory structures for the industry. The over-arching regulatory framework is provided by the Securities Industry Act of 1973, and its successor of 1983. This Act provides legal authority to curb excessive speculation, insider

trading, and other forms of share-rigging. It also includes provisions for licensing and regulation of dealers and for listing, and provides guidelines for the orderly functioning of the KLSE. In terms of listing and other matters the 1973 Act provided for the Capital Issues Committee (CIC) to fulfil the role of overall market regulator. The 1983 revision to the Act, apart from updating a number of the technical provisions to reflect the changing technical environment of the financial sector, formalized the role of the CIC as principal market regulator. The CIC has its secretariat within the Ministry of Finance, and is responsible, *inter alia*, for price-setting for all new share issues (other than bonus issues), and the determination of listing requirements for the KLSE.[48]

The most controversial aspect of the CIC's activity lies in the issue of share pricing for new issues. The CIC is avowedly risk-averse in its pricing policy, and consequently has a tendency to underprice new issues. It sets prices on the basis of pretax price/earnings (P/E) ratio guidelines. These cover a range from approximately 3.5 to 8.0 (the range for the financial sector is somewhat higher at 8–12). However, average market P/E ratios have been in the region of 30 (post the 1987 crash), and consequently new share issues priced on the basis of CIC P/E guidelines tend to be heavily 'underpriced', oversubscribed, and return very high early trading premia on the secondary market.[49] Consistent underpricing is not a phenomenon exclusive to the KLSE, but a common feature of privatization sales by risk-averse governments (see Chapter 4). However, systematic underpricing can have other important public finance and social welfare implications, through an erosion of the public sector's net worth. This issue will be dealt with in detail below.

Capital market and privatization

The use of public share issues as a means of asset sales has played a significant role in the Malaysian privatization programme. Proceeds from public sales totalled M$216.4m. out of a total of M$437.6m. (see Table 9.9), including the two largest sales up to mid-1990, MISC and MAS. Prices have been set by the CIC more or less within their recommended P/E ratio guidelines, and have subsequently been oversubscribed with high initial premia in secondary trading (Tables 9.21 and 9.22). More importantly, these initial premia were maintained over a significant period; after three months, the average premium over the issue price was still close to that which emerged in initial trading, as prices tended to stabilize towards the market P/E ratio, rather than revert to the CIC issue P/E ratio.

Aside from the high initial capital gains, it is also worth noting that in the case of Malaysia there has been only a relatively modest transfer of equity ownership to the private sector. In no case has there been a significant dilution of the public sector control through privatization, and in fact, when the role of the 'Golden Share' is taken into account, it seems as if public share issues have done nothing to transfer ownership and control to the private sector (Table 9.23). Unfortunately available data refer only to the distribution of shareholders following the primary issue but prior to the start of secondary market trade. Casual evidence does, however, point to a dramatic contraction in the number of individual shareholders through the realization of capital gains, and a consequent concentration of equity in the hands of the Bumiputra and non-Bumiputra institutions. For example, company accounts for MISC report a contraction in the number of shareholders from 60,000 at point of issue to only 5,000 following the first three months of secondary trading. This phenomenon is not unusual in share markets when systemic underpricing is prevalent; the same share behaviour is prevalent in the UK share sales through the stock exchange. However, one of the more striking

Table 9.21 Malaysian privatization share performance

Company	Trading Date	Issued (000s)	Issue Price	Traded Day 1	Turnover (%)	Price Day 1[a]	Premium (%)	Price Week1	Premium (%)	Price Month 1	Premium (%)	Price Month 3	Premium (%)
Malaysian Airline System Berhad	16/12/85	70,000	1.80	2,390	3.41	2.45	36.11	2.20	22.22	2.35	30.56	2.63	46.11
Malaysian Intl Shipping Corp	23/02/87	84,985	2.40	15,809	18.60	5.00	108.33	5.05	110.42	5.25	118.75	7.20	200.00
Sports Toto Malaysia Berhad	29/07/87	5,251	2.00	1,833	34.91	9.55	377.50	9.95	397.50	10.00	400.00	7.70	285.00
Tradewinds Malaysia Berhad	23/03/88	15,000	1.10	2,600	17.33	1.83	66.36	1.65	50.00	1.83	66.36	1.93	75.45
Sistem Televisyen Malaysia	25/04/88	6,618	2.00	1,228	18.56	6.05	202.50	5.00	150.00	5.10	155.00	5.30	165.00
Cement Manufacturers Sarawak	02/02/89	5,000	1.30	1,001	20.02	2.17	66.92	2.25	73.08	2.12	63.08	2.05	57.69

Source: KLSE Research Department.

Notes

a) Closing prices. Shares opened at MAS: M$3.50
    MISC: M$5.00
    Sports Toto: M$7.15
    Tradewinds: M$2.30
    TV3: M$6.10
    CMS: M$2.48

Table 9.22 *Malaysian public share issues*

Company	Issue Price	Price Day 1	Issue P/E[a]	Day 1 P/E[b]	CIC Pricing Guideline
MAS	1.80	2.45	5.90	8.03	4–8
MISC	2.40	5.00	4.90	10.21	4–8
TRADEWINDS	1.10	1.83	5.50	9.15	6–10
SPORTS TOTO	2.00	9.55	5.00	23.88	4–8
TV3	2.00	6.05	5.00	15.13	4–8
CEMENT SARAWAK	1.30	2.17	6.28	10.48	5–9

Source: KLSE Research Department.

Notes
a) Based on forecast dividend quoted in prospectus.
b) As Note a) but calculated at first-day trade price.

features of the Malaysian capital market is that concentration tends to revert back towards public, or quasi-public, shareholders. Given our earlier comments about the issue of risk absorption by these institutions, and their closeness to government in the implementation of the NEP, it raises the issue once more of the extent to which the privatization programme is in fact opening the economy to greater private sector control.

9.5.4 Capital market absorptive capacity

Estimates of the absorptive capacity of the capital market in any country are notoriously suspect, as they require an analysis not only of aggregate savings potential but also of the substitutability between savings instruments, on both a price and an institutional basis. Attempts have been made to assess the absorptive capacity of the equity market in anticipation of the Privatization Masterplan. The research attempting to assess the sustainable flow of new equity issues involves, in addition, an assessment of the structural limitations imposed on savings behaviour, institutional restrictions in the economy, and, in particular, the role of the NEP-fostered institutions. A recent study has been conducted by the Arab Malaysian Merchant Bank (AMMB), one of the merchant banks most closely associated with the privatization programme in Malaysia.

As noted above, gross national savings in Malaysia are high – about 30% of GDP. However, a large proportion of this is accounted for by contractual savings, mainly channelled into government securities, the Employees Provident Fund alone accounting for approximately 25% of GDP. In addition, the presence of the PNB's ASN unit trust schemes means that Bumiputra household financial savings are currently being tapped extensively. On the other hand, the recent reduction in the overall budget deficit has reduced public dis-saving substantially, and suggests that private sector savings are increasingly being directed towards private sector investment.

On the basis of this assessment of the levels of savings, the AMMB study concludes that there is excess demand in the capital market, that the market is supply-driven, and thus privatization will not crowd-out private investment. In 1989 net investment was M$2.4bn (M$1.1bn primary issues, M$1.3bn rights, M$0.03bn special Bumiputra issues), and it therefore estimates that the absorptive capacity is M$4bn per year in the equity market at 1989 prices. AMMB stresses a number of provisos in this analysis, the main ones being that the institutional investors, and in particular the EPF, are becoming more active in equity trading, and that

Table 9.23 Pre- and post-sale share distribution (%)

Pre-Sale Distribution

Company	Federal Govt	State Govt	Bumi Insts	Other Insts	Employees	Other Private	Total
MAS	90.0	10.0	0.0	0.0	0.0	0.0	100.0
MISC	36.8	20.0	8.0	5.2	0.0	30.0	100.0
Sports Toto	30.0	0.0	0.0	0.0	0.0	70.0	100.0
Tradewinds	66.3	0.0	0.0	30.5	0.0	3.2	100.0
Cement Sarawak	30.0	70.0	0.0	0.0	0.0	0.0	100.0

Post-Sale Distribution

Company	Federal Govt	State Govt	Bumi Insts	Other Insts	Employees	Other Private	Total
MAS	60.0	10.0	11.0	0.0	5.0	14.0	100.0
MISC	29.4	16.0	14.8	4.2	0.6	35.0	100.0
Sports Toto	30.0	0.0	3.8	0.0	5.0	61.3	100.0
Tradewinds	59.1	0.0	4.2	27.0	0.7	9.0	100.0
Cement Sarawak	30.0	54.4	4.3	0.0	1.4	9.9	100.0

Source: KLSE and Prospectuses.

privatization issues become more affordable to small investors, through lower par value shares or smaller bundles.

One of the main problems with the AMMB study is that the figure of M$4bn. cited as the annual absorptive capacity has been determined to a significant extent by the high level of new issues in 1987. Furthermore, the main source of growth during that period was not in new issues *per se*, but rather in rights issues – i.e. the expansion of existing stocks. To extrapolate these volume measures forward abstracts from these price effects and, importantly, ignores the relative rate of return on other forms of investment. Table 9.24 compares the relative return from different instruments, and indicates clearly the volatility of direct risk-capital investment compared to government paper. Most striking, however, is the rate of return on PNB/ASN investments. As noted above, this high nominal rate/low risk return can be maintained by PNB only if it can secure high-quality equity, can disintermediate risk away from the final equity holder, and can access monopoly rents.

Table 9.24 *Nominal rates of return by institution 1981–87 (%)*

	1981	1982	1983	1984	1985	1986	1987
PNB/ASN	20.0	18.0	18.1	17.2	17.2	10.1	10.1
Employee Provident Fund	8.0	8.0	8.5	8.5	8.5	8.5	8.5
Commercial Bank Deposits	7.0	6.5	6.0	7.5	6.0	6.0	4.0
20-Year Government Securities	–	–	–	8.6	8.6	8.6	7.6
KLSE Equity	13.9	−18.9	40.8	−19.3	−17.3	12.8	0.5
KLSE Equity (ex Dividend)	−4.6	−4.6	−3.0	−5.1	−5.5	−4.7	−4.7

Source: Economic Report of the Treasury; PNB, EPF, and KLSE Annual Reports.

On the basis of these comments, the AMMB estimate of absorptive capacity (for risk-capital investment) may seem on the high side. Even if it is reasonable, it remains low in comparison with the plans laid out in the Privatization Masterplan, especially in the proposals for the three large utilities, STM, LLN and KTM, which together could represent a public share issue of M$12–M$15bn over a period of 2–3 years. If this is the case, then privatization issues may well crowd-out other private sector issues, unless foreign capital and portfolio inflows are high. Moreover, as long as other capital market instruments continue to pay relatively high rates privatization equity will be taken up only if rates of return are kept high or, equivalently, issue prices are low. While the problems of underpricing have already been discussed and are clear, maintaining dividend yields may have even more damaging effects on the privatization programme. Many of the large SOEs planned for privatization are monopolistic, and dividends can be kept high for such companies only as long as monopoly pricing is maintained. If these monopoly profits are required to ensure that the capital market will absorb the issue then the government immediately faces a conflict between the efficiency gains from greater competition and the continued transfer of wealth through the capital market. The evidence from the first phase of the privatization programme would suggest that it has been the latter consideration which has predominated. However, efficiency considerations do figure in the debate, and it is to the regulation of enterprises in pursuit of efficiency gains that we finally turn.

9.6 Regulation and competition policy

This last section discusses the regulation of private sector commercial activities, and in particular the pricing decisions of privatized monopolies. Again, however, we are faced with the problem common to most of our country studies, namely that there is limited direct evidence on the government's thinking on, or capacity for, regulation prior to the privatization programme. Regulation has generally been internalized within government, with enabling legislation (for example, the Telecommunications Act 1950) vesting all powers of control and regulation in a government department, while competition policy elsewhere in the economy has, not unsurprisingly, been overshadowed by the concerns of the NEP.

The regulatory tradition in Malaysia

Under the NEP Malaysia is in some aspects a heavily regulated economy, and some evidence on the capacity for future market-based regulation of monopolies can be gleaned from the government's current regulation activity. However, this has generally been concerned with controlling market access in the case of the industrial sector, and with shaping asset-holding behaviour in the case of the capital market. It is industrial regulation we shall consider here.

The approach to regulation in Malaysia is clarified in its *Rules and Regulations Regarding Acquisitions, Mergers and Take-Overs* which states that 'the guidelines may be viewed as a means of restructuring the pattern of ownership and control of the corporate sector . . . and to encourage those forms of private investment which contribute to the development of the country, consistent with the objectives of the NEP' (Ministry of Finance, *Economic Report*, 1989/90). This approach has resulted in a heavy emphasis on the form of corporate ownership rather than on corporate performance *per se*, but whilst there is concern that the over-regulation of the economy in pursuit of NEP objectives has constrained growth and accentuated private sector risk aversion, the experience of recent decades suggests that regulation has been managed relatively judiciously. This is particularly so in the petroleum sector through the Petroleum Development Act 1974, and in the financial sector through the Securities Industry Act 1983, where the KLSE in particular and the capital market in general are regarded as accessible and well-managed markets.

It may also be noted that, outside the utilities and hydrocarbon sectors, the domestic economy is relatively competitive and thus, unlike other countries in this study, the need for a re-evaluation of existing competition policy in the light of the privatization programme is not as pressing. That there is a substantial capacity for regulation seems clear: whether the steps already taken point to the development of appropriate regulatory structures is less clear.

Regulation of the utilities

As with most privatization programmes covered in this study, the issue of post-privatization regulation received limited attention until quite late in the privatization programme. Most noticeable is the fact that, though the *Guidelines on Privatization* do not address the issue, the Privatization Masterplan does include proposals for a single unifying regulatory structure for all privatized enterprises (the Privatization Act). Events on the ground have preceded it, however, and there already exists a separate regulatory structure in the Telecommunications Act of 1989. This is very similar to the 1984 UK Telecommunications Act, and follows a number of regulation and competition structures employed in the UK. STM will retain a monopoly on the provision and leasing of lines, but competition will be allowed in the supply and installation of 'value-added networks', such as public telephone kiosks, facsimile equipment, dedicated computer lines, cellphones, and, significantly, the laying of fibre-optic cables. Price regulation for STM itself will be implemented by the Director General of Telecommunications, and the Act specifies the use of the RPI − X formula for price-setting, introduced in the UK for British Telecom.[50]

A number of issues present themselves with this form of regulation for the telecommunications industry in Malaysia. The first is the absence of timely and clear thinking on the structure and capacity of regulatory agencies for private sector monopolies (despite the fact that STM is now operating as a corporate entity). Though JTM has existed as a regulatory body since 1987, the industry has operated for almost 2 years without any formal regulatory structure. Even at present, there is a lack of clarity surrounding the exact structure of regulation as a whole in Malaysia. Whilst the drafting of the regulatory Act for the telecommunications industry implicitly envisaged a structure of related but independent regulatory bodies (the UK case), the Privatization Masterplan, on the other hand, proposes a uniform regulatory framework covering regulation of all utilities. It seems that, even if a decision is made to pursue the unified regulatory structure proposed by the PMP, a significant time lag may be expected before an operable structure is established.

Secondly, there is a perception that, in following the UK model, the government may well have underestimated the resource costs required to manage price regulation, not least in terms of the informational asymmetry between STM and its regulator, the Director General of Telecommunications. Finally, concern has been raised about the degree of competition in the private sector supply of equipment and other services. Casual evidence suggests that, though this end of the telecommunications market is not naturally monopolistic, entry-deterrence behaviour is prevalent, and concern has been expressed about the capacity, or willingness, of the JTM to avoid capture of this end of the market.

9.7 Conclusions

Privatization in Malaysia has so far presented us with an enigma. In terms of the baldest statistics, the privatization programme during the 1980s has had only a minimal impact on the balance between public and private, and in only a very small number of cases has there been any noticeable shift in the pattern of resource control. However, the programme seems relatively firmly entrenched in the policy matrix of the government, and, if implemented, the Privatization Masterplan may indeed involve a radical shift towards the private sector. The early evidence from the sale of STM would indicate that this process is now under way.

There are, however, a number of features of the Malaysian programme which separate it from others in the study. The first is that the basic structure of the Malaysian economy, and in particular its relatively open trade and capital orientation, mean that it has the potential to provide a structural competitive environment within which the gains from privatization can be realized. The private sector is relatively competitive, both domestically and internationally, the supply of skilled labour is good, and the macroeconomic regime is conducive to strong economic performance. In addition, there exist a high level of savings and a sophisticated financial sector capable of mobilizing these savings into risk capital.

Second, there exists capacity to manage a privatization programme professionally. Management expertise and regionally specialized consultancy services are available to undertake privatization, while the government itself commands sufficient human resources to suggest that a capacity to manage and regulate privatization exists.

However, thirdly, and most importantly, privatization in Malaysia does not exist within a vacuum. It is most accurately seen as a key element of the second phase of the New Economic Policy, and as such operates within the constraints established by the NEP. Within this environment the primacy of public sector intervention, particularly in the intermediation of risk, remains entrenched, and thus the real benefits of privatization are being compromised by continued public sector intervention in the private management of commercial risk.

Notes

1. 'Why Malaysia Means Business', *Euromoney*, February 1985.
2. As discussed further in section 9.2, data on the public sector for periods earlier than 1985–90 are sparse and many SOEs are not classified as public sector. These figures therefore tend to underestimate the true extent of public sector activity.
3. One of the anomalies of this new programme, which de-emphasizes the role of the state, is the stress put on the development of the Proton Saga car assembly plant as the jewel of the new industrial strategy. Proton is 100% government-owned.
4. The New Economic Policy was issued by the Department of National Unity on 18 March 1970 as a directive to all government departments and agencies guiding their preparation for the Second Malaysian Plan.
5. Much of which has been picked up by the widespread business interests of the UMNO, the main Malayan political party, and the majority member of the ruling coalition.
6. The holding agencies are organized under various Federal Ministries, the principal ones being the Ministry of Public Enterprises, the Prime Minister's Office, the Ministry of Primary Industries, and the Ministry of Regional Development. In addition, the Minister of Finance (Incorporated) holds equity directly in a small number of enterprises – in particular those which have been partially privatized.
7. Although these 50 account for a major share of the sector on most economic criteria.
8. Yusof (1989) notes that 'In the Malaysian story it seems fair to conclude that there was just not a very strong interest in arriving at an accurate estimate of the size of the public of private sector.'
9. A value of 100% represents equal amounts of debt and equity capital in total long-term liabilities.
10. Which, as noted, captures financial data on only approximately 50 of the SOEs.
11. CICU data extend back to 1980, but cover only about 40% of the full SOE sample. Average enterprise performance indicators are applied to the full SOE sector (assumed to be 1,000 enterprises).
12. Where accumulated losses exceed paid-up capital.
13. Since 1981 downstream licensing has been the responsibility of the Ministry of Trade and Industry.
14. The World Bank (1989c) finds average private sector profit rates for manufacturing of approximately 6.6% and public sector rates of only 1.9% over the 1981–5 period.
15. In terms of the NEP, all new share issues on the KLSE must include a 30% tranche reserved for the Bumiputra institutions.
16. The Plan was based on policies aimed at reviving private domestic investment following the slump in the period since 1985, and these have been relatively successful. Private investment fell by 8% in 1985 and by a further 16% in 1986, but has grown very strongly since then (5% 1987, 20% 1988, and 27% 1989).
17. A Build–Operate–Transfer (BOT) contract involves government agreeing with the private sector on (usually) the construction of a public or infrastructural asset. Instead of standard contracting or turn-key arrangements, the project is private sector-financed with the private sector recouping its outlay over a fixed period through tolls or other fees, the assets eventually revert to the public sector asset stock after a given period.
18. From discussions with officials the impression is gleaned that divestiture and closure through the UPSAK structure are seen as elements in the broader SOE reform brief. There is little sense of the politics of privatization emerging in this programme.
19. Although the Guidelines do make clear that issues of strategic significance to the country will be taken into consideration in considering the applications.
20. Only one major privatization was completed before the Guidelines were published – the Klang Port Authority container terminal. Most of the administrative arrangements subsequently adopted were a formalization of procedures adopted for the KCT sale.
21. *Malaysian Business* notes: 'Pro-privatization groups are said to have held their breaths when a heart attack seized Mahathir early this year, as concerned for the programme as for the Prime Minister's health. Privatization proposals froze and meetings at the EPU stalled. The momentum has since picked up in tandem with the PM's recovery' (*Malaysian Business*, 1–15 September 1989, p. 15).

22. After completion of the research for this chapter, two large sales were carried out by EPU: EON motor distributors, which raised M$56m. through public issue. The sale of 24% of the equity in Syarikat Telekom Malaysia (STM) in November 1990 STM raised M$2.35bn – almost five times the value of all other privatization issues put together – and was the biggest single listing ever on the KLSE (amounting to approximately 10% of the entire market's capitalization). However, no further details were available to the authors.

23. Although, as noted below, the purchasing company was majority-owned by the government.

24. This section draws heavily on Leeds (1989).

25. According to the KPA management, the initial M$111.6m. included an amortized amount for common services and overheads, although a fee is still paid for security and fire services supplied by KPA.

26. An important footnote to this is that, despite their initial opposition to privatization in principle, the main civil service union CUPACS has negotiated a deal whereby non-KCT employees of KPA can participate in any future employee participation in the share issue.

27. The ownership restriction apparently applies only to the 5.251 million shares issued on the KLSE, and not to the holdings of B&B Enterprises and Melawar.

28. The Malaysian Government forced a distribution whereby MAS retained all the fixed assets of the joint airline and the regional and domestic routes, leaving Singapore International Airways with only the international routes. SIA subsequently built up a modern fleet and one of the strongest international airlines in Asia.

29. Held 90% by the Minister of Finance (Incorporated), 5% by the State of Sarawak, and 5% by the State of Sabah. The authorized share capital was raised to M$1bn in September 1985.

30. The Chairman, Managing Director, Finance and Transport Ministry representatives and the representatives of Sabah and Sarawak.

31. The government also has a 40% equity stakes in United Motor Works Berhad.

32. The Moslem Pilgrim Trust – an Islamic financial institution.

33. According to the CICU database there are 20 SOEs in the shipping subsector. Of these 9 are active, including two shipping companies (MISC and PERNAS National Shipping Line) and a number of associated companies.

34. Quoted by the Assistant Company Secretary in interview.

35. Also, as will be noted in section 9.5, since MISC shares traded at a significant premium over their issue price, the market value of the company increased.

36. PERNAS is the largest of the SOE holding companies, accounting for 99 SOEs (CICU database).

37. TV3 was incorporated in 1983 and granted a licence to operate as Malaysia's only commercial TV station. The station serves Kuala Lumpur and the surrounding valley, and currently local production accounts for 40% of its output. It was established by a group of private sector investors (the main one of which was the *New Straits Times*, the leading newspaper in Malaysia). The company was listed in March 1988.

38. Only three of the smaller road sector BOTs have been completed and are charging toll fees. Unfortunately full details on the toll schemes and structures are not available.

39. Ailing enterprises are defined as those which had been making consistent losses over the previous five financial years.

40. Perwaja Steel, by far the worst performing of the 10, received an initial M$200m. capital injection.

41. The total nominal capital of the companies covered by the first UPSAK study totalled M$536m. – only 2% of the total paid-up capital of the SOE sector as a whole.

42. This is, in general, only possible for the sales involving public share issues as the objectives of the sale are listed in the Sale Prospectus.

43. Only in the case of Port Klang did the sale involve a statutory body as opposed to an SOE established in terms of the Companies Act. In the case of corporate SOEs, employees are not covered by government employment legislation.

44. Indeed, as one commentator noted to the author: 'It is difficult to understand what the purpose of the privatization programme is when the only majority sale has been of a betting company, and even then the government felt it necessary to issue itself a Golden Share!'

45. The KLSE is now the third largest of the IFC's 19 emerging equity markets worldwide.

46. The BSE was originally established as a share and unit trust company and became a functioning exchange in 1970. The BSE, which as its name suggests, quotes only Bumiputra-owned companies, is not covered by the Securities Industry Act, and is extremely small in comparison with KLSE, trading in only eight companies, with a trading turnover of a little over M$150,000 in 1988. Attempts have been made to rejuvenate the exchange, and, although the KLSE has made moves towards amalgamation, these have been rejected. It is consequently expected within the financial community that the BSE will gradually atrophy.

47. The Singapore exchange was also shut down at this time.
48. Main Board listing requires that a company has a 3–5 year profitable trading record, and a minimum capital of M$20m. The Second Board, formally introduced in 1989, is geared to smaller, less mature companies, and therefore requires only a 2–3 year trading record, and a minimum capital of M$5m. (up to a maximum of M$20m.). The Second Board is restricted to local companies, and listing fees are set at correspondingly lower rates than for the Main Board.
49. For example, the largest issue in 1989, by Southern Bank Berhad, was for 23.15 million shares at M$2.20, raising M$50.93m. Initial applications for the share totalled M$1.27bn, and at the end of the first five days of trade the share was trading at M$4.50 – a premium of 130%.
50. In terms of the UK telecommunications industry the first 5-year licence for BT embodied an allowable annual price increase for an index of BT's services equal to the rate of inflation (RPI) less 3% (X). This simply means that the company is committed to a 3% per annum efficiency gain in order to maintain real unit-cost increases constant. See Vickers and Yarrow (1988).

10 PAPUA NEW GUINEA

10.1 Introduction

Privatization in Papua New Guinea differs from virtually all the other countries in this book in that it has been promoted as a means not of addressing severe public finance problems but rather of developing a local non-traditional private sector and, more centrally, a local capital market. It has not developed out of an economic crisis, but has emerged as one element of a broader adjustment programme in the main free from the demands and conflicts of short term stabilization measures. All the same, the programme has met with only limited success and has not really helped to address any of the country's development objectives.

Papua New Guinea, which gained its independence from Australia in 1975, is an island economy, covering the eastern half of New Guinea and an extensive archipelago of smaller islands, and has a per capita income of US$810 (*World Development Report*, 1990). The population of approximately 3.75 million is widely dispersed, with almost 700 distinct language groups. This diversity is mirrored by the extreme segmentation of the economy and the lack of infrastructure between the main economic and population centres. The economy, however, enjoys an abundant endowment of natural resources, both agricultural and mineral, the latter ensuring that PNG is set to become one of the major mineral exporters. Outside the mineral sector, however, its isolation from product markets and the high costs of production mean that the economy is relatively undeveloped. Only 10% of the population is estimated to operate within the cash economy.

10.1.2 Economic developments 1975–90

At Independence, the economy was dominated by the agricultural sector (consisting principally of subsistence production plus cash-crop exports of coffee, cocoa, palm oil and copra). Bougainville Copper Limited (BCL), which was first established in 1972, had started production, however, and, along with other developments in the mineral sector, copper mining has been the dominant feature of the economy since Independence. The world recession hit the country hard during the early 1980s (see Table 10.1). Aggregate export commodity prices fell by 45% from 1980 to 1984, lowering the aggregate terms of trade by 54% in the period 1978–81, and occasioning a rise in the current account deficit to over 20% of GDP in 1981 and 1982. By 1983 world mineral prices had improved and real growth recovered to average around 5%, as the mining sector continued to expand (new facilities were opened at both BCL and Ok Tedi). Over the period, however, external debt had risen by 250% to well over 50% of GDP.

The positive developments which began to emerge in late 1988 and early 1989 were halted abruptly in May 1989 with the enforced closure of the BCL mine in

Table 10.1 *Macroeconomic indicators 1981–90*

	1970	1975	1980	1981	1982	1983	1984	1985	1986	1987	1988
GDP (Km.)	576.4	1,036.3	1,708.1	1,681.2	1,749.1	1,973.7	2,134.4	2,283.5	2,451.5	2,747.1	3,176.1
Real GDP growth (%)	7.2	5.9	1.1	–0.7	0.4	3.4	1.7	4.8	5.0	4.8	3.3
Domestic savings (% GDP)	6.1	13.8	15.1	6.6	11.0	14.5	15.9	13.1	17.2	17.1	18.3
Domestic investment (% GDP)	41.6	20.0	25.2	27.2	30.7	31.1	27.5	20.1	20.4	20.7	23.0
Budget deficit as % GDP	–	5.5	1.9	6.4	5.5	4.8	1.0	2.5	3.1	2.4	1.5
Current account deficit as % GDP	15.4	2.1	15.7	20.8	20.4	15.5	12.9	8.6	6.8	7.2	8.4
Terms of trade (1980 = 100)	123.7	108.7	100.0	86.0	91.1	95.1	102.5	94.8	91.7	84.4	85.3
External debt US$m.	36.0	275.0	510.0	639.0	768.0	956.0	1,011.0	1,098.0	1,239.0	1,471.0	1,137.0
Debt/GDP	5.7	21.3	29.2	48.7	72.3	77.0	81.7	90.5	77.6	77.0	66.5
Debt–service ratio	–	–	13.8	18.7	25.1	30.1	40.1	32.7	26.9	24.6	26.6
Inflation rate (%)	8.2	–1.1	2.8	–1.2	3.7	9.0	6.5	1.8	2.6	6.0	3.9
US$/Kina	0.89	0.76	0.67	0.67	0.74	0.83	0.89	1	0.97	0.91	0.88

Source: World Tables, 1989.

response to the worsening crisis on Bougainville.[1] At the time the shut-down was expected to be short-lived, but it lasted in the end for approximately 18 months, with the mine only re-opening in early 1991. The impact of the closure of the mine has been immense. There has been a sharp reduction in export earnings from the mine (previously the single biggest earner in the economy), which led the government to implement drastic expenditure cuts in the 1990/91 budget, to devalue the Kina by 8% in January 1990, and to enter into a US$34m. stand-by arrangement with the IMF. Indirectly, however, the crisis has retarded progress elsewhere in the mining sector, and has also created a crisis of confidence within the government on the future path of economic management. This is especially problematic given the importance of the mining sector and the size of the impending mineral boom, which will need careful economic management.

The structure of the economy
The mineral boom is likely to result in a significant growth in permanent income for the economy, with far-reaching implications for growth, fiscal policy, the balance of payments and exchange-rate management. Moreover, the expected Dutch Disease effects of the boom will directly impact on the development of the rest of the economy, particulary the manufacturing private sector. Even now the mineral sector dominates the economy, accounting for 15% of GDP and over 60% of total exports. During the period up to 1995, four medium- to large-sized gold fields and one major oil field are likely to be developed, along with some smaller projects. When full capacity has been reached it is likely that PNG will be the world's sixth largest gold producer, and also a medium-sized oil producer.

Investment expenditure to finance this boom is expected to total $3.2bn (in current prices) from 1990 to 1997, with peak investment being in 1991/92 at over $800m. This compares with total annual private sector non-mining investment in the period 1983–8 of $1.1bn. As a classic enclave sector, mineral production is highly import-dependent and capital-intensive. Net employment in the sector is small (BCL and Ok Tedi together employ less than 0.5% of the labour force), and hence the main impact of mineral production comes through its fiscal and monetary impact. The revenue impact of the boom is likely to be substantial, with current projections suggesting that revenue (tax and dividends) from minerals is likely to increase the share of mineral revenue in total revenue from 20% to 35% (4.6% of GDP to 9.8%) from 1988 to 1997. In tandem there is likely to be a major impact on the balance of payments: the mineral trade balance is expected to rise from $442m. in 1988 to $2.1bn in 1997, and the overall balance after amortization from $344m. to $1.2bn over the same period.

Outside the mineral sector, PNG is essentially an agricultural economy. Recent evaluations of the agricultural sector by the World Bank (1988b) suggest that it has a considerable growth capacity. It accounts for 35% of GDP, with cash crops accounting for 40% of total exports. Production of cash crops (coffee, cocoa, oil palm and copra) is dominated by the smallholder sector (66%), with the rest being plantation agriculture (mainly foreign-owned). In general, however, the constraints facing this sector are the same as for manufacturing sector (see below): principally problems of high real wages and extremely high transport costs.

As a result the non-traditional economy of PNG is small and rudimentary. Manufacturing accounts for only approximately 9% of GDP, with services[2] a further 21%. Virtually no manufacturing output is exported. Data from the National Statistical Office show that the sector is dominated by food-processing (accounting for 63% of manufacturing output and 45% of employment), with wood products and basic metal manufacture the only other significant sectors. Manufacturing has shown only meagre growth during the 1980s, with value-added in 1980–85 growing by an average of only 0.2% per annum. It is this sector, however, which must form the basis for non-boom growth and diversification in the face of the mineral boom, and hence the stimulation of manufacturing has formed the basis of the two-pronged privatization and capital market development strategy.

10.1.3 Macroeconomic policy framework

The goverment clearly understands the importance of the successful management of the boom. It emphasizes (1990a) that

> . . . structural adjustment policies will focus on the development of the non-mineral sector, as the mineral and petroleum sector requires little direct action by Government, other than to maintain the current [tight] fiscal regime and ensure stability. Significantly higher growth of the non-mineral sector requires a reduction in the cost structure of the economy and a focus on rural development within an environment of continued fiscal restraint.

This broad objective is to be pursued through (i) a continued re-direction of resources to the agricultural sector (identified as the sector most capable of employment generation); (ii) reduction in costs, and particularly real wages; and (iii) supply-side measures to develop the private sector and enhance domestic equity acquisition through privatization, the development of a local equity market, and further deregulation of foreign participation.

An important departure from the thrust of supply-side policies however concerns the mineral sector itself where the government reserves the right to take up to a 30% equity stake in new mineral projects and 22.5% in petroleum projects. In general, its stake has been lower (20% in BCL, Ok Tedi and Misima and 10% in Porgera), and in 1988 these holdings were consolidated in the Mineral Resources Development Corporation (MRDC). Though the exercise is costly (especially when there are other important investment needs in the country), and may result in the crowding-out of foreign private capital flows to the mineral sector by foreign debt flows to government, such equity participation is essentially political (especially in the light of the Bougainville crisis). As long as political perceptions about ownership rights and control concerning natural resource endowment persist, some form of public participation will be inevitable.

10.2 The SOE sector: history, performance and reform

The state-owned enterprise sector in Papua New Guinea is small, consisting of three main groups: commodity marketing boards for the main agricultural products (coffee, cocoa, copra); Commercial Statutory Authorities (CSAs) which cover the main utilities and financial institutions; and a number of commercial enterprises. By mid-1990 there were 10 CSAs and 31 other SOEs, 17 of which were majority-owned by the government (see Table 10.2).[3] Reform of the SOE sector has consisted of three components: the first a comprehensive financial reform programme for the CSAs; second an ad hoc programme for the financial institutions; and finally a programme of privatization concerned with smaller, principally non boom, SOEs. We shall deal with each in turn.

The reform of the Commercial Statutory Authorities

Each CSA is established in terms of an Act of Parliament, and comes under the direct regulation of the relevant line ministry and also the Investment Division of the Ministry of Finance and Planning. The recent history of the CSAs in PNG provides an interesting case study on the management of large state-owned enterprises within the public sector.[4]

Following the sluggish, but not poor, performance of the CSAs during the early 1980s, the National Executive Committee (NEC) established new operating guidelines for the sector in 1983.[5] These apply automatically to the four main CSAs (the Electricity Commission, (ELCOM), Postal and Telecommunications Corporation, (PTC), Air Niugini, and the PNG Harbours Board, (PNGHB)), but can be applied to any other CSA at the behest of the Minister for Finance, although as yet this step has not been taken. The main provisions are as follows:

i) new investments can be entertained only if the MFPD (Ministry of Finance, Planning and Development) is satisfied that they can generate a 10% internal rate of return. If a CSA wishes to undertake a non-commercial investment for social or political reasons it should make a submission to the NEC;

ii) overall rates of return are specified annually by the Minister for Finance in his Budget speech. Current rate of return targets stand at between 16% and 22% return on total assets;

iii) authorities are able to change their price level and structure in response to market conditions, with the approval of the government Price Controller;

iv) authorities receive no general exemptions from customs, stamp duty or import levy; and

v) authorities are required to pay dividends equal to 50% of after-tax profits (from 1984).

The financial impact of the policy has been dramatic (Table 10.3). The increase in operating profits across the sector as a whole since 1983 has been substantial, not just in the quick turnaround from the poor position of 1983 but maintaining a high growth rate thereafter. The main cause of this growth has not been rises in revenue, which has grown broadly in line with inflation, but rather tight containment of costs. The improvement has helped lift the rate of return on assets rapidly towards the levels set by the NEC. As a consequence, net operating cash flow to government has moved from a net deficit position of K10m. in 1981 to a net surplus of K23m. in 1987. This improvement has been recorded across all CSAs, although that of Air Niugini is by far the most marked.[6] The table also indicates the effect of the decision that CSAs will be liable for tax and duty.

While the impact of the revised policy towards the CSAs has improved the public finances, it is far from clear that this is an unambiguously beneficial process. Each CSA faces differing circumstances; the case of ELCOM can be used to consider some of the broader issues concerning the control of the SOE sector.

Table 10.2 *CSAs and SOEs: government equity participation as at 1990*

CSAs	% Govt equity	Value of shares at cost
National Airline Commission (Air Niugini)	100.0	7.91
PNG Banking Corporation	100.0	10.00
Agricultural Bank of PNG	100.0	26.18
Investment Corporation of PNG	100.0	5.58
Niugini Insurance Corporation	100.0	0.25
Bank of Papua New Guinea	100.0	15.00
Posts and Telecommunications Corporation	100.0	13.92
PNG Electricity Commission	100.0	42.98
PNG Harbours Board	100.0	7.83
PNG Water and Sewerage Board.	100.0	1.77
		518.45

Table 10.2 *continued*

SOEs	% Govt equity	Value of shares at cost	Sector	Notes
Cape Rodney Estates (Pty) Ltd	100.0	2.45	Agriculture	No dividends paid.
Energy Development Corporation	100.0	1.02	Water/Energy	In liquidation.
Food Marketing Corporation (Pty) Ltd	100.0	3.20	Services	In liquidation. No dividend.
Higaturu Transport (Pty) Ltd	100.0	0.60	Transport	Company is paying dividends.
Kagamuga Natural Products (Pty) Ltd	100.0	0.69	—	
Livestock Development Corporation	100.0	0.20	Agriculture	
Mineral Resource Development Co.	100.0	0.10	Mining	Targeted to absorb equity holdings in all mineral sector companies.
National Forest Products (Pty) Ltd	100.0	0.00	Agriculture	In liquidation – sale being sought.
National Plantation Management Agency	100.0	0.20	Agriculture	In liquidation. No dividend.
North Fly Highway Development Company	100.0	7.00	Transport	In preliminary development phase.
PNG Fish Marketing Corporation	100.0	0.40	Agriculture	In liquidation.
PNG Timber Holding (Pty) Ltd	100.0	0.00	Agriculture	
PNG Forest Products (Pty) Ltd	70.0	5.57	Agriculture	Joint venture with Inchape of Singapore.
Baimuru Fisheries Co. (Pty) Ltd	50.0	0.00	Agriculture	Joint venture with Gulf Provincial Govt. No dividend.
Hargy Oil Palms (Pty) Ltd	50.0	4.00	Agriculture	Joint venture with SIPEF (Belgium).
Higaturu Oil Palms (Pty) Ltd	50.0	11.50	Agriculture	Joint venture with CDC.
New Britain Palm Oil Development Ltd	50.0	2.50	Agriculture	Joint venture with Harrison & Crosfield (UK)
Celcure (Pty) Ltd	49.0	0.05	—	In liquidation.
Gogol Reforestation Co. (Pty) Ltd	49.0	0.09	Agriculture	No dividend paid.
Ramu Sugar Holding Ltd	48.9	12.43	Agriculture	No dividends paid.
Milne Bay Estates (Pty) Ltd	40.0	8.82	Mining	Joint venture with CDC (UK).
New Guinea Marine Products (Pty) Ltd	33.0	0.67	Mining	Joint venture with Hohsui & Nippon Suisan Kaisha (Japan).
Pacific Forum Line	31.7	2.70	Transport	Joint venture amongst all South Pacifican States.
Ok Tedi Mining Ltd	20.0	35.25	Mining	Joint venture. Dividends paid to MRSF.[a]
Open Bay Timber (Pty) Ltd	20.0	0.44	Agriculture	Joint venture with Kawa Lumber (Japan). No dividends.
Poliamba (Pty) Ltd	20.0	5.00	Manufacturing	
Star Mountain Holding Company (Pty) Ltd	20.0	11.75	Mining	Joint venture with Ok Tedi Associate. No dividends.
Bougainville Copper Ltd	19.1	75.70	Mining	Joint venture with CRA/RTZ. Dividends paid to MRSF.[a]
Stettin Bay Lumber (Pty) Ltd	16.6	0.15	Agriculture	Joint venture with Nissho Iwai (Japan).
Davara House (Pty) Ltd	3.0	0.05	Mining	Shares transferred from Agricultural Bank. No dividend.
PNG Shipping Corporation	0.0	0.00	Transport	Sold to Steamships Corp. in 1986 (see text).
		193.52		

Source: Ministry of Finance and Development Planning.

a) MRSF = Mineral Revenue Stabilization Fund.

Table 10.3   *CSA financial performance*

	1981	1982	1983	1984	1985	1986	1987
Revenue (Km.)	163.3	184.5	190.0	207.9	223.2	234.7	258.4
(% growth)		13.0	3.0	9.4	7.4	5.2	10.1
Costs (Km.)	147.9	156.8	176.5	181.9	188.7	188.2	202.3
(% growth)		6.0	12.6	3.1	3.7	-0.3	7.5
Operating profit (Km.)	15.4	27.7	13.5	26.0	34.5	46.5	56.1
(% growth)		79.9	-51.3	92.6	32.7	34.8	20.6
Return on investment (%)			7.5	9.8	12.5	15.4	
Flow of funds from CSAs (Km.):							
Tax	0.0	0.0	0.0	1.4	12.7	7.4	10.7
Dividend	0.0	0.0	0.0	0.0	2.8	2.4	11.0
Duty/Levy	0.2	0.2	0.3	0.9	0.7	1.0	1.4
Equity	7.8	4.0	2.3	-2.2	0.0	0.0	0.0
Subsidy	2.6	2.6	0.0	0.0	0.0	0.1	0.0
Net Govt Cash Flow (excl. investment)	-10.2	-6.4	-2.0	4.5	16.2	10.7	23.1

Source: Ministry of Finance and Planning.

ELCOM was established under the Electricity Supply Act of 1963 and is responsible for electricity generation and distribution across the country, although there are a number of operations (e.g. the mines) which are responsible for their own power generation. The Commission is technologically efficient, and benefits from the extensive use of hydroelectric power which cross-subsidizes other forms of generation. However, as a whole, PNG suffers from a geography and population distribution which militates against economies of scale in electricity generation.

Recent changes in government policy towards the CSAs have impacted on ELCOM in a number of ways. Following the 1983 NEC decision the financial picture of the Commission altered. The significant turnaround in its net cash flow to the government was due to the payment of taxes, but also came from lower costs for fuel imports and the start of various hydro schemes. ESCOM has been able to meet financial targets set by the government and has registered significant improvements in labour productivity in recent years, attained principally by shedding approximately 750 jobs.[7] However, capital productivity has not increased by the same amount, mainly because ELCOM is moving into marginal less productive areas.

Policy on pricing and investment has caused greater problems. The government has insisted on a uniform tariff policy, which involves very high subsidization of the rural consumer by the urban consumer. This is despite ELCOM having previously operated an (economically) efficient regional tariff. A more general problem concerns the setting of tariff charges by the government Price Controller. Although ELCOM's 5-year corporate plan includes an estimate of required tariff increases over the plan period, and although the government has approved the plan, the individual annual tariff increases must still be approved by the Price Controller, whose department has a poor delivery record; in the case of ELCOM, approval of the 1988 tariff increase was delayed by almost 18 months. ELCOM has repeatedly appealed for greater commercial orientation on the part of the Price Controller, but it is not clear that this has been heeded.

Investment policy and, in particular, the financial rate of return targets have brought further difficulties. The government has developed a policy which is applied to all CSAs, despite the diversity of their fixed asset bases. This form of regulation creates a distortionary Averch–Johnson effect where, with declining marginal efficiency of capital (on the rural electrification expansion, for example), the rate of return criterion is too strict. Applied to ELCOM in this way investment is constrained at a lower level than is efficient for the economy as a whole. With capital-intensive operations such as electricity supply, such regulation can result in capital under-investment, whereas in labour-intensive activities the rate of return may lead to an over-investment in capital. Given the relatively small number and the diversity of CSAs, a case-by-case approach based on an economic rate of return criterion may be optimal.

Moreover, the CSAs face considerable financing difficulties under the new arrangements. Until 1989 they were generally able to raise funds in commercial markets without a government guarantee. This practice has stopped, and its replacement, government on-lending to the CSAs (which accounts for approximately 60%–70% of total capital expenditure), is on particularly tight terms. For example, the government lends to ELCOM at 3% above its cost of capital on 15-year repayment terms with a five-year grace period. In response, ELCOM is now considering the possibility of raising money through local stock issues, although this is unlikely to succeed, given the high local interest rates.

The irony with respect to the concerns which this discussion of ELCOM illustrates is that the government has instituted exactly the kind of control regime advocated elsewhere in pursuit of increased financial efficiency in the SOE sector (for example in Kenya). The problems encountered in PNG highlight the central issue concerning the CSAs, namely that, as monopoly utilities, financial performance criteria will deviate from economic criteria. The government's ultimate objective ought to be the efficient allocation of resources. Across many activities this coincides with financial or market-based allocation, and such financial criteria are appropriate. In the case of the CSAs, where investment and pricing decisions are also determined on economic rather than financial grounds, the pursuit of narrow financial criteria must similarly be amended.

The CSA reform programme has achieved considerable and sustained financial and efficiency gains. This has been through the imposition on the Authorities of commercial operating principles by a government acting to maximize a clearly defined objective function. While there may be concerns that the objective function is too narrow in view of the divergence between economic and financial performance, the endeavour serves to underline the argument that performance improvements do not necessarily depend on changes in ownership.

The public sector financial institutions
Excluding the central bank, there are four public sector financial institutions, all of which are 100% government-owned, namely the PNG Banking Corporation, the Agricultural Bank of PNG, the Investment Corporation of PNG, and the Niugini Insurance Corporation. The character and performance of these institutions reflect many of the constraints of the PNG economy, most notably the thinness of the private sector and financial markets.

The Papua New Guinea Banking Corporation (PNGBC) was founded in 1974 on the eve of Independence and is the largest commercial bank in the country. It maintains a wide network of branches and agencies across the country and the islands (48 branches and 200 agencies), and accounts for approximately 50% of all banking activity in the economy.[8] Its financial performance has been robust, despite a low level of capitalization, and has been consistently profitable (Table 10.3). The loss in 1986 was occasioned by a severe liquidity crisis in 1985 which forced all the commercial banks to increase deposit rates. From 1986 onwards the liquidity conditions eased and the government moved towards greater interest-rate liberalization, accompanied by a rationalization of the PNGBC network (downgrading a number of branches to agencies and reducing staff levels) and of

Table 10.3 *Papua New Guinea Banking Corporation (Km.)*

	1982	1983	1984	1985	1986	1987	1988
Capital	10.00	10.00	10.00	10.00	10.00	10.00	10.00
Reserves	14.80	16.64	17.35	18.78	18.11	20.83	24.41
Total Shareholder Funds	24.80	26.64	27.35	28.78	28.11	30.83	34.41
Assets	272.17	339.07	376.91	401.64	447.17	436.64	468.63
of which: Loans	(184.82)	(214.44)	(259.41)	(297.46)	(326.63)	(327.37)	(342.03)
Deposits	223.91	275.69	304.56	320.01	387.08	370.29	388.44
Advances/Deposit Ratio (%)	82.54	77.78	85.18	92.95	84.38	88.41	88.05
Net profit	4.79	2.15	1.46	2.16	(2.02)	4.77	5.47
Dividend to Government	1.25	0.25	0.25	0.25	0.00	0.30	0.63
Return On Investment (%)	12.50	2.50	2.50	2.50	0.00	3.00	6.30
No. of Employees	1,300	1,324	1,376	1,413	1,463	1,340	1,250

Source: PNGBC Annual Reports.

the loan portfolio. By 1988 the corporation was again paying dividends to government. PNGBC is an efficient corporation (notwithstanding the costs carried in maintaining its extensive branch network), although there is some concern that its low level of capitalization has hampered development in key areas. The management, along with that of other financial institutions, is investigating the options for raising long-term capital from the domestic market in the absence of further government capital injections.

The Agricultural Bank of Papua New Guinea (AGBANK)[9] was established in 1965 as a development finance corporation to provide term lending to the agricultural, industrial and commercial sectors of the economy, and to support indigenization. AGBANK's lending is mainly in the agricultural sector (60%), with the remainder for hire-purchase and equipment finance (30%) and industrial, commercial and housing activities. All loans are to PNG nationals, or to companies with at least 75% PNG ownership. In addition to lending, the AGBANK has also built up a small portfolio of companies in which it holds equity, of which 10 are majority-controlled by AGBANK.

AGBANK's financial position is extremely weak due to an increasingly 'bad' portfolio and dangerously low (and worsening) operating margins (Table 10.4). An in-depth analysis of the cocoa and coffee sectors, following the collapse of these commodity prices in 1989, led to a special provision of K49m. made on the assumption that all coffee lending and 30% of cocoa lending was bad. Prior to this, however, the overall viability of the bank by 1987 was achieved through increased government subsidies, and in particular (in 1987) through the sale of equity in three subsidiary companies (see section 10.3 below). However, these three companies were amongst only six in the AGBANK investment portfolio which were returning a profit in 1987. Following the sale of these companies, the total losses of the portfolio were around K60,000 per annum. Furthermore, the fact that the portfolio is not paying dividends, and has a net asset value of only K273,000 raises severe questions about the realizable value of the K11.3m. investment by AGBANK in these companies. The outlook for AGBANK therefore looks grave. Following the sale of the subsidiary companies, its portfolio is increasingly less liquid, is generating considerably less income, and contains a dangerously high level of bad or doubtful debts. Only a recapitalization from government and other external creditors will stave off its collapse. At the time of writing the management was considering a domestic capital issue of around K30m.: however, there are severe doubts as to whether any financial institution would buy into the issue unless it were fully underwritten by the government.

The Investment Corporation (IC) was created in 1971 as a specialized development finance institution, with the specific aim of increasing the equity participation

Table 10.4 *Papua New Guinea Development Bank/Agricultural Bank of Papua New Guinea (Km.)*

	1979	1980	1981	1982	1983	1984	1985	1986	1987	1988	1989[a]
Capital	26.89	27.06	27.13	29.22	29.22	29.26	29.32	29.96	31.17	33.37	32.45
Reserves	0.00	0.00	0.00	6.58	6.58	6.58	6.58	8.08	12.08	24.48	26.29
Accumulated loss	(0.21)	(0.19)	(0.40)	(5.38)	(5.87)	(6.61)	(7.13)	(6.85)	(5.33)	(2.57)	(43.71)
Total shareholder funds	26.68	26.87	26.73	30.42	29.93	29.93	28.77	31.19	37.92	55.28	15.03
Income	3.49	4.15	4.87	4.11	6.24	4.66	6.08	6.82	8.29	9.48	8.82
Expenditure	3.15	3.94	4.86	9.08	6.73	5.23	6.44	7.14	10.58	9.06	51.83
Inc/(dec) bad debt prov	0.00	0.05	0.21	3.99	0.12	0.22	(0.70)	(0.03)	1.53	0.01	40.24
Operating profit/(loss)	0.34	0.21	0.01	(4.97)	(0.49)	(0.57)	(0.36)	(0.32)	(2.29)	0.42	(43.01)
Government subsidy	0.00	0.00	0.00	0.00	0.00	0.00	0.00	0.60	0.61	0.00	0.00
Other net income[b]	(0.18)	(0.19)	(0.22)	0.00	0.00	(0.17)	(0.17)	0.00	3.20	2.34	1.87
Net profit (loss)	0.16	0.02	(0.21)	(4.97)	(0.49)	(0.74)	(0.53)	0.28	1.52	2.76	(41.14)
Bad debt provision											
(as % of total loans)	4.00	4.50	4.10	12.80	11.70	12.10	18.00	14.00	10.70	10.60	50.51

Source: PNGDB & ABPNG Annual Reports.

Notes:
a) Estimate.
b) Principally depreciation charges. K3.2m. (1988) proceeds from sale of subsidiary companies.

of PNG individuals and institutions. In pursuit of this aim the Investment Corporation Fund (ICF) was set up in 1973. This is a unit trust, whose units are sold to PNG residents, and shares many of the characteristics of the PNB/ASN funds which feature heavily in the Malaysian privatization story (see Chapter 9). ICF is an open-ended investment company[10] managed on a fee basis by IC. It has approximately 25,000 unit holders, the majority of whom are individuals (including a number on payroll deduction schemes), although the largest by far are the main public sector superannuation funds, insurance companies and banking institutions. The ICF is dominated, however, by illiquid assets (although some of its investments are listed in Australia[11]), and this weakness has not only undermined the viability of IC's other development finance role, but has created a significant contingent liability for IC and for the government (the ultimate guarantor). The ICF has already averted one such crisis in the mid-1980s by extensive external borrowing, but it is clear that this is not sustainable. In 1990 it approached the government for a recapitalization to offset its liquidity crisis but without success. As with the other financial institutions, the corporation is also looking to raise funds through the local capital market, but these plans are in their early stages.

Finally, Niugini Insurance Corporation (NIC) is a 100% government-owned insurance company, established with an initial capital of K250,000 in 1977 under the Insurance Corporation Act. The corporation was fundamentally profitable and was targeted for privatization in 1988. It is dealt with in detail in section 10.3 below.

Though these public sector financial institutions enjoyed differing degrees of financial success, they had some important shared characteristics. The first was that (as with the CSAs) the narrowness of the private sector limited their operations, and restricted their opportunities for diversification.[12] Second, all the institutions were constrained by the weak capital market and their capacity to raise funds through debt issues. Support for capital market initiatives is consequently high amongst financial sector institutions.

Other equity holdings

Aside from the CSAs, the government holds a sizeable equity porfolio in 31 other companies. This portfolio is dominated by holdings in the minerals sector: the

K75.7m. in 19.1% of equity in BCL and K35.25m. in 20% of Ok Tedi account for 57% of total government equity participation.[13] With a few exceptions however, the enterprises are not performing well. A large number are paying no dividends (and indeed many have never paid dividends), while a significant number have been in liquidation for a sizeable period of time (see Table 10.2). More importantly for the privatization programme (since it is these non-CSAs that are likely to form the core of the government's privatization supply), it is generally only those enterprises in which the government is a minority shareholder in a majority foreign-owned and managed company which are performing satisfactorily. Of the 12 wholly-owned companies, only one has a dividend history, three are operating but not paying dividends and five are currently in liquidation. This does not provide a promising base from which to develop a privatization programme, to which we now turn.

10.3 The development of privatization structures

Two important National Executive Council (NEC) decisions (Nos 22/87 and 21/88) established privatization in PNG. The policy was proposed by the Ministry of Finance and Planning through an executive instrument (a Cabinet proposal) rather than as the outcome of manifesto promises or an extended political debate. Although there was no public debate (and even now public perceptions of the privatization programme are low), it is clear that an important impetus for the policy came from the donor community, and in particular the linking of privatization with the development of the capital market. The proposal under NEC decision 22/87 sought Cabinet approval to:

(1) begin a programme to sell the State's interests in a number of commercial enterprises in order to gain revenue and to reduce administrative costs; and
(2) to provide an opportunity for the Provinces, superannuation funds, and the people of Papua New Guinea to participate in the ownership of the enterprises as desired.

This first phase of the programme centred round a list of five companies identified for privatization. The list had originally been drawn up with the co-operation of the Centre for Privatization[14] in 1986, and consisted of National Forest Products Ltd, New Guinea Marine Products Ltd, Stettin Bay Lumber Products Ltd, Niugini Insurance Corporation, and BCL. The first privatization in PNG was in fact of the PNG Shipping Corporation and was undertaken in 1986 prior to the NEC's Decision 22/87 on privatization.

Papua New Guinea Shipping Corporation
The Papua New Guinea Shipping Corporation (PNGSC) sale in 1986 was the first sale by the government of an SOE. The sale was successful, uncontroversial and requires limited discussion. However, the example of PNGSC, and in particular its post-privatization performance, is illustrative of the relationships between ownership, market structure and performance in PNG.

The PNGSC was a small-scale shipping operation providing containerized cargo services from Papua New Guinea to Australia, and coastal services between Port Moresby, Lae and Rabaul. The government held 100% of the K3.68m. capital. In 1985, PNGSC made a net loss of K0.6m., and by 1986 was insolvent. At that time a deal was brokered by the Ministry of Finance,[15] which transferred the total equity to the Steamships Trading Company Ltd. The proceeds from the sale (which are unknown, but estimated to be around K900,000) were used to extinguish all claims of the company's creditors. There was no net revenue accruing to the government.

The purchaser, Steamships Trading Company Ltd, is the largest general transport and trading company in PNG. It is listed in Australia, with an issued capital of K15.5m. and total assets of K118m., the major holders of which are both Australian companies. Steamships' core activities are coastal shipping (freight and cargo), shipping agency, and stevedoring, although it holds in addition a diversified portfolio of trading, property and service interests in PNG. The company is profitable and employs in excess of 2,000 people, making it one of the largest employers in the country.

Upon acquisition PNGSC was integrated with the Shipping and Transport Division of Steamships. The operations of PNGSC were severely rationalized, with its coastal services being leased to another Steamships subsidiary company, Consort Line. The integration of the corporation into a larger, efficiently managed international shipping operation seems to have saved it from ultimate closure as management and operational efficiency has improved radically. Despite this it still faces problems arising from the structure of the economy and the manner of government price regulation. These severely compromise the long-term viability of the service. The fundamental problem is that containerized freight is a high-cost operation at the low volumes which arise from the lack of containerized export trade from PNG to Australia. Compounding this, all coastal shipping operations have been severely restricted through the refusal of the government Price Controller to allow freight rates to rise. Despite rising costs, there has been no increase in approved rates since 1984, a situation which has forced PNGSC and Steamships to reconsider the future of their coastal shipping operations.

Niugini Insurance Corporation

During the early 1980s NIC was profitable and efficient. However, between 1981 and 1986 the Corporation was faced with a number of adverse developments. Globally, the world recession (which resulted in the low level of capital investment in the economy) had an indirect impact on the insurance market, while, locally, the government passed the Motor Vehicle (Third Party) Insurance Act, under which all insurance companies were required to underwrite the operating deficit of the Motor Vehicle Insurance Trust (MVIT). As Table 10.5 indicates, the provision for the deficit on the MVIT borne by NIC rose from K43,000 in 1980 to over K1,033,000 in 1984, reflecting a MVIT deficit which itself rose by 2500% over the same period. This regulation created a considerable fixed cost in the market and acted as a disincentive to market growth. Furthermore, the government liberalized access to the insurance market, so that domestic companies, including the NIC, faced strong price competition especially for insurance in the mining sector. They also faced competition from large offshore insurers, many of whom were not charging actuarially fair premia in view of the high-risk environment (both geologically and socio-economically) in Papua New Guinea. Throughout the period, NIC along with the other companies in the sector argued strongly for the

Table 10.5 *Niugini Insurance Corporation: financial performance 1980–89 (K'000)*

	1980	1981	1982	1983	1984	1985	1986	1987	1988	1989
Capital	250	250	250	250	250	250	250	250	250	250
Reserves	1,356	1,531	1,476	1,256	1,403	1,923	2,326	2,898	3,150	3,794
Insurance inc	311	666	824	808	837	1,051	1,353	1,849	1,494	—
Insurance claims	298	630	964	922	758	1,108	1,372	1,621	1,734	—
U'writing profit/(loss)	13	36	(140)	(114)	79	(57)	(19)	228	(240)	—
Total profit/(loss)	79	174	(55)	(220)	148	516	653	572	251	645
Provision for MVIT	(43)	(76)	(341)	(773)	(1,033)	(637)	(267)	(267)	(235)	0

Source: Niugini Insurance Company Financial Statements.

underwriting provisions for MVIT to be abolished, and for greater preferential access to the domestic insurance market. From 1985 onwards a major restructuring of the MVIT was instituted and the burden of the deficit removed (temporarily) from the market. Post-1984, core underwriting performance picked up again, reaching a peak profit of K228,000 in 1987.

The attempted privatization of NIC was a sorry story, exposing some serious weaknesses in the planning, implementation and politics of privatization in PNG. Following NEC decision 22/87 the Minister for Finance, Julian Chan (the former prime minister), announced that the insurance company would be privatized. Domestic and international bids for a direct sale of the entire equity were invited, and a valuation exercise was undertaken. The final deadline for bids was set for March 1988, by which time a number of internationally reputable companies had responded. There was, however, no process of open tender and the company was eventually offered to an unknown group of Malaysian businessmen for K3m. The buyers seemed to have some experience in brokerage work, but were not recognized members of the international insurance market. Considerable confusion still remains concerning the process by which the contract was awarded.

The transfer date was set for July 1988. The Ministry of Finance and Planning proceeded to repeal the Insurance Corporation Act (1977) and create the new company, Nuigini Insurance (Pty) Ltd. Finally, it arranged for the transfer of employees and their pension liabilities to the private company. By the end of June 1988, when the sale was imminent, it became clear that the NIC's re-insurers were dissatisfied with the new buyers' credentials and indicated that they would not continue to re-insure the corporation. In early July the buyers requested a delay, reputedly on the grounds that they did not have the funds. The general election which occurred three days before the transfer date heralded a change of government and a change of Finance Minister. Immediately on taking office, the new Minister cancelled the offer for sale.

However, this pre-emptive action did not occur soon enough to stop NIC losing the confidence of its re-insurers and brokers. As Table 10.5 shows, this had an immediate and dramatic effect on the corporation's underwriting business. Insurance income fell for the first time in the corporation's history, turning the previous year's underwriting profit into a loss of K240,000. In November 1988 a new general manager was appointed and the process of reconstruction instituted. By early 1990 NIC had re-established its international reputation and had again become the leading domestic insurance company, although there remained some confusion about its legal status arising from the fact that, in preparation for privatization, the Insurance Corporation Act was repealed, but no new company was established.

The NIC fiasco highlighted a number of critical issues concerning the privatization programme in PNG, in particular the extremely damaging effect of ministers and officials attempting to conclude deals personally. This not only had the effect of attracting wholly inappropriate buyers, but more damagingly it undermined the reputation of the government and in particular its ability to manage a privatization programme. To an extent this point has been acknowledged in the attempt through NEC decision 21/88 to centralize the management of privatization within the Ministry of Finance and Planning. More recently, however, there have been a number of calls from private sector representatives and other economic commentators for the profile of the policy to be raised even further through the publication of a White Paper on privatization and the stipulation of clear unambiguous guidelines for tendering and sale.[16]

As far as NIC is concerned, privatization still remains an objective. The second attempt (which had not been instituted at the time of writing) was planned to be more cautious. The new tentative proposal involved an initial sale of only 49% of the equity, with the government remaining in control of 51% of the shares. The sale proposals were to involve an initial corporatization of the company, followed by a partial sale of the equity to PNG institutions.

The corporation's reaction to the proposal was positive, although it remains extremely cautious. It welcomed the new sale proposals principally as a means of creating a barrier against 'irresponsible' government interference in its commercial activities. However, it is clear that successful privatization of NIC (and the continued health of the entire PNG insurance market) requires a re-examination of the regulation of the sector, in terms of both protection against large offshore insurers and also the compulsory underwriting of the MVIT.

Other privatizations from the 'first five'
None of the other original five companies has been successfully privatized, although some progress has been made. The structure and status of each company as at mid-1990 is as follows. As noted earlier, the government has a 19.1% equity holding in Bougainville Copper Limited, with a nominal value of K75.7m. Under the initial plans of the divestiture programme, it was proposed that K5m. tranches of this equity should be progressively sold on the Australian Stock Exchange (and later on the PNG Exchange if it were to come into existence). However, due to the crisis on Bougainville and closure of the mine in May 1989, the programme was put in abeyance. Though the sale of BCL shares has not been carried out, important developments concerning equity participation in the mineral sector have occurred.

Having decided to sell its equity share in BCL, the government realized that, under BCL's original enabling legislation, this was non-transferrable, and divestiture plans therefore required legislative changes. This was achieved jointly with the creation of the Mineral Resource Development Corporation, which was created as a holding company for all government equity in the mineral sector. Following the disturbances on Bougainville, new measures were introduced to dissipate the concerns of local politicians and residents that the federal government was selling their natural inheritance to foreign companies. Under the auspices of the MRDC, 5% of BCL shares were transferred to the provincial government, and 5% to local landowners. These were to be transferred at cost (even though the initial demand was for the shares to be issued free), although the government stated that it would extend credit for the purchase of the first 2.5% of the equity.

New Guinea Marine Products (Pty) Ltd is a small distribution company in which the government has a 33% equity share worth K670,000, with the remainder of the equity held by Hohsui Corporation and Nippon Suisan Kaisha, both of Japan, who also provide the management. The company has been paying dividends. The government equity was originally offered as a private placement to the majority shareholders, but they declined the offer. New purchasers are currently being identified by the Commercial Investment Division of the Ministry of Finance and Planning.

National Forest Products (Pty) Ltd was established by the Department of Forestry to take over its Forest Products Commercial Division. The company has a nominal capital of only K2.00, and shareholders' equity of K300,000. It has not traded since 1986. Initial discussions have been held with Inchape of Singapore who would become joint-venture partners, but no sale proposal has yet emerged.

Stettin Bay Lumber Company Ltd (SBLC) is a joint venture with the Nissho Iwai Corporation of Japan. The government originally held 150,000 K1.00 shares in the company, which represented a 25% equity participation. This was enhanced in 1985 by a K850,000 bonus issue funded from the capitalization of accumulated profits. In 1987 the company made a new shares issue of K2m., raising the total capital to K6m. The government did not participate in the issue in order to reduce its equity participation which, as a consequence, now stands at 16.67%. No concrete plans have been developed to divest this remaining equity share.

AGBANK divestitures
In 1987 AGBANK disposed of three of its associated companies which, in its view, were 'mature and successful operations able to hold their place successfully in the Papua New Guinea economy and market place (*Annual Report*, 1986). The three companies, Niugini Table Birds (Pty) Ltd, Harambo Printers Ltd and Nationwide Car Rental Ltd, raised approximately K3.206m. for AGBANK and ensured that a net profit was returned for the year (despite an operating loss of K2.29m.). The companies were sold privately to the joint shareholders, who in each case were foreign. No other details are known about the sales or about their post-privatization performance.

Assessment, implications and outlook
The bald facts of the first four years of the privatization programme are far from impressive. Six enterprises were identified for sale: PNGSC was sold, NIC was almost sold, but then had to be rescued amidst a damaging fiasco; the BCL equity sale has been suspended; and negotiations have stalled on the other three sales. While it is clear that the turbulent circumstances on Bougainville have held up developments in privatizing the mining sector, the failure of the other sales is worrying. The problems have been largely systemic, and we shall deal with them in more detail in sections 10.4 and 10.5, but there is strong evidence that many of them have also stemmed from poor management and planning of the programme.

The most striking aspect of all the sales (both completed and planned) is the minimal role played by the domestic private sector. Though Steamships is a PNG-registered company, its management and shareholders are almost exclusively foreign. In the case of all the other companies, the main potential purchasers were all overseas companies. Even the proposed sale of BCL envisaged tranche sales on the Australian Stock Exchange, rather than placement with local institutions.[17] The outcome of the programme stands in strong contrast to the primary objective of NEC 22/87 which stated that 'the proposals should provide for the sale of shares primarily to pertinent Provincial Governments, the superannuation funds, and the Papua New Guinea public.' The ready jettisoning of the PNG public was partially explained by the second objective of privatization stated in NEC 21/88 relating to the maximization of government revenue from the sale. However, in this respect performance was similarly poor. No net proceeds flowed from the sale of PNGSC since all proceeds were applied immediately to extinguishing the company's outstanding liabilities to its creditors. Furthermore, the loss of insurance income and goodwill as a result of the abortive sale of NIC was actually translated into a loss to the government. Only with the sale of the AGBANK subsidiaries (which were not covered by the NEC privatization programme) was any revenue raised, although in this case it accrued to the bank and not directly to the government.

Most disturbing so far has been the amateurish manner in which the government has implemented the programme. Although some (distinctly non-neutral) technical assistance was contracted from the Centre for Privatization in identifying the candidates for sale, there seems to have been little systematic preparation of the companies for sale thereafter. The two privatization initiatives to date have been conducted in a covert manner, not through the Commercial Investment Division as required by the NEC but, apparently, by senior officials and ministers. In the case of PNGSC this seems to have resulted in the successful sale (from the point of view of the government) of a corporation which would otherwise have faced liquidation. In the case of NIC – a profitable company – the same covert approach yielded disastrous results.

NEC decision 21/88 did, however, strengthen the programme by authorizing the Minister of Finance to take sole charge of privatization.[18] In particular, it directed that he prepare a medium-term privatization programme based on a valuation of all government enterprises including the CSAs. This decision and the unilateral action by the incoming Minister, Paul Pora, over the NIC debacle, have put the management of the programme on a more solid footing. The Commercial Investment Division of the Ministry of Finance and Planning is now the sole co-ordinating body for the programme. However, the operations and policy advice of the CID reveal a number of worrying features and attitudes towards privatization, which are implicitly reflected in the policy approach to the CSAs and the other SOEs.[19] First, there is a tendency to see privatization as a 'quick fix', an easy programme to implement; and as a result there has been only a limited allocation of resources to the programme. In this respect the thinking is no different from that of many governments elsewhere in the world, but evidence is now widespread as to the considerable resource costs required to implement such programmes. There has as yet been no attempt to address the financial restructuring of companies before sale (although in most cases this has not occurred because the companies are joint ventures). There is a strong argument, of course, for the vendor selling the enterprise 'as-is', allowing the purchaser to undertake the restructuring as the new owners see fit. However, in an environment like PNG, only the foreign sector has the resources, technical expertise and, possibly, the lower risk aversion required to purchase such assets. A more risk-averse domestic sector may not come forward in such a situation, seeking rather to purchase assets which, though at a higher price, would be able to offer immediate profits. If this argument holds, and there is a genuine desire for enterprises to be sold to the domestic sector, then it behooves the government to undertake the necessary pre-privatization restructuring.

Second, there is the question of the method of sale. So far privatization has been limited to direct sales of equity to a single buyer. However, policy statements indicate a desire to consider public equity issues on the putative PNG Stock Exchange (and/or the Australian Exchange). Both these methods, while valid, are likely to preclude a large proportion of the domestic private sector. No attention has yet been paid to other forms of sale (leasing, management contracts, deregulation, franchising, employee or management buy-outs, etc.) which may enhance local participation. It is clear that the resolution of the Bougainville crisis will hinge crucially on how the national government chooses to address the ownership aspirations of the population there. It may be expected that, in resolving this issue, there will be a greater focus on mechanisms for increasing domestic participation in the economy. One particular initiative arising from the Bougainville crisis concerns the proposed transfer of equity from the government to the provincial government and local landowners. A scheme is currently being developed through the MRDC to allow such landowners to fund equity participation out of future dividend flows. While this is likely to be successful in the case of the mining sector, it is less likely to meet with acceptance in the non-mining sector, where the dividend flow is less secure. While evidence from other countries suggests that this form of financing can work, in general such schemes are underwritten either by the equity vendor (usually Employee Share Schemes funded through salary deductions), or by the commercial banking sector, itself underwritten by the government. In each of these cases, though the ownership objective is clearly being addressed, it is at the expense of revenue. At present the PNG Government does not seem to have clarified its policy position on this trade-off.

The conclusions to be drawn from the first phase of privatization in PNG are threefold. First, the development of privatization guidelines and operational procedures was weak and in part responsible for the disappointing record of implementation. Developments following NEC decision 21/88 have addressed some of these weaknesses, although, with no further privatizations having occurred since 1988, it is not possible to assess the effectiveness of the new structures. Second, there is little evidence that the government has addressed itself to the necessary trade-offs between the conflicting objectives of privatization. The policy at present emphasizes both wider ownership and revenue raising, and is directly linked to proposals for the establishment of a capital market. As has been shown already, these objectives cannot be simultaneously achieved. Finally, considerable emphasis was placed on the catalytic capacity of privatization in the development of the domestic private sector and the capital market. However, it rapidly became clear that such assumptions were wildly optimistic, and the absence of a capital market and the thinness of the domestic non-traditional private sector have, in fact, severely limited the scope of sales.

10.4 Private sector constraints to privatization

No matter how sophisticated the capacity of the privatization machinery in Papua New Guinea becomes, it is unlikely to overcome these two major constraints. The non-mining private sector is and will remain extremely small and dualistic, for a number of quite intractable reasons. First, as noted in the introduction, the topology and location of the country make it a very high-cost economy. As with some of the landlocked economies of southern Africa – in particular Malawi – transport and storage costs drive an enormous wedge between fob and cif prices. This transport wedge is inevitably shifted forwards on to domestic consumers for both final and, importantly, intermediate goods. PNG is thus faced with an immediate cost disadvantage in competing in non-mineral exports. One way in which such transport disadvantages can be overcome is, of course, through low unit labour costs. Again, however, this is not the case in PNG, where average wage costs are high. Data for 1983 show an average of US$88 per week in PNG, as opposed to $54 in Malaysia, $62 in Korea, $70 in Fiji, and $6 in Sri Lanka, and, although there are important policy changes aimed at introducing greater real wage flexibility into the economy, this is likely to have only a limited impact on export competitiveness. Similar problems exist for the primary product sector, where producers are fob price-takers. Given the rigidities of cost structures in the economy, and in particular the transport-cost wedge, the scope for profitable expansion of this sector is limited. Moreover, at a microeconomic level, faced with a rigid input cost structure, profit opportunities for potential acquirers of privatization equity are limited.

Government policy towards the CSAs compounds this problem. In an economy where the strongest linkage from the boom sector to the rest of the economy is through the fiscus, the argument for greater public subsidization of the critical infrastructural sector is strong. However, as noted in section 10.2, current policy towards the CSAs forces them to achieve certain financial rates of return. Given the conditions faced by the PNG economy, there is likely to be a significant difference between the financial and the economic rate of return. Public participation does not necessarily entail inefficiency in operation, as the recent experience of the CSAs has shown, but efficiency can co-exist with a pricing structure which reflects economic rather than financial costs.

As noted in section 10.1, one of the main implications of the fractured geography and prohibitive transport barriers is that the economy consists of very many small markets. Scope for expansion in these markets is limited, and in many cases it is impossible for industry to acquire minimum economic scale – even given the high cost of imported goods. Without this scope for economic, and in particular industrial, expansion, the natural dynamic for entrepreneurship and managerial development is limited. As with many of the smaller economies of Africa, there is an extremely limited tradition of the separation of ownership from management.

Very little evidence exists concerning the composition, concentration and efficiency of the private sector in PNG, although, from what there is, a number of factors do emerge (Tables 10.6 and 10.7). The first is that (for reasons alluded to above) PNG is a high-cost producer. Vertical linkages are limited and input costs have very high cif components which prevent the country being an effective exporter. In addition, manufacturing is generally small-scale, with almost 80% of factories employing less than 50 people. Only in the wood and food-processing subsectors are there a significant number of factories employing more than 50 people. In all, manufacturing employment accounted for only 32,000 employees in 1985, of whom 10% work in government-owned factory operations.[20] This is in contrast to approximately 150,000 in the public sector, and a similar proportion in the subsistence agriculture sector.

Table 10.6 also indicates that in many sectors there is no systematic difference between the public and privately owned enterprises except perhaps in food, beverages and tobacco and basic metals. The evidence on output per employee is mixed: in food, beverages and tobacco, and in wood products, output per employee is higher under government ownership, while in other sectors the reverse is the case. The data are, unfortunately, not sufficient to explain these differences, and to determine how much is due to differing labour productivity, and how much to differing capital intensity.

These data underline the main constraint to privatization, namely the limited scope of the private sector to provide either the competitive environment in which private ownership can be translated into economic welfare, or the managerial and entrepreneurial capacity required to achieve more efficient performance than can be achieved under public ownership. Having said this, though, there is also evidence that at the factory level there is a large number of comparably sized public and private enterprises. If savings could be appropriately mobilized then it would appear that a programme of sales of some of these small-scale government factory operations to the private sector would be entirely feasible. To a great extent these weaknesses have already been noted in connection with the privatization programme. Despite initial claims to the contrary, the government has been forced to look towards the foreign sector as the one most capable and likely to absorb divestiture.

10.4.1 *The foreign sector and foreign direct investment*

The foreign sector has been (and will continue to be) a major player in the PNG economy. Nevertheless there is an ambivalent attitude on the part of the government towards the sector, springing in part from the historical dominance of the country by Australian capital and skilled labour and, more recently, as a result of the Bougainville crisis. Consequently government policy towards foreign investment combines measures to enhance the inflow of foreign capital as well as to integrate local entrepreneurship with it. Foreign participation is thus welcomed, particularly in capital-intensive operations, but not so much in small-scale

Table 10.6 *Composition of industrial and commercial sectors*

Factory Operations[a]

	1981	1982	1983	1984	1985
No. of factories	722	697	688	693	705
Total employment	25,437	27,605	27,913	27,176	27,986
Value of output (Km.)	521.4	525.5	597.8	679.5	692.6
Output as % GDP	31.0	30.0	27.9	29.9	28.9
GDP (Km.)	1,681.2	1,749.1	2,143.8	2,269.4	2,397.4

Sectoral composition (1985)[b]

	No.	Employment	Output (Km.)	Employment per Enterprise	Output per Enterprise (Km.)	Output per Employee (k'000/person)
1. Government operations						
Manufacturing						
Food, beverages & tobacco	17	349	23.9	20.5	1.4	68.5
Textiles	0	0	0.0	0.0	0.0	0.0
Wood products	19	711	12.1	37.4	0.6	17.0
Paper products	3	194	1.3	64.7	0.4	6.7
Chemicals	0	0	0.0	0.0	0.0	0.0
Non-metallic minerals	0	0	0.0	0.0	0.0	0.0
Basic metals	20	855	5.9	42.8	0.3	6.9
TOTAL	59	2,109	43.2	35.7	0.7	20.5

Table 10.6 *continued*

	No.	Employment	Output (Km.)	Employment per Enterprise	Output per Enterprise (Km.)	Output per Employee (k'000/person)
Wholesale & retail	7	92	1.4	13.1	0.2	15.2
Construction	42	1,687	13.2	40.2	0.3	7.8
Transport	0	0	0.0	0.0	0.0	0.0
Other services	0	0	0.0	0.0	0.0	0.0
Total government	108	3,888	57.8	36.0	0.5	14.9
2. Non-government operations						
Manufacturing						
Food, beverages & tobacco	147	9,728	381.8	66.2	2.6	39.2
Textiles	16	458	3.6	28.6	0.2	7.9
Wood products	108	4,950	68.3	45.8	0.6	13.8
Paper products	26	1,057	17.9	40.7	0.7	16.9
Chemicals	22	637	26.0	29.0	1.2	40.8
Non-metallic minerals	18	597	16.6	33.2	0.9	27.8
Basic metals	127	4,233	90.1	33.3	0.7	21.3
TOTAL	464	21,660	604.3	46.7	1.3	27.9
Wholesale & retail	121	1,987	32.5	16.4	0.3	16.4
Construction	69	2,549	32.3	36.9	0.5	12.7
Transport	31	954	9.3	30.8	0.3	9.7
Other services	20	836	14.2	41.8	0.7	16.9
Total non-government	705	27,986	692.6	39.7	1.0	24.7
TOTAL ALL INDUSTRIES	813	31,874	750.4	75.7	1.5	39.6

Source: NSO Bulletin, 18 May 1989.

Notes
a) Excludes electricity-generating establishments.
b) Government operations include factory operations run by central and provincial governments as well as by SOEs.

Table 10.7 *Number of factories by employee size 1985*

Sector	< 5	5 < 20	21 < 50	> 50
Manufacturing				
Food, beverages & tobacco	21	40	40	46
Textiles	5	6	2	3
Wood products	15	48	23	22
Paper products	1	10	9	6
Chemicals	1	7	10	4
Non-metallic minerals	2	5	8	3
Basic metals	16	62	30	19
Total Manufacturing	61	178	122	103
Wholesale & retail	21	72	25	3
Construction	10	18	23	136
Transport	4	14	5	8
Other services	3	5	2	0
TOTAL	99	287	177	250

Source: NSO Bulletin, 18 May 1989.

operations, a process which, to an extent, has exacerbated the resource shifts from the non-mineral to the mineral sectors. The co-ordination and regulation of direct foreign participation is governed by the National Investment Development Authority (NIDA), although proposals were tabled in 1989 and 1990 for a new Foreign Investment Act, aimed at streamlining the foreign investment process and outlining the preferred and proscribed sectors of the economy. Missing from the Act is any clear policy on foreign participation in privatization; evidence from the first phase of the programme is that foreign participation is welcomed, and since many of the SOEs not totally government-owned are joint ventures with foreign companies, it is inevitable that they will continue to play a leading role in privatization as they will be the only ones capable of mobilizing the resources to acquire the equity. The tensions that this inevitably creates in terms of the political objectives of the privatization programme have added impetus to the development of a capital market, and it is to this issue that we now turn.

10.5 Capital market constraints to privatization

The development of a local capital market (stock exchange) has been at the forefront of PNG supply-side policies for quite some time,[21] and is symbiotically linked to privatization in the mind of the government. Privatization, it is felt, will be accelerated by the presence of a capital market, while capital market development will be stimulated by the privatization of government companies. In any assessment, there are three elements to consider. The first is the savings potential or absorptive capacity of the private sector, the second the question of the supply of equity, and the third the structure of the market. We shall deal with each in turn.

Background to the capital market initiative

A number of PNG-based public companies are already listed in Australia (see Table 10.8), dominated by the two largest mining and prospecting companies, Bougainville Copper Ltd and Ok Tedi Mining Corp. In addition, there is a small over-the-counter market, providing both primary and secondary trading facilities, but both are extremely rudimentary, unregulated and very thin. Since 1979 there have been a small number of primary issues (Table 10.9),

Table 10.8   *Papua New Guinea companies listed in Australia (1986)*

Company	Issued Capital (A$m.)
ANG Holdings Ltd	2.3
Austpac Gold N.L.	15.3
Bougainville Copper Ltd	401.0
Ok Tedi Mining Corp.	175.0
City Resources Ltd	42.8
Collins and Leahy Ltd	4.2
Dylup Investment Corp	2.3
Elf Acquitaine Ltd	16.3
Farmset Ltd	0.3
Foxwell Ltd	16.3
Keela-Wee Exploration Ltd	3.6
Koitaki Plantation Ltd	0.9
Niugini Mining Ltd	7.4
Oil Search Ltd	17.4
Pacific Arc Ltd	6.3
Placer Pacific Ltd	180.0
Steamships Trading Co.	15.5

Source: IFC (1986).

Table 10.9   *Share listings 1979–83 (K000)*

Company	Date	Issued	Take-up	Underwriter
Credit Corporation[a]	1979–85	29,805	21,939	None
Ramu Sugar Ltd	1979	25,000	20,460	None
Post Courier Merchant	1979	2,400	1,647	Offshore
Westpac	1980	450	450	None
Burns Philp (PNG) Ltd	1981	2,000		
Banque Indosuez	1983	1,550	1,530	RIFL
Niugini Lloyds	1983	1,530	1,530	RIFL
Kumul Kopi	1984	1,500	1,500	RIFL

Source: IFC (1986).

a) Three share issues.

the success of which has been mixed. The most successful listings have been in the two new overseas banks, Niugini Lloyds and Banque Indosuez, and Burns Philp (Papua New Guinea) Ltd (a long-established private Australian trading company).

The secondary market is significantly less well developed, although the companies which have handled the primary issues also provide market-making facilities in the secondary market. Only one company, however, Kina Securities, is an explicit market-maker providing 'dial-up' access to the Sydney Stock Exchange, and acting as local agent for a major Australian broking companies. The Investment Corporation provides some secondary trading to unit holders in the Investment Corporation Fund (see section 10.2 above), and a number of Australian companies maintain offshore trading links with Papua New Guinea. Trading volumes are extremely light, however.[22]

Savings capacity

We noted at the beginning of this chapter that the economy of PNG is very fractured and that only an estimated 10% of the population function within the
monetary economy. Within this economy aggregate gross domestic savings
averaged only 14% of GDP during the 1980s, and, as with Malawi, low rural
incomes mean that the bulk of household savings are for consumption-smoothing
purposes only. The IFC's 1986 Report suggests that, of the 200,000 taxpayers in
PNG, approximately 30,000 hold shares, but the vast majority do so through
payroll deduction schemes with the ICF. Active individual shareholders are thus
estimated to number about 13,000, plus some proportion of the large expatriate
community, capable in total of mobilizing some K40m. per annum.

The majority of investable savings are thus concentrated in a small number of
enterprises and financial institutions, in particular the pension funds. However,
these institutions adopt a cautious investment policy, preferring to hold the bulk
of their assets in government bonds and bank deposits, which, given PNG's
relatively tight monetary policy, pay high real rates of return (Table 10.10). Thus
the available pool of savings which may realistically be diverted towards new
equity investment is small.

Table 10.10 *Investments 1985 and 1988 (%)*

Institution	Equities 1985	1988	Property 1985	1988	Govt Securities 1985	1988	Term Deposits 1985	1988
Pension funds	15	14	22	12	36	21	21	45
Insurance companies	12	11	24	9	5	10	57	67
MVIT	5	8	0	2	0	10	95	80
TOTAL	13	12	19	10	26	18	39	55

Source: IFC (1986).

The supply of equities

Initial estimates of the number of firms listing on a PNG stock exchange were
highly optimistic. The IFC identified 271 potential listed companies, 20% of
which they expected to list (Table 10.11). With an average capitalization of
K2m. per company this provided an estimated initial market capitalization
of K100m.

Even to achieve this level of listings a number of concessions were considered
necessary. These included: tax breaks (a lower marginal rate was discussed for
listed companies); preferential access to money markets; and preferential access
to government contracting, for locally listed companies. In addition, there is also
a clear role for privatization. The IFC Report made the following recommendation (p. 27, para. 5.19):

> Should a programme to establish a stock exchange be initiated in Papua New Guinea,
> it clearly would be desirable for the Government to include a privatization policy,
> whereby companies would be earmarked for public distribution according to a pre-
> arranged schedule that takes into account such factors as the receptivity of the market,
> the size of the company, and its financial condition and management.

Market regulation and structure

At present the over-the-counter market is virtually unregulated, and there are no
provisions in the companies legislation to provide for the regulation of trade in
equity. There are no disclosure guidelines for the primary market; secondary

Table 10.11 *Potential listings on PNG Stock Exchange*

Companies already listed in Australia	16
Non-Australian public companies	23
Private companies	10
State-owned enterprises	4
Total	53

Source: IFC, 1986.

market prices are rarely published; there is a lack of supervision of secondary market activities; and there are no facilities for investor protection. Two new market structures have been considered: first, the establishment of an independent stock exchange in PNG, which would create its own legislation, dealing and operating rules; second, the possibility of an affiliation with the Sydney Stock Exchange, to increase the scope of potential demand and achieve credibility for the exchange and increased investor confidence. This would have dual listing through the creation of an affiliate along the lines of the second-board regional exchanges in Adelaide, Hobart and Brisbane.

Overall assessment
Though the IFC presented a cautiously optimistic picture in 1986, there are reasons to doubt the rapid development of a capital market. First, it will only function if there is a reasonable level of speculative investment by the players, and this is unlikely to come from domestic investors. Amongst potential investors, the main institutions are likely to be quite risk-averse, and, the smaller private investor sector even more so. Judging by experience elsewhere, small investors will respond to 'safe' investments – e.g. equity issues by commercial banks, or to investments which are greatly underpriced or underwritten. If the government's objective is to achieve asset transfer via high-profile share sales, this route is possible, but, as was argued in Chapter 5, it is unlikely to provide the dynamism required for sustainable capital market development. Despite the above analysis, however, the government remains of the opinion that public sector divestiture is a profitable means of developing the local capital market.

10.6 Conclusions

The story of privatization in Papua New Guinea is in some ways very similar to that in Malaŵi (see Chapter 13). Faced with an extremely narrow non-traditional sector, the governments have looked to privatization as a means of stimulating the private sector and in the process acting as a catalyst for the development of the financial sector, in particular the capital market. One important difference between the two countries, however, is that Papua New Guinea is doing this in the context of an imminent mineral sector boom, with its attendant Dutch Disease effects. The cost disadvantages faced by the non-mineral sector, arising from the small size and diffuse location of the PNG economy, will inevitably be exacerbated by the mineral boom, and will make the prospect of effective privatization increasingly difficult. Moreover, given recent concerns about the distribution of income and the role of foreign capital in the PNG economy, any policy such as privatization will immediately be confronted with extremely sensitive political issues.

In the light of this the management of privatization to date has not been impressive. The implicit structures are those of industrialized economies, while those sales which have been brokered have been exemplified by poor management and shoddy organization, and no attempt has yet been made to develop the policy in a manner consistent with the objectives and structures throughout Papua New Guinea.

The irony is that, through luck and good judgement, the government has managed to institute a successful management structure for the CSAs, which, although criticized for its excessive reliance on financial rather than economic criteria for performance evaluation, has illustrated the capacity of a small government to manage and regulate the SOE sector successfully. If the same attention is focused on the activities and future sales of the other enterprises in the government portfolio, a low-profile but successful programme of privatization may be possible.

Notes

1. The Bougainville crisis has been a feature of PNG economic and social history since the eve of Independence in 1975 when local island leaders declared UDI and established the Republic of the North Solomons. Provincial government was established in Bougainville only in April 1976. Clashes have occurred sporadically since then, principally over the issue of land-ownership claims and compensation payments. Events reached a head in 1989 when the national government dispatched troops to contain an outbreak of arson. In May 1989 BCL was closed temporarily as the Bougainville Republican Army, under the leadership of Francis Ona, issued a declaration demanding K10bn compensation and the secession of the island. The owners of BCL (RTZ) closed the mine permanently in June 1989 following the declaration of a State of Emergency, laying off 2,000 workers. Fighting countinued throughout 1989 and 1990, reaching a peak in early 1990, with unconfirmed reports that Ona had been killed. A ceasefire was agreed in February 1990, but this failed and the national government imposed a further economic blockade. An interim agreement was reached in August 1990 allowing New Zealand-brokered talks to open in Honiara, from which a peace treaty emerged in January 1991. Plans are now under way for the reconstruction of the island, the re-opening of the mine and the installation of a multinational peace team.
2. Commerce, finance, construction and transport.
3. In addition the Provincial Government Development Corporations also have equity participation in a number of smaller enterprises. These are not included here because of an absence of data.
4. As we noted earlier, public sector management (PSM) *per se* has nothing to do with privatization.
5. NEC decision No. 163/83 (1983).
6. One of the main reasons for the turnaround of Air Niugini's performance was the highly successful management contract/training agreement with KLM Dutch Airways from 1983 to 1987, and the development of joint service agreements with Singapore International Airlines.
7. For example, labour productivity rose from 150 mwh/employee to 240 mwh/employee between 1983 and 1989.
8. There are a number of other smaller financial institutions, but most only maintain head-office facilities in Port Moresby, and occasionally one or two branches at Lae and Rabaul.
9. Known as the Development Bank New Guinea until 1984.
10. The key feature of an open-ended investment company is that the company stands ready to repurchase its shares at net asset value. Shares in open-ended companies trade only at net asset value between the holder and the company: there is thus no secondary market in such shares. This contrasts with the closed-end company which has a fixed share issue which trades in a secondary market above or below net asset value depending on investors' expectations. The closed-end company has no redemption obligation.
11. The fact that only a small proportion of the shares in the ICF portfolio are listed creates extensive valuation problems. While the listed securities are revalued daily, the revaluation of unlisted securities relies more on 'managerial' information, analysts' expectations and annual (but often delayed) audited accounts.
12. The financing of the mineral sector is carried out almost entirely by offshore institutions.
13. This proportion will rise as government takes up equity in the other new mineral projects (Porgera, etc.). As noted earlier, the government has instituted a consolidation of equity participation in the mineral sector through the MRDC.

14. The Centre for Privatization has been the main contractor for the implementation of the USAID privatization support programme.
15. There are no financial details of the sale available within the Investment Division, which is responsible for the management of asset sales. Representatives of the Division claimed that the sale had been managed within the top levels of the Ministry of Finance.
16. Representations on these issues have been made by both the Institute of National Affairs (PNG), and the PNG Chamber of Commerce.
17. Although as noted above the crisis in Bougainville has somewhat altered this position.
18. The decision specifically directed individual ministers to refrain from moving to privatize companies and statutory bodies which come directly under them.
19. Interview with the authors, March 1990.
20. National Statistical Office, *Bulletin on Secondary Industries*, 1989.
21. Two major reports have been commissioned on the issue, one by the IFC in 1986 (the Robbins Report) and one by Daewoo Securities in 1989. The Commonwealth Secretariat are also in the process of revising the companies and securities legislation to accommodate a stock exchange initiative if and when a decision is made to proceed.
22. The IFC (1986) reported that there had been no trading at all in two of the listings, Westpac and Burns Philp (Papua New Guinea) Ltd between their issue and 1986.

11
SRI LANKA

11.1. Introduction

The economic history of Sri Lanka has been dominated by the twin objectives of poverty eradication and the reduction of unemployment, but, while achievement of the former has been relatively successful, it has been at the cost of sustainable macroeconomic performance. By the 1980s the economy was severely out of balance. The budget deficit was over 12% and the current account deficit almost 9% of GDP, while debt-service payments consumed almost 30% of export earnings. The origins of this parlous macroeconomic situation, which has been exacerbated by an increasingly protracted civil war in the north and east of the island, can be traced back to the early decades after Independence, and, in particular, to the period of centrally planned autarky from 1970 to 1977. The so-called '1977 Liberalizations' reversed these policies, but, though these measures have been relatively successful in stimulating output and employment in the private sector, the continued stagnation of the public sector has more than offset these gains. The country is currently undergoing a second wave of liberalization, and this time the focus is on public sector reform, central to which is the privatization of the large and inefficient state-owned enterprise sector.

Economic development to 1977

Rising unemployment in the 1950s and 1960s elicited strongly inward-looking economic policies aimed at agricultural self-sufficiency and import-substituting industrialization. Expansion of traditional subsistence agriculture[1] and state domination of the industrial sector characterized the economy during the three decades after Independence, and generated in their wake an extremely large and unwieldy public sector. The inward-looking stance in the agricultural sector, arising from over-valuation of the exchange rate and heavy taxation of export crops, saw a collapse in the production of Sri Lanka's mainstay exports of tea and rubber. In the industrial sector, the emphasis on import substitution, compounded latterly by the antagonism of Mrs Bandaranaike's government towards the private sector, led to a serious erosion of the economy's capital stock and caused private investment to slump. Capital flight and a managerial and entrepreneurial brain-drain undermined the capacity of the economy to function efficiently, and led to Sri Lanka's joining the ranks of the world's heavily aid-dependent economies. At the same time the public sector bureaucracy grew to unmanageable proportions and, as the World Bank noted, 'a whole generation of entrepreneurs grew to be more knowledgeable in the intricacies of the Government bureaucracy than of markets and consumer preferences' (World Bank, 1988a).

The macroeconomic impact of these developments was reflected principally in the budget deficit and the balance of payments (Table 11.1). The budget

Table 11.1 *Macroeconomic indicators (%)*

	1970–76	1977	1980	1981	1982	1983	1984	1985	1986	1987	1988	1989
Population growth	2.1	2.1	2.2	2.2	2.1	2.0	1.8	1.9	1.6	1.4	1.4	1.3
Real GDP growth	3.1	4.2	8.2	6.3	5.8	5.8	5.1	5.0	4.3	1.5	2.7	2.0
Share of manufacturing	18.0	23.1	17.7	16.2	14.4	14.0	14.9	14.7	15.2	16.0	15.4	15.3
Current account deficit	8.4	4.5	19.8	13.7	15.3	12.4	4.8	9.9	9.3	7.8	8.7	10.3
Budget deficit	6.1	4.6	18.3	12.5	14.2	10.8	6.7	9.5	12.2	11.1	15.6	12.5
Exchange rate (Rs/US$)	–	15.5	16.5	19.2	20.8	23.5	25.4	27.1	28.0	29.4	31.8	36.0
Gross domestic savings	–	15.5	14.0	14.1	15.4	16.7	21.7	13.9	14.4	15.5	14.4	10.7
Gross domestic investment	–	20.0	33.8	27.8	30.7	29.1	26.5	23.8	23.7	23.3	23.1	21.0
External debt/GDP	–	50.0	48.0	52.0	60.0	59.0	51.0	60.0	62.0	67.0	71.0	72.4
Debt-service ratio	–	13.5	17.0	19.5	21.9	24.2	17.6	22.5	26.7	27.6	28.9	24.4
Terms of trade	114.6	152.9	100.0	89.7	89.9	101.9	118.4	99.4	96.6	95.7	–	–

Source: World Bank, *World Tables*; Central Bank of Sri Lanka.

deficit, swollen by the cost of capital-intensive investment and by transfers to the unprofitable SOE sector, rose to 14% of GDP by 1977. Concurrently, the current account deficit also increased, from an average of around 5% of GDP in the 1960s to over 10% during the late 1970s and early 1980s, while the persistent over-valuation of the exchange rate reduced the competitiveness of non-traditional exports, and increased the cost of imported capital goods for the capital-intensive industrial sector.

The 1977 liberalizations and beyond
The collapse of Mrs Bandaranaike's Sri-Lankan Freedom Party in 1977 represented a watershed in the country's economic orientation. President Jayawardene had fought the election on a manifesto of reducing state domination of the economy. The 1977 budget therefore devalued the rupee and introduced a managed float for the exchange rate, and the removal of quantitative restrictions on imports and the decontrol of domestic prices and interest rates were also instituted. The immediate effect was a dramatic growth in private sector activity, especially in the manufacturing sector which grew at approximately 10% per annum from 1977 to 1988, compared to public sector manufacturing output which declined over the same period. Similarly the agricultural output of private estates grew rapidly over the period, while that of the public sector estates stagnated. In the industrial sector trade liberalization has proceeded at a steady pace since 1977 and has seen a significant reduction in effective protection across a wide range of tradable goods (see section 11.4 below). Trade liberalization has been supported by the creation of the Free Trade Zone in Colombo in 1979 and the establishment of the Greater Colombo Economic Commission, both of which have aimed to stimulate the export of non-traditional goods.

Recent economic developments
Despite the re-orientation of the economy since 1977, macroeconomic conditions remained precarious. Though growth continued at around 4–5% per annum during the 1980s, the fiscal and external deficits averaged 9.5% and 9.9% of GDP respectively, putting upward pressure on the domestic price level. Unemployment remained stubbornly high at 14% of the labour force, and was identified as one of the contributory factors in the current civil war which broke out in 1983. The civil war depressed investment levels and capital inflows (especially from tourism), while at the same time military expenditure rose rapidly, accounting for almost 5% of GDP by 1989. In 1986 the government announced a major stabilization programme which was later supported by an IMF Structural Adjustment Facility and extensive adjustment finance from the World Bank and other donors. In addition

to continued stabilization, the programme identified three particular supply-side adjustment measures: tariff and industrial policy reform; civil service rationalization and the enhancement of public sector efficiency; and SOE reform and privatization.

The continued security problems in Jaffna, compounded by the concern that the civil unrest has been fanned by the growing unemployment and poverty, has meant a much slower implementation of the reform programme than was expected. Rationalization of expenditure has not yet been achieved. The revenue base has continued to be eroded as a result of the security situation, while expenditure has been increasing owing to further military expenditure plus the high costs of poverty alleviation programmes.[2] By July 1989, fiscal crisis was imminent and, with civil unrest once again at a peak, the government was forced into dramatic stabilization efforts. The rupee was devalued against the US dollar, resulting in a 20% fall since December 1988; the Jana Saviya income-transfer programme was severely cut back and subsidies on wheat and fertilizers dramatically curtailed; and the public investment programme was reduced by almost 30%. Against this background, privatization emerged as one of the key supply-side measures in the government's attempt to maintain the momentum of the 1977 liberalization programme. Before considering the evolution of privatization policy we provide a brief survey of the SOE sector.

11.2 State-owned enterprises – structure and performance

11.2.1 The growth of the SOE sector

The SOE sector grew steadily during the 1950s and 1960s, with the nationalization of foreign-owned enterprises in the plantation, transport, petroleum and financial sectors. The most rapid growth, however, followed the 1970 general election victory of Mrs Bandaranaike's Sri Lankan Freedom Party. The subsequent enactment of the Government Business Undertakings Act and the Land Reform Act in 1971 paved the way for the creation of a large number of Government-Owned Business Undertakings (GOBUs), and accelerated the process of nationalization in the plantation sector. Central to this strategy was an emphasis on output and employment rather than efficiency, and on protection rather than competition. Private sector development was severely constrained by both the high level of protection afforded to public sector enterprises, and also by the always-present threat of expropriation by the state. By 1977 there were more than 250 SOEs covering all areas of economic activity. The 1977 liberalization programme brought a dramatic halt to the proliferation of SOEs, although a number, significantly in the financial sector, have been created since.

11.2.2 The size and structure of the SOE sector

Although no official statistics are available on the contribution of the sector to overall GDP, a number of studies suggest that it is in the region of 20%,[3] while national accounts data indicate that the sector accounts in addition for approximately 35% of gross fixed capital formation.[4] These figures compare with average figures for developing countries of 11% and 28% respectively (Nair and Filippides, 1988). The sector employed approximately 698,000 people in 1988, representing almost 40% of formal sector employment and 13% of total employment.

The impact of the sector on the central government budget is also significant, with transfers to SOEs accounting for well over 20% of expenditure throughout

Table 11.2 *Flow of funds to the SOE sector (Rsm.)*

	1980	1981	1982	1983	1984	1985	1986	1987	1988	1989
Current transfers to SOEs	1,582.7	363.4	845.4	1,275.0	1,081.5	751.3	1,936.1	1,264.3	2,140.4	1,919.4
Capital transfers to SOEs	6,086.0	7,174.0	10,653.0	10,422.0	13,681.0	13,441.0	14,874.0	11,198.0	9,683.0	9,429.0
Net lending to SOEs	806.7	402.6	627.4	657.4	382.0	751.5	2,170.1	2,705.4	4,794.9	6,615.3
Gross lending	806.7	569.3	718.1	800.6	901.3	997.2	2,671.2	3,159.3	5,091.8	7,160.0
Less: Repayments	–	(166.7)	(90.7)	(143.2)	(519.3)	(245.7)	(501.1)	(453.9)	(296.9)	(544.7)
Interest and dividends from SOEs	132.3	75.4	144.3	75.4	306.4	434.1	526.4	113.3	47.2	–
TOTAL FLOW OF FUNDS TO SOEs	8,475.4	7,940.0	12,125.8	12,354.4	15,144.5	14,943.8	18,980.2	15,167.7	16,618.3	17,963.7
Memorandum Items										
FoF as % of total expenditure	30.29	28.34	36.18	31.17	31.66	27.06	32.06	23.74	22.91	17.44
FoF as % of budget deficit	69.75	75.49	87.07	96.17	144.00	95.30	104.26	88.80	59.10	62.80
FoF as % of GDP	12.74	9.34	12.22	10.16	9.85	9.20	10.58	7.71	7.27	6.77

Source: Central Bank of Sri Lanka, *Review of the Economy 1988.*

Note: 1989 figures are budget estimates.

the 1980s (Table 11.2). Attempts in recent years to curtail such transfers have been relatively successful. Transfers remain large, accounting for over 100% of the budget deficit (10.6% of GDP) in 1986, and, even with the cutbacks in 1989, were still equivalent to 62% of the expected budget deficit.

By comparison, the external debt exposure of the SOE sector is moderate, representing only 6% of the total debt outstanding in 1989[5] (Table 11.3); and whilst the external debt to GDP ratio has risen from 62% in 1986 to 65% in 1989, the SOE share has fallen from almost 6% of GDP to less than 4% over the same period. Significantly, however, the bulk of SOE external debt is to commercial creditors at terms that are much less concessional than the debt incurred by the central government. The implicit grant element incurred by SOEs is also low, being approximately 5.5% for debt excluding that incurred by Air Lanka, and −12.33% when Air Lanka debt is included.[6] This compares with an all-creditor average grant element on new commitments from 1980 to 1987 of over 40%, for the government as a whole (World Bank, *World Debt Tables*, 1989).

The Public Enterprises Division of the Ministry of Finance identified 279 SOEs in existence at the end of 1989. Table 11.4 summarizes their distribution.

The majority are public corporations established either under the State

Table 11.3 *SOE external debt (Rsm.)*

	1986	1987	1988	1989
CENTRAL GOVERNMENT	88,759.8	112,805.3	125,552.4	155,126.7
− Mulilateral	24,547.7	31,118.4	36,088.2	47,392.7
− Bilateral	53,460.4	70,021.0	78,790.3	97,452.7
− Commercial	10,236.2	11,140.9	10,334.6	10,088.7
− Suppliers' credits	515.5	525.0	339.3	192.6
SOE (GUARANTEED)	8,496.9	9,702.6	8,009.2	9,691.9
− Multilateral	1,090.8	1,090.6	1,077.1	1,197.3
− Bilateral	0.0	0.0	0.0	0.0
− Commercial	7,400.6	8,606.1	6,925.7	8,494.6
− Suppliers' Credits	5.5	5.9	6.4	0.0
SOE (NON-GUARANTEED)	749.0	328.8	288.3	340.1
− Multilateral	0.0	0.0	0.0	0.0
− Bilateral	0.0	0.0	0.0	0.0
− Commercial	741.5	320.2	278.9	338.0
− Suppliers' credits	7.5	8.6	9.4	2.1
TOTAL	98,005.7	122,836.7	133,849.9	165,158.7
− Multilateral	25,638.5	32,209.0	37,165.3	48,590.0
− Bilateral	53,460.4	70,021.0	78,790.3	97,452.7
− Commercial	18,378.3	20,067.2	17,539.2	18,921.3
Suppliers' credits	528.5	539.5	355.1	194.7
DEBT SERVICE	11,658.0	14,539.0	17,662.0	0.0
− Principal	6,940.0	9,623.0	11,298.0	
− Interest	4,718.0	4,916.0	6,364.0	
Memorandum Items:				
External debt as % of GDP	61.90	66.10	70.40	65.30
Debt-service ratio	26.20	27.50	29.60	37.60
SOE debt as % of GDP	5.84	5.40	4.36	3.97

Source: Central Bank of Sri Lanka, *Review of the Economy 1988*.

Table 11.4 *Sectoral distribution of SOEs*

Sector	Public Corporations	Public Companies	GOBU	Total
1. Regulation	28	3	—	31
2. Human resources	50	1	—	51
3. Infrastructure	13	6	—	19
4. Commercial	69	66	10	145
5. Banking/finance	13	6	—	19
6. In liquidation	5	—	9	14
	178	82	19	279

Industries Corporations Act of 1957, or, in many cases, under specific statute. All public corporations fall under the aegis of the Finance Act of 1971, and are accountable to the Ministry of Finance. Public companies are enterprises established by the government in terms of the Companies Act, or converted from Corporations or GOBUs in terms of Act No. 23 of 1987 (see section 11.3 below). Generally the equity of a public company is held by a public corporation, although in a number of cases it is held directly by the Secretary to the Treasury. Government-Owned Business Undertakings (GOBUs) are the acquisitions through nationalization carried out by the government during the 1971–7 period, and are found solely in the commercial sector. GOBUs have an anomalous identity, the most notable feature being the absence of any legal persona in terms of company law.

The majority of SOEs are in tradeable sectors (commerce and banking and finance), and it is these sectors, as well as the infrastructure sector, that represent the focus for the privatization and SOE reform process. A detailed breakdown of the 145 commercial sector enterprises is given in Table 11.5:

Table 11.5 *Subsectoral distribution of commercial SOEs*

Sector	Public Corporations	Public Companies	GOBU	Total
Agriculture	15	2	—	17
Civil engineering	3	3	—	6
Energy	2	2	1	5
Manufacturing	16	24	6	46
Media	3	1	1	5
Other services	7	25	1	33
Road transport	11	—	—	11
Trading	12	9	1	22
	69	66	10	145

They are concentrated in manufacturing and services, and it is in these subsectors that the bulk of the public companies and GOBUs are found. As shown in Table 11.6, the government tends to wholly own SOEs, either directly or indirectly through another SOE. Only in a few cases does it hold a partial shareholding, and even then only in 7 cases is this a minority holding. This structure sets Sri Lanka apart from many other developing countries, and in part reflects the nature of growth of the sector, primarily through 'green-field' operations but also as a result of compulsory acquisition under the 1971 Acquisition of Business Undertakings Act and the 1975 compulsory purchase legislation. Rarely has the government entered into joint ventures with the private sector or foreign partners.[7]

Table 11.6 *Government ownership of SOEs*

Sector	Direct (100%)	Indirect (100%)	Majority (>50%)	Minority (<50%)
1. Regulation	28	3	–	–
2. Human resources	50	1	–	–
3. Infrastructure	13	6	–	–
4. Commercial	97	35	7	6
5. Banking & finance	12	3	3	1
	200	48	10	7

Detailed financial data on individual SOE performance for the period prior to 1977 are sparse, with comprehensive firm-level data only available from 1984 onwards. Table 11.7 provides summary data aggregated for the sector as a whole. Despite relatively tight control on employment, the aggregate rate of profit has shown a dramatic decrease from 1984 to 1988. While much of this decline has been caused by the worsening security situation, it is noticeable that the deterioration in performance is most marked in those subsectors where enterprises are not exposed to competition (i.e. the regulation, human resources, and infrastructure subsectors). Here the weighted average rate of profit fell from 2.41% in 1984 to –18.42% in 1988. The commercial enterprises which generally operate in a somewhat more competitive environment experienced a less dramatic fall in profits from 5% in 1984 to –0.54% in 1988, while banking and finance enterprises saw a rise in profits from 7% to 9.7% over the same period. Labour productivity, as proxied by sales per employee and profit per employee, shows a similar downward trend.

These aggregate figures do, however, mask a wide variety of performance. On the basis of pre-tax profit, there are a number of particularly poor performers including: the National Water Supply and Drainage Board (loss in 1988: Rs400m.); both state-owned tea plantations (combined loss in 1988: Rs820m.); Lanka Cement Ltd (loss in 1988: Rs100m.); Pelewatte Sugar Corporation (loss in 1988: Rs255m.); Sri Lanka Transport Boards (combined loss in 1988: Rs635m.); and Ceylon Shipping Corporation (loss in 1988: Rs374m.). Balancing these loss-making enterprises, however, are a number of high-performing SOEs including: Ceylon Mineral Sands Corporation (profit in 1988: Rs300m.); Sri Lanka Cement Corporation (profit in 1988: Rs28m.); Ceylon Glass Company (profit in 1988: Rs58m.); Lanka Milk Foods (profit in 1988: Rs60m.); Ceylon Electricity Board (profit in 1988: Rs1,135m.); Sri Lanka Port Authority (profit in 1988: Rs473m.).

Table 11.7 *SOE summary of financial performance (Rsm.)*

	1984	1985	1986	1987	1988
Sales	66,589.6	65,714.5	67,056.7	75,265.9	80,894.3
Net pre-tax income/profit	3,475.3	1,606.8	2,088.3	751.1	(197.8)
Cap. expenditure	18,057.6	20,027.3	16,970.3	15,741.2	16,517.7
Long-term liabilities	27,984.5	32,278.4	39,348.7	46,698.6	51,553.1
Long-term assets	157,403.4	180,761.1	199,132.1	227,328.3	265,094.7
Employment	689,861	689,453	683,248	695,650	693,031
Profit rate (%)	5.22	2.45	3.11	1.00	−0.24
Return on assets (%)	2.21	0.89	1.05	0.33	−0.07
Sales per employee	96,526.1	95,314.0	98,144.0	108,195.1	116,725.4
Profit per employee	5,037.7	2,330.5	3,056.4	1,079.7	(285.4)

Source: Ministry of Finance Public Enterprises Division.

It is noticeable that both the profitable and the loss-making enterprises are spread widely across all sectors, and no sector can be regarded as either unambiguously unprofitable or profitable. Similarly there is no clear relationship between profitability and corporate structure (i.e. it is not clear that public companies systematically perform better than public corporations).

A more comprehensive review compiled by the Ministry of Finance gives a 10-year series for a small sample of manufacturing sector companies (see Table 11.8). Particularly noticeable is the real value-added growth which from 1985 to 1987 managed to exceed real growth for the economy as a whole, in part due to improved labour productivity. However, the recovery was accompanied by a large rise in the debt–equity ratio, with firms increasing their leverage from 0.29 in 1978 to 1.16 in 1988, which, if continued, may put in question the sustainability of the profit improvement.

Though this evidence indicates some improvements in the manufacturing subsector, SOEs remain relatively inefficient (Table 11.7). For example, against an average utilization rate for the private sector of 75%, capacity utilization in the public sector has rarely exceeded 60%, with only the petroleum sector producing at near to full capacity. Similarly, indicators of operational efficiency in the transport sector indicate declining numbers of passengers and freight carried on domestic public transport systems (i.e. road, rail, and sea), and sharply rising unit costs. It was against this background that the focus of policy shifted towards reform measures for the public sector, and in particular the formulation of a privatization programme.

11.3 Privatization policy and experience

The explicit commitment to privatization dates only from 1987, although a number of important steps towards it were taken during the previous decade under the auspices of the Parliamentary Committee on Public Enterprises (COPE). The main developments were the creation, within the Public Enterprise Division of the Ministry of Finance, of a public enterprise audit and financial monitoring system, and the preparation of legislation to provide a unified legal framework for the SOE sector. In addition, a number of line ministries embarked on specific enterprise reform measures, some of which led to eventual divestiture (World Bank, 1988a). In 1983, the Ministry of Industries attempted to sell 40% of the Sri Lanka Rubber Manufacturing Company to its employees, and later to the general public. At that time there was no formal stock exchange (see section 11.5), and the issue was handled by the Colombo Brokers Association. The share issue met with very little response, however, with only 0.05% being taken up by the employees, yielding a mere Rs17,000 (US$425) to the government. In view of this lack of response, no further public listing was sought for the company. Concurrently the same ministry undertook the divestiture of elements of the Co-operative Wholesale Enterprise (CWE), a large and profitable conglomerate holding company with a turnover of approximately Rs4bn, and a workforce in excess of 4,500. Joint-stock companies were created to take over CWE operations in the areas of computer services, printing, motor distribution, and milk powder packaging. Initial plans envisaged the creation of subsidiary companies, followed by share issues to employees and the general public. In the case of three of the subsidiaries, Sathosa Computer Services Ltd, Sathosa Printers Ltd, and Sathosa Motors Ltd, however, no shares have been sold and 100% of the equity is held by the government through CWE. Shares in Lanka Milk Foods Ltd, on the other hand, were issued in 1983, and again in 1986. Public take-up in both cases was very poor. The first public issue of Rs2.6m. worth of shares (43% of the total equity), which was,

Table 11.8 *Financial performance of 15 selected manufacturing corporations*

	1978	1979	1980	1981	1982	1983	1984	1985	1986	1987
Value-added (Rsm.)	613,367	755,767	1,186,734	1,141,557	1,210,636	1,346,369	1,451,571	1,711,011	1,930,467	2,235,915
Employees	30,210	31,550	37,390	36,512	36,644	35,629	34,430	32,206	30,761	32,265
Cost of employment (Rsm.)	257,523	307,848	392,322	488,048	570,441	649,023	726,961	793,069	830,794	872,612
Op. profit/assets (%)	8.0	8.0	13.0	7.0	6.0	5.0	4.0	7.0	12.0	15.0
Value-added/assets (%)	23.0	24.0	31.0	28.0	26.0	28.0	29.0	33.0	35.0	40.0
Debt-equity ratio	29.0	24.0	24.0	36.0	46.0	78.0	105.0	118.0	136.0	116.0
Real profit/emp. (Rs)	7,214.0	6,238.0	7,413.0	2,819.0	2,324.0	1,570.0	883.0	1,803.0	3,006.0	2,974.0
Real VA/emp. (Rs)	20,303.0	17,897.0	16,981.0	11,519.0	9,437.0	8,227.0	6,704.0	8,302.0	8,816.0	8,169.0
GDP deflator	100.0	116.0	137.0	165.0	187.0	214.0	251.0	253.0	267.0	295.0
Real VA growth (%)	—	6.50	32.88	-20.17	-6.62	-2.91	-7.86	16.85	6.97	4.63
Real wage growth (%)	—	-1.06	-9.00	5.72	2.55	2.16	-0.94	15.62	3.99	-9.54
Real VA/emp. growth (%)	—	-11.85	-5.12	-32.16	-18.07	-12.82	-18.51	23.84	6.19	-7.34
Labour prod. growth (%)	—	-10.79	3.88	-37.88	-20.62	-14.98	-17.57	8.22	2.20	2.20
Real GDP growth (%)	—	6.30	5.81	5.77	5.08	5.00	5.10	5.00	4.35	1.50

Source: Ministry of Finance Public Enterprises Division.

again, handled through the Colombo Brokers Association, resulted in a take-up of only 12,000 shares (4.6%) and raised Rs120,000. The second issue was not subscribed for at all, and thus CWE retained 95% of the equity in the company as at 1989.

The Ministry of Industries' third divestiture attempt during this period, that of three tile factories, was similarly disappointing. A decision was made in the mid-1980s to sell the factories Noorani Tiles, Shaw Industries, and Vijaya Tile Works, following a period of extremely poor financial performance. All three had been nationalized under the 1971 Business Undertakings Act, and at the time of the decision they were all run by a so-called 'Competent Authority' (i.e. direct management by civil servants without a management board). Though the decision was made to sell the factories in the mid-1980s, the sale has not been finalized, and its details are not known.[8] However, it is known that the factories are currently non-operational but that local buyers have been identified.

In contrast, the Ministry of Textiles has been more successful with its reform programme for the National Textile Corporation. This has involved a programme of technical and financial restructuring for four textile mills, leading to their privatization. The eventual sale of the mills is due to occur from 1990 to 1992; the programme is discussed in greater detail below.

Finally, this period also witnessed important reforms in the transport sector, with the liberalization in 1979 of the bus system, which had been the monopoly of the nationalized Sri Lanka Road Transport Board since 1958. Entry to the industry is subject to government licence, but once in private operators have full freedom over routes, scheduling and fares. Competition is relatively strong, with private sector operators now controlling over 50% of the market. The retention of partial subsidization of public sector fares and government funding of losses by the SLTB (and the regional transport boards) has, however, distorted the market, resulting in excess capacity on a few profitable urban routes and excess demand on the protected, and subsidized, routes operated by the SLTB. Nevertheless, the government is committed to the gradual phasing-out of the final subsidies over time, and thus an efficient and competitive bus sector seems likely to emerge.

Notwithstanding these initiatives, even as late as 1985 the government still took a cautious stance on asset transfer as an element in the overall SOE reform programme, with the Minister of Finance stating in his 1985 budget speech:

> I want to make it clear that my remarks are only directed towards the improvement of the efficiency of the public corporations . . . In countries such as ours, the private sector is not developed enough to undertake heavy investments, especially in infrastructure. I do not believe that there is any magic in the private sector. The magic lies only in management.

11.3.1 The development of privatization structures 1987–90

The sentiments expressed in 1985 were soon revised, however, following the announcement in November 1986 of a three-year World Bank adjustment programme and the creation, in May 1987, of the Presidential Commission on Privatization (PCOP) by President Jayawardene.[9] The Commission, which consisted of both senior civil servants and representatives of the private sector, took over much of the work of COPE. Its first action was to establish guidelines for the privatization of SOEs, the prime requirement being that SOEs could be considered for privatization only when they were profitable: the rationalization of enterprises prior to sale was thus treated as a separate aspect of the SOE reform programme (see below). In addition, candidates for privatization did not include those in politically sensitive sectors, and had to be spread across ministries so as to retain 'Cabinet-level harmony'. In the light of earlier privatization initiatives by the Ministry of Industries, this firm orientation of the privatization programme towards the currently profitable commercial sector represented an attempt both to accelerate the sale of assets and to establish a reputation amongst potential investors as to the government's commitment to the policy.

A central element in establishing the framework for privatization was the enactment, in May 1987, of the 'Conversion of Government Owned Business Undertakings into Public Corporations Act, No. 22 of 1987' and the 'Conversion of Public Corporations or Government Owned Business Undertakings into Public Companies Act, No. 23 of 1987'. These Acts provided for the establishment of a statutorily independent corporate body to take over the operations of a GOBU or public corporation, and in particular for the transfer of the company's share capital to the Secretary of the Treasury. Significantly they also provided for the transfer of employees to the company, with the provision of compensation determined by the Cabinet for all those not offered such employment. By March 1990, Cabinet approval had been granted for the conversion of 24 GOBUs and public corporations, including all the remaining operational GOBUs and a number of the public corporations being considered for privatization.

In late 1989 the PCOP was disbanded, and its functions transferred to the newly created Public Investment Management Board (PIMB), established with World Bank support under the auspices of the Ministry of Finance, and consisting of the same members as its predecessor. However, whilst the PCOP undertook the whole range of privatization issues from selection of candidates to their eventual divestiture, PIMB's main focus was on the financial and operational restructuring of the manufacturing SOEs, a process referred to as 'commercialization', and the creation of an appropriate enabling environment for their privatization. In keeping with the thrust of its work, the PIMB was itself converted into a public company, the Public Investment Management Company (PIMC). In addition to the commercialization of each SOE,[10] PIMC will enter into Agency or Shareholder Agreements with enterprises (depending on whether the government is a majority or minority shareholder), designed to stipulate the obligations and requirements of the tripartite relationship between the PIMC, the company, and the government, covering such areas as reporting and audit requirements for the government, agreed performance targets for the company, and the evaluation of commercial and non-commercial activities.

The actual privatization of SOEs is, however, the responsibility of the Commercialization Division (CD) of the Ministry of Finance.[11] CD has been the main government institution in the privatization programme in Sri Lanka, principally through its function as secretariat to the Presidential Commission on Privatization/'People-ization', and as the implementing agency for the conversion of GOBUs and public corporations into public companies. It is also responsible for maintaining the link between the work of the PIMB/PIMC, the line ministries and the other agencies involved in privatization.[12]

11.3.2 Privatizations 1987–90

By mid-1990 only two sales had been completed, although a comprehensive 'pipeline' had been drawn up, and plans were under way to finalize the sale of 10 other enterprises by early 1991. This section reviews the two completed sales and the 'pipeline', while the following section discusses the 'commercialization' and preparation for sale of the Sri Lanka Telecommunications Department.

United Motors Lanka Limited

The sale of United Motors Limited (UML) was an important milestone in the privatization programme in Sri Lanka. Not only was it the first sale under the explicit banner of privatization, but it was also the first divestiture handled by the Commercial Division. As a result, while it was instrumental in establishing a number of ground-rules which are likely to be adopted in subsequent privatizations, it also served to highlight a number of economic and legal constraints inherent in the privatization programme.

Background and selection. UML was incorporated as a private company in 1945 to distribute and service a range of imported vehicles. Following a period of relative profitability, the company was taken over in 1972 as a GOBU in terms of the Business Acquisition Act. Despite the depressed market environment during the 1972–7 period, UML survived on the strength of government contracts. Following liberalization in 1977, it consolidated its role as principal supplier to the government and gradually expanded by strengthening its dealership arrangement with the Mitsubishi Corporation of Japan. On the eve of sale in 1989 it was employing almost 600 staff, and made a net profit of Rs20m. Since 1985 it had contributed an average of Rs5m. per annum to government revenue.[13] In view of this strong financial performance, and the strength of its links with Mitsubishi, United Motors was selected by the Presidential Commission as the first company to be privatized.

The sale was carried out entirely by the Commercialization Division. Following the valuation of the company, CD established a new capital structure and prepared the Memoranda and Articles of Association. On 9 May 1989 the GOBU United Motors Limited was converted into a public company, United Motors Lanka Limited, in terms of Act No. 23 of 1987, with an authorized share capital of Rs100m., denominated in 10 million Rs10 shares, all held by the Secretary to the Treasury.

Offer for sale. Of the 10 million shares, 500,000 (5%) were offered at par to the Mitsubishi Motor Corporation,[14] raising a total of Rs5m., and a further 500,000 were reserved for employees of the company. This portion of the equity was not an ESS as such, but rather an *ad hoc* addition to the sale designed to offset the liability incurred by the new company for compensation payments arising from the termination of contracts with employees of the GOBU. Legislation designed to transfer this liability automatically to government had not been promulgated at the time of the sale, and these shares were therefore paid into a trust fund out of which future gratuities were to be paid.

The remaining 90% of the shares were offered for sale at par on the Colombo Securities Exchange[15] starting on 5 July 1989, at a time of severe security problems and in the middle of a transport strike. The government nevertheless went ahead with the sale[16] with the result that only 3.3 million shares were taken up by the public (and of this 75% was taken up by the two state-owned insurance companies), with some 5.7 million left with the underwriters, the majority of whom are in fact government-owned institutions. Thus in total the government realized net proceeds of approximately Rs95m. (US$2.25m.), and fully divested itself of the enterprise.

Shares in UMLL were quoted at Rs17.50 as at the end of 1990, and the company paid an interim dividend of 5%, with a final dividend of a further 7.5% for 1989/90. There was, however, virtually no trade in the shares from July 1989 to mid-1990, since the underwriters, who formed the majority shareholders in UMLL, agreed not to release shares on to the market pending a revision of the capital structure of the company (see below).

Assessment. The prospectus for UML stated (p. 19) that the primary objectives of the sale were:

> in keeping with the present Government programme, to 'people-ize' selected state enterprises and thereby achieve the following: (a) to encourage a widespread share ownership in the public, and (b) to introduce and encourage greater efficiency in commercial and economic operations of the enterprise which would be achieved by relieving the enterprise of the public sector constraints which often surround its operational activities and financial requirements, giving it greater flexibility to operate in a market oriented environment.

Though the sale resulted in the complete divestiture of the company (albeit principally to public sector underwriters), the extent to which it achieved its objectives is limited. The primary objective of 'people-ization' was clearly not achieved since approximately 63% of the shares remained in the hands of underwriting institutions, and a further 22% were held by the two state-owned insurance companies. In terms of the second objective of freeing the business from the constraints of the public sector, the extent to which this has been achieved is less clear. It is obviously too early for any significant changes to be identified, but indications suggest that the shareholders are satisfied with management performance,[17] and the first-year dividend of 12.5% on par, combined with the premium on the share price, suggests that financial performance was also satisfactory.[18] In the absence of detailed financial figures for the post-privatization period, it is however impossible to evaluate this issue further.

In a number of other respects, concerns can be raised about the sale. First, aside from the obvious issue of whether it was wise to continue with the sale during a time of such severe civil unrest, it seems that, despite the commitment to 'people-ization', the government failed to market the issue actively. The prospectus was regarded as bland and unattractive, and the extensive branch network of the state banks was used only passively in encouraging share subscriptions; there were no financial incentives for these agencies to market the offer to their clients, nor were schemes employed to attract new investors to the share issue. Second, the decision to issue all the capital of the company as equity rather than to gear it in terms of equity and debt was viewed by market participants as showing a poor understanding of the capital market. The view of investors (shared by the underwriters[19]) seems to have been that, if the government had increased the company's leverage by issuing only 50% of the capital as equity, the dividend yield per share would have been sufficient to attract more individual equity participation. This question is of particular importance in Sri Lanka where investors tend to discount future capital gains very heavily in favour of short-term dividend yields. Finally, though a certain tranche of the equity was reserved for employees, this was effectively funded by government in lieu of pension obligations: no effort seems to have been made to encourage employee share participation, despite the fact that such measures had proved very successful in other, well-publicized, privatizations in other developing countries.

National Textile Corporation (Thulhiriya Mill)
Thulhiriya textile mill is one of four GOBU mills owned by the government under the National Textile Corporation (NTC). The sale of the mill was the first step in the final phase of the reform package initiated in the mid-1980s.

Following the 1977 liberalizations, which *inter alia* lifted the ban on imported textiles, the four mills operated by NTC (Thulhiriya, Pugoda, Veyangoda, and Mattegama) found themselves increasingly uncompetitive relative to imported textiles. Obsolete capital stock and inefficient management contributed to the accumulation of large losses from 1977 onwards. Reform initiatives were spear-headed by the Ministry of Textiles, and consisted of three elements. The initial phase involved the negotiation of management contracts with three overseas textile firms: Tootals of the UK and Bombay Dyeing Ltd and Lakshmi Ltd from India. All these contracts were signed in mid-1980. Concurrently the NTC assumed all the outstanding debts of the four mills (approximately Rs570m.). Thulhiriya Mill showed a dramatic improvement in performance, with the Rs26m. loss in 1980 being replaced by consistent profits from 1983 onwards. The management con-tract and restructuring also led to a marked increase in capacity utilization, output and employment, which rose from 2,500 in 1980 to almost 4,000 by 1985.

The second phase of the reform programme was the conversion of the GOBU mills into public companies, Thulhiriya and Veyangoda Mills in 1989 and Mat-tegama and Pugoda in 1990. The third stage is the sale of the mills and the eventual closure of the NTC. Thulhiriya Mill was sold in October 1989 on a private basis to a Korean firm, Kabul Spinning & Textile Co., for Rs275m. (US$7.5m.). The proceeds, which accrued to the NTC, were then used to restructure the debt of Veyangoda Mill prior to its sale.

The sale of the three remaining mills was scheduled to occur in 1990, starting with the Pugoda Mill. It was valued at Rs260m., of which Rs160m. was to be con-verted into long-term debt in favour of the government, with the balance to be issued in the form of equity – 60% to the incumbent management (Lakshmi Ltd), and 40% through a public issue on the Colombo Stock Exchange. The sale had not occurred at the time of writing. The final stage of the textile mill privatization programme will come with the closure of the NTC. Proceeds from the sale of the mills will be used to meet outstanding employment liabilities of the corporation, whilst the government will continue to honour its 1984 commitment to write off progressively the outstanding debts of the corporation (estimated to be Rs326m. at the end of 1989).

As with the sale of United Motors, the sale of the Thulhiriya Mill is too recent to allow any comprehensive assessment of the direct effect of privatization. How-ever, the NTC sale has proceeded smoothly, although the entire privatization has been long in execution, with the eventual sales occurring more than 10 years after the reform programme began. During this period there has been a significant turn-around in the financial and operational performance of all the mills, due, in the main, to three factors. The first was the introduction of new (foreign) management in 1980, and the second the financial support of the debt conversion by NTC itself. It was, however, the combination of these two factors with the improvements in the market environment through broader liberalization measures (particularly through exchange-rate alignment) which elicited improvements in performance.

The privatization pipeline

By mid-1990, following the successful GOBU and public corporation conversion programme, which brought the majority of viable commercial enterprises to a point where divestiture is possible, the government had, with the active sup-port of both the World Bank and USAID, established an ambitious medium-term pipeline of commercial enterprises targeted for privatization (Table 11.9).

A number of features emerge from the table. The most striking feature of the pipeline is its size, and the number of public share issues expected in the first year. Despite the fact that since 1987 the government had succeeded in selling only two enterprises, it was still expecting to privatize seven in the second half of 1990 alone, and a further 12 in the following two years. In fact, none of the sales in the pipeline were implemented in the remainder of 1990. This was in part due to the persistent security crisis, but it also reveals an excessively optimistic view of the likely speed

Table 11.9 *Privatization pipeline, 1990–93: firm and tentative proposals*

Company	Proposed date of sale	Method of sale	Expected revenue[a] Rsm.	Net asset value Rsm.
FIRM				
Ceylon Oxygen	1990 QI	Public	60	285.6
ITN	1990 QI	Public	20	55.8
Pugoda Textile Mill	1990 QIII	Public/Private	100	368.1
State Distillers	1990 QIII	Public	100	388.0
Hunas Hotel	1990 QIII	Private		7.9
Hotel Buhari	1990 QIII	Private		7.4
State Trading (Export) Co.	1991 QI	Private		146.9
TENTATIVE				
Ceylon Oils & Fats				296.3
Milco Ltd				50.8
Colombo Commercial Co. (Engineering)				116.4
Colombo Commercial Co. (Fertilizers)				450.0
Colombo Commercial Co. (Tea Trading)				91.0
Cey Nor Ltd				46.5
Ceylon Manufacturers and Merchants Trading Co.				49.9
Heavyquip Co. Ltd				5.4
State Printing Corporation				119.0
State Trading (General) Corp.				205.2
Paranathan Chemicals[20]				
TOTAL				3,398.7

Source: Commercialization Division (as planned March 1990).

a) Estimated revenue yield to government from equity sales.

of implementation. More worrying is the fact that, despite the failure of the United Motors issue in 1989, and although the Securities Council advised the government in 1989 that the absorptive capacity of the market was approximately Rs50m. to Rs100m. per annum in new issues (see section 11.5), the pipeline envisaged a placement of Rs220m. during the second half of 1900.

As was discussed in Chapter 5, attempts to accelerate privatization beyond the absorptive capacity of the economy can be ultimately counter-productive. We deal with this issue in the Sri Lankan context in sections 11.4 and 11.5 below, but first we conclude this section by examining the potentially most ambitious of all the privatization initiatives so far in Sri Lanka, that of telecommunications.

The commercialization of Sri Lanka Telecommunications Department
The proposed privatization of telecommunications represents a quantum leap in the privatization programme, even in comparison with the ambitious pipeline outlined above. If it were to proceed, it would move the programme away from the sale of medium-sized enterprises operating in fairly competitive markets to the privatization of a monopolistic utility. This move immediately raises questions not only about the absorptive capacity of the private sector, but also about the capacity of the capital market to mobilize the requisite resources from the private sector, and about the regulation of the industry as a private sector operation.

However, although ultimately the Ministry of Finance envisages full privatization of the Telecommunications Department, this is only a medium-term objective and the initial activity has focused on the 'commercialization' of the department. Significantly, though, all discussion of the eventual divestiture has been shelved following the strongly expressed opposition to such moves by the telecommunications union, UPTO.

The Telecommunications Department was formally converted into a public company, Sri Lanka Telecomms Ltd (SLT Ltd), in February 1990, but by the end of the year no detailed restructuring plans had been implemented. The restructuring programme envisaged the transfer of all the assets and approximately 90% of the current staff to SLT; following a valuation and capital restructuring programme, the remaining staff were to assume a regulatory function in terms of a revised Telecommunications Act.[21] The second phase of the privatization programme, the sale of some or all of the equity in the public corporation, has, as noted, not been openly discussed. However, in view of the scale of the enterprise (turnover from 1987 to 1990 averaged approximately Rs1.75bn), the option of seeking foreign equity participation has been raised.[22]

11.3.3 Summary and evaluation

By the end of the 1980s privatization had been established as an important element in macroeconomic policy and as a logical component of the liberalization programme set in train in 1977. In reality, however, the programme so far has been small and far from successful. Only two enterprises have been sold to the private sector, yielding revenue to government of Rs350m.[23] (approximately 1.2% of the budget deficit for 1989, or 0.13% of GDP), while the pipeline for the remainder of 1990 (even though it did not materialize) envisaged the transfer of a further six companies with a combined net asset value of only Rs892m. The impact of this programme on the budget deficit has thus far been marginal. It may be useful to contrast this with the public savings accruing from the reform of Air Lanka and Ceylon Shipping Corporation (CSC), which, while not representing a complete turnaround in performance, have seen a reduction in transfers from Rs2.7bn in 1986 to Rs0.5bn in 1989.

The direct efficiency impact of the privatization programme is similarly negligible, although significant improvements in performance have occurred in the enterprises being targeted for privatization (especially the textile mills). These improvements have come almost exclusively from the commercialization process, and in a number of cases from the effect of new management contracts. This mirrors the experience of many other countries where the most dramatic efficiency gains and performance improvements are enjoyed during the run-up to privatization.

Programme management has, however, been handicapped by poor inter-agency co-ordination, and excessive duplication. This has emerged for a number of reasons, many of which relate to the conflicting objectives of the donors in the programme. Although the PIMB/PIMC has taken over a large amount of the work of the PCOP it has not assumed the overall co-ordination role and, more importantly, no agency has assumed a lead in strategic policy direction or programme evaluation. Consequently both co-ordination and strategy have been delegated, by default, to the donors. Strategic policy direction and evaluation are functions which should fall to the Commercialization or Public Enterprises Division, but both seem, at present, to be following a reactive role in the privatization programme.[24]

The second concern is that the diversified structures which have been established to implement the privatization programme have, in a number of cases, actually increased government involvement in the enterprises. A pertinent example of this is the case of Cey-Nor Ltd, which was corporatized in 1990 and placed in the privatization pipeline. Prior to corporatization, Cey-Nor had to deal only with its line ministry, the Ministry of Agriculture and Fisheries. Currently, however, it is required to report regularly to four institutions: PIMB, the Ministry of Agriculture and Fisheries, the Ministry of Plan Implementation and the Ministry of Finance (both Commercialization and Public Enterprise Divisions). In an exercise designed to streamline and minimize the relationship between government and the SOEs this multiplicity of responsible agencies is damaging.

None the less, under the banner of 'people-ization', and with the vigorous support of President Premedasa, the programme was beginning to attract increasing support from the private sector, which regards it as a tangible indication of the government's commitment to the private sector as the main engine of growth in the economy. It may be noted, however, that discussions with private sector investors suggest that this confidence is somewhat fragile, and, though the government seems to have been at least partially absolved of the failure of the United Motors share issue, the success of subsequent issues is clearly essential to the maintenance of private sector confidence. In the final two sections we consider the extent to which the private sector and the capital market can provide the conditions for successful privatization, if such confidence is maintained.

11.4 The structure of the private sector

As with many developing countries, whilst an understanding of the composition and structure of the private sector is central to assessing the capacity of the domestic economy to create an environment conducive to privatization, comprehensive industry data for Sri Lanka are weak. Aggregate data on industry structure and protection are published regularly, but invariably there is no breakdown between public sector and private sector, or firm-level or even detailed sector-level analysis. Recourse to sample-based data is thus required, which focus only on the manufacturing sector.[25] Most firms in the manufacturing sector in Sri Lanka are extremely small, with 85% having less than five employees; only about 500 employ more than 100 people. Importantly, this figure contains virtually all the foreign-owned companies and joint-venture operations. Concentration ratios, based on these employment data, are thus high, and confirm the popular view that in many areas the private sector in Sri Lanka is not particularly competitive.

It is also significant that, of all the SOEs in the manufacturing sector (145), only about 10 employ less than 100 people, and the average employment is over 500. SOEs dominate in a number of subsectors, in particular chemicals, non-metallic minerals, base metal products, and paper. More importantly, employment data for the manufacturing sector SOEs targeted for privatization show that only in the case of the two hotels does the sale involve a transfer of enterprises which do not dominate their sectors.

However, even if SOEs in aggregate account for a large share of output and employment in many sectors, there are a number of sectors which, among themselves, could provide a competitive market. This is particularly so in the manufacturing, trading, and services sectors. Moreover, though in a number of areas SOEs may dominate the domestic market, an important determinant of the effect of competition is the degree of import protection.

As noted earlier, a central part of the 1977 reforms involved the removal of virtually all quantitative restrictions and their replacement with a tariff-based trade policy. However, in 1986 the multi-banded tariff structure was replaced with a four-band system. Prior to the introduction of this new structure, Sri Lanka's average unweighted nominal tariff was 20.2%, which was lower than many other countries in Asia with the exception of Malaysia (Table 11.10), and almost 50%

Table 11.10 *Nominal and effective protection rates*

(a)	Average nominal tariff rate	Year
Sri Lanka	20.2	1987
South Korea	21.9	1985
Indonesia	23.0	1984
Malaysia	13.6	1982
Philippines	29.0	1984
Thailand	34.0	1985

(b) Sri Lanka nominal and effective protection 1979–87

	1979	1981	1983	1985	1987
Average nominal rate (%)	16	n.a.	36	n.a.	20
Average effective rate (%)	50	61	56	97	107

of all dutiable items attracted a tariff of less than 10%. However, detailed research on the manufacturing sector suggests not only that these nominal protection rates mask much higher rates of effective protection, even exceeding 100% by 1987, but that the average rate of protection has in fact increased since the abolition of QRs in 1977.[26]

In addition to competing with the domestic economy, the foreign sector is also involved in the privatization through direct foreign investment. Whilst DFI has been welcomed in Sri Lanka, its role in the privatization programme has remained somewhat ambiguous. The general principles behind the attitude to DFI, recently reiterated in the government's 1990 Industrial Strategy Paper, centre on the development of an export-oriented sector, with a strong emphasis on technology transfer and employment generation. Foreign investments which would be directly competitive, or which might crowd-out domestic producers, are not generally encouraged. Most foreign investment consequently occurs through joint-venture operations, although foreign participation is generally limited to 49%. In terms of the privatization programme, however, although the policy on 'people-ization' specifically emphasizes the role of domestic investors, foreign participation has been welcomed. This is evidenced in the NTC reform programme, and to a lesser extent the United Motors sale supports this view. Significant foreign participation is also expected in the sale of the other textile mills, and of Ceylon Oxygen and the State Trading (Export) Company. Furthermore, in anticipation of future foreign participation in privatization, the 100% tax on asset transactions by non-residents, imposed under the Finance Act of 1963, was waived in June 1990. Shares traded in companies in the GCEC Export Processing Zone were exempted in 1980, as were all transactions between non-residents in 1988, and a specific waiver was granted to the Mitsubishi Corporation for its share acquisition in United Motors Lanka Limited.

Conclusion

In the first decade since liberalization, the domestic private sector in Sri Lanka remained concentrated and highly protected from import competition. The sector is populated by small firms, the majority employing fewer than 5 people, with most large firms being either state- or foreign-owned. Despite these weaknesses, little attention has been paid to the issues of competition policy and regulation. Although recent tariff reforms, and the relaxation of restrictions on foreign equity participation, have served to expose the economy to some greater degree of external competition, there is no comprehensive competition policy with respect to the domestic market. Historically, regulation has been based on quantitative controls, and has been designed principally to control access to the market by, for example, foreign firms rather than to control market behaviour itself. Elsewhere it has been internalized within the public sector. There is thus only limited indication of the capacity for market-based regulation. The one area where such regulation is proceeding is in the capital market, although, as noted below, this has not yet met with much success.

11.5 Capital market constraints to privatization

The recent focus on the role of the privatization programme in promoting wider share ownership in Sri Lanka, and the proposed public share issues in Ceylon Oxygen, the ITN Television Network, Pugoda Mill and the State Distillers have highlighted the role of the Colombo Stock Exchange. This section therefore examines the capacity of the CSE to provide the mechanism for mobilization of household and corporate sector savings for investment, and to provide a mechanism through which shareholders can enforce market discipline on enterprise management.

11.5.1 Background
The Colombo Stock Exchange began formal trading in December 1985, although there had been stock and commodity trading in Colombo since the end of the nineteenth century. Stock trading was carried out before 1985 on a 'call-over' basis by the Colombo Brokers Association, but this was replaced by the CSE with an 'open out-cry' system in which trading takes place on a floor open to the public. Table 11.11 summarizes the size and performance of the CSE from its inception to the end of 1990. The most striking feature is its extremely modest size, both in absolute terms and in relation to the domestic economy. Average daily turnover barely exceeded US$25,000 in 1989 (Malaysia's daily turnover averaged US$31m. and Pakistan's US$860,000), and market capitalization was only 8% of GDP (compared with 125% for the KLSE). Nevertheless there are 176 listed companies on the Exchange, although in many there is little or no trade. In 1989 alone, only 9 companies had their shares traded on more than half the trading days, while 12% of all companies were not traded at all during the year. Those few companies in which the government is a shareholder engage in this low level of activity, with each share (other than Lanka Milk) trading on average only 10 days a year (Table 11.12). Net new listings have totalled four companies since the exchange opened in 1985, with only 21 new issues coming to the market in that period.[27] Though comprehensive data on new issues are not available, it is instructive to note that in 1988, whilst a number of the financial sector issues were oversubscribed (especially the Seylan Bank and Union Carbide issues), the average take-up was only about 50%, with the majority of stock being held by institutional investors.

The market is thus very concentrated: in 1988 trade in the shares of the top 5 companies[28] accounted for 52.7% of total turnover, and that of the top 25 for 80.5%. One of the reasons for this co-existence of a large number of listed companies and very low turnover lies in the tax structure. Prior to April 1990 all companies with more than 20% of their equity listed on the CSE were eligible for a reduced rate of corporate taxation. Concerned that listing is undertaken principally in pursuit of this tax concession, rather than in the interests of broad-based ownership, the government revised the eligibility criteria, so that companies

Table 11.11 *Colombo securities market*

	1985	1986	1987	1988	1989	1990
Market capitalization (Rsm.)	9,873.60	11,812.30	18,460.30	15,693.80	17,087.30	36,879.9
Annual turnover (Rsm.)	79.00	140.40	335.50	380.00	225.80	1,563.04
Shares traded (m.)	4.77	6.09	17.32	13.20	12.22	41.69
Average no. of daily transactions	18	37	65	55	71	203
Companies traded (% of total)	83.14	76.30	89.88	87.50	90.91	93.71
New listings	2	6	4	8	2	1
De-listings	0	5	9	0	2	2
Companies listed	172	173	168	176	176	175
All Share Index (1/1/85 = 100)	122.22	141.38	217.97	172.44	179.49	384.39
Sensitive Index (1/1/85 = 100)[a]	158.92	218.19	384.12	309.56	341.74	680.31
New share issues	3	5	4	10	1	1
Offer value of new issues (Rsm.)	87.45	130.5	205.9	201.49	33.00	7.00
Memorandum Item:						
Turnover as % of capitalization	0.80	1.19	1.82	2.42	1.32	4.24
Capitalization of % of GDP	5.98	6.46	9.22	6.97	7.67	–
New Issues as % of capitalization	0.89	1.10	1.12	1.28	0.19	0.02
New Issues as % of turnover	110.72	92.95	61.37	53.02	14.61	0.45

Source: Colombo Securities Exchange.

a) Sensitivity Index covers companies most traded.

qualify for the reduced level of taxation only if there are more than 200 shareholders and the top five shareholders hold less than 60% of the equity. It is expected that these new criteria will exclude approximately 75% of all listed companies.

Throughout the period, and despite the political uncertainty, the market performed relatively well, with both turnover and market price indices increasing steadily from 1985 to 1988. The market experienced a sharp reversal in 1988 with the collapse of confidence and flare-up of political uncertainty prior to the General Election.[29] It revived slightly in 1989, and the first half of 1990 saw an unprecedented surge in trading, fuelled by the removal of the 100% tax on share transactions by non-nationals in June 1990.

The market faces serious regulatory problems. The CSE operates an extremely liberal listing regime and companies seeking quotation on the market need have no past performance record.[30] Liberal access is matched by correspondingly weak regulation of trading, and there are widespread perceptions of insider trading. The creation of credible market regulation falls under the auspices of the Securities Council (SC), which was established in 1987 with the purpose of

> the creation and maintenance of a market in which securities can be traded in an orderly and fair manner; the protection of the financial interest of investors; the regulation of the market to ensure that professional standards are maintained; and the operation of a compensation fund to protect investors from financial loss arising from the failure of a licensed stock broker. (Act No. 36 of 1987, Section 12.)

Though the Council has been in existence for almost two years, it has not yet established a reputation for effective regulation, and the elimination of insider trading has yet to be addressed.

11.5.2 Absorptive capacity

Preliminary research commissioned by the Securities Council to assess the capacity of the market concludes that, if good-quality investment opportunities are available, then private savings will be forthcoming. Frequently cited examples are the

Table 11.12 *Performance of CSE listed companies with government shareholding*

Company	Govt equity (%)	Sector	1988 Turnover	Transactions	Days traded	1989 Turnover	Transactions	Days traded
Lanka Cement	89.2	Manuf	127,788	41	24	82,538	22	13
Pelwatte Sugar	48.9	Manuf	5,400	3	2	74,975	13	9
Elephant Lite Co.	30.0	Chem	395,355	37	17	20,130	8	5
Ceylon Hotels Co.	57.0	Hotel	216,528	34	27	431,546	23	12
Trans Asia Hotels	?	Hotel	6,725	7	6	1,900	2	2
Asian Hotel Corporation	99.0	Hotel	8,500	4	4	2,138	5	4
Colombo Drydock	97.0	Transport	19,000	5	4	10,938	8	7
Lanka Milk Foods	98.0	Food	1,054,608	236	97	568,975	161	72
TOTALS			1,833,904	367		1,193,140	242	

Source: Colombo Securities Exchange.

recent issues by Sampath and Seylan banks, both of whose Rs50m. issues were greatly oversubscribed. Consequently, it is suggested that, *ceteris paribus*, new issues of Rs50m. to Rs100m. per annum could safely be attracted on to the market: as already noticed, however, this is much less than the value of privatization issues planned for 1990.

These estimates are suspect for a number of reasons. First, the only consistently successful sector in terms of new issues on the CSE was the financial sector (and Union Carbide). New issues in the trading and manufacturing sectors have been distinctly less successful. Given that the prospective public issues in the privatization programme are principally in these latter sectors, reference to financial sector oversubscriptions may not be entirely useful. Second, high levels of domestic financing of the budget deficit have tended to push money market interest rates to a level where equity investment has been increasingly crowded out. Although the CSE enjoyed considerable growth in the first half of 1990, this was, as noted above, mainly in response to the abolition of the 100% tax on foreign equity transactions, and was relatively short-lived.

The size and structure of the CSE thus raises considerable doubts about its capacity to mobilize savings and provide secondary market trading. With a few exceptions, primary share issues have not met with great success, while secondary trading is very limited. Despite this, and although attempts to date to float public issues have not met with much success, the government seems to be committed to privatization through public share issues, both in pursuit of the objectives of 'people-ization' and as a means of deepening the capital market itself. An important step has been taken with the creation of the Securities Council, but it has not yet established itself as a credible regulator of the market. Rapid divestiture of public sector equity on the market is therefore unlikely to be successful.

11.6 Conclusions

Privatization in Sri Lanka has not proceeded smoothly. This was mainly due to the extremely adverse political and economic circumstances of the period, when the government not only sought to implement austere stabilization and adjustment measures but did so in the context of a civil war. Structural constraints, common to most low-income developing countries, have also meant that, even without such circumstances, privatization would not have been straightforward. Sri Lanka's economy remains poor and savings levels are low, while savings mobilization is constrained by the limitations of a narrowly based equity market.

The government has nevertheless established a complex, and somewhat unco-ordinated, institutional structure to manage the privatization programme, and has embarked on an ambitious programme which envisages the divestiture of over 20 enterprises in the three years from 1989 to 1992. By the end of 1990, however, only the first two enterprises had been sold, while the remainder of the 'pipeline' was subject to significant delays, not least in the case of those enterprises identified for sale through public share issues. On the other hand, the parallel objective of reforming the SOE sector has met with more success, particularly in the transport sector, and in the case of the National Textile Corporation has led to the ultimate privatization of the enterprises concerned.

Further progress in privatization and the form that it takes face a number of constraints. Significant limitations to competition exist in the domestic private sector, and, as yet, there is no regulatory regime to combat monopolistic practices. However, with many subsectors being populated by numerous medium-sized SOEs, effective competition could be elicited by the (more or less) simultaneous sale of similar enterprises. The limiting factor in pursuit of this option is the weakness in the mobilization of domestic savings. Aggregate savings rates are low, while the crowding-out effects from deficit financing and fiscal distortions in the financial system have reduced the attractiveness of equity investment. Moreover, the capital market is very narrowly based and centred on a small number of investors. Resources for privatization are concentrated in the hands of a small number of established domestic companies and, importantly, the foreign sector. President Premadasa's attempt to establish the doctrine of 'people-ization' represented an attempt to remedy this situation, but the initial evidence from the sale of United Motors suggests that, without more radical measures to effect wider share ownership, ownership of privatized SOEs will necessarily be concentrated and will involve high levels of foreign participation. In the Sri Lankan context, then, it seems clear that attempts to accelerate the privatization programme, or indeed to use it to accelerate the development of the capital market, may be politically as well as economically counter-productive.

Notes

1. From 1956 to 1977 the average nominal rate of protection on the producer price for rice (the staple commodity) was 83% of the border price, while implicit taxes on export commodities (tea, rubber and cotton) were kept at approximately 30% of the border price.
2. Three main programmes are in existence, covering approximately 45% of the population. These are the National Food Stamps Programme, the schools midday meal programme, and the Jana Saviya Programme – which is an income transfer programme aimed at providing consumption and investment support to low-income families.
3. See *inter alia* USAID (1988). These figures, however, understate the true size of the SOE sector as they exclude a number of key operations which would, in most cases, be considered under the SOE sector, but which in Sri Lanka are classified as Government Departments, and consequently part of the central government's activities. These are what are referred to as the government trading enterprises, and include two major enterprises, the Posts and Telecommunications Department and the Sri Lanka Railways.
4. Based on 1982 data, the last year in which SOE capital formation was reported separately from that of the private sector.
5. Nair and Filippides (1988) report an average share for 99 developing countries of 18.6%.
6. Estimates based on loans outstanding as at end 1989.
7. The main exceptions being the Development Finance Corporation of Ceylon, where the other shareholders are Bank of Ceylon (19%), People's Bank (19%), the Dutch and German aid agencies (10% each) and IFC (12%).
8. Whilst the World Bank (1988a) details arrangements for the sale and refers to approximate valuations, no further reference to the three factories can be found in official data – although the PED classifies them as being 'Under Sales Agreement'. However, there is no evidence that any of the companies are trading, and discussions with officials have failed to cast any light on the issue.
9. Following the election of President Premadasa in February 1989, the Commission became known as the Presidential Commission on People-ization. People-ization, as defined by President Premadasa, reflects the link between the twin objectives of privatization and of the transfer of ownership to domestic individuals as opposed to institutions or foreign operators.
10. This will involve the development of restructuring plans for companies covering balance-sheet restructuring, redeployment and retrenchment of labour and management, expansion or closure of activities, etc.
11. The reason for the, apparently artificial, division between CD and the PIMB/PIMC is partly to do with the role of the external donors' funding of the restructuring/privatization programme. Direct support for the privatization work of the PCOP was provided by USAID, for training and technical assistance on the preparation for sale of SOEs and also for meeting severance pay and gratuity liabilities arising out of privatization. The funding was to total $7.9m., over five years from 1989. Following the dissolution of the Commission, USAID declined to combine its assistance to the government with that of the World Bank to PIMB, and consequently its support has been targeted directly through the Commercialization Division. This was because USAID felt that

PIMB was not sufficiently committed to privatization but rather included strengthening of existing public sector institutions within its brief.

12. As will be noted below, the CD seems to be fully involved only when the privatization process involves a public listing of equity. In cases where it involves private sales or management contract and leasing agreements the initiative for the programme seems to lie with the responsible line ministry.

13. In terms of Section 8 (2) of the 1985 Inland Revenue (Amendment) Act, since from 1986 all public corporations (and GOBUs) were required to pay tax on deemed dividends equal to 25% of net profit.

14. As will be discussed in section 11.5, all transfer of shares to a non-resident attract a tax of 100%. However, a waiver was granted by the Minister for Finance exempting the sale of shares from government to Mitsubishi from the tax.

15. The Colombo Securities Exchange operates par-based primary trading whereby all new issues are at par (always Rs10 per share).

16. Apparently most officials and advisers involved with the sale were keen to delay the issue. Political expediency prevailed in order to indicate that industrial action and security problems would not halt the implementation of the government's economic policy.

17. The management offered their resignation *en bloc* to the major shareholders in March 1990, but it was not accepted.

18. In 1988 UML paid Rs4.99m., which would equate approximately to a dividend rate of 10% (based on issued share capital and a profit retention rate of 50%).

19. Interview with the authors.

20. This company has acted as a trading company and ceased chemical manufacture many years ago. The government, supported by certain donors, is recommending closure, but the North East District Corporation have put in a tentative proposal to re-establish the company as a manufacturing operation.

21. Although the draft Act was not available for examination, indications suggest that it is based on the UK Telecommunications Act 1984.

22. This speculation has centred principally on the involvement of Cable and Wireless of the UK which, in addition to being one of the dominant telecommunications enterprises in Asia (principally in Hong Kong), has also played an important role in the privatization of telecommunications in the Carribean (see Chapter 7).

23. This excludes the proceeds from the sale of the GOBU tile factories. Note also that the proceeds from the Thulhiriya sale were to be directed towards the capital restructuring of the other NTC textile mills.

24. Unfortunately it seems that the PED's role in the actual restructuring process is marginal, despite its responsibility for the primary financial database, its established analytical experience with the SOE sector, and its strong cadre of qualified financial analysts.

25. The only sector for which comprehensive data exist.

26. G. Wignaraja, 'Industrial Exports in a Semi-Open Economy: Firm-Level Analysis in Sri Lanka', Doctoral Thesis, Oxford University (forthcoming).

27. The value of new issues quoted in Table 11.12 represents the nominal value of the issue, rather than the amount taken up. As the ratio to turnover would suggest, a significant proportion of new issues were not taken up.

28. Carsons (Services); Hattons National Bank (Finance); Hayleys (Trading); Mercantile Leasing (Finance); Sampath Bank (Finance).

29. The effect of political uncertainty on the market was exacerbated by its impact on a sizeable number of investors who took severe losses on margin trading in the tourism sector.

30. Contrast this with the Malaysian case where companies on the main board need to show a 5 year profit and dividend track record before listing.

12   KENYA

12.1 Introduction

Kenya provides an intriguing case-study in privatization. As an economy it exhibits many of the structural constraints which characterize most sub-Saharan African countries, but it also serves to highlight the delicate politics of privatization in adjustment. At the outset we may note that to all intents and purposes there has been no privatization to speak of in Kenya, in spite of the fact that the policy has been on the agenda for most of the 1980s and has repeatedly featured in the adjustment lending programmes from the donor community. We begin this case-study with a summary of the Kenyan economy and the role of the SOEs. We then examine the process by which the government moved towards a policy of reform and privatization and how this policy has emerged in practice, and conclude with an assessment of the impact of the economic structure on the implementation of privatization in Kenya.

12.1.1 Macroeconomic structure and performance

Kenya is a low-income East African open economy heavily dependent on agricultural exports, principally coffee and tea. The population is estimated at around 23 million with a growth rate of 4% per annum – one of the highest in the world (Central Bureau of Statistics, 1990). The population is principally African, though there is a small, but economically powerful, group of Kenyan-Asians and Europeans. GDP per capita was $370 in 1988. The economy is dominated by agriculture (30% of GDP), with the industrial sector accounting for a further 20%. The bulk of non- agricultural economic activity is centred along the Nairobi–Mombasa corridor and despite the relatively low per capita income, the economy is regarded as one of the more developed in sub-Saharan Africa.

Kenya was one of the principal British settler colonies in Africa and from the early twentieth century has been an important export-crop producer. Its more recent economic history reflects this orientation. The first post-Independence decade 1963–73 was characterized by a remarkable degree of growth, stability and industrialization. Real GDP growth averaged 6.6% per annum and the manufacturing sector grew rapidly, accounting for some 15% of total GDP by the end of the decade. The oil price shock of 1973, however, applied a sharp brake to the economy which was at that time beginning to feel the effects of rising import costs and also a reversal in private capital flows. Stabilization attempts were initiated in 1975 under an IMF loan but these were abandoned following the coffee boom of 1976–7. This boom (which saw coffee prices rise by over 400%) generated a current account surplus of over 10% of GDP whilst real growth recovered to earlier levels, even exceeding 8% in 1977. Despite the opportunity presented by the temporary coffee boom, failure to address the fundamental weaknesses of the

323

Table 12.1 *Macroeconomic indicators 1970–1989*

	1970–74	1975–79	1980	1981	1982	1983	1984	1985	1986	1987	1988	1989
GDP growth (%)	5.00	4.50	5.34	3.98	2.58	1.06	1.99	4.14	5.78	4.92	5.20	5.90
Gross savings (% of GDP)	17.90	16.10	18.67	19.49	18.33	20.13	22.05	24.85	22.09	18.82	20.10	19.40
Gross investment (% of GDP)	25.40	23.90	23.66	23.98	19.29	18.76	18.34	19.92	22.55	22.93	23.82	23.36
Investment-savings (% of GDP)	7.50	7.80	5.00	4.50	0.97	-1.37	-3.71	-4.93	0.46	4.11	3.71	3.96
Real growth GDP/capita	1.50	1.00	1.29	-0.06	-1.45	-2.94	-2.08	-0.06	1.86	1.20	1.57	1.41
Current revenue as % GDP	–	–	22.48	22.45	21.48	21.12	20.24	20.27	20.03	21.01	21.25	25.67
Current surplus as % GDP	–	–	2.60	1.21	-2.19	-1.10	-1.50	-1.62	-1.02	-1.93	-1.28	-0.12
Budget deficit as % GDP	–	–	4.58	6.61	7.88	5.02	4.88	6.35	4.41	6.61	3.31	3.64
Interest as % current exp.	–	–	9.19	10.59	14.46	17.17	18.18	18.20	21.68	19.35	21.40	21.70
Interest as % GDP	–	–	1.83	2.25	3.42	3.82	3.95	3.99	4.56	4.44	4.82	6.20
Composition of Investment												
Government (%)	–	–	20.67	20.44	18.95	14.22	19.02	22.50	19.87	21.79	23.82	20.09
SOE (%)	–	–	24.50	24.01	26.06	23.99	22.80	17.68	23.03	16.59	16.57	19.45
Private (%)	–	–	54.83	55.55	54.99	61.79	58.18	59.82	57.09	61.61	59.61	60.46

Source: CBS, *Economic Survey* (various issues).

economy at this time meant that Kenya entered the 1980s in a state of severe disequilibrium (Table 12.1). By 1981 the budget deficit had reached 9.5% of GDP; real growth fell back to less than 3% by 1982; and the deficit on the current account exceeded 12% of GDP. Domestic inflation peaked in 1980 at 20% per annum.

During the 1980s frequent adjustment measures were instituted. Nevertheless, though stabilization objectives were met, only limited supply-side adjustment eventuated. Real growth began to recover, touching almost 6% in 1986, whilst at the same time the budget deficit had been reduced to 4.4% of GDP from a peak of almost 8% in 1982, and domestic inflation fell back rapidly from its high in 1981 to around 10% in 1984, and to as low as 4% in 1986.

Performance since then has been mixed. Real growth, following the 1986 coffee boom, averaged 5% per annum to 1989, while gross investment recovered to approximately 23% of GDP. Aggregate national savings of 20% of GDP have remained relatively high throughout the decade and are almost twice as high as the sub-Saharan African average of 12%. The budget deficit has averaged approximately 5% of GDP from 1985 to 1990; although lower than the levels attained in the early 1980s, this remains significantly above the target of 2.5% of GDP set in Sessional Paper No. 1 of 1986 (Table 12.2). Improvements in the fiscal position have, in the main, come from reductions in capital expenditure and, in particular, from a market reduction in transfer payments to SOEs (which fell from 1.5% of GDP in 1984 to less than 0.5% in 1988). Control of current expenditure is, however, confounded by high debt-service costs, which now account for over 20% of current expenditure and almost 5% of GDP – a rise of almost 300% since 1977/78. External debt rose extremely rapidly during the late 1970s and into the 1980s, from 25% of GDP in 1980 to over 50% by 1987, with debt service rising from 3.2% of GDP to 5.4% over the same period (Table 12.3). The government, and in particular the parastatals, borrowed heavily from commercial sources, at high rates of interest, as illustrated by the fact that, while in 1980 the grant element on new loans was 52%, this fell to only 15.3% in 1981. Measures taken during the mid-1980s, however, reduced private exposure and improved the concessionality of borrowing. Combined with Kenya's re-eligibility for loans from the International Development Association and their consequent impact on co-financing terms, the concessionality of external borrowing increased dramatically, raising

Table 12.2 *Target growth rates 1988–2000 (%)*

GDP at factor cost		5.9
Agriculture		5.3
Manufacturing		7.5
Trade		5.5
Government		5.4
Other sectors		6.7
Population		3.7
GDP per capita		2.1
Budget Projections	Share of GDP	Growth p.a.
Total revenue	24.0	6.1
Deficit target	2.5	0.7
Expenditure limit	22.8	5.1
—Recurrent	16.1	5.1
—Development	6.7	5.1

Source: Sessional Paper No. 1 of 1986.

Table 12.3 *Medium- and long-term external debt (Ksh. m.)*

	1980	1981	1982	1983	1984	1985	1986	1987	1988	1989*
Outstanding debt										
Central government	8,994	11,846	17,136	25,170	31,304	37,173	46,547	57,160	61,412	58,935
SOEs	4,206	4,682	6,476	7,859	7,424	8,018	9,967	10,747	11,965	13,622
TOTAL	13,200	16,528	23,612	33,029	38,728	45,191	56,514	67,907	73,377	72,557
Debt service										
Central government										
Principal	722	996	1,382	1,716	2,314	3,044	2,770	3,426	3,960	
Interest	350	842	1,172	1,164	1,240	1,270	1,942	1,518	2,358	
Total	1,072	1,838	2,554	2,880	3,554	4,314	4,712	4,944	6,318	
SOEs										
Principal	236	302	472	654	770	748	924	1,106	1,046	
Interest	392	396	404	588	646	786	798	942	840	
Total	628	698	876	1,242	1,416	1,534	1,722	2,048	1,886	
Memorandum Items										
Growth of GoK debt (%)	—	31.71	44.66	46.88	24.37	18.75	25.22	22.80	7.44	-4.03
Growth of SOE debt (%)	—	11.32	38.32	21.36	-5.54	8.00	24.31	7.83	11.33	13.85
Growth of total debt (%)	—	25.21	42.86	39.88	17.25	16.69	25.06	20.6	8.06	-1.12
SOE debt as % of total	31.86	28.33	27.43	23.79	19.17	17.74	17.64	15.83	16.31	18.77
Total debt as % of GDP	25.09	27.32	34.07	43.18	44.11	45.97	48.47	51.33	48.06	49.48
Debt service as % GDP	3.23	4.19	4.95	5.39	5.66	5.95	5.52	5.28	5.37	
Debt service as % of exports	11.28	16.36	19.49	21.03	21.24	22.93	21.23	24.97	—	

Source: Ministry of Finance, Kenya External Debt Reporting System (KEDRES).

* denotes provisional figures.

the implicit grant element to over 60% in 1987 and 1988 (World Bank, *World Debt Tables*, 1990).

Sessional Paper No. 1 of 1986 on *Economic Management for Renewed Growth* outlined the government's medium-term adjustment programme and specified the conditions for a sustainable growth trajectory through to the end of the century (see Table 12.2). It stressed the importance not only of macroeconomic demand management and trade liberalization, but also of supply-side measures, including financial sector reform and continuance of the reform programme of the state-owned enterprise (SOE) sector. The adjustment programme has been strongly supported by the donor community, and in particular by the Bretton Woods institutions, with IDA/World Bank resources being provided through a series of sector adjustment loans (SECALs) for the agricultural, industrial, and financial sectors and also, more recently, through one of the first IMF Enhanced Structural Adjustment Facility loans.[1] As we shall see, though SOE reform is a recurring theme of these loans, this reform has occurred only to a limited extent.

To sum up. For many years Kenya has been portrayed as the success story of East and Southern Africa, and, as such, has been fêted by private investors and official donors alike. However, the government is now being forced to accept that the current performance is not sustainable and that further supply-side adjustment is required. Though the adjustment debate has gone on throughout the 1980s, progress has been slow, hindered in part by a reluctance on the part of the authorities to assume the political costs of adjustment and in part by a skilful management of relationships with the country's principal external creditors (Mosley, 1991). Very recent events – including the USAID moratorium on new assistance – indicate that time is running out for Kenya. Genuine adjustment is therefore more likely to occur; unlike many others in Africa, the Kenyan economy has greater depth of human resources and infrastructural capacity to sustain such adjustment measures.

12.2 The SOE sector

12.2.1 Extent and origins

The origins of the parastatal sector in Kenya extend back to the early 1900s with the creation of the railway system (then known as Uganda Railways) linking Mombasa with the inland cities of Nairobi and Kampala. By the time Kenya gained its Independence in December 1963, public ownership was widespread in the infrastructure, agricultural marketing, and development finance, serving to facilitate the country's role as an agricultural commodity exporter. From Independence until the late 1970s there was an increase in, and change in the direction of, public sector participation in the economy as attention shifted towards the role of the state in broader resource management. The fundamental tenets of this new view were crystallized in Sessional Paper No. 10 of 1966 on *African Socialism and its Application to Planning in Kenya*, which became the basis of the political economy for the subsequent two decades. African Socialism, used to describe a collective mixed economy in which centralized planning and control measures directed the financial and human resources of the economy, had at its core the principle of 'Kenyanization' – the rapid acceleration of the transfer of economic control from the hands of foreigners to Kenyans.

These aims were melded within an interventionist economic policy, one important element of which was public ownership. The Sessional Paper states (para. 32):

> In order to control effectively, sufficiently and not excessively in each case, many types and degrees of control are needed, ranging from none, through influence, guidance, and control of a few variables such as prices or quantities, to absolute control represented by State ownership and operation.

Similarly (paras 73–5):

> Nationalization is a useful tool that has already been used in Kenya and will be used
> again when circumstances require. Nationalization will be needed (i) when assets in
> private hands threaten the security or undermine the integrity of the nation; (ii) when
> productive resources are being wasted; (iii) when the operation of an industry by private
> concerns has a serious detrimental effect on the public interest; and (iv) when other less
> costly means of control are not available.

Under this broad umbrella was a further commitment to increase the state's
participation in the economy through direct investment, joint ventures with private investors (through the Development Finance Institutions (DFIs)), and the
creation of the state-owned trading and construction companies.

Though this policy established a broad mandate for public participation in the
economy, it was tempered by a clear view on the importance of performance monitoring and regulation. It was noted that: 'ownership can be abused whether public
or private, and ways must be found to control resource use in either case'. Similarly, it was made clear that nationalized industries and other commercial parastatals must be operated efficiently, and must cover their costs and earn profits
'at least equal to the taxes paid by equivalent private sector operations'. Despite
these concerns, the two decades since Sessional Paper No. 10 was adopted witnessed a burgeoning growth in the parastatal sector, with progressively weakening
financial performance and without a commensurate development of the government's monitoring, control and regulation functions.[2]

12.2.2 Size and performance of the SOE sector

The SOE sector[3] consists of approximately 342 institutions, of which 206
are commercial and financial enterprises, 10 are commodity boards, and the
remainder a series of regulatory, professional and developmental institutions
(Table 12.4). Approximately half are held through one of 12 holding companies (Table 12.5), the biggest, in terms of industrial holdings, being the
Industrial Development Bank and the Industrial Commercial Development
Corporation.

Best estimates suggest that, prior to the collapse of the East African Community
in 1977, the sector accounted for approximately 15% of GDP and a similar
proportion of gross capital formation. By 1984 its share of output had fallen
substantially, to around 8% of GDP, though the sector still accounted for 30%
of all public sector employment, 50% of public sector capital formation (equivalent
to 20% of total capital formation), and 20% of the external debt burden of
the economy.[4] As Table 12.4 shows, the sector spans a number of broad areas:
financial institutions; agricultural and other commodity boards; transport and
other utilities; regulatory and advisory bodies; and commercial (principally industrial) enterprises. We shall briefly discuss the main subsectors, but we can note in
advance the broad dichotomy between the financial and non-financial SOEs
(Table 12.6). While the sector as a whole more or less breaks even in terms of net
flows of funds, the table reveals the extent to which transfers to the non-financial
SOEs are financed by the profit remittances of the financial SOEs.

Transport, energy and communications[5]

Most of the major transport and communications utilities pre-date Independence,
having been established to serve the broader East African region as a whole
(i.e. Kenya, Uganda and Tanzania)[6] and to expedite the transportation of primary produce to markets overseas. Consequently the contraction of the market

Table 12.4 *State-owned enterprises*

Sector	Subsector	Majority Ownership	Minority Ownership	Total
DEVELOPMENT	Sectoral	9	0	9
INSTITUTIONS	National	3	0	3
	Regional	4	0	4
	Commodity Board	10	0	10
FINANCE	Banks	4	2	6
	Financial Insts	3	2	5
	Insurance	4	2	6
	Investment	1	1	2
COMMERCIAL	Sugar	5	0	5
	Tea	9	13	22
	Food Processing	5	12	17
	Livestock	2	2	4
	Textiles	6	12	18
	Plastics	0	8	8
	Beverages	2	1	3
	Engineering	1	12	13
	Fishing	1	3	4
	Chemicals	3	4	7
	Retail	4	3	7
	Tourism	15	16	31
	Mining	7	0	7
	Wood & Paper	1	6	7
	Construction	10	3	13
	Transport	8	2	10
	Vehicle Assembly	1	6	7
	Energy	4	0	4
REGULATION		55	0	55
PROFESSIONAL		11	0	11
MISCELLANEOUS		39	0	39
CO-OPERATIVES		5	0	5
TOTAL		232	110	342

Source: Government of Kenya, Working Party on Government Expenditure, 1982.

Table 12.5 *SOE holding company structure*

Holding Company	100%	51%–100%	25%–50%	<25%	Total
ICDC	10	11	23	16	60
IDB			4	23	27
Agricultural Development Bank	2	4			6
Kenya Commercial Bank	2				2
National Bank Kenya		1			1
Kenya National Insurance Co.	1		1		2
Kenya Re-Insurance	2				2
Kenya National Trading Co.	1	1			2
Kenya Tourism Dev. Co.	2	13	8	2	25
Kenya Tea Dev. Co.	9	8	1	21	39
Cotton Lint Seed Co.	5				5
Kenya Airways	2				2
TOTAL	36	38	37	62	173

Source: ibid.

Table 12.6 *Flow of funds to SOE sector 1983/4–1988/9 (Ksh.m.)*

	1983/84	1984/85	1985/86	1986/87	1987/88	1988/89
Revenue						
Dividends and Profits						
Financial SOEs	716.8	848.9	805.2	881.8	1,040.0	1,404.0
Non-Financial SOEs	106.3	56.2	109.9	161.7	160.0	216.0
Total	823.1	905.1	915.1	1,043.5	1,200.0	1,620.0
Expenditure						
Current Transfers						
Financial SOEs	0.0	0.1	0.0	0.0	0.0	0.0
Non-Financial SOEs	222.4	1,020.1	414.0	0.0	139.0	160.0
Total	222.4	1,020.2	414.0	0.0	139.0	160.0
Capital Transfers						
Financial SOEs	1.9	0.0	16.8	4.7	0.0	0.0
Non-Financial SOEs	17.2	56.6	23.2	0.0	0.0	0.0
Total	19.1	56.6	40.0	4.7	0.0	0.0
Equity Participation						
Financial SOEs	0.0	0.0	17.1	17.5	0.0	0.0
Non-Financial SOEs	10.2	107.4	192.6	140.0	142.6	334.0
Total	10.2	107.4	209.7	157.5	142.6	334.0
Net Lending						
Financial SOEs	(9.7)	392.4	141.9	5.5	(44.1)	20.0
Non-Financial SOEs	201.7	5.3	(96.0)	(64.6)	(63.8)	42.0
Total	192.0	397.7	45.9	(59.1)	(107.9)	62.0
Gross Flow of Funds						
Financial SOEs	(7.8)	392.5	175.8	27.7	(44.1)	20.0
Non-Financial SOEs	451.5	1,189.4	533.8	75.4	217.8	536.0
Total	443.7	1,581.9	709.6	103.1	173.7	556.0
Net Flow of Funds						
Financial SOEs	(724.6)	(456.4)	(629.4)	(854.1)	(1,084.1)	(1,384.0)
Non-Financial SOEs	345.2	1,133.2	423.9	(86.3)	57.8	320.0
Total	(379.4)	676.8	(205.5)	(940.4)	(1,026.3)	(1,064.0)
Net Flow of Funds as % of Total Expenditure						
Financial SOEs	−3.2	−1.7	−2.2	−2.4	−2.5	−2.6
Non-Financial SOEs	1.5	4.3	1.5	−0.2	0.1	0.6
Total	−1.7	2.6	−0.7	−2.7	−2.4	−2.0

Source: IMF, *Government Financial Statistics*, 1990.

area following the collapse of the East African Community had an adverse impact on the performance of these enterprises. In a number of cases this loss of market share has been aggravated by competition from other transport systems and has resulted in severe financial problems and a rise in unit operating costs to uneconomic levels. For example, for Kenya Railways the loss of the EAC traffic has been compounded by fierce competition from the road sector, and from the state-owned Kenya Pipeline Company (KPLC) which since 1980 has handled a major proportion of the lucrative oil transportation from Mombasa to Nairobi. KPLC has enjoyed a rate of profit on its operations of more than 25% per annum, while in contrast since 1978 KR has failed to break even, despite repeated debt reschedulings and conversions on the part of the government. Low earnings and minimal capital expenditure have taken their toll on operational efficiency, with locomotive and rolling stock availability declining to as low as 50% for locos and 80% for wagons, with a commensurate rise in turnaround time for freight traffic.

Similarly Kenya Airways' performance has been turbulent since its inception in

1978 (as the successor to the East African Airways), and remains plagued by poor financial and operational management and chronic overstaffing.[7] Load factors began to rise slightly in the early 1980s, but remained far below break-even point. By 1983 accumulated losses for the airline had reached over 140% of total assets. In the late 1980s a fleet modernization was undertaken at the insistence of IATA, and some progress has been made in improving operational efficiency. KA remains a serious problem for the government, however. Efforts have been made to identify a management contract partnership with a foreign airline operator, but as yet with no success.

The financial performance of the power generation and telecommunications utilities is considerably better, not least because of their protected monopoly positions. Kenya Power and Lighting (prior to 1983, East African Power and Lighting) was originally a private public company listed in London, but in 1970 the government acquired 100% control. During the first decade following Independence, KPL operated profitably in response to the strong growth in demand, but performance since 1978 has been weaker. Again, the loss of markets in neighbouring states depressed financial performance, and this was exacerbated by the costs of developing a high-cost, rural electrification programme.[8] The company is now faced with severe liquidity problems, even though price increases have been kept more or less in line with real operating costs (excluding debt-service costs) and operational productivity growth has been reasonable.

Finally, Kenya Posts and Telecommunications (formerly East African Posts and Telecommunications) traces its origins to the mid-1920s. Since Independence it has enjoyed a secure and profitable monopoly position providing postal and telecommunication services. More recently the corporation has launched a programme to establish a manufacturing capacity for telecommunication equipment for the domestic and East and Southern African markets.

Agriculture
Government involvement in the agricultural sector has been mainly through the commodity boards and the Agricultural Development Corporation and Agricultural Finance Corporation. The reform of agricultural enterprises is not the primary focus in this study and we shall not go into details on this sector. In section 12.3, however, we discuss the salient features of agricultural reform as they relate to the issue of privatization.

Financial SOEs
Financial sector development in Kenya is similar to that adopted by governments elsewhere in Anglophone Africa. Since Independence the government has expanded the commercial banking sector and developed a broad range of other financial institutions, although, unlike many other countries, it has not nationalized or even acquired equity in either of the two main resident British commercial banks, Barclays and Standard Chartered. In 1968 it established the National Bank of Kenya, and then in 1970 acquired 60% of the equity in Grindlays Bank, which had operated in Kenya since 1904. This new bank was renamed the Kenya Commercial Bank (KCB), which on the basis of an extensive branch network became the biggest single commercial bank in the country. Though the government acquired the remaining 40% of the equity in 1976, it retained a management contract with Grindlays until 1986. In 1987 KCB followed the other two large commercial banks in selling new equity to the public through the Nairobi Stock Exchange (see section 12.3).

In addition, the government rapidly established a variety of other development finance institutions, which have borne the brunt of long-term lending to industry and agriculture. Few of them have performed well. Though there is some evidence of internal inefficiencies and, in particular, skills shortages and deficiencies in project appraisal, the main problems facing the DFIs have been systemic, due mainly to the limited number of viable projects and a weak capital market, which precludes the easy divestiture of the loan portfolio. Compounding this are obvious moral hazard and adverse selection problems: the DFIs are approached by companies only after the commercial banks have rejected them, while, in a number of cases, the high interest rates charged by the DFIs (to cover the poor loan portfolio performance and their foreign-exchange liabilities) mean that only high-risk projects are attracted to them. Conversely successful enterprises in the loan portfolios tend to 'graduate' to the commercial banks which can provide funds at a lower rate, thereby worsening the overall portfolio position of the DFIs. By 1987 the rate of return on their portfolios had fallen to 1.3%. This crisis has reduced new DFI lending to a minimum. Unable to contract new capital, the DFIs have resorted to holding on to their profitable companies longer than would be optimal in order to use their dividend income to refinance losses elsewhere in the portfolio. Prompted by the NBFI crisis in the mid-1980s (see Killick and Mwega, 1990), the government embarked on a major restructuring process for the DFIs, aimed at strengthening the lending base, improving credit allocation, and, crucially, creating (once again) a clear division between their commercial and non-commercial functions. This will be dealt with in section 12.3 below.

Commercial and industrial enterprises

Although almost half of all SOEs (including regulatory bodies) are in the commercial sector, direct government participation has been relatively slight. Unlike all the other subsectors examined above, the majority of SOEs have had only a minority government participation, and in only 33 cases is there 100% equity control. Furthermore, the majority of commercial SOEs are held through government-owned holding companies, principally the DFIs, Industrial and Commercial Development Corporation (ICDC) and Industrial Development Bank (IDB), the Kenya Tea Development Agency (the holding company for government participation in 24 tea factories), and the Kenya Tourism Development Corporation (Table 12.5). In general, SOEs in the commercial sectors operate in competitive markets,[9] and the evidence on their performance relative to private enterprises produces some interesting results. Grosh (1990) suggests that, while there is very little difference between the performance of private manufacturing enterprises and those in which government has a majority control, neither group is as efficient as joint-venture operations in which the government takes a minority equity position (Table 12.7).

Table 12.7 *Profitability and performance of manufacturing firms*

	No.	*NPR*	*EPR*	*DRC*	*ROR*	*DRC (100%)*
Public	12	1.33	47%	1.41	15%	1.05
Quasi-Public	18	1.11	3%	0.96	11%	0.92
Private	43	1.16	22%	1.46	9%	0.96

Source: Grosh (1990).

Key:
NPR — Net Protection Rate.
EPR — Effective Protection Rate.
DRC — Domestic Resource Cost; DRC (100%) DRC at 100% capacity utilization.
ROR — Rate of Return.

Grosh argues that this questions the value of a privatization programme based solely on domestic purchases, and instead contends that public joint participation is a key determinant of performance. On the contrary, however, given that the bulk of private sector joint-venture partners are foreign, and that it is generally the private sector partner rather than the government which provides the management input into the company, the more pertinent issue is that of the role of foreign participation in the domestic private sector. This is most noticeable in the more competitive sectors such as textiles where quasi-public and private companies are clearly more efficient than their public counterparts. Across the sectors as a whole, it is in the textile sector that economies of scale are less and the demand more price-elastic, and it is here that the forces of competition can be expected to work most strongly. We shall return to this point in section 12.4.

Further evidence on this aspect of the sector is provided by the World Bank (1987b) which examines the relative performance of public and private sector enterprises in the textiles and sugar sectors, amongst others, where there is a mixture of public and private enterprises. Since in both sectors firms are principally export-oriented price-takers, this offers a good opportunity to assess internal efficiency directly.

The sugar industry in Kenya has failed to generate sizeable profits. Erratic cane supply and low levels of investment saw performance decline during the 1970s as private growers and millers left the industry. Despite this decline, the government launched a major expansion programme by adding three new mills, Mumias, Nzoia, and South Nyanza, aimed at returning Kenya to a position of self-sufficiency in sugar. As a result of this huge investment, sugar output tripled and the country briefly became a net exporter of sugar, although this position has once again been reversed. Within the sector, there are two privately owned sugar mills, and although these are operating at a low level of efficiency (mainly due to low utilization levels) there is evidence that their performance is better than to that of equivalent-vintage public sector mills. Whilst the World Bank study identifies managerial, financial and operational inefficiencies across the publicly owned mills as a major drawback, it also stresses the extent to which government involvement in the sector – through setting of cane prices, monopsony purchases through the Kenya National Trading Corporation, and control over distribution – has acted as such a disincentive to all growers and millers regardless of ownership that relative efficiency measures are virtually meaningless.[10] More generally, however, while a number of individual mills could be made financially viable, this is not possible for the industry as a whole at its current size, and rationalization and closure of capacity may therefore be necessary.

The textile sector provides a contrasting picture. The sector is extensive in Kenya and all forms of ownership are represented. In addition to approximately 18 SOE textile firms (of which 5 are majority-owned), there are some 30 private companies (a number of which have foreign participation). The private sector is dominated by Kenyan-Asians and this group also has a considerable management presence in the SOE sector. The sector is fairly mature and internally competitive, with low levels of market concentration and industry-wide labour productivity levels which, though lower than in many NICs, compare favourably with, for example, the textile sectors in India and Bangladesh.

There is, however, a marked difference between the financial performance of public and private sector firms. While most of the private sector firms have been profitable throughout the 1980s, the majority of public mills are in financial difficulties, with every public sector textile firm reporting operating losses in 1985. The causes are varied, but are mainly a combination of low investment levels, sub-optimal scale,[11] poor management, and excessively high capital gearing. The problems are compounded by the tendency for poor performance to be tolerated by the government; not only is performance weak, but reporting of it is sluggish. It may also be noted that the sector as a whole, though domestically competitive, faces problems in international markets because of high input costs occasioned by the pricing behaviour of the Cotton Lint and Seed Board which maintains producer prices at 160% of world prices.

The rejuvenation of the sector, not least in terms of its export competitiveness, rests to a great extent on the need to restructure input prices and, more importantly, for the sector to achieve greater scale economies in production. But there is also scope for divestiture, both through acquisition of SOEs by private operators, and also through closure of excess capacity. Privatization, as a means of reform, has been seen by many as an appropriate option for the textile sector.

Other sectors. Though this covers the bulk of commercial SOEs, the other main sectors are the tourism and service sectors, which have become central elements in the exchange-earning capacity of the economy in the 1980s. As Table 12.4 indicates, government participation in these sectors is widespread, but sadly there are very few comprehensive data. In general, the casual evidence suggests that the tourism sector is relatively competitive (domestically and internationally) and efficient and profitable (especially during the mid-1980s when Kenya emerged as a major tourist destination in Africa). Government participation is vested principally in a large number of joint-venture agreements, where international management participation is dominant.

Conclusion

The SOE sector is broad-based, with, at one extreme, a group of large, monolithic, utility companies providing the requisite services but at a low level of efficiency and riven with policy contradictions. There is little evidence of comprehensive reform measures amongst these enterprises. Elsewhere in the agricultural and financial sectors the SOEs are undergoing a degree of reform – although as with limited privatization – under the auspices of the donor community. At the other extreme there is a large commercial sector consisting of a broad range of firms of decidedly mixed efficiency, sections of which exhibit the competitive structures which would provide the appropriate conditions for a managed programme of privatization to emerge.

12.3 SOE reform and the development of privatization policy

12.3.1 Government policy

Despite the emphasis on commercial orientation and accountability established in the 1966 Sessional Paper on African Socialism, the actual policy stance towards the SOE sector was a mixture of benign neglect and malign intervention. The initial objectives of 'Kenyanization' and the use of SOEs as catalysts to stimulate industrial development were, unfortunately, overwhelmed by: government intervention in their operations in pursuit of employment and other non-commercial objectives; excessive measures taken to protect SOEs from effective competition, leading to high levels of managerial slack and operational inefficiency; the use of SOEs for the purposes of patronage; and the failure to dispose of commercial holdings to private investors. Moreover, concerns had been frequently raised about the weakness of SOE management – the list being headed by directionless senior management; concentration on political rather than commercial management issues; weak capacity for delegation, training, and junior management control; and fragile, often non-existent, internal information systems.

These internal problems were compounded by poor control and monitoring on the part of the government. Enabling legislation for the sector was diverse and extremely heterogeneous; reporting and accountability obligations were ill-defined; and goverment co-ordinating capacity was poor – the institutional framework of the Auditor General's Office, the Inspectorate of Statutory Bodies, and the Ministry of Finance Business Section were uniformly weak and virtually dormant throughout the 1970s. Along with the rest of the macroeconomy, tell-tale signs of weakness in government policy towards the SOE sector began to emerge in the mid-1970s, but it was not until the early 1980s that pressure for adjustment resulted in action.

The Ndegwa Committee

Reform initiatives have been partial in scope and long in gestation, and this was certainly the case with the Report of the Committee on the Review of Statutory Boards 1979 (the Ndegwa Committee). The Committee's terms of reference were to examine the financial, administrative and operational problems facing SOEs, and to recommend new control procedures. However, the Commitee restricted its attention to the 66 statutory bodies and excluded the host of non-statutory state-owned enterprises.

It produced three main recommendations. First, with a view to establishing general principles in terms of the performance and regulation of parastatals, it recommended that a State Corporations Act be enacted to come under the aegis of a putative Parastatals Advisory Committee, which would establish the guidelines and criteria for the creation of parastatals, the appointment of their boards and management, their reporting obligations to the government, etc. Second, it recommended that the hitherto dormant Inspectorate of Statutory Bodies, first created in 1966, be revived and, in particular, that it be involved in policy formulation as well as its traditional audit and review function; it was even suggested that the Inspectorate offer consultancy services to smaller line ministries in the 'good' management of SOEs. Third, the Committee recommended that the Business Section of the Ministry of Finance be upgraded to a full Investment Division with the objective of streamlining all government investments in or through SOEs. In particular, the new Division was to be responsible for setting investment guidelines for parent ministries, dividend and other investment targets, co-ordinating all external assistance, and pre-screening of all funding proposals from SOEs.

The first and third of the recommendations have been implemented – although with a substantial time lag. The State Corporations Act, eventually promulgated in 1986, covers the standard menu of co-ordination issues such as board composition, rules of appointments, reporting obligations, scope and authority of parent ministries, and co-ordinating the various roles of the Inspectorate, the Ministry of Finance, and the Auditor General. Once again, however, the Act covers only the statutory bodies and plays no role in monitoring the non-statutory SOEs, for which responsibility remains in the hands of the Ministry of Finance Investments Division.

The most marked outcome of the Act to date has been in the area of SOE external debt. In terms of the Act no SOE is allowed to borrow on its own account (except Kenya Airways, which makes use of commercial suppliers' credit), and all external borrowing has to be approved by the Ministry of Finance. As noted in section 12.1, before 1986 a significant number of SOEs were borrowing from commercial sources at market rates. This trend has since been reversed. As Table 12.8 shows, the terms on new debt (including SOE debt) have improved

Table 12.8 *Average terms of new debt commitments*

	1970	1980	1981	1982	1983	1984	1985	1986	1987	1988	1989
Official creditors											
Interest (%)	2.3	3.4	5.5	5.2	5.1	5.8	4.1	3.7	1.4	2.3	1.8
Maturity (yrs)	38.6	31.7	29.9	31.4	32.0	23.5	28.9	30.6	37.4	26.9	34.8
Grace (yrs)	8.4	8.0	7.1	7.2	7.2	5.2	9.4	7.1	10.3	8.6	8.8
Grant element (%)	64.8	54.1	37.1	40.2	42.4	29.3	48.7	50.8	73.2	61.3	68.9
Private creditors											
Interest (%)	7.2	7.8	14.5	8.9	9.0	8.4	9.9	6.4	7.5	7.9	8.2
Maturity (yrs)	18.0	10.6	9.2	14.8	15.0	10.6	11.9	12.6	8.6	8.5	8.3
Grace (yrs)	0.9	2.6	2.8	3.3	3.7	2.1	2.1	3.7	3.1	1.6	1.5
Grace element (%)	14.1	9.6	−19.0	6.0	5.4	4.5	1.8	19.5	9.7	7.6	5.6
All creditors											
Interest (%)	2.6	3.5	9.0	5.5	5.2	6.4	6.4	5.0	2.3	3.7	2.7
Maturity (yrs)	37.3	31.3	21.8	30.2	31.3	20.7	22.2	21.8	33.2	22.4	31.2
Grace (yrs)	7.7	7.9	5.4	6.9	7.0	4.5	6.5	5.4	9.2	6.9	7.8
Grant element (%)	58.7	53.2	15.3	37.7	40.8	23.8	30.2	35.5	63.8	48.2	60.3

Source: World Bank, *World Debt Tables* (various issues).

dramatically, although, as noted, this was also due to Kenya's re-admission to IDA in 1986.

Working Party on Government Expenditure and Task Force on Divestiture

Though briefly mentioned by the Ndegwa Committee, privatization proposals emerged only with the Report of the Working Party on Government Expenditure in 1982.[12] The WPGE (p. 7) argues that the economic crisis in Kenya was, in part, due to

> the proliferation of commercial activities by Government which has diverted scarce management talent away from the central function of Government. . . . Its solution requires a firm decision by Government to focus public expenditures and management talent on the essential functions of Government in order to ensure that they are per-formed efficiently, and that available resources are used for essential and productive services.

It argued that the over-extension of the SOE sector had imposed serious distortions on the economy in three main ways. First, the strategy of providing a wide range of services to a rapidly growing population had become too expensive, and the pursuit of employment objectives had worked to the detriment of producti-vity considerations; second, government investments in commercial and industrial activities absorbed an excessive proportion of the budget, with insufficient return; and, finally, government provision of services had directly discouraged private sector service provision. These problems emerged because government involve-ment in the process persisted beyond its optimal time period, to the extent that the original objectives of state participation were compromised. In particular, the WPGE pointed to the fact that the government had not attempted to dispose of its holdings in commercial enterprises to Kenyans. In consequence the fundamental aim of Kenyanization was achieved only through the second-best option of government trusteeship. Moreover, as government participation increased, SOE operations tended to become less autonomous and less commercial. Consequently, even to the extent that SOEs were used as instruments of wealth creation for Kenyans, they were seen to be doing so with ever diminishing efficiency.

Moreover, it was noted that most of the SOEs were not strategic. Since management was provided by foreign and Kenyan-Asian partners, government ownership was not achieving the goals of Kenyanization. In effect, the government was doing little other than underwriting risks which should (and could) be borne by the private sector. The WPGE recommended that the government should reduce its own commercial exposure. In particular, new public investments should be reduced to a minimum, some existing investments should be disposed of, and those parastatals and other investments whose retention in the public sector was considered essential should be more effectively administered. It consequently recommended the creation of a Task Force on Divestiture to conduct a review of all SOEs (statutory bodies and other government investments), in order to classify them into: those whose retention was essential to accelerated and equitable national development and the regulation of the private sector; those whose objectives had been achieved and which should be discontinued; those whose functions could be absorbed by parent ministries; and those whose functions could be more efficiently performed by the private sector. For the latter group, the Task Force was then required to devise an effective strategy and appropriate mechanisms for the divestiture of shares and assets.

The Task Force was duly constituted in 1983 and sat until late 1986. Though now disbanded, it has never published any of its findings[13] – mainly, it is assumed, because of the political sensitivity of their subject matter. Despite the tacit support of the external donors (in particular the World Bank and USAID) who have focused a large element of their adjustment lending towards SOE reform and privatization initiatives, the policy maintains an extremely low profile. SOE reform in general, and privatization in particular, remain highly politicized issues and are likely to do so as long as the SOEs are seen as important instruments in the process of political control. The core problems in implementing privatization in Kenya are not those of deficient absorptive capacity, savings mobilization, or even regulation capacity, but more deeply embedded problems of ethnicity. There is a deep-seated concern on the part of dominant political figures that commercial, financial and managerial capital is concentrated in the hands of foreigners, Kenyan-Asians and, to a lesser extent, members of the Kikuyu tribe. To the extent that the interventionist stance represented an attempt to redress this economic imbalance, privatization, at least as presented in the public debate, is seen predominantly as a volte-face, a rejection of patronage, and of 'Kenyanization'. As one observer put it: 'In Kenya, though the economics of privatization may well generate a positive sum, the politics of privatization is seen simply in terms of a zero sum game.' As long as this sentiment prevails in the minds of politicians and civil servants the outlook for privatization is likely to be limited.

Thus, though lip service has been paid to the principle of privatization throughout the 1980s, and though the general thrust of the earlier recommendations has been echoed in subsequent policy statements, including the important Sessional Paper No. 1 of 1986 on *Economic Management for Renewed Growth*, the strength of commitment to privatization displayed by the WPGE has not been maintained. This dilution of the privatization imperative has been reflected in the virtual absence of any genuine initiatives, and the consequently negligible impact of the policy alongside the broader SOE reform packages. Like many other countries, the most striking indirect effect of the emergence of a 'privatization debate' in Kenya is its 'threat effect' and the brake it applies on the creation of new SOEs. SOE growth (by numbers) has been virtually zero, while (as noted above) some considerable degree of control has been exerted over transfers to the SOE sector and some important reform measures have been accelerated.

In view of the sensitivity surrounding the privatization programme in Kenya, and in particular the report of the Task Force, it has been extremely difficult to establish even a basic catalogue of actual privatization initiatives or of the future pipeline for privatization. The following section, however, attempt to marshall what evidence there is on SOE reform measures and privatizations.

12.3.2 SOE reform measures

Since 1979 there have been a number of direct attempts to address the problems of the SOE sector as a whole (as well as a number of firm- and sector-specific reforms). This section reviews their developments while the next addresses the more specific issue of how privatization fits into this programme.

Agricultural sector reform[14]

One of the important political aspects of reform and privatization in the agricultural sector has been the extent to which reform measures which challenged the rents of important individuals and groups were effectively stymied. This occurred with the reforms promoted by World Bank in maize marketing, and with similar attempts to improve the operational efficiency of the Agricultural Finance Corporation. Unlike many other economies, such as Malaŵi, the Kenyan commodity marketing boards passed on border prices for produce to the growers, and in the case of maize the producer price in fact generally exceeded the border price. The beneficiaries were originally settler-farmers but, following Independence, these rents were generally earned by large-scale, and politically powerful, Kenyan maize farmers. Similarly the debtors of the AFC (which was set up in 1963 to finance land re-purchases) tended to be from the political elite. The AFC lent to customers at rates of interest generally 2% points below the commercial bank lending rate (which itself was strongly negative during most of the period), and as a result of poor debt enforcement the Corporation had a persistently high default rate on loans – averaging in excess of 50% in most years.

Though the 1982 World Bank SAL, the 1986 SECAL, and Sessional Paper No. 1 of 1986 called for urgent reform of maize pricing and the restructuring of the AFC, the wholescale restructuring of agricultural marketing envisaged has not materialized. A number of marketing boards, principally the Kenya Farmers Association (renamed as the Kenya Grain Growers Association), the Kenya Coffee Board, the Kenya Cotton Commission, the Kenya Tea Development Authority and the Kenya Meat Commission, have been restructured by increasing the representation of local grain-growing and livestock co-operatives. In general, however, there has been no radical change in the operating procedures of these bodies, or, apparently, in their pricing policies. Liberalization of grain trading has not proceeded as planned, although greater competition has been introduced through purchase rights being granted to the Kenya Grain Growers Cooperative Union, and the concern has been raised that the restructuring of the boards represents merely a further step in an extremely complex and delicate bargaining game between the World Bank and the Government of Kenya over the restructuring of a politically sensitive sector of the economy (see Mosley, 1991: 287–98).

Restructuring of the DFIs

Though still incomplete, the DFI restructuring programme is likely to be one of the successes to emerge from the first decade of SOE reform and privatization, and may generate the credibility necessary for the government to pursue effective SOE reform in other areas. In mid-1990 a report on the Development Finance Corporation of Kenya, the Industrial and Commercial Development Corporation, and the Industrial Development Bank had been submitted to the government and had received Cabinet approval in principle. The report consisted of a comprehensive audit of the portfolios of the three institutions, and an evaluation of the non-performing companies in each portfolio. On the basis of these exercises comprehensive restructuring plans were prepared for the DFIs. The government maintained the view that they should remain the primary venture-capital organizations in the economy, but, aware of the risks involved in this form of lending, the policy envisages more active portfolio management. An unambiguous profit orientation was re-emphasized, with each DFI being required to earn an 'acceptable' return on its capital (the DFIs currently earn less than 2% on their capital on average), a process which was encouraged by the proposed financial restructuring (mainly through improved gearing to match the future equity orientation in lending) and by the goverment's absorption of the foreign-exchange risk on the DFIs' own borrowing. Central to the restructuring were plans to promote a more rapid portfolio turnover, with a number of divestiture options being considered including private placements with private sector institutions, individual listings on the Nairobi Stock Exchange, and the creation of unit trusts. At the time of writing, however, no such divestiture plans had been prepared.

Assessment of SOE reform initiatives

In view of the long delay in the implementation of the recommendations of the Ndegwa Committee, the SOE reforms have occurred only slowly, and progress so far has concentrated on establishing an appropriate framework for monitoring the SOE sector. However, weak institutional structures for SOE management were far from being the central problem facing the sector. More important was the fact that the weaknesses that emerged in the 1980s resulted from a more fundamental tendency for the government to use the SOEs and their management to pursue non-commercial objectives. Consequently, though the institutional reforms are important to the efficient operation of the sector, the failure to address the more basic issue of exposing the SOEs to a more commercial market and regulatory environment has not been tackled with the same enthusiasm. As the World Bank (1987b) notes, in relation to the specific institution of the State Corporations Act:

> The Act concentrates too much on the issue of financial misdemeanours to the exclusion of creating mechanisms which will promote productivity and efficient corporate operations.

Notwithstanding these comments, the public finance impact of the SOE reforms has been impressive. As Table 12.6 indicated, in the period from 1984/5 to 1988/9 total transfers to non-financial SOEs (current transfers, capital transfers, equity participation and net lending) fell from 4.2% of total expenditure (1.4% of GDP) to 0.53% (0.25% of GDP). During the same period the SOE share of total external debt fell from 24% in 1982 to 16% in 1988, and its share of domestic credit similarly fell from around 7% of the total to 4% by 1989.

These figures represent, in essence, a concerted effort to erase some of the worse financial excesses from the public accounts. What has not been addressed, however, are the underlying policy weaknesses which have brought about these problems. In many sectors, for example the utilities, transport, sugar, and textiles, broader reform measures are required. Despite the State Corporations Act, there is apparently only a limited degree of co-ordination of policy. This is clearest in the transport sector, where KR's viability is being worsened by the pricing policy of the KPLC, while, in the textile sector, the maintenance of high input prices through the Lint and Cotton Board directly undermines the export competitiveness of the SOE (and private) firms. There is also evidence (for example, in KPL) that SOEs are still being required to take on marginal, or even non-commercial, investments in pursuit of government policy aims. Again, there is no suggestion that this is an unsuitable role for such enterprises to adopt; but rather it highlights the conflicting commercial and non-commercial objectives set for the enterprises. Finally, (as in the case of KA) there is clear evidence of extreme internal operational inefficiency which, because of the existence of 'soft' budget constraints, has not been eradicated by the competition faced by the airline.

12.3.3 Privatization methods and experience

With the government's reluctance to publish the report of the Task Force, it is not possible to provide much detail on the structure of the privatization process in Kenya, or on the nature of the privatization 'pipeline' (if one exists). However, a number of features do emerge. First, it is known that a general set of broad policy guidelines for privatization has been adopted by the Cabinet. Under these, however, the privatization programme has been decentralized so that individual ministers are 'required' to pursue privatization within these guidelines only as they see fit. It is suspected that these guidelines are essentially the principles set out by the WPGE, and that the decentralization of the privatization initiative has served to dilute the policy's significance (and to enhance the capacity of unsympathetic ministers to block sale moves). Second, experience so far suggests that enterprises considered for privatization are generally those in which government participation is through equity participation on the part of the DFIs. No indications yet suggest that the government is willing, or able, to tackle privatization in the large-scale infrastructure sector. Third, there is no systematic programme to identify and prepare candidates for privatization. On the contrary, privatization has emerged as a residual response to financial and operational failure on the part of government-owned commercial enterprises. Thus, whereas many other countries have attempted to raise the profile of privatization by well-publicized sales of profitable enterprises, the government of Kenya has kept the profile of the programme low, imbuing it with the air of a closing-down sale.

Though discussion in the WPGE and elsewhere has linked the privatization programme with public share sales through the Nairobi Stock Exchange (and thereby linked the policy closely with on-going capital market developments), there has been only one sale of shares to the public – that in Kenya Commercial Bank shares, which, as we note below, is not strictly a privatization. Otherwise two methods of sale have been employed. The first is the direct sale of assets to domestic (or possibly foreign) purchasers of specified enterprises, and the second is what has become known as the 'Receivership Method' through which the government has called in loans or lines of credit, forcing the closure and bankruptcy of the enterprise, and allowing the receiver to organize its sale to the private sector.

In terms of direct sales, the first and most widely publizised privatization initiative was the Uplands Bacon Factory, a 100% government-owned statutory body involved in meat processing since its establishment in 1946. The enterprise had never been profitable, however, and, following negotiations prior to the 1986 World Bank Agricultural Sector Credit, a commitment was made to sell it. Throughout 1986 and 1987 the government actively sought a buyer (or at least new management) for the factory, initially domestically, but latterly internationally (in particular in the European Community). No satisfactory bidders came forward and the factory was not sold. Following a period of closure, it is again in operation, but still under public ownership and management.[15]

A number of other enterprises, in which the government holds only a minority of the equity through the Development Finance Corporation of Kenya (itself 30.5% owned by ICDC), have also been identified as targets for divestiture by direct sale. These are Rift Valley Textiles and Kicomi (1983) Ltd in the textile sector, Ceramic Industries of East Africa, and Mugitex Manufacturers Ltd (see Table 12.9).

Table 12.9 *DFCK enterprises identified for sale*

Company	Sector	DFCK equity	Secured loans
Rift Valley Textiles	Textiles	Ksh. 2.4m (35.6%)	Ksh. 1.1m
Kicomi (1983) Ltd	Textiles	Ksh. 10.4m (36.8%)	Ksh. 21.2m
Mugitex Manufacturers	Metals	Ksh. 0.5m (41.6%)	Ksh. 0.1m
Ceramic Industries	Ceramics	Ksh. 2.5m (51.1%)	Ksh. 15.2m
TOTAL		Ksh. 15.8m	Ksh. 37.6m

Source: DFCK, *Annual Report*, 1988.

The selection has (apparently) been made by the board of DFCK itself, mainly on the basis that these companies are intrinsically profitable and have relatively good vintage capital. Since the government is only a minor shareholder in DFCK, and since in all cases except Ceramic Industries DFCK is only a minority share-holder in the company, the government's direct role in the sale of these enterprises is negligible. As with the sales effected by the DFIs in Malaŵi, these cannot be con-sidered as central to the privatization programme, but rather as part of the normal activities of a venture-capital company. However, even so no suitable buyers have yet been identified, and the companies remain in the DFCK portfolio.

The 'Receivership Method' has, in a perverse way, been a more successful method of privatization, although in most cases the process has not been con-cluded. The government, its holding company, or often a third creditor has initiated foreclosure, the company concerned has been put in the hands of the receiver, but no (acceptable) private operator has yet been found. Long delays have been encountered in the completion of the receivership process, and invariably the cost of the delay has been borne by the relevant DFI.[16] However, in other cases, enterprises have been sufficiently rationalized and management improved under the receivers for operations to start up again, and performance has improved. The prime example here is the Kenya National Transport Company Ltd (KENATCO). KENATCO was founded in 1964 by private owners, but was taken over by government in 1966 (100% of the equity is held by ICDC). The com-pany was involved in road haulage and taxi operations, but the closure of the Ugandan and Tanzanian borders in the 1970s undermined its financial viability and it was eventually put into receivership in 1983. Although there has been no new buyer and it therefore remains in public sector ownership, the receivers have established a new company, Kenatco Taxis Ltd (also 100% ICDC-owned), which now operates a successful urban taxi service in Nairobi. Efforts are still under way to divest the company fully to private sector owners.

By mid-1990 there were a number of SOEs in receivership and identified as pos-sible candidates for privatization. In addition to Kenatco Taxis Limited, buyers are being sought for the rump of KENATCO (government equity participation is 100% and valued at Ksh. 6.9m.), Kenya Fishing Industries Ltd (100% equity, valued at Ksh. 10.9m.), and Yuken Textiles Ltd (100% equity, valued at Ksh. 18.6m.). Direct ICDC equity participation in these enterprises thus totals Ksh. 36.4m. No private sector buyers had been identified at that time for these enterprises but the ICDC management believe that new owners will eventually be found.

The autonomous nature of the 'receivership model' has effectively transformed privatization into a passive, indirect response to enterprise failure. As the World Bank (1987b) has noted:

> it appears that the Kenyans have inadvertently hit upon a halfway measure to divestiture. In effect the Government is allowing receivership status to be used as a form of privatization of management.

By following this route, the government has distanced itself from the privatization and has developed a mechanism to achieve the basic aim of privatization without conflicting with the politically sensitive issues of Kenyanization. It remains the case, however, that the sticking point has been the identification of new owners and managers of the enterprises other than the receivers themselves, and it is still unclear whether 'suitable' buyers with the capital to purchase the equity are likely to be forthcoming.

The Kenya Commercial Bank sale

The most recent privatization, and the only one that has, in fact, been completed successfully, was the sale of equity in the Kenya Commercial Bank in 1988. Strictly speaking, however, given that it was a new share issue designed to raise additional capital for the bank, and did not involve any sale of equity by the government, there was no privatization. None the less, the issue did bring the private sector in as joint owners of the bank. The decision to sell equity to the public was taken, somewhat opportunistically, following the immensely successful Barclays Bank of Kenya's public share issue in April 1986. Barclays was the first new issue on the market since 1984, and the largest single issue in the history of the Nairobi Stock Exchange, raising Ksh. 90m. for the bank. Barclays Bank shares were distributed widely through the branch network, and the 5 million shares were oversubscribed by 500%. The KCB management therefore sought permission to finance its own forthcoming capital requirement through the issue of 7.5 million Ksh. 10 shares, representing 20% of the total issued capital, to the public through a listing on the Nairobi Stock Exchange. Government permission was granted and the share issue (and listing) proceeded in July 1988. The Barclays issue was, in retrospect, greatly 'underpriced', not least because, being the first new share issue for some time, there was no clear indication of what the prospective demand would be. KCB, however, was able to use the Barclays share price to set its issue price, and the shares were offered at Ksh. 20, raising a total of Ksh. 150m. As with Barclays the issue was oversubscribed, but by only 22%. KCB introduced a rationing scheme which, unlike the Barclays issue, limited the initial number of shareholders to only 75,000 applicants each receiving 100 shares. Secondary trading has been relatively light, but by 1989 KCB was trading at around Ksh. 30 per share, representing a premium on the issue price of 50%. During the same period the NSE all-share index actually fell by approximately 15%. The success of this first equity issue was followed in September 1990 by a further 20% capital increase, which now leaves the government with a 60% equity stake in the bank.[17]

The KCB share issue was more a matter of opportunity than of strategic planning. The sale has had an indirect fiscal effect through the substitution of a government capital injection by private capital, but it has not radically altered the nature of the Bank's management or of the board of directors and, as with other such sales (for example, NCB in Jamaica), the overall performance of the bank has not changed. Moreover, in view of the fact that the sale was precipitated in no small measure by the Barclays Bank initiative, it is difficult to conclude that KCB's apparent 'political' success has been used to overcome more widespread political opposition to the privatization programme.

12.3.4 Summary and outlook

It remains somewhat premature to talk of a privatization programme in Kenya. The main policy emphasis has been on improving the performance of SOEs as a whole, while privatization, where it has occurred, has been a residual, reactive process.

In view of the extreme secrecy and political sensitivity surrounding the policy of privatization in Kenya, it is difficult to assess how, if at all, the programme will develop. Though the policy is seen by technocrats as an important, if not essential, element of a broad SOE reform process, and although it has been embodied in official policy statements throughout the 1980s, there is, in reality, no genuine political commitment to it. Privatization is still basically anathema to many Kenyan politicians, is seen as the antithesis of 'Kenyanization' and as an unacceptable challenge to the prevailing system of patronage and control in the economy. Without a strong 'political' commitment to privatization (as is evident in, say, Malaysia, Sri Lanka and Jamaica) the technical and economic arguments, which are in some sectors quite compelling, are being stifled. This lack of political commitment does, however, explain the emergence of the 'Receivership' method of privatization. Nevertheless, it remains the view of donors, commentators, and many policy-makers within the government that current fiscal imbalances mean that further, more aggressive action is required. As the World Bank (1987b) notes:

> The Government's efforts to improve the performance of SOEs will, at best, take a long time to implement and there is a possibility that these efforts will lead to very little change in performance. On the other hand, Kenya can no longer afford to place increasingly scarce resources into unproductive hands . . . The logical conclusion is that if Government cannot make the parastatals run efficiently, and if it cannot afford to subsidize their operations, the remaining option is divestiture.

The following sections sets these specific political constraints to one side and addresses the question of whether, if political attitudes towards the policy alter, the private sector can generate the resources and provide the competitive environment through which the extraction of performance and efficiency gains from privatization can be achieved.

12.4 Private sector structures

As became increasingly evident from the previous section, privatization in Kenya, if it is to expand in scope, is most likely to be confined to the manufacturing, services and financial sectors, rather than the utilities. This section will therefore attempt to draw together some evidence on the structure of these sectors of the economy.

12.4.1 Background to the manufacturing sector

One of the distinguishing features of the Kenyan economy, in comparison with many others in sub-Saharan Africa, is the relative dynamism of the private manufacturing and services sector. Though the economy remains predominantly agricultural, the period since Independence saw a dramatic rise in the manufacturing sector. It now accounts for approximately 13% of GDP, as compared with approximately 8% at Independence, and from 1975 to 1985 it grew at an average of 6% per annum. The sector employs approximately 185,000 people, 22% of whom are employed in SOEs. The dominant subsectors are food-processing (accounting for 30% of employment and 30% of value-added), textiles and clothing (17% of employment and 7% of value-added), and beverages and tobacco (4% of employment and 11% of value-added).

12.4.2 Ownership structure

The Kenyan private sector hosts a variety of ownership forms. Most noticeable is the sizeable number of foreign-owned firms, many of which pre-date Independence. Most of these are relatively efficient and well integrated into other sectors of the economy, although newer foreign-owned companies – those attracted initially by the prospect of high protection levels and easy access to the EAC market – have proved less profitable and, since many are now operating at low capacity, have relatively low levels of efficiency. New foreign direct investment is at historically low levels and, outside the financial sector, there is, in fact, net disinvestment at present.

Kenyan-Asians have been by far the most dynamic entrepreneurs in post-Independence Kenya, providing high-quality managerial, financial and technical inputs into the economy. They are the dominant force in the medium-scale manufacturing sector, especially in textiles, where re-investment of profits is high.[18] The Kenyan-Asian community has, however, been the target of considerable antagonism, not least following the attempted *coup d'état* in 1982, and, though they remain the one group most able to acquire and manage industrial public enterprises profitably, their direct participation in the privatization programme is likely to be discouraged.

The African private sector remains an important part of the economy, accounting for about 10% of value-added and a similar proportion of employment. However, the bulk of this activity is concentrated in small and micro-enterprises. There is an almost total absence of African joint-stock enterprises, and there has been a very low rate of 'graduation' from small- to medium-sized enterprises, despite widespread fiscal and institutional support (principally through the Kenyan Industrial Estates). The inevitable consequences of this for privatization are twofold. First, there is the modest level of capital accumulation generated by this group. Aggregate savings from the sector are not insubstantial, but in general they do not consist of savings which could be readily directed into sizeable capital accumulation. Second, the sector is not yet capable of acting as seed-bed for the managerial capacity necessary to run relatively large-scale SOEs. Consequently, since most SOEs are large- and medium-sized enterprises, the immediate economic environment in which privatized enterprises will function is shaped by foreign and Kenyan-Asian companies.

12.4.3 Performance of manufacturing sector

Whether SOEs, when transferred to the private sector, can increase their operational efficiency greatly depends on the structure and efficiency of the private sector. The World Bank study (1987b, 52–3) presents a comprehensive picture of the average efficiency and degree of protection in Kenyan manufacturing, concluding that 'certainly by African standards Kenyan industry stands out as being among the most competitive and efficient', although the averages reveal a significant disparity across subsectors (Table 12.10). Capacity utilization ranged from 42% in the electrical equipment sector to 96% for textiles. Similarly the widespread use of quantitative restrictions and tariffs in response to balance-of-payments crises during the 1970s has resulted in high and variable levels of protection. Effective protection rates ranged from highly protected sectors such as iron and steel products, cement and textiles to low levels in the paper and wood products and beverages and tobacco sectors.

The World Bank study also suggests that large firms (i.e. those employing

Table 12.10 *Manufacturing sector efficiency and protection, 1987 (%)*

	Import content	NRP	ERP	Cap util	Short-run DRC	Long-run DRC	Rate of profit
Food processing	36	24	111	89	0.37	0.71	23
Beverages and tobacco	33	29	38	75	0.37	0.88	48
Textiles	62	46	126	96	0.99	2.13	19
Leather & footwear	44	37	80	53	2.03	2.9	−4
Paper & wood	11	22	6	93	0.57	1.58	11
Plastics and pharmaceuticals	93	48	129	72	0.76	1.72	26
Basic and other chemicals	81	50	211	86	0.86	1.46	21
Cement & glass	59	30	248	88	1.99	6.29	11
Iron & steel products	62	38	312	56	1.86	5.48	12
Electrical & transport	83	71	312	42	1.76	3.49	8
Average by value-added in sector	43	33	107	81	0.69	1.53	24

Source: World Bank, 1987b.

Notes:
NRP: Nominal Rate of Protection = (Output valued at domestic prices)/(output valued at world prices).
ERP: Effective Rate of Protection = (Value-added at domestic price)/(valued-added at world prices).
Short-run DRC: Domestic Resource Cost = (Labour costs)/(value-added at world prices).
Long-run DRC: Domestic Resource Cost = (Labour costs + annual capital costs)/(value-added at world prices).

more than 50 people) are more efficient, have lower import content and operate at higher capacity than small companies. Finally, the study reports measures of the degree of market concentration. Based on the Herfindahl Index measure of concentration,[19] the Bank suggests that approximately 38% of firms and 62% of sales are generated by monopolistic or oligopolistic producers. Most noticeable is the fact that oligopolistic firms are more highly protected and less inefficient than new monopolies. It is within this sector that many of the SOEs are found, and thus the removal of protection and other barriers to entry into these markets may be expected to induce improvements in efficiency.

12.4.4 Developments in the private sector
The shift towards structural adjustment in the 1980s served to re-orient industrial policy. The general objectives are embedded in Sessional Paper No. 1 of 1986 which states (para. 1.7):

> Government's strategy for industrialization must concentrate on two approaches. First, the domestic market for manufactured goods must be expanded markedly and this can only be done if incomes in the rural areas rise rapidly. Second, Kenya's industry must be restructured to become much more efficient, capable of competing against imported goods in Kenya with moderate protection and of exporting profitably within the PTA and further abroad.

Under this commitment the government has embarked on a number of reform measures aimed at enhancing industrial performance. The first was the creation, in 1986, of the Industrial Promotion Centre (IPC) as the vehicle for revitalizing direct foreign investment and the promotion of an aggressive export sector. The IPC serves as a 'one-stop' investment centre and acts as agent for the implementation of the goverment's investment promotion initiative. This is concentrated in three areas: manufacturing-in-bond,[20] management of the World Bank's Multilateral Investment Guarantee arrangements, and development of the new Export Processing Zones established in Mombasa and Nairobi.

The second element has been trade liberalization. Initial progress, under SALs I and II was weak, and was plagued by the continued use of trade restrictions as instruments of short-run external stabilization policy. Under the auspices of the 1988 Industrial Sector Credit, however, the government embarked on a comprehensive review of quantitative restrictions and tariffs, with the aim of reducing the number of items on restricted licence schedules and implementing an unrestricted licensing for all other goods; re-aligning tariffs to ensure a reduction of effective protection to a 'similar-good-similar-tariff' basis; reducing the number of tariff rates from 25 to 12; and a general move towards *ad valorem* tariffs. It is expected, however, that, given the slow progress in trade liberalization from 1980 to 1988, this revision will take a number of years to implement.

The third important innovation followed from the WPGE recommendations on competition policy and industrial regulation. The result of this initiative was the Restrictive Trade Practices, Monopolies and Price Control Act of 1989. The Act marks an important component in the shift towards greater private sector participation in the economy. In addition to supporting the trade liberalization process by moving to the complete decontrol of all domestic prices (other than those covered by specific monopoly provisions), the Act tackles competition policy by proscribing predatory trade practices undertaken 'with the intention of driving a competitor out of business, inducing a merger, forcing a product switch, or temporary closure'. Such predatory practices also include sales 'at prices which are found to be below their average variable cost'; collusive tendering; and collusive bidding. Similarly, monopoly power is deemed to exist if a company produces supplies or distributes to more than one-third of the market (by value), and the Act empowers the Minister to investigate 'any economic sector which he has reason to believe may feature one or more factors relating to unwarranted concentrations of economic power'.[21]

Similarly, any merger, acquisition or takeover which leads to a concentration of economic power requires the prior permission of the Minister. Mergers will be deemed advantageous if they lead to lower unit cost, more efficient resource use, increased export performance and greater employment, and disadvantageous if they reduce competition in domestic markets, etc., or if they encourage capital-intensive rather than labour-intensive operations. The competition policy embodied in this Act marks a landmark in the re-orientation of the Kenyan economy by introducing a market-based regulatory regime. However, at the time of writing the regulatory regime has yet to be put to the test, and the regulatory mettle of the government has not been challenged.

12.4.5 Summary
Macroeconomic evidence suggests that aggregate savings in Kenya are sufficient to absorb a sizeable programme of divestiture. However, savings are heavily skewed between African and non-African Kenyans, and the capacity for large-scale mobilization of speculative savings remains concentrated in the hands of Kenyan-Asians, although the capacity for the mobilization of small investor savings has received a fillip from the share issues by the commercial banks.

In addition, the structure of the private sector suggests that it has the capacity to provide a competitive environment in which private ownership of formerly public assets can elicit efficiency gains, at least for the industrial sectors. This possibility is enhanced by the fact that public sector involvement in some industrial subsectors (such as textiles) is so broad that the privatization of SOEs *en masse* could in itself form a potentially competitive market.

Second, though the private sector has historically been characterized by high levels of protection, recent moves to liberalize the trade regime are likely to generate a greater degree of competition from imports and thereby elicit efficiency improvements in the domestic economy. Similarly, greater access to the domestic sector by foreign capital and also the introduction of (potentially) aggressive competition policy will contribute to the competitiveness of the private sector.

Whether this potential can be effectively brought to bear depends crucially on the capacity to mobilize savings. As noted in Chapter 5, the presence of a functioning capital market can enhance the mobilization of savings and allow many of the problems of wealth concentration to be addressed in a manner which ameliorates the conflicting objectives of concentration of wealth and the extraction of efficiency gains from privatization. We now turn to the issue of capital markets and the mobilization of savings for privatization.

12.5 The capital market and resource mobilization

Like many other developing countries, Kenya has recently begun to pay greater attention to financial sector reform and the role of the capital market, in particular the Nairobi Stock Exchange (NSE).

12.5.1 Origins and development of NSE
Equity trading in Kenya has a long history covering the duration of the country's colonial and post-colonial history. Until the 1950s shares were traded by estate agents in Kenya, with those of a number of larger companies (and utilities) being directly listed in London, but in 1954 the NSE was established as a self-regulating body. The exchange consists of six broking companies and operates a daily call-over market.[22]

As Table 12.11 indicates, the NSE is a small market, with market capitalization averaging only marginally over 2% of GDP throughout the 1980s, although there was some increase after 1986 following the increased new issues. Throughout the decade there were only 7 new issues (as opposed to 6 in the 1974–8 period), although in contrast to the new issues in the 1970s the average size was much larger and total new capital raised from 1986 to 1989 was Ksh. 642m. (equivalent to about 7% of total market capitalization in 1989). Turnover in secondary markets is shockingly low, however, representing only approximately 0.1% of capitalization. The bulk of the trade on the NSE is in government paper, and the bulk of the debt issued by the government is held by financial SOEs, principally the National Social Security Fund. From 1973 to 1981, public sector institutions held approximately 80% of all debt issued on the market, with approximately 15% held

Table 12.11 *Nairobi Stock Exchange: 1980–89 (Ksh. m.)*

	1980	1981	1982	1983	1984	1985	1986	1987	1988	1989
Market capitalization	3,003	2,880	2,580	3,240	3,820	4,250	5,080	7,000	8,410	8,730
Mkt cap. as % GDP	2.7	2.2	1.7	2.0	2.0	2.0	2.0	2.5	2.6	2.5
Value of turnover	–	–	–	–	–	–	–	–	–	2
No. of listed companies	57	54	54	54	55	55	53	53	55	55
No. of new issues	–	–	–	–	1	–	1	1	3	1
Value of new issues	–	–	–	–	12	–	90	30	278	305
Market index (1980=100)	100.0	92.6	92.4	101.2	102.1	111.3	133.7	194.4	226.9	215.6

Source: Nairobi Stock Exchange Yearbook.

by other financial institutions and 5% by the corporate sector. None is held by private individuals.

The latter half of the 1980s saw a revival of interest in the equity market, stimulated mainly by the shares issued by the three major commercial banks, Barclays Bank of Kenya, the Kenya Commercial Bank and Standard Chartered Bank of Kenya. The Barclays and KCB issues (discussed in section 12.3) were followed in October 1989 by the Standard Chartered issue which raised Ksh. 305m. and is the single biggest share issue on the NSE.[23] These three issues (along with a rights issue by ICDC of Ksh. 126m. in 1988) represented an increase in new capital from 1986 to 1989 of Ksh. 703m., representing approximately 8% of the 1989 market capitalization.

12.5.2 Equity market regulation

The NSE has no formal corporate status and is not subject to any form of regulation. Concern has been expressed about the lack of transparency in the dealing process where brokers operate in a 'dual-capacity' mode – as agents for clients but also as market-makers on their own book. Concerns about the extent of insider trading constitute a major disincentive to equity trading in Kenya, to the extent that a number of fund managers have started to trade off the exchange. As a result, one of the objectives of the newly created Capital Markets Development Authority is to provide the NSE with a corporate identity and directly tackle the issue of the market's regulation and transparency. First announced in the 1988/89 Budget Speech, the Capital Markets Authority Act was tabled in 1989 to provide a regulatory framework for the development of the capital market in Kenya. The principal role of the CMA, as stated in the enabling act is:

(a) the development of all aspects of the capital markets with particular emphasis on the removal of impediments to, and the creation of incentives for, longer term investment in productive enterprise;

(b) the creation, maintenance and regulation, through implementation of a system in which the market participants are self-regulatory to the maximum practicable extent, of a market in which securities can be issued and traded in an orderly, fair and efficient manner.

The authority is new, however, and it is unlikely that any substantive progress will be made in the direct regulation of the market before 1992, while the CMA establishes itself and formulates detailed operational plans. Even when operational, it is unlikely that the CMA will focus entirely on the NSE. Its initial aims are seen to lie more in the need to develop secondary trading in the markets for government paper, and also to help to develop the DFI restructuring programme.

12.5.3 The NSE and privatization options

The evidence from the commercial bank share issues suggests that the NSE can play an important role in the privatization programme. Its importance may be threefold. The first is simply in providing a method of mobilizing domestic sales for privatization issues. The second is the extent to which this form of selling could be used profitably to overcome concerns about the distribution of ownership in the economy. The evidence from the Barclays Bank share issue in particular is that, if suitably priced and marketed, a wide share ownership can result in Kenya – even if this is possibly at the expense of deep secondary market trading. And, finally, if the evidence of other countries is anything to go by, the use of the capital market for privatization can serve as a key instrument in establishing the government's commitment to the programme.

However, if successful privatization is to be sustained in Kenya through public share sales, it is necessary that the regulatory structure be enhanced, and that parallel steps be taken to deepen the market, attract new players, and improve payment and trading systems. Despite its age, the stock market in Kenya is as yet too thin and too immature to be able to handle even a moderate-sized public share issue. The role of the NSE in privatization could be very important, not least in the divestiture of industrial and commercial companies to the private sector in a way that avoids extreme political concern about concentration of ownership. However, whether this can be fulfilled will depend crucially on the success with which the Capital Market Authority addresses the problems of market regulation and the promotion of secondary trading in equities.

12.6 Conclusions

The privatization debate in Kenya raises a number of important implications for privatization throughout Africa. Kenya is one of the few sub-Saharan African countries which enjoys an economic structure which could be conducive to a positive programme of privatization concentrated in the industrial and commercial sectors of the economy. The private sector is relatively deep, competitive and subject to only moderate levels of protection. It enjoys relatively high levels of management skills, good international market access, and a comparatively benign macroeconomic environment, not plagued by poor exchange-rate or monetary management. Furthermore, these conditions are gradually improving under the current adjustment programme. Kenya also enjoys a savings level higher than the SSA average and the mechanisms for mobilizing these savings are relatively well developed. Current policy is also addressing the need to deepen the capital market and improve financial intermediation. Against this background there exists an SOE sector which, though plagued in many cases by excessive interference and extremely poor management, consists of a large number of commercial and potentially competitive enterprises in the industrial sector. The SOEs are numerous and in a sizeable number of sectors do not enjoy sustainable monopoly positions. In other words, though far from perfect, Kenya offers an economic environment in which the supposed benefits of privatization, in terms of efficiency and competition, could be realized.

In some respects, it might have been expected that, faced with this environment, Kenya would have set the pace for privatization in Africa. That the policy remains low-key and attitudes to it remain hostile sharply underlines the fact that privatization is essentially a political process. Though there is strong support from technocratic elements in the civil service for a higher-profile privatization programme within a broader SOE reform package, support at the political level has never been forthcoming. Privatization remains a betrayal of the basic control function of government. The irony is that Kenya is one of the few countries in SSA where, in the industrial sector at least, privatization can play a significant role in assisting the process of reform, by concentrating goverment resources and enhancing the capacity of the private sector to meet the sustainable employment-generation objectives embodied in the government's own medium-term development strategy.

Notes

1. World Bank Agricultural Sector Credit (1986); World Bank Financial Sector Adjustment Credit (1989); IMF Structural Adjustment Facility (1988); IMF Enhanced Structural Adjustment Facility (1989).
2. One of the legacies of this uncontrolled growth is the absence of a comprehensive financial database for the sector as a whole. The Ministry of Finance recently established a comprehensive database for the larger enterprises (principally the utilities), but as yet it is not possible to obtain detailed data on the sector as a whole.
3. The term parastatal or public enterprise is used synonymously in Kenya. In the interest of consistency we shall use the term SOE throughout.
4. It should be noted, however, that even these figures probably underestimate the true extent of government participation since they refer almost exclusively to the statutory bodies and do not include the other goverment companies and investments (in particular the ones held through the DFIs).
5. This section draws heavily on the data in Grosh (1986).
6. For example, Kenya Railways and the East African Harbour Board were originally operated under the aegis of Uganda Railways, established in 1903.
7. Compared with its regional rival, Ethiopian Airlines, which operates 31 aircraft with a staff of 2,000, Kenya Airways operates 11 aircraft with a staff of 4,000, a sixfold difference.
8. The project was funded almost entirely through the account of KPL and its subsidiaries (the Kenya Power Company and the Tana and Taru River Development Authorities), so that the power-generating companies as a whole accounted for almost 28% of the total external debt of the SOE sector by 1989, over twice their share in the early 1980s.
9. Even though in some cases all other competitors are also SOEs.
10. The same conclusion emerges from some of the public vs private studies of highly regulated markets reviewed in Chapter 2.
11. All enterprises operate at below the estimated minimum economic scale for the sector, with the largest company (the public sector Kicomi Ltd) operating at approximately only 75% of the minimum economic scale.
12. The WPGE was also chaired by Philip Ndegwa who was the then Governor of the Central Bank of Kenya and, like the 1979 Committee, included Harris Mule (Permanent Secretary, Finance) and Simeon Nachaye (Permanent Secretary, Office of the President) as members. These three were widely regarded as the three most influential civil servants in Kenya in recent decades.
13. It is alleged that the World Bank and other donors have been asking for copies of the Task Force Report since 1986, but to no avail.
14. The details are well covered in Mosley *et al.* (1991).
15. There is a lack of clarity about the status of the Uplands Bacon Factory. Mosley *et al.* (1991) suggest that the enterprise is currently in operation, but the 1990 *Economic Survey* indicates that the factory remains closed.
16. The best-known case of this phenomenon is the Kenya Furfural Company, a joint-venture Ksh. 20m. brewing company owned jointly by Guinness of the UK and the DFCK. The company has been in liquidation since 1982, but no action has been taken on the future of the plant, nor have creditors been settled, since the receivers have not yet received a final decision to proceed with the receivership proceedings from the goverment shareholder.
17. No details have been obtained on this second share issue.
18. As a result of good exchange-rate management, Kenya has not experienced the levels of capital flight on the part of the Kenyan-Asian community which have so plagued other countries in the region.
19. Defined as $HI = (v^2 - 1)/n$ where v is the coefficient of variation and n the number of firms in the sector. Pure monopoly is 1,000 by construction, and as HI falls the sector becomes more competitive. Generally $HI < 200$ is taken to be competitive, with values between 200 and 1,000 indicating oligopolistic structures.
20. This is eligible to large companies which are 100% exporters. Eligible companies are entitled to full exemptions on duties and sales tax on all plant, equipment, raw materials, etc. More generally, other manufacturers are entitled to a 20% rebate on the fob value of exports if the domestic value-added exceeds 30%.
21. The Act states that 'unwarranted concentration of power' shall be deemed to be prejudicial to the public interest if its effect would be:- (a) to increase unreasonably the cost relating to the production, supply, or distribution of goods or the provision of any service; or (b)

to increase unreasonably the price at which goods are sold, or the profits derived from production, supply or distribution; or (c) to reduce or limit unreasonably competition in the production, supply or distribution of any goods; or (d) to result in a deterioration in the quality of supply.

22. The NSE does not have a trading floor, and market trading occurs in the New Stanley Hotel in Nairobi.

23. As at early 1990 the shares were trading at a premium of approximately 100% on the issue price.

13 MALAŴI

13.1 Introduction

Much of the discussion in this book has centred on the necessity of certain structural characteristics if privatization is to yield meaningful outcomes. Broadly, these are the existence of a (relatively) competitive private sector, an adequate level of private sector savings which can be effectively mobilized through the capital market, and a managerial and regulatory capacity through which the allocative inefficiencies of monopoly practice can be attenuated. While some of these features may be present in the larger countries in our study (for example, Malaysia, Jamaica, Sri Lanka, and Kenya), they are absent in Malaŵi. Their absence raises a number of important issues about the fundamental rationale for privatization in low-income economies. In the face of a virtually non-existent domestic private sector and very low domestic savings, the question is raised: What can realistically be expected as the outcome of a programme of privatization? If, however, privatization is pursued (through either domestic or external processes), the issue then is one of how a programme should be managed in the face of such constraints. In this respect Malaŵi offers a valuable insight into the problems of privatization in small economies, for, unlike many comparable economies, privatization in Malaŵi has enjoyed a relatively high degree of political support. Thus, in contrast to Kenya, the experience of Malaŵi is one in which the political commitment is present but the structure is unconducive, and to this extent provides an important case study for similar low-income economies.

13.1.2 Macroeconomic background

Malaŵi is a small, landlocked, predominantly agricultural country of approximately 8 million people. In line with a number of other African countries, during the first decade and a half following Independence in 1964 it enjoyed extremely favourable economic performance, even though the economy was (and still is) heavily dependent on the principal export commodity, tobacco. The first year after Independence saw a rapid expansion of the tobacco industry to fill the supply gap created by the declaration of UDI in neighbouring Rhodesia, thereby setting the pattern for the coming decade. Aided by favourable (and stable) terms of trade and strong capital inflows, the decade 1965–75 witnessed a 66% rise in per capita GDP. Domestic savings rose from around 8% of GDP to 14% in 1974 and 21% in 1978, while gross investment averaged around 25% throughout the period. Public sector investment was the driving force behind the GDP growth, with infrastructural investment providing the basis for export growth and increased industrialization. Malaŵi quickly acquired a reputation as a non-interventionist, market-based economy, free from the excessive price distortions so characteristic of many of its neighbours (see Gulhati, 1989; Harrigan, 1991).

Despite this impressive performance, Malaŵi remains one of the poorest countries in the world.[1] Primary agriculture accounts for 40% of GDP, 90% of exports, and almost 50% of the formal sector labour force. The manufacturing sector, in contrast, accounts for only 12% of GDP, and itself is dominated by food-processing, which accounts for approximately 40% of total manufacturing output, with textiles, pharmaceuticals, and chemicals accounting for 30% of the remainder.

Although Malaŵi has acquired a non-interventionist reputation, the economy has exhibited severe policy distortions in respect of the agricultural sector, and has been dominated by a small number of large quasi-public enterprises plus the anomalous Press Holdings, the country's main holding company, which is owned by the Life President, Dr Hastings Banda (see section 13.2). The ramifications of these distortions emerged in the reform and privatization debate in the later 1980s. Throughout the post-Independence period, and particularly during the 1970s, policy in the agricultural sector discriminated in favour of estate agriculture.[2] Incomes policies kept down labour costs for the estates, while the low prices paid to smalholder producers by the Agricultural Development and Marketing Corporation (ADMARC) ensured that they had a ready supply of labour. This policy, which effectively imposed punitive production taxes on smallholders, had a severely detrimental effect on smallholder production. Smallholders increasingly ceased production of ADMARC-controlled cash crops, while a growing number of them switched into wage employment on the large estates where their marginal revenue was higher. Moreover, under the aegis of Press Holdings and its participation in the financial sector, expansion of the estate subsector was financed through cheap commercial bank credit. The estate subsector accounted for over 50% of all bank lending by 1980 (Harrigan, 1991: 206).

The implications of this distortion were threefold. First, the subsidization of the estate tobacco subsector undermined efforts at diversification and, combined with the exposure of the financial and industrial sectors to changes in the fortunes of estate tobacco, left the economy excessively exposed to external trade shocks: the crisis of the 1980s was almost entirely the result of this exposure. Second, the tightly enforced incomes policy kept real wages low and suppressed capital accumulation by all agents other than ADMARC and Press Holdings, whose operations became increasingly capital-intensive. Savings levels (as Table 13.1 shows) were low throughout the 1970s, and even the modest increase during the early 1980s was generated mainly by Press and ADMARC. The third, and related, effect of the distortion was the concentration of the bulk of non-traditional investment in the hands of these holding companies. The interlinkages were extreme, and the effects were felt throughout the 1980s in three ways. First, commercial linkages across the whole economy were highly correlated with changes in external circumstances, and in particular world prices for tobacco. Second, and in contrast, these linkages allowed adjustment measures to proceed quickly and smoothly in Malaŵi. Unlike Kenya where the relationship between powerful technocrats and the politicians led to delay and sabotage in the implementation of economic policy, the autocratic nature of Malaŵi's political structure ensured that implementation, once agreed, proceeded apace. It was this that gained Malaŵi its reputation as a country prepared to embrace the structural adjustment message wholeheartedly. Thirdly, however, as Harrigan (1991) has argued, the excessive focus on the details of institutional reform across the 'troika' of ADMARC, the Malaŵi Development Corporation and Press Holdings was achieved at the expense of addressing the structural weaknesses in the economy as a whole. Low savings levels and a dormant (or non-existent) domestic private sector are the product of

Table 13.1 *Macroeconomic indicators 1970–90*

	1970	1975	1980	1981	1982	1983	1984	1985	1986	1987	1988	1989
GDP (market prices) (Km.)	n.k.	530	1,005	1,108	1,244	1,436	1,705	2,024	2,275	2,685	3,699	4,480
Real GDP growth (%)	0.47	4.18	0.23	−5.30	2.28	3.99	5.35	4.62	0.88	0.39	1.30	3.80
Gross domestic savings (%)	13.30	10.10	10.90	11.88	15.07	15.24	14.82	13.82	9.01	11.60	7.80	5.70
Gross domestic investment (%)	26.10	28.40	21.80	17.69	21.43	22.83	12.88	18.61	11.13	14.05	16.10	15.40
Budget deficit (%)	n.k.	n.k.	−15.80	−12.50	−15.60	−12.50	−10.20	−8.80	−8.70	−13.90	−8.70	−5.50
Terms of trade (1980=100)	125.6	118.1	100.0	93.9	93.2	95.1	93.7	93.7	86.8	88.3	91.1	84.6
External debt/GDP (%)	n.k.	n.k.	65.50	66.29	74.13	72.42	73.08	90.55	94.38	110.74	n.k.	n.k.
Debt service/exports of gds & srvs (%)	n.k.	n.k.	21.59	27.67	22.99	21.13	20.75	29.08	40.51	23.36	n.k.	n.k.

Sources: Government of Malaŵi, *Economic Report*; World Bank, *World Debt Tables.*

the fundamental nature of the management of the economic means of production, and the underlying distortions caused by the emphasis on estate agriculture.

Crisis and adjustment
The early 1980s saw a sharp reversal in Malaŵi's economic fortunes. The combination of a number of adverse external shocks (in particular, falling tobacco prices; rising prices for oil and other imports; and the disruption of transport routes through Mozambique (Gulhati, 1989)) dramatically worsened the terms of trade, which fell by 20% between 1978 and 1981, and continued to slide throughout the decade. Growth slumped in 1980 and 1981, and remained well below its 1970s average during the 1980s. The latter part of the decade also saw a sharp contraction in savings and investment, with the former falling back to the levels of the 1970s and the latter to around 17% of GDP. Attempts to maintain domestic aggregate demand in the face of these shocks drove the budget deficit to almost 16% of GDP in 1981, the majority of which was funded through external borrowing (see Table 1.31). This resulted in the external debt burden rising to over 110% of GDP by 1987, with the associated debt-service payments consuming approximately 30% of total export earnings.

Throughout the 1980s adjustment lending was a constant feature of the economic landscape. Beginning in 1979, Malaŵi received short-term balance-of-payments support from the IMF through three standby arrangements, one Compensatory Finance Facility loan, and one IMF Trust Fund loan, and in 1988 it became the first country to receive funds from the newly created IMF Enhanced Structural Adjustment Facility. In addition, three Structural Adjustment Loans (SALs) were negotiated with the World Bank between 1981 and 1986, and in 1988 a further World Bank Sectoral Adjustment Credit. Malaŵian privatization initiatives are grounded solely in the conditions attaching to the three SALs, and these will be discussed in detail in section 13.3.[3] But first we shall consider the structure and features of the SOE sector.

13.2 The SOE sector

The SOE sector in Malaŵi is, at first sight, relatively small. Prior to the start of the reforms in the 1980s, it consisted of 77 commercial statutory and non-statutory enterprises and approximately 15 non-commercial organizations, operating in all major areas of the economy. Of this total 24 are fully government-owned (see Table 13.2), 31 majority-owned through either ADMARC or MDC, and 22 minority-owned. Despite the relatively small number of SOEs, the sector accounted for approximately 25% of GDP, 20% of gross fixed capital formation, and 8% of total formal sector employment (*Economic Report*, 1990). However, even this understates the actual scale of the state's participation in the economy, since any such assessment must include Press Holdings which can be regarded as a privately owned state enterprise. The bulk of the directly held SOEs (by number) are standard utilities (water and sewerage, electricity supply, posts and telecommunications, transport, etc.) although there are a small number of commercial SOEs (excluding those held in the ADMARC and MDC portfolios), in particular the Malaŵi Book Service, Wood Industries Corporation (WICO) and Malaŵi Dairy Industries. As noted above, though all the SOEs have variously been the target for attention, the focus of reform has been the troika of Press Holdings, ADMARC and MDC which together form the heart of the economy.

Table 13.2 *State-owned enterprises*

Enterprise	Government ownership (%)
1. Directly held SOEs [a]	
Mining Investment and Development	100
Smallholder Sugar Authority	100
Smallholder Tea Authority	100
Smallholder Coffee Authority	100
Tobacco Control Commission	100
Kasungu Flue Cured Tobacco Authority	100
ADMARC	100
Blantyre Dairy	100
Malaŵi Dairy Industries	100
Wood Industries Corporation	100
Malaŵi Export Promotion Corporation	100
Air Malaŵi	100
Malaŵi Railways	100
Electricity Supply Commission	100
Malaŵi Broadcasting Corp	100
Blantyre Water Board	100
Lilongwe Water Board	100
Malaŵi Housing Corp	100
Malaŵi Book Services	100
Reserve Bank of Malaŵi	100
Malaŵi Development Corp	100
Indebank	100
Indefund	100
SEDOM	100
2. ADMARC associated companies [b]	
ADMARC Canning Co.	100.0
Auction Holdings Ltd.	100.0
Buwa Tobacco Estate	100.0
Cold Storage Company	100.0
Fincorp Malaŵi	100.0
Grain and Milling Company	100.0
Kasidizi Estate	100.0
Livilidizi Estate	100.0
Maldeco Fisheries	100.0
Mangani Estate	100.0
National Oils	100.0
PEW Ltd	87.0
National Seed Company	72.5
Cattle Feedlot Company	50.0
Chasato Estate	50.0
Dawanye Ltd	50.0
Manica Freight	50.0
Tobacco Estates Ltd	50.0
Cotton Ginners Ltd	49.0
David Whitehead & Sons	49.0
Sugar Corp of Malaŵi	49.0
Dwangwa Sugar	42.0
Malaŵi Tea Factory	40.0
United Transport Ltd	35.0
Optichem	33.5
National Bank of Malaŵi	33.0
Bank of Malaŵi	22.0

Table 13.2 *continued*

Enterprise	Government ownership (%)
3. MDC associated companies [b]	
Can Makers (MDC) Ltd	100.0
Cold Storage Company	100.0
Malaŵi Restaurants	100.0
Merolga Knitwear	100.0
Plastic Products Ltd	100.0
Development Finance Corp Malaŵi	88.0
Freshcold Fisheries	85.0
Packaging Industries	81.0
Brick and Tile Co.	67.0
IMEXCO	51.0
Jacaranda Properties	51.0
Match Co. (Malaŵi)	50.0
Portland Cement	50.0
Malaŵi Hotels	47.0
Malaŵi Distillers	41.0
Agrimal	40.0
Malaŵi Iron & Steel	40.0
National Oils	30.0
Pipe Extruders Ltd	30.0
David Whitehead & Sons	29.0
Carlsberg Malaŵi	27.0
B&C Metals	25.0
Encor Products	23.0
Commercial Bank of Malaŵi	20.0
Guthrie Corp (Malaŵi)	20.0
National Insurance Co.	20.0

Sources: Economic Report, 1989; ADMARC, *Annual Report 1983*; MDC *Annual Report 1983*.

a) As at December 1989; b) prior to asset swap and divestiture.

Press Holdings[4]

Press Holdings was established in 1969 as an investment holding company by the Malaŵian Congress Party and was given to the President, Dr Hastings Banda, who remains the sole shareholder. It is therefore not a state-owned enterprise as such but, given the nature of its ownership, its preferential access to domestic credit, and its intimate links to the public finances, neither does it conform to the standard model of a private sector enterprise. Indeed, the peculiar nature of the relationship between Press Holdings and the SOE sector led one observer to comment: 'Malaŵi's private sector is alive, doing well, and is owned by government'.[5] Press maintains a unique position as the country's largest single enterprise: it is the world's biggest flue-cured tobacco company, its group turnover is equivalent to 36% of GDP, and it accounts for 10% of total formal sector employment. Its non-agricultural activities span the entire economy. By the early 1980s there were 22 wholly owned Press subsidiaries and 23 enterprises in which shares were held jointly with ADMARC and MDC. Through this extensive portfolio Press enjoyed monopoly control in a number of sectors, most notably the wholesale, retail, export and import, and transport sectors and was also a joint shareholder with MDC and ADMARC in a number of the larger industrial and commercial enterprises. Moreover, though Press was the major shareholder in both domestic commercial banks, by 1980, because of its privileged status, it had become their largest debtor (by 1982 Press debt to the commercial banks amounted to K80m or 7% of GDP). In addition, it owed ADMARC K54m. and was a major external debtor and was also in debt to government through a series of external loan guarantees.

Agricultural Development and Marketing Corporation (ADMARC)

ADMARC was established in 1971 to develop the marketing and distribution of agricultural production from the small-scale sector. In addition, it was charged with promoting the agricultural and industrial sectors through its subsidiary role as an investment holding company. In pursuit of the former objective, ADMARC was granted monopsony control over all smallholder crop production. Large-scale estate production (principally tobacco) was exempt from the ADMARC monopsony, but otherwise the bulk of all maize, groundnuts, cotton and non-estate tobacco had to be sold to ADMARC through its extensive storage and marketing network. By keeping producer prices low relative to world border prices (in the case of smallholder maize, as low as 8% of the border price in 1976) (see Table 13.3), ADMARC accumulated extensive cash resources throughout the 1970s. These were then employed to invest in agricultural and industrial projects elsewhere in the economy. Throughout the 1970s ADMARC acquired an extensive portfolio of estate-based food-processing holdings and a wide range of non-agricultural equity holdings (see Table 13.2). By the early 1980s, while the portfolio was large and diversified, it contained many poorly performing companies, whose operations were sustained only by continued subventions from the corporation's profits on its crop trading.

Table 13.3 *ADMARC producer prices as ratio of border prices (%)*

	Tobacco[a]	Tea	Cotton	Maize	Groundnuts
1970	18	90	100		70
1971	16	84	63	32	65
1972	17	86	67	79	71
1973	15	86	52	33	75
1974	9	113	46	35	71
1975	14	94	60	10	76
1976	17	126	48	8	46
1977	19	70	51	n.k.	38
1978	21	103	57	n.k.	48
1979	24	103	47	n.k.	51
1980	26	88	42	n.k.	52
1981	18	91	45	n.k.	35
1982	13	97	118	73	57
1983	25	102	376	74	78
1984	25	98	79	62	79
1985	31	70	108	59	117
Average	19.25	93.81	84.94	46.50	64.31

Source: Gulhati, (1989).

a) Excludes estate production.

Malaŵi Development Corporation (MDC)

MDC was established in 1964 as a development finance corporation. It is similar to many such corporations created throughout sub-Saharan Africa, although unlike the majority in which international financial institutions have equity participation, its share capital is fully held by the Government of Malaŵi. The corporation's fortunes have been closely linked with those of Press and ADMARC, although MDC is probably the weakest of the three institutions, relying as it does

Table 13.4 *Flow of funds to parastatals (K'000)*

	1981/2	1982/3	1983/4	1984/5	1985/6	1986/7	1987/8	1988/9	1989/90
Curent transfers	17,110	21,720	34,590	25,320	31,460	39,740	38,610	80,250	91,350
Capital transfers	0	0	0	0	0	0	0	0	0
Net lending	4,190	5,250	700	2,470	6,060	4,890	2,230	3,740	4,070
Total flow of funds	21,300	26,970	35,290	27,790	37,520	44,630	40,840	83,990	95,420
Total expenditure	392,800	400,300	432,00	503,200	611,900	797,000	832,900	991,400	1,130,200
Budget deficit	129,600	114,300	112,300	109,400	122,200	252,400	171,500	(12,900)	37,300
FoF/Total exp (%)	5.42	6.74	8.17	5.52	6.13	5.60	4.96	8.47	8.44

Source: Economic Report 1989.

solely on earnings from its corporate portfolio. Poor project selection and weak management, combined with poor gearing (the debt–equity ratio was 3 : 1 1983), rendered MDC financially vulnerable. Prior to the asset swap in 1984 (see section 13.3), the MDC portfolio was diversified (see Table 13.2), but it currently consists mainly of industrial and commercial companies, plus a small number of service and tourism operations.

13.2.1 SOE performance

During the 1980s average net transfers to the parastatal sector (principally by way of operating subventions and net lending) represented approximately 6.5% of government expenditure (Table 13.4). Despite a drop in 1986–8, there was a discernible upward trend in this share during the decade, so that by 1989/90 transfers to the sector accounted for 8.5% of gross expenditure (approximately 2.2% of GDP). Tables 13.5 and 13.6, which cover much shorter time periods, analyse the cause of these transfers. Profit on operations (i.e. before depreciation and interest) was negligible across the sector as a whole, and consequently all capital expenditure had to be funded by borrowing – principally through domestic credit (on average domestic credit to the sector accounted for 15% of total credit) or direct loans from government.

Table 13.5 *Performance of SOEs (K'000)*

	1985/86	1986/87	1987/88	1988/89
Revenue	250,348	259,182	295,581	365,224
Operating expenditure	258,234	258,740	277,393	339,782
Gross profit	(7,886)	442	18,188	25,442
Interest	29,991	31,650	20,142	22,450
Operating surplus/(deficit)	(37,877)	(31,208)	(1,954)	2,992
Capex	50,718	51,697	92,389	136,579
Surplus/(deficit)	(88,595)	(82,905)	(94,343)	(133,587)
Surp/(def)/Total expenditure (%)	14.48	10.40	11.45	13.96
Interest/revenue (%)	11.98	12.21	6.81	6.15

Source: *Economic Survey* (various years).

These aggregate figures disguise a wide variety of performance, however (Table 13.6). For example, it is clear that the transport sector is fundamentally unprofitable. Malaŵi Railways has consistently been unable to make a gross profit, while Air Malaŵi, though making a net profit, has been unable to generate sufficient cash to finance capital expenditure. The cost of replacement of the Air Malaŵi fleet, which now has an average age of 35 years, must be borne entirely by the central government budget. The non-viability of this sector is due mainly to low utilization and high fixed costs of operation in both rail and air transport and is compounded in the case of the railways by the security situation in Mozambique. Over the data period, all other SOEs were generating profits from their operations, although almost all were still failing to generate sufficient cash to meet current debt-service and depreciation costs, let alone to finance capital expenditure. Moreover, the cash flow of the sector was uniformly bad. Based on the actual outturns for 1988/9 and the projected figures for 1989/90 only ADMARC was able to return a positive cash flow; all the other SOEs had negative cash flow on top of large accumulated losses. Thus, even though these detailed figures come at the end of a decade of adjustment and reform, there has been, with the exception of ADMARC, no fundamental improvement in the sector's profitability or its call on public finances. As we shall see, this unchanged position may be ascribed to two

Table 13.6 *SOE financial performance 1988–90 (K'000)*

Actual 1988/9

SOE	Revenue	Expend.	Gross Profit	Interest + Depr.	Net. Op Profit	Capital Expend.	Overall Profit	Cash Flow	Net Profit (% of Assets)	Debt
ADMARC	157,969	137,092	20,877	13,090	7,787	391	7,396	23,354	37.8	67,729
Malaŵi Railways	20,659	21,877	(1,218)	3,380	(4,598)	4,538	(9,136)	(3,234)	−4.6	66,481
ESCOM	49,185	14,892	34,293	20,320	13,973	43,813	(29,840)	(357)	6.0	157,298
Malaŵi Development Corp	5,712	1,229	4,483	2,161	2,322	5,065	(2,743)	(382)	125.2	28,680
Malaŵi Housing Corp	10,924	7,469	3,455	1,223	2,232	547	1,685	(696)	8.3	13,708
Air Malaŵi	47,414	45,254	2,160	722	1,438	1,051	387	(675)	33.5	5,180
Blanytre Water	10,856	6,283	4,573	3,682	891	4,040	(3,149)	(507)	2.7	30,226
Lilongwe Water	5,460	3,911	1,549	2,026	(477)	12,712	(13,189)	(82)	−0.6	30,915
Malaŵi Book Service	10,456	9,618	838	115	723	193	530	339	39.4	0
Wood Industries	5,347	5,947	(600)	1,852	(2,452)	2,457	(4,909)	(386)	−40.9	15,035
MIDCOR	1,868	2,621	(753)	303	(1,056)	1,206	(2,262)	(223)	−82.6	156
Malaŵi Dairy Industries	8,027	6,016	2,011	750	1,261	1,842	(581)	(303)	16.8	2,051
Totals	333,877	262,209	71,668	49,624	22,044	77,855	(55,811)	16,848	4.2	423,459

Provisional 1989/90

SOE	Revenue	Expend.	Gross Profit	Interest + Depr.	Net. Op Profit	Capital Expend.	Overall Profit	Cash Flow	Net Profit (% of Assets)	Debt
ADMARC	163,171	137,071	26,100	6,057	20,043	3,000	17,043	11,973	93.4	61,700
Malaŵi Railways	25,170	28,308	(3,138)	3,900	(7,038)	17,130	(24,168)	(2,566)	−6.4	77,434
ESCOM	75,051	22,198	52,853	28,548	24,305	18,500	5,805	1,397	10.6	160,000
Malaŵi Development Corp	6,163	1,721	4,442	2,046	2,396	6,713	(4,317)	(93)	119.9	29,588
Malaŵi Housing Corp	14,902	12,972	1,930	1,500	430	910	(480)	(1,115)	1.7	19,120
Air Malaŵi	50,663	45,779	4,884	1,668	3,216	2,685	531	(3,226)	59.3	5,180
Blanytre Water	18,001	11,046	6,955	6,903	52	3,136	(3,084)	334	0.2	26,883
Lilongwe Water	7,870	4,833	3,037	3,467	(430)	31,211	(31,641)	222	−0.4	62,738
Malaŵi Book Service	15,000	11,350	3,650	150	3,500	462	3,038	(234)	172.2	0
Wood Industries	7,351	6,357	994	1,936	(942)	187	(1,129)	28	−22.0	16,874
MIDCOR	2,343	2,683	(340)	750	(1,090)	1,740	(2,830)	(5)	−50.7	140
Malaŵi Dairy Industries	13,250	11,088	2,162	1,426	736	1,734	(998)	132	3.8	1,551
Totals	398,935	295,406	103,529	58,351	45,178	87,408	(42,230)	6,847	7.8	461,308

Source: Department of Statutory Bodies.

main factors. The first is that initial restructuring efforts were directed towards the troika, and within that it was Press Holdings, whose performance is not captured by the government budget, which was the main beneficiary of change. And, secondly, despite the large amounts of adjustment financing received by Malaŵi (most of which included elements aimed at restructuring the SOE sector), little was done to alter the economic environment in which the sector operated.

Aggregate financial flows themselves are not sufficient to indicate that the SOE sector was internally inefficient: in the case of Malaŵi, given the small (probably uneconomic) market size and the macroeconomic environment which it faces, the sector could be efficient while still loss-making. However, it is the case that the overall weaknesses in the financial performance of the SOE sector were compounded by internal inefficiencies and poor management. In the case of ADMARC, MDC and the transport sector, this showed up in high variable cost overheads, while elsewhere the general financial and planning systems were weak. Financial control, strategic and investment planning, and technical management were absent. A lack of accountability and clear management information systems rendered many of the SOEs inefficient, despite the fact that the level of political interference in their operations was less than in many other countries.[6] In addition, however, the successful operation of the sector was severely constrained by the chronic shortages of skilled indigengous managers and technical staff. For example, in 1986 civil service shortages (vacancies plus expatriates) were running at 35% for architects, engineers and surveyors, and 84% for senior administrative and management personal. Outside central goverment, the skilled staff which did exist were concentrated in a small number of enterprises (notably ADMARC) (*Economic Report*, 1989).

13.3 Privatization and liberalization

13.3.1 Adjustment lending and the push for enterprise reform
The programme of adjustment lending to Malaŵi from 1980 to 1986, consisting principally of three World Bank Structural Adjustment Loans,[7] embraced a wide-ranging set of reforms across five broad areas. The main thrust was towards the rebalancing of agricultural production between the estate and smallholder subsectors, to reverse the decline in smallholder production. This was complemented by exchange-rate and price liberalization, and a comprehensive reform of public finance, within which emphasis was placed on revenue enhancement and parastatal reform. Harrigan's (1991) comprehensive review of adjustment lending in the 1980s discusses these measures in detail and we shall therefore concentrate here on those reforms directed specifically at the SOE sector.

The dramatic downturn in the terms of trade following the collapse of tobacco prices in 1979 cruelly exposed the fundamental weaknesses in the financial positions of ADMARC, MDC and Press Holdings.[8] As Gulhati notes (1989: 17): 'the financial crisis of this triumvirate had a major adverse impact on the commercial banks, the government budget, and Malaŵi's external creditworthiness'. On top of the external shock to the economy, the preceding decade of poor management, over-rapid expansion, and soft financing had exposed the lack of control over operating costs and glaring inefficiencies, both of which severely weakened the internal management of the organizations. The continuation of ADMARC's monopsony power, however, meant that it was still financially viable, and radical reform of its industrial portfolio was not covered by the first SAL. The same was not the case with Press Holdings and MDC, both of which became the target of urgent financial restructuring. Again, given the importance of Press, its reform was emphasized.

Reform of Press Holdings

The reform programme for Press was rapidly implemented, not least because of the support it received from the sole shareholder, President Banda. Preliminary examination of the company's portfolio revealed a negative net worth of K40m. Under the restructuring plan, Press Holdings was closed down and a new company, Press Group Ltd, was established. All productive assets were transferred to a third organization, the Press Corporation, with the original liabilities (held by Press Group) converted into K 54m. worth of 25-year income notes to the government[9], issued to cover the goverment's absorption of Press Holdings' liabilities to itself, to external creditors, and to the two commercial banks. Thus the first action in the Press restructuring was to underwrite a sizeable proportion of the commercial banks' K80m. investment in the corporation and to transfer all external debt risk from the Press balance sheet. The profits generated by the new Press Corporation would then be used to pay dividends on and to redeem the income notes. Following this 'fire-fighting' exercise, steps were also taken to trim employment levels and restructure the senior management, while a rationalization of the investment portfolio proceeded in parallel. Several Press subsidiaries were closed down, while a large number were swapped with MDC and ADMARC (see below). The Press restructuring was financially successful and the corporation's performance improved dramatically from 1984, with its profit rate rising from K1.6m. (1.3% of turnover in 1984) to K56m. (11.9% of turnover) in 1988. As described below, much of this improvement was due to the favourable outcome of the asset swap with MDC and ADMARC. As Harrigan notes (1991: 239), there was concern that the rehabilitation of Press might well have been to the long-run detriment of the Malaŵian economy as a whole.

13.3.2 ADMARC/MDC/Press asset swap and privatization

Two separate elements have comprised the main privatization thrust in Malaŵi to date: the restructuring of the portfolios of the three main institutions through a comprehensive asset-swap programme, and a programme of direct privatization by ADMARC and MDC. In both cases the process resulted in some K14m. worth of assets changing hands.

The motivation for the restructuring was two-fold. First, the uncontrolled growth and poor financial management of their enterprises during the 1970s meant that the three portfolios were unstructured and overlaid with a complex web of cross-holdings. Rationalization was necessary if portfolio management was to become coherent. The second reason for the asset swap, as opposed to other forms of rationalization, goes to the heart of the problem facing Malaŵi, namely that there was insufficient private sector absorptive capacity to consider direct asset sales. In this respect the asset swap was a substitute for the more normal process of divestiture of mature investments by Development Finance Institutions (DFIs). In the absence of a private sector, divestiture was substituted, in the main, by the only option available, namely swaps between the three institutions. To refer to this as a privatization, as is frequently done, is thus somewhat inaccurate.

The swap programme

Although involving all three institutions, the asset-swap programme emerged principally as an element in the reform of Press. The view taken therefore was on how best to restructure Press Holdings' portfolio by swapping assets with ADMARC and MDC rather than as an optimal rationalization across all three portfolios. The asset-swap programme, implemented from 1984 to 1986, was conducted on a 'no-cash' basis, and involved a K7.9m. net value transfer between ADMARC and MDC, K4.9m. between Press and MDC, and a further K1m. in cash from

ADMARC to MDC (see Table 13.7). Following the swap, the three portfolios were more in line with the main activities of the corporations. ADMARC's portfolio concentrated on primary activities – fishing, agriculture, refrigerated storage, and also textiles; MDC held mostly industrial and commercial, manufacturing and trading companies; Press retained the most heterogeneous portfolio, although it managed to increase its holding in the profitable brewing sector.

Table 13.7 *Press–ADMARC–MDC share swap, 1984–7*

To: ADMARC	MDC	Press
From:		
ADMARC —	Portland Cement (24%) Bata Shoes Comm. Bank of Malaŵi (10%) (Value: K6.9m.)	

MDC   Cold Storage Co.
     (100%)
   Madelco (100%)
   National Oils (30%)
   David Whitehead & Sons
     (29%)
   (Value: K7.9m.)
	—	Carlsberg Brewery (27%)
		Malaŵi Distilleries (41%)
		Malaŵi Pharmacies
		   (100%)
		Imexco (Services) (100%)
		Guthrie Corp (20%)
		(Value: K4.9m.)

Press	Imexco (49%) Portland Cement (25%) (Value: K4.9m.)	

Sources: ADMARC, *Annual Reports*, 1983–87; MDC, *Annual Reports*, 1983–87.

Assessments of the swap differ. Though the immediate outcome was the efficient and rapid rationalization of three previously incoherent investment portfolios, many observers correctly concluded that the main benefits of the process accrued to Press at the expense of MDC and, to a lesser extent, ADMARC.[10] In particular, although the short-run effect was positive for MDC (in addition to the cash consideration from ADMARC, the restructuring was accompanied by a K13m. government debt conversion, and the acquisition of K5m. foreign-exchange exposure), but the long-run health of its portfolio is less rosy, and the ultimate viability of the corporation is, if anything, less certain. Cash-generation capacity is extremely limited, and the prospects for further expansions of the portfolio are negligible. In Harrigan's view (1991: 239):

> the series of share swaps with ADMARC and MDC had the effect of passing many of Press's problems, in the form of unprofitable subsidiaries, on to these parastatals. Hence by 1986 ADMARC, having inherited many of Press's problems, itself stood in urgent need of a large restructuring operation.

We are forced to conclude that this first element of the reform, while undoubtedly including some valuable rationalization, was essentially a stabilization exercise aimed at staunching the losses of Press Holdings and preventing the potentially disastrous collapse of the company. In the process, however, no substantive managerial changes occurred across the investment portfolios, nor did the programme have any discernible impact on the efficiency of enterprise management or, indeed, on the behaviour of the troika in their role as shareholders.

The divestiture programme

Parallel to the asset swap there was a series of smaller divestitures on the part of MDC and ADMARC. In many cases, however, these divestitures hardly qualify as privatizations, for two reasons. First, since both institutions were involved in development finance operations, the regular turnover of their portfolios through the sale of equity – usually directly to the majority shareholder – was central to their day-to-day activity. Second, in a large number of cases they were selling equity in companies in which they held only a minority stake. Consequently as a result of the divestiture there were no fundamental changes in the ownership or structure of the companies concerned.

The asset sales proceeded gradually over a period of six years from 1984 to 1989. It has not been possible to identify the cash proceeds from each individual sale through the company accounts of either buyer or seller, although the aggregate proceeds can be identified through sources-and-uses statements for the holding companies. On this measure, the value of MDC sales from 1984 to 1987 (excluding those involved in the swaps) totalled K6.4m. against a book value of K6.1m., and the ADMARC sales totalled K7.2m., against a book value of K9m. (Table 13.8). The total proceeds represented approximately 10% of the net book value of the portfolios in each corporation as at 1986 (MDC and ADMARC, *Annual Reports*, 1986).

One of the inevitable features of a series of sales such as these is that there is virtually no publicly available information with which to assess their terms and conditions. However, a number of important features are known. First, the sales were all negotiated privately, with the relevant seller actively involved in identifying purchasers. Identification of buyers and the negotiation of the terms of the sale were handled almost exclusively by ADMARC and MDC themselves, with no direct government involvement. Second, as a result, the buyer was often the majority shareholder in the enterprise. Thus few of the sales were accompanied by any change in the structure of the enterprise or, importantly, of its management. Privatization, then, did not contribute towards the crowding-in of new entrepreneurs or indeed of existing Malaŵian businesses. Third, of the 17 or so divestitures identified,[11] over 50% were sold to foreign buyers. Measured in terms of net book value, these sales accounted for 65% of the total proceeds. The foreign purchasers were all well established in Malaŵi or Southern Africa and were generally multinational corporations based in the UK, the US, Japan and South Africa. Fourth, though ADMARC managed to divest a number of small tea estates (most of them around 100 ha) to local entrepreneurs, few of the eventual purchasers had the capital available to acquire the estates. ADMARC itself financed these purchases through soft loans.[12] Excepting Malaŵi Motors, all of the other sales, including the profitable Kavuzi Tea Company and the National Seed Company, were acquired by foreign purchasers.

As suggested earlier, it is no more appropriate to consider the 'normal' turnover of DFI portfolios as a privatization than it is to view their asset swap as such. However, there are some lessons to be learned from the exercise. First, there is the difficulty of managing a successful divestiture/privatization programme when an active capital market is absent. Though it is possible to argue that sales of equity tranches to the existing private sector shareholder are optimal, this also suggests that the seller had difficulty in identifying other potential buyers. Selling smaller tranches to multiple purchasers is possible but, without a market mechanism through which to divest the tranches or to trade assets after divestiture, this greatly reduces the incentive to hold these assets. Hence, the seller is obliged to sell the total equity to a single purchaser who purchases not merely a speculative asset but, more importantly, full managerial control of the enterprise. This problem of the

Table 13.8 *ADMARC and MDC divestitures (excluding share swap)*

Company	Book Value (K)	Sector	Proceeds (K'000)	Buyer	
ADMARC					
1987					
Advanx (Blantyre) Ltd	103,800	Tyres		Local	
Lever Brother (Malaŵi) Ltd	575,000	Chemicals	2,865	Foreign	Lever Bros (UK)[a]
1988					
Buwa Tobacco Estates	240	Estate Agriculture		Local	
Kasikidzi Estate	200	Estate Agriculture		Local	
PEW Ltd	682,100	—	2,781	Foreign	
1989					
Kavuzi Tea Company	7,500,000	Estate Agriculture		Foreign	Commonwealth Development Corporation (UK)
Livilidzi Estate	100	Estate Agriculture		Local	
Mangazi Estate	72,364	Estate Agriculture		Local	
National Seed Company	832,000	Seed Co.	1,599	Foreign	Cargill Inc. (US)[a]
TOTAL PROCEEDS			7,245		
MDC					
1984					
Jacaranda	76,500	Property		Local	N/A
Malaŵi Motors	3,000,000	Distribution		Local	Mandala Ltd[b]
Radio & Electri Co.	325,000	Retail		Foreign	Okhai Japan Ltd[b]
Nzeru Radio Co.	350,000	Radio Assembly		Foreign	Gateway Industry (South Africa)
IMEXCO	853,000	Import/Export		Foreign	N/A
Plastic Products	721,000	Packaging		Foreign	MCE (Ltd) UK
Agrimal	376,000	Agric. Tools	4,989	Foreign	Chillington Tool Co. Ltd (UK)[b]
1987					
Guthrie Corp	768,000	Trading	1,453	Local	Press Holdings (outside swap)
TOTAL PROCEEDS			6,442		

Sources: ADMARC and MDC, Annual Reports.

Notes
a) Purchaser was joint shareholder and/or manager.
b) Purchaser was former joint shareholder.

indivisibility of equity sales in the absence of a capital market underlines the second problem, namely that in low-income economies, with limited indigenous capital accumulation (or indeed managerial capacity), foreign participation will dominate the divestiture programme. Finally, the Malaŵian experience does indicate that if the objective is simply to divest the portfolios of ADMARC and MDC, without consideration of the broader impact on the development of the domestic private sector, then this can be achieved straightforwardly. If the process is unencumbered by concerns of competition and income distribution, privatization can be implemented rapidly and successfully. The effects of this process, other than perhaps signalling an intention to impose greater financial discipline on the SOE sector, are unlikely to be significant, however.

13.3.3 Other SOE reform measures and privatization plans
These two initiatives, the asset swap and the ADMARC/MDC divestitures, are the full extent of the privatization programme to date in Malaŵi. No radical reform has occurred in the SOE sector, and its structure, conduct and performance remain almost wholly unchanged. However, in terms of the relationship between the sector and central government, there has been one important development (also under the auspices of the SAL programme), namely the creation of the Department of Statutory Bodies. Established under the Office of the President and Cabinet in 1981 to monitor and control all parastatals, the DSB has evolved into an effective co-ordinating and monitoring unit. All the major SOEs – 17 commercial enterprises[13] and 11 non-commercial enterprises[14] – come under its auspices.

Since 1982, the DSB has concentrated on establishing a coherent financial and human resource management system for each SOE. Corporate plans have been introduced for each enterprise; performance targets instituted; training programmes developed; and contract arrangements and employment conditions revised. Allied to this the DSB has overseen the implementation of new tariff structures for the non-commercial enterprises in line with the adjustment conditions of the SALs, and has undertaken comprehensive balance-sheet reconstruction for some of the larger ailing enterprises, most noticeably through liability swaps with central government to eliminate the SOEs' foreign-exchange risk. The immediate effect of this latter reform can be seen in Table 13.5, which shows increased gross profits following the introduction of new tariff structures, and the elimination of net losses, mainly through a dramatic reduction in interest costs. What is less clear is whether the DBS's efforts have resulted in any change in the fundamental efficiency of the SOE sector. No valuable quantitative data currently exist (although performance audits are being planned and undertaken by the DSB as part of the corporate plan programme), but anecdotal evidence[15] suggests that efficiency improvements are emerging slowly.

Liberalization of ADMARC grain trading
We noted earlier that wholesale reform of ADMARC was not a priority under the first SAL in 1981. The subsequent rationalization of the investment portfolio from 1984 to 1986 helped to address some weaknesses. Under the third SAL in 1985, a more comprehensive reform of ADMARC's core business was introduced, the principal element being the liberalization of smallholder crop marketing to allow competition via private sector marketing. The programme was introduced in 1986 with a $44m. supplement to the Third Structural Adjustment Loan.[16] The loan conditions had four components. First, the government was required to announce that private individuals could participate in crop trading. Second, the smaller ADMARC markets were to be closed (before liberalization there

were over 1,200 markets). Differential pricing was to be introduced to encourage smallholders to deliver their produce to the larger markets and thereby relieve ADMARC of excess transport costs. Finally, consumer subsidies were to be reduced.

The liberalization programme was introduced rapidly but, unlike the divestiture programme, there were considerable problems. Planning and administrative processes were excessively hurried (in order to meet the terms of the loan). The new operating procedures were not clearly elucidated, and fewer smallerholders responded to the new orientation than was initially expected. Licences were not prepared in time, with fewer private traders coming forward. Finally, the collection and analysis of production and distribution data were not satisfactory, and undermined ADMARC's capacity to ensure emergency food distribution.

These problems were compounded by the fact that the first two years of operations saw unusual crop conditions, especially in the maize sector where falling supply (as a result of low producer prices during the previous years), combined with the growth in the number of refugees from Mozambique, drove up prices. Planning weaknesses and food security problems then emerged as serious concerns. Other problems arose within the next few years: storage facilities in the private sector were found to be substandard, resulting in high losses; it was feared that liberalization of export licensing was undermining quality controls and jeopardizing export quotas; and many private traders were using the differential prices for rural and urban markets to earn undesirable arbitrage profits.

Nevertheless, the consensus on the reforms has been positive. The main concern about the grain liberalization is germane to all privatizations. The rapid introduction of the reform led to a large number of failures in planning and implementation. First, the time required for successful implementation was seriously underestimated. Second, the extent of retraining and development of systems required in a transition from centralized to decentralized, market-based, systems was not fully appreciated. And, third, there was the important issue of market regulation and control.

13.3.3 Assessment

Assessing privatization in Malaŵi immediately begs the question, what in reality has changed? Privatization in the strict sense has only constituted a very small element in the reform programme for the SOE sector, and has not contributed towards addressing the core problems in the economy. While assets have been transferred to the private sector, in the majority of cases these have been to the foreign sector or to Press Holdings. At no point has the programme actively promoted the crowding-in of the indigenous private sector. Domestic private sector participation has occurred only to a limited degree, and has been concentrated in the sale of small estates by ADMARC. Outside privatization there have been important developments in establishing a comprehensive monitoring structure for the SOE sector, and steps have been taken to absorb the worst excesses of poor financial management within the government budget. The impact of these reforms on public finances will certainly be felt in the short to medium term, but they are unlikely to change the underlying performance of the enterprises.

The focus of the reform process has been on strengthening the three major enterprises, Press, ADMARC and MDC. This concentration has meant failure to address the fundamental problem of the economy, namely the undiversified productive base. In fact, it is argued that the speed and success of the recapitalization of Press has retarded the development of the private sector, by perpetuating its overwhelming domination of the economy. A genuinely effective reform package would have required the dismantling of the Press group in its entirety: Press's central role in the political economy of Malaŵi means that such an option was not, and could not have been, entertained. However, the failure to break up the monopolistic dominance of Press serves to underline the fact that the issue at stake in considering privatization is not really that of ownership, or of the mechanics of sale, but rather that of the structure of the economy in which production and investment occur. The extreme concentration of ownership, savings and economic power and the way in which their evolution has shaped economic structures represent the fundamental constraints to successful privatization in Malaŵi. It is to these issues that we now turn.

13.4 The structure of the private sector and limits to competition

The structure of the domestic private sector in Malaŵi clearly represents the limiting factor for privatization at three levels. The first is the extent to which the domestic market is conducive to the competition through which efficiency gains can be achieved. Lower production costs increase the efficiency of import substitution and the competitiveness of non-traditional exports. The relevant issue is the extent to which private sector structures will promote welfare-enhancing efficiency. Second, there is the question of whether the privatization process will generate the conditions required to promote higher and more diversified investment and entrepreneurship: by exposing former SOEs to the constraints of the market, will additional profit-making opportunities arise to 'crowd-in' private investment? Third is the extent to which domestic resources are sufficient to absorb the divestiture of former SOEs and, if they are, whether the financial sector is capable of mobilizing these resources for such investment. This section starts by describing the structure of the domestic industrial sector, and then considers the extent to which privatization and other policies have encouraged the crowding-in of new investment and entrepreneurship. It concludes with an analysis of private sector investment capacity and the capacity for mobilizing domestic savings for investment.

The most comprehensive analysis of the industrial sector in Malaŵi is provided by the World Bank's 1989 *Industrial Sector Memorandum* (World Bank, 1989f). The picture which emerges is of a narrowly-based sector dominated by foreign and parastatal enterprises, which enjoys a considerable degree of protection from external competition. Given the size of the economy, and especially its limited transport network, this is not surprising. Moreover, very low income levels mean that considerations of minimum efficient size result in many sectors of the economy being natural monopolies. The evidence on concentration bears this out. Across all industrial sectors concentration is high in absolute terms, and also relative to comparable economies (Table 13.9).

Table 13.9 *Sales concentration index*[a] *1987 (%)*

	Malaŵi	*Kenya*
Competitive (H < 200)	11	36
Oligopolistic (200 < H < 1000)	86	49
Monopoly (H > 1000)	3	15

Source: World Bank, *Industrial Sector Memorandum*, 1989.

Note: a) Measured using Herfindahl Index $H + 1000 (V^2_{+1})/N$, where V = coefficient of variation of sales and N the number of firms in the subsector.

As Table 13.9 indicates, only 11% of formal sector industrial activity occurs in competitive industries, which is some three times less than in Kenya. Although fewer subsectors than in Kenya are purely monopolistic it remains the case that the bulk of industrial activity in Malaŵi occurs in markets where effective competition is limited. As with virtually all other economies covered in this book, this conclusion is reinforced by the fact that most, if not all, of the SOEs (plus many of the Press subsidiaries) operate in oligopolistic or monopolistic sectors. The SOEs enjoy monopoly control of areas such as the utilities, air and rail transport and communications. As already noted, Press has monopoly control of certain traditionally competitive sectors such as wholesale and retail, road transport and, significantly, export and import trade handling.

However, while domestic market size and entrenched entry-deterring capacity preclude the maintenance of a large number of efficient companies, import penetration may provide the necessary competition to facilitate contestability of markets and an efficient competitive outcome. In terms of the privatization debate, the important issue is the extent to which domestic barriers to competition are offset by trade policy. The World Bank survey reveals that, in comparison with many similar countries, rates of nominal and effective protection in Malaŵi are moderate. However, moderate still does not mean low, especially in terms of effective protection. Average nominal protection on outputs is approximately 36%, with the highest levels in the cement and footwear sectors and the lowest in food processing. However, the average rate of effective protection is 140%, resulting in a strong bias in favour of import substitution. Thus not only is the economy concentrated, but the adverse effects of this concentration are exacerbated by significant obstacles to external competition.

The effect of high protection and market concentration on industrial efficiency can be measured by the domestic resource cost coefficient (DRC), which measures the number of units of domestic resources used per unit of foreign exchange saved by producing output domestically. Efficient firms will have a DRC less than one. Two measures for the DRC are normally calculated, the short-run DRC, which measures the efficiency of production given that all capital costs are sunk and that no capital replacement is required, and the long-run DRC which includes the costs of replacement of capital stock. Table 13.10 reports estimated DRCs from the main industrial subsectors:

Table 13.10 *Industrial efficiency measures*

Product	Short-Run DRC	Long-Run DRC
Food-processing	0.73	1.86
Beverages and tobacco	0.15	0.63
Textiles	0.67	3.66
Leather and footwear	0.53	1.36
Wood and paper	0.80	1.64
Pharmaceuticals	0.33	1.22
Chemicals	0.95	1.98
Cement	1.47	3.22
Steel products	0.93	1.94
Misc	1.13	2.25
Average	0.49	1.65

Source: Ibid.

As the table indicates, while the majority of subsectors are efficient in the short run, this does not hold in the long run, so that on average for every US dollar of foreign exchange saved through not importing the firms were incurring US$1.65 in labour and capital costs. The large gap between the short- and long-run figures reflects the high cost of imported capital equipment when compared with the low real labour costs resulting from the government's incomes policy. A further reason for this inefficiency is the low level of capacity utilization, currently running at less than 50%. The World Bank has re-estimated that if the industrial sector were to utilize its capital stock fully the long-run DRC would drop below 1.00, indicating that the sector was efficient. Finally, the estimated DRC results show that, though inefficient in the long run, the industrial sector in Malaŵi ranks relatively close to Kenya and Zimbabwe where the average long-run DRCs are 1.53 and 1.27 respectively.

Earlier we noted that public sector companies are larger and more monopolistic than average. They are also considerably less efficient, and more heavily protected, than all private companies. Table 13.11 illustrates the difference between SOEs and private firms, both local and foreign, which means that within the private sector foreign-owned companies enjoy a lower level of protection, but operate more efficiently.

Table 13.11 *Relative protection and efficiency measures*

	NRP (%)	EPR (%)	Long-Run DRC
SOEs	33	278	2.16
Private local	40	146	1.24
Private foreign	31	93	0.87

Source: Ibid.

Trade policy did not become a priority until the end of the SAL period, when it was becoming clear that the reform and rationalization described above had not wrought any measurable changes in the nature of competition in the private sector. Thus, with the introduction of the ITPAC loan in 1988, the government began to rationalize the external tariff structure and to lower average tariff rates. At the time of writing, however, there had been no discernible supply-side response to these changes.

Although trade liberalization will increase competition in the industrial sector at the margin, it remains the case that Malaŵi is subject to high natural transport-cost barriers. Being landlocked, it has always faced high transport costs. However, the geopolitical environment of southern Africa in the 1980s has massively increased the transport cost element in all Malaŵian trade. The closure of the Beira corridor, delays and losses on the Dar es Salaam corridor, and the immense costs of the trade route to Durban have resulted in Malaŵian cif prices being some 67% higher than the equivalent fob prices. This price barrier has two effects. First, it puts extremely heavy additional costs on exporters of non-traditional goods with a high price elasticity of demand. The effect of this is that non-traditional industrial exports account for only 5% of total exports from Malaŵi. Second, it provides a natural import-substituting barrier. However, given the narrowness of the industrial base in Malaŵi, these higher prices are borne by all inputs and passed on directly to domestic consumers. Though the changing geopolitical circumstances will certainly improve transport security problems, non-traditional exporters still face considerable transport cost barriers, in terms of scale economies and the efficiency of the transport network.

The implications of all this evidence concerning the structure of the private sector are as follows. First, there is clear evidence that industrial efficiency and the capacity to compete at lower levels of effective protection are significantly higher in the private than the public sector. This is the *sine qua non* of privatization. However, there is further evidence that domestic producers are much less efficient than foreign producers. Second, as a result of the natural barriers to entry caused by high transport costs and of a relatively high level of tariff barriers, the domestic Malaŵian economy is well protected from the forces of external competition. And, third, the entire industrial sector, both public and private, is characterized by very high degrees of concentration, the principal effect of which is to ensure that monopolistic and oligopolistic firms are widespread. Consequently, in the absence of competition from the external sector and/or the absence of an effective body of competition policy and regulatory capacity, the scope for significant efficiency gains from privatization is limited.

No explicit regulation or competition policy exists for the industrial sector in Malaŵi. Implicitly, regulation has been internalized by the close relationship between the political and economic agents in the economy, but this means that regulation against excessive monopolistic power is non-existent. Moreover, price regulation has been driven not so much by the consumers' interests but as a necessary adjunct to the incomes policy aimed at keeping the cost of labour low to the estate sector. Regulation in the sense normally associated with the privatization debate therefore does not exist. The privatization debate in Malaŵi has emerged without consideration of issues of post-privatization regulation, despite the clear evidence that the private sector is highly concentrated reinforcing the conclusion that 'privatization' in Malaŵi during the 1980s has had very little to do with improving the efficiency and competitiveness of the domestic economy, but rather is concerned with the restitution of the financial viability and oligopolistic power of a small number of quasi-public enterprises.

13.4.1 The financial sector and domestic resource mobilization capacity

Finally we come to what is possibly the overriding constraint to privatization in Malaŵi at present, namely the lack of savings mobilization. As noted above, regardless of post-privatization performance, if the government is prepared to sell assets to foreign buyers it is possible to implement divestiture. Such is the level of domestic savings, however, that a programme which proscribed foreign equity participation would almost inevitably fail. We noted earlier, first, that the asset swap was a response to insufficient domestic demand and, second, that, when assets were sold to the domestic private sector by ADMARC, a large number were financed directly by the seller. Privatization is predicated on the saving and investment behaviour of the private sector, and for such savings to be directed towards the purchase of state assets three basic conditions need to be met. First, savings must be high enough in aggregate to absorb the assets. Second, the private sector must be willing to switch its investment from liquid low-risk capital assets (for example, deposits and cash) into illiquid risky assets. Third, mechanisms must exist to allow investments to be realized and to mobilize the savings of a large number of small agents into investment in a small number of large assets.

With reference to the first two issues, aggregate savings in Malaŵi are low, and their distribution is highly skewed. As Table 13.1 showed, while aggregate savings rose throughout the 1970s and early 1980s, they fell back to much lower levels by the latter part of the decade. The bulk of the population has very limited savings, much of which is mobilized through the (dynamic) informal sector mainly for consumption smoothing rather than for speculative purposes (see Chipeta and Makandiwire, 1991). Those agents and enterprises with high levels of savings come principally from the financial sector, certain commercial groups (such as

Press), and a small political elite close to the President. The cash balances or savings of many commercial enterprises have, however, been accumulated in response to restrictive import policies and are held in anticipation of trade liberalization, at which point they will be employed to purchase inputs and capital goods in order to raise capacity utilization. Moreover, within the financial sector, the savings of many institutions are 'forced' savings resulting from statutory regulations governing the accumulation of government stock, thus financing public sector borrowing.

On the third issue, namely the capacity of the financial sector to provide the necessary capital market functions for privatization, we note that, of all the countries studied in this book, the financial sector in Malaŵi is the most narrowly based and the least able adequately to mobilize domestic financial resources for privatization. There is no money or inter-bank market, and the capital market itself remains undeveloped. Some corporate securities are traded, but only on a very limited private placement basis. Most capital market activity is focused on government stock, but here the emphasis is purely on the primary issue: most stock is held to maturity by the initial purchasers, who are mainly public sector institutions. As at mid-1989, 52% of all outstanding stock was held by public sector institutions, a further 21% by commercial banks, and 16% by private insurance companies.

The Capital Market Development Act, promulgated in 1989, represents the first step towards establishing the basis for an active local capital and equity market, but this initiative, like many others in Africa, can only provide the regulatory and institutional framework in which market development may occur. Since its enactment a proposal has emerged for a putative divestiture Unit Trust – developed with the help of USAID – aimed at providing a financial instrument through which the ADMARC and MDC privatization process may be expedited. Though there is strong support for the initiative from its sponsors (in particular USAID) and from the Reserve Bank of Malaŵi, there is much caution on the part of ADMARC and the MDC. Whilst the unit trust is an attractive proposition for the divestiture of elements of their portfolios in a 'digestible' manner, there are a number of drawbacks. The first and most obvious is that, in the absence of an equity market, there is no market mechanism through which asset valuation can be readily effected: both ADMARC and MDC have expressed concern at the prospect that the full cost of the valuation exercise will be borne by them. The second is one of incentives: with government paper currently paying approximately 20% per annum, investors in the unit trust will require an extremely high return. This can be achieved by divesting only the very best elements of the portfolios to the Trust and, in all probability, at a hefty discount. These actions may indeed assist in the launch of the unit trust, but at the cost of seriously affecting the performance of the MDC and ADMARC portfolios. The reaction to the concept of a unit trust underlines a more fundamental issue concerning the importance of a functioning capital market for privatization. Whilst, trivially, it is true that asset sales do not require a formal market, the success of a privatization programme does require the existence of mechanisms in the economy through which private agents can make resource and portfolio allocation decisions in response to price signals. In other words, while a formal primary market may not be essential for privatization, some form of secondary market clearly is. In Malaŵi, both are absent.

The foregoing paragraphs have painted a rather depressing picture of the constraints to privatization in Malaŵi. Low levels of savings capacity and the absence of a financial sector mature enough to mobilize savings mean that the absorptive capacity of the private sector is limited. Distortionary macroeconomic policies and structural limitations to the economy render the private sector far from capable of providing efficiency-enhancing competition without an effective regulatory structure. And a shortage of skilled entrepreneurs, managerial capacity and venture capital limits the prospects for emerging small- and medium-scale entrepreneurs to compete with large-scale enterprises. That these factors are the same as those advanced twenty years ago in support of an aggressive programme of public ownership emphasizes the fact that questions of asset ownership are more irrelevant to the issue of fostering growth through productive investment than is commonly argued.

13.5 Conclusions

Given the fundamental constraints characterizing the economy, the question is immediately raised: is there a continued role for privatization in structural adjustment programmes in Malaŵi? The answer seems to be a qualified No. Privatization will of itself be neither a solution to the problem of SOE performance nor a stimulus to enhanced private sector development. The fulfilment of these objectives in Malaŵi relies much more heavily on deeper structural adjustment via eliminating the bias against non-estate production and creating incentives for entrepreneurial activity through the promotion of the small-scale sector. Gradual private sector development will be the catalyst for successful privatization rather than vice versa, and, as the private sector develops, effective privatization into the domestic private sector (from the ADMARC and MDC portfolios in the first instance) can emerge. The qualification, however, is that this is inevitably a slow process, and there may be a limited role for privatization in the medium term. In particular, in the case of Press Holdings, there remains an economic argument for the privatization of its portfolio of interests. Many of Press's investments are in potentially competitive sectors (such as retailing, services, and distribution), and as individual units will be sufficiently small-scale for the financing of their acquisition to be possible. Set within a broader programme of liberalization, such a privatization (or strictly anti-trust) programme may yet yield positive results.

Notes

1. The 1990 *World Development Report* ranks Malaŵi as the 6th poorest country in terms of 1988 GNP per capita (US$170), after Mozambique, Ethiopia, Chad, Tanzania and Bangladesh. Life expectancy, at 47 years, is lower than all countries except Chad (46), Angola (45), Niger (45), Guinea (43), and Sierra Leone (42).
2. Estate agriculture, as opposed to smallholder cultivation, is dominated by foreign capital and also by Press Holdings. Estate agriculture forms the basis of Dr Banda's own personal wealth.
3. A more general discussion of structural adjustment lending to Malaŵi is found in Harrigan, 1991.
4. This section draws heavily on Harrigan, 1991.
5. Quoted in *The Financial Times*, 20 November 1989.
6. See *The Financial Times*, 29 December 1989. The issue of political control is particularly interesting in the case of Press Holdings where, for fear of upsetting the President, management concealed information. The fear was justified when the chief executive was imprisoned following the exposure of financial weaknesses within the corporation.
7. SAL I (1981) $45m.; SAL II (1982) $55m.; SAL III (1985) $70m. plus $44m. co-financing.
8. The loss of tobacco revenue to Press was compounded by excessive drawings from the company and unsustainable leverage in the balance sheet.
9. Income notes are a form of non-voting capital instruments similar to debenture stock.
10. Among the three portfolios the jewels were seen as Carlsberg Brewery and Malaŵi Distillers, while the worst asset was the ailing Portland Cement Company. During the swap, Press managed to acquire all the equity in the first two and completely eliminated its exposure in the last.
11. The ADMARC divestiture included a number of smaller estate sales which we have been unable to trace. It is felt, however, that there is no fundamental change in the results.

12. Reported in *The Financial Times*, 12 December 1989.
13. Some of the enterprises classified as commercial do provide non-commercial services (e.g. Electricity Supply Commission (ESCOM) and Malaŵi Housing Corp.) but these non-commercial services are generally cross-subsidized from the commercial operations.
14. The main ones are ADMARC, Malaŵi Airways, ESCOM, Malaŵi Development Corp, Air Malaŵi, Wood Industries (WICO), the water boards of Lilongwe and Blantyre, Malaŵi Book Service, MIDCOR, Malaŵi Dairy Industries, and the smallholder authorities.
15. See 'Reforming the Parastatals', *The Financial Times*, 29 December 1989.
16. This section draws heavily on Christiansen and Stackhouse, 1989.

References and Source Materials

Agriculture Bank of Papua New Guinea. *Annual Report and Financial Statements of Agriculture Bank of Papua New Guinea* (various years).

Agriculture Bank of Papua New Guinea (1989). 'Projected Accounts and Actual Balance Sheets 1982–89' (unpublished).

Agricultural Development Marketing Corporation (Malaŵi). *Annual Accounts and Report* (various years).

Agro 21 (1989). *Land Divestment Policy Manual*.

Alchian, A. and Demsetz, H. (1972). 'Production, Information Costs and Economic Organization', *American Economic Review* 62, 777–95.

Arab-Malaysian Merchant Bank (1989). *The Kuala Lumpur Bankers Directory 1989*.

Arab-Malaysian Merchant Bank Group (1989). *Annual Report 1989*.

Asian Development Bank (1985). *Privatization: Policies, Methods and Procedures*. Manila.

Averch, H. and Johnson, L. (1962). 'Behaviour of the Firm under Regulatory Constraint', *American Economic Review* 52, 1052–69.

Aylen, J. (1987). 'Privatization in Developing Countries', *Lloyds Bank Review*, January.

Ayub, M.A. (1981). *Made in Jamaica: The Development of the Manufacturing Sector*. World Bank Staff Occasional Papers No. 31. Washington DC.

Ayub, M.A. and Hegstad, S.O. (1986). Public Industrial Enterprises Determinants of Performance. *Industrial and Finance Series* 17.

Backus, D. and Driffill, J. (1985). 'Inflation and Reputation'. *American Economic Review* 75, 530–38.

Balassa, B. (1981). *Adjustment to External Shocks in Developing Economies*. World Bank Staff Working Papers 472. Washington DC.

Balassa, B. (1987). *Public Enterprise in Developing Countries: Issues of Privatization*. Development Research Department 292. World Bank, Washington DC.

Bank Negara Malaysia (1989). *Annual Report 1988*.

Bank Negara Malaysia (1989). *Quarterly Bulletin*.

Bank Negara Malaysia (1989). *Monthly Statistical Bulletin*.

Bank Negara, Malaysia (1989). *Money and Banking in Malaysia*. Kuala Lumpur.

Bank of Jamaica. *Annual Report* (various years).

Bank of Jamaica (1985). *The Central Bank and the Jamaican Economy 1960–1985*. Kingston.

Bank of Jamaica. *Economic Bulletin* (various issues).

Bank of Jamaica (1990). *Programme for the Conversion of Jamaican External Debt into Equity Investment*. Kingston.

Bank of Jamaica (1990). 'The Jamaican Experience with Debt Equity Swaps as a Technique of External Debt Management' (unpublished).

Bank of Jamaica Research Department (1990). *Bank of Jamaica Statistical Digest*.

Bank of Papua New Guinea. *Report and Financial Statements of the Bank of Papua New Guinea* (various years).

Bank of Papua New Guinea (1990). *Quarterly Economic Bulletin* (December) (Abstract).

Bates, R. (1989). 'The Reality of Structural Adjustment' in S. Commander (ed.) *Structural Adjustment and Agriculture*. James Currey, London.

Baumol, W.J., Panzar, J. and Willig, R.D. (1982). *Contestable Markets and the Theory of Industry Structure*. Harcourt Brace Jovanovich, New York.

Bennett, K.M. (1986). 'An Analysis of Jamaica's Foreign Exchange Auction', *Social and Economic Studies*, 35 (4), 93–109.

Berg, E. and Shirley, M. (1987). *Divestiture in Developing Countries*. World Bank Discussion Papers 11. Washington DC.

Bhaskar, V. (1991). *Privatization in Developing Countries: Issues and the Evidence*. UNCTAD Discussion Paper. Geneva.

Bienen, H. and Waterbury, J. (1989). 'The Political Economy of Privatization in Developing Countries', *World Development* 17 (5), 617–32.

Bishop, M.R. and Kay, J.A. (1989). 'Privatization in the United Kingdom: Lessons from Experience', *World Development* 17 (15), 643–59.

Boardman, A. and Vining, A. (1989). 'Ownership and Performance in Competitive Environments: A Comparison of the Performance of Private, Mixed and State-Owned Enterprises', *Journal of Law and Economics* 32, 1–33.

Bouin, O. and Michalet, C.A. (1991). *Rebalancing the Public and Private Sectors: Developing Country Experience*. OECD, Paris.

Bourne, C. (1981). 'Issues of Public Financial Enterprise in Jamaica: The Case of the Jamaica Development Bank', *Social and Economic Studies* 30, 197–208.

Brown, A. and McBain, H. (1983). *Studies in Caribbean Public Enterprise*. Institute of Social and Economic Research, University of West Indies, Mona. Vol. 1, 85–157.

Business Times of Malaysia, 6 October 1989.

Business Times of Malaysia, 6 October 1990.

Candoy-Sekse, R. and Palmer, A.R. (1988). *Techniques of Privatization of State-Owned Enterprises*. World Bank Technical Paper No. 90, Vol. III. Washington DC.

Caribbean Cement Co. Ltd (1987). *Prospectus Caribbean Cement Co. Ltd., Offer for Sale*, Kingston.

Caribbean Cement Co. Ltd. *Annual Report* (various years), Kingston.

Caves, D.W. and Christensen, L.R. (1980). 'The Relative Efficiency of Public and Private Firms in a Competitive Environment: the Case of the Canadian Railroads', *Journal of Political Economy* 88, 958–76.

Cement Manufacturers Sarawak Berhad (1988). *Prospectus for Share Offer*, Kuala Lumpur.

Cement Manufacturers Sarawak Berhad (1989). 'Security's Turnover and Value Report' (unpublished).

Central Bank of Kenya (1990). *Economic Report for the year ended 30th June 1988*. Nairobi.

Central Bank of Sri Lanka. *Review of the Economy* Colombo (various years).

Central Bank of Sri Lanka (1988). *Annual Report 1988*.

Central Bank of Sri Lanka Statistics Department (1987). *Report on the Survey of Business Activities and Planned Investment in Sri Lanka 1984/85 to 1986/87*. Colombo.

Central Bank of Trinidad & Tobago (1989). *Handbook of Key Economic Statistics*.

Central Bank of Trinidad & Tobago (1989). *Quarterly Statistics Digest* VIII No. 111.

Central Bank of Trinidad & Tobago (1989). *Quarterly Economic Bulletin*.

Central Bank of Trinidad & Tobago (1990). *Annual Economic Survey 1988*.

Central Bureau of Statistics Ministry of Planning and National Development (1990). *Economic Survey*. Government of Kenya, Nairobi.

Cheng-Young, P. (1988). 'Jamaica Case Study', in: 'Investment in the A.C.P. States and Related Financial Flows'. Vol. 2, 'Case Studies', May (unpublished).

Chipeta, C. and Mkandiwire, M. (1991). *The Informed Financial Sector and Macroeconomic Adjustment in Malaŵi*. African Economic Research Consortium, Research Paper No. 4, Nairobi, May.

Christiansen, R.E. (1989). 'Editor's Introduction: Privatization Special Issue', *World Development* 17 (5), 597–600.

Christiansen, R.E. and Stackhouse, L.A. (1989). 'The Privatization of Agricultural Trading in Malaŵi', *World Development* 17 (5), 729–41.

City Bank (Trinidad and Tobago) Ltd (1990). *Trinidad & Tobago Investment Guide*.

Cook, P. and Kirkpartick, C. (1988). *Privatization in Less Developed Countries*. Wheatsheaf, Hemel Hempstead.

Crichton, N. and Farrell, J.W. (1988). 'Market Structure and Concentration in the Manufacturing Sector in Trinidad and Tobago', *Social and Economic Studies*. 37 (3), 151–92.

Daily Gleaner, The (1987). 'PNP raps debt swap programme', 16 August.

Daily Gleaner, The (1987). 'Debt–equity swap rules liberalized for US banks', and 'PNP advises caution in debt–equity swap plan', 15 September.

Davis, D.G. (1971). 'The Efficency of Public vs Private Firms: The Case of Australia's Two Airlines', *Journal of Law and Economics* 14, 149–65.

Davis, D.G. (1977) 'Property Rights and Economic Efficency: The Australian Airlines Revisited', *Journal of Law and Economics* 20, 223–6.

Deaton, A.S. (1989). 'Savings in Developing Countries', *World Bank Research Observer*.

Development Finance Company of Kenya Limited (1988). *1988 Annual Report & Accounts*.

Downer, R. (1986). 'National Investment Bank of Jamaica Ltd., Privatization Strategy' (unpublished).

Euromoney (1985). 'Why Malaysia Means Business' (February).

Faaland, J., Parkinson, J.R. and Saniman, R. (1990). *Growth and Ethnic Inequality: Malaysia's New Economic Policy*. Hurst and Company, London.

Financial Gleaner, The (1987). 'Debt conversion programme', 11 September.

Floyd, R.H., Gray, C.S. and Short, R.P. (1984). *Public Enterprises in Mixed Economies: Some Macroeconomic Aspects*. International Monetary Fund, Washington DC.

Forsyth, P.J. (1984). 'Airlines and Airports: Privatization, Competition and Regulation', *Fiscal Studies* 5 (1), 61–75.

Forsyth, P.J. and Hocking, R.D. (1980). 'Property Rights and Efficency in a Regulated Environment: The Case of Australian Airlines', *Economic Record* 56, 182–5.

Frischtak, C.R., Hadjimichael, B. and Zachau, U. (1989). *Competition Policies for Industrializing Countries*. World Bank Policy, Planning and Research Papers. Washington DC.

Galal, A. (1990). *Public Enterprise Reform: A Challenge for the World Bank*. World Bank, Policy, Planning and Research Papers 400.

Gelb, A. with R. Auty (1988). 'Trinidad and Tobago: Windfalls in a Small

Parliamentary Democracy' in A. Gelb and associates, *Oil Windfalls: Blessing or Curse?* Oxford University Press for the World Bank, Oxford.

Glade, W.P. (ed.) (1986). *State Shrinking: A Comparative Enquiry into Privatization.* University of Texas, Austen, Texas.

Glade, W.P. (1989). 'Privatization in Rent-Seeking Societies', *World Development* 17 (5), 673–83.

Glade, W.P. (1991). *Privatization of Public Enterprises in Latin America.* ICS Press, San Francisco, CA.

Government of Jamaica (1984). *Budget Speech 1984/85.*

Government of Jamaica (1984). *Ministry Paper No. 45: Kingston Metropolitan Region – Transport System.*

Government of Jamaica (1985). *Ministry Paper No. 33: Tax Reform: Phase II Corporation Income Taxation.*

Government of Jamaica (1985). *Ministry Paper No 36: Structural adjustment programme (Agricultural Sector).*

Government of Jamaica (1985). *Budget Presentation 1985–1986.*

Government of Jamaica, Administrative Staff College (1985). *Public Sector Register 1984/85.* Ministry of the Public Service, Kingston, Jamaica.

Government of Jamaica. *Public Sector Entities (Selected) Estimates of Revenue and Expenditure* (various years).

Government of Jamaica (1986). *Ministry Paper No. 2: Tax Reform: Phase 11 Corporation Income Taxation.*

Government of Jamaica (1987). *Ministry Paper No 9: Corporation Income Taxation. A Bill Entitled An Act to Amend the Income Tax Act.*

Government of Jamaica (1987). *Ministry Paper No. 17: Going for Growth, The Medium Term Economic Programme.*

Government of Jamaica (1987). *Ministry Paper No. 8: Acquisition of Part of Barnett Estate Montego Bay Free Zone – $6.5 Million.*

Government of Jamaica (1987). *Ministry Paper: Standby arrangement with the International Monetary Fund – letter of intent.*

Government of Jamaica (1987). *Ministry Paper No. 25: Investment Performance.*

Government of Jamaica (1988). *Ministry Paper No. 35: IMF Standby Agreement September 1988–November 1989.*

Government of Jamaica (1988). *Ministry Paper No. 18: Tax Relief to Encourage Expansion of the Equity Base of Companies.*

Government of Jamaica (1990). *Ministry Paper No. 33: National Investment Bank of Jamaica Ltd., Activities – 1989/90.*

Government of Jamaica (1990). *Ministry Paper No. 41: Jamaica Telephone Company – Developments Since 1980.*

Government of Jamaica (1990). *Ministry Paper No. 22: Review of Trade Promotion Activities.*

Government of Jamaica (1990). *Ministry Paper No. 27: National Development Bank of Jamaica Limited and Agricultural Credit Bank of Jamaica Limited – Activities 1989/90.*

Government of Jamaica (1990). *National Five Year Plan 1990–1995.*

Government of Jamaica (1990). *Ministry Paper No. 50: 1984 Stand-by arrangements with the International Monetary Fund.*

Government of Jamaica (1990). *Ministry Paper No. 30: Jampro Limited – Activities 1989/90.*

Government of Jamaica (1990). *Ministry Paper No. 32: Green Zones – Activities 1989/90.*

Government of Jamaica (1990). *Ministry Paper No. 38: The 5-year Development Plan 1990/91–1994/95.*

Government of Jamaica (1990). *Ministry Paper: Policy on Foreign Investment.*
Government of Jamaica. (various years). *Budget Presentation and Debate.*
Government of Jamaica (1990). *Ministry Paper No. 43: Port Authority of Jamaica – Development since 1980.*
Government of Jamaica (1990). *Ministry Paper No. 40: Trans Jamaican Airlines Limited.*
Government of Jamaica (1990). *Ministry Paper No. 44: Jamaica Merchant Marine Ltd., Development since 1980.*
Government of Jamaica (1991). 'Proposals for a Competition Act'.
Government of Kenya (1966). *Sessional Paper No. 10: African Socialism and its Application to Planning in Kenya.*
Government of Kenya, Report and Recommendations of the Committee appointed by His Excellency the President (the Ndegwa Committee) (1979). *Review of Statutory Boards.* Nairobi.
Government of Kenya (1989). *Development Plan 1989–1993.*
Government of Kenya (1989). *Budget Speech for the Financial Year 1989/90.*
Government of Kenya Working Party on Government Expenditures (1982). *Report and Recommendations of the Working Party.*
Government of Malaŵi (1989). *Economic Report 1989.*
Government of Malaysia (1985). *Guidelines on Privatization.* Economic Planning Unit.
Government of Malaysia (1987). *Malaysian Code on Take-overs and Mergers 1987.*
Government of Malaysia (1990). Telecommunications Act, 1950 (Revised 1970) (unpublished).
Government of Malaysia, Economic Planning Unit (1989). *Guidelines for the Regulation of Acquisition of Assets, Mergers and Take-overs.* Foreign Investment Committee.
Government of Papua New Guinea (1987a). Public Officers Superannuation Fund Financial Statements for the year ended 31.12.87 (unpublished).
Government of Papua New Guinea (1987b). Defence Force Retirement Benefits Fund Financial Statements for year ended 31.12.87 (unpublished).
Government of Papua New Guinea (1987c). Retirement Benefits Fund Financial Statements for the year ended 31.12.87 (unpublished).
Government of Papua New Guinea (1988). *Statement of Direct Investments, Capital Contributions and Equity Option Rights as at 31.12.88.*
Government of Papua New Guinea (1989). Central Government External Debt Outstanding Debt Service Payments by Creditor 1980–89 (unpublished).
Government of Papua New Guinea (1990a). *Economic Policies, Presented by Hon. Paul Pora on the occasion of the 1990 Budget.*
Government of Papua New Guinea (1990b). Central Government Expenditure (unpublished).
Government of Papua New Guinea (1990c). Central Government Revenue and Grants (unpublished).
Government of Papua New Guinea (1990d). Statement of Direct Investments, Capital Contributions and Equity Option Rights as at 31 March, 1990 (unpublished).
Government of Papua New Guinea, National Statistical Office (1985). *Secondary Industries 1985.*
Government of Papua New Guinea, National Statistical Office (1990). *National Economic Accounts, Gross Domestic Product and Expenditure 1983–88.*
Government of Trinidad and Tobago. *Budget Speech of the Hon. E.E. Williams.* Ministry of Finance (various years).

Government of Trinidad and Tobago (1979). *Report of the Committee to Review the Role and Functions of the PUC*.

Government of Trinidad and Tobago (1989). *White Paper on Tax Reform for Trinidad and Tobago, the Second Phase*.

Government of Trinidad and Tobago (1972). *White Paper No. 2 on Public Sector Participation in Industry*.

Government of Trinidad and Tobago Ministry of Planning and Mobilization (1988). *Restructuring for Economic Independence. Draft Public Sector Investment Programme 1989–1991*.

Griffith-Jones, S. (1988). 'Debt Crisis Management in the Early 1980s: Can Lessons be Learnt?', *Development Policy Review* 6 (1), 1–25.

Grosh, B. (1986). 'Economic Performance of Kenya Parastatals: Lessons from the first two decades of independence' (unpublished).

Grosh, B. (1990). 'Public, Quasi-Public and Private Manufacturing Firms in Kenya: the Surprising Case of a Cliché Gone Astray', *Development Policy Review* 8 (1), 43–57.

Gulhati, R. (1989). *Malaŵi: Promising Reforms, Bad Luck*. Economic Development Institute, World Bank, Washington DC.

Harewood, J. and R. Henry (1985), *Inequality in a Post-Colonial Society: Trinidad and Tobago 1956–81*, St. Augustine: ISER, the University of the West Indies.

Harrigan, J. (1991). 'Malaŵi' in Mosley *et al. Aid and Power*.

Heller, P.S. and Schiller, C. (1989). 'The Fiscal Impact of Privatization, with Some Examples from Arab Countries', *World Development* 17 (5), 757–68.

Hemming, R. and Mansoor, A.M. (1988). *Privatization and Public Enterprises*. IMF Occasional Paper No. 56, Washington DC.

Henry, R. (1989). 'Privatization and the State Enterprise Sector in Trinidad and Tobago: Market and Non-Market Issues in a Plural Politicial Economy'. University of the West Indies (unpublished).

Hill, H. (1982). 'State Enterprises in a Competitive Industry: an Indonesian Case Study'. *World Development* 10 (11), 1015–23.

Hock, T.L. (1986). 'The Industrial Drive towards NIC Status'. *Asian Finance*, 15 June.

Hoon Lim Siong (1989). 'Privatization: The Public Sector has much to sell', *Financial Times*, 29 September.

Hoon Lim Siong (1990). 'Malaysia tries to square the sell-off circle', *Financial Times*, 6 March.

Horch, H. and Popiel, P.A. (1989). *Securities Market Development in Korea*. Economic Development Institute, World Bank, Washington DC.

Horch, H. and Popiel, P.A. (1989). *Policies for Developing Financial Markets*. Economic Development Institute, World Bank, Washington DC.

Hughes, W. (1990). 'Industrial Performance in the Jamaican Aluminium Sector', unpublished PhD thesis.

Industrial and Commercial Development Corporation (1987). *Annual Report & Accounts 1987/1988*. Nairobi.

International Finance Corporation (1986). 'Capital Market Study: Creating a Stock Exchange in Papua New Guinea and Related Issues'. IFC, Washington DC (unpublished).

International Finance Corporation (1989). *Quarterly Review of Emerging Stock Markets* IFC, Washington DC.

International Finance Corporation (1989). *Annual Report 1989*.

International Finance Corporation (1991). *Emerging Stock Markets Factbook* IFC, Washington DC.

International Monetary Fund (1987). *Theoretical Aspects of the Design of Fund-Supported Adjustment Programs*. Occasional Paper 55, Washington DC.

Investment and Development Bank of Malaŵi (1988). *Annual Report*. Blantyre.

Investment Promotion Centre (1989). *Investor's Guide to Kenya (3 Vols) Volume I: General Overview*. Nairobi.

Investment Promotion Centre (1989). *Investor's Guide to Kenya Volume II: Investment Policies, Procedures, and Opportunities*. Nairobi.

Investment Promotion Centre (1989). *Investor's Guide to Kenya Volume III: Manufacturing Under Bond*. Nairobi.

Investment Promotion Centre (1989). *Investor's Guide to Kenya Volume IV: Statistical Tables and Opportunities*. Nairobi.

Iton, W. (1990). 'An Overview of Emerging Stock Markets: the Jamaican Stock Market Experience', Paper presented to Symposium on Capital Market Development and Privatization, Bombay, November.

Jamaica Ministry of Development, Planning and Production (1990). Ministry Paper No. 31, *Environmental Protection and Conservation*. Government of Jamaica.

Jamaica National Investment Promotion Ltd (1987). *Starting and Operating a Business in Jamaica*. Ritch & Associates Ltd, Kingston.

Jamaica Public Service Co. Ltd. *Annual Report* (various years). Kingston.

Jamaica Stock Exchange (1986). *The Jamaica Stock Exchange Yearbook* (various years) Kingston.

Jamaica Stock Exchange (1990). *Stock Market Review 1974–1984*. Kingston.

Jamaica Telephone Co., Ltd (1985). *Annual Report 1985*. Kingston.

Jampro Ltd, Research & Statistics Unit (1989). *Jampro Ltd* (unpublished).

Jayaasankaran, S. (1987). 'NEP New Focus in the 1990s', *Malaysian Business*, December.

Jayawardena, A.S. (1985). 'Privatisation in Sri Lanka' in Asian Development Bank, *Privatization, Methods, Policies and Procedures*.

Jones, L., Tandon. P. and Vogelsang, I. (1988). 'Net Benefits from Privatization: A Valuation Methodology'. Boston University (unpublished).

Jones, L., Tandon, P. and Vogelsang, I. (1990). *Selling Public Enterprises: A Cost-Benefit Methodology*. MIT Press, Cambridge, MA.

Kar, P. (1990). Capital Markets in India (unpublished).

Karanja, R.W. (1990). 'Privatisation in Kenya' in V.V. Ramanadham (ed.) *Privatization in Developing Countries*.

Kay, J.A. and Thompson, D.J. (1986). 'Privatization: A Policy in Search of a Rationale', *Economic Journal* 96, 18–32.

Kelegama, S. and Ganeshan, W. (1988). 'Labour Absorption in the Manufacturing Sector in Sri Lanka with special reference to the post-1977 period', *Upanathi* 3 (1), 1–29.

Kennedy, P.J. (1986). 'State Shrinkage: the Jamaican Experience' in W.P. Glade (ed.) *State Shrinking*.

Kenya Association of Manufacturers (1990). *Members List and International Standard Industrial Classification*. KAM, Nairobi.

Government of Kenya (1988). *Kenya Gazette Supplement Acts 1988*. Nairobi.

Killick, T. and Commander, S. (1988). 'State Divestiture as a Policy Instrument in Developing Countries', *World Development* 16, 1465–79.

Killick, T. and Commander, S. (1988). 'Privatization in Developing Countries: A Survey of the Issues' in P. Cook and C. Kirkpatrick (eds) *Privatization in Less Developed Countries*.

Killick, T. and Mwega, F. (1990). *Monetary Policy in Kenya*. ODI Working Paper No. 39. Overseas Development Institute, London.

Kim, K.S. (1981). 'Enterprise Performance in the Public and Private Sectors: Tanzanian Experiences 1970–75', *Journal of Developing Areas* 15, 471–84.

Kirby, M.G. and Albon, R.P. (1985). 'Property Rights, Regulation and Efficiency: A Further Comment on Australia's Two-Arlines Policy', *Economic Record* 61, 535–9.

Klang Port Authority (1990). *Guide to Port Klang Malaysia*.

KPMG Peat Marwick Policy Economics Group (1988). 'Phase 1 Report Initial Overview of the Trinidad & Tobago Tax System. III Draft' (unpublished).

Krueger, A.O. (1974). 'The Political Economy of the Rent-seeking Society', *American Economic Review* 64, 291–303.

Kuala Lumpur Stock Exchange (1990). Distribution of Shares (unpublished).

Kuala Lumpur Stock Exchange (1990). *Investing in the Stock Market in Malaysia*.

Leeds, R.S. (1987). *Privatization in Jamaica: two case studies*. John F. Kennedy School of Government, Harvard University, Cambridge, MA.

Leeds, R.S. (1989). 'Malaysia: Genesis of a Privatization Transaction', *World Development* 17 (5), 741–57.

Lim Quek Peck (1985). 'Why Malaysia Means Business', *Euromoney* (February).

Lim Soh Eng (1987). 'Privatization: Early Birds Get the Rewards', *Malaysian Business* (December).

Lin, E.Y. (1989). 'Malaysia: Developing Securities Markets'. Paper presented at Round Table on 'Innovations in Foreign Financing; Country and Debt Conversion Funds, Venture Capital Funds and Limited Resource Financing'. UK (unpublished).

Lingren, C.J., Leite, S.P., Hanson, J. and Hayward, P. (1986). 'Sri Lanka: A Survey of the Financial System'. IMF Central Banking Department (unpublished).

McBain, H. (1980). 'External Financing of the Water Commission of Jamaica', *Social and Economic Studies* 30 (1), 171–96.

Maddock, N. (1987). 'Privatizing Agriculture: Policy Options in Developing Countries', *Food Policy*, 12 (4) November.

Malawi Development Corporation. *Annual Reports* (various years).

Malaysia Ministry of Finance. *Economic Report* (various years).

Malaysian Airline System Berhad (1985). Prospectus for Share Offer.

Malaysian Airline System Berhad (1985). Security's Turnover and Value Report (unpublished).

Malaysian Airline System Berhad (1988). *1988/89 Annual Report*.

Malaysian Airline System Berhad (1988). *1988/89 Financial Statement*.

Malaysian Business (1987a). 'Implementation. Vague Master Plan', November.

Malaysian Business (1987b). 'Privatization, the Early Bird Gets the Reward', December.

Malaysian Business (1988). 'Privatisation Telekom Copes with Enterprise', July.

Malaysian Business (1989a). 'Privatisation: Going Nowhere Fast', May.

Malaysian Business (1989b). 'KTM Privatisation: Which Track?', 5 May.

Malaysian Business (1990a). 'Privatisation: The Debate Goes On', November.

Malaysian Business (1990b). 'Privatisation. Aye for Private Enterprise', November.

Malaysian International Shipping Corporation Berhad (1986). Prospectus for Share Offer.

Malaysian International Shipping Corporation Berhad (1986). Rights Issue Report (unpublished).

Malaysian International Shipping Corporation Berhad (1987). Security's Turnover and Value Report (unpublished).

Malaysian International Shipping Corporation Berhad (1988). *1988 Annual Report*.

Malaysian International Shipping Corporation Berhad (1990). *Charting Future Growth. A Profile of Shipping Excellence*.

Malaysian International Shipping Corporation Berhad (1990). *Unaudited Half Yearly Consolidated Results for the six months ended 30th June 1989*.

Mario, I. Blejer and Ke-Young, C. (1988). *Measurement of Fiscal Impact Methodological Issues*. IMF, Washington DC.

Marsden, K. and Therese, B. (1987). *Private Enterprise in Africa: Creating a Better Environment*. World Bank Discussion Papers 17, Washington DC.

Marshall, J. and Schmidt-Hebbel, K. (1989). *Economic and Policy Determinants of Public Sector Deficits*. World Bank Working Paper, Washington DC.

Mayer, C. (1988). 'Myths of the West: Lessons from Developed Countries for Development Finance' (unpublished).

Mayer, C.P. and Meadowcroft, S.A. (1986). 'Selling Public Assets: Techniques and Financial Applications', *Fiscal Studies* 6 (4), 42–55.

Mills, G.E. (1981). 'The Administration of Public Enterprises: Jamaica and Trinidad and Tobago', *Social and Economic Studies* 30 (1), 45–73.

Mills, G.E. (1988). 'Privatisation in Jamaica, Trinidad and Tobago' in V.V. Ramanadham (ed.) *Privatization in Developing Countries*.

Millward, R. (1988). 'Measured Sources of Inefficiency in the Performance of Private and Public Enterprises in LDCs' in P. Cook and G. Kirkpatrick (eds) *Privatization in Less Developed Countries*.

Minister for Finance and Planning, Government of Papua New Guinea (1988). For the Members of the National Executive Council Revised Privatization Strategy (unpublished).

Ministry of Finance and Planning, Sri Lanka (1987). '10 Year Performance 1978–1987' (unpublished).

Ministry of Industries, Sri Lanka (1989). *A Strategy for Industrialisation in Sri Lanka*. Colombo.

Morgan Grenfell & Co. Ltd (1984). 'Investment in Jamaica' (unpublished).

Mosley, P. (1991). 'Kenya' in Mosley *et al.* (eds) *Aid and Power*.

Mosley, P., Harrigan, J. and Toye, J. (1991). *Aid and Power: The World Bank and Policy-Based Lending* (2 volumes). Routledge, London.

Nair, G. and Filippides, A. (1988). *How Much Do State-owned Enterprises Contribute to Public Sector Deficits in Developing Countries and Why?* World Bank PPR Working Paper No. 45, Washington DC.

Nambawan Finance Ltd (1988). *Annual Report of Nambawan Finance Ltd., 1988*.

Nankani, H. (1988). *Techniques of Privatization of State-Owned Enterprises*. World Bank Technical Paper No. 89, Vol. II, Washington DC.

National Hotels and Properties Ltd. Financial Statements for National Hotels and Properties Ltd., and its subsidiaries (various years).

National Hotels and Properties Ltd (1988). *Auditors' Report and Consolidated Financial Statements*. Touche Ross. Kingston.

National Hotels and Properties Ltd (1989). *Auditors' Report and Consolidated Financial Statements*. Touche Ross. Kingston.

National Investment Bank of Jamaica Ltd (1986). *Prospectus N.C.B. Group Ltd., Offer for Sale*.

N.C.B. Group (Jamaica). *N.C.B. Group Ltd., Annual Report* (various years).

Nellis, J. and Kikeri, S. (1989). 'Public Enterprise Reform: Privatization and the World Bank', *World Development* 17 (5), 659–73.

Nellis, J.R. (1986). *Public Enterprises in Sub-Saharan Africa*. World Bank Discussion Papers 1, Washington DC.

Nellis, J.R. (1989). *Contract Plans and Public Enterprise Performance*. World Bank Discussion Papers 48, Washington DC.

New Straits Times Malaysia (1990). 'More Enterprise Needed', 19 March.

Nicholas, P. (1988). *The World Bank's Lending for Adjustment: An Interim Report*. World Bank Discussion Papers 34, Washington DC.

Niugini Insurance Corporation. *Annual Report* (various years).

Niugini Insurance Corporation (1985). *Auditors' Report to the Auditor-General: Finance Statements 31.12.85*.

Niugini Insurance Corporation. *Financial Statements* (various years).

Nunnemkamp, P. (1986). 'State Enterprises in Developing Countries', *Intereconomics* 21 (4).

Pacific Islands Monthly (1989). 'Share Market for PNG', July.

Papua New Guinea Banking Corporation. *Annual Report* (various years).

Papua New Guinea, Department of Finance and Planning (1989). *An Assessment of IFC Recommendations in relation to Financial Sector Institutional Reforms*.

Papua New Guinea Development Bank. *Annual Report & Financial Statement* (various years).

Papua New Guinea Electricity Commission (1988). *Papua New Guinea Electricity Commission 1988 Annual Report*.

Papua New Guinea, Ministry of Finance, Monetary, Fiscal and Trade Division (1989). *An Overview of the Public Enterprise Sector and Policy Initiatives for 1990*.

Papua New Guinea Motor Vehicles Insurance Trust various years. *Profit and Loss Statement*.

Papua New Guinea National Provident Fund various years. *Board of Trustees' National Provident Fund Annual Reports*.

Parker, J.C. (1989). 'Public Policy and Private Sector Interests in Kenya's Structural Adjustment Programs'. Paper prepared for Nairobi Chamber of Commerce (unpublished).

Patterson, P.J. (1987). 'Public/Private Sector Relationships: a Conceptual Framework'. Address to symposium – Jamaica Institute of Management, June (unpublished).

Paul, S. (1988). *Emerging Issues of Privatization and the Public Sector*. World Bank, Working Paper No. 80, Washington DC.

Perkins, F.C. (1982). 'Technology Choice, Industrialization and Development Experiences in Tanzania', *Journal of Development Studies* 19.

Permodalan Nasional Berhad (PNB) (1990). *Annual Report*. Kuala Lumpur.

Petrojam Ltd. Annual Report (various years) (unpublished). Kingston.

Petroleum Corporation of Jamaica (1987). Financial Forecast (unpublished).

Petroleum Corporation of Jamaica (1990). Petroleum Corporation of Jamaica Pioneers in Resource Development (unpublished).

Petroleum Corporation of Jamaica (1990). Exploring and Developing Energy Resources (unpublished).

Pfeffermann, G.P. (1988). 'Private Business in Developing Countries'. World Bank (unpublished).

Pirie, M. (1986). *Privatization in Theory and Practice*. Adam Smith Institute, London.

Planning Institute of Jamaica (1981). *Ministry Paper No. 9 Extended Fund Facility Arrangement with International Monetary Fund*. Government of Jamaica.

Planning Institute of Jamaica (1982). *Ministry Paper No. 43 Jamaica/IMF Programme*. Government of Jamaica.

Popiel, P.A. (1987). *Development of Money and Capital Markets*. Economic Development Institute, World Bank, Washington DC.

Popiel, P.A. (1988). *Recent Developments and Innovations in International Financial Markets*. Economic Development Institute, World Bank, Washington DC.

Port Klang Authorities (1988). *The Story of Port Klang*. Public Relations Department. Kuala Lumpur.

Port Klang Authority (1988). *Annual Report*. Kuala Lumpur.

Port Klang Authority (1988). *1988 Perangkaan Statistics*. Kuala Lumpur.

Port Klang Authority (1990). *Port Klang, The Gateway to Malaysia*.

Price Waterhouse (1971). *Doing Business in Jamaica*. Kingston.

Private Sector Organisation of Jamaica (1990). Privatization (unpublished).

Ramanadham, V.V. (1988). *Privatization in Developing Countries*. Routledge, London.

Rees, R. (1985). 'The Theory of Principal and Agent', *Bulletin of Economic Research* 37, 3–26.

Reliance Stockbrokers Ltd & Trinidad and Tobago Stocks & Shares Ltd (1988). *Offer for Sale: The National Commercial Bank of Trinidad & Tobago Ltd*.

Reserve Bank of Malaŵi (1989). *Financial and Economic Review*. Lilongwe.

Riddell, R.C. (1990). 'A Forgotten Dimension? The Manufacturing Sector in African Development', *Development Policy Review* 8 (1), 5–25.

Roth, G. (1987). *The Private Provision of Public Services in Developing Countries*. Oxford University Press, New York.

Ryan, S. (1985). 'Public Utilities in Trinidad and Tobago: Regulation and Performance'. Paper prepared for Third Annual Conference of the Trinidad and Tobago Economic Association (unpublished).

Salim, A.R. (1990a). *Issues and Problems in Privatization: A case study of the Telecommunications Department of Malaysia*. Institute for Social and International Studies, Kuala Lumpur.

Salim, A.R. (1990b). *Privatization and its effects on the Trade Unions and Workers*. Institute for Social and International Studies, Kuala Lumpur.

Salim, A.R. and Salleh, I.M. (1988). *Why the Jabatan Post should not be privatized*. Institute for Social and International Studies, Kuala Lumpur.

Salim, A.R. and Salleh, I.M. (1989). *Public Enterprise Management: Strategies for success. Privatization of Public Enterprises: an overview study of Malaysia*. Institute for Social and International Studies, Kuala Lumpur.

Salleh, I.M. and Salim, A.R. (1987). *Towards the Formulation of a Masterplan, Privatisation in Malaysia: some guiding principles and strategies*. Institute for Social and International Studies, Kuala Lumpur.

Sampson, C.I. (1988). A Strategy for Public Enterprises (unpublished).

Seprod Ltd (1985). *Prospectus for Share Offer*.

Seprod Ltd (1989). *1989 Annual Report*.

Shapiro, C. and Willig, R.D. (1990). *Economic Rationales for the Scope of Privatization*. Princeton University Discussion Paper 41, Princeton, NJ.

Shirley, M. (1983). *Managing State-Owned Enterprises*. World Bank Staff Working Papers 577, Washington DC.

Shirley, M. (1989a). *Improving Public Enterprise Performance: Lessons from South Korea*. World Bank PPR Working Paper 312, Washington DC.

Shirley, M. (1989b). *The Reform of State-Owned Enterprises: Lessons from World Bank Lending*. World Bank, PPR Paper No. 4, Washington DC.

Shirley, M. and Nellis, J. (1991). *Public Enterprise Reform: The Lessons of Experience*. Economic Development Institute, World Bank, Washington DC.

Sistem Televisyen Malaysia Berhad (1988). Security's Turnover and Value Report (unpublished).

Sistem Televisyen Malaysia Berhad (1988). Prospectus for Sale Offer.

Sports Toto Malaysia Berhad (1987). Security's Turnover and Value Report (unpublished).

Sports Toto Malaysia Berhad (1987). Prospectus for Share Offer.

Staatz, J.M., Dione, J. and Dembele, N.N. (1989). 'Cereals Market Liberalization in Mali', *World Development* 17 (5), 703-19.

Statistical Institute of Jamaica (1987). *National Income and Product 1987*.

Statistical Institute of Jamaica (1988). *National Income and Product, Preliminary Report 1988*.

Steamships Trading Co. (Papua New Guinea) Ltd (1989). *Annual Report 1989*.

Stebbing, P.W. (1984). 'Trends in the Balance of Payments since Independence', *Bank of Papua New Guinea Quarterly Economic Bulletin*, December.

Stone, C. (1989). 'A Survey of Jamaican Shareholders' (unpublished).

Swaby, R.A. (1980). 'The Rationale for State Ownership of Public Utilities in Jamaica', *Social and Economic Studies* 30, 75-107.

Swanson, D. and Wolde-Semait, T. (1989). *Africa's Public Enterprise Sector and Evidence of Reforms*. World Bank Technical Paper No. 95, Washington DC.

Telecommunications of Jamaica Ltd (1988). *Telecommunications of Jamaica Ltd., 1988 Offer for Sale*. The Accountant General.

The Democratic Socialist Republic of Sri Lanka (and Amendments). Inland Revenue Act, No. 28 of 1979.

The Democratic Socialist Republic of Sri Lanka (1987). Conversion of Government Owned Business Undertakings into Public Corporations Act, No. 22 of 1987.

The Democratic Socialist Republic of Sri Lanka (1987). Conversion of Public Corporations or Government Owned Business Undertakings into Public Companies Act, No. 23 of 1987.

Touche Ross, Ogle & Co. (1987). *Divestment of Government-Owned Enterprises, Executive Digest*.

Touche, Ross, Thorburn & Co. (1988). *Jamaica Tax & Investment Profile*. Touche Ross International.

Touche Ross, Ogle & Co. (1990). *Divestment of Government-Owned Enterprises, Capacity of the Equity Market 1986-90*.

Tradewinds (Malaysia) Berhad (1988). Prospectus for Share Offer.

Tradewinds (Malaysia) Berhad (1988). Security's Turnover and Value Report (unpublished).

Trinidad & Tobago Central Statistical Office (1987). *The National Income of Trinidad & Tobago 1966-1985*.

Trinidad & Tobago Central Statistical Office (1988). *Statistics at a Glance*.

Trinidad & Tobago External Telecommunications Company Ltd. *Report and Accounts* (various years).

Trinidad & Tobago Industrial Development Corporation (1988). *A Guide for Investors*.

Trinidad & Tobago Industrial Development Corporation (1989). *Trinidad & Tobago, Land of Opportunity, A Guide for Investors*.

Trinidad & Tobago Industrial Development Corporation (1989). *Trinidad & Tobago Investment Policy*.

Trinidad & Tobago Ministry of Finance. *Review of the Economy* (various years).

Trinidad & Tobago Ministry of Finance and the Economy (1988). *Trinidad & Tobago Government's Relationship with the International Monetary Fund. 1988*.

Trinidad & Tobago National Alliance for Reconstruction (1986). *Manifesto of the National Alliance for Reconstruction 1986.*

Trinidad & Tobago National Planning Commission (1988). *Restructuring for Economic Independence. Draft Medium Term Macro Planning Framework 1989–1995.*

Trinidad & Tobago Stock Exchange various years. *Annual Report.*

Trinidad Cement Ltd (1987). *Trinidad Cement Share Offer.*

Trinidad Cement Ltd (1989). *Trinidad Cement Share Offer Phase 11.*

Tyler, W.G. (1979). 'Technical Efficiency in Production in a Developing Country: An Empirical Investigation of the Brazilian Plastics and Steel Industries'. *Oxford Economic Papers* 31, 477–495.

United States Agency for International Development (1986). *Implementing A.I.D. Privatization Objectives.* AID Policy Determination Paper.

United States Agency for International Development (1988). 'Sri Lanka: Private Sector Policy Support' (unpublished).

van de Walle, N. (1989). 'Privatization in Developing Countries: A Review of the Issues', *World Development* 17 (5), 601–16.

Vernon, R. (1988). *A Technical Approach to Privatization Issues: Coupling Project Analysis with Rules of Thumb.* EDI Working Papers, World Bank, Washington DC.

Vernon-Wortzel, H. and Wortzel L.H. (1989). 'Privatization: Not the Only Answer', *World Development* 17 (5), 633–42.

Vickers, J. (1986). 'Signalling in a Model of Monetary Policy with Incomplete Information', *Oxford Economic Papers* 38, 443–5.

Vickers, J. and Wright, V. (1988). 'The Politics of Privatization in Western Europe'. *Western European Politics* 2 (4), 1–30.

Vickers, J. and Yarrow, G. (1988). *Privatization: An Economic Analysis.* MIT Press, Cambridge, MA.

Vickers, J. and Yarrow, G. (1991). 'Economic Perspectives on Privatization', *Journal of Economic Perspectives* 5 (2), 111–32.

Vuylsteke, C. (1988). *Techniques of Privatization of State-Owned Enterprises.* World Bank Technical Paper No. 88, Washington DC.

Waterson, M. (1984). *Economic Theory of the Industry.* CUP, Cambridge.

Woon, T.K. (1989). 'Privatization in Malaysia', *Asean Economic Bulletin*, 242–57.

World Bank, *World Development Report*, Oxford University Press, Oxford and New York (various years).

World Bank, *World Tables.* Johns Hopkins University Press, Baltimore, MD (various years).

World Bank (1987a) *Report and Recommendation of the President of the IBRD to the Executive Directors on a Proposed Loan to Jamaica for a Public Enterprise Sector Adjustment Operation.* World Bank, Washington DC.

World Bank (1987b). *Kenya: Industrial Sector Policies for Investment and Export Growth.* Report No. KE-6711 (2 vols), Washington DC.

World Bank (1988a). *Sri Lanka, A Break with the Past: The 1987–90 Program of Economic Reforms and Adjustment.* Report No. 7220-CE (2 vols), World Bank, Washington DC.

World Bank (1988b). *Papua New Guinea: Agricultural Assessment Review.* Report No. 7090-PNG, World Bank, Washington DC.

World Bank (1988c). *Papua New Guinea Policies and Prospects for Sustained and Broad-Based Growth.* A World Bank Country Study: The Main Report, Washington DC.

World Bank (1988d). *Kenya Recent Economic Development and Selected Policy Issues*. Washington DC.

World Bank (1988e). *Trinidad and Tobago: A Program for Policy Reform and Renewed Growth*. Washington DC.

World Bank (1989a). *Jamaica: Adjustment under Changing External Conditions*. Report No. 7753-JM, World Bank, Washington DC.

World Bank (1989c). *Malaysia Matching Risks and Rewards in a Mixed Economy Program*. A World Bank Country Study, Washington DC.

World Bank (1989d). *Papua New Guinea: Opportunities and Challenges for Accelerated Development*. Report No. 7707-PNG, Washington DC.

World Bank (1989e). *Memorandum to Sri Lanka Aid Group*.

World Bank (1989f) *Malaŵi Industrial Sector Memorandum*. Report No. 402-MAI, World Bank, Washington DC.

World Bank (1982). *Jamaica: Structural Adjustment, Export Development and Private Investment*. Washington DC.

World Bank (1986). *Jamaica Memorandum on Transport Public Sector Enterprises*. Washington DC.

World Bank Operations Evaluation Department (1989). *Program Performance Audit Report, Jamaica. Structural Adjustment Loans II and III and Overview of Structural Adjustment Loans I–III*. Washington DC.

Yotopoulos, P.A. (1989). 'The (Rip) Tide of Privatization: Lessons from Chile', *World Development* 17 (5), 683–703.

Yuen, N.C. and Wagner, N. (1989). 'Privatization and Deregulation in Asean: An Overview', *Asean Economic Bulletin*.

Yusof, Z.A. (1989). 'A Note on Rebalancing the Private and Public Sectors: The case of Malaysia.' Presented at OECD Symposium on Competition and Economic Development. Paris, October (unpublished).

Index

absorptive capacity, 101, 102, 258, 337, 369, 372
  capital market, 137, 167, 205, 265, 267, 313, 318, 320
  private sector 171, 176, 293, 346-7, 363, 373
accountability, 33, 34, 112, 226, 335, 362
accounting practices, 9, 169
adjustment, structural, 4, 8, 39, 45, 52, 65-6, 75, 92-102 *passim*, 108, 113, 162, 164, 177, 273, 276, 301, 308, 320, 325, 327, 345, 349, 353, 367, 374
Aerospace Industries of Malaysia (AIM), 237
Africa, 3, 7, 8, 31, 32, 49, 70, 71, 77, 82, 89
  see also individual countries
  sub-Saharan, 31, 323, 325, 343, 358
Agricultural Bank of PNG (AGBANK), 281, 287
Agricultural Development and Marketing Corporation (ADMARC), 35, 39, 73, 353, 355, 356, 358, 360, 362-8 *passim*, 372-4
agriculture, 35, 39-42 *passim*, 66, 73, 118, 151-3, 158, 178, 182, 198, 219, 273, 275, 276, 281, 290, 299, 323, 331, 338, 340, 353, 358, 362, 364, 367-8
  estates, 50, 353, 355, 358, 374n2
  plantations, 35, 73, 219, 275, 301, 305
agroprocessing, 107, 161
aid, 12, 24, 100, 299, 327 *see also* lending, adjustment
Air Jamaica, 50, 114, 155, 172n3
Air Lanka, 50, 303, 314
Air Malaŵi, 50, 360
Air Niugini, 50, 277, 297n6
AIROD, 230, 237, 249
Albon, R.P., 27
allocation, resource, 4, 6, 8, 19, 23, 33, 54, 63, 79, 89, 100, 140, 226, 280
aluminium, 27, 111
Arab Malaysian Merchant Bank, 255, 256, 265, 267
Arawak Cement Ltd, 197, 205
Aseambankers, 232
ASEAN, 215
Asia, 3, 32, 80, 259 *see also individual countries*
Australia, 27, 273, 283-4, 290, 293, 294

Auty, R., 177, 183, 190, 193
Averch-Johnson effect, 21, 69n36, 279
Ayub, M.A., 73, 160

B and B Enterprises Berhad, 234
Backus, D., 57-8
balance of payments, 10, 275, 299, 300
balance sheet restructuring, 7, 191, 367
bananas, 107, 152
Banda President, 353, 357, 363
Bandaranaike, Mrs 299-301 *passim*
Bangladesh, 28, 333
Bank of London and Montreal, 189
Bank of Nova Scotia, 126, 130, 131
banking/banks, 40-2 *passim*, 45, 80, 87, 90, 126, 164, 165, 183, 189, 203, 280-2, 304, 305, 331, 332 *see also individual headings*
bankruptcy, 340
Banks, Donald, 131
Banque Indosuez, 294
Barclays Bank, 111, 126, 331, 342, 348
Bates, R., 11-12
Baumol, W.J., 17
bauxite, 107, 110, 111
Bayesian framework, 58-60
Berg, E., 61
beverages, 344
Bhaskar, V., 28
Bienen, H., 24
Black Power, 34, 36n5, 181
Boardman, A., 27
Bobb, Central Bank Governor, 46, 188
Bombay Dyeing Ltd, 312
bonds, 9, 84-5, 90, 91, 262
bonus payments, 7, 165
borrowing, 33, 108, 280, 325, 360 *see also* credit; debt
Bougainville, 275, 276, 286-8 *passim*, 290, 297n1
Bougainville Copper Ltd (BCL), 273, 275, 276, 283, 286, 287, 293
Bouin, O., 27
Brazil, 27
brewing sector, 364
Brown, A., 110, 112, 170
Bruce, Central Bank Governor, 46, 188

400 Index